2024

北京统计年鉴
Beijing Statistical Yearbook

Beijing
Statistical
Yearbook

图书在版编目(CIP)数据

北京统计年鉴. 2024 = Beijing Statistical Yearbook 2024 : 汉、英 / 北京市统计局, 国家统计局北京调查总队编. -- 北京 : 中国统计出版社, 2024. 11. -- ISBN 978-7-5230-0637-5

Ⅰ. C832.1-54

中国国家版本馆CIP 数据核字第20242L5C22号

北京统计年鉴2024

作　　者/北京市统计局　国家统计局北京调查总队
责任编辑/李 冲
封面设计/高 立
出版发行/中国统计出版社有限公司
通信地址/北京市丰台区西三环南路甲6号　邮政编码/100073
发行电话/邮购 (010) 63376909　书店 (010) 68783171
网　　址/http://www.zgtjcbs.com
印　　刷/河北鑫兆源印刷有限公司
经　　销/新华书店
开　　本/880mm×1230mm 1/16
字　　数/1200千字
印　　张/34.25印张　彩插/1.5印张
版　　别/2024年12月第1版
版　　次/2024年12月第1次印刷
定　　价/350.00元

2023年的北京
BEIJING IN 2023

43760.7
地区生产总值(亿元)
Gross Domestic Product(100 million yuan)

2947.1
研究与试验发展
(R&D)经费内部支出(亿元)
Internal Expenditure on R&D(100 million yuan)

84.8
第三产业增加值占地区
生产总值比重(%)
Added Value of Tertiary Industry
as % of GDP(%)

387074
社会劳动生产率(元/人)
Overall Labor Productivity(yuan/person)

6181.1
一般公共预算收入(亿元)
General Public Budget Revenue
(100 million yuan)

200278
人均地区生产总值(元)
Per Capita Gross Domestic Product(yuan)

全市居民人均可支配收入(元)
Per Capita Disposable Income of
Households of the Whole City (yuan)
81752

居民消费价格指数(上年=100)
Consumer Price Index(preceding year=100)
100.4

2023年的北京
BEIJING IN 2023

2185.8
常住人口（万人）
Resident Population(10000 persons)

1332
常住人口密度（人/平方公里）
Resident Population Density(person/sq.km)

街
街道办事处（个）
Sub-district Office(unit)
165

镇
建制镇（个）
Designated Town(unit)
143

乡
建制乡（个）
Designated Township(unit)
35

区
社区居委会（个）
Community Neighborhood Committee(unit)
3568

村
村民委员会（个）
Villagers' Committee(unit)
3768

22433
公路里程（公里）
Length of Highway(km)

836
城市轨道交通运营线路长度（公里）
Length of Routes of Urban Rail Transit in Operation(km)

29739
公共汽电车运营线路长度（公里）
Length of Routes of Buses and trolley Buses in Operation(km)

758.9
机动车保有量（万辆）
Possession of Motor Vehicles (10000 units)

72113
全市集中供热面积（万平方米）
Area of Centralized Heating (10000 sq.m)

2016714
天然气供气总量（万立方米）
Supply Volume of Natural Gas(10000 cu.m)

709.4
自来水综合生产能力（万立方米/日）
General Production Capacity of Tap Water(10000 cu.m/day)

1358
全社会用电量（亿千瓦时）
Electricity Consumption (100 million kW·h)

6.73
研究与试验发展经费内部支出相当于地区生产总值比例(%)
Ratio of Internal Expenditure on R&D to GDP(%)

263
万人发明专利拥有量(件)
Invention Patent Ownership per 10000 Persons(piece)

8536.9
技术合同成交总额(亿元)
Total Volume of Transaction of Technological Contracts(100 million yuan)

4.87
每十万常住人口公共图书馆书刊文献外借册次 (万册次)
Number of Books and Periodicals Lent to Readers of Public Libraies per 100000 Resident Population(10000 copies-times)

5.99
每千常住人口医院床位数 (张)
Hospital Beds per 1000 Resident Population(unit)

1.03
每十万常住人口博物馆数 (个)
Number of Museums per 100000 Resident Population(unit)

6.12
每千常住人口执业(助理)医师数 (人)
Licensed Physicians & Physician Assistants per 1000 Registered Population(person)

9.1
每十万常住人口幼儿园数 (个)
Number of Kindergartens per 100000 Resident Population(unit)

14.7
平均每一专任教师负担小学生数 (人)
Average Number of Students in Primary School Instructed by a Full-time Teacher(person)

32.0
$PM_{2.5}$年平均浓度(微克/立方米)
Annual Average Concentration of $PM_{2.5}$(μg/cu.m)

16.9
人均公园绿地面积 (平方米)
Per Capita Park Green Area(sq.m)

190.0
人均水资源 (立方米)
Per Capita Water Resources(cu.m)

49.8
城市绿化覆盖率(%)
Urban Green Coverage(%)

北京一日
A DAY IN BEIJING

每日创造
Daily Production

169345.1
一般公共预算收入
(万元)
General Public Budget Revenue(10000 yuan)

218390.3
一般公共预算支出
(万元)
General Public Budget Expenditure(10000 yuan)

12462.3
发电量
(万千瓦时)
Electricity Generation (10000 kW·h)

2747
汽车生产量
(辆)
Output of Motor Vehicles(vehicle)

281829
移动电话机生产量
(台)
Output of Mobile Telephones(set)

3757.3
实际利用外商直接投资额
(万美元)
Amount of Foreign Direct Investment Actually Utilized (USD 10000)

5860
显示器生产量
(台)
Output of Display (set)

2889.9
第一产业
Primary Industry

1198923.3
地区生产总值(万元)
Gross Domestic Product (10000 yuan)

178783.3
第二产业
Secondary Industry

1017250.1
第三产业
Tertiary Industry

834692.2
地区货物进口值
(万元)
Total Imports of Local Enterprises (10000 yuan)

571.7
公共汽电车客运量
(万人次)
Passengers Traffic of Public Buses and Trolley Buses(10000 person-times)

164385.0
地区货物出口值
(万元)
Total Exports of Local Enterprises (10000 yuan)

946.2
城市轨道交通客运量
(万人次)
Passengers Traffic of Urban Rail Transit (10000 person-times)

157019.2
国内旅游收入
(万元)
Earnings from Domestic Tourism (10000 yuan)

454.8
国际旅游收入
(万美元)
Earnings from International Tourism (USD 10000)

24.6
民航客运量
(万人次)
Passengers Traffic of Civil Aviation (10000 person-times)

70.5
公路客运量
(万人次)
Passengers Traffic of Highway (10000 person-times)

41.2
铁路客运量
(万人次)
Passengers Traffic of Railway (10000 person-times)

每日生活
Daily Life

337
常住出生人口
(人)
Births (Resident Population)
(person)

367
常住死亡人口
(人)
Deaths (Resident Population)
(person)

376
登记结婚对数
(对)
Total Number of
Marriage Registration
(couple)

151
离婚对数
(对)
Total Number of Divorces
(couple)

224.0
全市居民人均
可支配收入(元)
Per Capita Disposable Income
of Residents of the Whole City
(yuan)

2.1
生活垃圾清运量
(万吨)
Volume of Domestic Garbage
Collected and Transported
(10000 tons)

396237.3
社会消费品零售总额 (万元)
Total Retail Sales of Consumer Goods
(10000 yuan)

86390.6 吃类商品(万元)
Food (10000 yuan)

穿类商品(万元)
Clothing(10000 yuan) **21394.5**

16939.8 烧类商品(万元)
Fuels(10000 yuan)

用类商品(万元)
Daily Use Articles(10000 yuan) **271512.3**

130.4
全市居民人均
消费支出(元)
Per Capita Consumption Expenditure
of Residents of the Whole City
(yuan)

630.4
污水处理量
(万立方米)
Sewage Disposal Volume
(10000 cu.m)

516.2
法人单位从业人员
平均工资(元)
Average Wages of Employed
Persons in Legal Entities
(yuan)

350.2
自来水销售总量
(万立方米)
Total Sales Volume
of Tap Water
(10000 cu.m)

543.3
居民家庭用天然气销售量
(万立方米)
Sales Volume of Natural Gas
for Household Consumption
(10000 cu.m)

9166.5
城乡居民生活用电量
(万千瓦时)
Household Electricity
Consumption of Urban and
Rural Residents
(10000 kW·h)

622.2
特快专递业务量
(万件)
Express Deliveries
(10000 pcs)

9259
电影放映场次
(场次)
Show Times of Films
(times)

总体经济
OVERALL ECONOMY

地区生产总值(亿元)
Gross Domestic Product (100 million yuan)

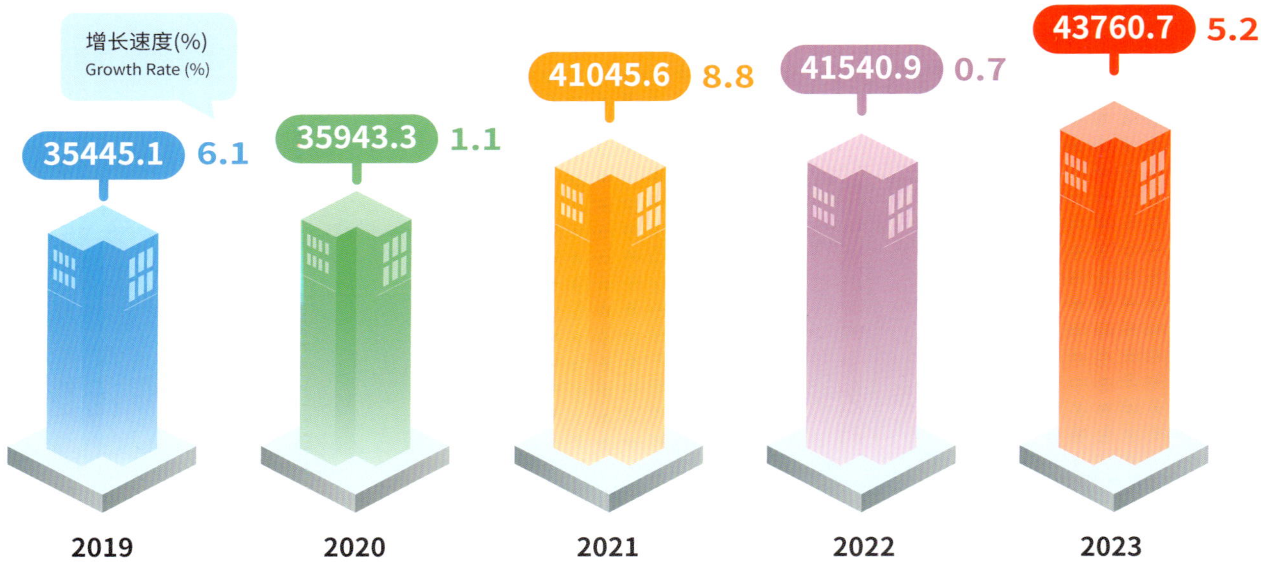

人均地区生产总值(元)
Per Capita Gross Domestic Product (yuan)

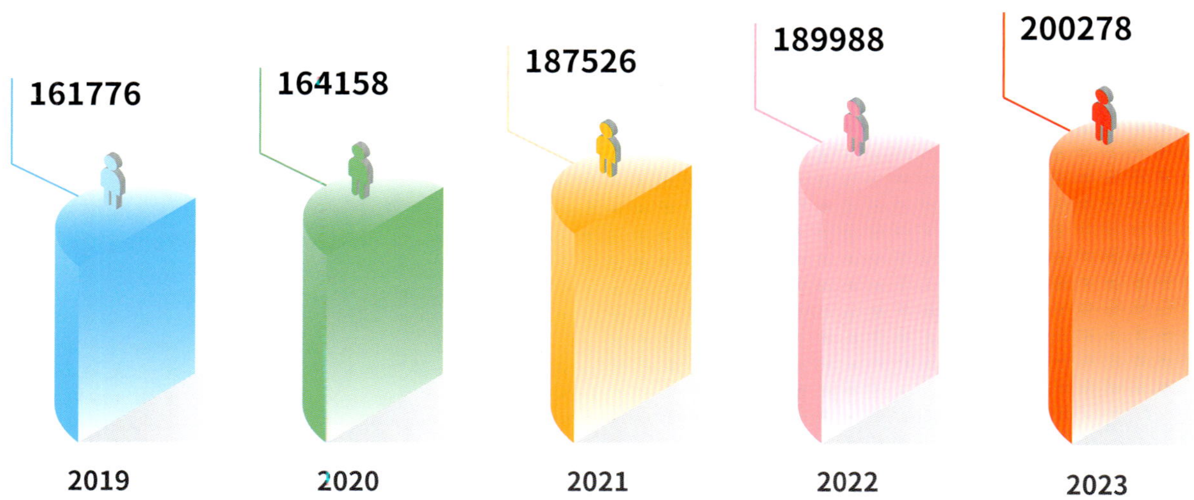

一般公共预算收入（亿元）
General Public Budget Revenue（100 million yuan）

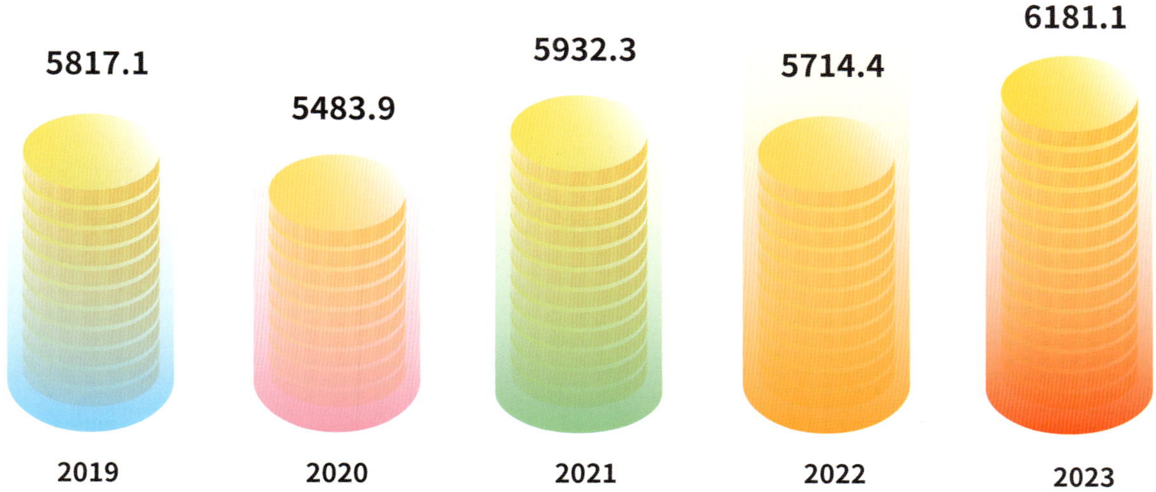

一般公共预算支出（亿元）
General Public Budget Expenditure（100 million yuan）

	2023	2022
一般公共服务 General Public Service	545.8	589.2
教育 Education	1227.9	1171.1
科学技术 Science and Technology	521.9	488.7
文化旅游体育与传媒 Culture, Tourism, Sport and Media	215.9	204.9
社会保障和就业 Social Security and Employment	1145.8	1067.8
卫生健康 Health Care	704.9	775.8
节能环保 Energy Conservation and Environmental Protection	220.7	222.9
交通运输 Transportation	373.1	395.3
城乡社区 Urban and Rural Community Affairs	929.6	808.6
农林水 Agriculture, Forestry and Water Conservancy	515.5	462.8
其他 Others	1570.2	1282.0
合计 Total	7971.2	7469.2

人口与就业
POPULATION AND EMPLOYMENT

常住人口(万人)
Resident Population (10000 persons)

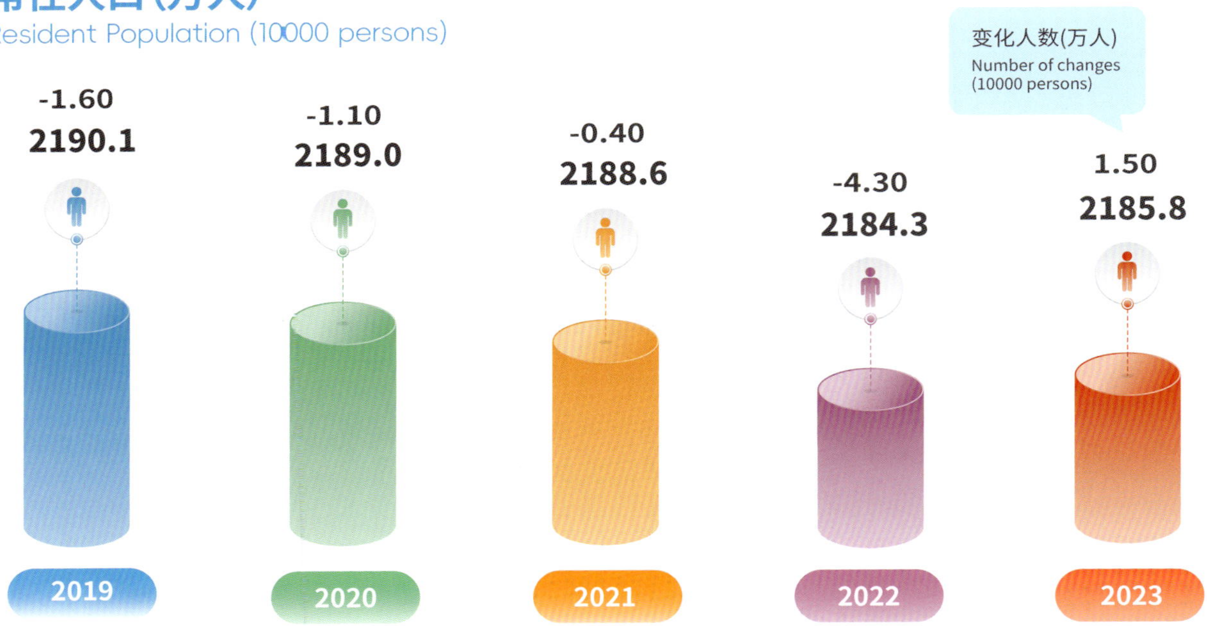

2023年常住人口分布(万人)
Distribution of Resident Population in 2023 (10000 persons)

法人单位从业人员年末人数（万人）
Number of Employed Persons in Corporate Units at Year-end (10000 persons)

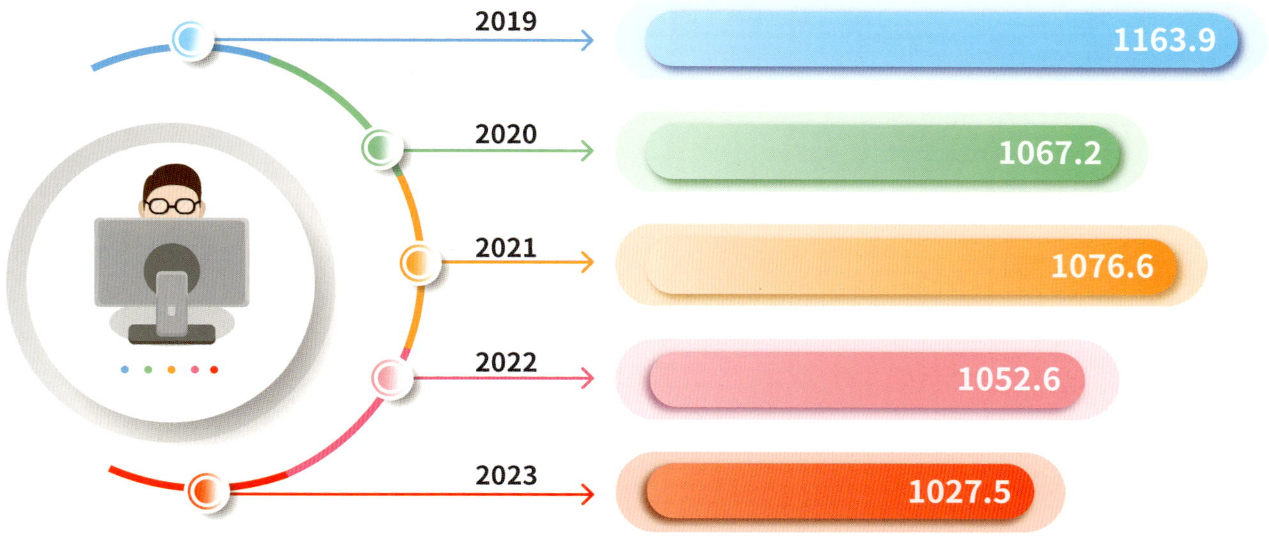

法人单位从业人员平均工资（元）
Average Wage of Employed Persons in Corporate Units (yuan)

价格指数
PRICE INDEX

价格指数（上年=100）
Price Index (preceding year=100)

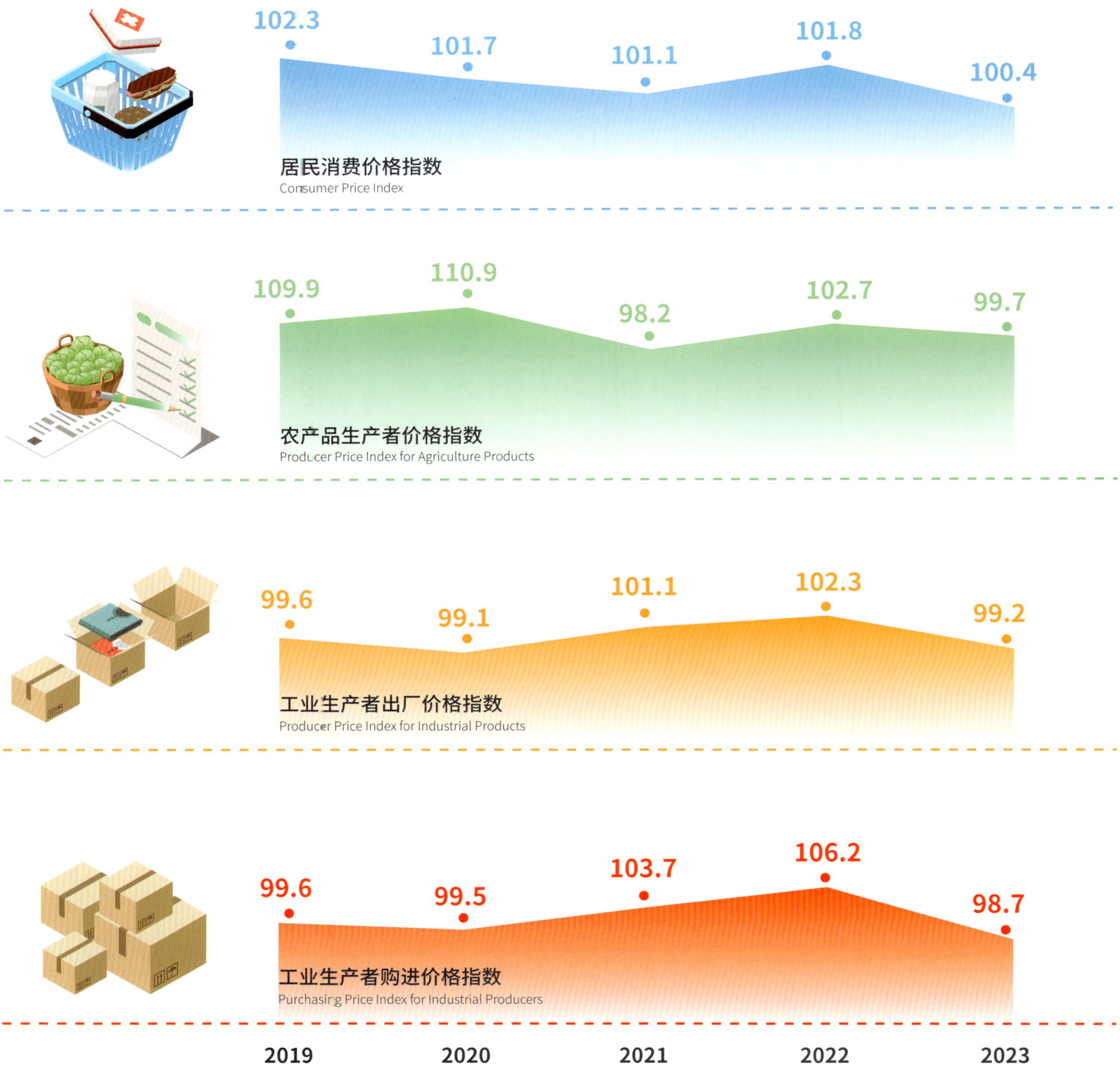

人民生活
PEOPLE'S LIVELIHOODS

居民人均可支配收入（元）
Per Capita Disposable Income of Households (yuan)

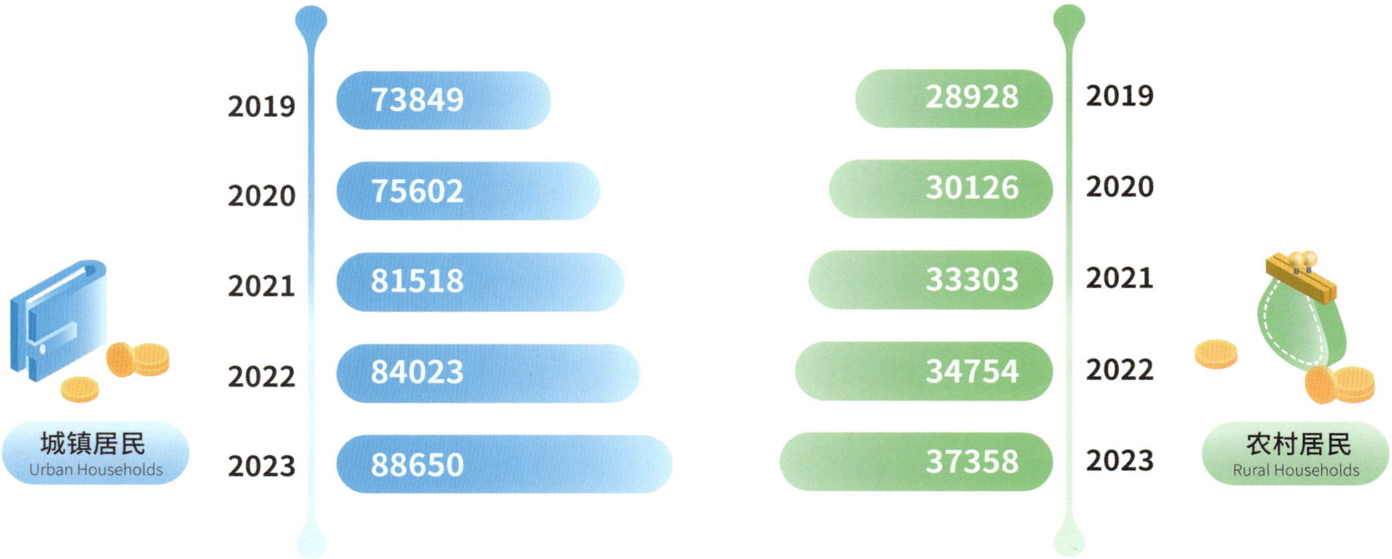

居民人均消费支出（元）
Per Capita Consumption Expenditure of Households (yuan)

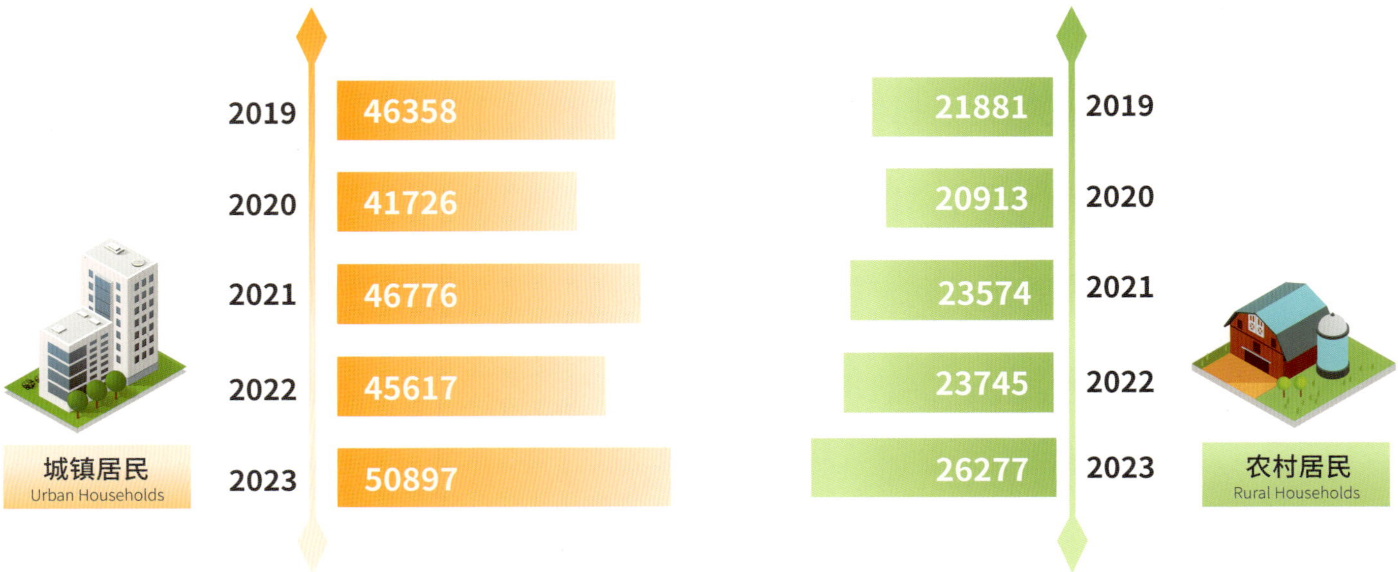

产业发展
INDUSTRY DEVELOPMENT

三次产业增加值结构(%)
Structure of Added Value of Three Industries (%)

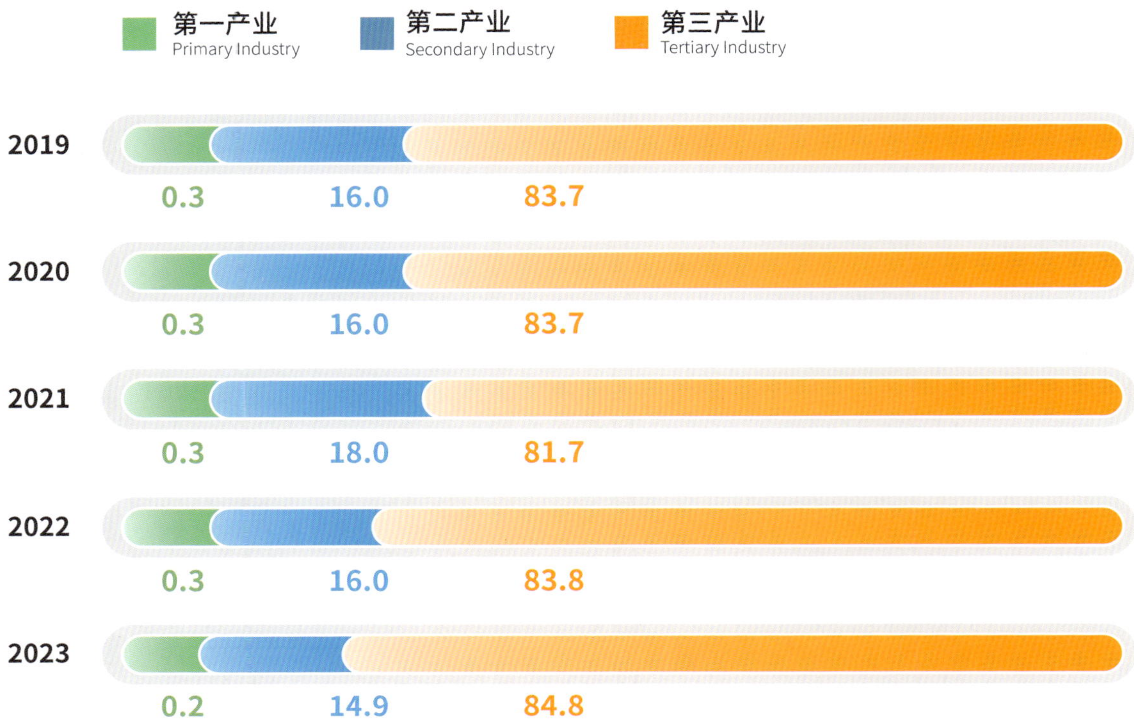

2023年数字经济和部分新兴产业增加值(亿元)
Added Value of Digital Economy and Some Emerging Industries (100 million yuan)

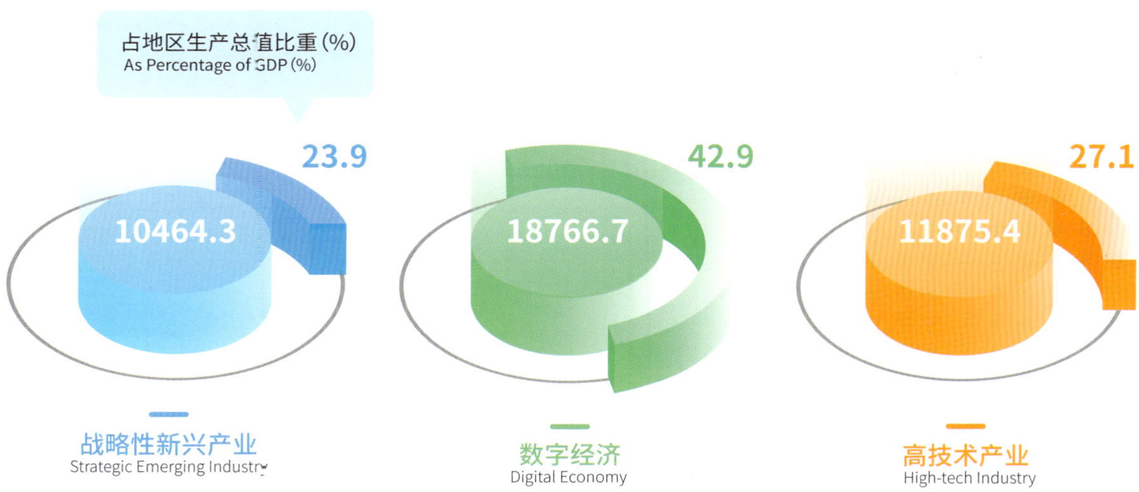

投资与消费
INVESTMENT AND CONSUMPTION

固定资产投资增长速度(%)
Growth Rate of Investment In Fixed Assets (%)

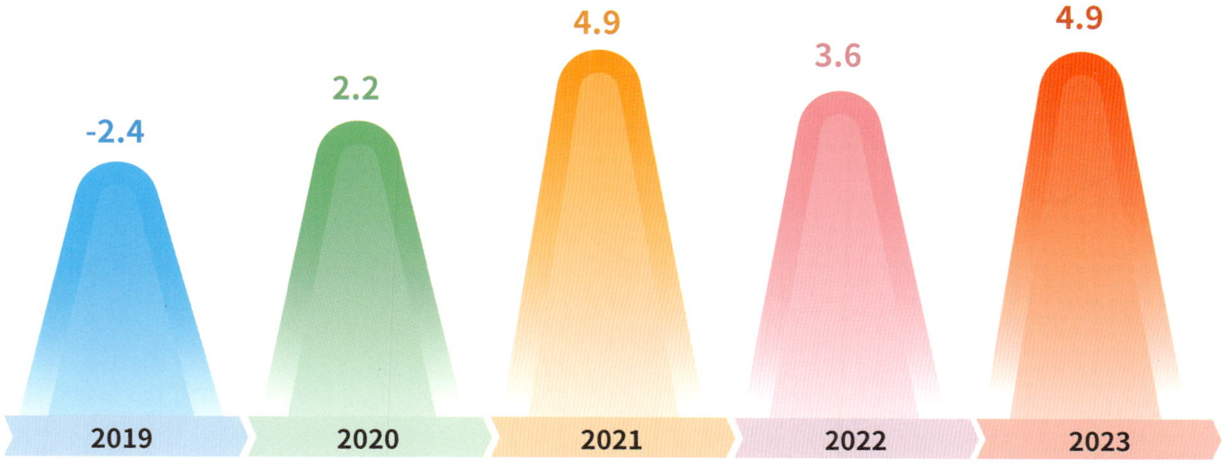

社会消费品零售总额(亿元)
Total Retail Sales of Consumer Goods (100 million yuan)

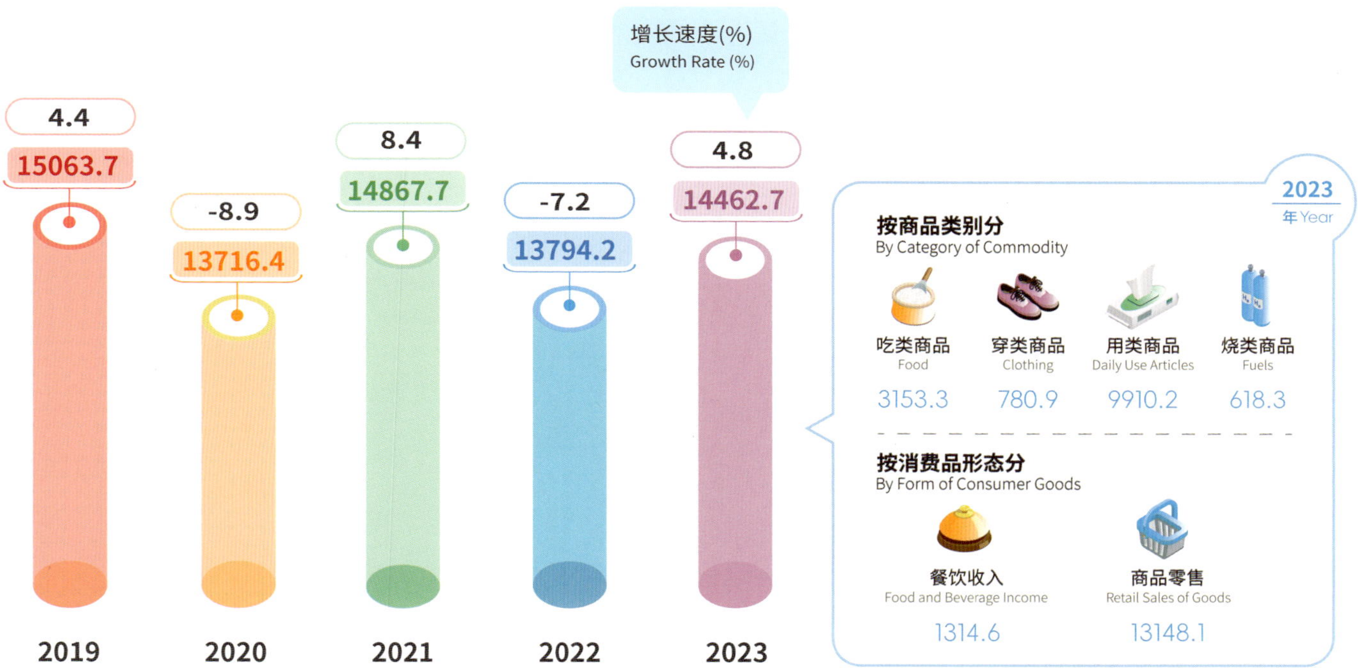

对外开放
OPENING TO THE OUTSIDE WORLD

货物进出口总值(亿元)
Total Value of Imports and Exports of Goods (100 million yuan)

新设外资企业数(个)
Number of Newly Established Foreign Invested Enterprises (unit)

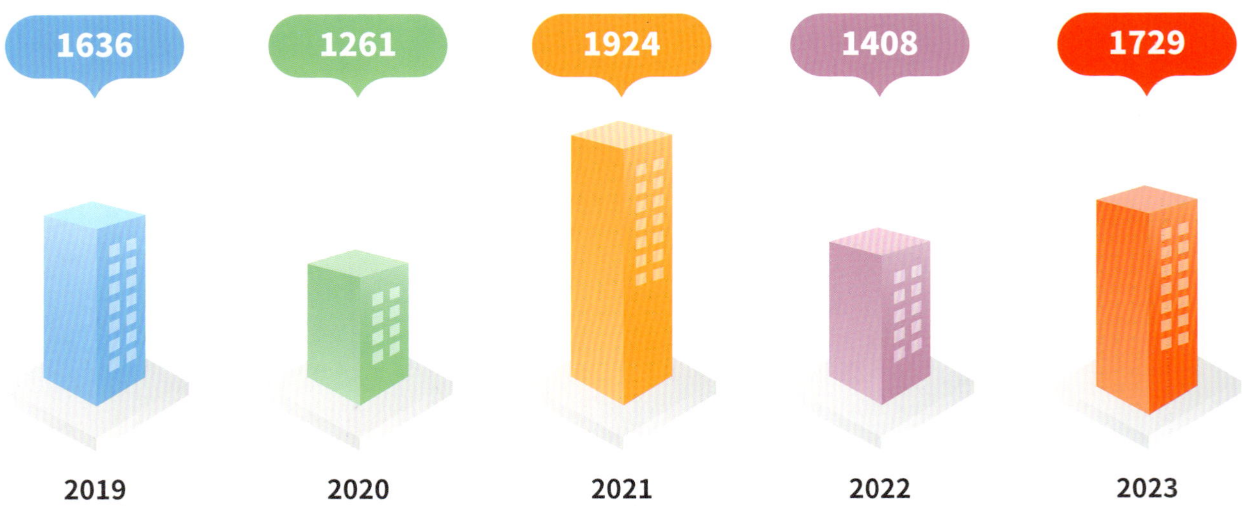

实际利用外商直接投资额(亿美元)
Amount of Foreign Direct Investment Actually Utilized (100 million yuan)

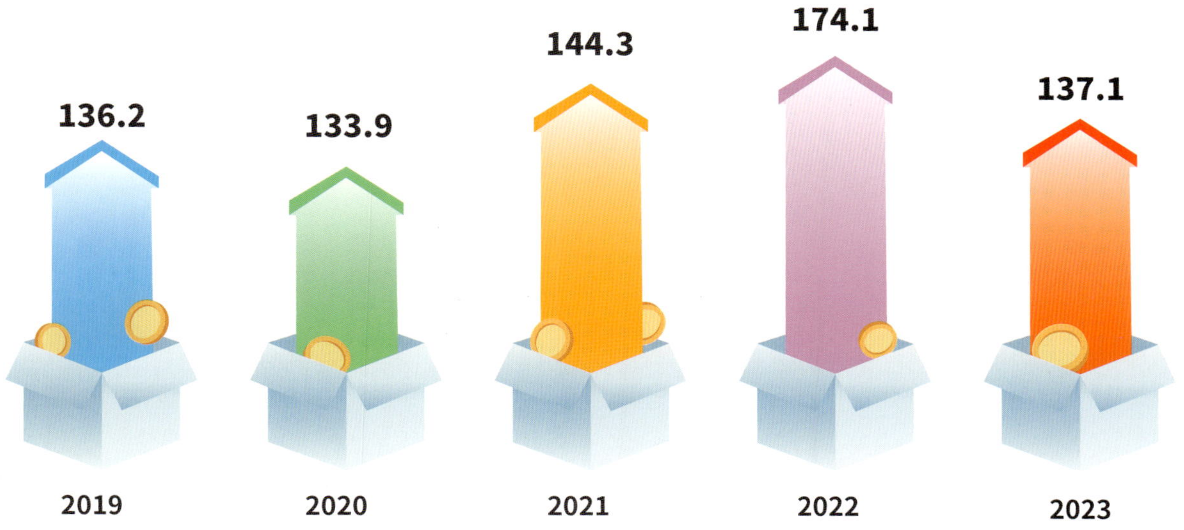

对外直接投资额(亿美元)
Amount of Outward Direct Investment (USD 100 million)

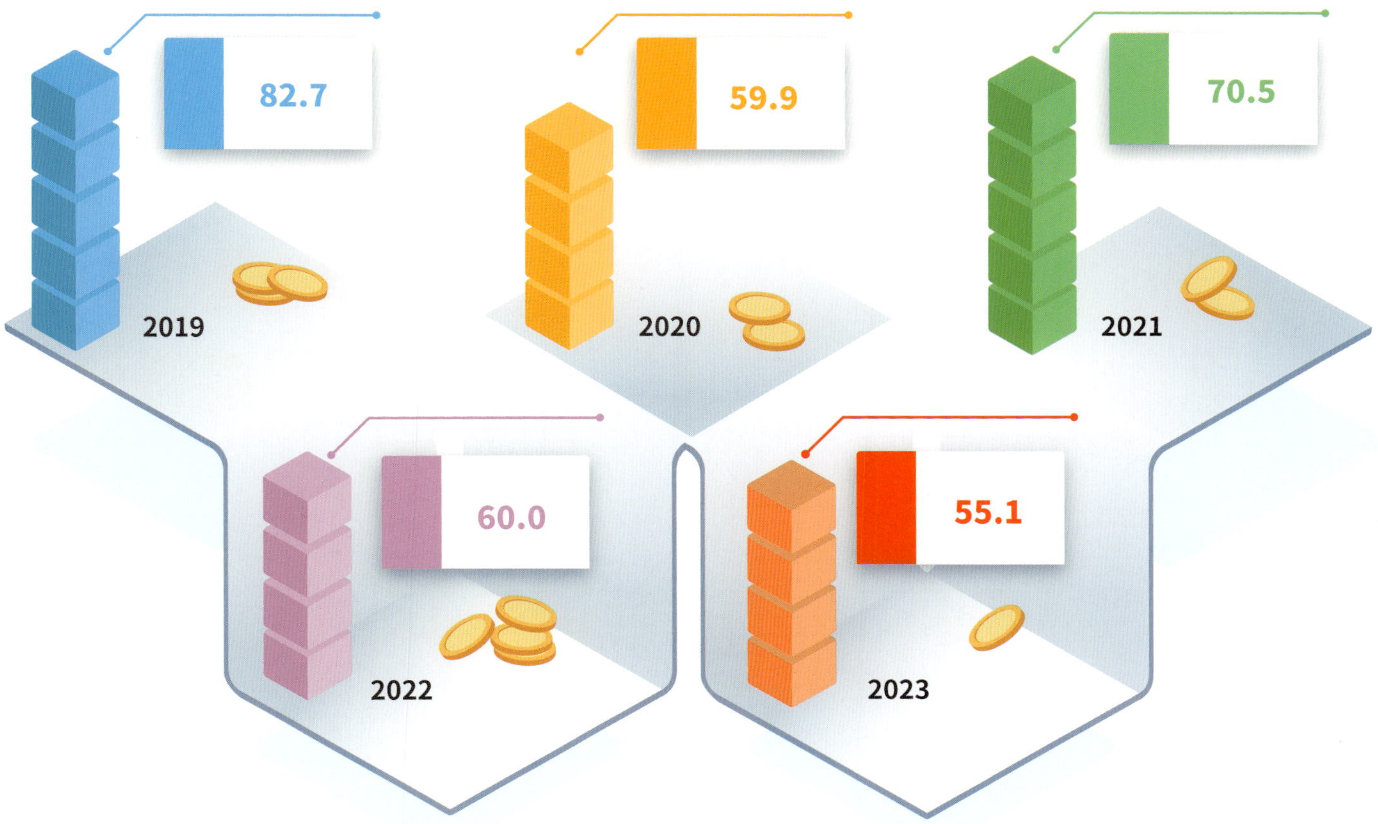

资源与环境
RESOURCE AND ENVIRONMENT

万元地区生产总值能耗（吨标准煤）
Energy Consumption per 10000 yuan of GDP (ton of SCE)

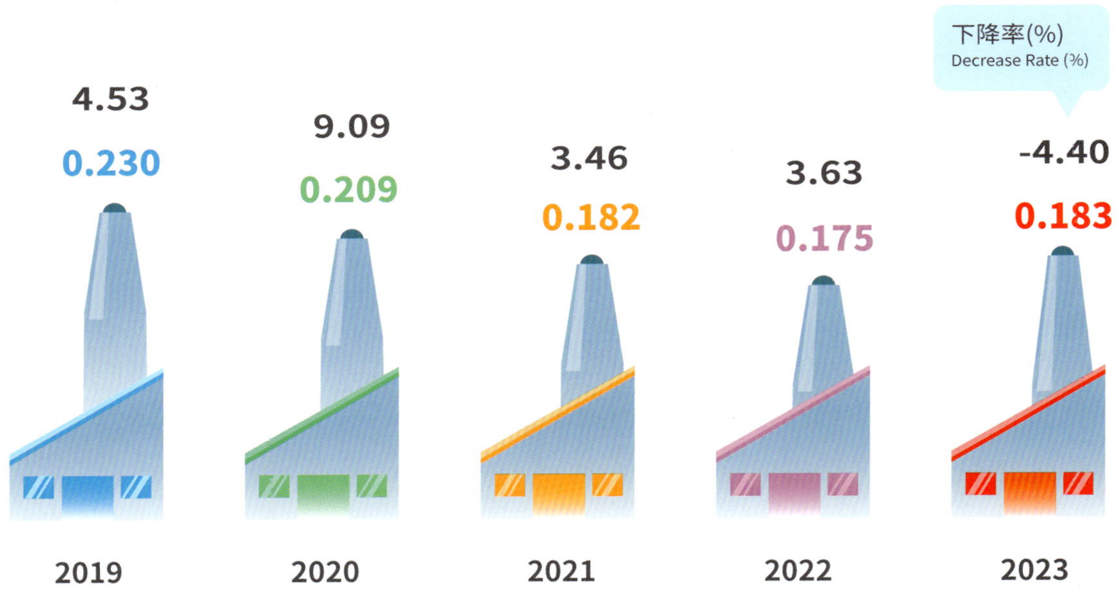

万元地区生产总值水耗(立方米)
Water Consumption per 10000 yuan of GDP (cu.m)

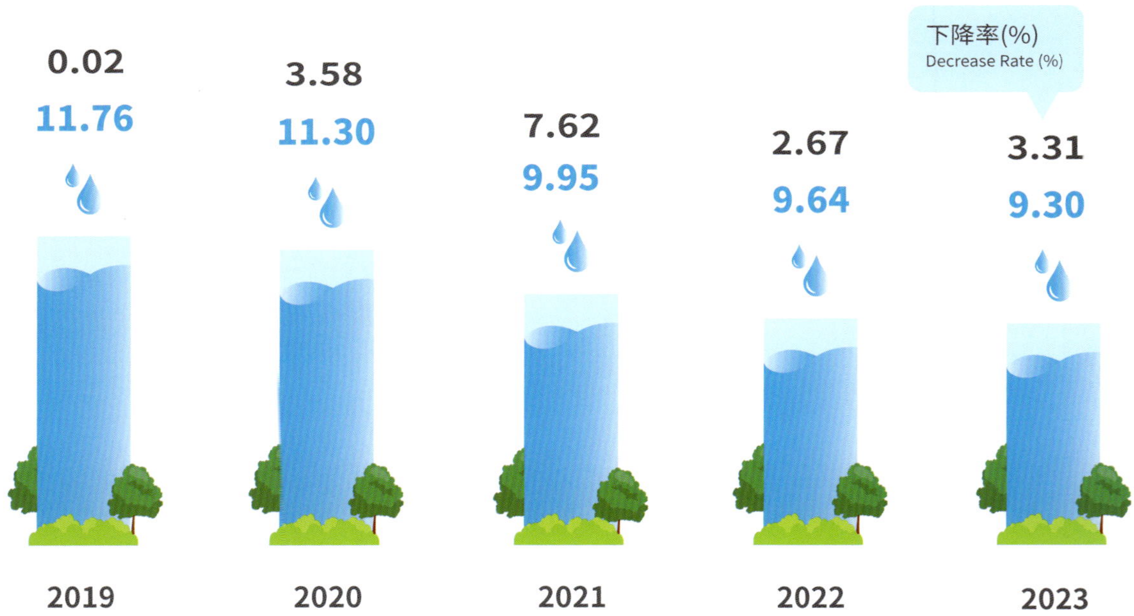

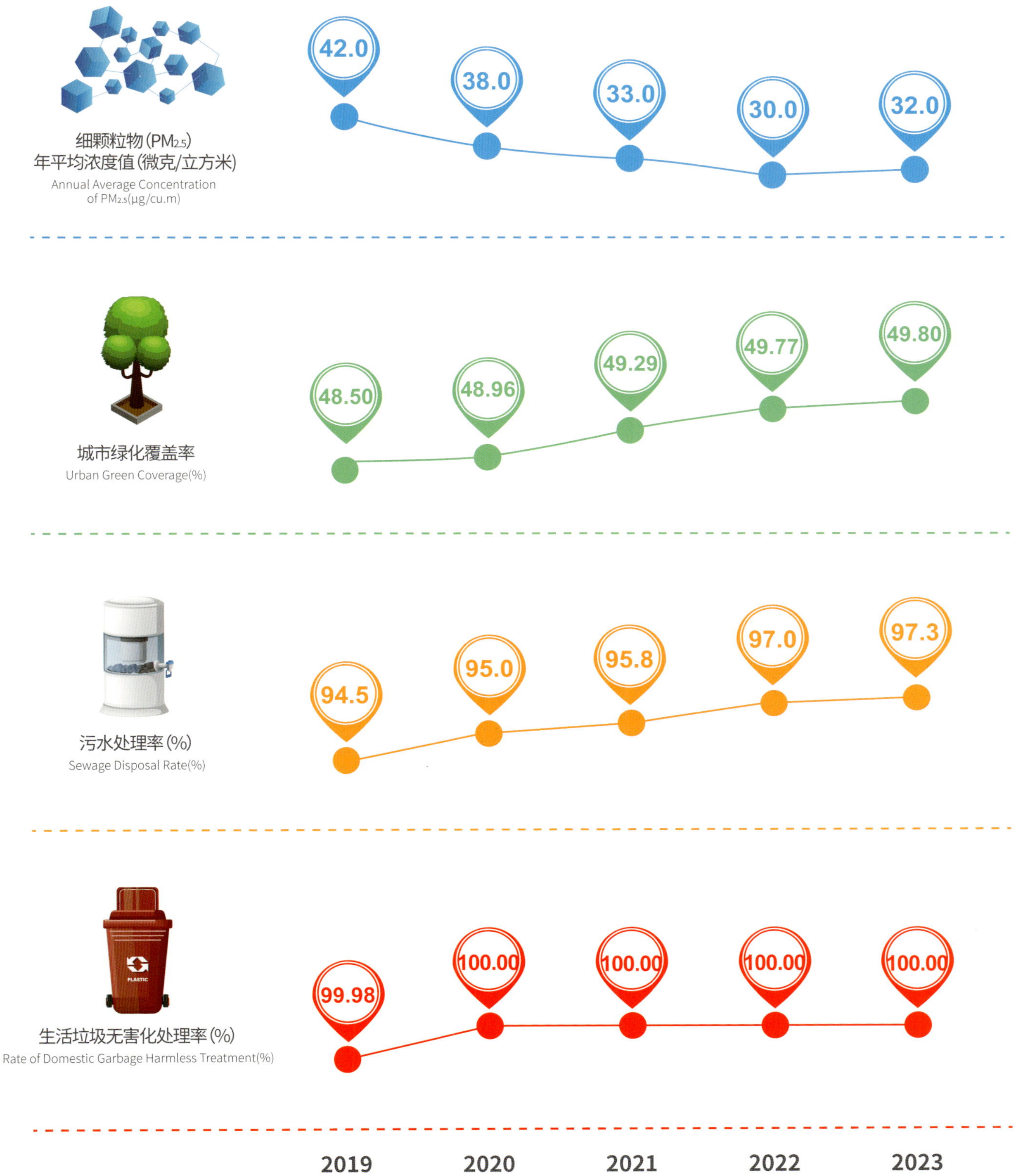
42.0
38.0
33.0
30.0
32.0
细颗粒物(PM2.5)
年平均浓度值(微克/立方米)
Annual Average Concentration
of PM2.5(μg/cu.m)
48.50
48.96
49.29
49.77
49.80
城市绿化覆盖率
Urban Green Coverage(%)
94.5
95.0
95.8
97.0
97.3
污水处理率(%)
Sewage Disposal Rate(%)
99.98
100.00
100.00
100.00
100.00
生活垃圾无害化处理率(%)
Rate of Domestic Garbage Harmless Treatment(%)
2019
2020
2021
2022
2023

科技创新
TECHNOLOGY INNOVATION

研究与试验发展(R&D)经费内部支出(亿元)
Internal Expenditure on R&D (100 million yuan)

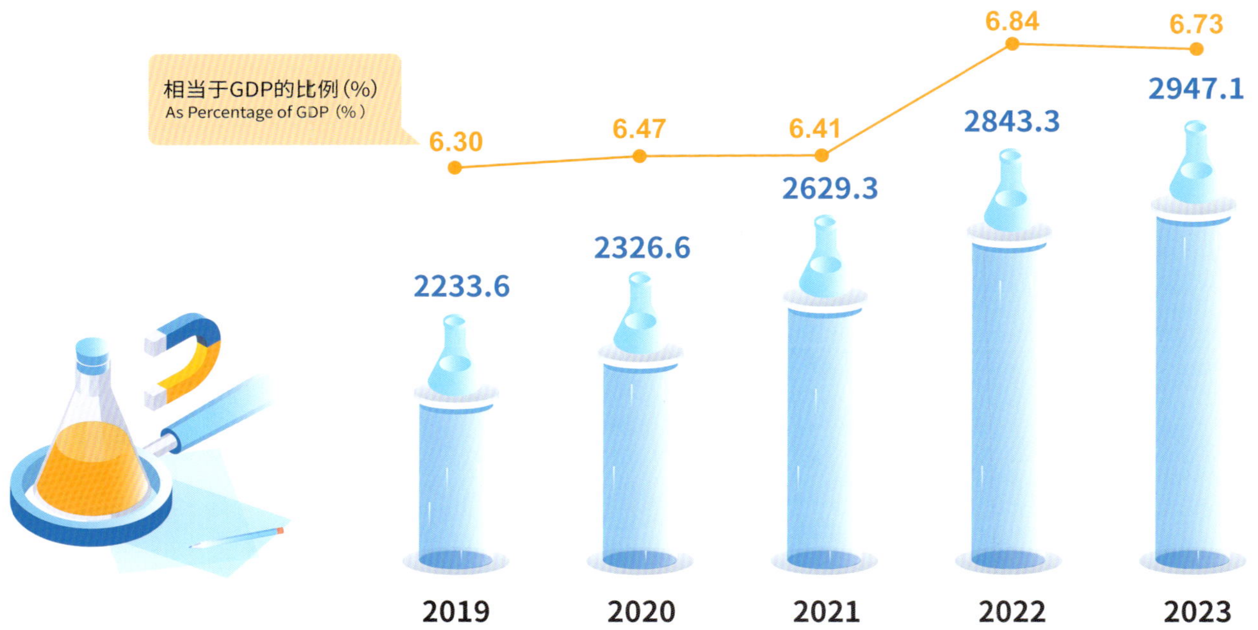

技术合同成交总额(亿元)
Total Volume of Transaction of Technical Contracts (100 million yuan)

专利和发明专利授权量(件)
Patent and Invention Patent Granted (piece)

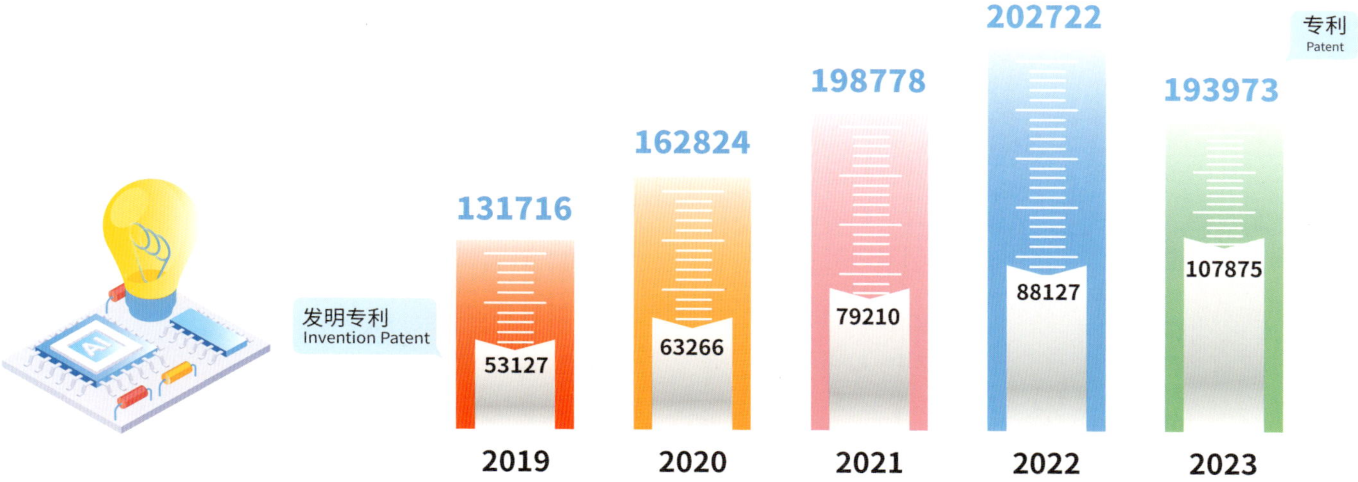

中关村国家自主创新示范区企业收入(亿元)
Revenue of Enterprise in Zhongguancun National Independent Innovation Demonstration Zone (100 million yuan)

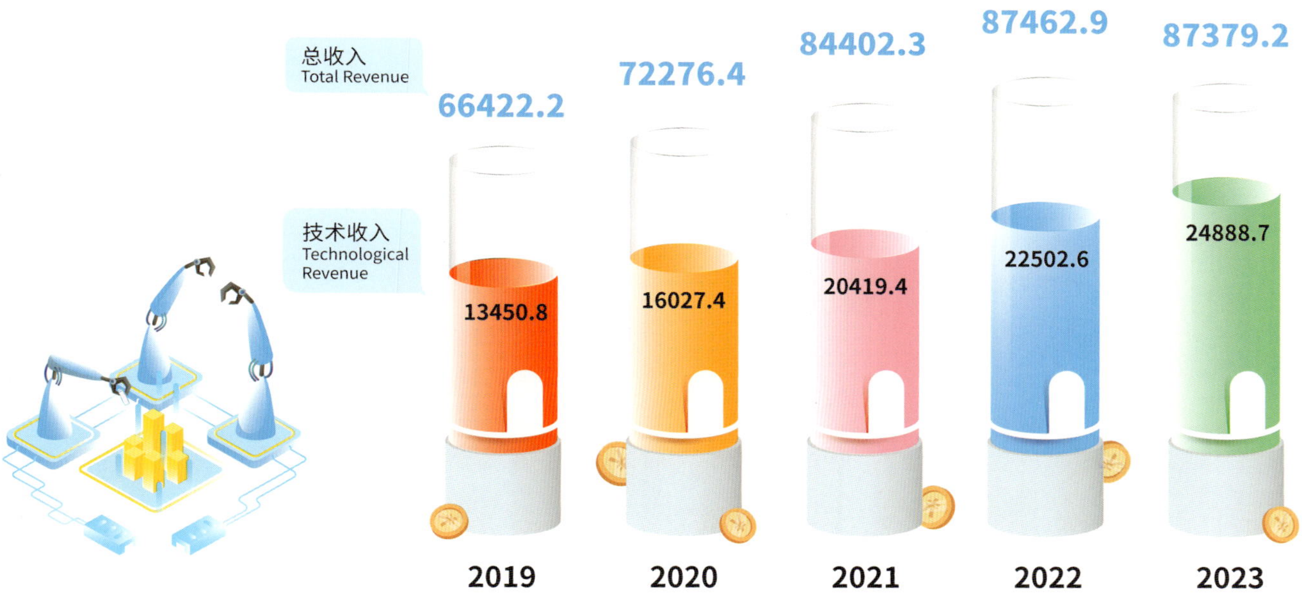

公共服务
PUBLIC SERVICE

教育
Education

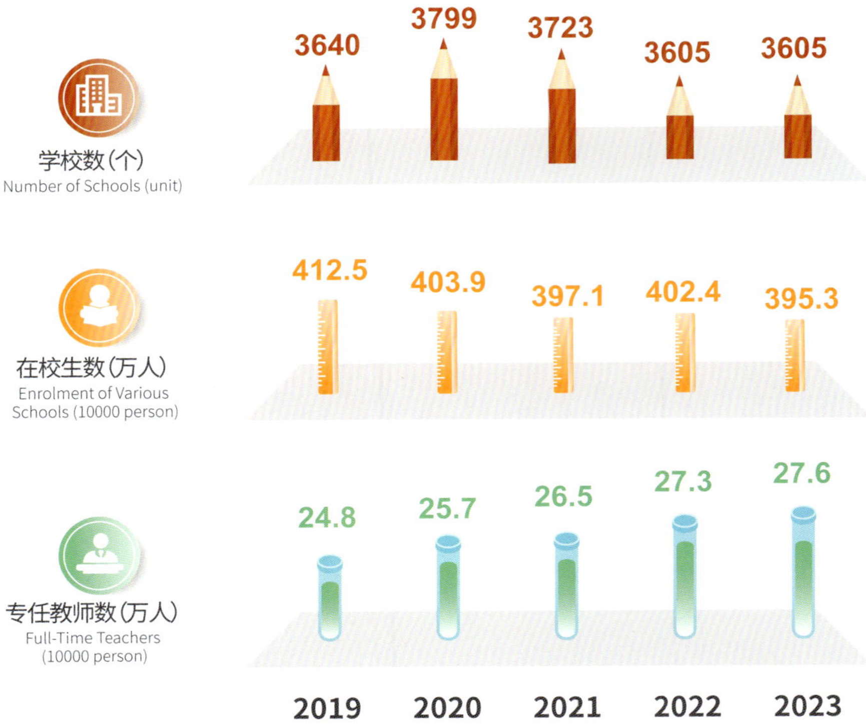

卫生
Health

每千常住人口执业(助理)医师数(人)
Licensed Physicians & Physician Assistants per 1000 Resident Population(person)

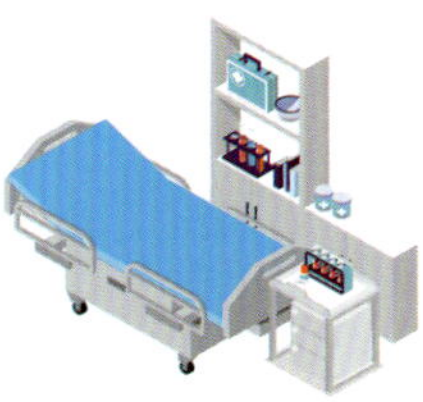

每千常住人口医院床位数(张)
Hospital Beds per 1000 Resident Population(unit)

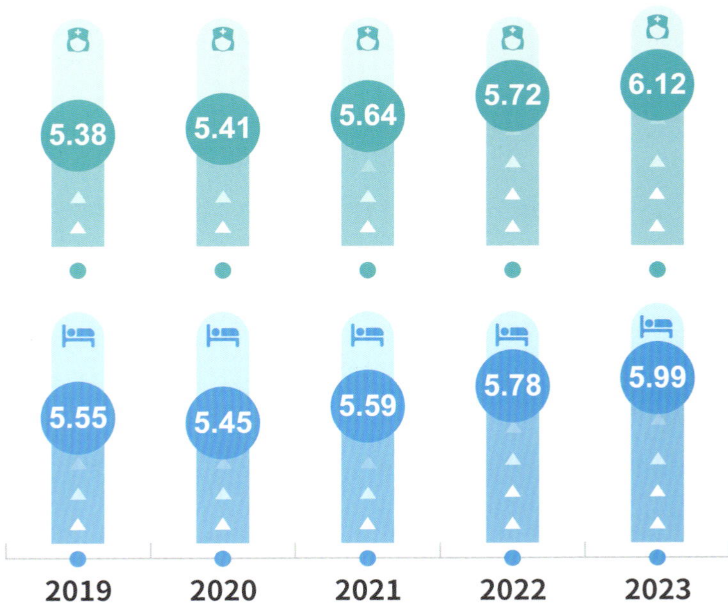

文化
Culture

指标 Indicator	2019	2020	2021	2022	2023
公共图书馆总藏数(万册、万件) Total Collections of Public Libraries (10000 copies)	7048	7241	7548	7819	8099
文物局系统内博物馆及文物保护管理机构参观人次(万人次) Visitors of Museums and Other Cultural Relics Preservation Agencies under the Municipal Cultural Heritage Bureau(10000 person-times)	2530.8	562.9	1019.0	413.3	1829.0
电影放映场次(万场次) Show Times of Films (10000 Times)	356.2	146.0	335.4	262.9	338.0

交通
Traffic

指标 Indicator	2019	2020	2021	2022	2023
公共汽电车客运量(万人次) Passengers Traffic of Public Buses and Trolley Buses (10000 person-times)	313366	182567	229634	172558	208656
城市轨道交通客运量(万人次) Passengers Traffic of Urban Rail Transit (10000 person-times)	396238	229400	308992	226331	345374

社会保障
SOCIAL SECURITY

指标 Item	2019	2020	2021	2022	2023
职工最低工资（元/月） Minimum Wages of Employed Persons (yuan/month)	2200	2200	2320	2320	2420
失业保险金最低标准（元/月） Minimum Unemployment Insurance (yuan/month)	1706	1816	2034	2034	2124
城乡居民最低生活保障标准（元/月） Minimum Living Allowance for Urban and Rural Residents (yuan/month)	1100	1170	1245	1320	1395
参加企业职工基本养老保险人数（万人） Participants of Basic Endowment Insurance for Enterprise Employed Persons (10000 persons)	1651.6	1679.9	1725.1	1764.7	1801.5
参加职工基本医疗保险人数（万人） Participants of Basic Medical Insurance for Employed Persons (10000 persons)	1682.5	1741.6	1486.0	1499.4	1504.7

注：自2021年9月起，"参加职工基本医疗保险人数"统计口径进行调整，去除6个月及以上未缴费人员，按调整后口径计算，2020年参加职工基本医疗保险人数为1450.7万人。

Note: Since September 2021, the statistical coverage of the "participants of basic medical insurance for employed persons" has been adjusted and those who failed to make payment for 6 months or more have been excluded. Calculated according to the adjusted coverage, the participants of basic medical insurance for employed persons totaled 14.507 million in 2020. Data for the previous years have not been adjusted according to the new caliber.

《北京统计年鉴 2024》
编辑委员会及编辑工作人员

使用指南

《北京统计年鉴》是一部按年连续出版的大型统计资料书，通过大量的统计数据记录北京市一年来经济社会发展变化情况，是国内外各界人士了解北京、认识北京的重要资料工具书。

一、关于框架结构

（一）总体结构

本年鉴整体框架保持稳定，彩页部分以图文并茂的形式反映北京市主要经济社会指标发展变化趋势；统计表是年鉴的主体内容，主要包括综合，国民经济核算，人口与就业，价格指数，人民生活，财政与税收，能源、资源和环境，城市公用事业，固定资产投资和房地产开发，对外经济贸易，农业及农村经济，工业，建筑业，第三产业，交通运输邮电业，批发和零售业、住宿和餐饮业，旅游业，金融业，科技，教育，卫生及社会服务，文化和体育，公共管理、社会保障和社会组织，开发区等 24 个章节，从多领域、多行业反映北京市经济和社会发展情况。

（二）章节结构

章节内结构：每一章节由简要说明、统计表和主要统计指标解释三部分组成。其中，简要说明在每一章节首页，主要介绍该章节的主要内容、统计范围、指标口径和历史数据调整方法；统计指标解释在每章节尾页，主要对本章节内所涉及的主要指标、计算方法等做简要解释。

统计表排列：每一章节从反映该领域主要情况出发编排统计表内容。统计表的排列顺序一般先是主要指标历史数据表，后为当年数据表。

二、关于使用方法

（一）年份

书名中标注的年份为出版年份，年鉴中最新数据为上一年数据。例如，《北京统计年鉴 2024》表示该年鉴为 2024 年出版，年鉴中最新数据年份截至 2023 年。

统计表名中的“年份”主要有三种标识方法，分别代表三种含义：一是“表格名称（****-****年）”表示表内所列数据是包含了这两个年份之间的各年资料；二是统计表名中未显示年份，表示表内所列数据为当年和上年两年数据；三是“表格名称（****年）”表示表内所列数据仅为某一年资料。

（二）符号

统计表中常见符号如下：

：表示总计中的其中项；有“#”号的分组指标表示总计的部分项目，无“#”号的分组指标则表示其中项之和等于总计。

‖ ：宾栏中的“‖”为分组符号，代表某个指标存在几种分组数据。

… ：表示该数据不足该表最小计量单位数。

空格：表示该项指标数据不详或没有数据。

*** ：在可能根据数据识别或者推断单个统计调查对象身份时，予以屏蔽处理，以“***”表示。

（三）数据

1.本年鉴各章节均包含历史数据表和当年数据表两部分。历史数据表中的历史数据原则上可以连续使用，部分历史数据有调整的，以最新出版的年鉴为准，使用时需留意简要说明、表下注释中对制度方法、口径范围等变化情况的说明。当年数据表中如指标的口径范围、计算方法以及与上年度数据相比变化较大时，也会在表下注释中进行说明。

2.与 2023 年版统计年鉴相比，主要做了如下修订：部分章节涉及的“按登记注册类型”分组调整为“按登记注册统计类别分”，对应调整分组项；在国民经济核算章节中增加“知识产权（专利）密集型产业增加值”数据；在人民生活章节中增加“全市居民家庭每百户拥有新能源汽车”数据；对人口与就业、价格指数、人民生活、工业、第三产业、交通运输邮电业、科技、卫生及社会服务、文化和体育、开发区等部分章节内容进行了调整。

（四）电子光盘

《北京统计年鉴》配有电子光盘，包括中文和英文两种语言的版本，辅助用户对数据进行加工处理。

（五）本年鉴中部分数据合计数或相对数由于单位取舍不同而产生的计算误差，均未作机械调整。

USER GUIDE

Beijing Statistical Yearbook is a large statistical book published continuously on a chronological basis. With a great deal of statistical data, this Yearbook gives a reflection of the economic and social development and changes in Beijing over the past year. It serves as an important reference book for domestic and foreign personnel in all circles to understand and know Beijing.

I. Framework Structure

(I) Overall Structure

The overall structure of *Beijing Statistical Yearbook* remains stable. In color pages, the development and changing trends of main economic and social indicators of Beijing have been presented with both illustration and pictures; statistical tables are the main part of this Yearbook, mainly including 24 chapters, i.e. General Survey; National Accounts; Population and Employment; Price Index; People's Living Conditions; Government Finance and Taxation; Energy, Resources and Environment; Public Utilities; Investment in Fixed Assets and Real Estate Development; Foreign Economic Relations and Trade; Agriculture and Rural Economy; Industry; Construction; Tertiary Industry; Transport, Post and Telecommunication Services; Wholesale and Retail Trade, Accommodation and Restaurants; Tourism; Finance; Science and Technology; Education; Health and Social Services; Culture and Sports; Public Management, Social Security and Social Organization; and Development Zones, reflecting the economic and social development situation across the city through multiple fields and industries.

(II) Structure of Chapters

Internal structure of chapters in this Yearbook: Each chapter is composed of the Brief Introduction, Statistical Tables and Explanatory Notes to Main Statistical Indicators. Thereinto, Brief Introduction appears on the first page of each chapter, mainly introducing the main content, statistical scope, indicator standards, method of adjustment to historical data in each chapter; Explanatory Notes to Statistical Indicators come on the last page of each chapter, mainly giving a brief explanation to the main indicators and calculation method, etc. involved in the chapter.

Arrangement of statistical tables: In each chapter, statistical tables are arranged for the purpose of reflecting the main conditions in the field. Generally speaking, main indicators historical data tables come before current year data tables.

II. How to Use

(I) Years

The year indicated in the title of the book is the year of publication. The latest data indicated in this Yearbook are data in the previous years. For example, this book is titled *2024 Beijing Statistical Yearbook*, which means it will be published in 2024 while the latest data in the book is by the end of 2023.

"Years" in the statistical tables are marked in three ways, each indicating a different meaning. Firstly, the statistical table is named "****** (AAAA- BBBB)", which refers to that the data listed in the table are those from the year of AAAA to BBBB; Secondly, the statistical table contains no years, indicating that the data listed in the table are those of current year and last year; Thirdly, the statistical table is named "****** (AAAA)", indicating that the data listed in the table are those of the year of AAAA.

(II) Symbols

Symbols in statistical tables include:

#: means that the item is included in the total. Grouped indicators marked with "#" are part of the total, while those without "#" mean that sum of included items equals to the total.

||: grouping symbol, means that there are multiple ways of grouping the indicators.

…: means that the figure is less than the minimum measurement unit of the table.

Blank: means that the figure is unknown or unavailable.

: When it is possible to identify or infer the identity of the individual statistical respondent based on the data, it shall be shielded and indicated with "".

(III) Data

1. Each chapter in this Yearbook consists of two parts: historical data tables and current year data tables. In principle, historical data that are shown in the historical data tables can be used continuously; for some historical data that have been adjusted, please refer to the latest yearbook; When using the data, it is necessary to refer to the Brief Introduction and the explanations on the change in method system, standards and scope in the Notes under the statistical tables. In the current year data tables, if the standards and scope, calculation method for the corresponding indicators, and certain data greatly differ from that of the previous year, they shall be explained in the Notes under the statistical tables.

2. Compared with the Statistical Yearbook of 2023 edition, there are mainly the following revisions: classification "By Registration Type" in some chapters is adjusted to "Classified by the Statistical Category of Registration", and the classified items have been adjusted accordingly; data on "added value of intellectual property right (patent) intensive industry" is added in the Chapter of "National Accounts"; data on "new energy vehicles per 100 households of the whole city" is added in the chapter of "People's Living Conditions"; adjustments have been made to the content of some chapters including Population and Employment, Price Index, People's Living Conditions, Industry, Tertiary Industry, Transport, Post and Telecommunication Services, Science and Technology, Health and Social Services, Culture and Sports, and Development Zones.

(IV) Electronic CD-ROM

Beijing Statistical Yearbook is provided with a CD-ROM, which contains Chinese and English versions of this Yearbook. The CD-ROM helps users in working with and processing the data.

(V) The sum of some statistics or some relative numbers in this Yearbook might have certain calculation errors because of the choice of different units of measurement. All the statistics have not undergone mechanical adjustment.

目 录

Contents

一、综合

GENERAL SURVEY

二、国民经济核算
NATIONAL ACCOUNTS

三、人口与就业
POPULATION AND EMPLOYMENT

四、价格指数
PRICE INDEX

五、人民生活
PEOPLE'S LIVING CONDITIONS

六、财政与税收
GOVERNMENT FINANCE AND TAX REVENUES

七、能源、资源和环境
ENERGY, RESOURCES AND ENVIRONMENT

八、城市公用事业
PUBLIC UTILITIES

九、固定资产投资和房地产开发
INVESTMENT IN FIXED ASSETS AND REAL ESTATE DEVELOPMENT

十、对外经济贸易
FOREIGN ECONOMIC RELATIONS AND TRADE

十一、农业及农村经济
AGRICULTURE AND RURAL ECONOMY

十二、工业
INDUSTRY

十三、建筑业
CONSTRUCTION

十四、第三产业
TERTIARY INDUSTRY

十七、旅游业
TOURISM

十八、金融业
FINANCE

十九、科技
SCIENCE AND TECHNOLOGY

二十、教育
EDUCATION

二十一、卫生及社会服务
HEALTH AND SOCIAL SERVICES

二十二、文化和体育
CULTURE AND SPORTS

二十三、公共管理、社会保障和社会组织
PUBLIC MANAGEMENT, SOCIAL SECURITY AND SOCIAL ORGANIZATION

二十四、开发区
DEVELOPMENT ZONES

01

综　合
GENERAL SURVEY

简要说明

一、主要内容

本章资料包括北京市行政区划，全市经济社会发展的主要指标以及“十四五”时期监测指标，法人及产业活动单位数，私营个体、非公经济、中小微型企业基本情况等。

二、有关统计标准的变化说明

（一）《国民经济行业分类》（GB/T 4754-2002）与《国民经济行业分类》（GB/T 4754-94）主要框架结构变化：

1.增加的门类：(1)信息传输、计算机服务和软件业；(2)租赁和商务服务业；(3)住宿和餐饮业；(4)水利、环境和公共设施管理业；(5)教育；(6)国际组织。

2.名称或范围进行调整的门类：(1)农、林、牧、渔业；(2)采矿业；(3)制造业；(4)交通运输、仓储和邮政业；(5)批发和零售业；(6)金融业；(7)科学研究、技术服务和地质勘查业；(8)居民服务和其他服务业；(9)卫生、社会保障和社会福利业；(10)文化、体育和娱乐业；(11)公共管理和社会组织。

3.取消的门类：(1)地质勘查、水利管理；(2)其他行业。

（二）《国民经济行业分类》（GB/T 4754-2011）与《国民经济行业分类》（GB/T 4754-2002）主要框架结构变化：

1.门类名称调整：(1)“电力、燃气及水的生产和供应业”更名为“电力、热力、燃气及水生产和供应业”；(2)“信息传输、计算机服务和软件业”更名为“信息传输、软件和信息技术服务业”；(3)“科学研究、技术服务和地质勘查业”更名为“科学研究和技术服务业”；(4)“居民服务和其他服务业”更名为“居民服务、修理和其他服务业”；(5)“卫生、社会保障和社会福利业”更名为“卫生和社会工作”；(6)“公共管理和社会组织”更名为“公共管理、社会保障和社会组织”。

2.门类顺序调整：(1)“批发和零售业”调至“交通运输、仓储和邮政业”之前；(2)“住宿和餐饮业”调至“交通运输、仓储和邮政业”之后。

3.门类范围调整：(1)农、林、牧、渔业；(2)制造业；(3)交通运输、仓储和邮政业；(4)信息传输、软件和信息技术服务业；(5)金融业；(6)租赁和商务服务业；(7)科学研究和技术服务业；(8)居民服务、修理和其他服务业；(9)教育；(10)卫生和社会工作；(11)文化、体育和娱乐业；(12)公共管理、社会保障和社会组织。

（三）《国民经济行业分类》（GB/T 4754-2017）与原（GB/T 4754-2011）门类名称和门类位次无调整。

Brief Introduction

I. Main Content

Statistics in this chapter mainly show the basic information of administrative divisions of Beijing, main indicators for social and economic development of the city, and monitoring indicators for the 14th Five-Year Plan, number of corporate and industrial entities, non-public economy, small-, medium- and micro-sized enterprises, etc.

II. Adjustment to Historical Statistics According to New Industrial Standards

(I) Changes to the main framework of the *Classification and Codes of National Economic Sectors (GB/T 4754-2002)* as compared with the previous version *(GB/T 4754-94)*:

1. Sectors added: (1) information transmission, computer service and software; (2) renting and leasing activities and business services; (3) accommodation and restaurants; (4) management of water conservancy, environment and public facilities; (5) education; (6) international organizations.

2. Sectors with name or range changed: (1) agriculture, forestry,animal husbandry and fishery; (2) mining; (3) manufacturing; (4) transport, storage and post; (5) wholesale and retail trade; (6) finance; (7) scientific research, technical service, geological prospecting; (8) resident service and other service; (9) health, social security, and social welfare; (10) culture, sports and recreation; (11) public administration and social organizations.

3. Sectors cancelled: (1) geological prospecting, water conservancy management; (2) other sectors.

(II)Compared with the previous *(GB/T 4754-2002)* version, the *Classification of National Economic Sectors (GB/T 4754-2011)* mainly involves the following framework changes:

1. Changes to the name of categories: (1) The "electric power, gas and water production and supply" is renamed "production and supply of electricity, heating , gas and water"; (2) the "information transmission, computer service and software" is renamed "information transmission, software and information technology services"; (3) the "scientific research, technical service and geological prospecting" is renamed "scientific research and development, technical services"; (4) the "resident service and other service" is renamed "resident services, repair and other services"; (5) the "health, social security and social welfare" is renamed "health and social works"; (6) "public administration and social organization" is renamed "public administration, social security and social organizations".

2. Changes to the order of categories: (1) the "wholesale and retail trade" is put before the "transport, storage and post"; (2) the "accommodation and catering" is put after the "transport, storage and post".

3. Changes to the scope of categories: (1) agriculture, forestry,animal husbandry and fishery; (2) manufacturing; (3) transport, storage and post; (4) information transmission, software and information technology services; (5) finance; (6) leasing and business services; (7) scientific research and technical service; (8) resident services, repair and other services; (9) education; (10) health and social works; (11) culture, sports and entertainment; (12) public administration, social security and social organizations.

(III) Compared with the previous *(GB/T 4754-2011)* version, no adjustment has been made in the name of categories and the order of categories in the *Classification of National Economic Sectors (GB/T 4754-2017)* version.

1-1 行政区划(2023年)
ADMINISTRATIVE AREAS(2023)

单位：个 (unit)

地 区	District	街道办事处 Sub-district Office	建制镇 Designated Town	建制乡 Designated Township	社区居委会 Community Neighborhood Committee	村民委员会 Villagers' Committee
全 市	**Total**	**165**	**143**	**35**	**3568**	**3768**
东城区	Dongcheng District	17			168	
西城区	Xicheng District	15			263	
朝阳区	Chaoyang District	24		19	606	144
丰台区	Fengtai District	24	2		367	56
石景山区	Shijingshan District	9			153	
海淀区	Haidian District	22	7		601	40
门头沟区	Mentougou District	4	9		122	178
房山区	Fangshan District	8	14	6	203	459
通州区	Tongzhou District	11	10	1	166	470
顺义区	Shunyi District	6	19		162	426
昌平区	Changping District	8	14		279	298
大兴区	Daxing District	8	14		238	437
怀柔区	Huairou District	2	12	2	36	284
平谷区	Pinggu District	2	14	2	51	272
密云区	Miyun District	2	17	1	96	330
延庆区	Yanqing District	3	11	4	57	374

资料来源：北京市民政局。
Source: Beijing Municipal Civil Affairs Bureau.

1-2 主要经济指标增长速度(1979-2023年)

单位：%

年 份 Year	地区生产总值比上年增长 YoY Growth Rate of Gross Domestic Product	农林牧渔业总产值比上年增长 YoY Growth Rate of Gross Output Value of Agriculture, Forestry, Animal Husbandry and Fishery	规模以上工业总产值比上年增长 YoY Growth Rate of Gross Output Value of Industry above Designated Size	固定资产投资比上年增长 YoY Growth Rate of Investment in Fixed Assets	社会消费品零售总额比上年增长 YoY Growth Rate of Total Retail of Consumer Goods
1979	9.7	7.0		17.3	20.6
1980	11.8	16.3		25.3	17.8
1981	-0.5	4.2		10.2	12.6
1982	7.4	12.8		5.5	6.6
1983	16.4	16.7		32.9	14.6
1984	17.4	13.3		29.2	22.5
1985	8.7	16.7	17.4	41.8	27.0
1986	8.0	8.5	3.8	13.0	15.3
1987	9.6	22.4	15.2	28.2	21.9
1988	12.8	52.9	27.9	19.7	35.5
1989	4.4	14.8	21.6	-14.4	15.2
1990	5.2	16.2	3.8	28.5	17.1
1991	9.9	9.0	16.7	7.1	18.3
1992	11.3	10.5	17.8	38.5	23.2
1993	12.3	18.8	35.7	54.3	22.4
1994	13.7	43.7	35.1	58.1	26.4
1995	12.0	13.9	-5.3	29.7	24.9
1996	9.3	2.7	6.5	4.2	12.5
1997	10.2	0.9	14.4	9.6	14.7
1998	9.6	2.5	7.0	20.2	14.5
1999	11.0	3.3	12.1	1.3	10.7
2000	12.0	4.4	30.2	10.8	10.7
2001	11.8	7.2	15.1	18.0	11.2
2002	11.8	5.6	10.7	18.5	10.3
2003	11.1	5.2	21.8	18.9	15.4
2004	13.3	4.5	30.0	17.2	15.7
2005	12.3	1.9	21.2	11.8	11.7
2006	12.8	0.4	18.2	19.3	14.0
2007	14.4	13.4	17.5	17.6	17.3
2008	9.0	11.6	7.9	-3.0	22.1
2009	10.0	3.6	6.0	26.2	16.8
2010	10.4	4.1	24.1	13.1	18.5
2011	8.1	10.7	5.9	13.3	14.6
2012	7.7	9.0	7.5	9.3	13.3
2013	7.7	6.6	11.4	8.8	10.0
2014	7.4	-0.4	6.2	7.5	9.4
2015	6.9	-12.3	-5.4	5.7	8.1
2016	6.9	-8.2	3.7	5.9	7.0
2017	6.8	-8.8	4.5	5.7	6.1
2018	6.7	-3.7	4.1	-9.9	3.5
2019	6.1	-5.1	3.6	-2.4	4.4
2020	1.1	-6.5	2.4	2.2	-8.9
2021	8.8	2.3	19.7	4.9	8.4
2022	0.7	-0.5	-4.5	3.6	-7.2
2023	5.2	-5.8	3.3	4.9	4.8

注：1.地区生产总值增长速度按不变价格计算。
2.自2011年起，固定资产投资统计起点由50万元调整至500万元。固定资产投资增长速度按可比口径计算。
3.2018年及以前，固定资产投资数据为全社会口径，自2019年起为不含农户口径，下同。
4.进出口总值增长速度为以美元计价的进出口总值增长速度，以人民币计价，2023年进出口总值增长0.06%。

ANNUAL GROWTH RATE OF MAIN ECONOMIC INDICATORS (1979-2023)

(%)

进出口总值比上年增长 YoY Growth Rate of Gross Value of Imports & Exports	居民消费价格指数(上年=100) Consumer Price Indices (Previous year=100)	城镇居民人均可支配收入 Per capita Disposable Income of Urban Households		农村居民人均可支配收入 Per capita Disposable Income of Rural Households	
		比上年名义增长 Nominal Growth Rate as Compared with That in the Previous year	比上年实际增长 Real Growth Rate as Compared with That in the Previous year	比上年名义增长 Normal Growth Rate as Compared with That in the Previous year	比上年实际增长 Real Growth Rate as Compared with That in the Previous year
	101.8	13.6	11.6	11.2	9.2
	106.0	20.8	14.0	16.2	9.6
	101.3	10.7	9.3	20.7	19.2
	101.8	1.1	-0.7	23.4	21.2
	100.5	5.2	4.7	20.1	19.5
16.3	102.2	17.5	15.0	27.9	25.2
-8.6	117.6	30.8	11.2	16.7	-0.8
-6.0	106.8	17.6	10.1	6.2	-0.6
-12.7	108.6	10.7	1.9	11.3	2.5
11.9	120.4	21.6	1.0	16.0	-3.7
-4.3	117.2	11.1	-5.2	15.8	-1.2
-17.4	105.4	19.1	13.0	5.4	-0.04
2.5	111.9	14.1	2.0	9.7	-2.0
3.1	109.9	17.8	7.2	10.5	0.6
11.7	119.0	38.8	16.6	19.8	0.7
3.5	124.9	43.4	14.8	27.5	2.1
28.2	117.3	22.6	4.5	34.3	14.5
-20.8	111.6	17.6	5.4	10.5	-1.0
3.7	105.3	6.6	1.2	2.8	-2.4
0.4	102.4	9.3	6.7	7.4	4.9
12.6	100.6	9.2	8.5	6.4	5.8
43.8	103.5	13.6	9.8	8.4	4.7
4.2	103.1	12.7	9.3	8.6	5.3
2.0	98.2	8.5	10.5	6.9	8.9
30.5	100.2	12.2	12.0	3.2	3.0
38.1	101.0	13.5	12.4	9.6	8.5
32.7	101.5	13.8	12.1	18.4	16.7
25.9	100.9	14.1	13.1	12.0	11.0
22.1	102.4	10.9	8.3	13.4	10.7
40.8	105.1	13.3	7.8	12.3	6.9
-20.9	98.5	9.0	10.7	8.9	10.6
40.4	102.4	9.6	7.0	13.0	10.4
29.1	105.6	13.2	7.2	11.1	5.2
4.8	103.3	10.8	7.3	11.8	8.2
5.4	103.3	10.6	7.1	11.3	7.7
-3.4	101.6	8.9	7.2	10.3	8.6
-23.1	101.8	8.9	7.0	9.0	7.1
-11.6	101.4	8.4	6.9	8.5	7.0
14.6	101.9	9.0	7.0	8.7	6.7
27.4	102.5	8.9	6.2	9.3	6.6
0.9	102.3	8.6	6.2	9.2	6.7
-19.5	101.7	2.4	0.7	4.1	2.4
40.6	101.1	7.8	6.6	10.5	9.3
16.0	101.8	3.1	1.3	4.4	2.6
-5.1	100.4	5.5	5.1	7.5	7.1

Note: a) The growth rates of GDP are calculated at constant price.

b) Since 2011, the statistical threshold of investment in fixed assets has been adjusted from RMB 500,000 to RMB 5 million. The growth rates of investment in fixed assets are calculated on a comparable basis.

c) In and before 2018, the data on investment in fixed assets were those of full coverage. Since 2019, the data were those that excluding rural households, the same below.

d) The growth rate of gross value of imports & exports refer to the growth rate of gross value of imports & exports calculated in USD. Calculated in RMB, the growth rate of gross value of imports & exports is 0.06% in 2023.

1-3 主要年份国民经济和社会发展总量指标

项　目		Item		1990
人口与就业		**Population and Employment**		
年末全市常住人口	(万人)	Year-end Resident Population	(10000 persons)	1086.0
#城镇人口		Urban Population		798.0
年末户籍人口	(万人)	Year-end Registered Population	(10000 persons)	1032.2
常住就业人口	(万人)	Resident Employed Population	(10000 persons)	
城镇非私营单位在岗职工平均工资	(元)	Average Wages of Employed Persons in Urban Non-Private Units	(yuan)	2653
年末实有城镇登记失业人员	(万人)	Year-end Number of Actual Registered Unemployed Persons in Urban Areas	(10000 persons)	1.67
国民经济核算		**National Accounts**		
地区生产总值	(亿元)	Gross Domestic Product	(100 million yuan)	500.8
人均地区生产总值	(元)	Per Capita Gross Domestic Product	(yuan)	4635
价格指数(上年=100)		**Price Indices (Preceding Year=100)**		
居民消费价格指数		Consumer Price Index		105.4
工业生产者出厂价格指数		Producer Price Index for Industrial Products		107.9
人民生活		**People's Livelihoods**		
全市居民人均可支配收入	(元)	Per Capita Disposable Income of Households of the Whole City	(yuan)	1741
全市居民人均消费支出	(元)	Per Capita Consumption Expenditures of Households of the Whole City	(yuan)	1469
财　政		**Government Finance**		
一般公共预算收入	(亿元)	General Public Budget Revenue	(100 million yuan)	
一般公共预算支出	(亿元)	General Public Budget Expenditure	(100 million yuan)	
能源、资源和环境		**Energy, Resources and Environment**		
能源消费总量	(万吨标准煤)	Total Energy Consumption	(10000 tons of SCE)	2709.7
水资源总量	(亿立方米)	Total Volume of Water Resource	(100 million cu.m)	36.9
城市绿化覆盖率	(%)	City Greening Coverage	(%)	28.0
城市公用事业		**City Public Utilities**		
全社会用电量	(亿千瓦时)	Electricity Consumption	(100 million kW·h)	150.5
自来水销售总量	(亿立方米)	Total Water Resources	(100 million cu.m)	5.3
居民燃气用户	(万户)	Households Gas Users	(10000 households)	176.1
公共交通客运量	(亿人次)	Passengers Traffic of Public Transport	(100 million person-times)	33.5
污水处理率	(%)	Sewage Disposal Rate	(%)	7.3

注：1.2015年常住人口数据根据北京市第七次全国人口普查结果进行了修订，下同。
2.2014年以前年末实有登记失业人员为城镇口径，2014—2019年调整为全市口径。自2020年9月起，对城镇登记失业人员相关统计口径进行调整，将离校未就业高校毕业生、领取失业补助金人员和领取一次性生活补助农民工纳入登记失业人员范围，下同。
3.地区生产总值绝对值按当年价格计算。2015年人均地区生产总值数据根据北京市第七次全国人口普查结果进行了修订，2023年为初步核算数据，下同。
4.城镇非私营单位在岗职工平均工资2000年及以前数据为职工口径，职工包括在岗职工和不在岗职工；自2001年起，调整为在岗职工口径。2007年及以前城镇单位在岗职工工资包括乡及乡以上独立核算法人单位，不包括乡镇企业和个体工商户；自2008年起不包括个体工商户的独立核算法人单位。
5.自2012年起，自来水数据口径调整为城镇公共供水。

AGGREGATE INDICATORS ON NATIONAL ECONOMIC AND SOCIAL DEVELOPMENT IN KEY YEARS

1995	2000	2005	2010	2015	2020	2022	2023
1251.1	1363.6	1538.0	1961.9	2188.3	2189.0	2184.3	2185.8
946.2	1057.4	1286.1	1686.4	1897.5	1916.4	1912.8	1919.8
1070.3	1107.5	1180.7	1257.8	1345.2	1400.8	1427.7	1431.2
			1067.3	1164.4	1163.8	1132.1	1129.0
8144	15726	34191	65683	113073	185026	215143	224562
2.19	3.32	10.57	7.73	9.16	29.02	36.39	35.74
1516.2	3277.8	7149.8	14964.0	24779.1	35943.3	41540.9	43760.7
12762	25014	47182	78307	113692	164158	189988	200278
117.3	103.5	101.5	102.4	101.8	101.7	101.8	100.4
107.3	102.5	101.3	102.2	96.9	99.1	102.3	99.2
5501	9230	16853	29228	48458	69434	77415	81752
4366	7644	13289	21834	33803	38903	42683	47586
	345.0	919.2	2353.9	4723.9	5483.9	5714.4	6181.1
	443.0	1058.3	2717.3	5737.7	7116.2	7469.2	7971.2
3533.3	4144.0	5049.8	6359.5	6802.8	6762.1	6896.9	7571.3
30.3	16.9	23.2	23.1	26.8	25.8	23.7	41.5
32.7	36.5	42.0	45.0	48.4	49.0	49.8	49.8
222.6	384.4	570.5	809.9	952.7	1140.0	1280.8	1357.8
6.8	7.5	7.2	8.9	10.4	11.2	12.3	12.8
219.8	291.9	462.6	634.2	885.7	902.2	973.6	993.3
37.2	40.7	51.8	69.0	73.8	41.2	39.9	55.4
19.4	39.4	62.4	81.0	87.9	95.0	97.0	97.3

Note: a)The data on resident population for 2015 have been revised according to the results of the Seventh National Population Census of Beijing, the same below.

b) The year-end number of actual registered unemployed persons before 2014 referred to the statistic in urban area and was adjusted to the statistic of the whole city from 2014 to 2019. The relevant statistical coverage of the registered unemployed persons in urban area was adjusted since September 2020, the unemployed college graduates, the personnel receiving unemployment compensation and the rural migrant workers receiving lump-sum living allowance were included in the list of registered unemployed persons; the same below.

c) The absolute values of GDP are calculated at current prices. The data on per capita GDP for 2015 have been revised according to the results of the Seventh National Population Census of Beijing, and the data for 2022 are the preliminary accounting data,the same below.

d) Data on average wages of employed persons in urban non-private entities in and before 2000 referred to that of staff and workers which included both fully employed staff and workers and the off-the-job ones. Since 2001, the data were adjusted to statistical range of fully employed staff and workers. In and before 2007, data on wages of employed persons in urban entities covered that of the legal entities with independent accounting at and above township level, excluding township enterprises and self-employed businesses;since 2008,such data have excluded that of the legal entities with independent accounting of self-employed businesses.

e) Since 2012, the statistical coverage of tap water data was adjusted to urban public water supply.

1-3 续表 1

项目		Item		1990
固定资产投资		**Investment in Fixed Assets**		
固定资产投资	(亿元)	Total Investment in Fixed Assets	(100 million yuan)	179.2
#基础设施投资		Infrastructure Investment		31.6
#房地产开发投资		Investment in Real Estate Development		22.5
对外经济贸易		**International Trade and Economic Cooperation**		
地区货物进出口总值	(亿美元)	Gross Value of Imports and Exports of Local Goods	(100 million USD)	236.4
地区货物进出口总值	(亿元)	Gross Value of Imports and Exports of Local Goods	(100 million yuan)	
实际利用外商直接投资额	(亿美元)	Amount of Foreign Direct Investment Actually Utilized	(100 million USD)	
农 业		**Agriculture**		
农林牧渔业总产值(当年价格)	(亿元)	Gross Output Value of Agriculture, Forestry,Animal Husbandry and Fishery(at current prices)	(100 million yuan)	70.2
工 业		**Industry**		
规模以上工业总产值(当年价格)	(亿元)	Gross Output Value of Industry above Designated Size (at current prices)	(100 million yuan)	625.9
规模以上工业主要财务指标		Principal Financial Indicators of Industry Enterprises Above Designated Size		
资产总计	(亿元)	Total Assets	(100 million yuan)	498.3
负债总额	(亿元)	Total Liabilities	(100 million yuan)	
营业收入	(亿元)	Businesses Revenue	(100 million yuan)	
利润总额	(亿元)	Total Profits	(100 million yuan)	48.9
建筑业		**Construction**		
建筑业总产值	(亿元)	Total Output Value of Construction	(100 million yuan)	94.7
交通运输邮电业		**Transport, Postal and Telecommunication Services**		
运 输		Transport		
货物周转量	(亿吨公里)	Freight Ton-Kilometers	(100 million ton-km)	268.8
旅客周转量	(亿人公里)	Passenger-Kilometers	(100 million passenger-km)	119.8
邮 电		Postal and Telecommunication Services		
邮政行业业务总量	(亿标准量)	Business Volume of Post Services	(volume in 100 million)	
电信业务总量	(亿元)	Business Volume of Telecommunication Services	(100 million yuan)	
固定电话用户	(万户)	Number of Fixed Telephone Subscribers	(10000 subscribers)	33.3
移动电话用户	(万户)	Number of Mobile Telephone Subscribers	(10000 subscribers)	0.3
批发和零售业、住宿和餐饮业		**Wholesale and Retail Trades, Hotels and Catering Services**		
社会消费品零售总额	(亿元)	Total Retail Sales of Consumer Goods	(100 million yuan)	345.1
旅游业		**Tourism**		
入境游客人数	(万人次)	Number of Overseas Visitor Arrivals	(10000 person-times)	100.0
国内游客人数	(万人次)	Domestic visitors	(10000 person-times)	
国际旅游收入	(亿美元)	Earnings from International Tourism	(USD 100 million)	6.6
国内旅游收入	(亿元)	Earnings from Domestic Tourism	(100 million yuan)	

注：1.自2011年起，固定资产投资统计起点由50万元调整至500万元。
2.2018年及以前固定资产投资为全社会口径，自2019年起为不含农户口径。
3.邮政行业业务总量与电信业务总量2000年及以前按1990年不变价格计算，2001—2010年按2000年不变价格计算，2011—2016年按2010年不变价格计算。2017—2020年，邮政行业业务总量按2010年不变价格计算，电信业务总量按2015年不变价格计算。自2021年起，邮政行业业务总量按2020年不变价格计算，电信业务总量按上年不变价格计算。

1—3 Continued 1

1995	2000	2005	2010	2015	2020	2022	2023
841.5	1297.4	2827.2	5493.5	7990.9			
156.1	351.9	610.7	1403.5	2174.5			
352.8	522.1	1525.0	2901.1	4226.3			
370.4	494.0	1255.1	3016.6	3194.2	3350.4	5465.0	5187.5
3108.2	4090.1	10331.9	20478.2	19827.7	23215.9	36445.5	36466.3
	16.8	35.3	53.4	127.2	133.9	174.1	137.1
164.4	188.6	239.3	328.0	368.2	263.4	268.2	252.6
1493.3	2842.0	6946.2	13699.8	17449.6	20879.3	23870.0	24652.2
2582.6	4612.7	12829.8	22750.6	38609.8	55167.0	66052.5	72994.0
1528.8	2676.4	4706.7	11548.1	18102.4	24193.8	29327.9	32590.1
			14807.1	19256.1	23849.0	27713.6	28950.6
85.3	127.1	413.5	1028.3	1597.7	1729.5	1998.7	1684.1
426.6	812.5	1894.0	5196.0	8436.7	12905.9	13726.8	14318.5
323.1	299.6	457.7	513.7	623.7	842.8	881.2	910.4
207.7	314.0	838.1	1399.5	1747.7	1015.0	573.3	1886.2
7.0	15.2	33.5	107.3	258.5	480.2	281.4	324.3
49.2	199.5	379.4	1066.8	923.4	3247.6	558.6	633.3
150.5	451.2	943.5	885.6	784.7	480.6	474.2	467.4
16.9	347.2	1459.8	2129.8	4051.6	3906.4	3926.9	4021.1
971.8	1760.3	3221.4	7273.0	12271.9	13716.4	13794.2	14462.7
207.0	282.1	362.9	490.1	420.0	34.1	24.1	116.8
6320.0	10186.0	12500.0	17900.0	26859.0	18352.4	18206.7	32736.9
21.8	27.7	36.2	50.4	46.1	4.8	4.4	16.6
352.6	683.0	1300.0	2425.1	4320.0	2880.9	2490.9	5731.2

Note: a) Since 2011,the statistical starting point of investment in fixed assets is changed from RMB 500,000 to RMB 5 million.
b)The data on investment in fixed assets in and before 2018 referred to that of the whole city; since 2019, the data refer to that excluding peasant households.
c) Business volume of postal and telecommunication services in and before 2000 was calculated at 1990 constant prices; that from 2001 to 2010 was calculated at 2000 constant prices; that of 2011-2016 was calculated at 2010 constant prices; since 2017 until 2020, the business volume of postal services was calculated at 2010 constant prices, and that of telecommunication services was calculated at the same price in 2015. Since 2021,the business volume of postal service was calculated at 2020 constant prices, and that of telecommunication services was calculated at the same price in the previous year.

1-3 续表 2

项目		Item		1990
金融业		**Financial Intermediation**		
金融机构(含外资)本外币存款余额	(亿元)	Balance of Local and Foreign Currency Deposits in Financial Institutions (Including Foreign Institutions)	(100 million yuan)	
金融机构(含外资)本外币贷款余额	(亿元)	Balance of Local and Foreign Currency Loans in Financial Institutions (Including Foreign Institutions)	(100 million yuan)	
原保险保费收入	(亿元)	Premiums Revenue	(100 million yuan)	
证券市场交易额	(亿元)	Trading Volume of Securities Market	(100 million yuan)	
科技		**Science and Technology**		
研究与试验发展经费内部支出	(亿元)	Internal Expenditure on R&D	(100 million yuan)	
技术合同成交总额	(亿元)	Total Volume of Transaction of Technological Contracts Concluded	(100 million yuan)	20.3
专利授权量	(件)	Patent Granted	(unit)	2268
教育		**Education**		
在校生数	(万人)	Patent Granted	(10000 persons)	
专任教师数	(万人)	Full-time Teachers	(10000 persons)	
卫生及社会服务		**Public Health and Social Services**		
卫生		Public Health		
医疗卫生机构个数	(个)	Health Care Institutions	(unit)	4953
医疗机构实有床位数	(万张)	Actual Number of Beds in Health Care Institutions	(10000 beds)	5.9
医疗卫生技术人员数	(万人)	Number of Health Care Technical Personnel	(10000 persons)	11.2
#执业(助理)医师		Licensed Physicians & Physician Assistants		5.1
注册护士		Registered Nurses		3.5
婚姻		Marriage		
登记结婚对数	(万对)	Number of Marriage Registration	(10000 couples)	9.3
离婚对数	(万对)	Number of Divorces	(10000 couples)	1.5
文化		**Culture**		
公共图书馆总藏数	(万册、万件)	Total Collections of Public Libraries	(10000 copies)	2205
博物馆及其他文物保护机构	(个)	Museums and Other Cultural Relic Protection and Administration Organizations	(unit)	
电影放映场次	(万场次)	Show Times of Films	(10000 times)	20.7
社会保障		**Social Security**		
参加企业职工基本养老保险人数	(万人)	Participants of Basic Endowment Insurance for Enterprise Workers	(10000 persons)	
参加职工基本医疗保险人数	(万人)	Participants of Basic Medical Insurance for Workers	(10000 persons)	

注：1.自2016年起，对专利相关数据的统计范围进行了调整。
2.2010年及以前，医疗卫生机构数据均不含村卫生室及驻京部队医院情况。自2011年起，包含村卫生室情况。自2012年起，除床位数外均包含驻京部队医院数据。
3.离婚对数包括在民政部门登记的对数以及经法院调离和判离的对数。
4."博物馆及其他文物保护机构"数据为北京市文物局系统内数据。
5.自2021年9月起，对参加职工基本医疗保险人数统计口径进行调整，去除6个月及以上未缴费人员，按调整后的口径计算，2020年参加职工基本医疗保险人数为1450.7万人。历史年份数据未按新口径进行调整。

1–3 Continued 2

1995	2000	2005	2010	2015	2020	2022	2023
	11526.0	28969.9	66584.6	128573.0	188081.6	218628.8	246430.0
	6407.9	15335.5	36479.6	58559.4	84308.8	97819.9	110835.5
	93.4	498.2	966.5	1403.9	2302.9	2758.5	3204.7
	14727.2	12930.0	129495.2	918064.8	1259914.7	1846185.7	2114284.5
	155.7	379.5	821.8	1384.0	2326.6	2843.3	2947.1
41.2	140.3	434.4	1579.5	3452.6	6316.2	7947.5	8536.9
4025	5905	10100	33511	94031	162824	202722	193973
238.0	229.9	226.4	330.0	373.4	403.9	402.4	395.3
17.7	16.7	17.5	20.7	22.6	25.7	27.3	27.6
4955	6176	7536	9511	10425	11211	12211	12518
6.7	7.1	7.9	9.3	11.2	12.7	13.4	13.9
11.6	11.6	12.0	17.1	25.7	30.4	32.2	34.3
5.4	5.2	5.1	6.6	9.6	11.9	12.5	13.4
3.7	4.0	4.3	6.7	11.4	13.5	14.3	15.3
8.6	8.0	9.7	13.8	16.6	11.4	9.1	13.7
2.0	2.7	3.4	4.4	8.2	8.2	4.4	5.5
2629	3020	3626	4613	5943	7241	7819	8099
51	53	73	79	77	80	58	50
9.2	12.2	22.6	74.3	198.1	146.0	262.9	338.0
261.1	391.6	520.0	982.5	1424.2	1679.9	1764.7	1801.5
		574.8	1063.7	1475.7	1741.6	1499.4	1504.7

Note: a) The statistical range of patent-related data was adjusted since 2016.

b) In and before 2010, data on health care institutions didn't cover the village clinics and the hospitals of troops stationed in Beijing. Since 2011, these data have covered village clinics. Since 2012, all the other data except for the data on the number of beds have covered the hospitals of troops stationed in Beijing.

c) Number of divorces includes those registered with civil affair authorities and those mediated and ruled in courts.

d) Data on museums and other cultural relics protection and administration organizations were the one under the jurisdiction of Beijing Municipal Cultural Heritage Bureau.

e) Since September 2021,the statistical coverage of the participants of basic medical insurance for workers was adjusted and those who failed to make payment for 6 months or more were removed. Calculated according to the adjusted coverage, the participants of basic medical insurance for workers totaled 14.507 million in 2020. Data for the previous years were not adjusted according to the new caliber.

1-4 主要年份国民经济和社会发展结构指标 COMPOSITION INDICATORS ON NATIONAL ECONOMIC AND SOCIAL DEVELOPMENT IN KEY YEARS

单位：% (%)

项 目	Item	1990	1995	2000	2005	2010	2015	2020	2021	2022	2023
人口与就业	**Population and Employment**										
常住人口	**Resident Population**										
按性别分	By Gender										
男	Male	50.2	50.1	52.1	50.6	51.6	51.5	51.1	51.1	51.0	50.9
女	Female	49.8	49.9	47.9	49.4	48.4	48.5	48.9	48.9	49.0	49.1
按城乡分	By Residence										
城 镇	Urban	73.5	75.6	77.5	83.6	86.0	86.7	87.5	87.5	87.6	87.8
乡 村	Rural	26.5	24.4	22.5	16.4	14.0	13.3	12.5	12.5	12.4	12.2
就 业	**Employment**										
常住就业人口	Resident Employed Population										
第一产业	Primary Industry					5.5	3.7	2.4	2.3	2.2	2.1
第二产业	Secondary Industry					23.6	18.9	16.7	16.7	16.4	16.2
第三产业	Tertiary Industry					70.9	77.4	80.9	81.0	81.4	81.7
国民经济核算	**National Accounts**										
地区生产总值	Gross Domestic Product										
第一产业	Primary Industry	8.7	4.8	2.4	1.2	0.8	0.6	0.3	0.3	0.3	0.2
第二产业	Secondary Industry	52.3	42.1	31.2	26.7	21.6	17.8	16.0	18.0	16.0	14.9
第三产业	Tertiary Industry	39.0	53.1	66.4	72.1	77.6	81.6	83.7	81.7	83.8	84.8
人民生活	**People's Livelihoods**										
城镇居民人均消费支出	Per Capita Consumption Expenditure of Urban Households										
#食品烟酒	Food, Tobacco and Liquor	54.2	48.5	35.8	29.4	26.8	22.1	21.0	20.8	21.1	20.8
衣 着	Clothing and Footwear	14.7	15.1	8.7	8.1	8.5	7.2	4.6	4.8	4.3	4.3
医疗保健	Health Care and Medical Services	1.4	2.9	7.0	9.8	6.4	6.5	9.0	9.9	9.4	9.1
交通通信	Transport and Communications	1.5	4.7	7.0	13.1	13.7	13.3	9.4	9.3	9.3	10.0
教育文化娱乐	Education, Culture and Recreation	11.6	10.2	14.8	14.7	11.5	11.0	7.2	7.8	7.2	8.2
农村居民人均消费支出	Per Capita Consumption Expenditure of Rural Households										
#食品烟酒	Food, Tobacco and Liquor	50.7	49.6	37.5	30.3	26.6	27.7	28.5	28.3	27.4	27.8
衣 着	Clothing and Footwear	9.5	10.9	7.0	6.4	5.9	6.3	5.0	5.4	4.7	4.7
医疗保健	Health Care and Medical Services	3.8	4.8	7.3	9.4	8.4	8.4	9.4	9.4	8.0	8.1
交通通信	Transport and Communications	1.7	4.1	7.0	11.9	11.7	13.5	14.0	14.4	13.8	13.3
教育文化娱乐	Education, Culture and Recreation	6.6	10.6	13.6	12.9	7.5	7.2	5.5	5.6	5.5	5.8
财 政	**Government Finance**										
一般公共预算收入	General Public Budget Revenue										
#增值税	Value-added Tax			13.3	10.6	8.9	15.2	30.1	29.4	23.0	30.4
个人所得税	Individual Income Tax			16.3	9.2	9.1	10.1	11.2	12.5	13.7	12.5
企业所得税	Corporate Income Tax			16.8	17.9	21.8	21.7	21.6	23.5	25.4	23.2

1-4 续表 1 Continued 1

单位：% (%)

项 目	Item	1990	1995	2000	2005	2010	2015	2020	2021	2022	2023
能源消费总量	**Total Energy Consumption**										
第一产业	Primary Industry	3.9	3.4	2.5	1.7	1.5	1.2	0.8	0.7	0.7	0.6
第二产业	Secondary Industry	63.5	65.9	58.5	46.8	37.2	28.0	25.9	23.8	24.2	21.6
第三产业	Tertiary Industry	19.0	17.9	26.1	35.1	41.7	48.7	48.0	49.8	48.1	52.1
生活消费	Household Consumption	13.6	12.8	12.9	16.4	19.5	22.1	25.3	25.7	27.0	25.7
投 资	**Investment**										
固定资产投资资金来源	Source of Capital for Investment in Fixed Assets										
中央预算资金	Central Budget	25.3	7.7	7.4	2.8	1.2	1.7	1.1	1.1	1.7	1.3
国内贷款	Domestic Loans	16.7	13.4	26.0	23.2	26.6	22.2	22.2	14.8	17.0	12.0
利用外资	Foreign Investment	11.2	20.5	3.6	1.6	0.5	0.1	0.1	0.2	0.1	0.05
债券、自筹和其他资金	Securities, Self-raised Funds and Others Funds	46.8	58.5	63.0	72.4	71.6	76.0	76.6	84.0	81.3	86.6
对外经济贸易	**International Trade and Economic Cooperation**										
海关出口商品(以美元计价)	Goods Exported at Customs (Calculated in USD)										
#一般贸易	General Trade		70.6	65.9	54.5	45.0	54.8	79.8	81.1	81.3	81.4
加工贸易	Processing Trade		21.3	29.6	39.6	42.1	28.0	5.4	5.1	4.4	4.1
海关进口商品(以美元计价)	Goods Imported at Customs (Calculated in USD)										
#一般贸易	General Trade		84.4	87.3	85.2	88.7	85.7	87.8	88.1	88.8	87.1
加工贸易	Processing Trade		5.2	3.5	8.2	5.9	7.7	3.9	3.4	3.9	4.3
农 业	**Agriculture**										
农林牧渔业产值	Gross Output Value of Agriculture, Forestry, Animal Husbandry and Fishery										
农 业	Farming	55.6	52.8	46.7	38.0	47.0	42.0	40.9	45.6	48.4	53.7
林 业	Forestry	1.3	1.6	2.8	5.2	5.1	15.6	37.1	32.9	32.3	26.1
牧 业	Animal Husbandry	39.9	41.8	46.4	50.5	42.6	36.9	17.2	17.2	15.8	16.6
渔 业	Fishery	3.3	3.7	4.1	3.6	3.5	3.2	1.6	1.6	1.4	1.6
农林牧渔专业及辅助性活动	Professional and Support Activities in Agriculture, Forestry, Animal Husbandry and Fishery				2.7	1.8	2.4	3.3	2.6	2.1	2.0
工 业	**Industry**										
规模以上工业总产值	Gross Output Value of Industry above Designated Size										
#医药制造业	Manufacture of Medicines	1.8	1.5	2.1	1.9	2.7	4.2	6.3	15.7	7.3	5.9
汽车制造业	Manufacture of Automobiles	7.8	11.6	3.9	11.8	15.9	22.3	19.8	13.7	14.2	14.5
计算机、通信和其他电子设备制造业	Manufacture of Computers, Communication and Other Electronic Equipment	6.0	10.4	32.9	25.6	16.3	12.1	13.8	15.0	14.7	13.6
电力、热力生产和供应业	Production and Supply of Electric Power and Heat Power	2.6	2.8	2.9	8.6	15.5	23.4	26.8	24.7	30.7	32.8
建筑业	**Construction**										
建筑业总产值	Total Output Value of Construction										
房屋建筑业	Construction of Buildings						51.3	54.2	54.4	55.9	52.8
土木工程建筑业	Civil Engineering						32.7	33.6	32.2	31.1	33.0
建筑安装业	Building Installation						7.9	6.3	6.5	6.4	6.8
建筑装饰、装修和其他建筑业	Building Decoration and Other Construction						8.1	5.9	6.9	6.6	7.4
交通运输业	**Transport**										
货运量(按运输方式分)	Freight Traffic (By Means of Transportation)										
铁 路	Railway	11.4	9.2	8.5	6.1	6.6	4.3	1.4	1.1	1.4	1.1
公 路	Highways	87.5	90.4	91.2	92.4	85.1	82.0	82.7	82.0	77.2	75.4
民 航	Civil Aviation	0.04	0.05	0.11	0.24	0.55	0.68	0.56	0.57	0.53	0.52
管 道	Petroleum and Gas Pipelines	1.0	0.3	0.2	1.2	7.7	13.0	15.4	16.3	20.8	23.0

注：1.自2017年起，将固定资产投资中原“国家预算内资金”调整为“中央预算资金”。
2.根据《国民经济行业分类》(GB/T 4754—2017)标准，自2018年起，将原“农林牧渔服务业”调整为“农林牧渔专业及辅助性活动”。

Note: a) Since 2017, under the Investment in Fixed Assets, the original "state budget" was adjusted to "central budget".
b) According to the standards in the Industrial Classification of the National Economy (GB/T 4754-2017), since 2018, the original "services to agriculture, forestry, animal husbandry and fishery" is adjusted to "professional and support activities in agriculture, forestry, animal husbandry and fishery".

1-4 续表 2 Continued 2

单位：% (%)

项目	Item	1990	1995	2000	2005	2010	2015	2020	2021	2022	2023
客运量(按运输方式分)	Passenger Traffic (By Means of Transportation)										
铁路	Railway	50.4	45.1	24.2	9.5	6.3	18.3	17.6	20.2	13.9	30.2
公路	Highways	46.7	47.7	70.7	85.3	89.7	71.4	67.7	66.3	75.3	51.7
民航	Civil Aviation	2.9	7.2	5.1	5.2	4.0	10.3	14.7	13.5	10.7	18.1
消费	**Consumption**										
社会消费品零售总额	Total Retail Sales of Consumer Goods										
吃类商品	Food	39.6	41.8	26.1	24.9	20.9	18.1	20.4	20.0	20.5	21.8
穿类商品	Clothing	13.2	14.3	9.2	8.4	7.6	6.1	5.1	5.6	4.8	5.4
用类商品	Daily Use Articles	44.8	42.0	59.7	59.0	64.9	71.4	71.2	70.4	70.5	68.5
烧类商品	Fuels	2.3	1.9	5.0	7.7	6.6	4.5	3.3	4.0	4.2	4.3
入境旅游	**Inbound Tourism**										
接待海外旅游人数	Inbound Overseas Visitor										
外国人	Foreigners	63.8	80.4	84.4	85.9	86.0	85.1	77.4	71.2	78.6	81.3
港澳台同胞	Chinese Compatriots from Hong Kong, Macao and Taiwan Province	34.7	17.5	15.6	14.1	14.0	14.9	22.6	28.8	21.4	18.7
科技	**Science and Technology**										
研究与试验发展(R&D)人员折合全时当量	Full-time Equivalent of R&D Personnel										
基础研究	Basic Research				12.9	15.2	16.8	22.3	22.3	22.6	22.9
应用研究	Applied Research				29.8	27.1	25.1	28.3	28.7	29.5	28.8
试验发展	Experimental Development				57.3	57.7	58.1	49.4	49.0	47.8	48.3
研究与试验发展(R&D)经费内部支出	Internal Expenditure on R&D										
基础研究	Basic Research				10.1	11.6	13.8	16.0	16.1	16.6	16.0
应用研究	Applied Research				27.8	26.4	23.0	24.5	25.0	25.7	25.5
试验发展	Experimental Development				53.1	62.0	63.2	59.4	58.9	57.7	58.4
教育	**Education**										
在校学生	Enrolment										
#普通本专科	Undergraduates		7.7	12.3	23.7	17.5	15.9	14.6	15.0	15.0	15.6
中等教育	Secondary Education		35.1	42.3	37.9	22.1	15.7	14.0	14.4	15.1	16.3
小学教育	Primary Education		42.3	32.3	21.8	19.8	22.8	24.6	26.1	26.9	29.4
专任教师	Full-time Teachers										
#高等教育	Higher Education		22.7	22.2	32.7	35.9	30.3	28.5	27.9	28.2	28.2
中等教育	Secondary Education		38.6	40.5	33.6	29.1	32.0	31.6	31.1	31.3	31.8
小学教育	Primary Education		37.9	36.8	25.3	23.9	22.1	22.0	22.3	22.2	22.3
卫生	**Public Health**										
卫生技术人员	Health Technical Personnel										
#执业(助理)医师	Licensed Physicians & Physician Assistants	45.6	46.7	44.6	42.4	38.6	37.6	39.0	38.9	38.8	39.0
注册护士	Registered Nurses	31.0	31.7	34.5	35.7	39.3	44.6	44.3	44.6	44.3	44.5

1-5 国民经济和社会发展主要比例和效益指标
MAIN PROPORTION AND EFFICIENCY INDICATORS ON NATIONAL ECONOMIC AND SOCIAL DEVELOPMENT

项目		Item		2023	2022
人口与就业		**Population and Employment**			
出生率	(‰)	Birth Rate	(‰)	5.63	5.67
死亡率	(‰)	Death Rate	(‰)	6.13	5.72
自然增长率	(‰)	Natural Growth Rate	(‰)	-0.50	-0.05
少儿抚养比	(%)	Children Dependency Ratio	(%)	16.65	16.60
老年抚养比	(%)	Elderly Dependency Ratio	(%)	22.01	20.76
城镇调查失业率	(%)	Surveyed Unemployment Rate in Urban Areas	(%)	4.4	4.7
国民经济核算		**National Accounts**			
人均地区生产总值	(元)	Per Capita Gross Regional Product	(yuan)	200278	189988
社会劳动生产率	(元/人)	Overall Labor Productivity	(yuan/person)	387074	362786
第一产业		Primary Industry		42965	42798
第二产业		Secondary Industry		353691	350165
第三产业		Tertiary Industry		402926	374328
人民生活		**People's Livelihoods**			
城镇与农村居民收入比例（以农村居民人均可支配收入为1）		Urban and Rural Households Income Ratio (Per Capita Disposable Income of Rural Households = 1)		2.37	2.42
能源消费		**Energy Consumption**			
能源消费弹性系数		Elasticity Ratio of Energy Consumption		1.90	0.00
电力消费弹性系数		Elasticity Radio of Electricity Consumption		1.17	5.39
万元地区生产总值能耗（可比价格）	(吨标准煤)	Energy Consumption per 10000 yuan of GDP (Constant Price)	(tce)	0.183	0.175
万元地区生产总值水耗（当年价格）	(立方米)	Water Consumption per 10000 yuan of GDP (Current Price)	(cu.m)	9.30	9.64
对外经济贸易		**International Trade and Economic Cooperation**			
进出口总值与地区生产总值之比（按人民币计算）	(%)	Proportion of Total Value of Imports & Exports to Gross Domestic Product (calculated by RMB)	(%)	83.33	87.73
工业（规模以上企业）		**Industry(Enterprise above Designated Size)**			
资产负债率	(%)	Asset-liability Ratio	(%)	44.65	44.40
流动资产周转率	(次)	Turnover Rate of Current Assets	(time)	0.95	1.01
成本费用利润率	(%)	Ratio of Profits to Cost	(%)	6.07	7.64
建筑业		**Construction**			
产值竣工率	(%)	Rate of Buildings Completed (by Output Value)	(%)	52.4	49.8
面积竣工率	(%)	Rate of Buildings Completed (by Floor Space)	(%)	15.7	15.4
邮电通信业		**Postal and Telecommunication Services**			
移动电话普及率	(户/百人)	Popularization Rate of Mobile Phones	(subscriber/100 persons)	184.0	179.8
固定电话主线普及率	(线/百人)	Popularization Rate of Main Line of Fixed Line Telephones	(line/100 persons)	21.4	21.7
科　技		**Science and Technology**			
研究与试验发展经费内部支出相当于地区生产总值比例	(%)	Ratio of Internal Expenditure on R&D to GDP	(%)	6.73	6.84
教　育		**Education**			
平均每一专任教师负担学生数		Average Number of Students Instructed by a Full-time Teacher			
#普通中学	(人)	Regular Secondary Schools	(person)	9.2	8.8
小学学校	(人)	Primary Schools	(person)	14.7	14.1
文　化		**Culture**			
每万人拥有公共图书馆	(个)	Public Libraries per 10000 persons	(unit)	0.01	0.01
每万人拥有博物馆	(个)	Museums per 10000 persons	(unit)	0.10	0.10
卫　生		**Public Health**			
每千常住人口医院床位数	(张)	Number of Beds at Hospitals per 1000 Resident Popula	(bed)	5.99	5.78
每千常住人口执业(助理)医师数	(人)	Number of Licensed Physicians & Physician Assistants per 1000 Resident Population	(person)	6.12	5.72

注：1.城镇调查失业率数据为年度均值。
　　2.人口相关指标为常住人口口径。

Note:a)The data on surveyed unemployment rate in urban areas are annual averages.
　　b)Relevant indicators on population refer to permanent population.

1-6 北京一日
A DAY IN BEIJING

项目	Item	2023	2022
每日创造	**Daily Production**		
地区生产总值 (万元/日)	Gross Domestic Product (10000 yuan/day)	1198923.3	1138105.8
第一产业	Primary Industry	2889.9	3054.5
第二产业	Secondary Industry	178783.3	181797.8
第三产业	Tertiary Industry	1017250.1	953253.4
一般公共预算收入 (万元/日)	General Public Budget Revenue (10000 yuan/day)	169345.1	156557.8
一般公共预算支出 (万元/日)	General Public Budget Expenditure (10000 yuan/day)	218390.3	204634.4
发电量 (万千瓦时/日)	Electricity Generated (10000 kW·h/day)	12462.3	12326.6
汽车生产量 (辆/日)	Output of Motor Vehicles (vehicle/day)	2747	2386
移动电话机生产量 (台/日)	Output of Mobile Phones (set/day)	281829	258343
显示器生产量 (台/日)	Output of Display (set/day)	5860	6401
公共汽电车客运量 (万人次/日)	Passenger Traffic of Public Buses and Trolley (10000 person-times/day)	571.7	472.8
城市轨道交通客运量 (万人次/日)	Passenger Traffic of Urban Rail Transit (10000 person-times/day)	946.2	620.1
铁路客运量 (万人/日)	Passenger Traffic of Railways (10000 persons/day)	41.2	10.7
公路客运量 (万人/日)	Passenger Traffic of Highways (10000 persons/day)	70.5	57.8
民航客运量 (万人/日)	Passenger Traffic of Civil Aviation (10000 persons/day)	24.6	8.2
国际旅游收入 (万美元/日)	Earnings from International Tourism (USD 10000/day)	454.8	120.8
国内旅游收入 (万元/日)	Earnings from Domestic Tourism (10000 yuan/day)	157019.2	68244.4
地区货物出口值 (万元/日)	Value of Exports of Local Goods (10000 yuan/day)	164385.0	161370.5
地区货物进口值 (万元/日)	Value of Imports of Local Goods (10000 yuan/day)	834692.2	837136.5
实际利用外商直接投资额 (万美元/日)	Total Amount of Foreign Direct Investment Actually Utilized (USD 10000/day)	3757.3	4769.2
每日生活	**Daily Life**		
社会消费品零售总额 (万元/日)	Retail Sales of Consumer Goods (10000 yuan/day)	396237.3	377924.5
吃类商品	Food	86390.6	77599.7
穿类商品	Clothing	21394.5	18000.3
用类商品	Daily Use Articles	271512.3	266401.0
烧类商品	Fuels	16939.8	15923.5
常住出生人口 (人/日)	Births (Resident Population) (person/day)	337	340
常住死亡人口 (人/日)	Deaths (Resident Population) (person/day)	367	343
登记结婚对数 (对/日)	Total Number of Marriage Registration (couple/day)	376	250
离婚对数 (对/日)	Total Number of Divorces (couple/day)	151	121
全市居民人均可支配收入 (元/日)	Per Capita Disposable Income of Residents of the Whole City (yuan/day)	224.0	212.1
全市居民人均消费支出 (元/日)	Per Capita Consumption Expenditure of Residents of the Whole City (yuan/day)	130.4	116.9
法人单位从业人员平均工资 (元/日)	Average Wages of Employed Persons in Legal Entities (yuan/day)	516.2	489.0
电影放映场次 (场次/日)	Show Times of Films (times/day)	9259	7201
特快专递业务量 (万件/日)	Express Deliveries (10000 pcs/day)	622.2	536.0
城乡居民生活用电量 (万千瓦时/日)	Household Electricity Consumption of Urban and Rural Residents (10000 kW·h/day)	9166.5	8792.4
居民家庭用天然气销售量 (万立方米/日)	Sales Volume of Natural Gas for Household Consumption (10000 cu.m/day)	543.3	560.8
自来水销售总量 (万立方米/日)	Total Sales Volume of Tap Water (10000 cu.m/day)	350.2	337.7
污水处理量 (万立方米/日)	Sewage Disposal Volume (10000 cu.m/day)	630.4	608.5
生活垃圾清运量 (万吨/日)	Volume of Domestic Garbage Collected and Transported (10000 tons/day)	2.1	2.0

注：离婚对数包括在民政部门登记的对数以及经法院调离和判离的对数。
Note: Number of divorces includes those registered with civil affair authorities and those mediated and ruled in courts.

1-7 "十四五"时期经济社会发展主要监测指标
MAIN MONITORING INDICATORS ON ECONOMIC AND SOCIAL DEVELOPMENT IN THE FOURTEENTH FIVE-YEAR PLAN PERIOD

项目	Item	"十四五"时期监测发展目标	Target of Development in the Monitoring in the 14th Five-Year Plan Period	2023
常住人口规模 (万人)	Resident Population (10000 persons)	≤2300	≤2300	2185.8
地区生产总值年均增速 (%)	Average Annual Growth Rate of GDP	5左右	5 or so	【4.8】
城市副中心和平原新城增加值占地区生产总值比重 (%)	Proportion of Added Value of Beijing Municipal Administrative Center and Plain New Towns to GDP (%)	>23	>23	21.4
全员劳动生产率 (万元/人)	Overall Labor Productivity (10000 yuan/person)	35左右	35 or so	38.7
全社会研究与试验发展经费支出占地区生产总值的比例 (%)	Ratio of Overall Expenditure on R&D to GDP (%)	6左右	6 or so	6.73
每万人口高价值发明专利拥有量 (件)	High-value Invention Patent Ownership per 10000 Persons (unit)	82左右	82 or so	137.0
数字经济增加值年均增速 (当年价格) (%)	Average Annual Growth Rate of added value of Digital Economy(Current Year's Prices) (%)	7.5左右	7.5 or so	【9.3】
全市居民人均可支配收入年均实际增速 (%)	Average Annual Real Growth Rate of Per Capita Disposable Income of Residents of the Whole City (%)	与经济增长基本同步	keeping pace with economic growth	【4.4】
实际利用外资规模 (亿美元)	Actual Utilization of Foreign Investment (USD 100 million)	累计830左右	accumulated 830 or so	455.6
生产生活用水总量 (亿立方米)	Total Volume of Water Consumed for Production and Daily Use (100 million cu.m)	<30	<30	25.3
地表水质量达到或好于Ⅲ类水体比例 (%)	Ratio of Surface Water to Category-III Water Body in Terms of Same or Better Quality (%)	达到国家要求	meeting the national requirements	76
细颗粒物($PM_{2.5}$)年均浓度值 (微克/立方米)	Average Annual Concentration of $PM_{2.5}$ (μg/cu.m)	达到国家要求	meeting the national requirements	32
森林覆盖率 (%)	Forest Coverage Rate (%)	45	45	44.9
单位地区生产总值能耗降幅 (%)	Decrease of Energy Consumption per Unit of GDP (%)	达到国家要求	meeting the national requirements	-4.40
每千常住人口执业(助理)医师数 (人)	Number of Licensed Physicians & Physician Assistants per 1000 of Resident Population (person)	5.6左右	5.6 or so	6.12
单位地区生产总值生产安全事故死亡率 (人/百亿元)	Death Rate of Work Accidents per Unit of GDP (person/10 billion yuan)	<0.9	<0.9	1.01
食品安全抽检合格率 (%)	Up-to-standard Rate of Food Security Spot Checks (%)	>98.5	>98.5	99.14
药品抽验合格率 (%)	Up-to-standard Rate of Drug Spot Checks (%)	>99	>99	99.96

注：【】内数值为"十四五"时期以来年均增速，实际利用外资数据为"十四五"以来累计数。

Note: Data in [ ] refer to the average annual growth rate since the 14th five-year plan period.The data on actual use of foreign capital are the cumulative numbers since the "Fourteenth Five-Year Plan" period.

1–8 四次经济普查法人单位基本情况

项　　目	Item	法人单位数(个) Total Number of Legal Entities (unit)			
		2004	2008	2013	2018
合　计	**Total**	**220947**	**267890**	**630545**	**988619**
按登记注册类型分	**By Status of Registration**				
内　资	Domestic Invested Enterprises	213857	258238	617359	973887
国　有	State-owned Enterprises	20722	15672	22094	17953
集　体	Collective-owned Enterprises	15879	9936	13845	15366
股份合作	Cooperative Enterprises	22180	10666	14456	6005
联　营	Joint Ownership	614	403	1363	350
有限责任公司	Limited Liability Corporations	31480	49555	149881	76162
股份有限公司	Share-holding Corporations Ltd.	3798	4602	5011	4475
私　营	Private	110531	161288	390809	835891
其　他	Others	8653	6116	19900	17685
港澳台商投资	Enterprises with Investment from Hong Kong, Macao and Taiwan	2257	2986	4960	5511
外商投资	Enterprises with Foreign Investment	4833	6666	8226	9221
按隶属关系分	**By Jurisdiction of Management**				
中　央	Central Government	10484	8728	9747	8732
地　方	Local	210463	259162	620798	979887
按行业分	**By Sector**				
农、林、牧、渔业	Agriculture, Forestry, Animal Husbandry and Fishery				413
采矿业	Mining	564	142	127	78
制造业	Manufacturing	30870	28786	33055	25684
电力、热力、燃气及水生产和供应业	Production and Supply of Electricity, Heating, Gas and Water	271	359	638	1193
建筑业	Construction	5878	9164	18486	35130
批发和零售业	Wholesale and Retail Trades	65084	85054	190704	273395
交通运输、仓储和邮政业	Transport, Storage and Post	3889	6022	14290	19176
住宿和餐饮业	Hotels and Catering Services	8705	10695	16323	34458
信息传输、软件和信息技术服务业	Information Transmission, Software and Information Technology	11611	15776	47602	77152
金融业	Financial Intermediation	672	1025	3811	12796
房地产业	Real Estate	8782	10955	17805	26885
租赁和商务服务业	Leasing and Business Services	32527	45003	134926	184764
科学研究和技术服务业	Scientific Research and Technical Services	13828	20451	71206	154187
水利、环境和公共设施管理业	Management of Water Conservancy, Environment and Public Facilities	1476	1719	3964	7346
居民服务、修理和其他服务业	Services to Households, Repair and Other Services	13001	10239	18735	36756
教　育	Education	5423	6242	11145	21236
卫生和社会工作	Health and Social Service	1745	2270	3810	6607
文化、体育和娱乐业	Culture, Sports and Entertainment	5856	7369	26784	53885
公共管理、社会保障和社会组织	Public Management, Social Security and Social Organization	10765	6619	17134	17478

注：1.本表2004年、2008年行业划分执行《国民经济行业分类》(GB/T 4754—2002)标准，2013年执行《国民经济行业分类》(GB/T 4754—2011)标准，2018年执行《国民经济行业分类》(GB/T 4754—2017)标准。
2.表中2018年资产总计、收入总计、企业利润、年末从业人员合计数包括铁路部门数据，不含分组数据。

BASIC STATISTICS ON CORPORATE UNITS IN THE FOURTH ECONOMIC CENSUS

资产总计(亿元) Total Assets (100 million yuan)				收入总计 (亿元) Total Income (100 million yuan)			
2004	2008	2013	2018	2004	2008	2013	2018
216316.9	**646673.0**	**1220785.2**	**2119561.6**	**30942.0**	**66702.8**	**140828.4**	**199152.1**
206314.5	623894.6	1166922.3	1985481.9	25986.1	52376.6	114828.6	162106.2
92836.4	280476.4	318572.3	828238.3	7729.4	11678.0	16652.3	24528.0
1711.4	1468.7	2684.0	5463.1	665.0	682.7	614.3	677.1
2953.8	625.6	1098.2	1359.5	387.2	310.8	446.6	322.6
130.8	101.9	107.7	62.6	63.0	29.5	45.6	14.7
45133.1	111630.9	225521.5	432145.1	8661.3	21588.4	62577.8	81395.9
58244.2	219733.8	587253.5	585069.2	4634.1	10644.3	18133.4	20911.1
4951.7	9085.3	29471.4	130690.4	3769.7	7155.3	15808.7	33206.9
353.2	772.2	2213.7	2453.5	76.4	287.7	550.0	1049.8
3558.1	7515.9	16959.1	38758.3	1110.0	3722.8	6725.3	15675.8
6444.2	15262.4	36903.9	56531.1	3845.8	10603.3	19274.5	20542.2
168110.5	532422.7	918654.6	1551884.8	13037.9	26806.7	58770.4	72168.2
48206.4	114250.3	302130.6	528886.5	17904.1	39896.0	82058.0	126156.0
			28.0				5.6
69.0	433.1	2927.1	3983.7	152.7	384.6	1419.2	553.3
6531.1	9981.8	17827.4	26713.7	5259.5	9703.6	14565.1	17012.0
6851.8	7317.3	13204.4	21867.4	813.1	1780.8	4070.5	5759.3
3199.9	7283.4	18021.1	35232.6	2083.4	4140.5	10244.9	15415.5
8103.0	17832.9	40399.0	62339.8	9636.2	24305.8	55353.5	66771.0
2494.3	4999.9	15176.9	54752.4	751.0	2378.1	4878.5	6396.0
777.7	1204.6	2048.6	2559.2	361.4	662.0	1020.8	1412.3
8734.8	11120.3	28206.2	55834.3	1347.0	2953.3	5719.9	13749.1
141269.9	474100.4	873336.5	1486292.5	4117.1	6199.0	16762.4	24901.7
10016.4	20042.3	47129.9	96972.5	1760.1	2518.3	4964.0	6526.8
19440.6	74670.8	117957.3	194326.7	1203.5	3575.7	10240.0	12313.4
2932.3	9569.2	24304.6	43862.1	1132.9	3785.8	6722.1	11717.8
714.0	929.3	2870.9	5839.4	88.9	216.5	413.9	1093.7
822.7	252.7	897.7	1075.3	266.8	137.5	316.2	535.0
1120.8	1990.3	3710.9	6591.7	490.1	852.0	692.0	2913.4
464.6	741.9	1338.2	2513.1	323.4	621.0	1146.7	2526.6
1083.2	1747.0	4367.3	9011.1	446.6	826.8	1360.7	2653.1
1690.9	2455.8	7061.4	9765.9	708.2	1661.5	938.0	6896.5

Note: a) In 2004 and 2008, the sectors in this table were classified in accordance with the standards in the Industrial Classification of the National Economy (GB/T 4754-2002); in 2013, the classification was carried out in accordance with the standards in the Industrial Classification of the National Economy (GB/T 4754-2011); and in 2018, the classification was carried out in accordance with the standards in the Industrial Classification of the National Economy (GB/T 4754-2017).

b) In 2018, the data on total assets, total income, enterprise profits and year-end total number of persons employed included that of the railway sector; however, the grouped data did not cover the data of the railway sector.

1-8 续表 Continued

项目	Item	企业利润(亿元) Profit of Enterprises (100 million yuan)				年末从业人员(万人) Employed Persons (10000 persons)			
		2004	2008	2013	2018	2004	2008	2013	2018
合 计	**Total**	**1989.0**	**5488.1**	**20566.8**	**24842.9**	**705.2**	**816.9**	**1111.3**	**1361.0**
按登记注册类型分	**By Status of Registration**								
内 资	Domestic Invested Enterprises	1460.7	4602.9	17673.4	19658.5	639.3	704.7	965.1	1199.4
国 有	State-owned Enterprises	806.5	1332.1	2880.4	4161.7	195.2	195.0	194.9	178.8
集 体	Collective-owned Enterprises	23.2	14.7	18.5	-19.4	43.6	26.5	21.7	16.7
股份合作	Cooperative Enterprises	26.2	6.8	6.6	7.8	28.6	14.0	12.2	5.9
联 营	Joint Ownership	1.2	-0.9	-0.4	0.3	2.4	1.3	1.1	0.5
有限责任公司	Limited Liability Corporations	393.4	1536.3	8916.4	9953.8	155.2	221.1	331.1	343.2
股份有限公司	Share-holding Corporations Ltd.	134.6	1630.4	5645.9	5682.8	39.3	62.4	80.8	92.1
私 营	Private	75.6	65.2	191.9	-139.9	162.4	170.6	300.6	537.5
其 他	Others	0.1	18.4	14.1	11.4	12.7	13.9	22.6	24.5
港澳台商投资	Enterprises with Investment from Hong Kong, Macao and Taiwan	188.0	113.1	649.4	910.8	20.4	39.0	55.1	73.6
外商投资	Enterprises with Foreign Investment	340.2	772.1	2244.0	3915.5	45.4	73.2	91.2	79.7
按隶属关系分	**By Jurisdiction of Management**								
中 央	Central Government	1083.5	3475.3	14647.9	16544.0	134.6	168.3	178.3	185.4
地 方	Local	905.5	2012.8	5918.9	7940.8	570.5	648.6	933.1	1167.2
按行业分	**By Sector**								
农、林、牧、渔业	Agriculture, Forestry, Animal Husbandry and Fishery				-0.4				0.2
采矿业	Mining	16.8	44.9	18.6	-69.9	4.1	5.1	6.9	3.6
制造业	Manufacturing	268.7	301.8	860.4	1095.6	148.8	134.7	138.5	96.8
电力、热力、燃气及水生产和供应业	Production and Supply of Electricity, Heating, Gas and Water	104.3	192.6	377.5	535.5	7.8	6.7	9.3	10.8
建筑业	Construction	46.9	87.7	436.5	498.0	69.7	54.7	65.5	96.5
批发和零售业	Wholesale and Retail Trades	221.7	726.5	1026.1	1456.0	83.2	94.3	147.8	161.4
交通运输、仓储和邮政业	Transport, Storage and Post	76.0	-3.3	275.2	776.3	43.0	69.5	68.6	71.5
住宿和餐饮业	Hotels and Catering Services	-0.3	7.1	-24.2	20.2	38.4	44.9	50.6	56.3
信息传输、软件和信息技术服务业	Information Transmission, Software and Information Technology	550.3	651.4	1830.7	2998.0	28.5	46.6	93.0	138.9
金融业	Financial Intermediation	237.6	1356.6	10964.5	12027.4	15.0	25.1	43.3	80.6
房地产业	Real Estate	126.2	316.2	819.7	899.4	31.9	41.0	56.4	73.0
租赁和商务服务业	Leasing and Business Services	244.8	1484.9	3192.2	4318.9	63.8	95.9	141.7	187.2
科学研究和技术服务业	Scientific Research and Technical Services	58.4	280.0	668.8	291.6	38.9	56.4	95.2	140.4
水利、环境和公共设施管理业	Management of Water Conservancy, Environment and Public Facilities	-0.3	5.2	21.2	9.0	7.5	9.3	12.9	18.4
居民服务、修理和其他服务业	Services to Households, Repair and Other Services	15.1	6.2	-1.0	-22.0	19.6	14.1	21.5	30.6
教 育	Education	-0.8	0.5	11.2	-26.1	38.7	43.1	53.1	67.1
卫生和社会工作	Health and Social Service	-0.3	0.5	0.5	-35.3	16.0	20.0	27.8	36.4
文化、体育和娱乐业	Culture, Sports and Entertainment	23.8	29.4	89.0	70.6	16.2	18.6	27.6	37.5
公共管理、社会保障和社会组织	Public Management, Social Security and Social Organization					34.1	36.6	51.8	54.1

1—9 规模(限额)以上法人单位基本情况(2023年)
BASIC STATISTICS ON CORPORATE UNITS ABOVE DESIGNATED SIZE(2023)

单位：个 (unit)

项 目	Item	法人单位数合计 Total Number of Corporate Units	单产业法人 Single-industry Corporates	多产业法人 Multi-industry Corporates
合 计	**Total**	**47207**	**37648**	**9559**
按登记注册类型分	**By Status of Registration**			
内 资	Domestic Invested Enterprises	42762	34690	8072
国 有	State-owned Enterprises	3460	3396	64
集 体	Collective-owned Enterprises	344	314	30
股份合作	Cooperative Enterprises	325	282	43
联 营	Joint Ownership	15	14	1
有限责任公司	Limited Liability Corporations	16979	13134	3845
股份有限公司	Share-holding Corporations Ltd.	1109	699	410
私 营	Private	20234	16558	3676
其他内资	Others	296	293	3
港澳台商投资	Enterprises with Investment from Hong Kong, Macao and Taiwan	1589	1072	517
与港澳台商合资经营	Joint Ventures	394	291	103
与港澳台商合作经营	Cooperative Enterprises	49	40	9
港澳台商独资	Solely-funded Enterprises	1066	698	368
港澳台商投资股份有限公司	Share-holding Corporations Ltd.	58	28	30
其他港澳台商投资	Others	22	15	7
外商投资	Enterprises with Foreign Investment	2856	1886	970
中外合资经营	Joint Ventures	729	532	197
中外合作经营	Cooperative Enterprises	58	46	12
外资企业	Solely-funded Enterprises	1957	1235	722
外商投资股份有限公司	Share-holding Corporations Ltd.	102	65	37
其他外商投资	Others	10	8	2
按机构类型分	**By Type of Institutions**			
企 业	Enterprises	43431	33903	9528
事业单位	Institutions	3227	3214	13
机 关	Government Units	2	2	
社会团体	Social Organization	12	12	
其他机构	Others	535	517	18

注：表中数据均为2023年1—12月定报数据，下同。
Note: The data in this table are all the regularly submitted data for January to December 2023,the same below.

1-10 国民经济各行业规模(限额)以上法人单位情况(2023年)
BASIC STATISTICS ON CORPORATE UNITS ABOVE DESIGNATED SIZE IN DIFFERENT SECTORS OF THE NATIONAL ECONOMY (2023)

单位：个 (unit)

行业	Sector	法人单位数 合计 Total Number of Corporate Units	单产业法人 Single-industry Corporates	多产业法人 Multi-industry Corporates
合计	**Total**	**47207**	**37648**	**9559**
农、林、牧、渔业	**Agriculture, Forestry, Animal Husbandry and Fishery**			
采矿业	**Mining**	**9**	**4**	**5**
煤炭开采和洗选业	Mining and Washing of Coal			
石油和天然气开采业	Extraction of Petroleum and Natural Gas	2		2
黑色金属矿采选业	Mining and Processing of Ferrous Metal Ores	2	1	1
有色金属矿采选业	Mining and Processing of Non-Ferrous Metal Ores			
非金属矿采选业	Mining and Processing of Non-metal Ores			
开采专业及辅助性活动	Professional and Support Activities for Mining	5	3	2
其他采矿业	Mining of Other Ores			
制造业	**Manufacturing**	**2901**	**2154**	**747**
农副食品加工业	Processing of Food from Agricultural Products	101	68	33
食品制造业	Manufacture of Foods	113	72	41
酒、饮料和精制茶制造业	Manufacture of Liquor, Beverages and Refined Tea	36	24	12
烟草制品业	Manufacture of Tobacco	1	1	
纺织业	Manufacture of Textile	9	5	4
纺织服装、服饰业	Manufacture of Textile, Wearing Apparel and Accessories	70	44	26
皮革、毛皮、羽毛及其制品和制鞋业	Manufacture of Leather, Fur, Feather and Related Products and Footwear	2	1	1
木材加工和木、竹、藤、棕、草制品业	Processing of Timber, Manufacture of Wood, Bamboo, Rattan, Palm and Straw Products	5	4	1
家具制造业	Manufacture of Furniture	34	21	13
造纸和纸制品业	Manufacture of Paper and Paper Products	27	22	5
印刷和记录媒介复制业	Printing and Reproduction of Recording Media	91	82	9
文教、工美、体育和娱乐用品制造业	Manufacture of Articles for Culture, Education, Arts and Crafts, Sport and Entertainment Activities	19	13	6
石油、煤炭及其他燃料加工业	Processing of Petroleum, Coal and Other Fuels	14	12	2
化学原料和化学制品制造业	Manufacture of Raw Chemical Materials and Chemical Products	132	105	27
医药制造业	Manufacture of Medicines	266	203	63
化学纤维制造业	Manufacture of Chemical Fibres	1		1
橡胶和塑料制品业	Manufacture of Rubber and Plastics Products	50	41	9
非金属矿物制品业	Manufacture of Non-metallic Mineral Products	169	129	40
黑色金属冶炼和压延加工业	Smelting and Pressing of Ferrous Metals	5	4	1

注：行业划分执行《国民经济行业分类》(GB/T 4754-2017)标准。

Note: Sectors in this table are classified in accordance with the standards in the Industrial Classification of the National Economy (GB/T 4754-2017).

1-10 续表 1 Continued 1

单位：个 (unit)

行 业	Sector	法人单位数 合 计 Total Number of Corporate Units	单产业法人 Single-industry Corporates	多产业法人 Multi-industry Corporates
有色金属冶炼和压延加工业	Smelting and Processing of Non-ferrous Metals	21	18	3
金属制品业	Manufacture of Metal Products	141	113	28
通用设备制造业	Manufacture of General Purpose Machinery	198	140	58
专用设备制造业	Manufacture of Special Purpose Machinery	377	292	85
汽车制造业	Manufacture of Automobiles	192	151	41
铁路、船舶、航空航天和其他运输设备制造业	Manufacture of Railway, Ship, Aerospace and Other Transport Equipments	73	53	20
电气机械和器材制造业	Manufacture of Electrical Machinery and Apparatus	222	162	60
计算机、通信和其他电子设备制造业	Manufacture of Computers, Communication and Other Electronic Equipment	303	210	93
仪器仪表制造业	Manufacture of Measuring Instruments and Machinery	188	137	51
其他制造业	Other Manufacture	7	7	
废弃资源综合利用业	Utilization of Waste Resources	12	9	3
金属制品、机械和设备修理业	Repair Service of Metal Products, Machinery and Equipment	22	11	11
电力、热力、燃气及水生产和供应业	**Production and Supply of Electricity, Heat, Gas and Water**	**164**	**133**	**31**
电力、热力生产和供应业	Production and Supply of Electric Power and Heat Power	109	93	16
燃气生产和供应业	Production and Supply of Gas	21	14	7
水的生产和供应业	Production and Supply of Water	34	26	8
建筑业	**Construction**	**2869**	**1968**	**901**
房屋建筑业	Construction of Buildings	519	292	227
土木工程建筑业	Civil Engineering	657	445	212
建筑安装业	Building Installation	622	428	194
建筑装饰、装修和其他建筑业	Building Decoration and Other Constructions	1071	803	268
批发和零售业	**Wholesale and Retail Trades**	**10777**	**8892**	**1885**
批发业	Wholesale Trade	8179	7118	1061
零售业	Retail Trade	2598	1774	824
交通运输、仓储和邮政业	**Transport, Storage and Post**	**830**	**573**	**257**
铁路运输业	Railway Transport	17	8	9
道路运输业	Road Transport	331	251	80
水上运输业	Water Transport	4	4	
航空运输业	Air Transport	34	17	17
管道运输业	Transport via Pipelines	3		3
多式联运和运输代理业	Intermodality and Forwarding Agency	294	179	115
装卸搬运和仓储业	Loading, Unloading and Storage	110	95	15
邮政业	Post	37	19	18
住宿和餐饮业	**Hotels and Catering Services**	**3320**	**2563**	**757**
住宿业	Hotels	1141	959	182
餐饮业	Catering Services	2179	1604	575
信息传输、软件和信息技术服务业	**Information Transmission, Software and Information Technology**	**4293**	**2994**	**1299**
电信、广播电视和卫星传输服务	Telecommunication, Radio and Television and Satellite Transmission Service	251	162	89
互联网和相关服务	Internet and Related Service	781	585	196
软件和信息技术服务业	Software and Information Technology	3261	2247	1014

1-10 续表 2 Continued 2

单位：个 (unit)

行业	Sector	法人单位数 合计 Total Number of Corporate Units	单产业法人 Single-industry Corporates	多产业法人 Multi-industry Corporates
金融业	**Financial Intermediation**	**2722**	**2714**	**8**
货币金融服务	Monetary and Financial Service	807	800	7
资本市场服务	Capital Market Service	1047	1047	
保险业	Insurance	594	593	1
其他金融业	Other Financial Activities	274	274	
房地产业	**Real Estate**	**4068**	**3307**	**761**
租赁和商务服务业	**Leasing and Business Services**	**5335**	**4134**	**1201**
租赁业	Leasing	199	150	49
商务服务业	Business Services	5136	3984	1152
科学研究和技术服务业	**Scientific Research and Technical Services**	**3801**	**2675**	**1126**
研究和试验发展	Research and Experimental Development	631	553	78
专业技术服务业	Professional Technical Services	1949	1208	741
科技推广和应用服务业	Science and Technology Popularization and Application Services	1221	914	307
水利、环境和公共设施管理业	**Management of Water Conservancy, Environment and Public Facilities**	**516**	**393**	**123**
水利管理业	Management of Water Conservancy	41	38	3
生态保护和环境治理业	Ecological Protection and Environmental Treatment	105	64	41
公共设施管理业	Management of Public Facilities	359	282	77
土地管理业	Management of Land	11	9	2
居民服务、修理和其他服务业	**Service to Households, Repair and Other Services**	**690**	**545**	**145**
居民服务业	Service to Households	196	143	53
机动车、电子产品和日用产品修理业	Repair of Motor Vehicles, Electronics and Household Products	198	159	39
其他服务业	Other Services	296	243	53
教育	**Education**	**1931**	**1824**	**107**
卫生和社会工作	**Health and Social Service**	**932**	**901**	**31**
卫生	Health	828	803	25
社会工作	Social Service	104	98	6
文化、体育和娱乐业	**Culture, Sports and Entertainment**	**2047**	**1872**	**175**
新闻和出版业	Journalism and Publishing Activities	508	444	64
广播、电视、电影和录音制作业	Radio, Television, Motion Picture and Audio Production Services	651	609	42
文化艺术业	Cultural and Art Activities	307	293	14
体育	Sports Activities	197	169	28
娱乐业	Entertainments	384	357	27
公共管理、社会保障和社会组织	**Public Management, Social Security and Social Organization**	**2**	**2**	
中国共产党机关	Organs of Communist Party of China			
国家机构	Government Agencies	1	1	
人民政协、民主党派	People's Political Consultative Conference and Democratic Parties			
社会保障	Social Security			
群众团体、社会团体和其他成员组织	Mass Organizations, Social Organizations and Other Membership Organizations	1	1	
基层群众自治组织及其他组织	Grass Roots Self-Governing Organization and Other Organizations			
国际组织	**International Organizations**			

1−11 规模(限额)以上企业法人单位情况(2023年)
STATISTICS ON CORPORATE ENTERPRISES ABOVE DESIGNATED SIZE (2023)

单位：个 (unit)

项 目	Item	法人单位合计 Total Number of Corporate Units
合 计	**Total**	**43431**
按成立时间分	**By Establishment Time**	
1949年以前	Before 1949	24
1950−1965	From 1950 to 1965	177
1966−1979	From 1966 to 1979	92
1980−1989	From 1980 to 1989	1172
1990年以后	After 1990	41966
按登记注册类型分	**By Status of Registration**	
内资企业	Domestic Invested Enterprises	38990
国有企业	State-owned Enterprises	232
集体企业	Collective-owned Enterprises	288
股份合作企业	Cooperative Enterprises	324
联营企业	Joint Ownership	14
有限责任公司	Limited Liability Corporations	16976
股份有限公司	Share-holding Corporations Ltd.	1109
私营企业	Private	20038
其他内资企业	Other Domestic Invested Enterprises	9
港澳台商投资企业	Enterprises with Investment from Hong Kong, Macao and Taiwan	1588
与港澳台商合资经营	Joint Ventures	394
与港澳台商合作经营	Cooperative Enterprises	49
港澳台商独资	Solely-funded Enterprises	1065
港澳台商投资股份有限公司	Share-holding Corporations Ltd.	58
其他港澳台商投资	Others	22
外商投资企业	Enterprises with Foreign Investment	2853
中外合资经营	Joint Ventures	729
中外合作经营	Cooperative Enterprises	57
外资企业	Solely-funded Enterprises	1955
外商投资股份有限公司	Share-holding Corporations Ltd.	102
其他外商投资	Other	10
按控股情况分	**By Holding Type**	
国有控股	State-holding	7646
集体控股	Collective-holding	1044
私人控股	Private-holding	30750
港澳台商控股	Holding by Investors from Hong Kong, Macao and Taiwan	1548
外商控股	Foreign-controlled Enterprises	2288
其 他	Others	155

1−12 全市私营个体经济基本情况
BASIC STATISTICS ON PRIVATE AND INDIVIDUAL ECONOMY

项 目	Item	私营 Private			个体 Individual		
		2023	2022	2023年为2022年% 2023 as % of 2022	2023	2022	2023年为2022年% 2023 as % of 2022
登记注册*	**Registered at Administration**						
户 数 (户)	Number of Business Entities (unit)	1908770	1739843	109.7	434142	420195	103.3
注册资本 (亿元)	Registered Capital (100 million yuan)	256999.7	236941.8	108.5	239.6	216.0	110.9
税收情况	**Taxes**						
税收收入合计（亿元）	Total Tax Revenue (100 million yuan)	2278.4	1907.1	119.5	2.9	3.4	85.7

注：*为期末时点数。
资料来源：北京市市场监督管理局、国家税务总局北京市税务局。
Note: Data with * indicate the accumulative data at end of the year.
Source: Beijing Municipal Administration for Market Regulation, Beijing Municipal Tax Service of State Taxation Administration.

1-13 规模以上非公经济主要指标(2022年)
MAIN INDICATORS OF NON-PUBLIC SECTORS OF THE ECONOMY ABOVE DESIGNATED SIZE (2022)

项　目	Item	单位数 (个) Number of Enterprises (unit)	收入合计 (亿元) Total Income (100 million yuan)	利润总额 (亿元) Total Profits (100 million yuan)	应交税金合计 (亿元) Taxes Payable (100 million yuan)	从业人员平均人数 (万人) Average Number of Persons Employed (10000 persons)
合　计	**Total**	**35452**	**101795.3**	**7078.8**	**2682.4**	**449.1**
按登记注册类型分	**Grouped by Registration Type**					
内　资	Domestic-funded	31263	52572.6	1471.4	1418.0	319.1
港澳台商投资	Hong Kong, Macao and Taiwan-funded	1518	23842.2	2560.9	459.3	57.8
外商投资	Foreign-funded	2671	25380.4	3046.5	805.2	72.3
按规模分	**Grouped by Size**					
#大型企业	Large-sized Enterprises	1248	44049.1	4915.2	1054.8	171.6
中小微型企业	Mini-, Small-, Mediume-sized Enterprises	30390	51491.2	1126.5	1285.1	233.2
中　型	Medium Size	6449	30415.7	809.8	739.8	125.8
小　型	Small Size	18861	16091.1	371.9	430.6	102.1
微　型	Mini Size	5080	4984.4	-55.1	114.6	5.3
按行业分	**Grouped by Sector**					
#制造业	Manufacturing	2411	10967.3	917.6	345.4	44.3
建筑业	Construction	2332	2697.3	39.4	74.8	16.5
批发和零售业	Wholesale and Retail Trade	9342	42171.8	1150.3	585.3	50.3
交通运输、仓储和邮政业	Transport, Storage and Post	649	3789.9	27.1	35.9	14.6
住宿和餐饮业	Accommodation and Restaurants	2782	834.3	-63.8	18.9	28.8
信息传输、软件和信息技术服务业	Information Transmission,Software and Information Technology Services	3820	21908.3	3062.9	660.5	97.5
金融业	Finance	1616	4266.6	1017.8	211.7	22.5
房地产业	Real Estate	2453	3094.1	-10.3	360.7	30.7
租赁和商务服务业	Renting and Leasing Activities and Business Services	4462	6521.1	559.6	195.9	76.3
科学研究和技术服务业	Scientific Research and Development, Technical Services	2641	2846.0	291.3	125.0	29.5
水利、环境和公共设施管理业	Management of Water Conservancy, Environment and Public Facilities	202	228.4	7.6	9.2	2.9
居民服务、修理和其他服务业	Resident Services, Repair and Other Services	631	203.7	0.2	8.4	10.3
教　育	Education	444	763.2	25.3	17.0	12.5
卫生和社会工作	Health and Social Works	363	417.4	-3.1	5.6	6.3
文化、体育和娱乐业	Culture, Sports and Entertainment	1229	540.8	7.5	20.3	4.7

注：1.本表不包含个体经营户数据。
2.按规模分组中的数据为非公企业法人单位数据。
3.行业划分执行《国民经济行业分类》(GB/T 4754—2017)标准。

Note: a) Data of the self-employed are not included in this table.
b) Data in the groups by size refer to those of the non-public corporate legal entities.
c) The sectors in this table are classified in accordance with the Standard in the Classification of National Economic Sectors(GB/T4754-2017).

1-14 规模以上中小微企业主要指标(2022年)
MAIN INDICATORS OF MICRO- SMALL- AND MEDIUM-SIZED ENTERPRISES ABOVE DESIGNATED SIZE (2022)

项 目	Item	单位数 (个) Number of Enter-prises (unit)	收入合计 (亿元) Total Income (100 million yuan)	利润总额 (亿元) Total Profits (100 million yuan)	应交税金合计 (亿元) Total Tax Payable (100 million yuan)	从业人员平均人数 (万人) Average Number of Employed Persons (10000 persons)
合 计	**Total**	**36981**	**79054.1**	**3611.3**	**2281.4**	**309.6**
按规模分	**Grouped by Size**					
中 型	Medium Size	8929	51009.7	2348.9	1362.9	177.7
小 型	Small Size	22078	21383.3	430.0	653.1	124.4
微 型	Micro Size	5974	6661.1	832.5	265.3	7.4
按登记注册类型分	**Grouped by Registration Type**					
内 资	Domestic-funded	33563	63887.5	2687.2	1846.4	268.6
港澳台商投资	Hong Kong, Macao and Taiwan-funded	1174	3820.4	213.7	143.8	14.9
外商投资	Foreign-funded	2244	11346.3	710.5	291.1	26.1
按行业分	**Grouped by Sector**					
#制造业	Manufacturing	2816	8406.2	672.8	378.1	43.6
建筑业	Construction	2543	2541.2	98.2	85.4	17.7
批发和零售业	Wholesale and Retail Trade	10371	39560.3	692.9	608.4	37.6
交通运输、仓储和邮政业	Transport, Storage and Post	783	2681.8	108.8	47.2	10.3
住宿和餐饮业	Accommodation and Restaurants	3207	530.0	-83.4	16.8	16.3
信息传输、软件和信息技术服务业	Information Transmission, Software and Information Technology Services	3778	11230.8	1134.8	306.9	42.9
房地产业	Real Estate	2414	2579.7	-103.8	296.9	22.0
租赁和商务服务业	Renting and Leasing Activities and Business Services	5163	6654.9	595.1	294.4	77.9
科学研究和技术服务业	Scientific Research and Development, Technical Services	3034	2628.7	350.3	125.4	22.8
水利、环境和公共设施管理业	Management of Water Conservancy, Environment and Public Facilities	300	353.9	18.6	14.0	2.7
居民服务、修理和其他服务业	Resident Services, Repair and Other Services	612	163.5	4.2	7.9	4.7
卫生和社会工作	Health Care and Social Works	28	9.3	-1.6	1.3	0.3
文化、体育和娱乐业	Culture, Sports and Entertainment	1771	1046.2	81.2	48.2	8.2

注：1. 本表中的企业规模划型标准执行《统计上大中小微型企业划分办法(2017)》。根据该《办法》的适用范围，在统计单位规模时，不含以下行业的单位：交通运输、仓储和邮政业中的铁路运输业，金融业，房地产业中的房地产租赁经营，教育，卫生和社会工作中的卫生。因此中小微企业数据不含以上行业数据。

2. 行业划分执行《国民经济行业分类》(GB/T 4754—2017)标准。

Note: a) In this table, enterprise size is identified in accordance with the *provisions stated in the Statistical Division Standards of Large, Medium-sized, Small and Micro Enterprises(2017)*. According to the scope of application of the measures, enterprises in the following sectors are not covered in the statistics of the size of enterprises: transport via railway in the sector of transport, storage and post; finance; real estate leasing management in the sector of real estate; education; health in the sector of health care and social works. Therefore, the data on micro, small and medium-sized enterprises do not include those related to the abovementioned sectors.

b) The sectors in this table are classified in accordance with the standards in *the Classification of National Economic Sectors(GB/T4754-2017)*.

主要统计指标解释

法人单位 指有权拥有资产、承担负债，并独立从事社会经济活动（或与其他单位进行交易）的组织。法人单位应同时具备以下条件：(1) 依法成立，有自己的名称、组织机构和场所，能够独立承担民事责任；(2) 独立拥有（或授权使用）资产或者经费，承担负债，有权与其他单位签订合同；(3) 具有包括资产负债表在内的账户，或者能够根据需要编制账户。

单产业法人 指仅包含一个产业活动单位的法人单位，该法人单位同时也是一个产业活动单位。

多产业法人 指由两个及以上产业活动单位组成的法人单位，这些产业活动单位接受法人单位的管理和控制。

登记注册类型 企业法人或企业产业活动单位的登记注册类型，按其在工商行政管理机关登记注册的类型填写。如企业登记注册类型发生变化，但未及时到工商部门变更登记，企业应根据变化后的实际情况填写。其他法人和产业活动单位的登记注册类型，按其主要经费来源和管理方式，根据实际情况，比照《企业登记注册类型与代码》填写。

国有企业 指企业全部资产归国家所有，并按《中华人民共和国企业法人登记管理条例》规定登记注册的非公司制的经济组织。不包括有限责任公司中的国有独资公司。

集体企业 指企业资产归集体所有，并按《中华人民共和国企业法人登记管理条例》规定登记注册的经济组织。

股份合作企业 指以合作制为基础，由企业职工共同出资入股，吸收一定比例的社会资产投资组建，实行自主经营，自负盈亏，共同劳动，民主管理，按劳分配与按股分红相结合的一种集体经济组织。

联营企业 指两个及两个以上相同或不同所有制性质的企业法人或事业单位法人，按自愿、平等、互利的原则，共同投资组成的经济组织称为联营企业。联营企业包括国有联营企业、集体联营企业、国有与集体联营企业和其他联营企业。

有限责任公司 指根据《中华人民共和国公司登记管理条例》规定登记注册，由两个以上，五十个以下的股东共同出资，每个股东以其所认缴的出资额对公司承担有限责任，公司以其全部资产对其债务承担责任的经济组织。有限责任公司包括国有独资公司、其他有限责任公司。

私营企业 指由自然人投资设立或由自然人控股，以雇佣劳动为基础的营利性经济组织。包括按照《公司法》《合伙企业法》《私营企业暂行条例》《个人独资企业法》规定登记注册的私营独资企业、私营合伙企业、私营有限责任公司、私营股份有限公司和个人独资企业。

其他企业 指上述类型之外的其他内资经济组织。

港澳台商投资企业 指港澳台地区投资者依照中华人民共和国有关涉外经济的法律、法规成立的企业，包括与港澳台商合资经营企业、与港澳台商合作经营企业、港澳台商独资经营企业、港澳台商投资股份有限公司、其他港澳台商投资企业。

外商投资企业 指外国企业或外国人依照中华人民共和国有关涉外经济的法律、法规成立的企业，包括中外合资经营企业、中外合作经营企业、外资企业、外商投资股份有限公司、其他外商投资企业。

非公经济 指资产由我国私人控股、港澳台商控股、外商控股的“非公有控股”经济成分的企业法人单位，以及主要经费来源于私人、港澳台资和外资的非企业法人单位和个体工商户。其中，私人、港澳台及外商控股是指由其绝对控股和相对控股的经济成分。

Explanatory Notes on Main Statistical Indicators

Legal Entity refers to any organization that has the right to own assets and bear liabilities, and conducts social and economic activities independently (or conducts transactions with other entities). A legal entity shall meet all of such conditions as: (1) established in accordance with law, having its own name, organization and site, capable of assuming civil responsibilities independently; (2) independently owning (or using under authorization) assets or outlays, assuming liabilities, having the right to sign contracts with other entities; (3) maintaining accounts including balance sheet, or capable of preparing accounts as needed.

Single-industry Legal Entity refers any legal entity conducting only one industrial activity. Such legal entity is also an industrial activity entity.

Multi-industry Legal Entity refers to any legal entity composed of two or more industrial activity entities which are managed and controlled by the legal entity.

Registration Type of an enterprise as legal person or as enterprise industrial activity entity shall be completed according to the type registered at the administration for industry and commerce. In the event of any change in registration type, and no registration alteration is made with the administration for industry and commerce in good time, the registration type shall be completed according to the actual situation. Registration type for other legal persons and industrial activity entities shall be completed according to the main source of outlays and management manner, pursuant to the actual conditions, and by referring to the *Type of Enterprise Registration and Code*.

State-owned Enterprise refers to non-corporation economic organizations where the entire assets are owned by the state and which have been registered in accordance with the *Regulation of the People's Republic of China on the Management of Registration of Corporate Enterprises*, excluding solely state-funded corporations in limited liability companies.

Collectively-owned Enterprise refer to economic organizations where the assets are owned collectively and which have been registered in accordance with the *Regulation of the People's Republic of China on the Management of Registration of Corporate Enterprises*.

Joint-equity Cooperative Enterprise refers to a form of collective economic organizations based on cooperative system, where capitals come mainly from employees as their shares, with certain proportion of capital from the public, where production is organized on the basis of independent operation, independent accounting for profits and losses, joint work, democratic management, and where the distribution system integrates distribution according to work with distribution according to capital share.

Associated Enterprise refers to organizations established by two or more corporate legal persons or institutional legal persons of the same or different ownership, through joint investment on the basis of voluntary participation, equality, and mutual benefits. They include state-owned associated enterprises, collectively-owned associated enterprises, state-collective associated enterprises and other associated enterprises.

Limited Liability Company refers to economic organizations established with investment from 2-50 shareholders and registered in accordance with the *Regulation of the People's Republic of China on the Management of Registration of Corporations*, each shareholder bearing limited liability to the corporation depending on its share of investment, and the corporation bearing liability to its debt to the maximum of its total assets. Limited liability companies include solely state-funded limited liability companies and other limited liability companies.

Private Enterprise refers to profit-making economic organizations established by natural persons or controlled by natural persons using employed labor. Private enterprises include solely private-funded enterprises, private partnership enterprises, private limited liability companies, private companies limited by shares, and private-funded enterprises registered in accordance with provisions in the *Company Law*, the *Partnership Enterprises Law*, the *Interim Regulations on Private Enterprises*, and the *Sole Proprietorship Enterprise Law*.

Other Enterprise refers to domestically funded economic organizations other than those mentioned above.

Hong Kong, Macao and Taiwan-invested Enterprise refers to enterprises established by investors from Hong Kong, Macao and Taiwan in accordance with laws and rules of the People's Republic of China on foreign-related businesses. They include joint ventures with investors from Hong Kong, Macao and Taiwan, cooperative enterprises with investors from Hong Kong, Macao and Taiwan, enterprises wholly funded by investors from Hong Kong, Macao and Taiwan, companies limited by shares and funded by investors from Hong Kong, Macao and Taiwan, and other enterprises funded by investors from Hong Kong, Macao and Taiwan.

Foreign-invested Enterprise refers to enterprises established by foreign enterprises or foreigners in accordance with laws and regulations of the People's Republic of China on foreign-related businesses. They include Sino-foreign joint ventures, Sino-foreign cooperative enterprises, foreign wholly-funded enterprises, foreign-funded companies limited by shares, and other foreign-funded enterprises.

Non-public Economy means corporate legal entities of "non-public sector of the economy" whose assets are controlled by Chinese individuals, investors from Hong Kong, Macao and Taiwan, and foreign investors, along with the non-corporate legal entities and self-employed operators whose main funds are from individuals, investors from Hong Kong, Macao and Taiwan, and foreign investors. Thereinto, enterprises controlled by individuals, investors from Hong Kong, Macao and Taiwan, and foreign investors mean economic sectors with absolute or relative control by such companies.

02

国民经济核算
NATIONAL ACCOUNTS

简要说明

一、主要内容

本章资料包括历年北京市地区生产总值、部分新兴产业增加值、各行业增加值、三次产业及三大需求贡献率、居民消费水平、社会劳动生产率等内容。

二、统计调查方法说明

地区生产总值是统计部门根据统计资料、财政决算资料、行政管理部门的行政记录资料和部门财务资料采用不同方法核算的数据。

三、关于历史数据调整的问题

按照国家统计局部署，2016 年开始实施地区研发支出核算方法改革，将研发支出未计入地区生产总值部分进行补充核算，并对历史数据进行了修订。

2018 年数据为北京市第四次全国经济普查数据，并根据普查结果对历史数据进行了修订。

2023 年的地区生产总值为初步核算数据，待最终核实数据确定后将在次年年鉴中进行更新。

四、有关统计标准的变化说明

（一）关于行业划分标准。本章行业划分执行《国民经济行业分类》（GB/T 4754-2017）标准。

（二）关于三次产业划分。三次产业分类依据国家统计局 2018 年修订的《三次产业划分规定》。第一产业是指农、林、牧、渔业（不含农、林、牧、渔专业及辅助性活动）。第二产业是指采矿业（不含开采专业及辅助性活动），制造业（不含金属制品、机械和设备修理业），电力、热力、燃气及水生产和供应业，建筑业。第三产业即服务业，是指除第一产业、第二产业以外的其他行业。

本章三次产业的分类均执行调整后的划分规定。

Brief Introduction

I. Main Content

Statistics in this chapter include the GDP of Beijing, added value of some emerging sectors, added value of different sectors, contribution rate of three industries and three demands, residents' consumption level and social labor productivity in previous years.

II. Statistical Survey Methods

The GDP of Beijing is calculated by the statistics department using different methods according to the statistical data and final financial account data as well as the administrative records of the administrative departments and the financial data of departments.

Ⅲ. Adjustment to Historical Statistics

In accordance with the deployment of the National Bureau of Statistics of the People's Republic of China (NBS), the reform of calculation method of regional R&D expenditure has been implemented since 2016, according to which supplementary accounting was carried out on the part of R&D expenditure not included in GDP data, and historical data were revised.

The data for 2018 were collected from the fourth national economic census in Beijing, and historical data were revised according to the census results.

The GDP data for 2023 were the preliminary accounting data and shall be updated in the yearbook of the following year after the final data verification and confirmation.

IV. Explanation on Changes of Statistical Standards

(I) Standard for Classification of Sectors.The standards in the *Classification of National Economic Sectors (GB/T 4754-2017)* have been implemented.

(II) Classification of Three Industries. The classification of three industries is based on the *Regulations on Three Industries Classification* revised by the National Bureau of Statistics in 2018. The primary industry refers to agriculture, forestry, animal production and hunting, fishing (excluding professional and supporting activities of agriculture, forestry, animal production and hunting, fishing). The secondary industry refers to mining and quarrying (excluding professional and support activities for mining), manufacturing (excluding repair of fabricated metal products, machinery and equipment), production and distribution of electricity, heating power, gas and water and construction. The tertiary industry refers to others excluding the primary and secondary industries.

The classification of three industries since 1978 as mentioned in this chapter has all been subject to the classification provisions after adjustment.

2-1 地区生产总值(1978-2023年)
GROSS DOMESTIC PRODUCT (1978-2023)

单位：亿元 (100 million yuan)

年份 Year	地区生产总值 Gross Domestic Product	按产业分 By Three Strata of Industry			按行业分 By Sector		人均地区生产总值(元) Per Capita Gross Domestic Product (yuan)	人均地区生产总值(美元) Per Capita Gross Domestic Product (USD)
		第一产业 Primary Industry	第二产业 Secondary Industry	第三产业 Tertiary Industry	#工业 Industry	#建筑业 Construction		
1978	108.8	5.6	77.2	26.0	70.2	7.2	1257	797
1979	120.1	5.2	85.0	29.9	77.4	7.8	1358	908
1980	139.1	6.1	95.6	37.4	86.9	8.9	1544	1009
1981	139.2	6.6	92.3	40.3	82.7	9.8	1526	895
1982	154.9	10.2	99.6	45.1	89.3	10.5	1671	883
1983	183.1	12.7	112.5	57.9	98.8	13.9	1943	983
1984	216.6	14.7	130.5	71.4	114.0	16.7	2262	972
1985	257.1	17.7	153.5	85.9	130.7	23.0	2643	900
1986	284.9	19.0	165.6	100.3	141.2	24.6	2836	821
1987	326.8	24.2	182.2	120.4	154.5	28.1	3150	846
1988	410.2	36.9	220.9	152.4	189.5	31.8	3892	1046
1989	456.0	38.3	251.8	165.9	212.8	39.4	4269	1134
1990	500.8	43.7	262.0	195.1	219.3	43.1	4635	969
1991	598.9	45.5	290.5	262.9	255.6	35.9	5494	1032
1992	710.2	48.7	343.4	318.1	291.3	53.2	6468	1173
1993	888.9	53.2	416.3	419.4	336.5	81.2	8030	1393
1994	1149.8	66.8	512.7	570.3	413.4	100.9	10280	1193
1995	1516.2	72.2	638.3	805.7	520.7	119.8	12762	1529
1996	1819.4	75.0	709.2	1035.2	570.0	141.6	14495	1743
1997	2118.1	77.2	774.8	1266.2	627.6	149.7	16949	2045
1998	2439.1	77.9	834.1	1527.1	661.5	175.1	19625	2371
1999	2759.8	78.4	900.0	1781.5	713.3	189.5	22054	2664
2000	3277.8	79.3	1023.7	2174.9	831.0	196.6	25014	3022
2001	3861.5	80.8	1127.2	2653.6	920.2	212.3	28097	3395
2002	4525.7	82.4	1235.1	3208.2	999.6	239.7	32231	3894
2003	5267.2	84.1	1456.4	3726.7	1195.1	276.1	36583	4420
2004	6252.5	85.4	1773.7	4393.4	1483.2	308.9	42402	5123
2005	7149.8	86.9	1907.4	5155.5	1600.5	326.8	47182	5760
2006	8387.0	87.2	2072.1	6227.7	1713.8	379.4	53438	6703
2007	10425.5	99.4	2413.4	7912.8	1989.1	448.5	63629	8368
2008	11813.1	111.4	2526.7	9175.1	2030.8	520.4	68541	9869
2009	12900.9	116.8	2736.4	10047.7	2182.6	580.3	71059	10402
2010	14964.0	122.8	3233.1	11608.1	2607.5	656.9	78307	11568
2011	17188.8	134.5	3563.3	13491.0	2859.6	738.1	86246	13353
2012	19024.7	148.4	3856.0	15020.3	3090.1	803.0	92758	14694
2013	21134.6	159.8	4168.3	16806.5	3336.6	872.0	100569	16240
2014	22926.0	159.2	4433.0	18333.9	3522.8	952.7	106732	17375
2015	24779.1	140.4	4419.8	20218.9	3458.9	1002.6	113692	18253
2016	27041.2	129.8	4665.8	22245.7	3635.5	1074.5	123391	18577
2017	29883.0	121.9	5049.4	24711.7	3885.9	1210.9	136172	20168
2018	33106.0	120.6	5477.4	27508.1	4139.9	1387.8	150962	22813
2019	35445.1	114.4	5667.4	29663.4	4243.3	1477.4	161776	23451
2020	35943.3	108.3	5739.1	30095.9	4255.1	1528.2	164158	23799
2021	41045.6	111.4	7389.0	33545.2	5855.1	1591.4	187526	29067
2022	41540.9	111.5	6635.6	34793.7	5115.5	1576.5	189988	28246
2023	43760.7	105.5	6525.6	37129.6	5008.5	1603.4	200278	28421

注：1.本表数据按当年价格计算。
2.人均地区生产总值按年平均常住人口计算。
3.2023年为初步核算数，下同。

Note: a) Data in this table are calculated at current prices.
b) Per capita GDP is calculated at average resident population.
c) The data for 2023 are the preliminary accounting data, the same below.

2-2 地区生产总值指数(1978−2023年)
INDICES OF GROSS DOMESTIC PRODUCT(1978-2023)

(上年=100) (preceding year=100)

年份 Year	地区生产总值 Gross Domestic Product	按产业分 By Three Strata of Industry			按行业分 By Sector		人均地区生产总值 Per Capita Gross Domestic Product
		第一产业 Primary Industry	第二产业 Secondary Industry	第三产业 Tertiary Industry	#工业 Industry	#建筑业 Construction	
1978	110.5	109.0	116.5	97.7	112.4	153.0	109.1
1979	109.7	105.0	109.1	113.2	110.1	108.4	107.4
1980	111.8	109.3	109.6	118.5	110.1	110.3	109.8
1981	99.5	109.2	96.3	106.0	95.3	106.4	98.3
1982	107.4	113.4	105.8	109.9	105.8	106.1	105.6
1983	116.4	107.5	113.6	124.2	111.5	132.3	114.5
1984	117.4	106.8	116.1	121.8	115.7	118.8	115.6
1985	108.7	106.3	111.0	104.4	109.1	124.7	106.9
1986	108.0	100.1	104.8	115.7	105.0	103.7	104.6
1987	109.6	113.4	105.6	116.7	105.5	106.3	106.1
1988	112.8	111.2	112.1	114.1	113.0	106.5	111.0
1989	104.4	101.1	108.9	97.3	108.4	112.2	103.1
1990	105.2	103.3	101.1	113.3	101.9	95.6	104.0
1991	109.9	103.7	107.5	114.5	112.6	81.6	108.9
1992	111.3	103.1	111.8	112.3	109.6	126.4	110.5
1993	112.3	103.2	112.8	113.3	110.2	128.8	111.4
1994	113.7	102.8	113.9	115.4	113.2	117.3	112.5
1995	112.0	92.0	107.4	120.7	107.3	107.8	105.4
1996	109.8	96.8	106.3	115.2	106.0	107.5	103.9
1997	110.2	103.0	107.7	113.4	108.2	105.3	110.7
1998	109.6	101.1	109.3	110.6	108.3	114.3	110.2
1999	111.0	102.5	111.7	111.0	112.4	108.3	110.2
2000	112.0	103.2	111.1	113.5	112.8	102.4	107.0
2001	111.8	103.6	109.0	113.4	109.0	106.7	106.6
2002	111.8	103.0	107.8	113.9	107.1	111.1	109.4
2003	111.1	98.5	110.2	111.9	111.4	110.7	108.4
2004	113.3	99.6	115.4	112.8	117.8	105.4	110.6
2005	112.3	98.4	109.7	113.8	110.4	106.6	109.3
2006	112.8	100.8	109.9	114.1	108.7	115.8	108.9
2007	114.4	102.0	111.9	115.5	112.1	111.0	109.6
2008	109.0	101.6	100.3	112.1	99.6	103.7	103.6
2009	110.0	104.6	110.0	110.1	108.2	118.3	104.5
2010	110.4	98.4	113.4	109.6	114.6	108.6	104.9
2011	108.1	100.9	106.6	108.6	107.5	102.9	103.6
2012	107.7	103.2	106.8	108.0	106.1	109.4	104.7
2013	107.7	103.0	107.7	107.8	107.3	109.4	105.2
2014	107.4	100.0	106.8	107.6	105.9	110.3	105.1
2015	106.9	89.2	102.8	108.2	100.2	112.4	105.4
2016	106.9	91.3	105.3	107.4	104.5	108.1	106.3
2017	106.8	95.2	104.2	107.4	105.0	101.7	106.7
2018	106.7	98.0	103.9	107.3	104.0	103.5	106.8
2019	106.1	95.0	103.9	106.5	103.0	105.4	106.2
2020	101.1	91.6	102.5	100.8	101.9	104.3	101.1
2021	108.8	102.8	123.2	106.1	131.5	100.1	108.9
2022	100.7	98.3	88.4	103.4	85.5	99.0	100.8
2023	105.2	95.4	100.4	106.1	100.3	100.8	105.2

注：本表数据按不变价格计算。
Note: Data in this table are calculated at constant prices.

2-3 地区生产总值指数(1978–2023年)
INDICES OF GROSS DOMESTIC PRODUCT(1978-2023)

(1978年=100) (year of 1978=100)

年 份 Year	地区生产总值 Gross Domestic Product	按产业分 By Three Strata of Industry			按行业分 By Sector		人均地区生产总值 Per Capita Gross Domestic Product
		第一产业 Primary Industry	第二产业 Secondary Industry	第三产业 Tertiary Industry	#工业 Industry	#建筑业 Construction	
1978	100.0	100.0	100.0	100.0	100.0	100.0	100.0
1979	109.7	105.0	109.1	113.2	110.1	108.4	107.4
1980	122.6	114.8	119.6	134.1	121.2	119.6	117.9
1981	122.0	125.4	115.2	142.1	115.5	127.3	115.9
1982	131.0	142.2	121.9	156.2	122.2	135.1	122.4
1983	152.5	152.9	138.5	194.0	136.3	178.7	140.1
1984	179.0	163.3	160.8	236.3	157.7	212.3	162.0
1985	194.6	173.6	178.5	246.7	172.1	264.7	173.2
1986	210.2	173.8	187.1	285.4	180.7	274.5	181.2
1987	230.4	197.1	197.6	333.1	190.6	291.8	192.3
1988	259.9	219.2	221.5	380.1	215.4	310.8	213.5
1989	271.3	221.6	241.2	369.8	233.5	348.7	220.1
1990	285.4	228.9	243.9	419.0	237.9	333.4	228.9
1991	313.7	237.4	262.2	479.8	267.9	272.1	249.3
1992	349.1	244.8	293.1	538.8	293.6	343.9	275.5
1993	392.0	252.6	330.6	610.5	323.5	442.9	306.9
1994	445.7	259.7	376.6	704.5	366.2	519.5	345.3
1995	499.2	238.9	404.5	850.3	392.9	560.0	363.9
1996	548.1	231.3	430.0	979.5	416.5	602.0	378.1
1997	604.0	238.2	463.1	1110.8	450.7	633.9	418.6
1998	662.0	240.8	506.2	1228.5	488.1	724.5	461.3
1999	734.8	246.8	565.4	1363.6	548.6	784.6	508.4
2000	823.0	254.7	628.2	1547.7	618.8	803.4	544.0
2001	920.1	263.9	684.7	1755.1	674.5	857.2	579.9
2002	1028.7	271.8	738.1	1999.1	722.4	952.3	634.4
2003	1142.9	267.7	813.4	2237.0	804.8	1054.2	687.7
2004	1294.9	266.6	938.7	2523.3	948.1	1111.1	760.6
2005	1454.2	262.3	1029.8	2871.5	1046.7	1184.4	831.3
2006	1640.3	264.4	1131.8	3276.4	1137.8	1371.5	905.3
2007	1876.5	269.7	1266.5	3784.2	1275.5	1522.4	992.2
2008	2045.4	274.0	1270.3	4242.1	1270.4	1578.7	1027.9
2009	2249.9	286.6	1397.3	4670.6	1374.6	1867.6	1074.2
2010	2483.9	282.0	1584.5	5119.0	1575.3	2028.2	1126.8
2011	2685.1	284.5	1689.1	5559.2	1693.4	2087.0	1167.4
2012	2891.9	293.6	1804.0	6003.9	1796.7	2283.2	1222.3
2013	3114.6	302.4	1942.9	6472.2	1927.9	2497.8	1285.9
2014	3345.1	302.4	2075.0	6964.1	2041.6	2755.1	1351.5
2015	3575.9	269.7	2133.1	7535.2	2045.7	3096.7	1424.5
2016	3822.6	246.2	2246.2	8092.8	2137.8	3347.5	1514.2
2017	4082.5	234.4	2340.5	8691.7	2244.7	3404.4	1615.7
2018	4356.0	229.7	2431.8	9326.2	2334.5	3523.6	1725.6
2019	4621.7	218.2	2526.6	9932.4	2404.5	3713.9	1832.6
2020	4672.5	199.9	2589.8	10011.9	2450.2	3873.6	1852.8
2021	5083.7	205.5	3190.6	10622.6	3222.0	3877.5	2017.7
2022	5119.3	202.0	2820.5	10983.8	2754.8	3838.7	2033.8
2023	5385.5	192.7	2831.8	11653.8	2763.1	3869.4	2139.6

注：本表数据按不变价格计算。

Note: Data in this table are calculated at constant prices.

2-4 地区生产总值指数(2000—2023年)
INDICES OF GROSS DOMESTIC PRODUCT(2000-2023)

(2000年=100) (year of 2000=100)

年份 Year	地区生产总值 Gross Domestic Product	按产业分 By Three Strata of Industry 第一产业 Primary Industry	第二产业 Secondary Industry	第三产业 Tertiary Industry	按行业分 By Sector #工业 Industry	#建筑业 Construction	人均地区生产总值 Per Capita Gross Domestic Product
2000	100.0	100.0	100.0	100.0	100.0	100.0	100.0
2001	111.8	103.6	109.0	113.4	109.0	106.7	106.6
2002	125.0	106.7	118.8	129.2	116.7	118.5	116.6
2003	138.9	105.1	129.5	144.6	130.0	131.2	126.4
2004	157.4	104.7	141.2	163.1	153.1	138.3	139.8
2005	176.8	103.0	153.9	185.6	169.0	147.4	152.8
2006	199.4	103.8	167.8	211.8	183.7	170.7	166.4
2007	228.1	105.9	182.9	244.6	205.9	189.5	182.4
2008	248.6	107.6	199.4	274.2	205.1	196.5	189.0
2009	273.5	112.5	217.3	301.9	221.9	232.5	197.5
2010	301.9	110.7	236.9	330.9	254.3	252.5	207.2
2011	326.4	111.7	258.2	359.4	273.4	259.8	214.7
2012	351.5	115.3	281.4	388.2	290.1	284.2	224.8
2013	378.6	118.8	306.7	418.5	311.3	310.9	236.5
2014	406.6	118.8	334.3	450.3	329.7	342.9	248.6
2015	434.7	106.0	364.4	487.2	330.4	385.4	262.0
2016	464.7	96.8	397.2	523.3	345.3	416.6	278.5
2017	496.3	92.2	432.9	562.0	362.6	423.7	297.2
2018	529.6	90.4	471.9	603.0	377.1	438.5	317.4
2019	561.9	85.9	490.3	642.2	388.4	462.2	337.1
2020	568.1	78.7	502.6	647.3	395.8	482.1	340.8
2021	618.1	80.9	619.2	686.8	520.5	482.6	371.1
2022	622.4	79.5	547.4	710.2	445.0	477.8	374.1
2023	654.8	75.8	549.6	753.5	446.3	481.6	393.6

注：本表数据按不变价格计算。
Note: Data in this table are calculated at constant prices.

2-5 地区生产总值构成(1978-2023年)
COMPOSITION OF GROSS DOMESTIC PRODUCT (1978-2023)

单位：% (%)

年 份 Year	地区生产总值 Gross Domestic Product	按产业分 By Three Strata of Industry			按行业分 By Sector	
		第一产业 Primary Industry	第二产业 Secondary Industry	第三产业 Tertiary Industry	#工业 Industry	#建筑业 Construction
1978	100.0	5.1	71.0	23.9	64.5	6.6
1979	100.0	4.3	70.8	24.9	64.4	6.5
1980	100.0	4.4	68.7	26.9	62.5	6.4
1981	100.0	4.7	66.3	29.0	59.4	7.0
1982	100.0	6.6	64.3	29.1	57.7	6.8
1983	100.0	6.9	61.4	31.6	54.0	7.6
1984	100.0	6.8	60.2	33.0	52.6	7.7
1985	100.0	6.9	59.7	33.4	50.8	8.9
1986	100.0	6.7	58.1	35.2	49.6	8.6
1987	100.0	7.4	55.8	36.8	47.3	8.6
1988	100.0	9.0	53.9	37.2	46.2	7.8
1989	100.0	8.4	55.2	36.4	46.7	8.6
1990	100.0	8.7	52.3	39.0	43.8	8.6
1991	100.0	7.6	48.5	43.9	42.7	6.0
1992	100.0	6.9	48.4	44.8	41.0	7.5
1993	100.0	6.0	46.8	47.2	37.9	9.1
1994	100.0	5.8	44.6	49.6	36.0	8.8
1995	100.0	4.8	42.1	53.1	34.3	7.9
1996	100.0	4.1	39.0	56.9	31.3	7.8
1997	100.0	3.6	36.6	59.8	29.6	7.1
1998	100.0	3.2	34.2	62.6	27.1	7.2
1999	100.0	2.8	32.6	64.6	25.8	6.9
2000	100.0	2.4	31.2	66.4	25.4	6.0
2001	100.0	2.1	29.2	68.7	23.8	5.5
2002	100.0	1.8	27.3	70.9	22.1	5.3
2003	100.0	1.6	27.7	70.8	22.7	5.2
2004	100.0	1.4	28.4	70.3	23.7	4.9
2005	100.0	1.2	26.7	72.1	22.4	4.6
2006	100.0	1.0	24.7	74.3	20.4	4.5
2007	100.0	1.0	23.1	75.9	19.1	4.3
2008	100.0	0.9	21.4	77.7	17.2	4.4
2009	100.0	0.9	21.2	77.9	16.9	4.5
2010	100.0	0.8	21.6	77.6	17.4	4.4
2011	100.0	0.8	20.7	78.5	16.6	4.3
2012	100.0	0.8	20.3	79.0	16.2	4.2
2013	100.0	0.8	19.7	79.5	15.8	4.1
2014	100.0	0.7	19.3	80.0	15.4	4.2
2015	100.0	0.6	17.8	81.6	14.0	4.0
2016	100.0	0.5	17.3	82.3	13.4	4.0
2017	100.0	0.4	16.9	82.7	13.0	4.1
2018	100.0	0.4	16.5	83.1	12.5	4.2
2019	100.0	0.3	16.0	83.7	12.0	4.2
2020	100.0	0.3	16.0	83.7	11.8	4.3
2021	100.0	0.3	18.0	81.7	14.3	3.9
2022	100.0	0.3	16.0	83.8	12.3	3.8
2023	100.0	0.2	14.9	84.8	11.4	3.7

注：本表数据按当年价格计算。
Note: Data in this table are calculated at current prices.

2-6 三次产业贡献率(1982−2023年)
SHARE OF THE CONTRIBUTIONS OF THE THREE STRATA OF INDUSTRY TO THE INCREASE OF THE GDP (1982-2023)

单位：% (%)

年 份 Year	地区生产总值 Gross Domestic Product	按产业分 By Three Strata of Industry			按行业分 By Sector	
		第一产业 Primary Industry	第二产业 Secondary Industry	第三产业 Tertiary Industry	#工业 Industry	#建筑业 Construction
1982	100.0	8.7	52.8	38.4	47.2	5.6
1983	100.0	2.3	54.6	43.1	41.3	13.2
1984	100.0	1.8	59.2	39.0	51.0	8.2
1985	100.0	3.1	80.6	16.3	58.5	22.1
1986	100.0	0.1	39.0	61.0	34.8	4.1
1987	100.0	5.4	36.8	57.8	31.2	5.6
1988	100.0	3.5	57.5	39.0	53.3	4.2
1989	100.0	1.0	121.1	-22.1	99.6	21.5
1990	100.0	2.4	12.8	84.8	19.8	-7.0
1991	100.0	3.3	39.8	56.9	55.8	-16.0
1992	100.0	2.2	53.6	44.1	37.9	14.9
1993	100.0	2.0	53.7	44.4	36.7	17.0
1994	100.0	1.5	52.3	46.3	41.7	10.5
1995	100.0	-4.3	31.9	72.2	26.3	5.6
1996	100.0	-1.7	31.7	70.0	25.5	6.3
1997	100.0	1.3	36.3	62.4	32.1	4.2
1998	100.0	0.5	45.5	54.0	34.0	11.6
1999	100.0	0.9	49.7	49.4	43.6	6.1
2000	100.0	1.0	43.4	55.6	41.9	1.5
2001	100.0	0.7	23.8	75.5	19.4	3.4
2002	100.0	0.6	20.2	79.2	14.8	5.4
2003	100.0	-0.3	27.0	73.3	24.4	5.5
2004	100.0	…	33.7	66.4	31.7	2.3
2005	100.0	-0.2	23.3	76.9	20.8	2.8
2006	100.0	0.1	20.7	79.2	15.2	5.7
2007	100.0	0.2	21.5	78.3	18.2	3.6
2008	100.0	0.2	0.8	99.0	-1.0	1.8
2009	100.0	0.4	23.4	76.2	15.8	7.9
2010	100.0	-0.1	30.2	70.0	26.6	3.9
2011	100.0	0.1	17.6	82.3	16.3	1.6
2012	100.0	0.3	18.7	81.0	13.8	5.1
2013	100.0	0.3	21.0	78.7	16.1	5.2
2014	100.0	…	19.4	80.6	13.5	6.0
2015	100.0	-1.0	8.5	92.6	0.5	7.9
2016	100.0	-0.7	13.8	86.9	9.2	4.7
2017	100.0	-0.3	10.8	89.5	9.9	1.0
2018	100.0	-0.1	10.0	90.2	8.0	2.1
2019	100.0	-0.3	10.7	89.6	6.5	3.4
2020	100.0	-2.9	38.2	64.6	23.0	15.3
2021	100.0	0.1	41.9	58.0	42.1	
2022	100.0	-0.7	-289.9	390.6	-288.0	-5.5
2023	100.0	-0.2	1.2	99.1	0.6	0.6

注：1.本表数据按不变价格计算。
2.产业贡献率指各产业增加值增量与地区生产总值增量之比。

Note: a) Data in this table are calculated at constant prices.
b) Share of the contributions of the three strata of industry to the increase of the GDP refers to the proportion of the increment of the value-added of each industry to the increment of GDP.

2-7 按产业、行业分地区生产总值(2001-2023年)

单位：亿元

项　　目	Item	2001	2002	2003	2004	2005	2006	2007	2008
地区生产总值	**Gross Domestic Product**	**3861.5**	**4525.7**	**5267.2**	**6252.5**	**7149.8**	**8387.0**	**10425.5**	**11813.1**
按产业分	**By Three Strata of Industry**								
第一产业	Primary Industry	80.8	82.4	84.1	85.4	86.9	87.2	99.4	111.4
第二产业	Secondary Industry	1127.2	1235.1	1456.4	1773.7	1907.4	2072.1	2413.4	2526.7
第三产业	Tertiary Industry	2653.6	3208.2	3726.7	4393.4	5155.5	6227.7	7912.8	9175.1
按行业分	**By Sector**								
农、林、牧、渔业	Agriculture, Forestry, Animal Husbandry and Fishery	81.8	82.9	84.6	87.4	88.7	88.8	101.3	112.8
工　业	Industry	920.2	999.6	1195.1	1483.2	1600.5	1713.8	1989.1	2030.8
建筑业	Construction	212.3	239.7	276.1	308.9	326.8	379.4	448.5	520.4
批发和零售业	Wholesale and Retail Trades	442.8	485.3	542.4	607.9	718.9	894.9	1155.1	1502.0
交通运输、仓储和邮政业	Transport, Storage and Post	227.6	249.2	271.1	303.4	333.9	373.5	412.5	408.4
住宿和餐饮业	Hotels and Catering Services	103.3	130.5	121.0	172.9	190.8	230.2	265.0	297.7
信息传输、软件和信息技术服务业	Information Transmission, Software and Information Technology	233.0	309.3	415.9	492.8	637.4	751.0	959.7	1117.6
金融业	Financial Intermediation	519.7	600.8	683.9	755.9	879.9	1036.1	1410.2	1648.5
房地产业	Real Estate	233.6	346.3	402.3	508.7	573.4	775.0	999.6	1037.8
租赁和商务服务业	Leasing and Business Services	146.4	230.1	250.4	294.6	379.9	474.4	679.4	836.1
科学研究和技术服务业	Scientific Research and Technical Services	195.2	230.4	273.1	305.3	373.3	459.7	591.8	720.3
水利、环境和公共设施管理业	Management of Water Conservancy, Environment and Public Facilities	27.3	29.8	33.6	37.5	43.5	50.9	57.7	66.1
居民服务、修理和其他服务业	Service to Households, Repair and Other Services	45.5	59.4	70.0	85.7	85.5	91.7	90.5	83.0
教　育	Education	160.8	174.5	225.7	288.5	312.9	347.3	406.7	451.0
卫生和社会工作	Health and Social Service	73.6	80.8	96.2	115.3	127.5	152.7	181.9	211.1
文化、体育和娱乐业	Culture, Sports and Entertainment	101.6	117.6	132.2	148.5	174.9	195.2	236.3	262.4
公共管理、社会保障和社会组织	Public Management, Social Security and Social Organizations	137.0	159.8	193.8	256.2	302.0	372.6	440.2	507.0
国际组织	International Organizations								

注：本表数据按当年价格计算。

GROSS DOMESTIC PRODUCT BY THREE STRATA OF INDUSTRY AND SECTOR(2001-2023)

(100 million yuan)

2009	2010	2011	2012	2013	2014	2015	2016	2017	2018	2019	2020	2021	2022	2023
12900.9	**14964.0**	**17188.8**	**19024.7**	**21134.6**	**22926.0**	**24779.1**	**27041.2**	**29883.0**	**33106.0**	**35445.1**	**35943.3**	**41045.6**	**41540.9**	**43760.7**
116.8	122.8	134.5	148.4	159.8	159.2	140.4	129.8	121.9	120.6	114.4	108.3	111.4	111.5	105.5
2736.4	3233.1	3563.3	3856.0	4168.3	4433.0	4419.8	4665.8	5049.4	5477.4	5667.4	5739.1	7389.0	6635.6	6525.6
10047.7	11608.1	13491.0	15020.3	16806.5	18333.9	20218.9	22245.7	24711.7	27508.1	29663.4	30095.9	33545.2	34793.7	37129.6
118.3	124.6	136.5	150.4	162.0	161.5	142.8	132.2	124.3	122.6	116.9	110.7	113.4	113.1	106.9
2182.6	2607.5	2859.6	3090.1	3336.6	3522.8	3458.9	3635.5	3885.9	4139.9	4243.3	4255.1	5855.1	5115.5	5008.5
580.3	656.9	738.1	803.0	872.0	952.7	1002.6	1074.5	1210.9	1387.8	1477.4	1528.2	1591.4	1576.5	1603.4
1606.6	1995.4	2256.9	2356.3	2483.2	2579.0	2506.7	2544.3	2703.7	2824.1	2867.5	2840.3	3126.7	3103.3	3073.1
449.2	570.4	637.3	635.5	670.6	724.8	739.8	790.8	901.0	1015.9	1010.8	844.4	900.9	879.5	1065.3
285.7	346.3	380.6	408.8	413.1	404.4	441.7	447.0	470.4	515.3	538.1	360.8	429.8	371.1	453.1
1165.3	1314.1	1611.7	1758.8	2015.8	2283.0	2600.0	3003.9	3508.2	4290.1	4879.6	5601.5	6770.5	7468.2	8514.4
1744.4	2038.1	2421.6	2783.2	3247.5	3736.8	4365.5	4784.7	5299.6	5951.3	6544.2	7057.1	7683.1	8061.6	8663.1
1319.1	1261.4	1358.2	1588.1	1731.5	1745.2	1899.2	2241.2	2420.5	2481.5	2603.8	2459.0	2603.6	2545.2	2612.0
886.2	1055.7	1285.5	1488.1	1746.9	1917.2	1987.1	2079.7	2226.4	2421.0	2599.3	2286.2	2591.0	2601.8	2710.0
808.2	940.2	1106.6	1245.9	1442.0	1628.9	1765.4	1980.0	2260.5	2578.3	2823.3	2973.9	3373.3	3504.9	3630.1
75.5	85.2	97.9	115.5	138.7	159.6	211.2	239.2	269.2	287.0	305.6	303.9	299.2	303.4	307.0
82.3	111.0	125.6	139.9	158.5	177.4	163.3	184.3	201.1	220.8	229.2	187.7	201.1	200.9	208.2
498.0	594.5	694.4	788.0	886.0	1000.1	1119.3	1263.9	1459.0	1603.4	1803.6	1899.2	1960.9	1934.7	1954.8
240.7	290.0	355.9	417.6	481.0	547.0	675.5	750.2	835.0	938.1	1015.1	1002.7	1103.3	1260.7	1290.0
275.4	313.9	361.6	430.1	482.4	508.1	568.5	612.7	657.4	728.1	749.7	651.7	795.0	791.7	836.1
583.1	658.9	760.7	825.6	866.8	877.6	1131.7	1277.1	1450.1	1600.9	1637.8	1581.0	1647.4	1708.9	1724.8

Note: Data in this table are calculated at current prices.

2-8 按产业、行业分地区生产总值指数(2001—2023年)

(上年=100)

项 目	Item	2001	2002	2003	2004	2005	2006	2007	2008
地区生产总值	**Gross Domestic Product**	**111.8**	**111.8**	**111.1**	**113.3**	**112.3**	**112.8**	**114.4**	**109.0**
按产业分	**By Three Strata of Industry**								
第一产业	Primary Industry	103.6	103.0	98.5	99.6	98.4	100.8	102.0	101.6
第二产业	Secondary Industry	109.0	107.8	110.2	115.4	109.7	109.9	111.9	100.3
第三产业	Tertiary Industry	113.4	113.9	111.9	112.8	113.8	114.1	115.5	112.1
按行业分	**By Sector**								
农、林、牧、渔业	Agriculture, Forestry, Animal Husbandry and Fishery	103.7	102.7	98.9	99.4	98.1	100.6	102.2	101.1
工 业	Industry	109.0	107.1	111.4	117.8	110.4	108.7	112.1	99.6
建筑业	Construction	106.7	111.1	110.7	105.4	106.6	115.8	111.0	103.7
批发和零售业	Wholesale and Retail Trades	112.5	109.2	111.3	111.1	117.8	118.1	122.5	125.4
交通运输、仓储和邮政业	Transport, Storage and Post	102.5	102.8	102.6	106.4	104.6	106.2	106.7	102.8
住宿和餐饮业	Hotels and Catering Services	109.3	117.5	90.9	135.8	107.2	115.8	108.0	98.3
信息传输、软件和信息技术服务业	Information Transmission, Software and Information Technology	113.5	119.8	124.4	112.0	121.8	111.6	116.8	115.4
金融业	Financial Intermediation	113.4	112.1	110.9	106.0	113.3	111.1	121.9	108.0
房地产业	Real Estate	132.4	131.6	111.9	119.3	109.3	123.1	106.3	95.7
租赁和商务服务业	Leasing and Business Services	106.7	132.6	103.5	109.5	122.0	117.6	124.3	123.6
科学研究和技术服务业	Scientific Research and Technical Services	127.6	113.2	112.2	108.6	115.3	115.5	118.5	119.1
水利、环境和公共设施管理业	Management of Water Conservancy, Environment and Public Facilities	95.2	102.5	104.3	104.2	113.5	110.7	104.8	115.1
居民服务、修理和其他服务业	Service to Households, Repair and Other Services	103.2	112.2	109.0	114.4	97.8	101.0	92.3	92.1
教 育	Education	125.6	109.7	128.1	124.5	107.6	106.9	111.6	110.3
卫生和社会工作	Health and Social Service	116.2	106.8	112.6	116.2	111.8	113.7	109.2	114.4
文化、体育和娱乐业	Culture, Sports and Entertainment	104.5	107.8	106.9	107.8	115.6	107.9	109.9	113.7
公共管理、社会保障和社会组织	Public Management, Social Security and Social Organizations	107.0	109.9	114.1	125.9	115.4	118.5	111.4	110.0
国际组织	International Organizations								

注：本表数据按不变价格计算。

INDICES OF GROSS DOMESTIC PRODUCT BY THREE STRATA OF INDUSTRY AND SECTOR(2001-2023)

(preceding year=100)

2009	2010	2011	2012	2013	2014	2015	2016	2017	2018	2019	2020	2021	2022	2023
110.0	**110.4**	**108.1**	**107.7**	**107.7**	**107.4**	**106.9**	**106.9**	**106.8**	**106.7**	**106.1**	**101.1**	**108.8**	**100.7**	**105.2**
104.6	98.4	100.9	103.2	103.0	100.0	89.2	91.3	95.2	98.0	95.0	91.6	102.8	98.3	95.4
110.0	113.4	106.6	106.8	107.7	106.8	102.8	105.3	104.2	103.9	103.9	102.5	123.2	88.4	100.4
110.1	109.6	108.6	108.0	107.8	107.6	108.2	107.4	107.4	107.3	106.5	100.8	106.1	103.4	106.1
104.6	98.6	100.9	103.2	103.0	100.1	89.4	91.5	95.3	97.7	95.1	92.3	102.3	98.3	95.4
108.2	114.6	107.5	106.1	107.3	105.9	100.2	104.5	105.0	104.0	103.0	101.9	131.5	85.5	100.3
118.3	108.6	102.9	109.4	109.4	110.3	112.4	108.1	101.7	103.5	105.4	104.3	100.1	99.0	100.8
109.3	121.5	109.2	103.7	105.3	105.4	98.4	103.0	107.0	100.8	101.9	97.9	107.6	98.8	99.1
101.5	111.1	104.7	105.3	105.6	105.7	102.8	105.4	110.9	105.9	100.8	87.5	103.0	95.5	120.3
97.0	115.7	102.7	99.7	97.2	99.5	100.5	100.5	102.3	102.2	99.9	72.4	115.0	86.2	121.1
104.9	109.8	123.0	106.9	108.9	112.2	111.9	112.3	113.5	119.0	112.9	114.5	111.3	110.2	113.5
106.7	109.4	108.1	112.5	112.5	113.2	118.4	109.3	107.7	107.6	109.5	104.9	105.1	106.2	106.7
123.2	86.8	94.3	114.5	103.1	98.8	105.2	106.7	99.5	100.8	106.2	99.1	103.3	97.6	102.3
111.8	111.4	118.4	109.5	109.9	106.5	98.5	101.8	103.7	103.7	104.4	85.9	103.8	99.2	104.0
118.8	108.6	107.6	107.8	111.5	110.3	112.4	108.6	109.8	108.9	106.4	100.3	106.8	102.4	103.4
120.4	105.6	106.0	106.9	106.7	112.8	113.6	109.3	110.7	103.8	103.8	99.1	94.4	101.4	101.1
104.5	126.1	112.9	104.4	103.6	113.5	102.5	109.7	103.4	104.4	100.7	86.2	102.9	99.3	102.9
109.4	111.2	103.7	106.0	106.3	110.4	111.8	108.8	108.6	106.8	109.6	105.3	100.4	97.4	100.5
114.1	112.7	108.5	108.7	112.1	111.4	114.3	107.7	108.1	109.2	105.8	94.3	106.6	113.8	102.1
107.5	106.6	106.4	109.4	106.3	102.2	103.7	106.9	102.8	106.0	102.1	89.5	113.8	99.5	104.3
112.5	107.5	103.8	104.8	103.9	99.2	110.3	109.1	108.8	107.5	98.6	98.6	101.7	103.2	100.5

Note: Data in this table are calculated at constant prices.

2-9 数字经济和部分新兴产业增加值(2016−2023年)
ADDED VALUE OF DIGITAL ECONOMY AND SOME EMERGING INDUSTRIES(2016-2023)

单位：亿元 (100 million yuan)

项　目	Item	2016	2017	2018	2019	2020	2021	2022	2023
地区生产总值	**Gross Domestic Product**	**27041.2**	**29883.0**	**33106.0**	**35445.1**	**35943.3**	**41045.6**	**41540.9**	**43760.7**
#数字经济	Digital Economy	9674.7	10852.6	12515.9	13609.2	14370.4	16596.3	17290.2	18766.7
#战略性新兴产业	Strategic Emerging Industry	5654.7	6619.8	7831.5	8441.9	8739.8	10597.1	10302.8	10464.3
#高技术产业	High-tech Industry	5888.8	6834.5	7996.0	8689.4	9514.9	11482.2	11083.2	11875.4
#生产性服务业	Producer Service Industry	13032.2	14549.2	16449.9	17806.1	18581.0	20741.9	21054.1	
#生活性服务业	Consumer Service Industry	6205.3	6839.0	7475.9	8043.5	7660.0	8637.6	8545.5	
#知识产权(专利)密集型产业	Intellectual Property (Patent) Intensive Industry			6310.4	6918.8	7558.4	10612.4	10092.3	10792.7

注：1.本表数据按当年价格计算。
　　2.知识产权(专利)密集型产业增加值根据2019年发布的统计分类标准进行测算。

Note: 1.Data in this table are calculated at current prices.
　　2.The added value of intellectual property (patent) intensive industry is calculated according to the statistical classification standards released in 2019.

2-10 支出法地区生产总值(1978−2023年)
GROSS DOMESTIC PRODUCT BY EXPENDITURE APPROACH (1978-2023)

单位：亿元 (100 million yuan)

年 份 Year	地区生产总 值 Gross Domestic Product	最终消费支 出 Final Consumption Expenditure	居民消费 Household Consumption	政府消费 Government Consumption	资本形成总 额 Gross Capital Formation	固定资本形成总额 Completed Fixed Assets	存货增加 Changes in Inventories	货物和服务净 流 出 Net Net Outflow of Goods and Services	最终消费率(消费率)(%) Final Consumption Rate (%)	资本形成率(投资率)(%) Capital Formation Rate (%)
1978	108.8	53.0	28.6	24.4	31.7	24.9	6.8	24.1	48.7	29.1
1979	120.1	55.4	31.5	23.9	37.0	29.1	7.9	27.7	46.1	30.8
1980	139.1	57.3	39.6	17.7	45.1	36.5	8.6	36.7	41.2	32.4
1981	139.2	61.8	44.2	17.6	50.5	40.2	10.3	26.9	44.4	36.3
1982	154.9	68.6	48.8	19.8	51.8	42.3	9.5	34.5	44.3	33.4
1983	183.1	77.6	54.6	23.0	62.9	56.1	6.8	42.6	42.4	34.4
1984	216.6	96.5	64.8	31.7	84.7	72.5	12.2	35.4	44.6	39.1
1985	257.1	127.1	88.7	38.4	150.6	102.7	47.9	-20.6	49.4	58.6
1986	284.9	161.1	109.9	51.2	178.8	116.0	62.8	-55.0	56.5	62.8
1987	326.8	181.5	124.3	57.2	201.2	148.6	52.6	-55.9	55.5	61.6
1988	410.2	222.6	161.9	60.7	251.1	177.7	73.4	-63.5	54.3	61.2
1989	456.0	244.0	176.1	67.9	271.5	151.9	119.6	-59.5	53.5	59.5
1990	500.8	269.7	194.1	75.6	296.5	195.0	101.5	-65.4	53.9	59.2
1991	598.9	302.6	225.7	76.9	327.3	208.8	118.5	-31.0	50.5	54.7
1992	710.2	342.2	261.2	81.0	415.5	289.2	126.3	-47.4	48.2	58.5
1993	888.9	446.7	355.5	91.2	537.3	446.1	91.2	-95.1	50.3	60.4
1994	1149.8	616.3	505.5	110.8	792.6	705.2	87.4	-259.1	53.6	68.9
1995	1516.2	848.4	675.1	173.2	1045.0	914.6	130.5	-377.2	56.0	68.9
1996	1819.4	1016.2	819.1	197.1	1074.9	981.5	93.4	-271.6	55.8	59.1
1997	2118.1	1207.5	998.9	208.7	1287.7	1080.5	207.2	-377.1	57.0	60.8
1998	2439.1	1318.0	1075.2	242.8	1439.3	1313.0	126.3	-318.3	54.0	59.0
1999	2759.8	1496.7	1184.5	312.2	1624.7	1334.9	289.9	-361.7	54.2	58.9
2000	3277.8	1654.4	1288.8	365.6	1836.0	1512.9	323.1	-212.6	50.5	56.0
2001	3861.5	1889.8	1417.4	472.4	2095.8	1728.3	367.4	-124.0	48.9	54.3
2002	4525.7	2279.3	1738.4	540.9	2541.8	2117.1	424.7	-295.4	50.4	56.2
2003	5267.2	2615.8	1977.5	638.3	2989.9	2635.0	354.9	-338.5	49.7	56.8
2004	6252.5	3054.4	2260.3	794.1	3478.3	3086.1	392.2	-280.3	48.9	55.6
2005	7149.8	3432.6	2521.1	911.5	3955.5	3494.8	460.7	-238.3	48.0	55.3
2006	8387.0	4112.5	2982.5	1130.1	4365.9	3880.8	485.1	-91.4	49.0	52.1
2007	10425.5	5087.3	3566.9	1520.4	4996.9	4428.7	568.2	341.3	48.8	47.9
2008	11813.1	6045.3	4137.3	1908.0	5335.7	4461.5	874.2	432.1	51.2	45.2
2009	12900.9	6991.8	4784.4	2207.4	5681.6	4910.1	771.5	227.5	54.2	44.0
2010	14964.0	8048.2	5634.1	2414.1	6873.2	5956.4	916.8	42.6	53.8	45.9
2011	17188.8	9516.9	6568.5	2948.4	7631.9	6670.1	961.8	40.0	55.4	44.4
2012	19024.7	10749.9	7398.0	3352.0	8508.4	7866.5	641.9	-233.5	56.5	44.7
2013	21134.6	12296.2	8471.5	3824.7	9218.1	8642.2	575.9	-379.7	58.2	43.6
2014	22926.0	13565.2	9219.9	4345.3	9633.4	8954.2	679.3	-272.6	59.2	42.0
2015	24779.1	14793.1	10118.8	4674.3	9910.8	9225.8	685.0	75.2	59.7	40.0
2016	27041.2	16134.7	11002.0	5132.6	10690.2	9951.8	738.4	216.4	59.7	39.5
2017	29883.0	17875.8	12064.4	5811.4	11784.3	10766.3	1018.0	222.9	59.8	39.4
2018	33106.0	20206.7	13478.1	6728.7	12527.8	11488.2	1039.7	371.5	61.0	37.8
2019	35445.1	21571.8	14536.2	7035.6	13463.4	12692.4	771.0	409.9	60.9	38.0
2020	35943.3	20722.2	13759.7	6962.5	14229.9	13542.8	687.1	991.2	57.7	39.6
2021	41045.6	23268.5	15804.9	7463.6	16198.3	15373.2	825.1	1578.8	56.7	39.5
2022	41540.9	23153.6	15425.1	7728.6	17132.4	16396.5	735.9	1254.8	55.7	41.2
2023	43760.7	24966.9	16711.2	8255.7	17838.5	17573.0	265.5	955.3	57.1	40.8

注：本表数据按当年价格计算。
Note: Data in this table are calculated at current prices.

2−11 支出法地区生产总值
GROSS DOMESTIC PRODUCT BY EXPENDITURE APPROACH

单位：亿元 (100 million yuan)

项　目	Item	2023	2022	指数(2022=100) Index (2022=100)
地区生产总值	**Gross Domestic Product**	**43760.7**	**41540.9**	**105.2**
最终消费支出	**Final Consumption Expenditure**	**24966.9**	**23153.6**	**106.2**
居民消费	Household Consumption	16711.2	15425.1	106.7
城镇居民	Urban Households	15581.7	14369.3	106.8
农村居民	Rural Households	1129.5	1055.8	105.5
政府消费	Government Consumption	8255.7	7728.6	105.2
资本形成总额	**Gross Capital Formation**	**17838.5**	**17132.4**	**104.2**
固定资本形成总额	Gross Fixed Capital Formation	17573.0	16396.5	107.4
存货增加	Increase in Inventories	265.5	735.9	45.7
货物和服务净流出	**Net Outflow of Goods and Services**	**955.3**	**1254.8**	**99.9**

注：本表总量数据按当年价格计算，指数按不变价格计算。
Note: Aggregate data in this table are calculated at current prices, while indices are calculated at constant prices.

2-12 三大需求贡献率(1982-2023年) CONTRIBUTION SHARE OF THE THREE COMPONENTS OF GDP TO THE INCREASE OF GDP(1982-2023)

单位：% (%)

年 份 Year	最终消费支出 Final Consumption Expenditure	资本形成总额 Gross Capital Formation	货物和服务净流出 Net Outflow of Goods and Services
1982	52.8	5.9	41.3
1983	18.3	44.6	37.1
1984	53.1	69.1	-22.2
1985	115.4	337.5	-352.9
1986	154.5	51.1	-105.5
1987	33.8	69.0	-2.8
1988	46.7	-10.8	64.1
1989	86.9	180.5	-167.4
1990	165.0	128.7	-193.7
1991	61.5	42.9	-4.4
1992	18.2	83.8	-1.9
1993	41.0	73.3	-14.2
1994	54.0	106.8	-60.8
1995	69.3	42.2	-11.5
1996	50.2	-25.2	75.1
1997	87.1	108.1	-95.1
1998	19.8	41.3	39.0
1999	56.1	68.9	-25.0
2000	30.5	46.2	23.2
2001	33.9	45.6	20.5
2002	72.2	68.9	-41.1
2003	40.0	69.4	-9.3
2004	39.7	43.5	16.8
2005	33.3	49.3	17.5
2006	63.0	27.6	9.4
2007	60.6	26.8	12.6
2008	87.4	10.1	2.5
2009	78.9	43.4	-22.3
2010	61.7	55.7	-17.4
2011	80.8	16.9	2.3
2012	74.0	50.9	-24.9
2013	67.0	43.4	-10.5
2014	73.3	25.0	1.7
2015	65.7	26.4	7.9
2016	62.2	31.3	6.5
2017	63.8	38.9	-2.7
2018	72.4	13.3	14.3
2019	56.1	37.9	6.0
2020	-327.2	218.6	208.6
2021	59.5	27.5	13.0
2022	-159.5	260.5	-1.0
2023	67.6	32.5	-0.1

注：1．三大需求指支出法地区生产总值的三大构成项目，即最终消费支出、资本形成总额、货物和服务净流出。
2．贡献率指三大需求增量与支出法地区生产总值增量之比。
3．本表数据按不变价格计算。

Note: a) Three components of GDP by expenditure approach are final consumption expenditure, gross capital formation and net outflow of goods and services.
b) Contribution share of the three components to the increase of the GDP refers to the proportion of the increment of the each component of GDP by expenditure approach to the increment of GDP.
c) Data in this table are calculated at constant prices.

2-13 居民消费水平(1978-2023年)
HOUSEHOLD CONSUMPTION LEVEL (1978-2023)

年 份 Year	居民消费水平(元) Household Consumption Level (yuan)			城乡消费水平对比(农村居民=1)	指数(1978年=100) Index (Year of 1978=100)			指数(上年=100) Index (Preceding Year=100)		
	全 市 All Households	城镇居民 Urban Households	农村居民 Rural Households	Urban/Rural Consumption Ratio (Rural Household=1)	全 市 All Households	城镇居民 Urban Households	农村居民 Rural Households	全 市 All Households	城镇居民 Urban Households	农村居民 Rural Households
1978	330	451	185	2.4	100.0	100.0	100.0	112.3	110.1	122.6
1979	356	464	221	2.1	117.5	114.5	120.8	117.5	114.5	120.8
1980	440	562	280	2.0	147.6	140.0	159.0	125.6	122.1	131.5
1981	485	590	338	1.7	160.3	144.8	189.4	108.6	103.6	119.2
1982	526	622	384	1.6	170.6	149.7	211.2	106.4	103.4	111.5
1983	579	674	432	1.6	175.4	151.2	222.6	102.8	101.0	105.4
1984	677	789	494	1.6	201.4	173.9	250.4	114.8	115.0	112.5
1985	912	1101	585	1.9	263.2	235.3	289.2	130.7	135.3	115.5
1986	1094	1284	749	1.7	312.9	272.0	365.8	118.9	115.6	126.5
1987	1198	1391	827	1.7	316.7	272.0	375.3	101.2	100.0	102.6
1988	1536	1779	1046	1.7	367.7	313.3	435.7	116.1	115.2	116.1
1989	1648	1874	1169	1.6	398.2	337.1	472.7	108.3	107.6	108.5
1990	1797	2045	1186	1.7	466.7	393.4	527.5	117.2	116.7	111.6
1991	2071	2330	1345	1.7	528.3	440.2	587.1	113.2	111.9	111.3
1992	2379	2701	1458	1.9	554.7	466.2	583.6	105.0	105.9	99.4
1993	3211	3749	1637	2.3	620.7	530.1	589.4	111.9	113.7	101.0
1994	4520	5321	2120	2.5	719.4	620.2	631.8	115.9	117.0	107.2
1995	5682	6520	3113	2.1	776.2	659.3	739.2	107.9	106.3	117.0
1996	6525	7508	3437	2.2	817.3	696.9	744.4	105.3	105.7	100.7
1997	7993	9341	3659	2.6	1001.2	866.9	795.0	122.5	124.4	106.8
1998	8652	10097	3900	2.6	1031.2	892.9	801.4	103.0	103.0	100.8
1999	9466	11032	4196	2.6	1123.0	970.6	860.7	108.9	108.7	107.4
2000	9835	11445	4314	2.7	1137.6	981.3	866.7	101.3	101.1	100.7
2001	10313	11903	4740	2.5	1147.8	981.3	923.0	100.9	100.0	106.5
2002	12380	14404	5073	2.8	1345.2	1159.9	961.8	117.2	118.2	104.2
2003	13734	15992	5336	3.0	1419.2	1223.7	964.7	105.5	105.5	100.3
2004	15328	17820	5786	3.1	1522.8	1309.4	1012.0	107.3	107.0	104.9
2005	16636	18877	6693	2.8	1591.3	1336.9	1120.3	104.5	102.1	110.7
2006	19003	21173	7613	2.8	1771.1	1459.9	1241.3	111.3	109.2	110.8
2007	21769	24103	9124	2.6	1930.5	1581.1	1411.4	109.0	108.3	113.7
2008	24005	26435	10548	2.5	2063.7	1680.7	1573.7	106.9	106.3	111.5
2009	26353	28871	12125	2.4	2247.4	1821.9	1773.6	108.9	108.4	112.7
2010	29483	32171	13642	2.4	2429.4	1962.2	1933.2	108.1	107.7	109.0
2011	32960	36032	13961	2.6	2584.9	2091.7	1877.1	106.4	106.6	97.1
2012	36076	39451	14912	2.6	2758.1	2229.8	1993.5	106.7	106.6	106.2
2013	40313	43674	19064	2.3	2940.1	2356.9	2380.2	106.6	105.7	119.4
2014	42918	46355	21001	2.2	3090.0	2470.0	2594.4	105.1	104.8	109.0
2015	46423	50085	22745	2.2	3287.8	2625.6	2752.7	106.4	106.3	106.1
2016	50195	54043	25031	2.2	3498.2	2788.4	2967.4	106.4	106.2	107.8
2017	54965	59189	27072	2.2	3690.6	2939.0	3130.6	105.5	105.4	105.5
2018	61458	66067	30575	2.2	3930.5	3121.2	3418.6	106.5	106.2	109.2
2019	66348	71235	32989	2.2	4201.7	3330.3	3654.5	106.9	106.7	106.9
2020	62842	67038	33611	2.0	3907.6	3077.2	3647.2	93.0	92.4	99.8
2021	72208	76976	38686	2.0	4939.2	3895.7	4471.5	126.4	126.6	122.6
2022	70549	75057	38817	1.9	4736.7	3736.0	4328.4	95.9	95.9	96.8
2023	76480	81311	42029	1.9	5058.8	3986.3	4622.7	106.8	106.7	106.8

注：1.本表居民消费水平数据按当年价格计算，指数按不变价格计算。
　　2.居民消费水平指按平均常住人口计算的人均居民消费支出。

Note: a) Data on household consumption level in this table are calculated at current prices, while indices are calculated at constant prices.
　　b) Household consumption level refers to per capita household consumption expenditure on the basis of average resident population.

2-14 社会劳动生产率(1978-2023年)
OVERALL LABOR PRODUCTIVITY (1978-2023)

单位：元/人 (yuan/person)

年 份 Year	社会劳动生产率 Overall Labor Productivity	第一产业 Primary Industry	第二产业 Secondary Industry	第三产业 Tertiary Industry
1978	2504	444	4484	1911
1979	2626	421	4556	2033
1980	2914	510	4750	2391
1981	2795	561	4316	2420
1982	2959	878	4437	2467
1983	3368	1094	4799	2998
1984	3909	1287	5347	3646
1985	4580	1671	6040	4268
1986	5002	1932	6331	4783
1987	5669	2569	6917	5501
1988	7046	4084	8309	6745
1989	7742	4270	9432	7140
1990	8203	4810	9564	7941
1991	9498	5014	10351	10145
1992	11068	5556	12236	11637
1993	13921	7111	14841	14808
1994	17798	9666	18590	18940
1995	22807	10036	23501	25077
1996	27453	10479	26708	31789
1997	32190	10757	29930	38674
1998	38170	10928	34495	46851
1999	44485	10733	40704	54598
2000	52958	10753	48241	65302
2001	61874	11212	53157	78046
2002	69194	11879	54745	89352
2003	76198	12910	63171	94215
2004	80294	13749	77352	90158
2005	82556	14049	82234	90091
2006	93308	14232	90784	102203
2007	111958	16399	106434	122898
2008	122823	17977	116034	134512
2009	130364	18653	134467	138876
2010	147436	19877	160731	154363
2011	159347	23018	142416	175197
2012	172529	26051	160635	186426
2013	187654	30155	181427	199247
2014	201194	32753	195932	212038
2015	214891	31339	198730	228231
2016	229942	30611	213048	243228
2017	251234	30354	233174	264934
2018	278096	32107	256310	292888
2019	298724	33740	267834	315216
2020	306252	36519	283482	319642
2021	353567	40513	381862	356902
2022	362786	42798	350165	374328
2023	387074	42965	353691	402926

注：1．本表数据按当年价格计算。
2．2010年及以前，社会劳动生产率为地区生产总值(增加值)与从业人员平均人数之比；自2011年起，社会劳动生产率为地区生产总值(增加值)与平均常住就业人口之比。

Note: a) Data in this table are calculated at current prices.
b) In and before 2010, the overall labor productivity referred to the ratio of GDP (the value added) to the average number of employed persons; since 2011, it refers to the ratio of GDP (the value added) to the average resident employed population.

主要统计指标解释

国内（地区）生产总值 是一个地区所有常住单位在一定时期内生产活动的最终成果。地区生产总值有三种表现形式，即价值形态、收入形态和产品形态。从价值形态看，它是所有常住单位在一定时期内所生产的全部货物和服务价值与同期投入的全部非固定资产货物和服务价值的差额，即所有常住单位的增加值之和；从收入形态看，它是所有常住单位在一定时期内创造的各项收入之和，包括劳动者报酬、生产税净额、固定资产折旧和营业盈余；从产品形态看，它是所有常住单位在一定时期内最终使用的货物和服务价值与货物和服务净出口（净流出）价值之和。在实际核算中，地区生产总值有三种计算方法，即生产法、收入法和支出法。三种方法分别从不同的方面反映地区生产总值及其构成。

最终消费率（消费率） 通常指一定时期内最终消费支出占国内（地区）生产总值的比重，一般按现行价格计算。

$$\text{最终消费率（消费率）}=\frac{\text{最终消费支出}}{\text{国内（地区）生产总值}}\times 100\%$$

资本形成率（投资率） 通常指一定时期内资本形成总额占国内（地区）生产总值的比重，一般按现行价格计算。

$$\text{资本形成率（投资率）}=\frac{\text{资本形成总额}}{\text{国内（地区）生产总值}}\times 100\%$$

数字经济及部分新兴产业统计划分标准：

1. **数字经济** 是指以数据资源作为关键生产要素、以现代信息网络作为重要载体、以信息通信技术的有效使用作为效率提升和经济结构优化的重要推动力的一系列经济活动。本分类将数字经济产业范围确定为：01 数字产品制造业、02 数字产品服务业、03 数字技术应用业、04 数字要素驱动业、05 数字化效率提升业等 5 个大类。数字经济是以《国民经济行业分类》（GB/T 4754-2017）为基础，对国民经济行业分类中符合数字经济产业特征的和以提供数字产品（货物或服务）为目的的相关行业类别活动进行再分类。

2. **战略性新兴产业** 是以重大技术突破和重大发展需求为基础，对经济社会全局和长远发展具有重大引领带动作用，知识技术密集、物质资源消耗少、成长潜力大、综合效益好的产业，包括：新一代信息技术产业、高端装备制造产业、新材料产业、生物产业、新能源汽车产业、新能源产业、节能环保产业、数字创意产业、相关服务业等9大领域。战略性新兴产业是以《国民经济行业分类》（GB/T 4754-2017）为基础，对其中符合“战略性新兴产业”特征的有关活动进行再分类。

3. **高技术产业** 包括高技术制造业和高技术服务业。高技术制造业是指国民经济行业中 R&D 投入强度相对高的制造业行业，包括：医药制造，航空、航天器及设备制造，电子及通信设备制造，计算机及办公设备制造，医疗仪器设备及仪器仪表制造，信息化学品制造等 6 大类。高技术服务业是采用高技术手段为社会提供服务活动的集合，包括信息服务、电子商务服务、检验检测服务、专业技术服务业的高技术服务、研发与设计服务、科技成果转化服务、知识产权及相关法律服务、环境监测及治理服务和其他高技术服务等 9 大类。高技术产业是以《国民经济行业分类》（GB/T 4754-2017）为基础，对国民经济行业分类中符合高技术产业范畴相关活动的再分类。

4. **生产性服务业** 指为生产活动提供的研发设计与其他技术服务，货物运输、通用航空生产、仓储和邮政快递服务，信息服务，金融服务，节能与环保服务，生产性租赁服务，商务服务，人力资源管理与职业教育培训服务，批发与贸易经纪代理服务，生产性支持服务。生产性服务业是以《国民经济行业分类》（GB/T 4754-2017）为基础，对国民经济行业分类中符合生产性服务业特征有关活动的再分类。

5. **生活性服务业** 是指满足居民最终消费需求的服务活动。分类范围包括十二大领域：居民和家庭服务，健康服务，养老服务，旅游游览和娱乐服务，体育服务，文化服务，居民零售和互联网销售服务，居民出行服务，住宿餐饮服务，教育培训服务，居民住房服务，其他生活性服务等。生活性服务业是以《国民经济行业分类》（GB/T 4754-2017）为基础，对国民经济行业分类中符合生活性服务业特征有关活动的再分类。

6.**知识产权（专利）密集型产业** 指发明专利密集度、规模达到规定的标准，依靠知识产权参与市场竞争，符合创新发展导向的产业集合，包括信息通信技术制造业，信息通信技术服务业，新装备制造业，新材料制造业，医药医疗产业，环保产业，研发、设计和技术服务业等七大类。知识产权（专利）密集型产业是以《国民经济行业分类》（GB/T 4754-2017）为基础，对国民经济行业分类中符合知识产权（专利）密集型产业特征的有关活动进行再分类。

Explanatory Notes on Main Statistical Indicators

Gross Domestic (Regional) Product represents the final results of all resident units in an area from their productive activities over a given period of time. It is expressed in three different perspectives respectively, namely value, income, and product. From the value perspective, it refers to the total value of all goods and services produced by all resident units during a certain period of time, minus the total value of input of goods and services of the nature of non-fixed assets; in other words, it is the sum of added value of all resident units. From the income perspective, it is the sum of incomes created by all resident units during a certain period of time, including compensation for labors, net taxes on production, depreciation of fixed assets and operating surplus. From the product perspective, it refers to the value of all goods and services for final demand by all resident units plus the net exports (net outflow) value of goods and services during a certain period of time. In actual national accounting, gross regional product is calculated in three methods, namely production method, income method and expenditure method, which reflect the gross regional product and its composition from different angles.

Final Consumption Rate (Consumption Rate) It usually refers to the proportion of final consumption in GDP (GRP) within a certain period, and is generally calculated at current price.

Final Consumption Rate (Consumption Rate) = Final Consumption / GDP (GRP) × 100%

Capital Formation Rate (Investment Rate) It usually refers to the proportion of total capital formation in GDP (GRP) within a certain period, and is generally calculated at current price.

Capital Formation Rate (Investment Rate) = Total Capital Formation / GDP (GRP) ×100%

Standards for the Statistical Classification of Digital Economy and Some Emerging Industries:

1. **Digital Economy** refers to a series of economic activities that take data resources as the key production factors, modern information network as the important carrier, and the effective use of information and communication technology as the important driving force for efficiency improvement and economic structure optimization. The industrial scope of digital economy is determined as the following 5 categories in this classification: 01 Digital product manufacturing industry, 02 Digital product service industry, 03 Digital technology application industry, 04 Digital elements driving industry, 05 Digital efficiency promotion industry. Digital economy is the re-classification of activities in related industry categories in the national economic sectors that are in line with the characteristics of digital economy and aim at providing digital products (goods or services) based on the *Classification of National Economic Sectors (GB/T 4754-2017)*.

2. **Strategic Emerging Industries** refer to the industries that are based on major technological breakthroughs and major development needs, play important leading and driving role in the overall economic and social situation and in the long-term development, are knowledge and technology intensive, consume little material resources, with great growth potential and good comprehensive benefits. The strategic emerging industries include 9 major areas which are respectively the new generation of information and technology industry, high-end equipment manufacture industry, new material industry, bioindustry, new-energy automobile industry, new energy industry, energy conservation and environmental protection industry, digital creative industry and related services industry. The strategic emerging industries are the re-classification of related activities that are in line with the characteristics of "strategic emerging industries" based on the *Classification of National Economic Sectors (GB/T 4754-2017)*.

3. **High-tech Industry** includes high-tech manufacturing industry and high-tech service industry. High-tech manufacturing industry refers to the manufacturing industry with a relatively high intensity of R&D input among the national economic sectors. It includes 6 major categories which are respectively manufacture of medicines, manufacture of aircrafts and spacecrafts, manufacture of electronic and communication equipment, manufacture of computers and office equipment, manufacture of medical equipment and appliance and measuring instrument and meter, and manufacture of information chemical products. High-tech service industry means the collection of services provided to society by adopting high-tech means. It includes 9 categories which are respectively information services, e-commerce services, inspection and testing services, high-tech service in professional technique services, R&D and design services, services for transformation of scientific and technological achievements, intellectual property right and related legal services, environmental monitoring and governance services, and other high-tech services. The high-tech industry is the re-classification of related activities that are in line with the categories of high-tech industry in the national economic sectors based on the *Classification of National Economic Sectors (GB/T 4754-2017)*.

4. **Producer Service Industry** refers to the R&D and design and other technology services, cargo transportation, general aviation production, storage and express mail services, information services, financial services, energy conservation and environmental protection services, productive leasing services, business services, human resource management and vocational education and training services, wholesale and trading agency services, and the productive support services

provided for production activities. The producer service industry is the re-classification of related activities that are in line with the characteristics of producer service industry in the national economic sectors based on the *Classification of National Economic Sectors (GB/T 4754-2017)*.

5. Consumer Service Industry refers to the service activities to meet the final consumption demands of residents. The scope of classification covers 12 areas which are respectively resident and household services, healthcare services, pension services, tourism, sightseeing and entertainment services, sport services, cultural services, resident retail and Internet sales services, resident trip services, accommodation and restaurants services, education and training services, resident housing services, and other consumer-oriented services, etc. The consumer service industry is the re-classification of related activities that are in line with the characteristics of consumer service industry in the national economic sectors based on the *Classification of National Economic Sectors (GB/T 4754-2017)*.

6. Intellectual Property (Patent) Intensive Industry refers to a collection of sectors in which the intensity and scale of invention patents meet prescribed standards that rely on intellectual property rights in market competition, and pursue innovation development. They include seven major categories: information and communications technology manufacturing, information and communications technology service, new equipment manufacturing, new material manufacturing, medicine and medical care, environmental protection, and research and development, designing, and technology service. Based on the Classification of National Economic Sectors *(GB/T 4754-2017)*, intellectual property (patent) intensive industry is a reclassification of relevant activities in the categories of national economic sectors that meet the characteristics of intellectual property (patent) intensive industry.

03

人口与就业
POPULATION AND EMPLOYMENT

简要说明

一、主要内容

人口部分包括历年北京市常住人口和户籍人口的分组资料、新中国成立以来已开展的七次人口普查数据、1990年以后的人口变动情况抽样调查数据。就业部分包括分三次产业的常住就业人口数据、法人单位从业人员及工资情况、城镇非私营单位在岗职工人数及工资的分组情况、城镇登记失业及新增就业情况等。

二、统计调查方法说明

（一）关于人口数据。1953年、1964年、1982年、1990年、2000年、2010年和2020年分别进行了七次人口普查，1987年、1995年、2005年、2015年进行了1%人口抽样调查，从1982年开始进行人口变动抽样调查。

（二）关于劳动工资数据。劳动工资统计采用全面调查和抽样调查相结合的方法。

三、有关行业划分的变化说明

2011年以前执行《国民经济行业分类》（GB/T 4754-2002）标准，2012-2017年执行《国民经济行业分类》（GB/T 4754-2011）标准，2018年起执行《国民经济行业分类》（GB/T 4754-2017）标准。

四、“城镇人口”和“乡村人口”口径变化情况

本章中1978-1989年“城镇人口”和“乡村人口”数据为户籍管理统计中的“非农业人口”和“农业人口”口径；1990-1999年根据1990年、2000年两次人口普查数据进行调整；2000年为国家统计局1999年发布的《关于统计上划分城乡的规定(试行)》中的“城镇人口”和“乡村人口”口径，2001-2005年为该口径的推算数；2006-2008年为国家统计局2006年发布的《关于统计上划分城乡的暂行规定》中的“城镇人口”和“乡村人口”口径的推算数；2009年及以后国家统计局每年对《统计用区划代码和城乡分类代码》进行更新维护，“城镇人口”和“乡村人口”的划分均按当年的城乡分类标准进行推算。

Brief Introduction

I. Main Content

Population statistics include classified data for permanent population and registered population in Beijing in previous years, statistics of population from seven population censuses since the founding of the People's Republic of China, and statistics of sample survey on population changes after 1990. Employment statistics include data on permanent employed population in three industries, employed persons and wages in legal entities, classified statistics for the number and wage of fully employed staff and workers in urban non-private entities, registered unemployment and new employment in urban areas.

II. Statistical Survey Methods

(I) Data on Population. Seven population censuses were conducted respectively in 1953, 1964, 1982, 1990, 2000, 2010 and 2020; 1% population sample surveys were conducted respectively in 1987, 1995, 2005 and 2015; and sample surveys on population changes have been conducted since 1982.

(II) Data on Employment Wage The combined method of comprehensive survey and sample survey is adopted in the employment wage statistics.

III. Changes in the Classification of Sectors

The standards in the *Classification of National Economic Sectors (GB/T 4754-2002)* were implemented before 2011. The standards in the *Classification of National Economic Sectors (GB/T 4754-2011)* were implemented from 2012 to 2017. The standards in the *Classification of National Economic Sectors (GB/T 4754-2017)* are implemented since 2018.

IV. Changes in the Terms of Urban Population and Rural Population

The data on urban population and rural population for the period from 1978 to 1989 as mentioned in this chapter refer to the non-agricultural population and agricultural population in the household registration statistics; the data had been adjusted from 1990 to 1999 in accordance with the data on two population censes which were conducted respectively in 1990 and 2000; that of 2000 referred to the urban population and rural population in the *Regulations on the Statistical Division of Rural and Urban Areas (Trial)* issued by the National Bureau of Statistics in 1999; the data of 2001 to 2005 were estimated on the same basis; the data of 2006 to 2008 were the estimated figures of the urban population and rural population in the *Provisional Regulations on the Statistical Division of Rural and Urban Areas* issued by the National Bureau of Statistics in 2006; the National Bureau of Statistics of China has carried on update and maintenance of the *Division Codes and Urban-rural Classification Codes for Statistical Use* since 2009; the division of urban population and rural population had all been estimated and calculated in accordance with the urban-rural classification standards for each year.

3-1 七次人口普查人口基本情况
BASIC STATISTICS ON POPULATION IN SEVEN CENSUSES

项目	Item	1953	1964	1982	1990	2000	2010	2020
常住人口　（万人）	**Resident Population　(10000 persons)**	**276.8**	**759.7**	**923.1**	**1081.9**	**1356.9**	**1961.2**	**2189.3**
按城乡分	**By Residence**							
城镇人口	Urban Population	205.8	425.8	597.0	794.5	1052.2	1685.9	1916.6
乡村人口	Rural Population	71.0	333.9	326.1	287.4	304.7	275.3	272.7
按性别分	**By Gender**							
男	Male	159.8	391.1	467.1	559.3	707.4	1012.6	1119.5
女	Female	117.0	368.6	456.0	522.6	649.5	948.6	1069.8
常住人口性别比（女=100）	**Sex Ratio of the Resident Population　(Female=100)**	**136.5**	**106.1**	**102.4**	**107.0**	**108.9**	**106.8**	**104.7**
家庭户规模　（人／户）	**Family Size　(person/household)**			**3.7**	**3.2**	**2.9**	**2.5**	**2.3**
各年龄组人口比重　（%）	**Proportion of Population by Age Group　(%)**							
0-14岁	Age 0-14	30.1	41.5	22.4	20.2	13.6	8.6	11.9
15-59岁	Age 15-59	64.3	51.9	69.1	69.7	73.9	78.9	68.5
60岁及以上	Age 60 and Over	5.6	6.6	8.5	10.1	12.5	12.5	19.6
#65岁及以上	Age 65 and Over	3.3	4.1	5.6	6.3	8.4	8.7	13.3
总抚养比　（%）	**Gross Dependency Ratio　(%)**	**50.2**	**83.8**	**38.9**	**36.1**	**28.2**	**20.9**	**33.6**
老年抚养比	Elderly Dependency Ratio	5.0	7.5	7.8	8.6	10.8	10.5	17.8
少儿抚养比	Children Dependency Ratio	45.2	76.3	31.1	27.5	17.4	10.4	15.8
民族人口	**Population by Ethnic Group**							
汉　族　（万人）	Han Nationality　(10000 persons)	260.0	731.2	890.8	1040.5	1298.4	1881.1	2084.5
占常住人口比重　（%）	Percentage to Resident Population　(%)	93.9	96.2	96.5	96.2	95.7	95.9	95.2
少数民族　（万人）	Ethnic Minority　(10000 persons)	16.8	28.5	32.3	41.4	58.5	80.1	104.8
占常住人口比重　（%）	Percentage to Resident Population　(%)	6.1	3.8	3.5	3.8	4.3	4.1	4.8
每十万人口拥有的各种受教育程度人口　（人）	**Population with Various Education Attainment Per 100000 Persons　(person)**							
大专及以上	Junior College and Above		4359	4866	9300	16839	31499	41980
高中和中专	Senior Secondary/Secondary Technical School		4513	17646	18978	23165	21220	17593
初　中	Junior Secondary School		11768	29086	30551	34380	31396	23289
小　学	Primary School		31883	26197	22579	16963	9956	10503
文盲人口及文盲率	**Illiterate Population and Illiteracy Rate**							
文盲人口　（万人）	Illiterate Population　(10000 persons)		168.9	114.7	94.3	57.8	33.3	17.2
文盲率　（%）	Illiteracy Rate　(%)		34.2	16.0	10.9	4.9	1.9	0.9
平均预期寿命　（岁）	**Life Expectancy at Birth　(year)**			**71.9**	**72.9**	**76.1**	**80.2**	**82.5**

注：1.1953年数据按当年区划统计。
2.1964年的文盲人口数为12周岁及以上文盲和半文盲人口，1982年、1990年、2000年、2010年、2020年的文盲人口数为15周岁及以上文盲和半文盲人口。文盲率是指15周岁及以上人口中，文盲人口和半文盲人口所占比重。
3.本表常住人口与表3-2相同的年份数据不同，是因为本表数据为普查时点数，表3-2为年末时点数。1953年、1964年、1982年、1990年普查时点为7月1日零时；2000年、2010年、2020年普查时点为11月1日零时。

Note: a) Data for 1953 are statistics by district division of the year.
b) Data on illiterate population in 1964 covered the illiterate and semi-illiterate population aged 12 and over, and data for 1982,1990,2000, 2010 and 2020 covered those aged 15 and over. Illiteracy rate refers to the percentage of illiterate and semi-illiterate people to total aged 15 and over.
c) This table has different data from Table 3-2 in terms of the resident population, because this table uses the data at the time point of the census, while in Table 3-2, the year end is taken as the time point for statistics. The time point of the census in 1953,1964,1982 and 1990 was 12 o'clock midnight, July 1st; the time point of the census in 2000, 2010 and 2020 was 12 o'clock midnight, November 1st.

3-2 常住人口(1978-2023年)
RESIDENT POPULATION (1978-2023)

单位：万人 (10000 persons)

年份 Year	常住人口 Resident Population	#常住外来人口 Resident Migrant Population	按性别分 By Gender 男 Male	女 Female	按城乡分 By Urban Area and Rural Area 城镇人口 Urban Population	乡村人口 Rural Population	常住人口密度(人/平方公里) Resident Population Density (person/sq.km)	常住人口出生率(‰) Birth Rate of Resident Population (‰)	常住人口死亡率(‰) Death Rate of Resident Population (‰)	常住人口自然增长率(‰) Natural Growth Rate of Resident Population (‰)
1978	871.5	21.8	443.2	428.3	479.0	392.5	519	12.93	6.12	6.81
1979	897.1	26.5	454.6	442.5	510.3	386.8	534	13.67	5.92	7.75
1980	904.3	18.6	457.8	446.5	521.1	383.2	538	15.56	6.30	9.26
1981	919.2	18.4	465.9	453.3	533.3	385.9	547	16.93	6.02	10.91
1982	935.0	17.2	474.0	461.0	544.0	391.0	556	20.04	5.68	14.36
1983	950.0	16.8	483.0	467.0	557.0	393.0	565	15.63	5.49	10.14
1984	965.0	19.8	491.0	474.0	570.0	395.0	574	16.74	5.53	11.21
1985	981.0	23.1	500.0	481.0	586.0	395.0	584	15.45	5.75	9.70
1986	1028.0	56.8	524.0	504.0	621.0	407.0	612	15.82	4.47	11.35
1987	1047.0	59.0	525.0	522.0	637.0	410.0	623	17.29	5.40	11.89
1988	1061.0	59.8	534.0	527.0	650.0	411.0	631	14.43	5.08	9.35
1989	1075.0	53.9	538.0	537.0	664.0	411.0	640	12.84	5.35	7.49
1990	1086.0	53.8	545.0	541.0	798.0	288.0	646	13.04	5.81	7.23
1991	1094.0	54.5	547.0	547.0	808.0	286.0	651	8.03	5.82	2.21
1992	1102.0	57.1	554.0	548.0	819.0	283.0	656	9.22	6.11	3.11
1993	1112.0	60.8	559.0	553.0	831.0	281.0	662	9.35	6.16	3.19
1994	1125.0	63.2	564.0	561.0	846.0	279.0	669	8.96	5.76	3.20
1995	1251.1	180.8	627.0	624.1	946.2	304.9	744	7.92	5.12	2.80
1996	1259.4	181.7	639.0	620.4	957.9	301.5	749	8.02	5.34	2.68
1997	1240.0	154.5	628.7	611.3	948.3	291.7	738	7.91	6.02	1.89
1998	1245.6	154.1	630.6	615.0	957.7	287.9	741	6.00	5.30	0.70
1999	1257.2	157.4	636.4	620.8	971.7	285.5	748	6.50	5.60	0.90
2000	1363.6	256.1	710.9	652.7	1057.4	306.2	811	6.20	5.30	0.90
2001	1385.1	262.8	722.1	663.0	1081.2	303.9	824	6.10	5.30	0.80
2002	1423.2	286.9	743.1	680.1	1118.0	305.2	847	6.60	5.73	0.87
2003	1456.4	307.6	761.2	695.2	1151.3	305.1	867	5.06	5.15	-0.09
2004	1492.7	329.8	779.9	712.8	1187.2	305.5	910	6.13	5.39	0.74
2005	1538.0	357.3	778.7	759.3	1286.1	251.9	937	6.29	5.20	1.09
2006	1601.0	403.4	817.6	783.4	1350.2	250.8	976	6.22	4.94	1.28
2007	1676.0	462.7	850.8	825.2	1416.2	259.8	1021	8.16	4.83	3.33
2008	1771.0	541.1	900.2	870.8	1503.6	267.4	1079	7.89	4.59	3.30
2009	1860.0	614.2	949.8	910.2	1581.1	278.9	1133	7.66	4.33	3.33
2010	1961.9	704.7	1013.0	948.9	1686.4	275.5	1196	7.27	4.29	2.98
2011	2023.8	749.9	1044.1	979.7	1744.6	279.2	1233	8.28	4.26	4.02
2012	2077.5	792.1	1073.7	1003.8	1792.7	284.8	1266	9.02	4.30	4.72
2013	2125.4	831.6	1097.9	1027.5	1836.1	289.3	1295	8.89	4.50	4.39
2014	2171.1	858.3	1118.8	1052.3	1878.0	293.1	1323	9.69	4.89	4.80
2015	2188.3	862.5	1126.2	1062.1	1897.5	290.8	1333	7.89	4.91	2.98
2016	2195.4	858.8	1126.1	1069.3	1904.8	290.6	1338	9.23	5.16	4.07
2017	2194.4	855.5	1123.9	1070.5	1907.7	286.7	1337	8.97	5.24	3.73
2018	2191.7	848.2	1122.2	1069.5	1908.8	282.9	1336	8.13	5.50	2.63
2019	2190.1	843.5	1120.5	1069.6	1913.1	277.0	1335	7.98	5.40	2.58
2020	2189.0	839.6	1119.4	1069.6	1916.4	272.6	1334	6.98	4.59	2.39
2021	2188.6	834.8	1117.7	1070.9	1916.1	272.5	1334	6.35	5.39	0.96
2022	2184.3	825.1	1114.2	1070.1	1912.8	271.5	1331	5.67	5.72	-0.05
2023	2185.8	824.0	1113.3	1072.5	1919.8	266.0	1332	5.63	6.13	-0.50

注：1978—1981年为户籍统计数，含暂住人口。自1990年起为人口变动情况抽样调查推算数。其中，1982年、1990年、2000年、2010年、2020年为人口普查推算数；1995年、2005年、2015年为1%人口抽样调查推算数；1983—1989年数据根据1982年、1990年两次人口普查数据进行了修订；2006—2009年数据根据2010年人口普查结果进行了修订；2011—2019年数据根据2010年、2020年两次人口普查结果进行了修订。

Note: Figures for 1978-1981 are from household registrations and cover temporary residents. Data since 1990 are estimated on the bases of the annual national sample survey on population changes. Specifically, data for 1982, 1990, 2000, 2010 and 2020 are the census estimates; data for 1995, 2005 and 2015 are estimated from sample surveys on 1% of the population; data for 1983-1989 are revised in accordance with the data from the population censuses in 1982 and 1990; data for 2006-2009 are revised in accordance with the results of the population census in 2010, and data for 2011-2019 are revised in accordance with the results of the population censuses in 2010 and 2020.

3-3 常住人口年龄构成情况(2010-2023年)
AGE COMPOSITION OF RESIDENT POPULATION (2010-2023)

单位：万人 (10000 persons)

年 份 Year	0-14	15-59	60岁及以上 Aged 60 and Over	#65岁及以上 Aged 65 and Over
2010	168.7	1547.2	246.0	171.0
2011	186.8	1564.2	272.8	184.7
2012	200.7	1581.5	295.3	196.7
2013	208.8	1610.5	306.1	205.0
2014	226.5	1601.5	343.1	227.5
2015	234.7	1587.4	366.2	241.2
2016	243.8	1572.8	378.8	252.6
2017	249.1	1550.7	394.6	264.7
2018	252.0	1532.1	407.6	273.0
2019	253.4	1518.4	418.3	280.4
2020	259.1	1500.0	429.9	291.2
2021	264.7	1482.3	441.6	311.6
2022	264.0	1455.2	465.1	330.1
2023	262.5	1428.5	494.8	346.9

注：表中2010年数据为北京市第六次全国人口普查推算数，2020年数据为北京市第七次全国人口普查推算数；2011—2019年数据根据年度人口抽样调查数据推算，并根据2010年和2020年两次人口普查结果进行了修订；2021—2023年数据为年度人口抽样调查推算数。

Note: Data for 2010 in this table are estimated from the Sixth National Population Census in Beijing, and data for 2020 are estimated from the Seventh National Population Census in Beijing; data for 2011-2019 are estimated on the basis of the sample surveys on population and have been revised in accordance with the results of the population censuses in 2010 and 2020. Data for 2021 -2023 are the estimates from the sample survey on population.

3-4 常住人口总量及人口密度(按地区分)(2023年)
TOTAL POPULATION AND DENSITY OF RESIDENT POPULATION (BY DISTRICT) (2023)

地 区	District	常住人口（万人）Resident Population (10000 persons)	#常住外来人口 Resident Migrant Population	城镇人口 Urban Population	乡村人口 Rural Population	常住人口密度（人／平方公里）Resident Population Density (person/sq.km)
全 市	**Total**	**2185.8**	**824.0**	**1919.8**	**266.0**	**1332**
东城区	Dongcheng District	70.3	14.9	70.3		16794
西城区	Xicheng District	109.9	21.8	109.9		21749
朝阳区	Chaoyang District	344.6	124.5	343.7	0.9	7572
丰台区	Fengtai District	201.1	62.7	199.9	1.2	6576
石景山区	Shijingshan District	56.4	15.6	56.4		6689
海淀区	Haidian District	312.5	105.0	305.5	7.0	7255
门头沟区	Mentougou District	39.7	11.6	36.5	3.2	274
房山区	Fangshan District	131.2	44.3	103.3	27.9	659
通州区	Tongzhou District	184.5	89.1	135.2	49.3	2036
顺义区	Shunyi District	132.7	60.2	92.5	40.2	1301
昌平区	Changping District	227.2	132.6	187.3	39.9	1691
大兴区	Daxing District	199.4	101.0	162.4	37.0	1924
怀柔区	Huairou District	44.0	15.3	33.1	10.9	207
平谷区	Pinggu District	45.6	7.2	28.1	17.5	480
密云区	Miyun District	52.4	10.7	35.0	17.4	235
延庆区	Yanqing District	34.3	7.5	20.7	13.6	172

注：本表数据为人口抽样调查推算数据，为年末数。
Note: Figures in this table are the year-end estimated figures on the basis of the sample survey on population.

3-5 常住人口自然变动(按地区分)(2023年)
NATURAL CHANGE OF RESIDENT POPULATION (BY DISTRICT) (2023)

地　区	District	出生人数 (人) Number of Births (person)	死亡人数 (人) Number of Deaths (person)	自然增加人数 (人) Natural Increase of Population (person)	出生率 (‰) Birth Rate (‰)	死亡率 (‰) Death Rate (‰)	自然增长率 (‰) Natural Growth Rate (‰)
全　市	**Total**	**122935**	**133999**	**-11064**	**5.63**	**6.13**	**-0.50**
东城区	Dongcheng District	2714	7307	-4593	3.86	10.38	-6.52
西城区	Xicheng District	5546	10531	-4985	5.04	9.57	-4.53
朝阳区	Chaoyang District	18128	18247	-119	5.26	5.30	-0.04
丰台区	Fengtai District	10967	13844	-2877	5.45	6.88	-1.43
石景山区	Shijingshan District	3496	5832	-2336	6.20	10.34	-4.14
海淀区	Haidian District	15001	11673	3328	4.80	3.74	1.06
门头沟区	Mentougou District	2254	5588	-3334	5.68	14.08	-8.40
房山区	Fangshan District	8883	10046	-1163	6.77	7.66	-0.89
通州区	Tongzhou District	9710	14681	-4971	5.27	7.96	-2.69
顺义区	Shunyi District	6826	5892	934	5.15	4.44	0.71
昌平区	Changping District	15352	10554	4798	6.76	4.65	2.11
大兴区	Daxing District	14347	6465	7882	7.20	3.24	3.96
怀柔区	Huairou District	2246	3040	-794	5.10	6.91	-1.81
平谷区	Pinggu District	2496	4039	-1543	5.47	8.86	-3.39
密云区	Miyun District	3124	3788	-664	5.95	7.22	-1.27
延庆区	Yanqing District	1845	2472	-627	5.36	7.19	-1.83

注：本表数据为人口抽样调查推算数据。
Note: Figures in this table are estimated figures on the basis of the sample survey on population.

3–6 常住人口年龄构成(2023年)
AGE COMPOSITION OF RESIDENT POPULATION (2023)

年龄组 Age Group	常住人口数 (万人) Resident Population (10000 persons)	占常住人口比重 (%) Proportion to Resident Population (%)
合 计 Total	**2185.8**	**100.0**
0–4	74.4	3.4
5–9	106.6	4.9
10–14	81.5	3.7
15–19	56.1	2.6
20–24	104.5	4.8
25–29	164.1	7.5
30–34	220.1	10.1
35–39	227.5	10.4
40–44	188.5	8.6
45–49	141.2	6.5
50–54	171.3	7.8
55–59	155.2	7.1
60–64	147.9	6.8
65–69	137.8	6.3
70–74	92.4	4.2
75–79	49.2	2.2
80–84	33.0	1.5
85岁及以上 Aged 85 and Over	34.5	1.6

注：本表数据为人口抽样调查推算数据，为年末数。
Note: Figures in this table are the year-end estimated figures on the basis of the sample survey on population.

3-7 常住人口受教育程度(2023年)
EDUCATION ATTAINMENT OF RESIDENT POPULATION (2023)

单位：人 (person)

项 目	Item	调查人口合计 Total Surveyed Population	男 Male	女 Female
15岁及以上人口	**Population Aged 15 and Over**	**463279**	**228719**	**234560**
#小 学	Primary Schools	24385	9469	14916
初 中	Junior Secondary Schools	89411	46266	43145
普通高中	Senior Secondary Schools	79776	40400	39376
大学专科	College Students	96512	48305	48207
大学本科	Undergraduates	127815	63035	64780
硕士研究生	Postgraduates with Master's Degree	32599	15927	16672
博士研究生	Postgraduates with Doctor's Degree	5142	3025	2117

注：本表数据为人口抽样调查样本数据。
Note: Figures in this table are the sample figures from the sample survey on population.

3-8 常住人口家庭户规模(2023年)
FAMILY SIZE OF RESIDENT POPULATION (2023)

地 区	Area	调查家庭总户数(户) Total Number of Surveyed Households (household)	家庭户规模所占比重(%) Percentage of Various Sized Family (%)				
			一人户 One Person	二人户 Two Persons	三人户 Three Persons	四人户 Four Persons	五人及以上户 Five Persons and Over
全 市	**Total**	**206335**	**26.8**	**34.2**	**22.3**	**9.7**	**7.0**
城 镇	Urban	174444	26.9	33.8	23.3	9.8	6.3
乡 村	Rural	31891	26.5	36.8	16.9	9.1	10.8

注：本表数据为人口抽样调查样本数据。
Note: Figures in this table are the sample figures from the sample survey on population.

3-9 常住就业人口规模及构成(2010—2023年)
RESIDENT EMPLOYED POPULATION AND ITS COMPOSITION (2010-2023)

单位：万人 (10000 persons)

年份 Year	常住就业人口 Resident Employed Population	第一产业 Primary Industry	第二产业 Secondary Industry	第三产业 Tertiary Industry	构成(%)(合计=100) Composition (%) (Total=100) 第一产业 Primary Industry	第二产业 Secondary Industry	第三产业 Tertiary Industry
2010	1067.3	58.3	252.1	756.9	5.5	23.6	70.9
2011	1090.1	58.6	248.3	783.2	5.4	22.8	71.9
2012	1115.3	55.3	231.8	828.2	5.0	20.8	74.3
2013	1137.2	50.7	227.7	858.8	4.5	20.0	75.5
2014	1141.8	46.5	224.8	870.5	4.1	19.7	76.2
2015	1164.4	43.1	220.0	901.3	3.7	18.9	77.4
2016	1187.6	41.7	218.0	927.9	3.5	18.4	78.1
2017	1191.3	38.6	215.1	937.6	3.2	18.1	78.7
2018	1189.6	36.5	212.3	940.8	3.1	17.8	79.1
2019	1183.5	31.3	210.9	941.3	2.6	17.8	79.5
2020	1163.8	28.0	194.0	941.8	2.4	16.7	80.9
2021	1158.0	27.0	193.0	938.0	2.3	16.7	81.0
2022	1132.1	25.1	186.0	921.0	2.2	16.4	81.4
2023	1129.0	24.0	183.0	922.0	2.1	16.2	81.7

注：表中数据根据2010年、2020年两次人口普查数据以及人口抽样调查和劳动力调查数据推算。

Note: Figures in this table are estimated on the basis of the two population censuses respectively in 2010 and 2020 as well as the sample survey on population and the labor force survey.

3-10 户籍人口(1978-2023年)
REGISTERED POPULATION (1978-2023)

单位：万人 (10000 persons)

年 份 Year	户籍户数(万户) Registered Households (10000 households)	户籍人口 Registered Population	#60岁及以上人口 Population Aged 60 and Over	按性别分 By Gender 男 Male	女 Female	按户籍性质分 By Type of Household Register 非农业户 Non-Agricultural	农业户 Agricultural	户籍人口出生人数 Births of Registered Population	户籍人口死亡人数 Deaths of Registered Population	户籍人口自然增加人数 Natural Increase of Registered Population
1978	205.5	849.7		432.1	417.5	467.0	382.6	10.9	5.2	5.7
1979	214.6	870.6		441.1	429.4	495.2	375.4	11.8	5.1	6.7
1980	223.2	885.7		448.4	437.3	510.4	375.3	13.7	5.5	8.2
1981	234.8	900.8		456.6	444.2	522.6	378.2	15.1	5.4	9.7
1982	245.0	917.8		465.5	452.3	534.0	383.8	18.2	5.2	13.1
1983	255.1	933.2		474.7	458.5	547.1	386.0	14.5	5.1	9.4
1984	263.1	945.2		481.2	464.0	558.1	387.0	13.2	5.1	8.1
1985	274.1	957.9		488.0	469.9	572.5	385.4	11.8	5.2	6.6
1986	284.6	971.2		495.5	475.7	586.8	384.4	12.9	5.2	7.8
1987	299.4	988.0		504.1	483.9	601.0	387.0	16.9	5.3	11.6
1988	310.8	1001.2		510.4	490.8	614.3	387.0	15.3	5.5	9.8
1989	322.5	1021.1		520.3	500.8	630.6	390.5	19.0	5.7	13.3
1990	335.0	1032.2		525.3	507.0	640.2	392.1	14.0	6.3	7.7
1991	343.1	1039.5		528.5	511.1	648.4	391.2	9.2	5.7	3.5
1992	349.3	1044.9		530.8	514.1	656.3	388.6	8.3	6.2	2.2
1993	354.6	1051.2		533.9	517.3	668.7	382.5	7.9	6.3	1.6
1994	360.3	1061.8		538.9	522.8	683.8	377.9	8.5	6.3	2.2
1995	365.7	1070.3		543.0	527.3	696.9	373.5	8.5	6.2	2.3
1996	370.9	1077.7		546.8	530.9	709.7	368.0	7.8	6.7	1.2
1997	375.7	1085.5		550.4	535.1	722.7	362.9	7.6	6.7	0.9
1998	383.4	1091.5		552.6	538.9	733.6	357.8	6.7	7.5	-0.8
1999	390.3	1099.8		556.7	543.1	747.2	352.6	6.3	6.2	0.1
2000	397.9	1107.5		560.1	547.4	760.7	346.8	7.2	7.8	-0.5
2001	405.3	1122.3		567.3	555.0	780.2	342.2	6.0	5.3	0.7
2002	416.3	1136.3		574.7	561.6	806.9	329.4	6.0	5.2	0.8
2003	427.6	1148.8		581.0	567.9	830.8	318.0	4.5	5.8	-1.3
2004	439.8	1162.9		587.2	575.7	854.7	308.2	6.6	6.2	0.4
2005	451.7	1180.7		596.0	584.7	880.2	300.5	7.5	7.0	0.5
2006	463.7	1197.6		604.2	593.4	905.4	292.2	7.7	5.1	2.6
2007	473.0	1213.3	210.3	612.0	601.3	929.0	284.3	9.9	5.2	4.8
2008	481.2	1229.9	218.6	620.0	609.9	950.7	279.2	10.6	5.1	5.5
2009	488.7	1245.8	228.7	627.5	618.9	971.9	273.9	10.9	6.2	4.7
2010	496.1	1257.8	237.2	632.8	625.0	989.5	268.3	10.2	9.1	1.1
2011	503.1	1277.9	250.5	642.4	635.6	1013.8	264.2	12.5	5.3	7.2
2012	509.2	1297.5	266.1	651.7	645.8	1039.3	258.2	14.5	5.7	8.8
2013	516.2	1316.3	283.2	660.4	655.9	1065.0	251.4	13.6	5.7	7.9
2014	522.6	1333.4	301.0	668.3	665.1	1089.8	243.6	17.2	7.6	9.6
2015	529.2	1345.2	318.0	673.3	671.9	1111.3	233.8	12.3	7.3	4.9
2016	538.2	1362.9	334.4	681.5	681.4	1132.0	230.9	20.5	8.9	11.6
2017	543.1	1359.2	336.4	676.8	682.4	1131.7	227.5	18.6	26.5	-7.9
2018	548.8	1375.8	352.3	684.2	691.6	1152.3	223.5	15.7	10.1	5.6
2019	554.4	1397.4	371.1	694.7	702.7	1176.3	221.2	15.3	4.9	10.4
2020	557.6	1400.8	378.8	694.9	705.9	1185.0	215.8	11.7	15.8	-4.1
2021	560.7	1413.5	388.6	700.9	712.7	1200.7	212.8	10.3	11.7	-1.4
2022	564.1	1427.7	414.4	708.1	719.6	1216.3	211.4	8.6	3.0	5.6
2023	564.8	1431.2	431.9	708.3	722.9	1224.3	207.0	9.3	20.4	-11.0

资料来源：北京市公安局。
Source: Beijing Municipal Public Security Bureau.

3-11 户籍人口年龄构成(2023年)
AGE COMPOSITION OF REGISTERED POPULATION (2023)

年龄组 Age Group	户籍人口(人) Registered Population (person)			占人口比重(%) Proportion (%)		
	合计 Total	男 Male	女 Female	合计 Total	男 Male	女 Female
合计 Total	**14312385**	**7083353**	**7229032**	**100.0**	**49.5**	**50.5**
0-4	527930	273311	254619	3.7	1.9	1.8
5-9	849641	438993	410648	5.9	3.1	2.9
10-14	655509	338741	316768	4.6	2.4	2.2
15-19	512360	264139	248221	3.6	1.8	1.7
20-24	511063	263219	247844	3.6	1.8	1.7
25-29	624597	318781	305816	4.4	2.2	2.1
30-34	865594	432430	433164	6.0	3.0	3.0
35-39	1187120	588776	598344	8.3	4.1	4.2
40-44	1220474	612516	607958	8.5	4.3	4.2
45-49	899947	442738	457209	6.3	3.1	3.2
50-54	1088411	540357	548054	7.6	3.8	3.8
55-59	1050590	523208	527382	7.3	3.7	3.7
60-64	1226775	611259	615516	8.6	4.3	4.3
65-69	1163836	561337	602499	8.1	3.9	4.2
70-74	824620	389987	434633	5.8	2.7	3.0
75-79	452772	206175	246597	3.2	1.4	1.7
80-84	310104	132218	177886	2.2	0.9	1.2
85-89	230820	98680	132140	1.6	0.7	0.9
90岁及以上 Aged 90 and Over	110222	46488	63734	0.8	0.3	0.4

资料来源：北京市公安局。
Source: Beijing Municipal Public Security Bureau.

3-12 户籍人口变动情况
CHANGES OF REGISTERED POPULATION

单位：人 (person)

项　目	Item	2023	2022
自然变动	**Natural Changes**		
自然增加	Natural Increase	-110353	55772
非农业人口	Non-agricultural Population	-81485	60721
农业人口	Agricultural Population	-28868	-4949
出　生	Births	93166	86044
非农业人口	Non-agricultural Population	86081	79166
农业人口	Agricultural Population	7085	6878
死　亡	Deaths	203519	30272
非农业人口	Non-agricultural Population	167566	18445
农业人口	Agricultural Population	35953	11827
机械变动	**Non-natural Changes**		
机械增加	Non-natural Increase	145058	85649
非农业人口	Non-agricultural Population	144731	84917
农业人口	Agricultural Population	327	732
市外迁入	Inflow	208854	139923
非农业人口	Non-agricultural Population	208429	139091
农业人口	Agricultural Population	425	832
迁往市外	Outflow	63796	54274
非农业人口	Non-agricultural Population	63698	54174
农业人口	Agricultural Population	98	100

资料来源：北京市公安局。
Source: Beijing Municipal Public Security Bureau.

3-13 全市法人单位按登记注册统计类别分从业人员年末人数(2008-2023年)
NUMBER OF EMPLOYED PERSONS IN CORPORATE UNITS AT YEAR-END BY STATISTICAL CETEGORY OF REGISTRATION(2008-2023)

单位：万人 (10000 persons)

年 份 Year	合 计 Total	内 资 Domestic Invested Units	港澳台投 资 Units with Funds from Hong Kong, Macao and Taiwan	外商投资 Foreign Funded Units
2008	812.0	705.7	33.5	72.8
2009	822.3	714.5	36.6	71.2
2010	865.3	748.0	42.4	74.9
2011	907.7	767.0	50.6	90.1
2012	951.4	804.4	54.3	92.7
2013	981.9	829.7	56.1	96.1
2014	1010.5	857.3	58.7	94.5
2015	1050.7	900.4	59.7	90.6
2016	1089.7	946.9	61.2	81.6
2017	1120.6	975.7	65.2	79.7
2018	1121.7	977.3	67.7	76.7
2019	1163.9	1018.3	71.1	74.5
2020	1067.2	922.1	73.3	71.8
2021	1076.6	927.8	73.5	75.3
2022	1052.6	904.9	70.5	77.2
2023	1027.5	882.5	71.3	73.7

3-14 全市法人单位从业人员年末人数及工资情况(2023年)
NUMBER OF EMPLOYED PERSONS IN CORPORATE UNITS AT YEAR-END AND THEIR WAGES(2023)

项　目	Item	从业人员年末人数(万人) Number of Employed Persons at Year-end (10000 persons)	从业人员工资总额(亿元) Total Wages of Employed Persons (100 million yuan)	从业人员平均工资(元) Average Wage of Employed Persons (yuan)
合　计	**Total**	**1027.5**	**19555.0**	**188413**
按登记注册统计类别分	**By Statistical Category of Registration**			
内　资	Domestic Invested Units	882.5	15579.5	174857
国　有	State-owned Units	150.7	3478.0	231908
私　营	Private Units	271.9	2925.1	105931
其他内资	Others	459.9	9176.4	197394
港澳台投资	Units with Funds from Hong Kong,Macao and Taiwan	71.3	2034.7	281474
外商投资	Foreign Funded Units	73.7	1940.8	260128
按城镇非私营、城镇私营分	**By Urban Non-Private Units and Urban Private Units**			
城镇非私营	Urban Non-Private Units	755.6	16629.9	218312
城镇私营	Urban Private Units	271.9	2925.1	105931
按国民经济行业分	**By Sector of National Economy**			
农、林、牧、渔业	Agriculture, Forestry, Animal Husbandry and Fishery	1.9	14.0	73125
采矿业	Mining	2.4	48.0	197171
制造业	Manufacturing	72.7	1278.7	173569
电力、热力、燃气及水生产和供应业	Production and Supply of Electricity, Heating, Gas and Water	10.2	211.6	210234
建筑业	Construction	63.6	854.7	132283
批发和零售业	Wholesale and Retail Trades	97.8	1501.6	151871
交通运输、仓储和邮政业	Transport, Storage and Post	53.0	803.2	150469
住宿和餐饮业	Hotels and Catering Services	43.8	298.1	68377
信息传输、软件和信息技术服务业	Information Transmission, Software and Information Technology	132.9	3987.6	294515
金融业	Financial Intermediation	60.3	2135.5	353584
房地产业	Real Estate	56.5	646.7	112325
租赁和商务服务业	Leasing and Business Services	142.3	2024.5	140983
科学研究和技术服务业	Scientific Research and Technical Services	92.1	1897.6	202148
水利、环境和公共设施管理业	Management of Water Conservancy, Environment and Public Facilities	14.1	169.2	115713
居民服务、修理和其他服务业	Service to Households, Repair and Other Services	20.4	132.3	65170
教　育	Education	56.0	1247.1	219949
卫生和社会工作	Health and Social Service	39.5	940.8	242108
文化、体育和娱乐业	Culture, Sports and Entertainment	25.5	526.0	204912
公共管理、社会保障和社会组织	Public Management, Social Security and Social Organizations	42.5	837.8	197846
国际组织	International Organizations			

3-15 规模以上企业法人单位按岗位分就业人员平均工资(2017-2023年) AVERAGE WAGE OF EMPLOYED PERSONS IN CORPORATE ENTERPRISES ABOVE DESIGNATED SIZE BY POSITION (2017-2023)

单位：元 (yuan)

项目	Item	2017	2018	2019	2020	2021	2022	2023
就业人员平均工资	Average Wage of Employed Persons	114379	126476	138978	150380	169410	180797	186020
中层及以上管理人员	Management Personnel at Middle Level and Above	288654	319343	332942	350464	386650	411034	425637
专业技术人员	Professional and Technical Personnel	156876	175614	189165	201236	225668	239333	242566
办事人员和有关人员	Office Clerks and Related Personnel	95130	100722	110416	115603	132097	136881	144532
社会生产服务和生活服务人员	Social Production Services and Life Services Personnel	68611	73836	82255	86132	95832	101667	110088
生产制造及有关人员	Production, Manufacturing and Related Personnel	74063	82620	90090	99493	109340	114621	117398

注：统计范围包括全市规模以上工业(含采矿业，制造业，电力、热力、燃气及水生产和供应业)、有资质的建筑业、限额以上批发和零售业、限额以上住宿和餐饮业、有开发经营活动的全部房地产开发经营业、规模以上服务业(含交通运输、仓储和邮政业，信息传输、软件和信息技术服务业，租赁和商务服务业，科学研究和技术服务业，水利、环境和公共设施管理业，居民服务、修理和其他服务业，教育，卫生和社会工作，文化、体育和娱乐业，以及物业管理、房地产中介服务等行业)共16个行业门类的企业法人单位。不包括农、林、牧、渔业，金融业，公共管理、社会保障和社会组织三个行业门类。

Note: The statistical scope include corporate enterprises in 16 classes of sectors in the industry above designated size (including mining; manufacturing; production and supply of electricity, heating, gas and water), qualified construction, wholesale and retail trades above designated size, hotels and catering services above designated size, all real estate development business with development and operating activities , and service sector above designated size (including transport, storage and post; information transmission, software and information technology; leasing and business services; scientific research and technical services; management of water conservancy, environment and public facilities; service to households, repair and other services; education; health and social service; culture, sports and entertainment; property management and real estate agency service, etc.) in Beijing. The following three classes of sectors are excluded: agriculture, forestry, animal husbandry and fishery; financial intermediation; public management, social security and social organization.

3-16 城镇非私营单位在岗职工年末人数及工资情况(1978-2023年)
NUMBER AND WAGES OF FULLY EMPLOYED STAFF AND WORKERS IN URBAN NON-PRIVATE UNITS AT YEAR-END (1978-2023)

年份 Year	在岗职工年末人数(万人) Number of Fully Employed Staff and Workers at Year-end (10000 persons)	在岗职工工资总额(亿元) Total Wages of Fully Employed Staff and Workers (100 million yuan)	在岗职工平均工资(元) Average Wage of Fully Employed Staff and Workers (yuan)
1978	291.6	18.7	673
1979	311.9	22.4	742
1980	326.5	26.9	848
1981	344.4	28.3	837
1982	360.1	30.5	863
1983	371.9	33.8	931
1984	375.4	40.4	1086
1985	382.3	50.7	1343
1986	397.9	58.0	1488
1987	405.2	66.7	1670
1988	410.4	81.2	2000
1989	418.4	96.3	2312
1990	454.9	118.9	2653
1991	470.0	132.2	2877
1992	476.6	158.5	3402
1993	467.3	218.9	4780
1994	471.8	306.5	6540
1995	470.9	382.0	8144
1996	460.6	442.4	9579
1997	465.3	514.8	11019
1998	450.1	558.2	12285
1999	438.0	614.5	13778
2000	434.2	695.5	15726
2001	400.3	777.3	19155
2002	434.2	950.9	21852
2003	436.3	1098.9	25312
2004	446.4	1315.1	29674
2005	448.4	1520.1	34191
2006	453.1	1805.5	40117
2007	478.9	2194.3	46507
2008	526.1	2874.3	54913
2009	560.4	3227.2	58140
2010	587.7	3789.1	65683
2011	640.3	4778.6	75834
2012	670.4	5657.9	85307
2013	695.5	6502.0	93997
2014	708.8	7293.3	103400
2015	724.8	8225.2	113073
2016	733.5	9005.0	122749
2017	756.4	10182.8	134994
2018	762.1	11562.8	149843
2019	727.8	12627.3	173205
2020	687.4	12692.8	185026
2021	708.4	14283.2	201504
2022	704.3	15356.5	215143
2023	710.4	16104.7	224562

注：1.2007年及以前城镇非私营单位是指除私营单位以外乡及乡以上独立核算法人单位，不包括乡镇企业和个体工商户。自2008年起是指不包括个体工商户的独立核算法人单位，下同。
2.表中2000年及以前数据为职工口径，职工包括在岗职工和不在岗职工，下同。

Note: a) Urban non-private units in and before 2007 referred to legal entities with independent accounting at and above township level other than the private units, excluding township enterprises and self-employed businesses. Since 2008, they referred to corporate units with independent accounting excluding self-employed businesses, the same below.
b) Data for and before 2000 in this table are counted in terms of the statistical range of employees which include both the fully employed staff and workers and the off-the-job ones, the same below.

3-17 城镇非私营单位在岗职工年末人数及工资情况(2023年)
NUMBER OF FULLY EMPLOYED STAFF AND WORKERS IN URBAN NON-PRIVATE UNITS AT YEAR-END AND THEIR WAGES (2023)

项目	Item	年末人数(人) Year-end Number (person)	工资总额(亿元) Total Wages (100 million yuan)	平均工资(元) Average Wage (yuan)
合计	**Total**	**7104273**	**16104.7**	**224562**
按登记注册统计类别分	**By Statistical Category of Registration**			
内资	Domestic Invested Units	5786138	12293.6	210714
国有	State-owned Units	1446847	3417.5	236939
其他内资	Others	4339291	8876.1	202101
港澳台投资	Units with Funds from Hong Kong,Macao and Taiwan	653897	1976.2	297671
外商投资	Foreign Funded Units	664238	1834.9	272466
按国民经济行业分	**By Sector of National Economy**			
农、林、牧、渔业	Agriculture, Forestry, Animal Husbandry and Fishery	13877	11.1	79603
#农业	Farming	2214	1.7	75826
采矿业	Mining	23476	47.5	197069
制造业	Manufacturing	546337	1042.9	188299
电力、热力、燃气及水生产和供应业	Production and Supply of Electricity, Heating, Gas and Water	92929	205.2	221710
建筑业	Construction	404777	666.5	161962
批发和零售业	Wholesale and Retail Trade	522226	1055.1	199936
批发业	Wholesale Trade	337183	803.5	235576
零售业	Retail Trade	185043	251.6	134808
交通运输、仓储和邮政业	Transport, Storage and Post	470038	756.6	160057
#铁路运输业	Railway Transport	86546	150.3	171394
道路运输业	Road Transport	196263	236.8	119705
邮政业	Post	60732	97.5	162011
住宿和餐饮业	Hotels and Catering Services	221769	195.6	88152
住宿业	Hotels	71520	70.1	97725
餐饮业	Catering Services	150249	125.5	83581
信息传输、软件和信息技术服务业	Information Transmission, Software and Information Technology	990504	3341.4	331175
金融业	Financial Intermediation	442446	1890.4	424561
房地产业	Real Estate	415731	545.1	128613
租赁和商务服务业	Leasing and Business Services	745051	1340.6	178649
租赁业	Leasing	11813	22.6	185163
商务服务业	Business Services	733238	1318.0	178541
科学研究和技术服务业	Scientific Research and Technical Services	616094	1500.2	240243
水利、环境和公共设施管理业	Management of Water Conservancy, Environment and Public Facilities	113003	149.1	127557
居民服务、修理和其他服务业	Service to Households, Repair and Other Services	60411	53.0	88980
#居民服务业	Service to Households	19673	20.9	109771
教育	Education	481199	1138.1	234869
卫生和社会工作	Health and Social Service	346315	886.0	259176
#卫生	Health	326771	863.0	267855
文化、体育和娱乐业	Culture, Sports and Entertainment	186087	448.5	240107
#文化艺术业	Cultural and Art Activities	33244	64.9	196483
体育	Sports Activities	16768	27.1	162627
公共管理、社会保障和社会组织	Public Management, Social Security and Social Organization	412003	831.8	202509
国际组织	International Organizations			

3-18 国民经济各行业城镇非私营单位在岗职工平均工资
AVERAGE WAGES OF FULLY EMPLOYED STAFF AND WORKERS IN URBAN NON-PRIVATE UNITS IN DIFFERENT SECTORS OF NATIONAL ECONOMY

单位：元 (yuan)

项 目	Item	2023	2022
合　计	**Total**	**224562**	**215143**
农、林、牧、渔业	**Agriculture, Forestry, Animal Husbandry and Fishery**	**79603**	**80082**
#农、林、牧、渔专业及辅助性活动	Professional and Support Activities in Agriculture, Forestry, Animal Husbandry and Fishery	118184	92301
采矿业	**Mining**	**197069**	**167262**
煤炭开采和洗选业	Mining and Washing of Coal	108333	
石油和天然气开采业	Extraction of Petroleum and Natural Gas	330223	322668
黑色金属矿采选业	Mining and Pressing of Ferrous Metal Ores	157320	160177
有色金属矿采选业	Mining and Processing of Non-Ferrous Metal Ores	383591	
非金属矿采选业	Mining and Processing of Non-metal Ores		
开采专业及辅助性活动	Professional and Support Activities for Mining	214754	162430
其他采矿业	Mining of Other Ores		152926
制造业	**Manufacturing**	**188299**	**182181**
农副食品加工业	Processing of Food from Agricultural Products	103956	108883
食品制造业	Manufacture of Foods	127174	123318
酒、饮料和精制茶制造业	Manufacture of Liquor, Beverage and Refined Tea	117791	111761
烟草制品业	Manufacture of Tobacco	349154	324856
纺织业	Manufacture of Textile	88614	89957
纺织服装、服饰业	Manufacture of Textile, Wearing Apparel and Ornament	88277	84991
皮革、毛皮、羽毛及其制品和制鞋业	Manufacture of Leather, Fur, Feather and Related Products, and Footwear	60364	67072
木材加工和木、竹、藤、棕、草制品业	Processing of Timber, Manufacture of Wood, Bamboo, Rattan, Palm and Straw Products	85121	83269
家具制造业	Manufacture of Furniture	112323	114553
造纸和纸制品业	Manufacture of Paper and Paper Products	117640	120056
印刷和记录媒介复制业	Printing and Reproduction of Recording Media	143964	135280
文教、工美、体育和娱乐用品制造业	Manufacture of Articles for Culture, Education, Arts and Crafts, Sport and Entertainment Activities	104576	102020
石油、煤炭及其他燃料加工业	Processing of Petroleum, Coal and Other Fuels	213067	208770
化学原料和化学制品制造业	Manufacture of Raw Chemical Materials and Chemical Products	159981	151193
医药制造业	Manufacture of Medicines	222658	223390
化学纤维制造业	Manufacture of Chemical Fibres	95080	107535
橡胶和塑料制品业	Manufacture of Rubber and Plastics Products	112044	105960
非金属矿物制品业	Manufacture of Non-metallic Mineral Products	134012	123470
黑色金属冶炼和压延加工业	Smelting and Pressing of Ferrous Metals	125947	127845

3-18 续表 1 Continued 1

单位：元 (yuan)

行业	Sector	2023	2022
有色金属冶炼和压延加工业	Smelting and Processing of Non-ferrous Metals	171984	158463
金属制品业	Manufacture of Metal Products	139843	125705
通用设备制造业	Manufacture of General Purpose Machinery	176777	169559
专用设备制造业	Manufacture of Special Purpose Machinery	204567	193991
汽车制造业	Manufacture of Automobiles	176997	168381
铁路、船舶、航空航天和其他运输设备制造业	Manufacture of Railway, Ship, Aerospace and Other Transport Equipments	230320	206086
电气机械和器材制造业	Manufacture of Electrical Machinery and Apparatus	199862	192711
计算机、通信和其他电子设备制造业	Manufacture of Computers, Communication and Other Electronic Equipment	251717	247713
仪器仪表制造业	Manufacture of Measuring Instruments and Machinery	203096	195384
其他制造业	Other Manufacture	139129	125263
废弃资源综合利用业	Utilization of Waste Resources	168678	131690
金属制品、机械和设备修理业	Repair Service of Metal Products, Machinery and Equipment	181011	183797
电力、热力、燃气及水生产和供应业	**Production and Supply of Electricity, Heating, Gas and Water**	**221710**	**208131**
电力、热力生产和供应业	Production and Supply of Electric Power and Heat Power	244302	228231
燃气生产和供应业	Production and Supply of Gas	192338	181028
水的生产和供应业	Production and Supply of Water	143552	137463
建筑业	**Construction**	**161962**	**153310**
房屋建筑业	Construction of Buildings	168973	165154
土木工程建筑业	Civil Engineering	169415	164280
建筑安装业	Building Installation	147793	141512
建筑装饰、装修和其他建筑业	Building Decoration and Other Constructions	121305	98995
批发和零售业	**Wholesale and Retail Trades**	**199936**	**194297**
批发业	Wholesale Trade	235576	234485
零售业	Retail Trade	134808	119941
交通运输、仓储和邮政业	**Transport, Storage and Post**	**160057**	**147103**
铁路运输业	Railway Transport	171394	159408
道路运输业	Road Transport	119705	111769
水上运输业	Water Transport	282467	290906
航空运输业	Air Transport	226173	215906
管道运输业	Transport via Pipelines	295999	267711
多式联运和运输代理业	Intermodality and Forwarding Agency	179791	190024
装卸搬运和仓储业	Loading, Unloading and Storage	121066	140524
邮政业	Post	162011	131595
住宿和餐饮业	**Hotels and Catering Services**	**88152**	**81321**
住宿业	Hotels	97725	90188
餐饮业	Catering Services	83581	76538
信息传输、软件和信息技术服务业	**Information Transmission, Software and Information Technology**	**331175**	**319550**
电信、广播电视和卫星传输服务	Telecommunication, Radio and Television and Satellite Transmission Service	293968	275454
互联网和相关服务	Internet and Related Service	381783	364949
软件和信息技术服务业	Software and Information Technology	324806	313985

3-18 续表 2 Continued 2

单位：元 (yuan)

行　　业	Sector	2023	2022
金融业	**Financial Intermediation**	**424561**	**413725**
货币金融服务	Monetary and Financial Service	410489	396593
资本市场服务	Capital Market Service	518557	518381
保险业	Insurance	330625	330320
其他金融业	Other Financial Activities	538940	493752
房地产业	**Real Estate**	**128613**	**127894**
租赁和商务服务业	**Leasing and Business Services**	**178649**	**173232**
租赁业	Leasing	185163	191202
商务服务业	Business Services	178541	172910
科学研究和技术服务业	**Scientific Research and Technical Services**	**240243**	**234723**
研究和试验发展	Research and Experimental Development	284970	280682
专业技术服务业	Professional Technical Services	220717	216462
科技推广和应用服务业	Science and Technology Popularization and Application Services	231361	223631
水利、环境和公共设施管理业	**Management of Water Conservancy, Environment and Public Facilities**	**127557**	**121869**
水利管理业	Management of Water Conservancy	223764	210915
生态保护和环境治理业	Ecological Protection and Environmental Treatment	193413	186924
公共设施管理业	Management of Public Facilities	108301	103618
土地管理业	Management of Land	262122	246661
居民服务、修理和其他服务业	**Service to Households, Repair and Other Services**	**88980**	**83101**
居民服务业	Service to Households	109771	99909
机动车、电子产品和日用产品修理业	Repair of Motor Vehicles, Electronics and Household Products	111728	100383
其他服务业	Other Services	66922	66562
教　育	**Education**	**234869**	**220707**
卫生和社会工作	**Health and Social Service**	**259176**	**236398**
卫　生	Health	267855	244747
社会工作	Social Service	116876	101903
文化、体育和娱乐业	**Culture, Sports and Entertainment**	**240107**	**231090**
新闻和出版业	Journalism and Publishing Activities	255577	244701
广播、电视、电影和录音制作业	Radio, Television, Motion Picture and Audio Production Services	305258	302156
文化艺术业	Cultural and Art Activities	196483	178871
体　育	Sports Activities	162627	147651
娱乐业	Entertainment	174363	173867
公共管理、社会保障和社会组织	**Public Management, Social Security and Social Organization**	**202509**	**199796**
中国共产党机关	Organs of Communist Party of China	191730	209402
国家机构	Organs of State	203211	199827
人民政协、民主党派	People's Political Consultative Conference and Democratic Parties	213479	217264
社会保障	Social Security	187837	217242
群众团体、社会团体和其他成员组织	Mass Organizations, Social Organizations and Other Membership Organizations	192666	174168
基层群众自治组织	Grass Roots Self-Governing Organizations		
国际组织	**International Organizations**		

3−19 城镇登记失业率和城镇新增就业人数(1979−2023年)
REGISTERED UNEMPLOYMENT RATE IN URBAN AREA AND NEWLY EMPLOYED PERSONS IN URBAN AREA (1979-2023)

单位：万人 (10000 persons)

年 份 Year	年末实有登记失业人员 Year-end Number of Actual Registered Unemployed Persons	年末城镇登记失业率(%) Year-end Registered Unemployment Rate in Urban Area(%)	城镇新增就业人数 Newly Employed Persons in Urban Area
1979	4.96	1.60	
1980	8.67	1.60	
1981	8.36	1.28	
1982	7.03	1.62	
1983	4.20	1.09	
1984	2.03	0.54	
1985	1.61	0.40	
1986	1.25	0.30	
1987	2.24	0.45	
1988	1.58	0.40	
1989	1.71	0.40	
1990	1.67	0.30	
1991	1.92	0.40	
1992	1.72	0.36	
1993	1.92	0.41	
1994	1.91	0.41	
1995	2.19	0.46	
1996	2.80	0.58	
1997	3.29	0.73	
1998	2.95	0.66	
1999	2.80	0.62	
2000	3.32	0.76	
2001	5.19	1.18	
2002	6.02	1.35	
2003	6.96	1.43	
2004	6.46	1.30	
2005	10.57	2.11	24.85
2006	10.40	1.98	27.24
2007	10.63	1.84	30.48
2008	10.33	1.82	32.99
2009	8.16	1.44	34.33
2010	7.73	1.37	37.42
2011	7.89	1.39	37.75
2012	7.20	1.27	35.77
2013	6.81	1.21	33.23
2014	8.77	1.31	33.62
2015	9.16	1.39	34.65
2016	9.14	1.41	36.93
2017	9.22	1.43	35.35
2018	10.24	1.40	33.27
2019	9.35	1.30	35.10
2020	29.02	2.56	26.10
2021	37.19	3.23	26.90
2022	36.39	3.12	26.10
2023	35.74	3.08	28.10

注：1.2014年以前年末实有登记失业人员为城镇口径，自2014年起调整为全市口径。
2.自2020年9月起，对城镇登记失业人员相关统计口径进行调整，将离校未就业高校毕业生、领取失业补助金人员和领取一次性生活补助农民工纳入登记失业人员范围。

资料来源：北京市人力资源和社会保障局。

Note: a) The year-end number of actual registered unemployed persons before 2014 refers to the statistical coverage in urban area and has been adjusted to the statistical coverage of the whole city since 2014.
b) The relevant statistical coverage of the registered unemployed persons in urban area has been adjusted since September 2020,the unemployed college graduates, the personnel receiving unemployment compensation and the rural migrant workers receiving lump-sum living allowance were included in the list of registered unemployed persons.

Source: Beijing Municipal Human Resources and Social Security Bureau.

主要统计指标解释

户籍人口 指公民依照《中华人民共和国户口登记条例》已在其经常居住地的公安户籍管理机关登记了常住户口的人。

常住人口 指在某地区实际居住半年以上的人口。

常住外来人口 指不具有本市户籍户口，来自北京市行政区划以外的省、自治区、直辖市，且在京居住半年以上的人口。

出生率 指在一定时期内（通常为一年）出生人数与同期平均人数(或期中人数)之比，一般用千分比表示。计算公式：

$$出生率=\frac{年出生人数}{年平均人数}\times1000‰$$

出生人数是指活产，即脱离母体时（不管怀孕月数），有过呼吸或其他生命现象的活婴儿总和。年平均人数是年初、年末人口数的平均数，也可用年中人口数代替。

死亡率 指在一定时期内（通常为一年）死亡人数与同期平均人数（或期中人数）之比，一般用千分比表示。计算公式：

$$死亡率=\frac{年死亡人数}{年平均人数}\times1000‰$$

自然增长率 指在一定时期内（通常为一年）人口自然增加数（出生人数减死亡人数）与该时期内平均人数（或期中人数）之比，一般用千分比表示。计算公式：

$$自然增长率=\frac{年出生人数-年死亡人数}{年平均人数}\times1000‰$$

人口自然增长率=人口出生率－人口死亡率

常住就业人口 指在常住人口中，年满 16 周岁，为取得报酬或经营利润，在调查周内从事了 1 小时（含 1 小时）以上劳动的人口；或由于在职学习、休假等原因在调查周内暂时未工作的人口；或由于停工、单位不景气等原因临时未工作的人口。

从业人员 指在各级国家机关、党政机关、社会团体及企业、事业单位中工作，取得工资或其他形式的劳动报酬的全部人员。包括：在岗职工、聘用的离退休人员以及在单位中工作的港澳台及外籍人员、兼职人员、借用的外单位人员和第二职业者。不包括本单位的不在岗职工。

在岗职工 指在本单位工作并由单位支付工资的人员，以及有工作岗位，但由于学习、病伤产假（六个月以内）等原因暂未工作，仍由单位支付工资的人员。

在岗职工工资总额 与在岗职工指标相对应，根据 1990 年 1 月 1 日的国家统计局令（一号）修订，指单位在报告期内直接支付给本单位在岗职工的劳动报酬总额。包括基础工资、职务工资、级别工资、工龄工资、计件工资、奖金、各种津贴和补贴、交通补贴、洗理费、书报费、旅游费、过节费、伙食补助、住房补贴、住房提租补贴、由单位从个人工资中直接为其代扣或代缴的个人所得税、房水电费以及住房公积金和社会保险基金个人缴纳部分等。

在岗职工平均工资 指企业、事业、机关等单位的在岗职工在一定时期内的人均劳动报酬。它表明一定时期在岗职工工资收入的高低程度，是反映在岗职工工资水平的主要指标。计算公式为：

$$\begin{matrix}在岗职工\\平均工资\end{matrix}=\frac{报告期实际支付的全部在岗职工工资总额}{报告期全部在岗职工平均人数}$$

从业人员平均工资 指企业、事业、机关等单位的从业人员在一定时期内的人均劳动报酬。计算公式为：

$$从业人员平均工资=\frac{报告期实际支付的全部从业人员劳动报酬总额}{报告期全部从业人员平均人数}$$

年末实有登记失业人员 指年末实有的登记失业人员总数，包括城镇登记失业人员和城市化建设地区的登记失业农民（失地农民）。

年末城镇登记失业率 指年末城镇登记失业人数与城镇从业人数和城镇登记失业人数二者之和的比。计算公式如下：

$$城镇登记失业率=\frac{年末实有登记失业人数}{城镇从业人数+年末实有登记失业人数}\times100\%$$

Explanatory Notes on Main Statistical Indicators

Registered Population refers to persons who have registered their permanent residence with the public security register authority of their habitual residence according to the *Households Registration Regulations of PRC.*

Permanent Population refers to persons actually living for more than half a year at a place.

Permanent Migrant Population refers to persons who have no permanent residence registration in Beijing, come from other provinces, autonomous regions and municipalities, and have stayed in Beijing for more than half a year.

Birth Rate refers to the ratio of the number of births to the average population (or mid-period population) during a certain period of time (usually a year), which is often expressed in ‰. The following formula is used:

Birth Rate = Annual Number of Births/Annual Average Number of Population×1,000‰

Number of births refers to live births, i.e. the births when babies has breathed or shown any vital phenomena regardless of the length of pregnancy. Annual average number of population is the average of the number of population at the beginning of the year and that at the end of the year. Sometimes it is substituted with the mid-year population.

Death Rate refers to the ratio of the number of deaths to the average population (or mid-period population) during a certain period of time (usually a year), which is often expressed in ‰. The following formula is used:

Death Rate= Annual Number of Deaths/Annual Average Number of Population×1,000‰

Natural Growth Rate refers to the ratio of the natural growth of population (births minus deaths) to the average population (or mid-period population) during a certain period of time (usually a year), which is often expressed in ‰. The following formula is used:

Natural Growth Rate = (Annual Number of Births - Annual Number of Deaths)/Annual Average Number of Population×1,000‰

Natural Growth Rate of Population = Birth Rate - Death Rate

Permanent Employed Population refers to persons aged 16 and over, among the permanent population, who perform some work for compensation or business gains for one hour or more during the reference period; or persons temporarily out of work for the reasons of in-service study or on holiday, etc.; or persons temporary out of work for the reasons of shutdown or recession of the entity, etc.

Employed Persons refer to all persons working in government agencies, Party and political organs, social groups, enterprises and public institutions at all levels, and receiving wages or labor remuneration in other forms. They include: fully employed staff and workers, retired persons employed, persons from Hong Kong, Macao, Taiwan and foreign countries who are employed, part-time employees, employees transferred from other entities, and employees with a second job. They exclude employees that are not on the job in the entity.

Fully Employed Staff and Workers refer to persons working in the entity and paid by the entity, as well as persons having a job in the entity, but not working temporarily due to study, illness, injury or maternity leaves (less than 6 months) and other reasons, and still paid by the entity.

Total Wages of Fully Employed Staff and Workers correspond to the indicator of Fully Employed Staff and Workers. The indicator was revised in accordance with No. 1 Decree of the National Bureau of Statistics dated January 1, 1990, referring to the total wages directly paid by an entity to fully employed staff and workers of the entity during the reporting period. It consists of basic wage, post wage, wage of a rank, seniority wage, piece rate wage, bonus, allowances and subsidies, traffic subsidy, washing and haircutting allowance, books and newspaper allowance, travel benefit, festival bonus, food subsidy, housing subsidy, subsidy for incremental house rent, as well as personal income tax, water and electricity fees and the personally payable portion of housing accumulation fund and social security fund withheld directly by the employer from the employee's wage.

Average Wage of Fully Employed Staff and Workers refers to the per-capita labor remuneration of fully employed staff and workers in enterprises, public institutions and government agencies within a given period of time. It shows the level of wage income of fully employed staff and workers within a given period of time, serving as a main indicator reflecting the level of wage of fully employed staff and workers. The following formula is used:

Average Wage of Fully Employed Staff and Workers = Total Wages of All Fully Employed Staff and Workers Actually Paid in the Reporting Period / Average Number of All Fully Employed Staff and Workers in the Reporting Period

Average Wage of Employed Persons refers to the per-capita labor remuneration of employed persons in enterprises, public institutions and government agencies within a given period of time. The following formula is used:

Average Wage of Employed Persons = Total Labor Remuneration of All Employed Persons Actually Paid in the Reporting Period / Average Number of All Employed Persons in the Reporting Period

Period-end Actual Registered Unemployed Persons refer to the total number of actual unemployed persons registered at the end period, including unemployed persons registered in urban regions and the unemployed peasants registered in urbanization regions (land-lost peasants).

Year-end Registered Unemployment Rate in Urban Area refers to the ratio of urban registered unemployed persons at year end to the sum of urban employed persons and urban registered unemployed persons. The following formula is used:

Registered Unemployment Rate in Urban Area
=Number of Actual Registered Unemployed Persons at Year End / (Urban Employed Persons + Number of Actual Registered Unemployed Persons at Year End) × 100%

04

价格指数
PRICE INDEX

简要说明

一、主要内容

本章价格指数资料，反映生产、流通、消费与投资的价格变动趋势和变动幅度。主要包括居民消费价格指数农产品生产者价格指数、工业生产者出厂价格指数、工业生产者购进价格指数、固定资产投资价格指数、住宅销售价格指数。

二、调查方法

（一）居民消费价格指数

编制居民消费价格指数的资料采用抽样调查和重点调查相结合的方法取得，即在全市选择不同的区域，按照布局合理的原则抽选价格调查点，由国家确定调查商品和服务项目，在此基础上按照消费量大、价格变动趋势有较强代表性的原则选择调查样本，对其市场价格进行定期调查，以样本推算总体。

抽选价格调查点。按照布局合理等原则，将不同区域各种类型的商场、农贸市场、服务网点分别按销售额、成交额和经营规模为标志，从高到低排队，依据所需调查点的数量进行等距抽样。

选择代表规格品。代表商品和服务项目由国家确定，代表规格品由各省市按照有关原则选择。选择原则：（1）消费量较大；（2）价格变动趋势和变动程度有较强的代表性，即选中规格品的价格变动特征与未选中规格品之间价格变动的相关性愈高愈好；（3）选中的规格品之间，性质相隔愈远愈好，价格变动特征的相关性愈低愈好；选中的工业消费品必须是合格产品，产品包装上有注册商标、产地、规格等级等标识。目前，居民消费价格调查按用途划分为 8 个大类，268 个基本分类，价格资料的采集采取定人、定点、定时直接调查的方法采集价格资料或者由选中的调查对象协助填报。

权数资料来源与计算。居民消费价格指数的权数根据城市居民家庭生活消费支出调查资料整理计算。按照国家统计局统一要求，自 2021 年 1 月起，北京流通消费价格统计专业执行新的《流通和消费价格统计报表制度》，其中居民消费价格调查项目目录重新进行了修订调整。

（二）工业生产者出厂价格指数和工业生产者购进价格指数

工业生产者出厂价格是工业品第一次出售时的出厂价格。该项调查采用重点调查与典型调查相结合的调查方法。根据代表性原则，抽选年主营业务收入 2000 万元以上的企业作为调查对象。经国家统计局审定，可酌情补充部分年主营业务收入 2000 万元以下的企业。

工业生产者购进价格是工业企业作为中间投入的价格。调查对象主要从填报工业生产者出厂价格的企业中选择。

选择代表企业的原则：（1）按工业行业选择调查企业，原则上应覆盖重点中类行业；（2）优先选择大型企业作为调查对象，并适当选择一些其他企业；（3）选择生产正常、稳定的企业作为调查对象。

选择代表产品的原则：（1）按工业行业选择基本分类和代表产品；（2）选择对国计民生影响大的产品；（3）选择生产较为稳定的产品；（4）选择有发展前景的产品；（5）选择具有地方特色的产品。

权数的确定。编制工业生产者出厂价格小类及以上的权数资料来源于工业统计中分行业工业销售产值数据资料；基本分类的权数资料来源于独立的工业生产者出厂价格权数专项调查。购进价格大类权数主要参考分行业的投入产出数据，其他分类权数来源于独立的工业生产者购进价格权数专项调查。一般情况下，工业生产者权数专项调查每五年进行一次。

根据国家统计制度要求，2021 年开始使用 2020 年作为新一轮的对比基期，新基期的调查分类目录、代表规格品和调查企业均有调整，分类权数也有变化，以反映工业生产结构的最新变动。

（三）固定资产投资价格指数

固定资产投资价格调查采用重点调查、典型调查和非传统数据替代相结合的方法。固定资产投资价格调查所涉及的价格是构成固定资产投资额实体的实际购进价格（或结算价格）。调查的内容包括构成当年建筑工程实体的钢材、木材、水泥、地方建筑材料、电料、化工材料等主要建筑材料价格，投入的劳动力价格（单位工资）和各种施工机械使用费用；设备工器具购置和其他费用投资价格。

选择建筑安装工程调查点的原则：（1）样本单位应具有一定覆盖面；（2）投资经济活动代表性强；（3）兼顾不同经济类型；（4）选择重点工程；（5）兼顾不同工程类别。

选择其他费用调查点的原则：在选择其他费用调查点时，所遵循的原则与建筑安装工程调查点的原则基本相同，特别是要注意选择那些投资额大的工程。但由于其他费用不易取得，所以在实际操作过程中，应同时在建设单位、施工单位开展重点调查，并辅以典型调查（从有关管理部门取得资料）。

权数的确定。固定资产投资价格指数的计算权数是建筑安装工程、设备工器具购置和其他费用三者前三年投资完成额的平均比重。

（四）住宅销售价格指数

住宅销售价格调查包括新建商品住宅销售价格和二手住宅销售价格调查。

新建商品住宅销售价格的调查方法：新建商品住宅销售面积、金额等资料直接采用当地房地产管理部门的网签数据。新建商品住宅的网签数据内容主要包括：住宅项目（楼盘）名称、项目地址、幢号、总层数、所在层数、房屋结构、建筑面积、成交总价（合同金额）、签约时间等。

二手住宅销售价格的调查方法：二手住宅销售价格调查为非全面调查，采用重点调查与典型调查相结合的方法，按照房地产经纪机构上报的方式收集基础数据。

（五）农产品生产者价格指数

农产品生产者价格调查采取抽样调查和重点调查相结合的调查方法。抽取 360 个农产品生产和出售的农业生产经营单位及行政村作为调查对象。对一些区域性比较强的农产品采取在主产区主观选样的方法选择农业生产经营单位及行政村作为调查对象。

由于北京市林业产品（树苗）产值比重较少，不足 1%，根据国家统计局统计制度要求，不需要进行林业产品生产者价格调查。

Brief Introduction

I. Main Content

Price indexes in this chapter reflect the trend and rate of changes in prices of production, circulation, consumption and investment, mainly consisting of consumer price index (CPI), producer price index for farm products, producer price index for industrial products (PPI), purchasing price index for industrial producers, price index for investment in fixed assets, and selling price index of residential houses.

II. Survey Methods

(I) Consumer Price Index (CPI)

Data for compilation of the consumer price index are collected through a combination of sample surveys and surveys of key units. Different areas are selected across the city, and price survey sites are selected in accordance with the principle of reasonable layout. Commodity and service items for survey are determined by the country. On this basis, survey samples are selected according to the principle of large quantity of consumption, and strong representativeness in price change trend. Regular surveys are conducted to collect data on their market prices. General indexes are inferred on the basis of the sample data.

The selection of price survey sites: By adopting the principle of reasonable layout, an equidistant sampling is conducted for department stores, agricultural product trade markets and service outlets in different types and in different areas by their sales value, transaction value and operational scale, which will be ranked in a descending order based on the number of survey sites required.

The selection of representative specifications: Representative commodities and service items are determined by the country. Representative specifications are selected by provinces and cities according to relevant principles. Principles for selection: (1) large quantity of consumption; (2) strongly representative trend and extent of price changes, which means the characteristics of price changes of selected specifications shall be highly correlated with price changes of those that are not selected; (3) selected specifications shall be different in their nature and least correlated in the characteristics of price changes between each other; the selected industrial consumer goods must be qualified products, with registered trademark, origin, specifications, grade and other marks on the their package. At present, data are collected under 268 basic headings in 8 categories in the consumer price surveys according to their specific purposes. Collection of price data: Price data are collected through direct surveys by designated personnel at designated sites on periodic basis, or the selected respondents should assist in filling in the price data.

Source and calculation of the weights: CPI weights are calculated according to survey information on living expenditures of urban residents. According to the uniform requirement of the National Bureau of Statistics, since January 2021, the new *Circulation and Consumption Price Statistical Reporting System* has been implemented for statistics of circulation and consumption price in Beijing, of which, the survey catalogues of consumer prices of household have been revised and adjusted.

(II) Producer Price Index for Industrial Products (PPI) and Purchasing Price Index for Industrial Producers

The producer price for industrial products refers to the producer's price of industrial products when sold for the first time. This survey program is a combined use of the methods of surveys of key units and surveys of typical units. According to the principle of representativeness, enterprises with annual main business income of more than RMB 20 million are selected as the enterprises for survey. After the examination and approval by the National Bureau of Statistics, some enterprises with annual main business income below RMB 20 million may be supplemented as appropriate.

Purchasing price for industrial producers refers to the price of intermediate inputs of industrial enterprise. Enterprises for survey are selected among those that have submitted the producer price for industrial products.

Principles for selecting the representative enterprises: (1) Enterprises to be covered in the survey are selected by industrial sectors. In principle, the key branch should be covered; (2) Large-sized enterprises should be preferred to be selected for the survey, with appropriate selection of some other enterprises at the same time; (3) Enterprises selected should be those with normal and stable production.

Principles for selecting representative products: (1) basic headings and representative products shall be selected by industrial sectors; (2) the selected products should have significant impact on the national economy and people's livelihood; (3) the production of the products selected should be relatively more stable; (4) the prospects of the products selected should be promising; (5) the products selected should be representative to the localities.

Determination of weights: Weights data used for compiling producer price for industrial products of small class and above come from data of industrial sales value collected by sectors in industrial statistics; weights data in basic headings come from independent special survey on the weights of producer price for industrial products. Weights data of purchasing price of large class are mainly with reference to the input-output data by sectors, and the weights data of other headings come from independent special survey on the weights of purchasing price for industrial producers. In general, the special survey on the weights of industrial producers is conducted once every five years.

According to the requirements of the national statistical system, since 2021, 2020 shall be taken as a new round of comparison base period; in the new base period, the survey classification catalogues, the representative specifications and the enterprises for survey have all been adjusted, and the classification weights have been changed as well so as to reflect the latest changes in the industrial production structure.

(III) Price Index for Investment in Fixed Assets

A combined method of key survey, typical survey and nontraditional data substitution is used for the survey of data on prices of investment in fixed assets. The prices collected in the surveys on prices of investment in fixed assets are the actual purchasing prices (or settlement prices) of entities of investment in fixed assets. The survey covers the prices of main construction materials that constitute the architectural engineering entities in the year, such as steel, timber, cement, local construction materials, electric parts and chemical materials; the prices of labor input (wages) and costs of use of construction machines; the purchasing price of equipment, tools and instruments as well as other expenditures.

Principles for selecting survey sites of construction and installation projects: (1) the sample unit shall have certain coverage; (2) the economic activity of investment should have strong representativeness; (3) different economic types should be considered; (4) key projects shall be selected; (5) attention should be given to various types of projects.

Principles for selecting survey sites of other expenditures: in the selection of survey sites of other expenditures, the same principles shall be followed as in the selection of survey sites of construction and installation projects. Especially projects with larger amount of investment shall be selected. Since it is not easy to obtain data on other expenditures, during the actual data gathering operations, key survey on builders and construction units should be conducted concurrently with survey on typical units (with information from administration units).

Determination of weights: Weights used for calculating the price index for investment in fixed assets are determined according to the average proportion of investment amount of construction and installation projects, purchase of equipment, tools and instruments and other expenditures completed in the previous three years.

(IV) Selling Price Index of Residential Houses

The surveys on selling price of residential houses include the surveys on new commercial residential house selling price and the second-hand residential house selling price.

Survey method of new commercial residential house selling price: Data of area and amount, etc. of new commercial residential houses are taken directly from the online contract signing data recorded by local real estate authorities. Online contract signing data of new commercial residential house mainly consist of the name of residential project (building), project location, building number, total number of floors, floor number, house structure, building area, total price of transaction (contractual amount), and date of contract signing, etc.

Survey method of second-hand house selling price: Survey of second-hand house selling price is incomplete survey conducted with the combined method of key survey and typical survey. Basic data are collected in accordance with the manner of reporting by real estate brokerage agencies.

(V) Producer Price Index for Farm Products

A combined method of sample survey and key survey was used for the survey of producer prices of farm products. 360 entities and administrative villages producing and selling farm products are sampled. For some regional farm products, data on agricultural production and operation units and administrative villages are collected with the method of subjective sampling in main production areas.

As the proportion of output value of forestry products (saplings) in Beijing is relatively small, taking no more than 1%, so no survey on producer price for forestry products is conducted according to statistical requirements of National Bureau of Statistics.

4–1 各种价格指数(1978–2023年)
PRICE INDICES (1978-2023)

(上年=100) (preceding year=100)

年 份 Year	居民消费价格指数 Consumer Price Index	农产品生产者价格指数 Producer Price Index for Agriculture Products	工业生产者出厂价格指数 Producer Price Index for Industrial Products	工业生产者购进价格指数 Purchasing Price Index for Industrial Producers	固定资产投资价格指数 Price Index for Investment in Fixed Assets
1978	100.6				
1979	101.8	109.5			
1980	106.0	105.5			
1981	101.3	109.4			
1982	101.8	101.9			
1983	100.5	101.8			
1984	102.2	102.3			
1985	117.6	117.6			
1986	106.8	108.1			
1987	108.6	116.1			
1988	120.4	123.2			
1989	117.2	106.8			
1990	105.4	101.9	107.9	114.8	
1991	111.9	101.7	105.8	111.7	107.3
1992	109.9	102.4	100.9	103.3	112.2
1993	119.0	107.0	121.8	133.2	126.6
1994	124.9	133.4	112.9	118.7	116.2
1995	117.3	130.6	107.3	106.7	113.9
1996	111.6	101.5	100.7	100.3	108.2
1997	105.3	92.8	101.1	103.4	102.7
1998	102.4	93.6	95.1	98.1	100.8
1999	100.6	97.5	97.7	95.8	99.9
2000	103.5	95.0	102.5	100.0	101.0
2001	103.1	102.0	99.4	100.5	100.6
2002	98.2	92.4	96.6	97.1	100.4
2003	100.2	102.5	101.5	104.7	102.2
2004	101.0	106.2	103.0	114.2	104.3
2005	101.5	102.9	101.3	111.4	100.7
2006	100.9	99.1	99.1	105.5	100.4
2007	102.4	114.4	99.7	105.0	102.8
2008	105.1	112.3	103.3	115.8	107.8
2009	98.5	98.3	94.4	88.6	97.1
2010	102.4	106.5	102.2	110.5	102.5
2011	105.6	110.7	102.3	108.4	105.7
2012	103.3	104.7	98.4	98.7	101.3
2013	103.3	104.7	97.4	97.8	99.9
2014	101.6	99.7	99.1	98.8	100.0
2015	101.8	99.8	96.9	93.7	97.6
2016	101.4	99.7	98.1	98.5	99.7
2017	101.9	96.2	100.7	104.4	104.7
2018	102.5	103.6	100.0	100.8	103.8
2019	102.3	109.9	99.6	99.6	102.1
2020	101.7	110.9	99.1	99.5	
2021	101.1	98.2	101.1	103.7	
2022	101.8	102.7	102.3	106.2	
2023	100.4	99.7	99.2	98.7	

注：1.自2011年起，"工业品出厂价格指数"更名为"工业生产者出厂价格指数"，"原材料、燃料、动力购进价格指数"更名为"工业生产者购进价格指数"，下同。
2.自2013年起，"农产品生产价格指数"更名为"农产品生产者价格指数"。
3.自2020年起，国家统计局取消固定资产投资价格统计，下同。

Note: a) Since 2011, the "producer price index for manufactured goods" has been replaced by the "producer price index for industrial products", and the "purchasing price index for raw materials, fuel and power" has been replaced by the "purchasing price index for industrial producers", the same below.
b) Since 2013, the "production price index for agricultural products" has been replaced by the "producer price index for agricultural products".
c) Since 2020, the National Bureau of Statistics has cancelled the statistics for fixed assets investment price, the same below.

4-2 各种价格定基指数(1978-2023年)
FIXED-BASE PRICE INDICES (1978-2023)

年份 Year	居民消费价格指数(1978=100) Consumer Price Index (year of 1978=100)	工业生产者出厂价格指数(1990=100) Producer Price Index for Industrial Products (year of 1990=100)	工业生产者购进价格指数(1990=100) Purchasing Price Index for Industrial Producers (year of 1990=100)	固定资产投资价格指数(1990=100) Price Index for Investment in Fixed Assets (year of 1990=100)
1978	100.0			
1979	101.8			
1980	107.9			
1981	109.3			
1982	111.3			
1983	111.8			
1984	114.3			
1985	134.4			
1986	143.5			
1987	155.8			
1988	187.6			
1989	219.9			
1990	231.8	100.0	100.0	100.0
1991	259.4	105.8	111.7	107.3
1992	285.1	106.8	115.4	120.4
1993	339.3	130.0	153.7	152.4
1994	423.8	146.8	182.4	177.1
1995	497.1	157.5	194.7	201.7
1996	554.8	158.6	195.2	218.3
1997	584.2	160.4	201.9	224.2
1998	598.2	152.5	198.0	226.0
1999	601.8	149.0	189.7	225.7
2000	622.9	152.7	189.7	228.0
2001	642.2	151.8	190.7	229.4
2002	630.6	146.6	185.1	230.3
2003	631.9	148.8	193.8	235.3
2004	638.2	153.3	221.4	245.5
2005	647.8	155.3	246.6	247.2
2006	653.6	153.9	260.2	248.2
2007	669.3	153.5	273.3	255.1
2008	703.4	158.6	316.3	275.0
2009	692.8	149.8	280.3	266.9
2010	709.4	153.1	309.7	273.6
2011	749.1	156.6	335.7	289.2
2012	773.8	154.1	331.3	293.0
2013	799.3	150.1	324.0	292.7
2014	812.1	148.7	320.1	292.7
2015	826.7	144.1	299.9	285.7
2016	838.3	141.4	295.4	284.8
2017	854.2	142.4	308.4	298.2
2018	875.6	142.4	310.8	309.5
2019	895.7	141.9	309.5	316.0
2020	910.9	140.6	307.8	
2021	920.9	142.2	319.0	
2022	937.2	145.5	338.9	
2023	940.9	144.4	334.3	

4-3 居民消费价格分类指数(2023年)
CONSUMER PRICE INDICES BY CATEGORY (2023)

项目	Item	2022 =100
居民消费价格指数	**Consumer Price Index**	**100.4**
#非食品价格指数	Non-food Price Index	100.6
#服务项目价格指数	Price Index for Services	101.2
#消费品价格指数	Price Index for Consumer Goods	99.7
食品烟酒	**Food, Tobacco and Alcohol**	**100.1**
食品	Food	99.0
粮食	Grain	99.6
薯类	Tubers	99.9
豆类	Beans	100.2
食用油	Edible Oil and Fats	101.3
菜及食用菌	Vegetables and Edible Mushrooms	94.0
#鲜菜	Fresh Vegetables	93.1
畜肉类	Meat of Livestock	93.5
禽肉类	Meat of Poultry	101.4
水产品	Aquatic Products	100.6
蛋类	Eggs	99.8
#鸡蛋	Egg	99.3
奶类	Milk and Other Dairy Products	98.3
干鲜瓜果类	Fruits and Nuts	104.1
#鲜果	Fresh Fruits	104.0
糖果糕点类	Candy and Cake	103.4
调味品	Flavoring	101.2
其他食品类	Other Foods	100.5
茶及饮料	Tea and Beverages	102.3
烟酒	Tobacco and Alcohol	102.3
卷烟	Cigarettes and Cigars	103.8
酒类	Alcohol	100.6
在外餐饮	Dining Out	101.7
衣着	**Clothing**	**100.6**
服装	Garments	100.8
鞋类	Footwear	100.0
居住	**Residence**	**100.3**
租赁房房租	Rent of Rental Housing	100.3
住房保养维修及管理	Housing Maintenance and Management	101.1
水电燃料	Water, Electricity and Fuels	100.0
自有住房	Own Housing	100.2
生活用品及服务	**Articles for Daily Use and Services**	**100.3**
家具及室内装饰品	Furniture and Interior Decorations	99.8
家具	Furniture	99.3
室内装饰品	Interior Decorations	103.5
家用器具	Home Appliances	99.9
大型家用器具	Large Home Appliances	100.2
小家电	Small Home Appliances	98.3
家用纺织品	Home Textiles	100.3
家庭日用杂品	Daily Use Household Articles	100.1
个人护理用品	Personal-care Supplies	100.2
家庭服务	Household Services	102.2
交通通信	**Transport and Communication**	**98.3**
交通	Transport	97.9
交通工具	Transport Facility	94.8
交通工具用燃料	Fuels for Transport Facility	94.5
交通工具使用和维修	Use and Maintenance of Transport Facility	100.9
交通费	Traffic Fee	104.8
通信	Communications	99.6
通信工具	Communications Devices	99.2
通信服务	Communications Services	99.9
邮递服务	Mail Service	99.3
教育文化娱乐	**Education, Culture and Recreation**	**102.8**
教育	Education	100.6
教育用品	Educational Articles	100.0
教育服务	Education Services	100.7
文化娱乐	Culture and Recreation	104.8
文娱耐用消费品	Durable Consumer Goods for Culture and Recreation	98.0
其他文娱用品	Other Articles	100.2
文化娱乐服务	Services for Culture and Recreation	102.7
旅游	Touring	110.2
医疗保健	**Health Care**	**100.2**
药品及医疗器具	Medicine and Medical Instruments	100.5
中药	Traditional Chinese Medicines	104.2
西药	Western Medicine	98.8
滋补保健品	Nourishing Health Care Products	100.4
医疗卫生器具	Medical and Health Instruments	99.0
保健器具	Health Care Instruments	99.5
医疗服务	Medical Services	100.0
其他用品及服务	**Other Articles and Services**	**104.2**
其他用品类	Other Articles	106.1
首饰手表	Jewelry and Watches	110.0
母婴用品	Maternal and Infant Articles	97.2
其他杂项用品	Other Miscellaneous	99.1
其他服务	Other Services	102.5
在外住宿	Outside Accommodation	110.1
美容美发洗浴	Beauty Salon and Bath	100.9
养老服务	Pension Services	102.4
金融及保险服务	Financial and Insurance Services	100.2
中介法律及其他服务	Intermediary Legal and Other Services	102.1

4-4 农产品生产者价格指数
PRODUCER PRICE INDICES FOR FARM PRODUCTS

(上年=100) (preceding year=100)

项　　目	Item	2023	2022
总 指 数	**General Index**	**99.7**	**102.7**
农业产品	Agriculture Products	102.1	103.3
#粮　食	Grain	96.1	116.1
蔬菜及食用菌	Vegetable and Edible Mushrooms	100.4	99.5
林业产品	Forestry Products		
畜牧业产品	Animal Husbandry Products	94.6	102.0
#肉　牛	Beef Cattle	93.9	101.1
肉　羊	Mutton Sheep	92.9	94.2
奶产品	Milk Products	98.3	99.1
猪	Hogs	92.2	100.7
肉禽(毛重)	Poultry (Gross Weight)	89.9	106.3
禽　蛋	Eggs	96.0	105.4
渔业产品	Fishery Products	103.9	99.3

4-5 工业生产者出厂价格及购进价格指数(2000-2023年)

(上年=100)

年 份 Year	工业生产者出厂价格指数 Producer Price Index for Industrial Products (PPI)	轻工业 Light Industry	重工业 Heavy Industry	生产资料 Means of Production	生活资料 Consumer Goods	工业生产者购进价格指数 Purchasing Price Index for Industrial Producers	燃料、动力类 Fuel and Power
2000	102.5	98.0	104.2	103.4	98.8	100.0	104.3
2001	99.4	99.6	99.4	99.4	99.6	100.5	101.7
2002	96.6	97.6	96.4	96.4	97.9	97.1	102.3
2003	101.5	98.0	104.5	102.2	99.1	104.7	109.6
2004	103.0	100.2	105.3	103.7	100.6	114.2	120.0
2005	101.3	98.7	103.3	101.9	99.1	111.4	117.1
2006	99.1	97.9	99.6	99.0	99.3	105.5	113.1
2007	99.7	100.7	99.2	99.3	101.3	105.0	105.1
2008	103.3	101.8	104.0	103.8	101.3	115.8	132.3
2009	94.4	96.2	93.6	93.3	99.1	88.6	85.1
2010	102.2	98.7	103.8	102.7	100.3	110.5	121.3
2011	102.3	104.6	102.0	102.5	101.6	108.4	117.8
2012	98.4	101.1	98.0	97.8	101.0	98.7	99.0
2013	97.4	100.7	96.9	96.7	100.5	97.8	96.4
2014	99.1	100.8	98.8	98.7	100.9	98.8	99.4
2015	96.9	100.0	96.4	96.1	99.9	93.7	85.6
2016	98.1	101.8	97.6	98.0	98.3	98.5	98.0
2017	100.7	99.3	100.9	101.5	99.4	104.4	108.4
2018	100.0	99.9	100.0	100.4	99.3	100.8	102.0
2019	99.6	103.6	99.1	99.6	99.6	99.6	99.5
2020	99.1	103.8	98.5	98.9	99.5	99.5	98.5
2021	101.1	99.9	101.4	102.1	99.1	103.7	106.1
2022	102.3	99.2	102.9	104.3	98.1	106.2	115.7
2023	99.2	99.9	99.1	100.0	97.6	98.7	100.2

注：根据统计制度规定，我国工业生产者价格统计调查每五年进行一次基期轮换，2021年1月开始编制和发布以2020年为基期的价格指数。与上轮基期相比，新基期的调查分类目录、代表规格品和调查企业均有调整，分类权数也有变化，以反映工业生产结构的最新变动。

PRODUCER PRICE INDICES FOR INDUSTRIAL PRODUCTS AND PURCHASING PRICE INDICES FOR INDUSTRIAL PRODUCERS (2000-2023)

(preceding year=100)

黑色金属材料类 Ferrous Metals	有色金属材料和电线类 Nonferrous Metals and Cables	化工原料类 Raw Chemical Materials	木材及纸浆类 Timber and Paper Pulp	建筑材料及非金属类 Building Materials and Non-metals	其他工业原材料及半成品类 Other Industrial Materials and Semi-finished Products	农副产品类 Agricultural Products	纺织原料类 Textile Materials
100.5	106.9	103.4	94.8	101.9	98.4	94.5	91.5
100.3	97.9	97.6	98.3	99.5	98.8	103.5	100.6
96.4	96.1	99.3	102.5	97.6	92.3	93.6	97.8
110.9	101.4	107.3	100.6	99.0	95.2	114.3	98.1
124.5	120.9	111.1	100.7	105.8	103.8	122.3	102.8
108.3	123.3	114.9	103.6	101.8	102.8	96.3	106.2
96.7	138.3	104.1	100.3	99.4	98.0	101.3	100.9
115.6	112.2	106.7	101.7	103.5	95.3	138.6	99.2
128.5	97.9	108.3	108.5	115.2	94.9	132.6	101.5
79.8	81.1	82.3	97.0	99.4	95.3	88.2	97.6
115.4	121.6	111.7	104.2	102.7	99.0	106.6	102.8
112.7	115.2	112.7	105.7	103.0	98.9	128.8	108.2
92.2	96.7	102.5	99.0	93.9	98.8	98.5	100.8
94.6	92.1	98.6	98.4	94.2	98.9	102.2	99.6
95.3	95.3	99.2	99.9	96.8	98.9	97.5	100.7
87.2	93.7	94.1	99.0	95.7	98.4	103.1	99.8
99.7	97.2	96.6	99.1	100.6	98.3	112.8	99.8
111.3	123.4	102.9	101.4	106.3	99.9	93.0	101.9
105.7	105.8	101.5	101.1	105.0	98.8	90.7	100.8
100.4	97.2	97.0	98.4	99.3	99.4	111.9	100.2
101.4	100.0	96.4	99.3	99.0	99.3	119.7	100.2
114.7	113.1	105.1	99.9	100.0	100.3	89.8	98.1
97.7	107.8	103.2	99.4	105.3	99.6	101.3	101.0
95.3	99.3	94.9	98.9	93.1	98.9	94.8	99.3

Note: According to the statistical system, the statistical survey of industrial producer price in China is subject to the alternation of base period once every five years, and the price indices with 2020 as the base period were started to be compiled and published since January 2021. Compared with the previous base period, the survey classification catalogues, the representative specifications and the enterprises for survey have all been adjusted in the new base period, and the classification weights have been changed as well so as to reflect the latest changes in the industrial production structure.

4-6 工业生产者出厂价格指数
PRODUCER PRICE INDICES FOR INDUSTRIAL PRODUCTS

(上年=100) (preceding year=100)

项　　目	Item	2023	2022
总指数	**General Index**	**99.2**	**102.3**
按轻、重工业分	**By Light Industry and Heavy Industry**		
轻工业	Light Industry	99.9	99.2
以农产品为原料	Using Farming Products as Raw Materials	99.5	101.6
以非农产品为原料	Using Non-agricultural Products as Raw Materials	100.1	97.8
重工业	Heavy Industry	99.1	102.9
采　掘	Excavation	101.2	94.9
原材料	Raw Materials	100.8	108.4
加　工	Processing	97.8	99.1
按生产、生活资料分	**By Capital Goods and Consumer Goods**		
生产资料	Means of Production	100.0	104.3
采　掘	Excavation	101.2	94.9
原材料	Raw Materials	100.8	108.5
加　工	Processing	99.0	100.1
生活资料	Consumer Goods	97.6	98.1
食　品	Foods	100.7	102.0
衣　着	Clothing	95.4	94.7
一般日用品	Articles for Daily Use	100.1	96.7
耐用消费品	Durable Consumer Goods	95.9	97.5

4-7 工业生产者出厂价格指数(按行业分)
PRODUCER PRICE INDICES FOR INDUSTRIAL PRODUCTS (BY SECTOR)

(上年=100) (preceding year=100)

项　　目	Item	2023	2022
总指数	**General Index**	**99.2**	**102.3**
石油和天然气开采业	Extraction of Petroleum and Natural Gas	104.6	120.7
黑色金属矿采选业	Mining and Processing of Ferrous Metal Ores	95.5	82.0
开采专业及辅助性活动	Professional and Support Activities for Mining	102.5	101.2
农副食品加工业	Processing of Food from Agricultural Products	97.0	103.5
食品制造业	Manufacturing of Foods	101.2	101.3
酒、饮料和精制茶制造业	Manufacturing of Alcohol, Beverages and Refined Tea	101.0	102.3
烟草制品业	Manufacturing of Tobacco	104.1	102.5
纺织业	Manufacturing of Textiles	98.8	101.0
纺织服装、服饰业	Manufacturing of Textile Wearing Apparel and Accessories	95.4	94.7
家具制造业	Manufacturing of Furniture	98.3	101.3
造纸和纸制品业	Manufacturing of Paper and Paper Products	98.7	100.4
印刷和记录媒介复制业	Printing and Reproduction of Recorded Media	99.7	99.3
文教、工美、体育和娱乐用品制造业	Manufacturing of Articles for Culture, Education, Arts and Crafts, Sports and Entertainment Activities	111.0	101.6
石油、煤炭及其他燃料加工业	Processing of Petroleum, Coal and Other Fuels	94.8	129.0
化学原料和化学制品制造业	Manufacturing of Raw Chemical Materials and Chemical Products	95.5	97.8
医药制造业	Manufacturing of Medicines	99.1	96.4
橡胶和塑料制品业	Manufacturing of Rubber and Plastic Products	98.5	97.8
非金属矿物制品业	Manufacturing of Non-metallic Mineral Products	96.9	104.7
黑色金属冶炼和压延加工业	Smelting and Pressing of Ferrous Metals	93.0	91.3
有色金属冶炼和压延加工业	Smelting and Processing of Non-ferrous Metals	82.8	117.7
金属制品业	Manufacturing of Metal Products	98.4	105.0
通用设备制造业	Manufacturing of General Purpose Machinery	99.8	101.1
专用设备制造业	Manufacturing of Special Purpose Machinery	100.1	99.6
汽车制造业	Manufacturing of Automobiles	99.6	100.0
铁路、船舶、航空航天和其他运输设备制造业	Manufacturing of Railway, Ship, Aerospace and Other Transport Equipments	100.0	100.3
电气机械和器材制造业	Manufacturing of Electrical Machinery and Apparatus	99.7	100.5
计算机、通信和其他电子设备制造业	Manufacturing of Computers, Communication and Other Electronic Equipment	93.0	95.5
仪器仪表制造业	Manufacturing of Measuring Instruments and Machinery	106.0	99.1
其他制造业	Other Manufacturing	102.6	109.0
废弃资源综合利用业	Utilization of Waste Resources	90.3	105.2
金属制品、机械和设备修理业	Repair Service of Metal Products, Machinery and Equipment	102.8	99.6
电力、热力生产和供应业	Production and Supply of Electric Power and Heat Power	102.0	107.0
燃气生产和供应业	Production and Supply of Gas	96.6	102.0
水的生产和供应业	Production and Supply of Water	100.0	100.0

4-8 工业生产者购进价格指数
PURCHASING PRICE INDICES FOR INDUSTRIAL PRODUCERS

(上年=100) (preceding year=100)

项 目	Item	2023	2022
总指数	**General Index**	**98.7**	**106.2**
燃料、动力类	Fuel and Power	100.2	115.7
黑色金属材料类	Ferrous Metals	95.3	97.7
#钢 材	Steel Products	95.8	98.3
其 他	Others	92.0	93.7
有色金属材料和电线类	Nonferrous Metals and Cables	99.3	107.8
化工原料类	Raw Chemical Materials	94.9	103.2
木材及纸浆类	Timber and Paper Pulp	98.9	99.4
建筑材料及非金属类	Building Materials and Non-metals	93.1	105.3
其他工业原材料及半成品类	Other Industrial Materials and Semi-finished Products	98.9	99.6
农副产品类	Agricultural Products	94.8	101.3
纺织原料类	Textile Materials	99.3	101.0

4-9 住宅销售价格指数(2023年各月)
SELLING PRICE INDICES FOR RESIDENTIAL HOUSES (EACH MONTH OF 2023)

(上年同月=100) (same month of previous year=100)

项 目	Item	1月 Jan.	2月 Feb.	3月 Mar.	4月 Apr.	5月 May	6月 Jun.
新建商品住宅	**New Commercial Residential Houses**	**105.2**	**104.7**	**104.6**	**104.5**	**104.3**	**103.5**
90平方米及以下	90sq.m and below	104.6	104.6	104.5	104.2	104.5	104.0
90-144平方米	90-144sq.m	104.5	104.0	103.6	104.0	104.0	103.2
144平方米以上	Above 144sq.m	106.0	105.2	105.3	105.1	104.3	103.4
二手住宅	**Second-hand Residential Houses**	**104.3**	**104.4**	**103.8**	**103.3**	**102.8**	**101.5**
90平方米及以下	90sq.m and below	103.9	104.3	103.7	103.0	102.6	101.2
90-144平方米	90-144sq.m	104.1	103.8	103.6	103.4	102.8	101.4
144平方米以上	Above 144sq.m	105.6	105.4	104.5	103.9	103.5	102.5

4-9 续表 Continued

(上年同月=100) (same month of previous year=100)

项 目	Item	7月 Jul.	8月 Aug.	9月 Sep.	10月 Oct.	11月 Nov.	12月 Dec.
新建商品住宅	**New Commercial Residential Houses**	**103.5**	**102.8**	**102.9**	**102.1**	**101.9**	**101.7**
90平方米及以下	90sq.m and below	103.7	102.5	102.3	101.7	101.5	101.4
90-144平方米	90-144sq.m	102.9	102.2	102.2	101.6	101.0	100.7
144平方米以上	Above 144sq.m	103.6	103.3	103.7	102.7	102.6	102.4
二手住宅	**Second-hand Residential Houses**	**100.6**	**100.8**	**101.1**	**99.8**	**98.6**	**97.8**
90平方米及以下	90sq.m and below	100.2	100.6	101.1	99.6	98.0	96.8
90-144平方米	90-144sq.m	100.8	100.5	100.9	99.7	98.9	99.1
144平方米以上	Above 144sq.m	101.4	101.9	101.7	100.7	99.5	98.2

主要统计指标解释

居民消费价格指数 是度量消费商品及服务项目价格水平随着时间而变动的相对数，反映一定时期内居民家庭购买的消费品及服务价格水平的变动趋势和变动程度。居民消费价格指数变动率通常被用来作为反映通货膨胀（或紧缩）程度的指标。

工业生产者出厂价格指数 是反映全部工业产品出厂价格总水平变动程度的相对数。其中包括工业企业售给商业、外贸、物资部门的产品，还包括售给工业和其他部门的生产资料以及直接售给居民的生活消费品。通过工业生产者价格指数能观察工业产品出厂价格变动对工业总产值的影响。

工业生产者购进价格指数 是反映全部工业原材料、燃料、动力购进价格总水平变动程度的相对数。用其可以观察和研究工业企业原材料价格变动对生产的影响，以及企业对原材料涨价的消化能力和承受能力，为制定价格政策提供依据。

固定资产投资价格指数 是反映固定资产投资额价格变动程度的相对数。固定资产投资额由建筑安装装饰工程投资完成额，设备、工器具购置投资完成额和其他费用投资完成额三部分组成。编制固定资产投资价格指数可以准确地反映固定资产投资中涉及的各类投资品和取费项目价格变动幅度，消除按现价计算的固定资产投资指标中的价格变动因素，真实地反映固定资产投资的规模、速度、结构和效益，为国家科学地制定、检查固定资产投资计划，提高宏观调控水平，为完善国民经济核算体系提供科学、可靠的依据。

住宅销售价格指数 是反映住宅销售价格总水平变动趋势和程度的相对数。包括新建商品住宅销售价格指数和二手住宅销售价格指数。

农产品生产者价格指数 是指农产品生产者价格总水平变动程度的相对数。农产品生产者价格是指农产品生产者第一次出售其产品时的单位产品价格。

Explanatory Notes on Main Statistical Indicators

Consumer Price Index (CPI) is a relative number measuring the changes in prices of consumer goods and service over time, reflecting the trend and degree of changes in prices of consumer goods and service purchased by households over a period of time. The change rate of CPI is usually used for reflecting the level of inflation (or deflation).

Producer Price Index for Industrial Products (PPI) is a relative number reflecting the degree of changes in general producer prices of all industrial products, covering products sold by industrial enterprises to commercial, foreign trade and materials companies, as well as production materials sold to industrial and other enterprises, and consumer goods directly sold to consumers. It can be used to observe the impact of changes in producer prices of industrial products on gross industrial output value.

Purchasing Price Index for Industrial Producers is a relative number reflecting the degree of changes in the overall level of prices of all industrial raw materials, fuels and power. It can be used to observe and study the impact of changes in prices of raw materials in industrial enterprises on their production, as well as the enterprises' capacity of digesting and bearing the rising prices of raw materials, thus providing basis for formulating price policies.

Price Index for Investment in Fixed Assets is a relative number reflecting the degree of changes in prices of investment in fixed assets. The investment in fixed assets consists of three components, i.e. the completed investment in construction, installation and decoration projects, the completed investment in purchasing equipment, tools and instruments, and the completed investment in other expenditures. The compilation of the price index for investment in fixed assets can accurately reflect the range of changes in prices of various investment varieties and charging items involved in the investment in fixed assets, can remove the factor of price change in the indicators for investment in fixed assets calculated at current price, can truly reflect the size, growth, structure, and efficiency of investment in fixed assets, can provide scientific and reliable basis for the state to scientifically formulate and inspect the plans for investment in fixed assets, improve the level of macro control and improve the national economic accounting system.

Selling Price Index of Residential Houses is a relative number reflecting the trend and degree of changes in the overall level of house selling prices, including newly built commercial residential house selling price index and second-hand house selling price index.

Producer Price Index for Farm Products is a relative number reflecting the degree of changes in the overall producer prices of farm products. Producer price of farm products refers to the price of unit product at which the producers of farm products sell their products for the first time.

05

人民生活
PEOPLE'S LIVING CONDITIONS

简要说明

一、主要内容

本章资料反映北京市居民生活现状及变化情况，分为全市居民生活、城镇居民生活和农村居民生活三部分，主要包括家庭基本情况、家庭收入和消费支出情况、居住状况和耐用消费品拥有量等。

二、调查方法

城乡居民生活状况调查方法和方案由国家统计局统一制定，采用抽样调查的方法，按对全市及分区居民主要收支指标有代表性的原则在全市城乡住户中抽取样本，并按一定的周期对样本进行轮换以保证其代表性。对抽中的住户采用日记账和问卷相结合的方式采集数据。

三、本章资料的调查范围

城镇住户调查的口径范围：2000−2003 年为 1000 户城市居民，覆盖城八区；2004−2006 年为 2000 户城市居民，覆盖城八区；2007 年为 3000 户城镇居民，覆盖所有区县；2008−2012 年为 5000 户城镇居民，覆盖所有区县。

农村住户调查的口径范围：2000−2002 年为 2710 户，覆盖 14 个郊区县；2003 年为 2670 户（石景山区全部农民转居民，40 个样本取消），覆盖 13 个郊区县；2004−2012 年为 3000 户，覆盖 13 个郊区。

城乡住户调查一体化：2013 年，根据国家统计局实施城乡住户调查一体化改革的要求和《住户收支与生活状况调查方案》的有关规定，国家统计局北京调查总队对全市城乡住户进行了统一的样本抽取，城乡住户调查样本量共计 10000 户。

按照国家统计局要求，自 2015 年起，北京按照改革后的新口径发布全市和分城乡的居民收支数据。与老口径相比，新口径的差异主要体现在三个方面：一是对居民收支指标口径进行了调整，将反映居民收入的核心指标由原来的城镇居民人均可支配收入和农村居民人均纯收入统一为人均可支配收入；二是按照国家城乡划分标准，将城镇地区的村委会由原来的农村划入城镇进行统计；三是在分城乡的居民收支数据基础上，增加了全体居民的人均可支配收入、人均消费支出数据。

Brief Introduction

I. Main Content

Statistics in this chapter reflect the living conditions of residents in Beijing and their changes, consisting of three parts, including the living conditions of the residents of the whole city, urban residents and rural residents. Figures include the basic family situation, household income and consumption expenditure, housing conditions and number of durable consumer goods in possession.

II. Method of Survey

Methods and plans of survey for living conditions of urban and rural residents are designated by National Bureau of Statistics. The method of sampling survey is adopted to take samples across urban and rural residents of the whole city following the principle of selecting representative residents in terms of major income and expenditure indicators across the city and the districts. Samples are changed in certain periods to ensure their representativeness. For selected residents, statistics are gathered through journals and questionnaires.

III. Scope of Survey

Scope of survey for urban residents: In 2000-2003, the survey covered 1,000 urban households in 8 urban districts; in 2004-2006, covered 2,000 urban households in 8 urban districts; in 2007 covered 3,000 urban households in all districts and counties; in 2008-2012, covered 5,000 households in all districts and counties.

Scope of survey for rural residents: In 2000-2002, the survey covered 2,710 households in 14 suburban districts and counties; in 2003, covered 2,670 households (All rural residents became urban residents in Shijingshan District, so 40 samples were cancelled.) in 13 suburban districts and counties; in 2004-2012, covered 3,000 households in 13 suburban districts.

Integration of survey on urban and rural residents: in 2013, according to the requirements of the National Bureau of Statistics on carrying out integrated reforms of urban and rural resident survey, and *Survey Plan on Income and Expenditure, and Living Conditions of Households*, the NBS Survey Office in Beijing took a total of 10,000 samples of urban and rural residents in an integrated way.

According to requirements of National Bureau of Statistics, since 2015, Beijing has started to issue data on income and expenditure of residents in the city and residents in urban and rural areas according to new standards after the reform. As compared with former standards, the new standards mainly show differences in the following 3 aspects: first, standards on resident income and expenditure indicators are adjusted. Core indicators reflecting resident income are unified from original per capita disposable income of urban residents and per capita net income of rural residents to per capita disposable income; second, according to national standards on division of urban and rural areas, village committees in urban areas that were classified into rural areas are now classified into urban areas; third, based on data on resident income and expenditure in urban and rural areas, data on per capita disposable income and per capita consumption expenditure of residents in Beijing are added.

5-1 全市居民家庭生活基本情况(1978-2023年)
BASIC LIVING CONDITIONS OF HOUSEHOLDS OF THE WHOLE CITY (1978-2023)

年份 Year	人均可支配收入(元) Per Capita Disposable Income (yuan)	人均可支配收入实际增长(%) Real Growth Rate of Per Capita Disposable Income (%)	人均消费支出(元) Per Capita Consumption Expenditure (yuan)	#食品烟酒 Food, Tobacco and Liquor	全市居民家庭恩格尔系数(%) Engel Coefficient of Households of the Whole City (%)	全市居民人均住房建筑面积(平方米) Per Capita Floor Space of Houses in Whole City (sq.m)
1978	302		281	169	60.1	
1979	344	11.9	321	191	59.5	
1980	412	13.0	390	214	55.0	
1981	469	12.4	428	240	56.1	
1982	507	6.2	463	264	57.1	
1983	561	10.0	496	278	56.2	
1984	682	18.9	572	315	55.1	
1985	854	6.5	757	376	49.6	
1986	971	6.4	900	444	49.3	
1987	1078	2.2	974	502	51.5	
1988	1292	-0.4	1234	614	49.7	
1989	1457	-3.8	1312	705	53.7	
1990	1741	13.4	1469	787	53.6	
1991	1975	1.3	1578	846	53.6	
1992	2303	6.1	1882	981	52.1	
1993	3126	14.0	2514	1198	47.7	
1994	4419	13.2	3502	1636	46.7	
1995	5501	6.1	4366	2125	48.7	
1996	6429	4.7	4972	2317	46.6	
1997	6837	0.9	5629	2466	43.8	
1998	7472	6.7	6099	2515	41.2	
1999	8155	8.4	6670	2620	39.3	
2000	9230	9.4	7644	2750	36.0	
2001	10399	9.3	8150	2885	35.4	
2002	11300	10.7	9480	3061	32.3	
2003	12628	11.5	10451	3131	30.0	
2004	14342	12.5	11672	3490	29.9	
2005	16853	15.8	13289	3912	29.4	
2006	19296	13.5	15123	4228	28.0	
2007	21458	8.6	15933	4572	28.7	
2008	24371	8.1	17447	5157	29.6	
2009	26571	10.7	19381	5561	28.7	
2010	29228	7.4	21834	5853	26.8	
2011	33176	7.5	24298	6086	25.0	
2012	36817	7.5	26562	6574	24.8	
2013	40830	7.4	29176	7008	24.0	
2014	44489	7.3	31103	7468	24.0	
2015	48458	7.0	33803	7584	22.4	33.23
2016	52530	6.9	35416	7609	21.5	34.02
2017	57230	6.9	37425	7549	20.2	34.23
2018	62361	6.3	39843	8065	20.2	34.86
2019	67756	6.3	43038	8489	19.7	34.52
2020	69434	0.8	38903	8374	21.5	34.56
2021	75002	6.8	43640	9307	21.3	35.59
2022	77415	1.4	42683	9223	21.6	35.85
2023	81752	5.2	47586	10142	21.3	37.01

注：本表数据为城乡住户调查一体化改革后的可比口径数据，下同。
Note: Figures in this table are that of comparable standard after the reform to the integration of survey of urban and rural residents, the same below.

5-2 全市居民家庭基本情况(2015−2023年)
BASIC DATA ON HOUSEHOLDS OF THE WHOLE CITY (2015-2023)

项目	Item	2015	2016	2017	2018	2019	2020	2021	2022	2023
平均每户常住人口 (人)	Average Resident Population Per Household (person)	2.8	2.7	2.7	2.8	2.8	2.8	2.8	2.8	2.5
平均每户就业人口数 (人)	Average Employed Population Per Household (person)	1.4	1.3	1.3	1.3	1.3	1.2	1.3	1.2	1.1
平均每一就业者负担人数 (人)	Average Dependents Per Employed Person (person)	1.6	1.6	1.6	1.6	1.7	1.7	1.7	1.7	1.8

5-3 全市居民家庭人均收支情况(2015−2023年)
PER CAPITA INCOME AND CONSUMPTION EXPENDITURE OF HOUSEHOLDS OF THE WHOLE CITY (2015-2023)

单位：元 (yuan)

项目	Item	2015	2016	2017	2018	2019	2020	2021	2022	2023	2023年为2022年% 2023 as % of 2022
人均可支配收入	**Per Capita Disposable Income**	**48458**	**52530**	**57230**	**62361**	**67756**	**69434**	**75002**	**77415**	**81752**	**105.6**
工资性收入	Income of Wages and Salaries	30241	33114	35217	37687	41214	41439	45675	47758	51632	108.1
经营净收入	Net Business Income	1421	1396	1408	1201	1201	812	940	903	1026	113.6
财产净收入	Net Income from Property	7499	8230	9306	10612	11257	11789	12460	12418	12280	98.9
转移净收入	Net Income from Transfer	9297	9790	11299	12861	14084	15394	15927	16336	16814	102.9
人均消费支出	**Per Capita Consumption Expenditure**	**33803**	**35416**	**37425**	**39843**	**43038**	**38903**	**43640**	**42683**	**47586**	**111.5**
食品烟酒	Food, Tobacco and Liquor	7584	7609	7549	8065	8489	8374	9307	9223	10142	110.0
衣着	Clothing and Footwear	2426	2433	2238	2176	2230	1804	2104	1861	2053	110.3
居住	Housing	10350	11188	12295	14110	15751	15711	16847	17170	18668	108.7
生活用品及服务	Household Equipments, Furnishings and Services	2098	2327	2492	2372	2387	2146	2560	2193	2352	107.3
交通通信	Transport and Communications	4490	4702	5034	4767	4979	3789	4227	4129	4858	117.7
教育文化娱乐	Education, Culture and Recreation	3635	3687	3917	3999	4311	2766	3348	3008	3799	126.3
医疗保健	Health Care and Medical Services	2229	2456	2900	3275	3740	3513	4285	3982	4276	107.4
其他用品及服务	Miscellaneous Goods and Services	991	1015	1000	1079	1151	800	962	1117	1438	128.7

5-4 全市居民家庭每百户主要耐用消费品拥有量(2023年)
MAIN DURABLE GOODS OWNED PER 100 HOUSEHOLDS OF THE WHOLE CITY(2023)

项　　目		Item		全市居民 Households of the Whole City	城镇居民 Urban Households	农村居民 Rural Households
家用汽车	(辆)	Automobile	(unit)	51	51	52
新能源汽车	(辆)	New Energy Vehicles	(unit)	4	4	3
摩托车	(辆)	Motorcycle	(unit)	4	4	7
助力车	(台)	Electric Bicycle	(set)	27	21	65
洗衣机	(台)	Washing Machine	(set)	99	98	103
电冰箱(柜)	(台)	Refrigerator	(set)	102	101	109
微波炉	(台)	Microwave Oven	(set)	72	74	61
彩色电视机	(台)	Color TV Set	(set)	105	104	115
空调	(台)	Air Conditioner	(set)	190	188	200
热水器	(台)	Water Heater	(set)	99	98	104
烤箱	(台)	Oven	(set)	15	15	17
洗碗机	(台)	Dishwasher	(set)	6	7	2
排油烟机	(台)	Kitchen Ventilator	(set)	92	92	90
固定电话	(线)	Fixed-line Telephone	(set)	21	21	17
移动电话	(部)	Mobile Phone	(set)	217	216	226
计算机	(台)	Computer	(set)	74	79	43
照相机	(台)	Camera	(set)	23	25	6
乐器	(架)	Musical Instrument	(set)	13	14	6
健身器材	(台)	Fitness Equipment	(set)	9	9	9
空气净化器（含新风系统）	(台)	Air Purifier (with Fresh Air System)	(set)	27	29	11
地面清洁电器	(台)	Ground Cleaning Appliance	(set)	27	29	16

5−5 全市居民家庭居住构成情况(2023年)
COMPOSITION OF HOUSING CONDITIONS FOR HOUSEHOLDS OF THE WHOLE CITY (2023)

单位：% (%)

项 目	Item	全市居民 Households of the Whole City	城镇居民 Urban Households	农村居民 Rural Households
居住空间样式	**Style of Living Space**	**100.0**	**100.0**	**100.0**
单栋楼房占比重	Individual Storied Buildings	4.3	2.8	14.3
单栋平房占比重	Individual Single-storey Buildings	13.7	6.6	63.6
四居室及以上单元房占比重	Four-bedroom and above Flat	1.8	2.0	
三居室单元房占比重	Three-bedroom Flat	18.9	21.2	3.0
二居室单元房占比重	Two-bedroom Flat	41.7	47.0	4.9
一居室单元房占比重	One-bedroom Flat	11.0	11.9	4.3
筒子楼或连片平房占比重	Tube-shaped Apartment or Closely Grouped Single-storey Buildings	8.5	8.4	9.4
其他占比重	Others	0.1		0.6
房屋来源	**Housing Source**	**100.0**	**100.0**	**100.0**
租赁公房占比重	Public Houses Rented	5.7	6.5	0.1
租赁私房占比重	Private Houses Rented	18.3	18.6	15.9
自建住房占比重	Self-built Houses	16.8	8.5	75.1
购买商品房占比重	Purchased Commercial Houses	29.0	32.8	2.5
购买房改住房占比重	Purchased Houses from Housing Reform	11.3	12.8	0.5
购买保障性住房占比重	Purchased Indemnificatory Housing	4.5	5.1	0.1
拆迁安置房占比重	Resettlement Housing	9.1	9.9	3.9
继承或获赠住房占比重	Housing under Inheritance or Donation	1.0	1.2	0.1
免费借用房占比重	Free Borrowed Houses	2.7	2.9	0.9
雇主提供免费住房占比重	Free Housing Supplied by Employers	1.4	1.5	0.8
其他来源占比重	Others	0.2	0.2	0.0
取水位置	**Water-taking Location**	**100.0**	**100.0**	**100.0**
住宅内管道取水	Water-taking through Pipes in the House	94.9	96.3	85.6
住宅内其他方式取水	Water-taking by Other Means in the House	0.7	0.7	0.4
院内管道取水	Water-taking through Pipes in the Yard	3.8	2.4	13.2
院内其他方式取水	Water-taking by Other Means in the Yard	0.1	0.1	0.3
其他位置取水	Water-taking from Other Locations	0.5	0.5	0.5
饮用水来源情况	**Source of Drinking Water**	**100.0**	**100.0**	**100.0**
经过净化处理的自来水占比重	Tap Water via Purification Treatment	93.9	95.9	80.2
受保护的井水和泉水占比重	Protected Well Water and Spring Water	5.2	3.3	18.8
不受保护的井水和泉水占比重	Unprotected Well Water and Spring Water	0.1	0.0	0.9

5-5 续表 continued

单位：% (%)

项　　目	Item	全市居民 Households of the Whole City	城镇居民 Urban Households	农村居民 Rural Households
江河湖泊水占比重	Water from Rivers and Lakes			
收集雨水占比重	Collecting Rainwater			
桶装水占比重	Barreled Water	0.7	0.8	0.1
其他占比重	Others			
住户厕所类型	**Toilet Type of Households**	**100.0**	**100.0**	**100.0**
水冲式卫生厕所占比重	Water-flushing Sanitary Toilets	99.2	99.6	97.0
卫生旱厕占比重	Sanitary Pit Toilet	0.7	0.4	2.7
普通旱厕占比重	Common Pit Toilet	0.1		0.3
住户厕所使用情况	**Toilet Use Conditions of Households**	**100.0**	**100.0**	**100.0**
本住户独用占比重	Exclusive Use by One Household	93.0	92.8	94.4
几户合用占比重	One Toilet Shared by Several Households	3.2	3.3	2.5
公用厕所占比重	Communal Toilet	3.8	3.9	3.0
主要炊用能源状况	**Main Cooking Energy Conditions**	**100.0**	**100.0**	**100.0**
柴草占比重	Firewood			0.4
煤炭占比重	Coal			
罐装液化石油气占比重	Bottled LPG	18.5	11.6	66.2
管道液化石油气占比重	Pipeline LPG			
管道煤气占比重	Pipeline Gas			
管道天然气占比重	Pipeline Natural Gas	73.7	81.0	22.9
电占比重	Electricity	6.5	6.2	8.7
燃料用油占比重	Oil Used in Fuel			
沼气占比重	Marsh Gas	0.1		0.6
其他占比重	Others			
无炊用行为占比重	Non-cooking Behaviors	1.2	1.2	1.1
住宅外道路路面状况	**Pavement Conditions of Roads Outside Houses**	**100.0**	**100.0**	**100.0**
水泥或柏油路面的户数占比重	Cement or Tar-coated Surface	96.9	97.4	93.6
沙石或石板等硬质路面的户数占比重	Hard Surface Paved with Sand and Stones or Slates	2.9	2.4	6.4
其他路面的户数占比重	Other Pavements	0.2	0.2	

5-6 全市居民家庭主要食品人均消费量(2023年)
PER CAPITA CONSUMPTION OF MAJOR FOODS OF HOUSEHOLDS OF THE WHOLE CITY (2023)

单位：公斤 (kg)

项　目	Item	全市居民 Households of the Whole City	城镇居民 Urban Households	农村居民 Rural Households
粮　食	Grain	81.7	76.2	116.8
豆　类	Beans and Products	8.7	8.3	10.9
蔬菜及菜制品	Vegetables and Vegetable Products	100.0	97.4	116.8
植物油	Vegetable Oil	5.5	5.2	7.6
猪　肉	Pork	16.3	15.1	23.8
牛羊肉	Beef and Mutton	6.4	6.4	6.4
禽　类	Poultry	6.5	6.5	6.7
蛋类及其制品	Eggs and Egg Products	15.5	15.0	18.5
奶及奶制品	Milk and Dairy Products	18.5	19.1	14.4
水产品	Aquatic Products	9.1	9.1	9.1
食　糖	Sugar	0.8	0.8	1.2

5-7 城镇居民家庭生活基本情况(1978-2023年)
BASIC LIVING CONDITIONS OF URBAN HOUSEHOLDS (1978-2023)

年份 Year	人均可支配收入(元) Per Capita Disposable Income (yuan)	人均可支配收入实际增长(%) Real Growth Rate of Per Capita Disposable Income (%)	人均消费支出(元) Per Capita Consumption Expenditure (yuan)	#食品烟酒 Food, Tobacco and Liquor	城镇居民家庭恩格尔系数(%) Engel Coefficient of Urban Households (%)	每一城镇就业者负担人数(人) Dependents Per Urban Employed Person (person)	城镇居民人均住房建筑面积(平方米) Per Capita Floor Space of Houses in Urban Areas (sq.m)
1978	365		360	211	58.7	1.86	6.70
1979	415	11.6	409	237	57.9	1.83	6.73
1980	501	14.0	490	271	55.3	1.80	7.06
1981	555	9.3	511	295	57.7	1.72	7.48
1982	561	-0.7	535	318	59.3	1.66	7.92
1983	591	4.7	574	338	58.8	1.65	8.37
1984	694	15.0	667	379	56.8	1.63	8.72
1985	908	11.2	923	467	50.6	1.66	9.09
1986	1068	10.1	1067	543	50.9	1.66	9.20
1987	1182	1.9	1148	605	52.7	1.65	9.75
1988	1437	1.0	1456	743	51.1	1.71	10.30
1989	1597	-5.2	1520	841	55.3	1.52	10.74
1990	1902	13.0	1646	892	54.2	1.52	11.17
1991	2170	2.0	1748	955	54.7	1.47	11.64
1992	2556	7.2	2135	1126	52.8	1.43	12.09
1993	3547	16.6	2940	1405	47.8	1.42	12.45
1994	5085	14.8	4134	1919	46.4	1.41	12.85
1995	6235	4.5	5020	2436	48.5	1.41	13.34
1996	7332	5.4	5730	2672	46.6	1.41	13.82
1997	7813	1.2	6532	2854	43.7	1.43	14.36
1998	8536	6.7	7069	2906	41.1	1.40	14.96
1999	9322	8.5	7712	3030	39.3	1.41	15.88
2000	10590	9.8	8866	3174	35.8	1.41	16.75
2001	11939	9.3	9443	3352	35.5	1.39	17.62
2002	12949	10.5	11050	3558	32.2	1.41	19.22
2003	14535	12.0	12122	3627	29.9	1.39	19.71
2004	16502	12.4	13487	4026	29.9	1.44	21.49
2005	18775	12.1	14851	4363	29.4	1.39	22.03
2006	21415	13.1	16869	4692	27.8	1.40	23.65
2007	23752	8.3	17682	5058	28.6	1.40	24.77
2008	26918	7.8	19253	5684	29.5	1.40	26.90
2009	29329	10.7	21230	6125	28.9	1.40	27.69
2010	32132	7.0	23999	6437	26.8	1.40	28.94
2011	36365	7.2	26467	6610	25.0	1.50	29.38
2012	40306	7.3	28949	7123	24.6	1.40	29.26
2013	44564	7.1	31632	7515	23.8	1.50	31.31
2014	48532	7.2	33717	8007	23.7	1.50	31.54
2015	52859	7.0	36642	8091	22.1	1.50	31.69
2016	57275	6.9	38256	8070	21.1	1.56	32.38
2017	62406	7.0	40346	8003	19.8	1.58	32.56
2018	67990	6.2	42926	8577	20.0	1.61	33.08
2019	73849	6.2	46358	8951	19.3	1.63	32.54
2020	75602	0.7	41726	8751	21.0	1.68	32.60
2021	81518	6.6	46776	9720	20.8	1.69	33.40
2022	84023	1.3	45617	9645	21.1	1.71	33.63
2023	88650	5.1	50897	10584	20.8	1.69	34.58

5-8 城镇居民家庭基本情况(2015-2023年)
BASIC DATA ON URBAN HOUSEHOLDS (2015-2023)

项　目	Item	2015	2016	2017	2018	2019	2020	2021	2022	2023
平均每户常住人口 （人）	Average Resident Population Per Household (person)	2.7	2.6	2.6	2.8	2.7	2.7	2.7	2.7	2.4
平均每户就业人口数 （人）	Average Employed Population Per Household (person)	1.3	1.3	1.2	1.2	1.2	1.1	1.2	1.1	1.0
平均每一就业者负担人数 （人）	Average Dependents Per Employed Person (person)	1.5	1.6	1.6	1.6	1.6	1.7	1.7	1.7	1.7

5-9 城镇居民家庭人均收支情况(2015-2023年)
PER CAPITA INCOME AND CONSUMPTION EXPENDITURE OF URBAN HOUSEHOLDS (2015-2023)

单位：元 (yuan)

项　目	Item	2015	2016	2017	2018	2019	2020	2021	2022	2023	2023年为2022年% 2023 as % of 2022
人均可支配收入	**Per Capita Disposable Income**	**52859**	**57275**	**62406**	**67990**	**73849**	**75602**	**81518**	**84023**	**88650**	**105.5**
工资性收入	Income from Wages and Salaries	32568	35701	37883	40489	44327	44620	49150	51295	55487	108.2
经营净收入	Net Business Income	1337	1292	1293	1073	1034	685	795	756	861	113.9
财产净收入	Net Income from Property	8492	9310	10520	11983	12690	13152	13869	13791	13616	98.7
转移净收入	Net Income from Transfer	10462	10972	12710	14445	15798	17145	17704	18181	18686	102.8
人均消费支出	**Per Capita Consumption Expenditure**	**36642**	**38256**	**40346**	**42926**	**46358**	**41726**	**46776**	**45617**	**50897**	**111.6**
食品烟酒	Food, Tobacco and Liquor	8091	8070	8003	8577	8951	8751	9720	9645	10584	109.7
衣　着	Clothing and Footwear	2651	2643	2429	2346	2391	1924	2235	1977	2180	110.3
居　住	Housing	11252	12128	13347	15391	17235	17163	18382	18605	20261	108.9
生活用品及服务	Household Equipments, Furnishings and Services	2273	2511	2633	2496	2569	2307	2745	2322	2454	105.7
交通通信	Transport and Communications	4860	5078	5396	5033	5229	3925	4358	4261	5072	119.0
教育文化娱乐	Education, Culture and Recreation	4028	4055	4325	4402	4738	3021	3665	3272	4151	126.9
医疗保健	Health Care and Medical Services	2370	2630	3088	3476	3974	3755	4610	4303	4608	107.1
其他用品及服务	Miscellaneous Goods and Services	1117	1141	1125	1205	1271	880	1061	1232	1587	128.8

5-10 城镇居民家庭每百户主要耐用消费品拥有量(1978-2023年) MAIN DURABLE GOODS OWNED PER 100 URBAN HOUSEHOLDS (1978-2023)

年 份 Year	热水器 (台) Water Heater (set)	洗衣机 (台) Washing Machine (set)	彩 色 电视机 (台) Color TV Set (set)	电冰箱 (台) Refrige-rator (set)	照相机 (台) Camera (set)	空 调 (台) Air Conditioner (set)	计算机 (台) Computer (set)	移动电话 (部) Mobile Phone (set)	家用汽车 (辆) Automobile (unit)
1978					8				
1979		…			10				
1980		2		…	11				
1981		12	2	2	13				
1982		19	2	3	17				
1983		29	4	7	21				
1984		42	8	15	29				
1985		58	32	42	35				
1986		76	51	62	47				
1987		83	58	72	56				
1988		86	70	81	60				
1989		90	81	89	62				
1990		93	91	96	67				
1991		93	97	102	73	…			
1992	17	96	101	101	77	1			
1993	23	100	107	101	82	2			
1994	39	103	112	104	85	5			
1995	45	100	114	104	87	12			
1996	52	101	119	105	87	14			
1997	58	101	124	104	88	27	12	1	1
1998	65	102	133	105	95	34	15	3	1
1999	67	100	141	103	95	50	24	13	3
2000	74	103	146	107	96	70	32	28	3
2001	78	102	149	107	101	90	45	62	3
2002	84	99	148	102	100	107	56	94	4
2003	85	99	147	100	103	119	68	134	7
2004	94	102	151	103	100	136	79	165	13
2005	97	105	153	104	109	147	89	190	14
2006	98	107	155	105	113	157	96	206	18
2007	99	102	147	108	99	157	92	207	20
2008	95	99	134	103	82	152	86	191	23
2009	98	100	138	104	89	163	97	213	30
2010	98	100	140	103	92	169	104	221	34
2011	97	100	138	103	85	171	104	215	38
2012	99	101	141	103	90	179	112	226	42
2013	99	100	140	103	85	180	110	225	43
2014	99	101	141	104	88	186	114	229	45
2015	93	96	130	98	65	161	107	220	47
2016	93	95	127	97	58	166	103	223	49
2017	92	95	126	97	58	168	105	224	50
2018	99	100	124	103	46	179	100	226	52
2019	99	101	125	103	47	182	101	230	53
2020	100	101	125	104	47	187	96	232	54
2021	100	101	122	103	36	205	91	237	60
2022	100	101	122	103	37	206	90	237	60
2023	98	98	104	101	25	188	79	216	51

5-11 农村居民家庭生活基本情况(1978-2023年)
BASIC LIVING CONDITIONS OF RURAL HOUSEHOLDS (1978-2023)

年份 Year	人均可支配收入(元) Per Capita Disposable Income (yuan)	人均可支配收入实际增长(%) Real Growth Rate of Per Capita Disposable Income (%)	人均消费支出(元) Per Capita Consumption Expenditure (yuan)	#食品烟酒 Food, Tobacco and Liquor	农村居民家庭恩格尔系数(%) Engel Coefficient of Rural Households (%)	每一农村劳动力负担人数(人) Dependents Per Rural Labor Force (person)	农村居民人均住房面积(平方米) Per Capita Living Space of Rural Residents (sq.m)
1978	225		185	117	63.2	2.15	9.20
1979	250	9.2	205	131	63.9	2.16	9.67
1980	290	9.6	253	138	54.5	2.13	10.09
1981	351	19.2	313	164	52.4	2.14	12.35
1982	433	21.2	362	190	52.5	1.97	13.01
1983	519	19.5	384	194	50.5	1.82	14.24
1984	664	25.2	435	223	51.3	1.79	14.22
1985	775	-0.8	510	240	47.1	1.64	16.48
1986	823	-0.6	644	292	45.3	1.66	17.41
1987	916	2.5	706	341	48.4	1.64	18.38
1988	1063	-3.7	883	408	46.2	1.63	19.23
1989	1231	-1.2	976	484	49.6	1.62	20.09
1990	1297	-0.04	981	497	50.7	1.61	20.62
1991	1422	-2.0	1100	537	48.8	1.59	21.92
1992	1572	0.6	1149	559	48.7	1.58	22.67
1993	1883	0.7	1255	587	46.8	1.51	23.70
1994	2401	2.1	1584	780	49.2	1.49	24.42
1995	3224	14.5	2336	1158	49.6	1.47	24.74
1996	3562	-1.0	2565	1191	46.4	1.45	25.74
1997	3662	-2.4	2693	1202	44.7	1.48	27.39
1998	3932	4.9	2873	1215	42.3	1.44	27.64
1999	4183	5.8	3123	1226	39.3	1.43	28.65
2000	4533	4.7	3426	1286	37.5	1.51	28.91
2001	4921	5.3	3553	1222	34.4	1.52	31.01
2002	5259	8.9	3733	1239	33.2	1.48	32.58
2003	5429	3.0	4149	1260	30.4	1.45	33.95
2004	5948	8.5	4619	1406	30.4	1.46	34.21
2005	7041	16.7	5318	1611	30.3	1.45	36.94
2006	7888	11.0	5728	1731	30.2	1.42	39.10
2007	8948	10.7	6403	1924	30.0	1.40	39.54
2008	10052	6.9	7289	2189	30.0	1.40	39.40
2009	10942	10.6	8904	2365	26.6	1.39	39.42
2010	12368	10.4	9262	2460	26.6	1.39	40.62
2011	13742	5.2	11086	2895	26.1	1.38	48.63
2012	15365	8.2	11888	3197	26.9	1.40	49.08
2013	17101	7.7	13564	3786	27.9	1.49	51.35
2014	18867	8.6	14535	4048	27.9	1.50	52.42
2015	20569	7.1	15811	4372	27.7	1.60	43.03
2016	22310	7.0	17329	4667	26.9	1.62	44.50
2017	24240	6.7	18810	4653	24.7	1.68	44.89
2018	26490	6.6	20195	4802	23.8	1.70	46.26
2019	28928	6.7	21881	5542	25.3	1.76	47.19
2020	30126	2.4	20913	5968	28.5	1.86	47.08
2021	33303	9.3	23574	6664	28.3	1.75	49.61
2022	34754	2.6	23745	6503	27.4	1.76	50.16
2023	37358	7.1	26277	7301	27.8	1.95	52.59

5-12 农村居民家庭基本情况(2015-2023年)
BASIC DATA ON RURAL HOUSEHOLDS (2015-2023)

项　　目	Item	2015	2016	2017	2018	2019	2020	2021	2022	2023
平均每户常住人口　（人）	Average Resident Population Per Household (person)	2.9	3.0	2.9	3.1	3.0	3.0	3.1	3.1	2.6
平均每户整半劳动力　（人）	Average Full/Semi Labor Force Per Household (person)	2.3	2.4	2.4	2.3	2.4	2.5	2.5	2.5	2.1
平均每一劳动力负担人口　（人）	Average Dependents Per Labor Force (person)	1.6	1.6	1.7	1.7	1.8	1.9	1.8	1.8	1.9

5-13 农村居民家庭人均收支情况(2015-2023年)
PER CAPITA INCOME AND CONSUMPTION EXPENDITURE OF RURAL HOUSEHOLDS (2015-2023)

单位：元 (yuan)

项　　目	Item	2015	2016	2017	2018	2019	2020	2021	2022	2023	2023年为2022年% 2023 as % of 2022
人均可支配收入	**Per Capita Disposable Income**	**20569**	**22310**	**24240**	**26490**	**28928**	**30126**	**33303**	**34754**	**37358**	**107.5**
工资性收入	Income from Wages and Salaries	15491	16637	18223	19827	21376	21174	23434	24928	26819	107.6
经营净收入	Net Business Income	1959	2062	2140	2021	2262	1613	1874	1850	2090	113.0
财产净收入	Net Income from Property	1204	1350	1570	1877	2127	3103	3443	3556	3681	103.5
转移净收入	Net Income from Transfer	1915	2260	2307	2765	3163	4236	4552	4420	4768	107.9
人均消费支出	**Per Capita Consumption Expenditure**	**15811**	**17329**	**18810**	**20195**	**21881**	**20913**	**23574**	**23745**	**26277**	**110.7**
食品烟酒	Food, Tobacco and Liquor	4372	4667	4653	4802	5542	5968	6664	6503	7301	112.3
衣　着	Clothing and Footwear	996	1095	1025	1088	1200	1036	1265	1108	1241	112.0
居　住	Housing	4636	5199	5588	5951	6298	6453	7020	7910	8411	106.3
生活用品及服务	Household Equipments, Furnishings and Services	993	1157	1595	1580	1230	1121	1377	1360	1692	124.4
交通通信	Transport and Communications	2140	2306	2730	3078	3385	2924	3388	3282	3487	106.2
教育文化娱乐	Education, Culture and Recreation	1145	1342	1314	1436	1587	1143	1317	1307	1534	117.4
医疗保健	Health Care and Medical Services	1336	1347	1699	1992	2247	1973	2212	1900	2132	112.2
其他用品及服务	Miscellaneous Goods and Services	193	217	206	268	392	295	331	375	479	127.7

5-14 农村居民家庭每百户主要耐用消费品拥有量(1985-2023年)
MAIN DURABLE GOODS OWNED PER 100 RURAL HOUSEHOLDS (1985-2023)

年 份 Year	洗衣机 (台) Washing Machine (set)	彩 色 电视机 (台) Color TV Set (set)	电冰箱 (台) Refrige-rator (set)	照相机 (台) Camera (set)	空 调 (台) Air Conditioner (set)	计算机 (台) Computer (set)	移动电话 (部) Mobile Phone (set)	家用汽车 (辆) Automobile (unit)
1985	23	7	2	2				
1986	39	12	5	4				
1987	48	15	9	5				
1988	56	20	14	7				
1989	61	25	19	8				
1990	63	29	23	8				
1991	69	42	36	11				
1992	73	46	40	14				
1993	76	56	47	15				
1994	80	65	53	17	1			
1995	81	74	63	21	2			
1996	83	79	67	21	2			
1997	84	85	72	25	3			
1998	85	92	75	26	5			
1999	86	101	81	29	9			
2000	85	107	84	26	20	7	14	3
2001	91	112	86	29	27	12	30	5
2002	94	116	91	32	35	16	52	6
2003	94	116	94	32	39	22	77	6
2004	96	119	96	35	47	27	102	8
2005	97	129	100	37	63	36	139	10
2006	97	131	100	38	72	41	161	10
2007	99	134	104	37	78	46	182	11
2008	101	137	104	39	89	52	201	12
2009	101	138	105	42	98	58	212	12
2010	103	139	107	42	107	64	224	16
2011	99	134	104	37	108	63	231	19
2012	99	136	103	37	113	67	235	21
2013	95	132	102	32	123	74	221	34
2014	97	132	103	32	127	75	222	35
2015	90	131	95	21	118	69	230	32
2016	94	138	101	20	135	74	243	38
2017	94	138	103	21	141	74	244	38
2018	100	136	111	13	168	66	248	45
2019	102	136	112	12	180	65	249	45
2020	103	137	113	12	185	67	251	47
2021	108	135	118	12	225	62	268	56
2022	108	136	118	13	225	62	268	57
2023	103	115	109	6	200	43	226	52

主要统计指标解释

可支配收入 指调查户在调查期内获得的、可用于最终消费支出和储蓄的总和，即调查户可以用来自由支配的收入。可支配收入既包括现金，也包括实物收入。按照收入的来源，可支配收入包含四项，分别为：工资性收入、经营净收入、财产净收入和转移净收入。计算公式为：

可支配收入＝工资性收入+经营净收入+财产净收入+转移净收入

其中：经营净收入=经营收入-经营费用-生产性固定资产折旧-生产税

财产净收入=财产性收入-财产性支出

转移净收入=转移性收入-转移性支出

工资性收入 指就业人员通过各种途径得到的全部劳动报酬和各种福利，包括受雇于单位或个人、从事各种自由职业、兼职和零星劳动得到的全部劳动报酬和福利。

经营净收入 指住户或住户成员从事生产经营活动所获得的净收入，是全部经营收入中扣除经营费用、生产性固定资产折旧和生产税之后得到的净收入。计算公式为：

经营净收入=经营收入-经营费用-生产性固定资产折旧-生产税

财产净收入 指住户或住户成员将其所拥有的金融资产、住房等非金融资产和自然资源交由其他机构单位、住户或个人支配而获得的回报并扣除相关的费用之后得到的净收入。财产净收入不包括转让资产所有权的溢价所得，计入“非收入所得”。

转移净收入 指国家、单位、社会团体对住户的各种经常性转移支付和住户之间的经常性收入转移，在扣减调查户对国家、单位、住户或者个人的经常性或义务性转移支付后的净收入。

计算公式为：转移净收入=转移性收入-转移性支出

转移性收入 指国家、单位、社会团体对住户的各种经常性转移支付和住户之间的经常性收入转移。包括养老金或退休金、社会救济和补助、政策性生产补贴、政策性生活补贴、救灾款、经常性捐赠和赔偿、报销医疗费、住户之间的赡养收入，以及本住户非常住成员寄回带回的收入等。转移性收入不包括住户之间的实物馈赠。

转移性支出 指调查户对国家、单位、住户或个人的经常性或义务性转移支付。包括缴纳的税款、各项社会保障支出、赡养支出、经常性捐赠和赔偿支出以及其他经常转移支出等。

消费支出 指住户用于满足家庭日常生活消费需要的全部支出，包括用于消费品的支出和用于服务性消费的支出。根据用途不同，消费支出可划分为食品烟酒、衣着、居住、生活用品及服务、交通通信、教育文化娱乐、医疗保健、其他用品及服务八大类。根据来源不同，消费支出可划分为现金消费支出、实物消费支出（含自产自用、来自单位或雇主、来自政府和其他社会组织）。

农村居民家庭整半劳动力 指农村常住居民家庭成员中有劳动能力并经常参加实际劳动的人员，是生产的基本要素指标之一，是发展生产增加农民家庭收入的重要源泉。按规定，农村男18周岁至50周岁、女18周岁至45周岁为整劳动力；男16周岁至17周岁、51周岁至60周岁，女16周岁至17周岁、46周岁至55周岁为半劳动力。农民家庭整半劳动力既包括在上述规定劳动年龄内和在劳动年龄以外有劳动能力并经常参加实际劳动的男女整半劳动力，也包括农民家庭常住人员中属于职工的劳动力，但不包括在劳动年龄内已丧失劳动能力的人员。

现住房总建筑面积 指调查户现住房的总建筑面积。现住房计算总建筑面积时以房屋产权证或租赁证为准，建筑面积也可按使用面积×1.333计算得出，应扣除住房中专门用于出租的建筑面积。

恩格尔系数 随着家庭和个人收入增加，收入中用于食品方面的支出比例将逐渐减小，这一定律被称为恩格尔定律，反映这一定律的系数被称为恩格尔系数。计算公式为：

$$\text{恩格尔系数}=\frac{\text{食品支出总额}}{\text{家庭或个人消费支出总额}}\times 100\%$$

Explanatory Notes on Main Statistical Indicators

Disposable Income refers to the total income at the disposal of sampled households gained during the survey, which can be used for final consumption expenditure and savings. Disposable income includes cash and income in kind. By income source, disposable income can be divided into 4 types, namely wage income, net business income, net property income and net transfer income. The following formula is used:

Disposable Income = wage income + net business income + net property income + net transfer income

Of which: Net business income = business income - business expense - depreciation of productive fixed assets - production tax

Net property income = property income - property expenditure

Net transfer income = transfer income - transfer expenditure

Wage Income refers to all payments of labor and various welfares earned by employed persons through all channels, including all payments of labor and welfare gained from institutional or individual employers, various freelance work, part-time job, and scattered work.

Net Business Income refers to the net income of a family or family members from productive and operating activities. It is the net income of all operating income deducting business expense, depreciation of productive fixed assets and production tax. The following formula is used:

Net business income = business income - business expense - depreciation of productive fixed assets - production tax

Net Property Income refers to the net income of a family or family members earned by deducting relevant expenses from returns of their financial assets, non-financial assets (such as house) and natural resource delivered to other institutions, families or individuals for management. Net property income does not include income from premium of property ownership transfer and it shall be regarded as non-revenue proceeds.

Net Transfer Income refers to net income after deducting recurrent or compulsory transfer payment of sampled households to the nation, institutions, households or individuals from various recurrent transfer payments by the nation, institutions, social groups to households and recurrent income transfer among households.

The following formula is used: Net transfer income = transfer income - transfer expenditure

Transfer Income refers to various recurrent transfer payment from the nation, institutions and social groups to households, along with recurrent income transfer among households, including retirement pension, social relief and allowance, policy production subsidiary, policy living subsidiary, disaster relief fund, recurrent donation and compensations, medical expense reimbursement, alimony income among households and income mailed or brought by non-permanent members of such household, etc. Transfer income does not include physical donation among households.

Transfer Expenditure refers to the recurrent or compulsory transfer payment made by the sampled households to the nation, institutions, households or individuals, including tax payment, various social security expenditures, alimony expenditure, recurrent donation and compensation expenditure and other recurrent transfer expenditure, etc.

Consumption Expenditure refers to total expenditures of households for consumption in daily life, including expenditures on consumer goods and services. By usage, it includes 8 categories, i.e. expenditures on food, tobacco and liquor, clothing, housing, living articles and services, transportation and communication, educational, cultural and recreational services, healthcare and medical services, and other goods and services. By source, it includes cash consumption and physical consumption (including self-produced and self-used products and those from institutions or employers, government and other social organizations).

Full/Semi Labor Force in Rural Households refers to persons among permanent family members in rural households who are capable of working and work frequently. This is one of the indicators for basic production elements, and an important source for production development and increase of farmer's household income. As stated in regulations, rural males aged 18-50 and females aged 18-45 are full labor force. Males aged 16-17 and 51-60 and females aged 16-17 and 46-55 are semi labor force. Full/Semi Labor Force in Rural Households includes the male and female full/semi labor force within the above-mentioned range age as well as those beyond such range of ages who are capable of working and work frequently; also include labor force among permanent members in rural households who are employees. But it excludes persons who are within the range of labor age but incapable of working.

Total Building Area of Current Houses refers to the total building area of house resided by the surveyed households, which is calculated on the basis of the property ownership certificate or lease certificate. The building area can also be calculated as the usable floor space multiplied by 1.333, which shall deduct the building area of the house specially used for lease.

Engel Coefficient Along with the increase in household and personal income, a gradually smaller proportion of income is used for purchase of food. This law is called Engel's law, and the coefficient reflecting such law is called Engel's Coefficient. The following formula is used:

$$\text{Engel Coefficient} = \frac{\text{expenditure on food}}{\text{total household or individual consumption expenditure}} \times 100\%$$

06

财政与税收
GOVERNMENT FINANCE AND TAX REVENUES

简要说明

一、主要内容

本章资料包括北京市政府预算收支情况，北京市税收收入情况。

二、有关情况的说明

地方政府预算收支包括一般公共预算收支、政府性基金预算收支、国有资本经营预算收支和社会保险基金预算收支情况，相关数据为决算数。2015 年，财政部门对财政收支统计口径进行了调整，将 11 项政府性基金收入纳入一般公共预算收入。2016 年，根据财政部、国家税务总局《营业税改征增值税试点实施办法》，在全国全面推开营改增试点。因此，自 2019 年起，“营业税”无数据。

2017 年及以前，税收收入情况包括国税收入和地税（费）收入。自 2018 年起，根据机构改革要求，北京市地方税务局与北京市国家税务局合并为国家税务总局北京市税务局，取消“国税收入”和“地税（费）收入”，统一使用税收收入。

Brief Introduction

I. Main Content

Statistics in this chapter include budgetary revenue and expenditure of Beijing Municipal Government and the tax revenues of Beijing.

II. Condition Explanation

Local government budgetary revenue and expenditure includes general public budgetary revenue and expenditure, governmental fund budgetary revenue and expenditure, budgetary revenue and expenditure of state-owned capital operation, and social insurance fund budgetary revenue and expenditure; the relevant data are final accounts. In 2015, the financial department adjusted the statistical caliber of financial revenue and expenditure, and incorporated 11 governmental fund revenues into general public budgetary revenue. In 2016, the pilot program of replacing business tax with value-added tax was implemented in an all-round manner throughout the country in accordance with the *Measures for Implementation of the Pilot Program of Replacing Business Tax with Value-added Tax* issued by the Ministry of Finance and the State Taxation Administration. Therefore, there has been no data on business tax since 2019.

In and before 2017, the statistics for tax revenues included state tax revenues and local tax revenues. Since 2018, according to the institutional reform requirements, Beijing Local Taxation Bureau and Beijing Municipal Bureau of State Taxation have been merged into Beijing Municipal Tax Service of the State Taxation Administration; the state tax revenue and local tax revenue are cancelled and uniformly replaced with tax revenue.

6-1 地方政府预算收入(1978-2023年)

单位：亿元

年 份 Year	一般公共预算收入 General Public Budget Revenue	税收收入 Tax Revenue	#增值税 Value-added Tax	#房产税 House Property Tax	#土地增值税 Land Appreciation Tax	#契税 Deed Tax	#营业税 Business Tax
1978		18.25					
1979		19.41					
1980		21.22					
1981		24.22					
1982		25.81	0.05				
1983		38.03	1.30				
1984		43.91	2.20				1.23
1985		59.99	4.79				10.23
1986		60.83	7.61				13.19
1987		67.77	9.09				15.42
1988		84.04	15.10				21.11
1989		91.09	16.75				25.33
1990		94.23	16.47				27.95
1991		100.58	19.53				30.78
1992		110.54	22.29				35.86
1993		148.19	42.30				52.07
1994		120.53	25.54				45.63
1995		163.40	27.22				64.46
1996		201.32	29.53				81.61
1997	182.32	235.82	32.67				97.54
1998	229.45	272.23	37.58				113.00
1999	281.37	315.10	39.72				128.86
2000	345.00	372.79	45.96				149.05
2001	454.17	475.00	59.00				181.35
2002	533.99	539.87	66.69				227.79
2003	592.54	588.96	75.26	30.79	3.07	20.40	263.69
2004	744.49	726.50	68.88	31.97	1.85	43.68	333.16
2005	919.21	886.13	97.60	35.21	2.38	60.68	383.76
2006	1117.15	1076.82	117.80	43.29	5.67	64.87	460.99
2007	1492.64	1435.67	134.84	51.75	24.34	80.30	601.06
2008	1837.32	1775.58	158.34	63.84	34.67	82.97	651.78
2009	2026.81	1913.97	179.73	73.98	54.16	103.16	752.60
2010	2353.93	2251.59	210.01	83.83	85.86	134.27	855.40
2011	3006.28	2854.63	237.76	99.40	121.29	136.17	1071.51
2012	3314.93	3124.75	314.00	110.72	132.07	126.58	1152.74
2013	3661.11	3514.52	574.89	122.54	187.24	177.49	1034.79
2014	4027.16	3861.29	646.69	140.22	214.33	192.52	1068.64
2015	4723.86	4263.91	716.12	152.06	174.86	210.23	1186.13
2016	5081.26	4452.97	1214.34	198.22	177.35	254.29	584.41
2017	5430.79	4676.68	1657.88	273.11	288.99	197.46	14.02
2018	5785.92	4988.83	1792.96	299.52	209.13	245.30	8.48
2019	5817.10	4822.98	1820.90	354.43	225.37	225.19	
2020	5483.89	4643.87	1653.11	308.47	259.30	231.20	
2021	5932.31	5164.64	1742.86	342.86	247.43	245.09	
2022	5714.36	4867.07	1315.00	336.63	335.09	219.91	
2023	6181.10	5357.09	1877.13	368.50	223.15	225.17	

资料来源：北京市财政局。

BUDGETARY REVENUE OF LOCAL GOVERNMENT (1978-2023)

(100 million yuan)

#个人所得税 Individual Income Tax	#企业所得税 Corporate Income Tax	#城市维护建设税 City Maintenance and Construction Tax	非税收入 Non-Tax Revenue	政府性基金预算收入 Governmental Fund Budget Revenue	国有资本经营预算收入 Budget Revenue of Government Capital Operation	社会保险基金预算收入 Social Insurance Fund Budget Revenue
0.02	1.76					
0.05	1.43					
0.07	11.70					
0.13	12.70					
0.34	16.18	2.16				
0.97	20.46	2.51				
1.54	21.87	2.70				
1.23	27.70	3.37				
1.53	24.31	3.74				
2.02	22.55	4.35				
2.56	20.59	4.77				
3.15	19.08	5.13				
4.30	14.20	6.57				
9.24	21.70	7.18				
16.21	29.67	10.42				
22.67	37.22	11.36				
28.76	41.05	12.74	-53.50	27.59		
36.49	41.42	14.12	-42.78	32.56		
45.88	45.99	15.27	-33.74	39.07		
56.38	58.03	17.35	-27.79	53.39		
79.52	86.07	20.53	-20.83	53.51		
61.29	100.00	24.91	-5.88	66.97		
57.21	93.70	28.85	3.58	73.40		
73.34	121.70	34.72	17.99	85.55		
84.52	164.76	38.83	33.08	88.14		
102.28	213.86	45.17	40.33	118.63		
135.20	309.34	56.63	56.97	389.40		
171.33	497.52	63.95	61.75	444.71		
177.84	430.42	71.28	112.84	651.96		
215.33	513.09	80.00	102.34	1456.98	46.26	1011.23
272.90	683.71	145.65	151.65	1352.82	52.74	1254.17
281.49	752.47	160.34	190.18	1197.92	60.87	1664.60
333.84	802.12	177.41	146.59	1841.76	63.21	1988.63
383.52	915.84	187.24	165.87	3122.91	64.46	2251.68
478.12	1024.73	204.36	459.95	2028.37	61.60	2667.13
571.26	1095.23	221.64	628.29	1316.47	64.75	3446.83
643.20	1229.80	225.41	754.11	3132.76	61.63	3587.41
728.46	1287.74	245.58	797.09	2009.26	65.41	4186.00
544.16	1228.53	234.98	994.12	2216.30	74.99	4734.44
611.91	1182.49	222.05	840.02	2317.35	80.81	4237.43
743.28	1395.07	245.61	767.66	2705.73	78.09	5545.52
784.59	1449.32	217.69	847.29	2227.46	89.22	5610.78
772.81	1434.81	232.99	824.01	2110.31	68.76	6424.87

Source: Beijing Municipal Finance Bureau.

6-2 地方政府预算支出(1997-2023年)

单位：亿元

年份 Year	一般公共预算支出 General Public Budget Expenditure	#一般公共服务 General Public Services	#教育 Education	#科学技术 Science and Technology	#文化旅游体育与传媒 Culture, Tourism, Sport and Media	#社会保障和就业 Social Security and Employment	#卫生健康 Health Care
1997	236.39						
1998	280.68						
1999	355.19						
2000	443.00						
2001	559.11						
2002	628.35						
2003	734.80						
2004	898.28						
2005	1058.31						
2006	1296.84	159.95	209.21	70.14	40.51	149.22	100.95
2007	1649.50	179.56	263.00	90.74	53.62	179.28	118.95
2008	1959.29	196.27	316.30	112.19	61.11	209.33	145.05
2009	2319.37	212.21	365.67	126.31	74.75	234.29	166.63
2010	2717.32	239.57	450.22	178.92	79.36	275.90	186.82
2011	3245.23	261.38	520.08	183.07	87.01	354.88	225.49
2012	3685.31	286.57	628.65	199.94	141.37	424.31	256.06
2013	4173.66	297.12	681.18	234.67	154.71	469.13	276.13
2014	4524.67	272.23	742.05	282.71	163.90	509.01	322.29
2015	5737.70	300.12	855.67	287.80	188.50	700.48	370.52
2016	6406.77	367.20	887.38	285.78	198.35	716.21	397.95
2017	6824.53	493.24	964.62	361.76	208.96	795.38	427.87
2018	7471.43	512.40	1025.51	425.87	245.43	835.65	490.09
2019	7408.19	499.43	1137.18	433.42	279.32	972.98	534.41
2020	7116.18	527.10	1138.29	410.96	225.11	1055.86	605.64
2021	7205.12	532.65	1147.83	449.45	220.06	1054.19	632.67
2022	7469.15	589.25	1171.12	488.70	204.95	1067.80	775.82
2023	7971.25	545.81	1227.90	521.91	215.87	1145.82	704.86

注：自2019年起，原“文化体育与传媒”更名为“文化旅游体育与传媒”，原“医疗卫生与计划生育”更名为“卫生健康”，下同。
资料来源：北京市财政局。

BUDGETARY EXPENDITURE OF LOCAL GOVERNMENT (1997-2023)

(100 million yuan)

#节能环保 Energy Conservation and Environment Protection	#交通运输 Transportation	#城乡社区 Urban and Rural Community Affairs	#农林水 Agriculture, Forestry and Water Conservancy	政府性基金预算支出 Governmental Fund Budget Expenditure	国有资本经营预算支出 Budget Expenditure of Government Capital Operation	社会保障基金预算支出 Social Security Fund Budget Expenditure
20.14	7.05	153.26	88.62	114.74		
29.27	33.09	187.43	102.51	418.15		
35.47	80.35	199.84	121.77	441.64		
54.04	147.07	347.82	142.01	501.50		
60.85	154.99	294.30	158.64	1347.65	47.74	811.92
94.51	199.12	339.27	187.34	1329.71	67.46	986.99
113.54	243.76	430.76	222.69	1118.45	62.68	1268.73
138.17	231.79	510.67	297.62	1798.81	66.95	1490.34
213.36	214.55	567.40	343.67	2559.09	63.99	1672.32
303.26	295.63	995.39	424.78	2281.30	61.72	1896.03
363.38	353.48	1120.37	443.55	1432.09	45.63	2497.23
458.44	446.48	1034.14	518.35	2461.60	58.86	2594.95
399.45	462.99	1246.22	576.04	2560.27	52.80	3011.72
308.81	401.59	1074.61	584.62	2960.23	52.24	3755.05
236.90	327.97	872.94	497.33	3470.47	57.89	4124.84
249.24	362.70	860.00	497.87	3462.81	53.26	4675.51
222.90	395.25	808.60	462.79	2642.10	64.54	4285.02
220.67	373.10	929.61	515.53	2737.06	47.17	4264.13

Note: Since 2019, the original "culture, sport and media" has been changed to "culture, tourism, sport and media"; and the original "medical and health care, and family planning" has been changed to "health care". The same applies to the following table.

Source: Beijing Municipal Finance Bureau.

6-3 地方政府预算收入
BUDGETARY REVENUE OF LOCAL GOVERNMENT

单位：亿元 (100 million yuan)

项　　目	Item	2023	2022
一般公共预算收入	**General Public Budget Revenue**	**6181.10**	**5714.36**
#增值税	Value-added Tax	1877.13	1315.00
房产税	House Property Tax	368.50	336.63
土地增值税	Land Appreciation Tax	223.15	335.09
契税	Deed Tax	225.17	219.91
个人所得税	Individual Income Tax	772.81	784.59
企业所得税	Company Income Tax	1434.81	1449.32
城市维护建设税	City Maintenance and Construction Tax	232.99	217.69
耕地占用税	Farm Land Occupation Tax	5.81	2.74
罚没收入	Penalty Receipts	73.96	60.75
行政事业性收费收入	Charge of Administrative and Institutional Units	65.91	58.81
政府性基金预算收入	**Governmental Fund Budget Revenue**	**2110.31**	**2227.46**
国有资本经营预算收入	**Budget Revenue of Government Capital Operation**	**68.76**	**89.22**
社会保险基金预算收入	**Social Insurance Fund Budget Revenue**	**6424.87**	**5610.78**

资料来源：北京市财政局。
Source: Beijing Municipal Finance Bureau.

6-4 地方政府预算支出
BUDGETARY EXPENDITURE OF LOCAL GOVERNMENT

单位：亿元 (100 million yuan)

项　　目	Item	2023	2022
一般公共预算支出	**General Public Budget Expenditures**	**7971.25**	**7469.15**
#一般公共服务	General Public Services	545.81	589.25
教　育	Education	1227.90	1171.12
科学技术	Science and Technology	521.91	488.70
文化旅游体育与传媒	Culture, Tourism, Sport and Media	215.87	204.95
社会保障和就业	Social Security and Employment	1145.82	1067.80
卫生健康	Health Care	704.86	775.82
节能环保	Energy Conservation and Environment Protection	220.67	222.90
交通运输	Transportation	373.10	395.25
城乡社区	Urban and Rural Community Affairs	929.61	808.60
农林水	Agriculture, Forestry and Water Conservancy	515.53	462.79
政府性基金预算支出	**Governmental Fund Budget Expenditure**	**2737.06**	**2642.10**
国有资本经营预算支出	**Budget Expenditure of Government Capital Operation**	**47.17**	**64.54**
社会保险基金预算支出	**Social Insurance Fund Budget Expenditure**	**4264.13**	**4285.02**

资料来源：北京市财政局。
Source: Beijing Municipal Finance Bureau.

6-5 地税税费收入分税种、分行业完成情况(2010-2017年)
LOCAL TAX REVENUE BY CATEGORY AND SECTOR (2010-2017)

单位：亿元 (100 million yuan)

项　　目	Item	2010	2011	2012	2013	2014	2015	2016	2017
地税税费收入	**Local Tax Revenue**	**2104.9**	**2666.6**	**2865.3**	**3061.6**	**3387.8**	**3868.2**	**3261.8**	**3683.1**
按税种分	**By Category**								
#增值税	Value-added Tax							44.6	41.5
营业税	Business Tax	855.4	1071.5	1152.7	1032.4	1067.9	1186.1		
企业所得税	Corporate Income Tax	173.2	210.5	221.0	258.1	333.9	374.1	479.8	555.9
个人所得税	Individual Income Tax	536.3	681.3	703.5	834.5	958.8	1195.3	1428.1	1608.0
按行业分	**By Sector**								
第一产业	Primary Industry	3.7	4.0	4.9	5.0	7.7	7.9	7.4	7.8
第二产业	Secondary Industry	235.2	303.1	326.2	348.5	388.5	408.7	345.5	386.4
#制造业	Manufacturing	101.8	138.4	150.4	160.7	179.4	206.3	219.5	235.8
电力、燃气及水的生产和供应业	Production and Supply of Electricity, Gas and Water	15.7	19.4	21.2	25.2	28.9	29.2	35.1	37.5
建筑业	Construction	109.9	134.4	144.6	154.0	171.7	166.5	85.1	106.6
第三产业	Tertiary Industry	1866.0	2359.5	2534.1	2708.1	2991.6	3451.6	2908.9	3288.9
#交通运输、仓储和邮政业	Transport, Storage and Post	51.4	64.0	60.6	38.1	40.5	46.4	47.1	52.5
信息传输、计算机服务和软件业	Information Transmission, Computer Services and Software	98.0	125.5	132.8	123.7	141.8	147.1	171.1	192.0
批发和零售业	Wholesale and Retail Trades	111.4	159.4	169.3	188.8	206.2	230.1	244.2	283.9
金融业	Financial Intermediation	276.4	366.4	446.7	478.0	599.5	763.0	411.2	429.4
房地产业	Real Estate	437.4	520.4	525.4	659.3	734.2	745.7	841.7	938.0

资料来源：国家税务总局北京市税务局。
Source: Beijing Municipal Tax Service of State Taxation Administration.

6-6 国税税收收入分税种、分行业完成情况(2010-2017年)
STATE TAX REVENUE BY CATEGORY AND SECTOR (2010-2017)

单位：亿元 (100 million yuan)

项 目	Item	2010	2011	2012	2013	2014	2015	2016	2017
国税税收收入	**State Tax Revenue**	**4346.8**	**5332.5**	**6339.4**	**7470.9**	**8325.2**	**8655.2**	**9378.5**	**9605.7**
按税种分	**By Category**								
#增值税	Value-added Tax	868.3	961.7	1096.0	1456.3	1659.8	1710.5	2486.2	3286.1
营业税	Business Tax	145.4	161.3	191.3	203.7	80.7	150.7		
企业所得税	Corporate Income Tax	2642.0	3506.5	4252.0	5024.4	5757.3	5937.2	5976.0	5373.9
按行业分	**By Sector**								
第一产业	Primary Industry	5.8	0.7	0.3	2.6	0.9	2.5	4.3	4.5
第二产业	Secondary Industry	779.1	881.1	843.8	1069.3	1159.4	1182.2	1198.0	1339.7
#制造业	Manufacturing	623.2	709.2	764.6	832.0	889.5	963.2	960.7	985.3
电力、燃气及水的生产和供应业	Production and Supply of Electricity, Gas and Water	105.2	103.5	131.0	261.4	194.1	171.1	169.2	203.2
建筑业	Construction	30.1	45.3	54.8	57.0	50.9	63.9	170.2	260.3
第三产业	Tertiary Industry	3561.9	4450.8	5495.3	6399.0	7164.8	7470.5	8176.1	8261.5
#交通运输、仓储和邮政业	Transport, Storage and Post	157.9	209.2	212.1	245.1	242.6	242.6	189.4	239.3
信息传输、计算机服务和软件业	Information Transmission, Computer Services and Software	30.8	105.9	245.9	373.2	296.2	285.0	306.3	371.4
批发和零售业	Wholesale and Retail Trade	1081.6	1410.8	1314.6	1451.0	1474.0	1420.6	1468.5	1645.7
金融业	Financial Intermediation	1831.2	2158.0	3034.0	3500.2	4153.2	4401.4	4828.6	4115.7
房地产业	Real Estate	107.6	122.3	111.6	157.0	156.9	104.3	274.9	380.9

资料来源：国家税务总局北京市税务局。
Source: Beijing Municipal Tax Service of State Taxation Administration.

6−7 税收收入情况(2017−2023年)
STATISTICS ON TAX REVENUE(2017-2023)

单位：亿元 (100 million yuan)

项 目	Item	2017	2018	2019	2020	2021	2022	2023
税收收入	**Tax Revenue**	**12403.9**	**12655.5**	**13098.1**	**12805.9**	**13990.9**	**13633.4**	**15113.3**
按税种分	**By Category**							
#增值税	Value-added Tax	3327.6	3595.3	3629.9	3252.4	3541.3	2774.1	3883.2
企业所得税	Corporate Income Tax	5929.8	5727.5	6501.1	6467.5	6922.2	7195.9	7645.5
个人所得税	Individual Income Tax	1610.3	1824.2	1363.1	1553.1	1885.7	1994.2	1968.3
按行业分	**By Sector**							
第一产业	Primary Industry	11.7	11.2	12.6	10.5	9.5	9.1	12.0
第二产业	Secondary Industry	1665.8	1808.3	1746.4	1601.6	1744.4	1768.2	1857.7
#制造业	Manufacturing	1179.0	1202.5	1222.7	1189.8	1258.4	1204.2	1146.7
电力、热力、燃气及水生产和供应业	Production and Supply of Electricity, Heating, Gas and Water	235.9	213.6	186.0	127.6	121.4	124.2	198.3
建筑业	Construction	354.0	367.3	351.2	325.0	342.8	321.7	351.3
第三产业	Tertiary Industry	10726.4	10836.0	11339.1	11193.8	12237.0	11856.1	13243.6
#交通运输、仓储和邮政业	Transport, Storage and Post	286.0	344.7	354.7	144.7	247.9	141.5	260.3
信息传输、软件和信息技术服务业	Information Transmission, Software and Information Technology	550.4	630.7	664.6	700.6	976.6	973.4	1249.1
批发和零售业	Wholesale and Retail Trades	1324.5	1529.1	1243.9	1098.0	1470.5	1186.8	1338.2
金融业	Financial Intermediation	4515.4	4252.7	5217.0	5710.4	5669.6	5676.3	6094.2
房地产业	Real Estate	1302.1	1175.8	1203.1	1122.3	1167.7	1136.5	1086.7

注：本表税收收入不含各项非税收入，2017年为同口径数据。
资料来源：国家税务总局北京市税务局。
Note: Tax revenue in this table doesn't include the non-tax revenues. That of 2017 is the data of the same caliber.
Source: Beijing Municipal Tax Service of State Taxation Administration.

主要统计指标解释

财政部分

一般公共预算收入　是通过一定的形式和程序，由各级财政部门组织并纳入预算管理的各项收入。

政府性基金预算收入　是按规定收取，转入或通过当年财政安排，由财政管理并具有指定用途的政府性基金预算收入等。

国有资本经营预算收入　指国家以所有者身份依法取得国有资本收益，并对所得收益进行分配而发生的各项收支预算，是政府预算的重要组成部分。

社会保险基金预算收入　社会保险基金预算是指社会保险经办机构根据国家预算管理和社会保险相关法律法规编制的、经规定程序审批的具有法律效力的年度基金财务收支计划。

税收收入　包括增值税、营业税、企业所得税、个人所得税、资源税、城市维护建设税、房产税、印花税、城镇土地使用税、土地增值税、车船税、耕地占用税、契税等。

非税收收入　包括专项收入、行政事业性收费、罚没收入和其他收入。

一般公共预算支出　是各级财政部门对集中的一般预算收入有计划地分配和使用而安排的支出。

政府性基金预算支出　是各级财政部门用基金预算收入安排的支出。

一般公共服务支出　指政府提供基本公共管理与服务的支出，包括人大事务、政协事务、政府办公厅（室）及相关机构事务、发展与改革事务、统计信息事务、财政事务、税收事务、审计事务、海关事务、人力资源事务、纪检监察事务、人口与计划生育事务、商贸事务、知识产权事务、工商行政管理事务、国土资源事务、海洋管理事务、测绘事务、地震事务、气象事务、民族事务、宗教事务、港澳台侨事务、档案事务、共产党事务、民主党派事务及工商联事务、群众团体事务、彩票事务等。

教育支出　指政府教育事务支出，包括教育行政管理、学前教育、小学教育、初中教育、普通高中教育、普通高等教育、初等职业教育、中专教育、技校教育、职业高中教育、高等职业教育、广播电视教育、留学生教育、特殊教育、干部继续教育、教育机关服务等。

科学技术支出　指用于科学技术方面的支出，包括科学技术管理事务、基础研究、应用研究、技术研究与开发、科技条件与服务、社会科学、科学技术普及、科技交流与合作等。

文化旅游体育与传媒支出　指政府在文化、文物、体育、广播影视、新闻出版等方面的支出。

社会保障和就业支出　指政府在社会保障与就业方面的支出，包括社会保障和就业管理事务、民政管理事务、财政对社会保险基金的补助、补充全国社会保障基金、行政事业单位离退休、企业改革补助、就业补助、抚恤、退役安置、社会福利、残疾人事业、城市居民最低生活保障、其他城镇社会救济、农村社会救济、自然灾害生活救助、红十字事务等。

卫生健康支出　指政府医疗卫生与计划生育管理方面的支出。

节能环保支出　指政府环境保护支出，包括环境保护管理事务支出、环境监测与监察支出、污染治理支出、自然生态保护支出、天然林保护工程支出、退耕还林支出、风沙荒漠治理支出、退牧还草支出、已垦草原退耕还草、能源节约利用、污染减排、可再生能源和资源综合利用等支出。

交通运输支出　指政府交通运输和邮政业方面的支出，包括公路运输支出、水路运输支出、铁路运输支出、民用航空运输支出、邮政业支出等。

城乡社区支出　指政府城乡社区事务支出，包括城乡社区管理事务支出、城乡社区规划与管理支出、城乡社区公共设施支出、城乡社区住宅支出、城乡社区环境卫生支出、建设市场管理与监督支出等。

农林水支出　指政府农林水事务支出，包括农业支出、林业支出、水利支出、扶贫支出、农业综合开发支出等。

税收部分

税费收入　指由税务局征缴的各项税收收入和罚没收入。包括企业所得税、个人所得税、资源税、房产税、契税、城市维护建设税等。

税收收入　指由税务局征缴的各项税收收入。包括增值税、消费税、企业所得税、个人所得税、城市维护建设税等。

企业所得税　是对中国境内全部企业的生产经营所得和其他所得征收的一种税。

增值税　指以商品或劳务销售额为计税依据并实行扣除已征税款制度的一种流转税。

个人所得税　是对个人（自然人）取得的各项应税所得征收的一种税。

Explanatory Notes on Main Statistical Indicators

Finance

General Public Budgetary Revenue refers to the revenue organized by finance authorities at all levels in certain form and through certain procedures and involved in budgetary management.

Governmental Fund Budgetary Revenue refers to governmental fund budgetary revenues collected, transferred or allocated by government finance in the current year in accordance with regulations, and regulated by government finance and used for specific purpose.

Budgetary Revenue of State-owned Capital Operation refers to the state-owned capital income of the country as the owner and all kinds of income and expenditure budgets resulted from the allocation of the income. It is an important part of governmental budget.

Social Insurance Fund Budgetary Revenue refers to a legally effective annual financial revenue and expenditure plan of fund formulated by social insurance agencies in accordance with relevant laws and regulations of state budget management and social insurance as well as specified approval procedures.

Tax Revenue includes value-added tax, business tax, corporate income tax, individual income tax, resource tax, urban maintenance and construction tax, house property tax, stamp tax, urban land use tax, land appreciation tax, tax on vehicles and boat operation, farm land occupation tax, deed tax, etc.

Non-tax Revenue includes special program receipts, charge of administrative and institutional units, income of fines and confiscation, and other non-tax revenues.

General Public Budgetary Expenditure refers to the expenditure arranged by finance authorities at all levels from the general budgetary revenue according to the planned distribution.

Governmental Fund Budgetary Expenditure refers to the expenditure arranged by finance authorities at all levels according to the fund budget revenue.

Expenditure for General Public Services refers to the spending on the basic public management and services provided by the government, including the expenses on affairs of Beijing Municipal People's Congress, CPC Beijing Municipal Committee, General Office of Beijing Municipal Government and relative institutions, development and reform, statistical information, finance, taxation, audit, customs, human resources, discipline inspection and supervision, population and family planning, commerce and trade, intellectual property, administration for industry and commerce, land and resources, oceanic administration, surveying and mapping, earthquake, weather, ethnics, religions, Hong Kong, Macao, Taiwan, and Overseas Chinese, archive administration, Chinese Communist Party, democratic parties, federation of industry and commerce, mass organizations, and lottery, etc.

Expenditure for Education refers to the spending of government on education, including the expenses on the administration of education, pre-school education, primary education, junior high school education, senior high school education, general higher education, primary vocational education, secondary vocational education, technical school education, vocational senior high school education and higher vocational education, radio and television education, overseas student education, special education, continuing education for management personnel, and services for education authorities, etc.

Expenditure for Science and Technology refers to the spending on science and technology (S&T), including the expense on the administration of S&T, basic research, applied research, technology research and development, conditions and services of S&T, popularization of social science and S&T, exchanges and cooperation of S&T, etc.

Expenditure for Cultural，Tourism Sport and Media refers to the spending on culture, cultural relics, sports, radio, films, television, press and publication, etc.

Expenditure for Social Security and Employment refers to the spending on social security and employment, including the expenses on social security and employment administration affairs, civil affairs, budgetary subsidy on the social insurance funds, subsidy on National Social Security Fund, subsidy on retirees of administrative and institutional units, subsidy on enterprise reform, subsidy on employment, pension, reemployment of ex-serviceman, social welfare, the handicapped undertakings, subsistence allowances for urban residents, other urban social relief, rural social relief, relief for natural disasters, affairs of Red Cross, etc.

Expenditure for Health refers to the spending of government on health care and family planning.

Expenditure for Energy Conservation and Environmental Protection refers to the spending of government on environmental protection, including the expenses on administration of environmental protection, environment monitoring and supervision, pollution control, natural and ecological protection, projects of natural forest protection, reforestation, control of sand storms, returning pasture and grazing land to grassland, energy conservation and utilization, emission reduction, comprehensive utilization of renewable energy and resources, etc.

Expenditure for Transportation refers to the spending of government on transportation and postal services, including the expenses on highway transportation, waterway transportation, railway transportation, civil aviation transportation and postal services, etc.

Expenditure for Urban and Rural Community refers to the spending of government on urban and rural community affairs, including the expenses on administration of urban and rural communities, planning and management of urban and rural communities, public facilities in urban and rural communities, residential houses in urban and rural communities, sanitation in urban and rural communities, management and supervision of construction markets, etc.

Expenditure for Agriculture, Forestry and Water Conservancy refers to the spending of government on agriculture affairs, forestry affairs, water conservancy affairs, poverty alleviation and comprehensive agricultural development, etc.

Taxes

Local Tax Revenue refers to the revenue of taxes levied and collected by tax authorities at all levels, including corporate income tax, personal income tax, resource tax, house property tax, deed tax, urban maintenance and construction tax, etc.

State Tax Revenue refers to the revenue of taxes levied and collected by tax authorities at all levels, including value-added tax, excise tax, corporate income tax, individual income tax, urban maintenance and construction tax, etc.

Corporate Income Tax is a sort of tax levied against income of China domestic enterprises from their production and operation and other income.

Value-Added Tax is a sort of commodity turnover tax based on commodity and service sales, with a system of deduction of tax levied.

Personal Income Tax is a sort of tax levied against taxable income earned by individuals (natural persons).

07

能源、资源和环境
ENERGY, RESOURCES AND ENVIRONMENT

简要说明

一、主要内容

本章资料包括北京市能源生产与消费情况、万元地区生产总值能耗、能源平衡表、能源消费弹性系数和北京地区用电量情况、气象情况、水资源情况、排水及节水情况、园林绿化及森林情况、大气环境、固体废物处置情况等。

二、能源统计范围及测算方法

（一）关于统计范围。能源部分统计范围为全社会口径。

（二）关于测算方法。第二、三产业限额以上法人单位能源消费统计采取全面调查、限额以下法人单位能源消费情况根据普查年度数据资料推算、农林牧渔业、居民生活能源消费统计根据农林牧渔中间消耗和能源供应部门的能源供应资料核算。

三、关于历史数据调整的问题

2004年能源消费数据为北京市第一次全国经济普查数据，1995-2003年的能源消费数据根据第一次全国经济普查的数据结果进行了修订。

2008年能源消费数据为北京市第二次全国经济普查数据，1995-2007年的能源消费数据根据第二次全国经济普查的数据结果进行了修订。

2010年，根据北京市第六次全国人口普查的数据结果对2006-2010年的人均指标数据进行了修订。

2013年能源消费数据为北京市第三次全国经济普查数据。2005-2012年的能源生产量、能源消费总量、万元地区生产总值能耗及下降率，以及2010-2012年的能源消费构成、能源消费弹性系数、平均每万元地区生产总值能源消费量、人均生活用能源、主要能源日均消费量数据已根据第三次全国经济普查的数据结果进行了修订。

2018年能源消费数据为北京市第四次全国经济普查数据。2015-2017年的能源消费数据根据第四次全国经济普查的数据结果进行了修订。1992-2017年的万元地区生产总值能耗及下降率、万元地区生产总值水耗及下降率、能源消费弹性系数、平均每万元地区生产总值能源消费量中使用的地区生产总值数据，根据北京市第四次全国经济普查的数据结果进行了修订。

2020年，根据北京市第七次全国人口普查的数据结果对2011-2019年的人均指标数据进行了修订。

四、有关统计标准的变化说明

（一）关于行业划分。2012年以前，执行《国民经济行业分类》（GB/T 4754-2002）标准。2012-2017年执行《国民经济行业分类》（GB/T 4754-2011）标准。自2018年起，执行《国民经济行业分类》（GB/T 4754-2017）标准。

（二）关于三次产业划分。2003年，根据《国民经济行业分类》（GB/T 4754—2002），国家统计局印发了《国家统计局关于印发〈三次产业划分规定〉的通知》（国统字〔2003〕14号）。2012年，根据国家质检总局和国家标准委颁布的《国民经济行业分类》（GB/T 4754—2011），国家统计局对2003年《三次产业划分规定》进行了修订。主要在以下方面作出调整：一是将门类“农、林、牧、渔业”中的“农、林、牧、渔服务业”，“采矿业”中的“开采辅助活动”，“制造业”中的“金属制品、机械和设备修理业”等三个大类一并调整到第三产业。调整后，第一产业为4个大类；第二产业为2个门类和36个大类；第三产业为15个门类和3个大类。二是明确第三产业即为服务业。

本章2012年及以后三次产业的分类执行调整后的划分规定。

Brief Introduction

I. Main Content

Statistics in this chapter include the energy production and energy consumption in Beijing, energy consumption in regions with RMB 10,000 of GDP, energy balance sheet, energy consumption elasticity coefficient, electricity consumption in Beijing, meteorology, water resources, water drainage and water saving, landscaping and forest, atmospheric environment, solid waste disposal, etc.

II. Scope of Statistics and Calculation Method for Energy

(I) Scope of Statistics. Statistics on energy cover the entire society.

(II) Calculation Method. Comprehensive survey is adopted on energy consumption of legal entities above designated size in the secondary and tertiary industries, and energy consumption of legal entities below designated size are estimated and calculated on the basis of the annual census data; statistics on energy consumption in agriculture, forestry, animal production and hunting, fishing and statistics on household energy consumption are calculated based on the information on intermediate consumption in agriculture, forestry, animal production and hunting, fishing and based on the energy supply data of the energy supply departments.

III. Adjustment to Historical Data

Data on energy consumption for 2004 were collected from the first national economic census in Beijing; data on energy consumption for the period between 1995 and 2003 had been revised according to the data of the first national economic census.

Data on energy consumption for 2008 were collected from the second national economic census in Beijing; data on energy consumption for the period between 1995 and 2007 had been revised in accordance with the data of the second national economic census.

In 2010, the per-capita index data from 2006 to 2010 were revised in accordance with the results of the sixth national population census in Beijing.

Data on energy consumption for 2013 were collected from the third national economic census in Beijing. Data on energy production, total energy consumption, energy consumption per RMB 10,000 of GDP and the decrease rate for the period between 2005 and 2012, and the data on composition of energy consumption from 2010 to 2012, the data on energy consumption elasticity coefficient, average energy consumption per RMB 10,000 of GDP, per-capita energy consumption for living, daily average consumption of main energy, have been revised in accordance with the results of the third national economic census.

Data on energy consumption for 2018 were collected from the fourth national economic census in Beijing. Data on energy consumption for the period between 2015 and 2017 had been revised according to the results of the fourth national economic census. Data on energy consumption per RMB 10,000 of GDP and the decrease rate, water consumption per RMB 10,000 of GDP and the decrease rate, energy consumption elasticity coefficient, and the GDP data for energy consumption per RMB 10,000 of GDP, for the period between 1992 and 2017 have been revised in accordance with the results of the fourth national economic census in Beijing.

In 2020, the per-capita index data from 2011 to 2019 were revised in accordance with the results of the seventh national population census in Beijing.

IV. Changes in Relevant Statistical Standards

(I) Classification of Sectors. The standards in the *Classification of National Economic Sectors (GB/T 4754-2002)* were implemented before 2012. The standards in the *Classification of National Economic Sectors (GB/T 4754-2011)* were implemented from 2012 to 2017. The standards in the *Classification of National Economic Sectors (GB/T 4754-2017)* are implemented since 2018.

(II) Classification of Three Industries. According to the *Classification of National Economic Sectors (GB/T 4754-2002),* the National Bureau of Statistics issued the *Notice of the National Bureau of Statistics on the Issuance of the 'Regulations on Three Industries Classification'* (G.T.Z. [2003] No. 14) in 2003. According to the *Classification of National Economic Sectors* (GB/T 4754-2011) promulgated by the General Administration of Quality Supervision, Inspection and Quarantine of the People's Republic of China and the Standardization Administration of the People's Republic of China, the National Bureau of Statistics revised the *Regulations on Three Industries Classification* of 2003 version in 2012. Adjustments were mainly made in the following aspects: Firstly, the "service activities for agriculture, forestry, animal husbandry and fishing" in the category of "agriculture, forestry, animal production and hunting, fishing", the "mining support service activities" in the category of "mining and quarrying", and the "repair of fabricated metal products, machinery and equipment" in the category of "manufacturing" were adjusted to the Tertiary Industry. After adjustment, the Primary Industry fell into 4 categories; the secondary industry fell into 2 classes and 36 categories; and the Tertiary Industry fell into 15 classes and 3 categories. Secondly, the Tertiary Industry was defined as the service industry.

The classification of three industries since 2012 as mentioned in this chapter has all been subject to the classification provisions after adjustment.

7-1 能源生产量(2005-2023年) ENERGY PRODUCTION (2005-2023)

年份 Year	一次能源合计(万吨标准煤) Total Primary Energy (10000 tce)	#原煤(万吨) Raw Coal (10000 tons)	#水电(亿千瓦时) Hydropower (100 million kW·h)	#风电(亿千瓦时) Wind Power (100 million kW·h)	#光伏发电(亿千瓦时) Photovoltaic Power (100 million kW·h)
2005	679.5	945.2	4.0		
2006	460.6	642.1	4.1		
2007	466.1	648.8	4.2		
2008	414.2	578.5	4.5	0.9	
2009	475.7	641.3	4.4	1.4	
2010	499.9	500.1	4.3	3.1	
2011	500.3	500.1	4.5	3.1	
2012	507.2	493.1	4.2	3.1	
2013	541.7	500.1	4.7	3.3	0.1
2014	514.0	457.5	6.8	2.8	0.1
2015	545.6	450.1	6.6	2.6	0.5
2016	445.8	317.6	12.2	3.3	1.1
2017	416.9	255.0	11.2	3.5	2.0
2018	611.5	176.2	9.9	3.5	3.1
2019	691.1	36.1	10.2	3.4	4.8
2020	576.8		11.5	3.7	6.2
2021	385.6		13.7	4.0	6.2
2022	440.2		9.4	5.0	9.1
2023	348.4		8.4	4.8	11.0

7-1 续表 Continued

年份 Year	二次能源合计(万吨标准煤) Secondary Energy (10000 tce)	#汽油(万吨) Gasoline (10000 tons)	#煤油(万吨) Kerosene (10000 tons)	#柴油(万吨) Diesel Oil (10000 tons)	#燃料油(万吨) Fuel Oil (10000 tons)	#液化石油气(万吨) Liquefied Petroleum Gas (10000 tons)	#热力(万百万千焦) Heat (10 billion kilo-joule)	#电力(亿千瓦时) Electricity (100 million kW·h)
2005	2772.6	142.2	12.4	154.7	64.5	47.3	11335.7	209.8
2006	2632.9	145.6	11.6	167.1	57.9	23.0	12181.6	209.7
2007	2767.9	160.4	36.4	244.7	36.7	41.0	12686.9	224.2
2008	3104.9	202.3	85.2	354.8	28.6	42.9	13650.5	244.7
2009	3146.9	242.1	111.6	314.8	28.0	28.8	14226.1	241.9
2010	3397.8	247.7	116.1	314.5	33.7	29.0	15345.0	262.0
2011	3080.9	245.3	126.4	309.3	21.3	27.2	14795.5	256.1
2012	3135.6	255.2	132.9	274.5	18.4	31.9	15400.5	283.3
2013	3000.2	223.9	99.4	194.7	16.9	28.1	14893.6	326.7
2014	3314.3	287.4	152.3	219.8	4.7	32.1	15055.4	351.6
2015	3460.4	296.3	160.0	180.4	1.4	34.0	15819.7	412.5
2016	3267.7	260.5	149.8	152.5	0.7	41.3	16091.9	419.0
2017	3316.6	271.0	190.8	156.6	3.6	41.6	16473.3	376.2
2018	3523.4	276.2	187.6	159.8	4.2	42.4	18380.0	432.1
2019	3601.5	285.5	191.3	173.1	0.7	46.1	18195.2	443.0
2020	3311.2	207.8	103.1	160.4	4.8	29.3	19774.0	436.1
2021	3392.0	227.3	106.3	140.0	3.6	52.7	19178.1	448.7
2022	3426.2	201.7	76.2	169.5	1.1	105.5	20563.7	443.6
2023	3461.1	210.3	120.5	153.7	2.7	137.5	20078.5	447.4

7-2 能源消费总量及构成情况(2010—2023年)
TOTAL ENERGY CONSUMPTION AND ITS COMPOSITION(2010-2023)

年份 Year	能源消费总量(万吨标准煤) Total Energy Consumption (10000 tce)	占能源消费总量的比重(%) Proportion to Total Energy Consumption (%)						非化石能源占能源消费总量的比重(%) Proportion of Non-fossil Energy to Total Energy Consumption
		煤炭 Coal	石油 Petroleum	天然气 Natural Gas	一次电力 Primary Electricity	电力净调入(+)调出(-)量 Net Amount of Electricity Transferred in (+) / out (-)	其他能源 Other Energy	
2010	6359.49	29.59	30.94	14.58	0.45	24.35	0.09	
2011	6397.30	26.66	32.92	14.02	0.45	25.62	0.33	
2012	6564.10	25.22	31.61	17.11	0.42	25.38	0.26	
2013	6723.90	23.31	32.19	18.20	0.35	24.99	0.96	
2014	6831.23	20.37	32.56	21.09	0.41	24.03	1.54	
2015	6802.79	13.05	33.79	29.18	0.40	21.71	1.88	
2016	6916.72	9.22	33.14	31.88	0.66	23.37	1.73	4.60
2017	7088.33	5.06	34.00	32.00	0.65	26.15	2.14	7.20
2018	7269.76	2.77	34.14	34.17	0.61	25.68	2.63	7.80
2019	7360.32	1.81	34.55	34.01	0.67	25.79	3.17	7.90
2020	6762.10	1.50	29.27	37.16	0.84	26.96	4.26	10.40
2021	7103.62	1.44	28.66	36.15	0.90	28.70	4.15	11.96
2022	6896.89	1.02	23.06	38.92	0.92	31.73	4.35	14.25
2023	7571.35	0.63	27.53	35.75	0.86	31.29	3.94	14.32

注：2023年非化石能源占能源消费总量的比重为初步核算数据。
Note: The data on proportion of non-fossil energy to total energy consumption in 2023 are the preliminary accounting data.

7-3 能源消费总量及万元地区生产总值能耗(1980-2023年) TOTAL ENERGY CONSUMPTION AND ENERGY CONSUMPTION PER 10000 YUAN OF GDP (1980-2023)

单位：万吨标准煤 (10000 tons of SCE)

年份 Year	能源消费总量 Total Energy Consumption	第一产业 Primary Industry	第二产业 Secondary Industry	第三产业 Tertiary Industry	生活消费 Residential Consumption	万元地区生产总值能耗（吨标准煤） Energy Consumption Per 10000 Yuan of GDP (ton of SCE)	万元地区生产总值能耗下降率(%) Decrease Rate of Energy Consumption Per 10000 Yuan GDP (%)
1980	1907.7	66.8	1400.3	297.6	143.0	13.715	
1981	1902.6	53.3	1339.4	334.9	175.0	13.668	-0.23
1982	1920.4	55.7	1346.2	338.0	180.5	12.398	6.02
1983	1984.7	73.4	1379.4	313.6	218.3	10.839	11.22
1984	2144.1	85.8	1470.9	347.3	240.1	9.899	7.98
1985	2211.4	90.7	1488.3	351.6	280.8	8.601	5.12
1986	2400.0	95.7	1612.0	380.4	311.9	8.424	-0.49
1987	2475.8	89.0	1647.8	424.7	314.3	7.576	5.88
1988	2612.6	111.7	1748.1	412.2	340.6	6.369	6.45
1989	2653.2	114.4	1735.9	427.0	375.9	5.818	2.73
1990	2709.7	105.7	1720.1	515.3	368.6	5.411	2.92
1991	2872.0	126.7	1807.6	542.0	395.7	4.795	3.56
1992	2987.5	143.6	1888.1	552.4	403.4	4.877	6.54
1993	3264.6	133.6	2150.9	561.0	419.1	4.745	2.69
1994	3385.9	143.6	2234.1	574.8	433.4	4.329	8.78
1995	3533.3	120.4	2328.4	632.7	451.8	4.033	6.83
1996	3734.5	110.8	2477.0	698.1	448.6	3.882	3.76
1997	3719.2	95.7	2369.6	799.8	454.1	3.508	9.64
1998	3808.1	96.2	2400.5	856.4	455.0	3.277	6.58
1999	3906.6	86.9	2370.7	971.8	477.2	3.029	7.57
2000	4144.0	104.8	2424.8	1080.9	533.5	2.868	5.29
						(1.264)	
2001	4229.2	105.4	2366.6	1196.2	561.0	1.154	8.71
2002	4436.1	103.0	2414.6	1334.5	584.0	1.083	6.18
2003	4648.2	99.9	2476.7	1391.0	680.6	1.021	5.69
2004	5139.6	85.6	2664.2	1638.0	751.8	0.997	2.41
2005	5049.8	85.4	2363.7	1771.7	829.0	0.872	4.33
						(0.706)	
2006	5399.3	91.1	2421.2	1962.8	924.2	0.669	5.21
2007	5747.7	95.1	2434.6	2198.4	1019.6	0.623	6.96
2008	5786.2	95.2	2215.6	2394.3	1081.1	0.575	7.63
2009	6008.6	97.1	2206.5	2527.3	1177.7	0.543	5.63
2010	6359.5	98.5	2364.1	2654.4	1242.5	0.521	4.12
						(0.425)	
2011	6397.3	98.3	2160.1	2818.9	1320.0	0.396	6.94
2012	6564.1	98.1	2082.1	2967.0	1416.9	0.377	4.74
2013	6723.9	97.3	2079.2	3109.1	1438.3	0.358	4.93
2014	6831.2	91.7	1998.4	3236.5	1504.6	0.339	5.40
2015	6802.8	84.6	1902.7	3312.6	1502.9	0.316	6.18
						(0.275)	
2016	6916.7	80.4	1870.8	3414.4	1551.1	0.261	4.91
2017	7088.3	72.0	1844.2	3519.3	1652.8	0.251	4.04
2018	7269.8	60.7	1835.2	3681.4	1692.4	0.241	3.88
2019	7360.3	55.8	1850.7	3762.5	1691.4	0.230	4.53
2020	6762.1	50.9	1751.5	3246.9	1712.8	0.209	9.09
						(0.188)	
2021	7103.6	50.3	1690.1	3534.2	1829.0	0.182	3.46
2022	6896.9	48.1	1670.9	3314.8	1863.0	0.175	3.63
2023	7571.3	47.2	1636.7	3941.9	1945.5	0.183	-4.40

注：1.本表能源消费量指标按等价值计算，万元地区生产总值能耗下降率按不变价格计算。
2.1992年以前万元地区生产总值能耗按当年价格计算；自1992年起按不变价格计算。更换基期年份计算两个不变价格数据，括号内数据按新基期价格计算。
3.第一产业中包含农林牧渔专业及辅助性活动能源消费；2017年及以前，第二产业中包含开采专业及辅助性活动，金属制品、机械和设备修理业的能源消费，下同。
4.2023年万元地区生产总值能耗及其下降率为初步核算数据，下同。

Note: a) Energy consumption in this table is calculated in terms of equal value. Decrease rate of energy consumption per 10000 yuan of GDP is calculated at constant prices.
b) Energy consumption per 10000 yuan of GDP before 1992 was calculated at current prices; figures in and after 1992 have been calculated at constant prices. Two figures at constant prices were calculated for the year in which the base period was changed. Figures in brackets are calculated at the price of new base period.
c) In the primary industry, the energy consumption in the professional and support activities in agriculture, forestry, animal husbandry and fishery were included; the energy consumption in the professional and support activities for mining, repair service of metal products, machinery and equipment were included in the secondary industry in and before 2017, the same below.
d) The data for 2023 on the energy consumption per 10000 yuan of GDP and its decrease rate are the preliminary accounting data, the same below.

7—4 按产业、行业分能源消费总量
TOTAL ENERGY CONSUMPTION BY THREE STRATA OF INDUSTRY AND SECTOR

单位：万吨标准煤 (10000 tce)

项　目	Item	2023	2022
能源消费总量	**Total Energy Consumption**	**7571.3**	**6896.9**
按产业分	**By Three Strata of Industry**		
第一产业	Primary Industry	47.2	48.1
第二产业	Secondary Industry	1636.7	1670.9
第三产业	Tertiary Industry	3941.9	3314.8
生活消费	Residential Consumption	1945.5	1863.0
按行业分	**By Sector**		
#采矿业	Mining	1.4	1.2
制造业	Manufacturing	1110.8	1129.3
电力、热力、燃气及水生产和供应业	Production and Supply of Electricity, Heat, Gas and Water	427.5	438.6
建筑业	Construction	103.4	106.7
批发和零售业	Wholesale and Retail Trades	255.6	241.9
交通运输、仓储和邮政业	Transport, Storage and Post	1321.9	875.7
住宿和餐饮业	Hotels and Catering Services	247.8	197.8
信息传输、软件和信息技术服务业	Information Transmission, Software and Information Technology	343.5	335.1
金融业	Financial Intermediation	77.4	77.2
房地产业	Real Estate	512.1	492.3
租赁和商务服务业	Leasing and Business Services	226.5	200.3
科学研究和技术服务业	Scientific Research and Technical Services	214.9	208.3
水利、环境和公共设施管理业	Management of Water Conservancy, Environment and Public Facilities	76.3	85.3
居民服务、修理和其他服务业	Service to Households, Repair and Other Services	47.9	44.4
教　育	Education	266.7	247.2
卫生和社会工作	Health and Social Service	118.7	117.0
文化、体育和娱乐业	Culture, Sports and Entertainment	91.8	82.0
公共管理、社会保障和社会组织	Public Management, Social Security and Social Organization	121.5	93.0

7-5 按产业、行业分万元地区生产总值能耗(2000−2023年)
ENERGY CONSUMPTION PER 10000 YUAN OF GDP BY THREE STRATA OF INDUSTRY AND SECTOR(2000-2023)

单位：吨标准煤 (tce)

年 份 Year	万元地区生产总值能耗 Energy Consumption Per 10000 yuan of GDP	按产业分 By Three Strata of Industry			按行业分 By Sector	
		第一产业 Primary Industry	第二产业 Secondary Industry	第三产业 Tertiary Industry	#工 业 Industry	#交通运输、仓储和邮政业 Transport, Storage and Post
	地区生产总值按2000年不变价格计算 GDP at 2000 constant price					
2000	1.264	1.322	2.369	0.497	2.836	1.420
2001	1.154	1.284	2.121	0.485	2.525	1.653
2002	1.083	1.218	2.007	0.475	2.397	1.732
2003	1.021	1.199	1.868	0.443	2.202	1.798
2004	0.997	1.032	1.742	0.462	2.003	2.162
2005	0.872	1.046	1.409	0.439	1.619	2.091
	地区生产总值按2005年不变价格计算 GDP at 2005 constant price					
2005	0.706	0.983	1.239	0.344	1.422	1.502
2006	0.669	1.041	1.155	0.334	1.341	1.806
2007	0.623	1.065	1.037	0.324	1.201	1.968
2008	0.575	1.048	0.941	0.315	1.089	2.262
2009	0.543	1.022	0.852	0.302	0.989	2.294
2010	0.521	1.054	0.805	0.289	0.923	2.228
	地区生产总值按2010年不变价格计算 GDP at 2010 constant price					
2010	0.425	0.802	0.731	0.229	0.852	1.711
2011	0.396	0.793	0.627	0.224	0.724	1.723
2012	0.377	0.767	0.566	0.218	0.658	1.717
2013	0.358	0.738	0.525	0.212	0.611	1.725
2014	0.339	0.696	0.472	0.205	0.554	1.716
2015	0.316	0.720	0.437	0.194	0.527	1.733
	地区生产总值按2015年不变价格计算 GDP at 2015 constant price					
2015	0.275	0.603	0.430	0.164	0.516	1.689
2016	0.261	0.627	0.402	0.157	0.484	1.684
2017	0.251	0.590	0.380	0.151	0.454	1.605
2018	0.241	0.507	0.364	0.147	0.434	1.631
2019	0.230	0.491	0.353	0.141	0.425	1.664
2020	0.209	0.489	0.326	0.121	0.398	1.325
	地区生产总值按2020年不变价格计算 GDP at 2020 constant price					
2020	0.188	0.470	0.305	0.108	0.387	1.266
2021	0.182	0.452	0.239	0.111	0.283	1.320
2022	0.175	0.440	0.267	0.100	0.328	1.055
2023	0.183	0.452	0.261	0.112	0.321	1.324

7-6 按产业、行业分万元地区生产总值能耗下降率(2001—2023年)
DECREASE RATE OF ENERGY CONSUMPTION PER 10000 YUAN OF GDP BY THREE STRATA OF INDUSTRY AND SECTOR(2001-2023)

单位：% (%)

年 份 Year	万元地区生产总值能耗下降率 Decrease Rate of Energy Consumption per 10000 yuan of GDP	按产业分 By Three Strata of Industry			按行业分 By Sector	
		第一产业 Primary Industry	第二产业 Secondary Industry	第三产业 Tertiary Industry	#工 业 Industry	#交通运输、仓储和邮政业 Transport, Storage and Post
2001	8.71	2.92	10.45	2.43	10.94	-16.41
2002	6.18	5.12	5.39	2.04	5.07	-4.76
2003	5.69	1.53	6.91	6.83	8.15	-3.79
2004	2.41	13.97	6.77	-4.40	9.03	-20.27
2005	4.33	-2.46	7.52	-2.98	7.64	-4.09
2006	5.21	-5.87	6.83	2.87	5.66	-20.22
2007	6.96	-2.31	10.16	3.00	10.49	-8.99
2008	7.63	1.52	9.27	2.83	9.34	-14.92
2009	5.63	2.50	9.50	4.12	9.15	-1.43
2010	4.12	-3.10	5.51	4.16	6.63	2.89
2011	6.94	1.09	14.29	2.19	15.07	-0.73
2012	4.74	3.34	9.73	2.56	9.10	0.37
2013	4.93	3.69	7.29	2.78	7.13	-0.46
2014	5.40	5.73	10.01	3.28	9.32	0.50
2015	6.18	-3.44	7.37	5.38	4.96	-0.98
2016	4.91	-4.07	6.67	4.00	6.13	0.27
2017	4.04	5.94	5.38	4.06	6.32	4.70
2018	3.88	15.90	4.22	2.50	4.38	-1.61
2019	4.53	3.33	2.94	4.08	1.98	-2.04
2020	9.09	0.33	7.61	14.39	6.51	20.37
2021	3.46	3.83	21.69	-2.50	26.92	-4.26
2022	3.63	2.70	-11.80	9.31	-15.98	20.08
2023	-4.40	-2.89	2.40	-12.06	2.10	-25.50

注：表内万元地区生产总值能耗下降率按不变价格计算。
Note: Decrease rate of energy consumption per 10000 yuan of GDP in the table is calculated at constant prices.

7-7 电力平衡表
ELECTRICITY BALANCE SHEET

单位：亿千瓦时 (100 million kW·h)

项　　目	Item	2023	2022
可供本地区消费的能源量	**Total Energy Available for Local Consumption**	**910.98**	**838.89**
加工转换投入(-)产出(+)量	**Input (-) or Output (+) in Processing and Conversion**	**446.86**	**443.38**
火力发电	Thermal Power	447.40	443.57
供　热	Heating	-0.54	-0.19
煤炭洗选	Washing of Coal		
炼　焦	Coking		
炼油及煤制油	Petroleum Refining and Coal-to-liquids		
#油品再投入量(-)	Oil Product Re-input (-)		
制　气	Gas Production		
#再投入量(-)	Re-input (-)		
天然气液化	Natural Gas Liquefaction		
煤制品加工	Coal Product Processing		
回收能	Recovery of Energy		
损失量	**Losses**	**37.36**	**46.47**
#运输和输配损失	Losses in Transportation and Transmission	37.36	46.47
终端消费量	**Final Consumption**	**1319.88**	**1234.14**
农、林、牧、渔业	Agriculture, Forestry, Animal Husbandry and Fishery	15.53	15.48
工　业	Industry	237.33	232.82
#用作原料、材料	Use as Materials		
建筑业	Construction	24.51	25.76
交通运输、仓储和邮政业	Transport, Storage and Post	67.86	59.92
批发和零售业、住宿和餐饮业	Wholesale and Retail Trades, Hotels and Catering Services	126.12	107.81
其　他	Other Sectors	513.95	471.42
居民生活	Household Consumption	334.58	320.92
平衡差额	**Balance**	**0.60**	**1.66**
消费量合计	**Total Energy Consumption**	**1357.78**	**1280.80**

7-8 综合能源平衡表(标准量)
COMPREHENSIVE ENERGY BALANCE SHEET (STANDARD VOLUME)

单位：万吨标准煤 (10000 tons of SCE)

项　目	Item	2023	2022
可供本地区消费的能源量	**Total Energy Available for Local Consumption**	**7571.06**	**6899.82**
加工转换投入(−)产出(+)量	**Input (-) or Output (+) in Processing and Conversion**	**-93.78**	**-86.02**
火力发电	Thermal Power		
供　热	Heating	-80.14	-78.88
煤炭洗选	Washing of Coal		
炼　焦	Coking		
炼油及煤制油	Petroleum Refining and Coal-to-liquids	394.36	386.30
#油品再投入量(−)	Oil Product Re-input (-)	-414.23	-409.65
制　气	Gas Production	2.51	6.90
#再投入量(−)	Re-input (-)	-23.18	-20.33
天然气液化	Natural Gas Liquefaction		
煤制品加工	Coal Product Processing		
回收能	Recovery of Energy	26.92	29.65
损失量	**Losses**	**151.90**	**180.22**
#运输和输配损失	Losses in Transportation and Transmission	99.89	124.99
终端消费量	**Final Consumption**	**7325.67**	**6630.65**
农、林、牧、渔业	Agriculture, Forestry, Animal Husbandry and Fishery	47.21	48.12
工　业	Industry	1294.00	1302.80
#用作原料、材料	Use as Materials	215.07	205.83
建筑业	Construction	103.37	106.73
交通运输、仓储和邮政业	Transport, Storage and Post	1321.90	875.74
批发和零售业、住宿和餐饮业	Wholesale and Retail Trades, Hotels and Catering Services	503.41	439.68
其　他	Other Sectors	2110.25	1994.56
居民生活	Household Consumption	1945.52	1863.01
平衡差额	**Balance**	**-0.29**	**2.94**
消费量合计	**Total Energy Consumption**	**7571.35**	**6896.89**

7-9 能源平衡表(实物量简表)(2023年)
ENERGY BALANCE SHEET (PHYSICAL VOLUME SIMPLE EDITION) (2023)

单位：万吨 (10000 tons)

项目	Item	原煤 Raw Coal	洗精煤 Washed Coal	其他洗煤 Other Washed Coal	煤制品 Coal Products	焦炭 Coke	原油 Crude Oil	汽油 Gasoline	煤油 Kerosene
可供本地区消费的能源量	**Total Energy Available for Local Consumption**	**54.77**			**7.20**	**0.19**	**791.36**	**200.05**	**518.51**
加工转换投入(－)产出(＋)量	**Input (-) or Output (+) in Processing and Conversion**	**-35.79**					**-790.40**	**210.31**	**120.54**
火力发电	Thermal Power	-13.62							
供热	Heating	-22.18							
煤炭洗选	Washing of Coal								
炼焦	Coking								
炼油及煤制油	Petroleum Refining and Coal-to-liquids						-790.40	210.31	120.54
#油品再投入量(－)	Oil Product Re-input (-)								
制气	Gas Production								
#再投入量(－)	Re-input (-)								
天然气液化	Natural Gas Liquefaction								
煤制品加工	Coal Product Processing								
回收能	Recovery of Energy								
损失量	**Losses**						**0.96**		
#运输和输配损失	Losses in Transportation and Transmission								
终端消费量	**Final Consumption**	**18.98**			**7.20**	**0.19**		**410.36**	**639.05**
农、林、牧、渔业	Agriculture, Forestry, Animal Husbandry and Fishery	0.67						1.55	
工业	Industry	18.27				0.19		4.89	0.05
#用作原料、材料	Use as Materials								
建筑业	Construction							6.65	
交通运输、仓储和邮政业	Transport, Storage and Post	0.03						17.99	638.36
批发和零售业、住宿和餐饮业	Wholesale and Retail Trades, Hotels and Catering Services							12.68	
其他	Other Sectors							27.64	0.64
居民生活	Household Consumption				7.20			338.97	
平衡差额	**Balance**								
消费量合计	**Total Energy Consumption**	**54.77**			**7.20**	**0.19**	**791.36**	**410.36**	**639.05**

7-9 续表 1 Continued 1

单位：万吨 (10000 tons)

项目	Item	柴油 Diesel Oil	燃料油 Fuel Oil	石脑油 Naphtha	润滑油 Grease Oil	石蜡 Oilfin	溶剂油 Solvent Oil	石油沥青 Oil Asphalt	石油焦 Petroleum Coal
可供本地区消费的能源量	**Total Energy Available for Local Consumption**	**-31.57**	**-2.39**	**38.17**	**0.56**	**0.02**		**18.94**	**-44.08**
加工转换投入(-)产出(+)量	**Input (-) or Output (+) in Processing and Conversion**	**153.45**	**2.51**	**-12.69**				**7.53**	**44.08**
火力发电	Thermal Power	-0.15							
供热	Heating	-0.11	-0.16						
煤炭洗选	Washing of Coal								
炼焦	Coking								
炼油及煤制油	Petroleum Refining and Coal-to-liquids	153.71	2.67	137.49				7.53	44.08
#油品再投入量(-)	Oil Product Re-input (-)			-150.17					
制气	Gas Production								
#再投入量(-)	Coke Re-input (-)								
天然气液化	Natural Gas Liquefaction								
煤制品加工	Coal Product Processing								
回收能	Recovery of Energy								
损失量	**Losses**								
#运输和输配损失	Losses in Transportation and Transmission								
终端消费量	**Final Consumption**	**121.88**	**0.12**	**25.48**	**0.56**	**0.02**		**26.47**	
农、林、牧、渔业	Agriculture, Forestry, Animal Husbandry and Fishery	1.77							
工业	Industry	10.31	0.01	25.48	0.56	0.02		26.47	
#用作原料、材料	Use as Materials			25.48	0.55	0.02		26.47	
建筑业	Construction	12.85							
交通运输、仓储和邮政业	Transport, Storage and Post	72.29							
批发和零售业、住宿和餐饮业	Wholesale and Retail Trades, Hotels and Catering Services	3.46	0.06						
其他	Other Sectors	21.19	0.04						
居民生活	Household Consumption								
平衡差额	**Balance**								
消费量合计	**Total Energy Consumption**	**122.14**	**0.28**	**175.66**	**0.56**	**0.02**		**26.47**	

7-9 续表 2 Continued 2

单位：万吨 (10000 tons)

项目	Item	液化石油气 Liquefied Petroleum Gas	炼厂干气 Refinery Gas	其他石油制品 Other Petroleum Products	天然气(亿立方米) Natural Gas (100 million cu.m)	液化天然气 Liquefied Natural Gas	热力(万百万千焦) Heat (10 billion kilo-joule)	电力(亿千瓦时) Electricity (100 million kW·h)	其他能源(万吨标准煤) Other Energy (10000 tce)
可供本地区消费的能源量	**Total Energy Available for Local Consumption**	**-15.01**		**-51.46**	**199.43**	**18.14**	**862.99**	**910.98**	**267.28**
加工转换投入(-)产出(+)量	**Input (-) or Output (+) in Processing and Conversion**	**28.86**	**63.83**	**178.89**	**-130.93**	**-0.40**	**20199.07**	**446.86**	**-141.95**
火力发电	Thermal Power	-0.01	-0.05	-0.15	-70.00		-186.00	447.40	-140.32
供热	Heating	-0.28	-1.49	-5.76	-59.19	-0.40	20078.53	-0.54	-0.32
煤炭洗选	Washing of Coal								
炼焦	Coking								
炼油及煤制油	Petroleum Refining and Coal-to-liquids	94.46	76.20	248.96					-37.28
#油品再投入量(-)	Oil Product Re-input (-)	-65.32		-64.16					
制气	Gas Production		-10.82						19.51
#再投入量(-)	Re-input (-)				-1.74				
天然气液化	Natural Gas Liquefaction								
煤制品加工	Coal Product Processing								
回收能	Recovery of Energy						306.54		16.46
损失量	**Losses**				**3.95**			**37.36**	
#运输和输配损失	Losses in Transportation and Transmission							37.36	
终端消费量	**Final Consumption**	**13.84**	**63.83**	**127.43**	**64.55**	**17.74**	**21062.06**	**1319.88**	**127.23**
农、林、牧、渔业	Agriculture, Forestry, Animal Husbandry and Fishery	0.04			0.02			15.53	0.06
工业	Industry	0.32	63.83	127.43	11.06	1.49	4234.05	237.33	4.38
#用作原料、材料	Use as Materials		3.54	112.71					
建筑业	Construction	0.20			0.29		146.49	24.51	0.32
交通运输、仓储和邮政业	Transport, Storage and Post	0.18			1.31	16.25	510.66	67.86	6.32
批发和零售业、住宿和餐饮业	Wholesale and Retail Trades, Hotels and Catering Services	1.23			7.02		1340.06	126.12	4.65
其他	Other Sectors	1.37			25.02		8638.53	513.95	46.24
居民生活	Household Consumption	10.49			19.83		6192.27	334.58	65.27
平衡差额	**Balance**							**0.60**	**-1.90**
消费量合计	**Total Energy Consumption**	**79.45**	**76.20**	**197.50**	**199.43**	**18.14**	**21248.06**	**1357.78**	**305.16**

7–10 能源平衡表(标准量简表)(2023年)

ENERGY BALANCE SHEET (STANDARD VOLUME SIMPLE EDITION) (2023)

单位：万吨标准煤 (10000 tce)

项目	Item	合计 Total	原煤 Raw Coal	洗精煤 Washed Coal	其他洗煤 Other Washed Coal	煤制品 Coal Products	焦炭 Coke	原油 Crude Oil	汽油 Gasoline	煤油 Kerosene
可供本地区消费的能源量	**Total Energy Available for Local Consumption**	**7571.06**	**41.64**			**3.81**	**0.18**	**1130.54**	**294.35**	**762.94**
加工转换投入(−)产出(+)量	**Input (-) or Output (+) in Processing and Conversion**	**-93.78**	**-27.21**					**-1129.17**	**309.45**	**177.36**
火力发电	Thermal Power		-10.35							
供　热	Heating	-80.14	-16.86							
煤炭洗选	Washing of Coal									
炼　焦	Coking									
炼油及煤制油	Petroleum Refining and Coal-to-liquids	394.36						-1129.17	309.45	177.36
#油品再投入量(−)	Oil Product Re-input (-)	-414.23								
制　气	Gas Production	2.51								
#再投入量(−)	Re-input (-)	-23.18								
天然气液化	Natural Gas Liquefaction									
煤制品加工	Coal Product Processing									
回收能	Recovery of Energy	26.92								
损失量	**Losses**	**151.90**						**1.36**		
#运输和输配损失	Losses in Transportation and Transmission	99.89								
终端消费量	**Final Consumption**	**7325.67**	**14.43**			**3.81**	**0.18**		**603.80**	**940.30**
农、林、牧、渔业	Agriculture, Forestry, Animal Husbandry and Fishery	47.21	0.51						2.28	
工　业	Industry	1294.00	13.89				0.18		7.20	0.07
#用作原料、材料	Use as Materials	215.07								
建筑业	Construction	103.37							9.78	
交通运输、仓储和邮政业	Transport, Storage and Post	1321.90	0.02						26.47	939.28
批发和零售业、住宿和餐饮业	Wholesale and Retail Trades, Hotels and Catering Services	503.41							18.66	
其　他	Other Sectors	2110.25							40.68	0.95
居民生活	Household Consumption	1945.52				3.81			498.75	
平衡差额	**Balance**	**-0.29**								
消费量合计	**Total Energy Consumption**	**7571.35**								

7-10 续表 1 Continued 1

单位：万吨标准煤 (10000 tce)

项 目	Item	柴油 Diesel Oil	燃料油 Fuel Oil	石脑油 Naphtha	润滑油 Grease Oil	石蜡 Oilfin	溶剂油 Solvent Oil	石油沥青 Oil Asphalt	石油焦 Petroleum Coal
可供本地区消费的能源量	**Total Energy Available for Local Consumption**	**-46.00**	**-3.42**	**57.26**	**0.79**	**0.03**		**25.20**	**-49.52**
加工转换投入(-)产出(+)量	**Input (-) or Output (+) in Processing and Conversion**	**223.59**	**3.59**	**-19.03**				**10.03**	**49.52**
火力发电	Thermal Power	-0.22							
供 热	Heating	-0.17	-0.23						
煤炭洗选	Washing of Coal								
炼 焦	Coking								
炼油及煤制油	Petroleum Refining and Coal-to-liquids	223.97	3.82	206.23				10.03	49.52
#油品再投入量(-)	Oil Product Re-input (-)			-225.26					
制 气	Gas Production								
#再投入量(-)	Re-input (-)								
天然气液化	Natural Gas Liquefaction								
煤制品加工	Coal Product Processing								
回收能	Recovery of Energy								
损失量	**Losses**								
#运输和输配损失	Losses in Transportation and Transmission								
终端消费量	**Final Consumption**	**177.59**	**0.17**	**38.23**	**0.79**	**0.03**		**35.23**	
农、林、牧、渔业	Agriculture, Forestry, Animal Husbandry and Fishery	2.58							
工 业	Industry	15.03	0.01	38.23	0.79	0.03		35.23	
#用作原料、材料	Use as Materials			38.23	0.78	0.03		35.23	
建筑业	Construction	18.72							
交通运输、仓储和邮政业	Transport, Storage and Post	105.34							
批发和零售业、住宿和餐饮业	Wholesale and Retail Trades, Hotels and Catering Services	5.04	0.09						
其 他	Other Sectors	30.88	0.06						
居民生活	Household Consumption								
平衡差额	**Balance**								
消费量合计	**Total Energy Consumption**								

7-10 续表 2

单位：万吨标准煤

项目	Item	液化石油气 Liquefied Petroleum Gas	炼厂干气 Refinery Gas
可供本地区消费的能源量	**Total Energy Available for Local Consumption**	**-25.74**	
加工转换投入(-)产出(+)量	**Input (-) or Output (+) in Processing and Conversion**	**49.47**	**100.30**
火力发电	Thermal Power	-0.02	-0.08
供热	Heating	-0.47	-2.35
煤炭洗选	Washing of Coal		
炼焦	Coking		
炼油及煤制油	Petroleum Refining and Coal-to-liquids	161.94	119.73
#油品再投入量(-)	Oil Product Re-input (-)	-111.98	
制气	Gas Production		-17.01
#再投入量(-)	Re-input (-)		
天然气液化	Natural Gas Liquefaction		
煤制品加工	Coal Product Processing		
回收能	Recovery of Energy		
损失量	**Losses**		
#运输和输配损失	Losses in Transportation and Transmission		
终端消费量	**Final Consumption**	**23.73**	**100.30**
农、林、牧、渔业	Agriculture, Forestry, Animal Husbandry and Fishery	0.06	
工业	Industry	0.56	100.30
#用作原料、材料	Use as Materials		5.56
建筑业	Construction	0.35	
交通运输、仓储和邮政业	Transport, Storage and Post	0.31	
批发和零售业、住宿和餐饮业	Wholesale and Retail Trades, Hotels and Catering Services	2.11	
其他	Other Sectors	2.36	
居民生活	Household Consumption	17.99	
平衡差额	**Balance**		
消费量合计	**Total Energy Consumption**		

7-10 Continued 2

(10000 tce)

其他石油制品 Other Petroleum Products	天然气 Natural Gas	液化天然气 Liquefied Natural Gas	热力 Heat	电力 Electricity	其他能源 Other Energy
-61.75	**2674.79**	**31.87**	**29.43**	**2435.42**	**267.28**
214.67	**-1797.11**	**-0.70**	**688.79**	**1194.64**	**-141.95**
-0.18	-1038.56		-6.34	1196.08	-140.32
-6.91	-735.37	-0.70	684.68	-1.44	-0.32
298.75					-37.28
-76.99					
					19.51
	-23.18				
			10.45		16.46
	50.65			**99.89**	
				99.89	
152.92	**827.03**	**31.17**	**718.22**	**3528.56**	**127.23**
	0.21			41.52	0.06
152.92	141.75	2.61	144.38	634.48	4.38
135.25					
	3.69		5.00	65.51	0.32
	16.76	28.56	17.41	181.43	6.32
	89.99		45.70	337.18	4.65
	320.53		294.57	1373.99	46.24
	254.09		211.16	894.46	65.27
				1.61	**-1.90**

7-11 分行业能源消费总量和主要能源品种消费量(2023年)

单位：万吨

项　目	Item	能源消费总量(万吨标准煤) Total Energy Consumption (10000 tce)	煤　炭 Coal
合　计	**Total**	**7571.35**	**61.97**
农、林、牧、渔业	Agriculture, Forestry,Animal Husbandry and Fishery	47.21	0.67
采矿业	Mining	1.43	
煤炭开采和洗选业	Mining and Washing of Coal		
石油和天然气开采业	Extraction of Petroleum and Natural Gas	0.04	
黑色金属矿采选业	Mining and Processing of Ferrous Metal Ores	0.68	
有色金属矿采选业	Mining and Processing of Non-Ferrous Metal Ores		
非金属矿采选业	Mining and Processing of Nonmetal Ores		
开采专业及辅助性活动	Professional and Support Activities for Mining	0.71	
其他采矿业	Mining of Other Ores		
制造业	Manufacturing	1110.79	18.27
农副食品加工业	Processing of Food from Agricultural Products	17.59	
食品制造业	Manufacture of Foods	25.75	
酒、饮料和精制茶制造业	Manufacture of Liquor, Beverages and Refined Tea	22.93	
烟草制品业	Manufacture of Tobacco	1.13	
纺织业	Manufacture of Textile	0.49	
纺织服装、服饰业	Manufacture of Textile, Wearing Apparel and Accessories	3.72	
皮革、毛皮、羽毛及其制品和制鞋业	Manufacture of Leather, Fur, Feather and Related Products and Footwear	0.10	
木材加工和木、竹、藤、棕、草制品业	Processing of Timber, Manufacture of Wood, Bamboo, Rattan, Palm, and Straw Products	0.44	
家具制造业	Manufacture of Furniture	2.50	
造纸和纸制品业	Manufacture of Paper and Paper Products	5.85	
印刷和记录媒介复制业	Printing and Reproduction of Recording Media	15.98	
文教、工美、体育和娱乐用品制造业	Manufacture of Articles for Culture, Education, Arts and Crafts, Sport and Entertainment Activities	1.54	
石油、煤炭及其他燃料加工业	Processing of Petroleum, Coal and Other Fuels	468.01	
化学原料和化学制品制造业	Manufacture of Raw Chemical Materials and Chemical Products	47.95	
医药制造业	Manufacture of Medicines	69.69	
化学纤维制造业	Manufacture of Chemical Fibers	1.09	
橡胶和塑料制品业	Manufacture of Rubber and Plastics Products	5.75	
非金属矿物制品业	Manufacture of Non-metallic Mineral Products	91.76	18.27

注：1.各行业能源消费总量不等于各品种能源消费量(标准煤)的简单加总(有能量重复计算部分)。
　　2.各行业能源消费总量相加不等于合计，差额部分是不能分到具体行业的太阳能光热利用量。

TOTAL ENERGY CONSUMPTION AND CONSUMPTION OF MAIN ENERGY VARIETIES BY SECTOR (2023)

(10000 tons)

汽 油 Gasoline	煤 油 Kerosene	柴 油 Diesel Oil	燃料油 Fuel Oil	液 化 石油气 Liquefied Petroleum Gas	液 化 天然气 Liquefied Natural Gas	天然气 (亿立方米) Natural Gas (100 million cu.m)	热 力 (万百万千焦) Heat (10 billion kilo-joule)	电 力 (亿千瓦时) Electricity (100 million kW·h)
410.36	**639.05**	**122.14**	**0.28**	**79.45**	**18.14**	**199.43**	**21248.06**	**1357.78**
1.55		1.77		0.04		0.02		15.53
0.03		0.41				0.07	3.68	0.21
						0.07		0.02
0.01							3.67	0.17
							0.01	
0.02		0.41						0.03
4.30	0.05	8.93	0.01	65.89	1.48	15.92	4216.46	170.67
0.16		0.33		0.01	0.21	0.33	61.76	3.77
0.15		0.39		0.01	0.13	0.64	73.07	5.26
0.10		0.10				0.92	49.91	3.47
						0.04		0.23
0.01							0.41	0.16
0.09		0.01			0.01	0.06	14.38	0.82
							0.07	0.03
0.02		0.01					3.85	0.10
0.09		0.02			0.03	0.02	2.99	0.73
0.08		0.06			0.07	0.13	1.69	1.45
0.22		0.16				0.15	42.51	4.49
0.04						0.01	8.21	0.39
0.02		0.06		65.67		7.27	2522.08	22.48
0.16		0.22		0.02	0.07	0.17	236.34	10.82
0.30		0.10		0.01	0.64	1.30	351.54	14.72
						0.04	0.06	0.23
0.07		0.08		0.02		0.03	5.92	1.83
0.19		5.74	0.01	0.01	0.30	1.10	103.27	7.32

Note: 1.The data on total energy consumption of all sectors is not equal to the simple sum of consumption (SCE equivalent) of all energy varieties (There is the double-counted part of energy).
2.The total energy consumption of all sectors is not equal to the sum, and the difference is reflected in the utilization of the solar thermal which cannot be classified into the specific sectors.

7-11 续表

单位：万吨

项　　目	Item	能源消费总量（万吨标准煤）Total Energy Consumption (10000 tce)	煤　炭 Coal
黑色金属冶炼及压延加工业	Smelting and Pressing of Ferrous Metals	19.14	
有色金属冶炼及压延加工业	Smelting and Processing of Non-ferrous Metals	4.61	
金属制品业	Manufacture of Metal Products	9.93	
通用设备制造业	Manufacture of General Purpose Machinery	17.92	
专用设备制造业	Manufacture of Special Purpose Machinery	20.65	
汽车制造业	Manufacture of Automobiles	72.74	
铁路、船舶、航空航天和其他运输设备制造业	Manufacture of Railway, Ship, Aerospace and Other Transport Equipments	18.56	
电气机械和器材制造业	Manufacture of Electrical Machinery and Apparatus	16.06	
计算机、通讯和其他电子设备制造业	Manufacture of Computers, Communication and Other Electronic Equipment	131.71	
仪器仪表制造业	Manufacture of Measuring Instruments and Machinery	6.06	
其他制造业	Other Manufacture	4.49	
废弃资源综合利用业	Utilization of Waste Resources	0.99	
金属制品、机械和设备修理业	Repair Service of Metal Products, Machinery and Equipment	5.66	
电力、燃气及水的生产和供应业	Production and Supply of Electricity, Gas and Water	427.45	35.79
电力、热力生产和供应业	Production and Supply of Electric Power and Heat Power	302.22	35.79
燃气生产和供应业	Production and Supply of Gas	52.89	
水的生产和供应业	Production and Supply of Water	72.34	
建筑业	Construction	103.37	
批发和零售业	Wholesale and Retail Trades	255.65	
交通运输、仓储和邮政业	Transport, Storage and Post	1321.90	0.03
住宿和餐饮业	Hotels and Catering Services	247.76	
信息传输、软件和信息技术服务业	Information Transmission, Software and Information Technology	343.53	
金融业	Financial Intermediation	77.39	
房地产业	Real Estate	512.15	
租赁和商务服务业	Leasing and Business Services	226.49	
科学研究和技术服务业	Scientific Research and Technical Services	214.86	
水利、环境和公共设施管理业	Management of Water Conservancy,Environment and Public Facilities	76.32	
居民服务、修理和其他服务业	Service to Households, Repair and Other Services	47.93	
教　育	Education	266.65	
卫生和社会工作	Health and Social Service	118.68	
文化、体育和娱乐业	Culture, Sports and Entertainment	91.80	
公共管理、社会保障和社会组织	Public Management, Social Security and Social Organization	121.55	
居民生活	Household Consumption	1945.52	7.20

7-11 Continued

(10000 tons)

汽 油 Gasoline	煤 油 Kerosene	柴 油 Diesel Oil	燃料油 Fuel Oil	液 化 石油气 Liquefied Petroleum Gas	液 化 天然气 Liquefied Natural Gas	天然气 (亿立方米) Natural Gas (100 million cu.m)	热 力 (万百万千焦) Heat (10 billion kilo-joule)	电 力 (亿千瓦时) Electricity (100 million kW·h)
0.01		...				0.90	0.81	2.87
0.02		0.01				0.04	4.77	1.45
0.28		0.13	...	0.01		0.11	24.94	2.58
0.33	...	0.07		0.07	0.01	0.12	65.80	4.87
0.51		0.23		0.02	0.01	0.12	96.33	5.50
0.25		0.81		0.02		1.58	63.48	18.02
0.20	...	0.05		...	0.01	0.09	119.66	4.84
0.34		0.05		...		0.09	34.08	4.71
0.27	...	0.04	...	...		0.55	249.79	43.20
0.21		0.01		...		0.03	38.11	1.51
0.04	...	0.11		...		0.02	36.99	1.03
0.01		0.05	...	...		...	0.06	0.33
0.15	0.04	0.09		...		0.10	3.59	1.42
0.56		1.23	0.16	0.04	0.41	129.97	199.92	104.35
0.33		1.06	0.16	0.01	0.40	125.83	164.24	78.22
0.10		0.01		0.01	...	4.03	5.98	0.42
0.13		0.16		0.02	0.01	0.11	29.69	25.71
6.65	...	12.85	...	0.20		0.29	146.49	24.51
11.73	...	3.35	0.01	0.44		0.96	669.23	73.77
17.99	638.36	72.29	...	0.18	16.25	1.31	510.66	67.86
0.95	...	0.11	0.05	0.79		6.06	670.83	52.36
2.71		0.47	...	0.10		0.42	433.57	118.55
0.84		0.02		...		0.22	313.88	23.38
2.06		0.22	...	0.09		10.98	1786.84	112.45
8.38	0.03	10.27	0.01	0.32		1.33	905.95	55.62
6.01	0.60	1.47	0.01	0.22		1.82	1218.58	51.11
1.42		6.43		0.05		0.51	67.29	20.59
1.45		1.10	...	0.06		1.19	203.84	7.56
1.01	0.01	0.44	0.01	0.14		5.38	1645.45	49.25
0.79		0.08	0.01	0.08		1.55	628.47	27.52
1.15		0.31	...	0.11		0.80	510.22	22.56
1.84		0.39		0.20		0.83	924.45	25.36
338.97				10.49		19.83	6192.27	334.58

7-12 能源消费弹性系数(2000-2023年)
ELASTICITY RATIO OF ENERGY CONSUMPTION (2000-2023)

年份 Year	能源消费比上年增长 (%) Growth Rate of Energy Consumption over Preceding Year (%)	电力消费比上年增长 (%) Growth Rate of Electricity Consumption over Preceding Year (%)	能源消费弹性系数 Elasticity Ratio of Energy Consumption	电力消费弹性系数 Elasticity Ratio of Electricity Consumption
2000	6.08	9.53	0.51	0.79
2001	2.06	5.68	0.17	0.48
2002	4.89	9.54	0.41	0.81
2003	4.78	5.71	0.43	0.51
2004	10.57	10.60	0.79	0.80
2005	7.44	11.16	0.60	0.91
2006	6.92	9.16	0.54	0.72
2007	6.45	9.06	0.45	0.63
2008	0.67	4.90	0.07	0.55
2009	3.84	7.15	0.38	0.71
2010	5.84	9.49	0.56	0.91
2011	0.59	2.21	0.07	0.27
2012	2.61	5.91	0.34	0.77
2013	2.44	4.42	0.32	0.57
2014	1.60	2.72	0.22	0.37
2015	0.31	1.91	0.04	0.28
2016	1.67	7.25	0.24	1.05
2017	2.48	4.57	0.36	0.67
2018	2.56	7.08	0.38	1.06
2019	1.25	2.10	0.21	0.35
2020	-8.13	-2.24	0.00	0.00
2021	5.05	8.13	0.57	0.92
2022	-2.91	3.88	0.00	5.39
2023	9.78	6.01	1.90	1.17

7-13 平均每万元地区生产总值能源消费量(2010-2023年) AVERAGE ENERGY CONSUMPTION PER 10000 YUAN OF GDP (2010-2023)

年 份 Year	能源总消费量 (吨标准煤) Total Energy Consumption (tce)	煤 炭 (千克) Coal (kg)	电 力 (千瓦时) Electricity (kW·h)	石 油 (千克) Petroleum (kg)	天然气 (立方米) Natural Gas (cu.m)
	地区生产总值按2010年不变价格计算 GDP at 2010 constant price				
2010	0.425	169.07	537.23	90.59	49.98
2011	0.396	140.04	508.04	89.50	45.45
2012	0.377	125.10	499.50	82.02	52.85
2013	0.358	107.57	484.10	78.89	52.64
2014	0.339	86.14	463.00	76.30	56.40
2015	0.316	54.06	441.32	73.48	68.14
	地区生产总值按2015年不变价格计算 GDP at 2015 constant price				
2015	0.275	47.02	383.89	63.92	59.28
2016	0.261	31.99	385.10	59.58	61.26
2017	0.251	17.33	377.06	58.52	58.16
2018	0.241	9.15	378.40	56.55	62.23
2019	0.230	5.71	364.28	54.73	59.15
2020	0.209	4.17	352.41	42.16	59.26
	地区生产总值按2020年不变价格计算 GDP at 2020 constant price				
2020	0.188	3.76	317.23	37.95	53.35
2021	0.182	3.34	315.13	35.44	49.27
2022	0.175	2.01	325.03	27.63	50.83
2023	0.183	1.50	327.67	34.34	48.73

7-14 人均生活用能源(2010-2023年)
HOUSEHOLD ENERGY CONSUMPTION PER CAPITA (2010-2023)

年 份 Year	合 计 (千克标准煤) Total (kgce)	煤 炭 (千克) Coal (kg)	电 力 (千瓦时) Electricity (kW·h)	液化石油气 (千克) Liquefied Petroleum Gas (kg)	天然气 (立方米) Natural Gas (cu.m)	汽 油 (升) Gasoline (liter)
2010	650.2	173.6	729.1	11.3	53.1	164.9
2011	662.4	166.9	726.3	10.6	52.6	167.4
2012	690.9	158.5	789.2	9.3	56.3	173.9
2013	684.4	147.0	747.3	9.8	56.8	179.9
2014	700.4	136.6	787.9	10.9	59.2	181.3
2015	689.5	125.3	801.8	11.5	63.1	192.7
2016	707.7	109.8	891.6	12.0	58.5	196.5
2017	753.0	82.4	993.4	11.8	74.7	205.1
2018	771.7	34.7	1168.9	10.9	64.3	223.1
2019	772.0	22.2	1148.4	8.6	66.6	231.5
2020	782.3	16.4	1277.9	4.9	72.4	206.8
2021	835.6	8.7	1308.4	4.8	80.2	237.3
2022	852.1	5.4	1467.8	5.5	93.9	185.6
2023	890.4	3.3	1531.2	4.8	90.8	212.5

注：本表人均生活用能源按常住人口年平均数计算。2011—2019年数据根据北京市第七次全国人口普查结果进行了修订。

Note: Data on household energy consumption per capita in the table are calculated with the data on the annual average resident population. Data from 2011 to 2019 have been revised based on the results of the Seventh National Population Census in Beijing.

7-15 全社会用电量情况(1978-2023年)
TOTAL ELECTRICITY CONSUMPTION IN BEIJING (1978-2023)

单位：万千瓦时 (10000 kW·h)

年份 Year	全社会用电量 Electricity Consumption	第一产业 Primary Industry	第二产业 Secondary Industry			第三产业 Tertiary Industry	城乡居民生活用电 Household Electricity Consumption		
				工业 Industry	建筑业 Construction			城市 Urban	乡村 Rural
1978	735000	48993	570621	570621		94555	20831	11022	9809
1979	802317	52134	620262	620262		107437	22484	11495	10989
1980	854638	65283	648496	648496		116947	23912	12441	11471
1981	867153	80027	643976	643976		121883	21267	9452	11815
1982	925700	104842	657060	657060		139403	24395	10820	13575
1983	956293	92601	687937	687937		151290	24465	12320	12145
1984	1029420	105234	716653	716653		177455	30078	16025	14053
1985	1106255	111110	746324	746324		210622	38199	22479	15720
1986	1181155	105688	851519	835725	15794	175090	48858	31008	17850
1987	1285023	77909	923797	899760	24037	224747	58570	35063	23507
1988	1378574	83809	970885	943383	27502	248446	75434	48624	26810
1989	1421817	100151	979216	949629	29587	258067	84383	56120	28263
1990	1504785	93049	1014037	986356	27681	302775	94924	65262	29662
1991	1613977	93256	1061207	1032064	29143	348769	110745	77575	33170
1992	1759611	101985	1155514	1123835	31679	375874	126238	88621	37617
1993	1924978	107010	1243115	1206001	37114	429835	145018	103579	41439
1994	2054504	101134	1307898	1262961	44937	479679	165791	119025	46766
1995	2225922	102099	1403864	1341398	62466	538936	181022	130897	50125
1996	2443709	111904	1496968	1422590	74378	617286	217551	158474	59077
1997	2636078	120444	1529201	1449129	80072	721774	264659	196641	68018
1998	2762080	108267	1548485	1457149	91336	811283	294045	220543	73502
1999	2972629	121242	1581977	1478523	103454	912834	356576	276642	79934
2000	3844266	130865	2172604	2066892	105712	1064322	476475	385396	91079
2001	3999415	131811	2105819	1978673	127146	1222471	539314	439058	100256
2002	4399637	137370	2293735	2145292	148443	1342490	626042	517386	108656
2003	4676056	107372	2418419	2250525	167894	1447344	702921	574623	128298
2004	5131804	104234	2593504	2391414	202090	1628731	805335	647474	157861
2005	5705364	114308	2795753	2605832	189921	1906093	889210	706405	182805
2006	6115719	122550	2943550	2744127	199423	2090888	958731	768884	189847
2007	6670089	133557	3091374	2881807	209567	2378399	1066759	862604	204155
2008	6897189	136065	2943893	2763399	180494	2654140	1163091	949878	213213
2009	7391465	157310	3027974	2853018	174956	2918229	1287952	982720	305232
2010	8099029	168992	3278682	3081364	197319	3258009	1393346	951811	441535
2011	8217055	170368	3109174	2894464	214708	3490143	1447370	945588	501782
2012	8742835	181391	3209078	2980645	228430	3734022	1618344	1370932	247412
2013	9131113	185749	3345854	3110626	235229	4029145	1570365	1347401	222964
2014	9370485	185633	3352904	3129060	223846	4139319	1692629	1457398	235231
2015	9527169	185031	3238220	3030638	207583	4356332	1747586	1496078	251508
2016	10202704	196243	3343189	3129675	213514	4708959	1954313	1664539	289774
2017	10668904	112930	3323724	3105551	218276	5063019	2169231	1842219	327012
2018	11423809	106382	3316045	3073165	253012	5437818	2563564	2106181	457383
2019	11663964	98872	3254317	2990649	263949	5794810	2515964	2049447	466517
2020	11399700	90673	2944549	2696395	248451	5566552	2797925	2306966	490959
2021	12329152	94160	3077101	2811754	265681	6294023	2863869	2356386	507482
2022	12808016	91235	3051841	2794799	257647	6455725	3209216	2666550	542666
2023	13577778	91978	2996442	2752332	245051	7143598	3345760	2770619	575140

注：1.1985年以前农、林、牧、渔和水利业用电量中，只包含农业排灌、农副业和社队企业的用电量。
2.1980年以前的城市居民用电量以全市市政用电量的 1/10计算。
3.2000年以前工业用电量不包含输配损失和发电企业自产自用电量。
4.自2018年起，行业划分执行《国民经济行业分类》(GB/T 4754—2017)标准，为保证数据可比，对2017年数据进行了修订。

资料来源：国网北京市电力公司。

Note: a) Before 1985, electricity consumption by agriculture, forestry, animal husbandry and fishery and water conservancy only included the electricity consumption by farming irrigation, agricultural and sideline products, and village enterprises.
b) Before 1980, electricity consumption by urban households was one-tenth of the total electricity consumption by municipal administration in Beijing.
c) Before 2000, electricity consumption by industry excluded transmission and distribution losses and electricity generated and consumed by power generating enterprises.
d) Sectors are classified in accordance with the standards in the Industrial Classification of the National Economy (GB/T 4754-2017) since 2018. In order to keep the data comparable, the data of 2017 have been revised.

Source: State Grid Beijing Electric Power Company.

7-16 水资源情况(2001-2023年)

单位：亿立方米

项　目	Item	2001	2002	2003	2004	2005	2006	2007
全年水资源总量	**Total Water Resources in the Year**	**19.2**	**16.1**	**18.4**	**21.4**	**23.2**	**22.1**	**23.8**
地表水资源量	Surface Water Resources	7.8	5.3	6.1	8.2	7.6	6.7	7.6
地下水资源量	Groundwater Resources	15.7	14.7	14.8	16.5	15.6	15.4	16.2
人均水资源(立方米)	**Per Capita Water Resources (cu.m)**	**139.7**	**114.7**	**127.8**	**145.1**	**153.1**	**140.6**	**145.3**
水资源配置量	**Water Resources Allocation**	**38.9**	**34.6**	**35.8**	**34.6**	**34.5**	**34.3**	**34.8**
按来源分	By Source							
地表水	Surface Water	11.7	10.4	8.3	5.7	7.0	6.4	5.7
地下水	Groundwater	27.2	24.2	25.4	26.8	24.9	24.3	24.2
再生水	Recycled Water			2.1	2.0	2.6	3.6	5.0
南水北调水	Water Transit from South to North							
全年用水总量	**Water Use in the Year**	**38.9**	**34.6**	**35.8**	**34.6**	**34.5**	**34.3**	**34.8**
按用途分	By Purpose							
农业用水	Water Used by Agriculture	17.4	15.5	13.8	13.5	13.2	12.8	12.4
工业用水	Water Used by Industry	9.2	7.6	8.4	7.7	6.8	6.2	5.8
生活用水	Water Used by Households and Service	12.0	10.8	13.0	12.8	13.4	13.7	13.9
生态环境用水	Water for the Eco-environment	0.3	0.8	0.6	0.6	1.1	1.6	2.7
万元地区生产总值水耗(立方米)	**Water Consumption per 10000 yuan of GDP (cu.m)**	**100.81**	**76.50**	**67.97**	**55.26**	**48.25**	**40.90**	**33.38**
万元地区生产总值水耗下降率(%)	**Decrease Rate of Water Consumption per 10000 yuan of GDP (%)**	**13.81**	**20.46**	**6.92**	**14.82**	**11.08**	**11.86**	**11.32**

注：1.本表人均水资源按常住人口年平均数计算。2011—2019年数据根据北京市第七次全国人口普查结果进行了修订。
2.自2020年起，原“全年供水总量”更名为“水资源配置量”。
3.万元地区生产总值水耗按当年价格计算，下降率按不变价格计算。如按不变价格计算，2023年万元地区生产总值水耗为9.82立方米。
4.2023年万元地区生产总值水耗及下降率为初步核算数。
资料来源：除人均数据、万元地区生产总值水耗及其下降率以外，其他数据来自北京市水务局。

WATER RESOURCES(2001-2023)

(100 million cu.m)

2008	2009	2010	2011	2012	2013	2014	2015	2016	2017	2018	2019	2020	2021	2022	2023
34.2	**21.8**	**23.1**	**26.8**	**39.5**	**24.8**	**20.3**	**26.8**	**35.1**	**29.8**	**35.5**	**24.6**	**25.8**	**61.3**	**23.7**	**41.5**
12.8	6.8	7.2	9.2	18.0	9.4	6.5	9.3	14.0	12.0	14.3	8.6	8.3	31.6	7.4	21.9
21.4	15.1	15.9	17.6	21.6	15.4	13.8	17.4	21.1	17.7	21.1	16.0	17.5	29.7	16.4	19.6
198.5	**120.3**	**120.8**	**134.5**	**192.6**	**118.1**	**94.3**	**122.8**	**160.0**	**135.6**	**161.7**	**112.1**	**117.6**	**280.1**	**108.6**	**190.0**
35.1	**35.5**	**35.2**	**36.0**	**35.9**	**36.4**	**37.5**	**38.2**	**38.8**	**39.5**	**39.3**	**41.7**	**40.6**	**40.8**	**40.0**	**40.7**
5.5	4.6	4.6	5.5	5.2	4.8	8.5	2.9	2.9	3.6	3.0	6.6	8.5	4.4	5.9	6.2
22.9	21.8	21.2	20.9	20.4	20.1	19.6	18.2	17.5	16.6	16.3	15.5	13.5	13.9	12.2	12.4
6.0	6.5	6.8	7.0	7.5	8.0	8.6	9.5	10.0	10.5	10.8	11.5	12.0	12.0	12.1	12.8
0.7	2.6	2.6	2.6	2.8	3.5	0.8	7.6	8.4	8.8	9.3	8.1	6.6	10.5	9.9	9.3
35.1	**35.5**	**35.2**	**36.0**	**35.9**	**36.4**	**37.5**	**38.2**	**38.8**	**39.5**	**39.3**	**41.7**	**40.6**	**40.8**	**40.0**	**40.7**
12.0	12.0	11.4	10.9	9.3	9.1	8.2	6.5	6.1	5.1	4.2	3.7	3.2	2.8	2.6	2.5
5.2	5.2	5.1	5.0	4.9	5.1	5.1	3.8	3.8	3.5	3.3	3.3	3.0	2.9	2.4	2.8
14.7	14.7	14.7	15.6	16.0	16.3	17.0	17.5	17.8	18.3	18.4	18.7	17.0	18.4	18.6	19.0
3.2	3.6	4.0	4.5	5.7	5.9	7.2	10.4	11.1	12.6	13.4	16.0	17.4	16.7	16.4	16.4
29.71	**27.52**	**23.50**	**20.92**	**18.86**	**17.21**	**16.35**	**15.42**	**14.35**	**13.22**	**11.87**	**11.76**	**11.30**	**9.95**	**9.64**	**9.30**
7.45	**8.08**	**10.28**	**5.38**	**7.37**	**5.89**	**4.05**	**4.70**	**4.98**	**4.70**	**6.75**	**0.02**	**3.58**	**7.62**	**2.67**	**3.31**

Note: a) Data on per capita water resources in the table are calculated in terms of the annual average resident population. Data for 2011-2019 have been revised in accordance with the results of the Seventh National Population Census in Beijing.

b) Since 2020, the original "total water supply in the year" has been changed to "water resources allocation".

c) Water consumption per 10 000 yuan of GDP is calculated at current prices, and decrease rate is calculated at constant prices. If calculated at constant prices, the water consumption per 10 000 yuan of GDP in 2023 was 9.82 cubic meters.

d) The data on water consumption per 10 000 yuan of GDP and its decrease rate in 2023 are the preliminary accounting data.

Source: Except for the per capita data and the data on water consumption per 10 000 yuan of GDP and its decrease rate, all the other data are from Beijing Water Authority.

7-17 分行业规模以上工业用水量情况
WATER USE OF INDUSTRIAL ENTERPRISES ABOVE DESIGNATED SIZE BY SECTOR

项目	Item	用水量(万立方米) Water Use (10000 cu.m)		重复用水率(%) Reuse Rate of Water(%)	
		2023	2023年为2022年% 2023 as % of 2022	2023	2022
合计	**Total**	**24645.5**	**103.4**	**95.5**	**95.6**
采矿业	**Mining**	**747.1**	**72.8**	**92.6**	**91.9**
煤炭开采和洗选业	Mining and Washing of Coal				
石油和天然气开采业	Extraction of Petroleum and Natural Gas	2.5	95.4		
黑色金属矿采选业	Mining and Processing of Ferrous Metal Ores	645.0	73.2	93.6	92.9
有色金属矿采选业	Mining and Processing of Non-Ferrous Metal Ores				
非金属矿采选业	Mining and Processing of Nonmetal Ores				
开采专业及辅助性活动	Professional and Support Activities for Mining	99.6	70.5		
其他采矿业	Mining of Other Ores				
制造业	**Manufacturing**	**12764.0**	**105.3**	**95.2**	**95.7**
农副食品加工业	Processing of Food from Agricultural Products	484.9	104.3	75.9	77.6
食品制造业	Manufacture of Foods	675.2	104.2	90.5	89.0
酒、饮料和精制茶制造业	Manufacture of Liquor, Beverages and Refined Tea	1593.3	107.7	58.6	61.7
烟草制品业	Manufacture of Tobacco	16.6	106.7	98.2	98.5
纺织业	Manufacture of Textile	1.6	79.4		
纺织服装、服饰业	Manufacture of Textile, Wearing Apparel and Accessories	46.4	91.2	0.5	0.4
皮革、毛皮、羽毛及其制品和制鞋业	Manufacture of Leather, Fur, Feather and Related Products and Footwear	0.5	264.2		
木材加工和木、竹、藤、棕、草制品业	Processing of Timber, Manufacture of Wood, Bamboo, Rattan, Palm and Straw Products	0.1	76.8		
家具制造业	Manufacture of Furniture	26.9	80.3	4.9	3.5
造纸和纸制品业	Manufacture of Paper and Paper Products	49.6	95.9	71.0	70.5
印刷和记录媒介复制业	Printing and Reproduction of Recording Media	160.9	95.6	67.4	63.7
文教、工美、体育和娱乐用品制造业	Manufacture of Articles for Culture, Education, Arts and Crafts, Sport and Entertainment Activities	15.7	116.2		
石油、煤炭及其他燃料加工业	Processing of Petroleum, Coal and Other Fuels	1953.6	112.0	98.6	98.8
化学原料和化学制品制造业	Manufacture of Raw Chemical Materials and Chemical Products	276.3	94.5	98.5	98.6
医药制造业	Manufacture of Medicines	1537.7	101.0	83.3	80.9
化学纤维制造业	Manufacture of Chemical Fibers	10.8	110.5	97.2	97.5
橡胶和塑料制品业	Manufacture of Rubber and Plastics Products	37.8	101.8	95.6	96.5
非金属矿物制品业	Manufacture of Non-metallic Mineral Products	693.2	95.1	86.6	86.4
黑色金属冶炼和压延加工业	Smelting and Pressing of Ferrous Metals	176.3	100.6	97.8	97.8
有色金属冶炼和压延加工业	Smelting and Pressing of Non-ferrous Metals	57.2	110.9	95.2	95.4
金属制品业	Manufacture of Metal Products	79.2	101.1	38.3	19.5
通用设备制造业	Manufacture of General Purpose Machinery	174.5	93.8	89.2	90.9
专用设备制造业	Manufacture of Special Purpose Machinery	267.9	104.9	47.6	55.3
汽车制造业	Manufacture of Automobiles	796.3	99.0	93.1	93.3
铁路、船舶、航空航天和其他运输设备制造业	Manufacture of Railway, Ship, Aerospace and Other Transport Equipments	66.7	99.2	94.5	94.3
电气机械和器材制造业	Manufacture of Electrical Machinery and Apparatus	151.3	102.8	11.9	14.9
计算机、通信和其他电子设备制造业	Manufacture of Computers, Communication and Other Electronic Equipment	3201.4	110.6	93.3	95.3
仪器仪表制造业	Manufacture of Measuring Instruments and Machinery	55.8	102.1	1.0	0.5
其他制造业	Other Manufacture	5.2	85.5		
废弃资源综合利用业	Utilization of Waste Resources	17.5	108.3		
金属制品、机械和设备修理业	Repair Service of Metal Products, Machinery and Equipment	133.6	109.4		
电力、热力、燃气及水生产和供应业	**Production and Supply of Electricity, Heat, Gas and Water**	**11134.4**	**104.2**	**95.8**	**95.7**
电力、热力生产和供应业	Production and Supply of Electric Power and Heat Power	6674.5	103.2	97.3	97.1
燃气生产和供应业	Production and Supply of Gas	33.6	96.4		
水的生产和供应业	Production and Supply of Water	4426.3	105.8	79.6	79.7

注：重复用水率=重复用水量/(用新水量+重复用水量)×100%。
Note: Reuse Rate of Water = Volume of Water Used Repeatedly / (Volume of New Water Used + Volume of Water Used Repeatedly)×100%.

7-18 气象情况(1978-2023年)
METEOROLOGY (1978-2023)

年 份 Year	降水量 (毫米) Precipitation (mm)	平均气温(℃) Average Temperature (℃)			日照时数(时) Hours of Sunshine (hour)	平均风速(米/秒) Average Wind Speed (meter/second)	平均气压(百帕) Average Air Pressure (100 pa)	大风日数(日) Days of Strong Wind (day)	雨日数(日) Days of Rain (day)
			最高 Highest	最低 Lowest					
1978	664.8	11.6	37.5	-14.4	2865.4	2.6	1012.8	35	64
1979	718.4	11.1	35.9	-15.4	2667.4	2.5	1012.2	33	63
1980	380.7	11.0	35.1	-15.4	2920.8	2.5	1012.7	29	83
1981	393.2	12.3	38.1	-14.0	2803.9	2.5	1010.8	15	92
1982	544.4	12.8	37.3	-14.3	2825.1	2.6	1010.5	26	92
1983	489.9	13.0	37.2	-15.0	2844.3	2.4	1010.3	29	100
1984	488.8	11.9	36.1	-14.9	2767.6	2.4	1010.6	18	90
1985	721.0	11.5	35.1	-15.2	2511.9	2.2	1010.4	12	104
1986	665.3	12.1	38.5	-15.4	2804.1	2.3	1010.7	21	96
1987	683.9	12.3	36.1	-15.5	2631.9	2.4	1010.3	23	102
1988	673.3	12.7	38.1	-13.2	2558.1	2.4	1010.8	17	96
1989	442.2	13.2	35.8	-11.0	2626.2	1.9	1011.1	3	78
1990	697.3	12.7	37.5	-14.8	2325.0	1.9	1010.6	12	113
1991	747.9	12.5	35.7	-12.6	2536.6	2.1	1010.8	8	98
1992	541.5	12.8	37.5	-8.7	2712.5	2.2	1011.0	6	100
1993	506.7	13.0	35.8	-13.0	2669.8	2.6	1010.8	12	91
1994	813.2	13.7	37.2	-11.5	2470.5	2.5	1010.1	9	92
1995	572.5	13.3	35.0	-9.2	2519.1	2.6	1010.3	16	89
1996	700.9	12.7	36.0	-10.0	2418.7	2.6	1011.0	16	103
1997	430.9	13.1	38.2	-14.0	2596.5	2.5	1012.9	11	76
1998	731.7	13.1	37.2	-14.2	2420.7	2.3	1012.5	10	93
1999	266.9	13.1	41.9	-12.2	2594.0	2.4	1012.5	7	86
2000	371.1	12.8	39.4	-15.0	2667.2	2.5	1012.7	10	83
2001	338.9	12.9	39.6	-17.0	2611.7	2.4	1012.9	10	78
2002	370.4	13.2	41.1	-12.8	2588.4	2.3	1012.7	15	84
2003	444.9	12.9	37.6	-15.0	2260.2	2.5	1013.3	6	93
2004	483.5	13.5	38.9	-12.9	2515.4	2.4	1012.6	12	94
2005	410.7	13.2	38.9	-11.5	2576.1	2.4	1012.8	5	79
2006	318.0	13.4	37.3	-14.7	2192.7	2.2	1012.5	5	86
2007	483.9	14.0	37.3	-11.7	2351.1	2.2	1012.6	5	78
2008	626.3	13.4	36.3	-13.5	2391.4	2.2	1012.6	8	100
2009	480.6	13.3	39.6	-12.2	2511.8	2.2	1011.9	15	86
2010	522.5	12.6	40.6	-16.7	2382.9	2.3	1012.2	14	88
2011	720.6	13.4	35.9	-11.6	2485.7	2.2	1013.2	3	82
2012	733.2	12.9	38.0	-13.7	2450.2	2.2	1012.2	3	85
2013	578.9	12.8	38.2	-14.1	2371.1	2.1	1012.2	3	71
2014	461.5	14.1	41.1	-11.2	2344.1	2.1	1013.0	8	77
2015	458.6	13.7	38.9	-9.2	2420.2	2.1	1013.2	7	99
2016	669.1	13.8	37.8	-15.2	2502.1	2.1	1013.1	2	86
2017	576.2	14.2	38.5	-10.1	2600.1	2.1	1013.1	4	78
2018	546.5	13.6	39.9	-13.9	2483.7	2.0	1013.2	3	73
2019	406.3	13.8	38.0	-14.4	2542.3	2.1	1013.1	8	65
2020	527.1	13.8	37.8	-12.8	2527.4	2.0	1013.1	4	96
2021	698.4	13.6	37.2	-19.6	2292.2	1.9	1012.4	8	109
2022	585.4	13.4	39.2	-11.3	2579.1	1.9	1012.8	5	77
2023	630.8	14.3	41.1	-16.7	2568.1	2.0	1012.3	6	69

资料来源：北京市气象局。
Source: Beijing Meteorological Service.

7-19 气 象(2023年)
METEOROLOGY (2023)

月 份 Month	降水量 (毫米) Precipitation (mm)	平均气温(℃) Average Temperature (℃)	日照时数(时) Hours of Sunshine (hour)	平均风速(米/秒) Average Wind Speed (meter/second)	平均气压(百帕) Average Air Pressure (100 pa)	大风日数(日) Days of Strong Wind (day)	雨日数(日) Days of Rain (day)
全 年 Total	**630.8**	**14.3**	**2568.1**	**2.0**	**1012.3**	**6**	**69**
1	1.2	-2.5	218.3	2.0	1023.1	1	2
2	6.4	1.6	166.0	1.8	1024.1	1	3
3	0.3	10.7	242.0	2.4	1015.0	1	3
4	21.0	15.2	184.1	2.5	1009.8		8
5	14.3	21.9	212.4	2.2	1006.2		11
6	15.7	28.4	313.1	2.1	999.9		5
7	321.7	29.0	232.8	2.1	999.0	1	10
8	104.6	27.3	198.4	1.7	1002.0		14
9	119.8	22.7	189.3	1.4	1009.6		6
10	3.7	15.6	233.9	1.4	1015.0		6
11	8.0	4.8	200.5	2.1	1020.1	1	1
12	14.1	-3.5	177.3	1.7	1024.3	1	

注：1.年极端最高气温41.1℃，出现日期6月22日。
2.年极端最低气温-16.7℃，出现日期1月25日。
资料来源：北京市气象局。
Note: a) Annual utmost highest air temperature is 41.1℃, seen on the June 22th .
b) Annual utmost lowest air temperature is -16.7℃, seen on the January 25th.
Source: Beijing Meteorological Service.

7-20 污水处理及环境卫生(1978-2023年)
SEWAGE DISPOSAL AND ENVIRONMENTAL SANITATION (1978-2023)

年份 Year	污水管道长度(公里) Length of Sewage Pipes (km)	污水处理能力(万立方米/日) Sewage Disposal Capacity (10000 cu.m/day)	污水处理率(%) Sewage Disposal Rate (%)	再生水利用量(万立方米) Recycled Water Used (10000 cu.m)	生活垃圾无害化处理能力(吨/日) Harmless Treatment Capacity of Domestic Garbage (ton/day)	生活垃圾产生量(万吨) Domestic Garbage Generated (10000 tons)	生活垃圾清运量(万吨) Volume of Domestic Garbage Collected and Transported (10000 tons)	生活垃圾无害化处理率(%) Rate of Domestic Garbage Harmless Treatment (%)	粪便清运量(万吨) Volume of Excrement Collected and Transported (10000 tons)
1978	290	23.2	7.6				107.2		88.9
1979	309	23.2	10.2				128.0		89.4
1980	334	23.2	9.4				147.0		95.1
1981	347	25.2	10.8				174.0		97.6
1982	365	25.2	10.9				204.7		99.3
1983	411	25.2	10.2				221.4		99.5
1984	568	25.2	10.0				235.4		98.8
1985	706	25.2	10.0				248.1		142.2
1986	747	26.4	8.9				274.4		167.5
1987	805	26.4	7.7				298.3		181.0
1988	770	26.4	7.4				319.9		190.0
1989	860	26.4	6.6				337.0		196.0
1990	904	30.4	7.3				384.1		210.0
1991	968	30.4	6.6				397.1		210.3
1992	1036	4.5	1.2				430.9		216.0
1993	1064	4.5	3.1				446.3		220.6
1994	1122	24.5	9.6				467.2		238.1
1995	1065	58.5	19.4				483.9		258.4
1996	1597	58.5	21.2				483.0		268.0
1997	1635	58.5	22.0				490.0		279.0
1998	1712	58.5	22.5				495.1		295.6
1999	1754	58.5	25.0				505.0		298.0
2000	1852	128.5	39.4		6550		295.6	56.40	274.0
2001	2163	143.5	42.0		6750		309.3	82.15	301.0
2002	2658	180.6	45.0		8750		321.4	86.36	311.7
2003	2903	215.0	50.1		9400		361.4	91.31	268.0
2004	2909	255.0	53.9		10050	495.5	405.9	93.78	175.0
2005	2521	324.0	62.4	23816	10350	536.9	454.6	95.96	171.7
2006	3398	331.0	73.2	36088	10350	585.1	538.3	92.45	175.7
2007	4357	348.0	76.2	49501	10350	619.5	600.9	95.70	189.1
2008	4458	329.4	78.9	60000	12148	672.8	656.6	97.71	206.8
2009	4495	356.0	80.3	64999	13680	669.1	656.1	98.22	211.2
2010	4479	365.0	81.0	68014	16680	634.9	633.0	96.95	194.4
2011	4765	369.4	82.0	71012	16930	634.4	634.4	98.24	207.5
2012	5735	388.5	83.0	75003	17530	648.3	648.3	99.12	207.2
2013	6363	393.0	84.6	80108	21971	671.7	671.7	99.30	220.7
2014	6536	425.0	86.1	86620	21971	733.8	733.8	99.59	216.1
2015	7157	439.5	87.9	94826	27321	790.3	790.3	99.80	204.7
2016	7889	612.0	90.0	100398	24341	872.6	872.6	99.84	204.0
2017	10207	665.6	92.4	105085	24341	924.8	924.8	99.88	214.3
2018	12147	670.6	93.4	107633	28591	975.7	975.7	99.94	201.1
2019	13188	679.2	94.5	115152	32711	1011.2	1011.2	99.98	198.0
2020	14920	687.9	95.0	120133	33811	797.5	797.5	100.00	201.7
2021	16132	707.9	95.8	120315	33861	784.2	784.2	100.00	209.4
2022	18050	712.1	97.0	120540	31461	740.6	740.6	100.00	211.5
2023	18997	721.6	97.3	127697	28426	758.9	758.9	100.00	218.5

注：1.污水处理能力等指标自1992年起为污水无害化处理情况，1992年以前为污水简易处理情况。
2.生活垃圾无害化处理率按清运量计算。

资料来源：北京市水务局、北京市城市管理委员会。

Note: a) The data on sewage disposal capacity and other indicators since 1992 have been about harmless disposal of sewage, and those before 1992 were about simple disposal of sewage.

b) The rate of domestic garbage harmless treatment is calculated in terms of the volume collected and transported.

Source: Beijing Water Authority, Beijing Municipal Commission of Urban Management.

7-21 排水及节水
WATER DRAINAGE AND SAVING

项　目	Item	2023	2022
排　水	**Water Drainage**		
污水处理能力　(万立方米/日)	Sewage Disposal Capacity (10000 cu.m/day)	721.6	712.1
污水年处理量　(万立方米)	Annual Disposal Volume of Sewage (10000 cu.m)	230109	222087
#污水厂	Disposed by Sewage Disposal Plants	222670	214661
污水处理率　(%)	Sewage Disposal Rate (%)	97.3	97.0
污水排放总量　(万立方米)	Total Volume of Sewage Drainage (10000 cu.m)	236454	228913
排水管道长度　(公里)	Length of Drainage Pipelines (km)	29929	28939
污水管	Sewage Pipes	18997	18050
雨水管	Rain Pipes	9470	9398
雨污合流管	Rain-sewage Sewer	1462	1491
再生水利用量　(万立方米)	Volume of Recycled Water Used (10000 cu.m)	127697	120540
节　水	**Water Saving**		
节水量　(万立方米)	Volume Saved (10000 cu.m)	9346	7373
节水措施　(项)	Water Saving Measures Implemented (unit)	56	63

资料来源：北京市水务局。
Source: Beijing Water Authority.

7-22 环境卫生
MUNICIPAL ENVIRONMENTAL SANITATION

项　目	Item	2023	2022
工作量	**Work Load**		
清扫街道面积　(万平方米/日)	Area of Cleaned Streets (10000 sq.m/day)	17804	17812
生活垃圾无害化处理能力　(吨/日)	Harmless Treatment Capacity of Domestic Garbage (ton/day)	28426	31461
生活垃圾清运量　(万吨)	Volume of Domestic Garbage Collected and Transported (10000 tons)	758.9	740.6
生活垃圾无害化处理量　(万吨)	Volume of Domestic Garbage Harmlessly Treated (10000 tons)	758.9	740.6
生活垃圾无害化处理率	Rate of Domestic Garbage Harmless Treatment	100.0	100.0
(按清运量计算)　(%)	(Calculated by Volume of Garbage Collected and Transported) (%)		
餐厨垃圾处理量　(万吨)	Volume of Kitchen Garbage Treated (10000 tons)	75.2	58.1
粪便清运量　(万吨)	Volume of Excrement Collected and Transported (10000 tons)	218.5	211.5
环卫机械数量　(辆)	**Number of Environmental Sanitation Machinery (unit)**	**12291**	**12159**
环卫设施	**Environmental Sanitation Facilities**		
公共厕所　(座)	Public Lavatories (unit)	7122	6435

资料来源：北京市城市管理委员会。
Source: Beijing Municipal Commission of Urban Management.

7-23 环境保护(2000-2023年)
ENVIRONMENTAL PROTECTION (2000-2023)

年份 Year	可吸入颗粒物 (PM_{10}) 年平均浓度值 (微克/立方米) Annual Average Concentration of PM_{10} (μg/cu.m)	细颗粒物 ($PM_{2.5}$) 年平均浓度值 (微克/立方米) Annual Average Concentration of $PM_{2.5}$ (μg/cu.m)	二氧化硫 (SO_2) 年平均浓度值 (微克/立方米) Annual Average Concentration of SO_2 (μg/cu.m)	二氧化氮 (NO_2) 年平均浓度值 (微克/立方米) Annual Average Concentration of NO_2 (μg/cu.m)	化学需氧量 (COD) 排放量 (万吨) COD Emission Volume (10000 tons)	二氧化硫 (SO_2) 排放量 (万吨) SO_2 Emission Volume (10000 tons)	区域环境噪声平均值 (分贝) Average Value of Urban Environment Noise (db)	道路交通干线噪声平均值 (分贝) Average Value of Road Traffic Noise (db)
2000	162		71	71	17.9	22.4	53.9	71.0
2001	165		64	71	17.0	20.1	53.9	69.6
2002	166		67	76	15.3	19.2	53.5	69.5
2003	141		61	72	13.4	18.3	53.6	69.7
2004	149		55	71	13.0	19.1	53.8	69.6
2005	142		50	66	11.6	19.1	53.2	69.5
2006	161		53	66	11.0	17.6	53.9	69.7
2007	148		47	66	10.7	15.2	54.0	69.9
2008	122		36	49	10.1	12.3	53.6	69.6
2009	121		34	53	9.9	11.9	54.1	69.7
2010	121		32	57	9.2	11.5	54.1	70.0
2011	114		28	55	19.3	9.8	53.7	69.6
2012	109		28	52	18.7	9.4	54.0	69.2
2013	108	89.5	27	56	17.8	8.7	53.9	69.1
2014	116	85.9	22	57	16.9	7.9	53.6	69.1
2015	102	80.6	14	50	16.2	7.1	53.3	69.2
2016	92	73.0	10	48	8.7	3.3	54.3	69.3
2017	84	58.0	8	46	8.2	2.0	53.2	69.3
2018	78	51.0	6	42	5.6	1.1	53.7	69.6
2019	68	42.0	4	37	5.1	0.6	53.7	69.6
2020	56	38.0	4	29	5.4	0.2	53.6	69.0
2021	55	33.0	3	26	4.9	0.1	53.7	69.0
2022	54	30.0	3	23	4.5	0.1	52.8	68.7
2023	61	32.0	3	26	11.9	0.1	53.5	68.5

资料来源：北京市生态环境局。
Source: Beijing Municipal Ecology and Environment Bureau.

7-24 环境保护 ENVIRONMENTAL PROTECTION

项目		Item		2023	2022
水环境		**Water Environment**			
废水排放		Discharge of Wastewater			
#工业废水排放量	(万吨)	Industrial Wastewater Discharge Volume	(10000 tons)	8616.61	8103.50
化学需氧量(COD)排放量	(吨)	COD Discharged	(ton)	118718	44834
#工业废水中COD排放量		Discharged COD in Industrial Wastewater		1360	1335
氨氮排放量	(吨)	Ammonia Nitrogen Discharged	(ton)	9727	2040
#工业废水中氨氮排放量		Discharged Ammonia Nitrogen in Industrial Wastewater		26	23
大气环境		**Atmosphere Environment**			
二氧化硫(SO_2)排放量	(吨)	SO_2 Emission Volume	(ton)	1063	1078
#工业二氧化硫排放量		Emission of Industrial SO_2		896	799
氮氧化物排放量	(吨)	Emission of Nitrogen Oxides	(ton)	97921	74180
#工业氮氧化物排放量		Emission of Industrial Nitrogen Oxides		9428	9765
颗粒物排放量	(吨)	Particulate Matter Emissions	(ton)	5465	4124
#工业颗粒物排放量		Industrial Particulate Matter Emissions		1633	1622
固体废物		**Solid Wastes**			
一般工业固体废物产生量	(万吨)	Common Industrial Solid Wastes Generated	(10000 tons)	182.46	171.44
一般工业固体废物综合利用量	(万吨)	Integrated Reuse of Common Industrial Solid Wastes	(10000 tons)	173.67	143.26
一般工业固体废物处置量	(万吨)	Common Industrial Solid Wastes Disposed	(10000 tons)	8.92	28.17
危险废物产生量	(吨)	Hazardous Wastes Generated	(ton)	273363	271234
生态环境		**Ecological Environment**			
自然保护区个数	(个)	Number of Nature Reserves	(unit)	21	21
#国家级自然保护区		National Nature Reserves		2	2
自然保护区面积	(万公顷)	Area of Nature Reserves	(10000 hectares)	13.8	13.8

注：1.根据国家关于排放源统计的核算办法和要求，2023年生活源核算方法和口径改变，化学需氧量(COD)排放量、氨氮排放量2023年数据与2022年数据不可比。

2.自2020年起，原“烟(粉)尘排放量”更名为“颗粒物排放量”。

资料来源：北京市生态环境局、北京市园林绿化局。

Note: a)According to the national unified accounting methods and requirements on the statistics of emission source, the accounting standard and caliber for domestic emission source changed in 2023, the data on COD Emission Volume and Ammonia Nitrogen Discharge for 2023 was incomparable to that for 2022.

b)Since 2020, the original “Smoke and Dust Emission” has been changed to “Particulate Emissions”.

Source: Beijing Municipal Ecology and Environment Bureau, Beijing Municipal Forestry and Parks Bureau.

7−25 园林绿化情况(1978−2023年)
STATISTICS FOR LANDSCAPING (1978-2023)

年 份 Year	年末公园绿地面积 (公顷) Park Green Area (year-end) (hectare)	人均公园绿地面积 (平方米) Per Capita Park Green Area (sq.m)	城市绿化覆盖率 (%) Urban Green Coverage (%)	绿地面积 (公顷) Green Area (hectare)
1978	2693	5.1	22.3	
1979	2693	5.1	22.3	
1980	2746	5.1	20.1	
1981	2751	5.1	20.1	
1982	2779	5.1	20.1	
1983	2823	5.1	20.1	
1984	2878	5.1	20.1	
1985	3263	4.9	22.1	
1986	3606	5.1	22.9	
1987	3570	5.1	22.9	
1988	4074	5.8	25.0	
1989	6910	6.0	26.0	
1990	7110	6.1	28.0	
1991	4279	6.4	28.4	
1992	4213	6.7	30.3	
1993	4452	7.8	31.3	
1994	5221	7.9	32.4	
1995	5017	7.5	32.7	
1996	5147	7.5	33.2	
1997	5408	7.8	34.2	
1998	6351	9.0	35.6	
1999	6457	9.1	36.3	
2000	7140	9.7	36.5	26680
2001	7554	10.1	38.8	30224
2002	7907	10.7	40.6	32572
2003	9115	11.4	40.9	38475
2004	10446	11.5	41.9	36755
2005	11365	12.0	42.0	38877
2006	11788	12.0	42.5	45495
2007	12101	12.6	43.0	46320
2008	12316	13.6	43.5	46993
2009	18070	14.5	44.4	61695
2010	19020	15.0	45.0	62672
2011	19728	15.3	45.6	63541
2012	21178	15.5	46.2	65540
2013	22215	15.7	46.8	67048
2014	28798	15.9	47.4	80223
2015	29503	16.0	48.4	81305
2016	30069	16.1	48.4	82113
2017	31019	16.2	48.4	83501
2018	32619	16.3	48.4	85286
2019	35157	16.4	48.5	88704
2020	35720	16.6	49.0	92683
2021	36397	16.6	49.3	93127
2022	36900	16.9	49.8	93558
2023	37238	16.9	49.8	94136

资料来源：北京市园林绿化局。
Source:Beijing Municipal Forestry and Parks Bureau.

7-26 森林情况(2005-2023年)
STATISTICS FOR FORESTS (2005-2023)

年 份 Year	森林面积 (公顷) Forest Area (hectare)	森林覆盖率 (%) Forest Coverage Rate (%)	活立木蓄积量 (万立方米) Total Stock of Standing Trees (10000 cu.m)	森林蓄积量 (万立方米) Forest Stock (10000 cu.m)	森林火灾次数 (次) Number of Forest Fires (times)
2005	619243.2		1521.4	1295.3	9
2006	626006.3	35.9	1521.4	1295.3	13
2007	636565.7	36.5	1559.5	1368.9	8
2008	641368.3	36.5	1574.0	1394.4	
2009	658914.1	36.7	1810.3	1406.2	2
2010	666050.7	37.0	1854.7	1435.4	4
2011	673411.8	37.6	1899.4	1468.7	3
2012	691341.1	38.6	1943.3	1499.0	1
2013	716456.1	40.1	1993.4	1536.8	
2014	734530.6	41.0	2109.1	1669.9	1
2015	744956.1	41.6	2149.3	1701.1	3
2016	756000.7	42.3	2180.0	1724.6	4
2017	767665.1	43.0	2211.1	1749.8	3
2018	777603.5	43.5	2246.8	1798.0	1
2019	791972.0	44.0	2306.2	1850.0	8
2020	848313.9	44.4	3064.2	2520.7	8
2021	852720.9	44.6	3830.0	3164.6	
2022	855655.3	44.8	3924.1	3373.8	1
2023	853184.7	44.9	4078.5	3479.2	7

资料来源：自2019年起，森林火灾数据来源于北京市应急管理局，其余年份及其他指标数据均来源于北京市园林绿化局。
Source: Since 2019, the data on forest fires have been provided by Beijing Emergency Management Bureau; the data for other years and other indicator data are provided by Beijing Municipal Forestry and Parks Bureau.

主要统计指标解释

能源生产量 能源生产量是反映能源生产规模、构成、生产成果的重要指标。按能源的成因分为一次能源（亦称天然能源）生产量和二次能源（亦称人工能源）生产量。

一次能源生产量 指报告期内企业将自然界现存的能源资源经过开采而产出的合格产品数量，主要包括原煤、原油、天然气、水电等。

二次能源生产量 指报告期内经过各种加工转换设备生产出的另一种形式的各种合格的能源产品数量。如火电、热力、洗煤、焦炭、各种石油制品、焦炉煤气、其他煤气等。

能源消费总量 指一定地域（行政或地理区域）内，国民经济各行业和居民家庭在一定时期所消费的各种能源的总和。能源消费总量包括终端能源消费量、能源加工转换损失量、能源运输和管理过程的损失量三部分。

能源消费总量（等价值） 是电力按等价热值计算的能源消费总量。等价热值是能源统计中经常使用的一个热值概念，是指加工转换产出的某种二次能源所投入的一次能源的量，即获得一个度量单位的某种二次能源所消耗的以热值表示的一次能源。

能源加工转换投入产出量 能源具有由一种能量形式转换为另一种能量形式及耗用过程中可用一种能源替代另一种能源的特征。为提高能源的利用价值和效率，对能源进行加工、转换，产出适合生产和生活需要的更高级的能源产品。在加工转换投入(-)产出(+)量中，“-”表示能源加工转换的投入量，“+”表示二次能源的产出量。

投入量 是指为生产二次能源产品，所投入到能源加工转换设备的各种能源数量。在表中以负数表示。

产出量 是指各种能源（一次能源或少量再投入的二次能源）经过加工转换后，产出的各种二次能源产品（包括不作为能源使用的副产品，联产品）数量。

加工转换损失量 是指在能源加工、转换过程中损失的能量（能源），即能源加工、转换过程中投入的能源和产出的二次能源之间的差额。

损失量 指能源在经营管理和生产、输送、分配、储存等过程中发生的损失以及由于自然因素等原因造成的损失数量。不包括加工转换损失量。

终端消费量 是指能源消费环节的最后一个环节的能源消费，包括直接用作燃料、原材料和动力的各种能源的消费。它们的消费过程体现了能源消费的终止，不会再重新作为能源投入使用。终端消费量不包括用于能源加工转换投入量、加工转换损失量和损失量。

能源消费弹性系数 指能源消费总量增长率与地区生产总值增长率的比值。

电力消费弹性系数 指电力消费量增长率与地区生产总值增长率的比值。

平均每万元地区生产总值能源消费量 能源总消费量或分品种能源消费量与地区生产总值之比。

人均生活用能量 指用于生活消费的各种能源数量与人口总数之比。

垃圾无害化处理能力 指垃圾无害化处理场（厂）按工艺设计每天所能处理生活垃圾的数量。垃圾无害化处理场（厂）必须是按照有关技术、环境、卫生标准和规范进行设计、建设、运行、维护和管理的各种生活垃圾处理设施，主要包括卫生填埋场、堆肥厂和焚烧厂等。

大风日数 指出现瞬时风速达到或超过 17.0m/s（或目测估计风力达到或超过 8 级）大风的天数。

水资源总量 指降水形成的地表和地下水总量，是当地自产水资源，不包括入境水量。

排水管道长度 指所有排水总管、干管、支管、检查井及连接井进出口等长度之和。计算时应按单管计算，即在同一条街道上如有两条或两条以上并排的排水管道时，应按每条排水管道的长度相加计算。

污水处理能力 指污水处理厂（或处理装置）每昼夜处理污水量的设计能力。

污水处理量 指污水处理厂（或污水处理装置）处理装置实际处理的污水量。包括物理处理量、生物处理量和化学处理量。

污水处理率 指污水处理量与污水排放总量的比率。计算公式：

$$\text{污水处理率}=\frac{\text{污水处理量}}{\text{污水排放总量}}\times 100\%$$

生活垃圾清运量 指报告期内收集和运送到各垃圾处理场（厂）的垃圾的数量。

粪便清运量 指报告期内收集和运送到各粪便处理场（厂）的粪便的数量。

生活垃圾无害化处理量 指报告期内简易处理场和各种垃圾无害化处理场（厂）处理垃圾的总量。垃圾简易处理量指垃圾简易填埋场所处理的垃圾总量。垃圾无害化处理量指垃圾无害化处理场（厂）所处理的垃圾总量。

生活垃圾无害化处理率 指报告期垃圾无害化处理量与垃圾产生量的比率。计算公式：

$$\text{垃圾无害化处理率}=\frac{\text{垃圾无害化处理量}}{\text{垃圾产生量}}\times 100\%$$

在统计时，如果生活垃圾产生量不易取得，可用清运量代替。

化学需氧量（COD）排放量 指工业 COD 排放量、农业 COD 排放量、生活 COD 排放量及集中式治理设施（不含污水厂）COD 排放量之和。

二氧化硫（SO_2）排放量 指报告期内工业 SO_2 排放量生活 SO_2 排放量及集中式治理设施（不含污水厂）SO_2 排放量之和。

工业固体废物综合利用量 指报告期内企业通过回收、加工、循环、交换等方式，从固体废物中提取或者使其转化为可以利用的资源、能源和其他原材料的固体废物量（包括当年利用的往年工业固体废物贮存量）。如用做农业肥料、生产建筑材料、筑路等。

公园绿地 指城市中向公众开放的，以游憩为主要功能，有一定的游憩设施和服务设施，同时兼有健全生态、美化景观、科普教育、应急避险等综合作用的绿化用地，包括：综合公园、社区公园、专类公园和游园四个种类。

绿化覆盖率 指报告期末区域内绿化覆盖面积与区域面积的比率。

计算公式：

$$绿化覆盖率=\frac{区域内绿化覆盖面积}{区域面积}\times 100\%$$

森林面积 指乔木林面积、竹林面积与特殊灌木林面积之和。

活立木蓄积量 指一定范围土地上全部树木蓄积的总量，包括森林蓄积、疏林蓄积、散生木蓄积和四旁树蓄积。

森林蓄积量 指一定森林面积上存在着的林木树干部分的总材积，以立方米为计量单位。

森林火灾次数 指发生在城市市区外的一切森林、林木和林地的火灾次数，包括森林火警、一般灾害、重大灾害和特大灾害。

Explanatory Notes on Main Statistical Indicators

Energy Production is an important indicator reflecting the size, composition and results of energy production. By the cause of formation, it consists of the production of primary energy (also known as natural energy) and that of secondary energy (also known as artificial energy).

Production of Primary Energy means up-to-grade products produced by primary energy producers in the reporting period through extraction of existing energy in the nature, mainly including raw coal, crude oil, natural gas, hydroelectricity, etc.

Production of Secondary Energy means various up-to-grade energy products in another form that are made from primary energy with various processing and converting equipment in the reporting period, including thermal power, heating power, washed coal, coke, various petroleum products, coke oven gas and other gases, etc.

Total Energy Consumption means the total consumption of various energies by national economic sectors and resident households in a specific region (administrative or geographic). Total energy consumption can be divided into three parts: end-use energy consumption, loss during energy processing and conversion and loss during energy transport and management.

Total Energy Consumption (in Equivalent Caloricity) means the total consumption of electric power calculated in equivalent caloricity. Equivalent caloricity is a caloricity concept frequently used in statistics of energy. It means the quantity of primary energy input for a secondary energy produced through processing and conversion, i.e. the primary energy in terms of caloricity which is consumed to produce one measuring unit of a secondary energy.

Input and Output of Energy Processing and Conversion One form of energy can be converted into another form of energy. And in consumption, one sort of energy can be replaced with another. In order to improve the energy use value and efficiency, energy is processed and converted to produce energy products at higher levels which are suitable for productive and living needs. In the processing and conversion input (-) and output (+), "-" means the input for energy processing and conversion. And "+" means the output from energy processing and conversion.

Input means the volume of energy put into the energy processing and converting equipment in order to produce secondary energy products. It is shown as a negative number in the table.

Output means the volume of secondary energy products (including byproducts and multi-products that cannot be used as energy) from processing and conversion of energy sources (primary energy or a small amount of secondary energy re-input).

Loss during Processing and Conversion means the energy lost in the processing and conversion of energy, namely the difference between the energy input and the secondary energy output during energy processing and conversion.

Energy Loss means the loss of energy during operation, management, production, transportation, distribution and storage, as well as the loss due to natural factors and other reasons. It excludes the loss during processing and conversion.

End-use Energy Consumption means the energy consumption in the last section of energy consumption, including the consumption of various energy sources used as fuel, raw materials and power. Such consumption represents the end of energy consumption, and the energy will not be put into use again as energy. End-use energy consumption does not include the input for energy processing and conversion, loss during the processing and conversion of energy, and energy loss.

Elasticity Coefficient of Energy Consumption means the ratio of growth rate of total energy consumption to the growth rate of GDP.

Elasticity Coefficient of Electric Power Consumption means the ratio of growth rate of electric power consumption to the growth rate of GDP.

Average Energy Consumption per RMB 10,000 of GDP means the ratio of total energy consumption or energy consumption by variety to GDP.

Per-capital Energy Consumption by Households means the ratio of quantity of energy consumed by households to the total population.

Harmless Disposal Capacity of Waste means the daily quantity of domestic waste that can be disposed at harmless disposal facilities (sites) according to the process designed. Harmless disposal facilities (sites) must be domestic waste disposal facilities, including landfills, manure yards, incineration facilities and so on, which are designed, built, operated and managed in accordance with relevant technological, environmental, and sanitary standards and criterion.

Total Water Resources means the total volume of surface water and underground water caused by rainfall, which is locally generated water resources and excludes inbound water.

Number of Windy Days means the number of days with an instantaneous wind speed of 17.0 m/s or more (or with visually estimated force 8 or above wind).

Length of Sewage Pipes means the total length of all main drainage pipes, trunk pipes, branch pipes, access manholes, and connector well entrances and exits, and so on. The length of single pipes shall be included, i.e. if there are two or more drainage pipes parallel on a street, the length of every pipe shall be included.

Sewage Treatment Capacity means the designed capacity

of sewage disposal day and night for a sewage disposal plant (or facility).

Volume of Sewage Treated means the volume of sewage actually disposed by sewage disposal plants (or sewage disposal facilities), consisting of physical volume, biological volume and chemical volume of waste water disposed.

Sewage Treatment Rate means the ratio of sewage disposed to the total discharge of sewage. The formula is:

Sewage Disposal Rate = Volume of Sewage Disposed / Total Discharge of Sewage × 100%

Domestic Waste Removed and Transported means the quantity of waste collected and transported to waste treatment sites (plants) in the reporting period.

Excrement Removed and Transported means the quantity of excrement collected and transported to waste treatment sites (plants) in the reporting period.

Volume of Harmless Disposal of Domestic Waste means the total volume of waste disposed by simple disposal sites and harmless waste disposal sits (plants) in the reporting period. Simple disposal of waste means the total volume of waste by simple landfills. Harmless waste disposal means the total volume of waste disposed by harmless waste disposal sites (plants).

Rate of Harmless Disposal of Domestic Waste means the ratio of harmless waste disposal to the waste produced in the reporting period. The formula is:

Rate of Harmless Disposal of Domestic Waste = Harmless Waste Disposal / Waste Produced × 100%

In practical statistics, if it is hard to get figures on the volume of domestic waste produced, the volume removed and transported may be used.

COD Emission Volume means the sum of industrial COD emission, agricultural COD emission, domestic COD emission, and COD emissions from centralized treatment facilities (excluding sewage disposal plants).

SO_2 Emission Volume means the sum of industrial SO_2 emission, domestic SO_2 emission, and SO_2 emissions from centralized treatment facilities (excluding sewage disposal plants) in the reporting period.

Industrial Solid Waste Utilized means the volume of solid wastes from which useful materials can be extracted or which can be converted into usable resources, energy or other materials by means of reclamation, processing, recycling and exchange (including utilizing in the year the stocks of industrial solid wastes of the previous year). Examples of such utilizations include fertilizers, building materials and road materials.

Green Land and Parks means the green land open to the public, with main function of recreation, having some recreational facilities and service facilities, and simultaneously exerting the synthetic action in ecosystem health, landscaping, science popularization education, emergency avoidance, etc. They can be classified into four types of parks: comprehensive parks, community parks, special use parks and recreational parks.

Green Land Coverage means the ratio of area of green land in a region to the total area of the region in the reporting period. The formula is:

Green Land Coverage = Area of Green Land in a Region / Total Area of the Region × 100%

Forest Area means the sum of high-forest area, bamboo forest area and special shrub area.

Total Stock of Standing Trees mean the total stock of all trees on specific area of land, including trees in forest, trees in sparse forest, scattered trees and trees planted by the side of villages, farm houses and along roads and rivers.

Forest Stock means the total volume of timber of forest tree trunks growing on specific area of forest, which are measured in cubic meters.

Number of Forest Fires means the number of all fires occurring in forests, woods, woodlands outside the urban districts, including forest fires, general fires, severe fires and fire disasters.

08

城市公用事业
PUBLIC UTILITIES

简要说明

主要内容

本章资料反映北京市城市公用事业的综合水平，主要包括：公路、城市道路及桥梁情况，水、气、热等供应及消费情况，城市公共交通情况，市政主要设施情况。

Brief Introduction

Main Content

Statistics in this chapter show the overall level of urban public utilities in Beijing, which consist: Highways,urban roads and bridges Water, gas and heating supply and consumption, Urban public transport , Main public facilities.

8-1 公路、城市道路及桥梁(1978-2023年)
HIGHWAYS, URBAN ROADS AND BRIDGES (1978-2023)

年 份 Year	境内道路总里程(公里) Total Length of Highways and Roads (km)	公路里程(公里) Length of Highways (km)	#高速公路 Express-ways	城市道路里程(公里) Length of Urban Roads (km)	#快速路 Rapid Roads	#主干路 Trunk Roads	城市道路面积(万平方米) Area of Urban Roads (10000 sq.m)	城市道路桥梁(座) Number of Bridges (unit)	#立交桥 Overpasses
1978		6562		2078			1611	351	2
1979		7278		2131			1618	348	2
1980		7487		2185			1664	351	6
1981		7566		2234			1742	342	8
1982		7683		2671			2098	408	9
1983		8058		2820			2265	431	10
1984		8271		2928			2393	440	11
1985		8482		2979			2485	460	16
1986		8995		3038			2559	479	16
1987		9103		3087			2631	510	22
1988		9124		3151			2701	522	23
1989		9371		3235			2815	552	27
1990		9648	35	3276			2905	562	33
1991		10259	63	3308			3134	569	40
1992		10827	71	3189			3212	595	55
1993		11260	99	3285			3398	596	64
1994		11532	112	3316			3470	616	75
1995		11811	113	3194			3494	582	84
1996		12084	114	3665			3807	646	133
1997		12306	144	3637			4061	693	140
1998		12498	190	3721			4214	715	138
1999		12825	230	3753			4353	787	141
2000		13600	268	4126			4921	834	149
2001		13891	335	4312			6062	891	160
2002		14359	463	5444			7645	1051	180
2003	18239	14453	499	3055			5345	848	119
2004	19010	14630	525	4067	219	834	6417	949	271
2005	19015	14696	548	4073	239	922	7437	964	304
2006	25377	20503	625	4380	232	955	7286	1079	376
2007	25765	20754	628	4421	236	960	7632	1230	377
2008	26921	20340	777	6143	242	755	8940	1738	381
2009	27436	20755	884	6204	242	805	9179	1765	393
2010	27907	21114	903	6312	263	855	9395	1855	411
2011	28446	21347	912	6258	263	861	9164	1885	418
2012	28585	21492	923	6271	263	865	9236	1950	413
2013	28808	21673	923	6295	269	953	9611	1998	414
2014	29209	21849	982	6426	383	965	10002	2042	422
2015	29069	21885	982	6423	383	969	10029	2069	427
2016	29282	22026	1013	6374	390	970	10275	2088	431
2017	29463	22226	1013	6359	390	984	10347	2094	435
2018	29429	22256	1115	6203	390	998	10328	2156	435
2019	29531	22366	1168	6156	390	1006	10459	2165	437
2020	29537	22264	1173	6147	390	1020	10654	2184	437
2021	29631	22320	1177	6168	397	1028	10741	2203	439
2022	29716	22363	1196	6209	397	1040	10892	2203	441
2023	30063	22433	1211	6265	397	1059	11081	2230	441

注：1.境内道路总里程为全市道路和公路里程之和(剔除道路、公路交叉重复部分)。
2.道路及桥梁1978—1981年统计范围为城八区及通县；1982—2002年统计范围为城八区及14个县城；2003—2009年统计范围为城八区和北京经济技术开发区。自2010年起城市道路及其附属设施统计范围为城六区。
3.自2008年起道路数据为北京市城市道路普查数据。

资料来源：北京市交通委员会。

Note: a) Total length of highways and roads means the sum of the length of roads and highways across the city (excluding the overlapped parts of roads and highways).
b) Statistics for roads and bridges covered 8 urban districts and Tongzhou County in 1978-1981; the coverage was extended to 8 urban districts and 14 counties in 1982-2002; in 2003-2009, the coverage included 8 urban districts and Beijing Economic-Technological Development Area; since 2010, statistics for urban roads and the auxiliary facilities have been confined to 6 urban districts.
c) Since 2008, statistics for roads and highways have been from the data of Beijing Urban Road Census.

Source: Beijing Municipal Commission of Transport.

8–2 城市公共交通(1978–2023年)

年 份 Year	公共交通运营线路条数(条) Number of Routes of Public Transportation in Operation (line)	公共汽电车 Public Buses and Trolley Buses	城市轨道交通 Urban Rail Transit	公共交通运营线路长度(公里) Length of Routes of Public Transportation in Operation (km)	公共汽电车 Public Buses and Trolley Buses	城市轨道交通 Urban Rail Transit	公共交通运营车辆(辆) Number of Public Transportation Vehicles in Operation (unit)
1978	119	118	1	1427	1403	24	2743
1979	121	120	1	1469	1446	24	2997
1980	123	122	1	1479	1455	24	3113
1981	127	126	1	1525	1501	24	3375
1982	139	138	1	1678	1654	24	3620
1983	151	150	1	1820	1797	24	3907
1984	164	162	2	1939	1899	40	4221
1985	191	189	2	2312	2272	40	4583
1986	200	198	2	2574	2534	40	4576
1987	194	192	2	2382	2342	40	4776
1988	199	197	2	2445	2405	40	4787
1989	207	205	2	2525	2485	40	4890
1990	216	214	2	2654	2614	40	5160
1991	223	221	2	2755	2715	40	5182
1992	262	260	2	3379	3338	42	5223
1993	268	266	2	3532	3491	42	5213
1994	284	282	2	4117	4075	42	5319
1995	300	298	2	4538	4497	42	5367
1996	399	397	2	7317	7276	42	6828
1997	667	665	2	14011	13969	42	10479
1998	690	688	2	14929	14888	42	10819
1999	750	748	2	16566	16513	54	12509
2000	682	680	2	15639	15585	54	14191
2001	555	553	2	13180	13126	54	15420
2002	592	589	3	15835	15760	75	17580
2003	620	616	4	16131	16017	114	17445
2004	621	617	4	15247	15133	114	19343
2005	626	622	4	18328	18214	114	19471
2006	624	620	4	18582	18468	114	20489
2007	649	644	5	17495	17353	142	20525
2008	679	671	8	18057	17857	200	23221
2009	701	692	9	18498	18270	228	23730
2010	727	713	14	19079	18743	336	24011
2011	764	749	15	19832	19460	372	24478
2012	795	779	16	19989	19547	442	25831
2013	830	813	17	20153	19688	465	27590
2014	895	877	18	20776	20249	527	28331
2015	894	876	18	20740	20186	554	28311
2016	895	876	19	20392	19818	574	27892
2017	908	886	22	19898	19290	608	30966
2018	910	888	22	19881	19245	637	29732
2019	1181	1158	23	28331	27632	699	29459
2020	1231	1207	24	29145	28417	727	30727
2021	1244	1217	27	29363	28580	783	30189
2022	1318	1291	27	30971	30174	797	30739
2023	1312	1285	27	30575	29739	836	30897

注：自2006年5月1日起，公共汽电车、城市轨道交通售票采取刷卡方式，并陆续进行了票制票价改革，客运量统计口径方法相应调整，因此与历史数据不可比。

资料来源：本表自2005年起数据来源于北京市交通委员会。

URBAN PUBLIC TRANSPORTATION (1978-2023)

公共汽电车 Buses and Trolley Buses	城市轨道交通 Urban Rail Transit	公共交通客运量（万人次） Passenger Traffic of Public Transport (10000 person-times)	公共汽电车 Public Buses and Trolley Buses	城市轨道交通 Urban Rail Transit	出租小汽车 Taxis Service 运营车辆（辆） Vehicles in Operation (unit)	客运量（万人次） Passenger Traffic (10000 person-times)
2627	116	172559	169465	3094		
2889	108	205703	200918	4785		
3001	112	236998	231477	5521		
3259	116	263944	257478	6466		
3500	120	284175	276922	7253		
3753	154	302501	294301	8200		
4037	184	324437	314132	10305		
4398	185	335227	321264	13963		
4371	205	328770	312990	15780		
4524	252	330417	311190	19227		
4535	252	337094	306396	30698		
4587	303	306435	275383	31052		
4857	303	334673	296495	38178		
4877	305	344525	307438	37087		
4900	323	348770	305959	42811		
4890	323	335378	286268	49110		
4984	335	353289	299993	53296		
4984	383	371579	315777	55802		
6427	401	349847	305433	44414		
10044	435	391182	346676	44507		
10382	437	418825	372494	46331		
12018	491	426706	378483	48223		
13604	587	406691	363213	43478		
14803	617	449720	402850	46870		
16939	641	492122	443880	48242		
16753	692	426628	379380	47248		
18451	892	499830	439130	60700		
18503	968	517769	449793	67976	66000	65000
19522	967	468225	397919	70306	66646	64121
19395	1130	488138	422645	65493	66646	64111
21507	1714	592523	470863	121660	66646	69000
21716	2014	658785	516517	142268	66646	68000
21548	2463	689788	505144	184645	66646	69000
21628	2850	722552	503272	219280	66646	69600
22146	3685	761578	515416	246162	66646	69862
23592	3998	804775	484306	320469	67046	69946
23667	4664	815849	477180	338668	67546	66828
23287	5024	738384	406003	332381	68284	58750
22688	5204	734953	369019	365934	68484	47665
25624	5342	713396	335595	377801	68484	39378
24076	5656	703818	318975	384843	70035	34021
23010	6449	709604	313366	396238	71517	33110
23948	6779	411967	182567	229400	74875	17427
23079	7110	538626	229634	308992	79600	21451
23465	7274	398889	172558	226331	70230	18669
23385	7512	554030	208656	345374	71456	23867

Note: Since May 1, 2006, public buses and trolley buses and rail transit tickets have been sold by card swiping. Ticket system and prices have also been subject to reform successively. The statistical coverage and methods for passenger traffic are adjusted accordingly, so these figures are not comparable with historical data.

Source: Since 2005, data in this table have been provided by Beijing Municipal Commission of Transport.

8-3 城市供水、供气及供热(1978-2023年)
URBAN WATER SUPPLY, GAS SUPPLY AND HEATING(1978-2023)

年 份 Year	全市集中供热管道长度(公里) Length of Pipelines for Centralized Heating in Beijing (km)	全市集中供热面积(万平方米) Area of Centralized Heating (10000 sq.m)	#住 宅 Residence	煤 气 销售量(万立方米) Sales Volume of Coal Gas (10000 cu.m)	液化石油气 销 售 量(吨) Sales Volume of Liquefied Petroleum Gas (ton)	天然气 销售量(万立方米) Sales Volume of Natural Gas (10000 cu.m)
1978				32687	97255	
1979				32113	114350	
1980				34935	128990	
1981				36309	134771	
1982				36748	149805	
1983				37319	150058	
1984				38710	156421	
1985				41678	169720	
1986				44542	182239	
1987				47594	178205	
1988				49595	177112	287
1989				56056	175814	1805
1990		3702		59508	172688	3544
1991		4560		66111	174326	5062
1992		5281		73615	174694	6040
1993		5730		80163	177065	6702
1994		7056		80409	173105	7623
1995		7537		85201	177637	11003
1996		7838		88356	185304	13504
1997		8399		76429	172879	16565
1998		9102		68998	174464	32619
1999		9992		61846	188450	64833
2000		10860		46719	190571	95919
2001		14729		33960	182188	150585
2002		18172		21077	234680	176504
2003		25108		23991	311657	208837
2004		28150	18962	17714	431660	250326
2005	6272	31736	22218	16776	356551	294279
2006	7013	34977	23158	9763	415268	389202
2007	10424	37203	23697		319631	441327
2008	11948	42501	26738		289576	578626
2009	12156	44240	27694		332693	645356
2010	12224	46715	32305		299392	677009
2011	11734	50794	34563		394437	726229
2012	11031	52555	35104		379371	883385
2013	11192	54591	36806		453546	956852
2014	12038	56786	38085		531556	1088999
2015	12207	58465	39031		523391	1427808
2016	13545	61136	41084		489473	1538425
2017	60169	60751	42215		457024	1577065
2018	60549	62932	43460		448107	1807388
2019	60166	63928	44419		395029	1823476
2020	63740	65935	45486		292445	1779490
2021	65376	68378	46596		413474	1868398
2022	68277	71301	48400		156291	1946384
2023	66496	72113	49105		122796	1977184

注：1.自2017年起，全市集中供热管道长度数据包含一级、二级管网数据，2016年及以前只包含一级管网数据。
2.自2006年6月起，全市煤气家庭用户已全部置换为天然气用户，因此自2007年起煤气销售量无数据。
3.2011—2021年，液化石油气销售量数据包含市内销售量数据和市外销售量数据，自2022年起，液化石油气销售量数据不包含市外销售量及作为化工原料的销售量数据，下同。
4.2019—2021年，天然气销售量数据包含市内销售量数据和市外销售量数据，自2022年起，天然气销售量数据不包含市外销售量数据，下同。

资料来源：北京市城市管理委员会、北京市水务局。

Note: a) Since 2017, the figures on length of pipelines for centralized heating in Beijing have included that of the primary and secondary heating network; in and before 2016, the said figures included the primary network data only.

b) Since June 2006, all households using coal gas in Beijing have started to use natural gas. Therefore, there are no data on sales volume of coal gas since 2007.

c) The sales volume data of liquefied petroleum gas (LPG) in 2011-2021 included both in-the-city and out-of-city sales. Starting from 2022, LPG sales volume data excluded out-of-city sales and sales as raw chemical materials, the same applies to the following table.

d) The natural gas sales volume data in 2019-2021 included both in-the-city and out-of-city sales. Starting from 2022, the natural gas sales volume data excluded out-of-city sales, the same below.

Source: Beijing Municipal Commission of Urban Management, Beijing Water Authority.

8-3 续表 Continued

年 份 Year	居 民 燃气用户 (万户) Gas Using Households (10000 households)	自来水综合 生产能力 (万立方米/日) Production Capacity of Tap Water (10000 cu.m/day)	自来水供水 管道长度 (公里) Length of Tap Water Supply Pipelines (km)	自 来 水 售 水 量 (万立方米) Sales Volume of Tap Water (10000 cu.m)
1978	65.2	134	2926	32664
1979	76.7	151	3083	36232
1980	80.3	163	3272	38933
1981	85.1	167	3435	41634
1982	88.0	164	4216	41136
1983	90.9	166	4452	42778
1984	96.9	167	4622	43716
1985	102.3	176	4927	45601
1986	153.6	188	5079	46695
1987	160.9	185	5257	47680
1988	165.4	189	5550	50059
1989	172.6	206	5647	50145
1990	176.1	215	5770	52718
1991	184.7	221	5947	56107
1992	192.4	226	6130	58704
1993	197.5	234	6367	60794
1994	210.3	242	6727	67977
1995	219.8	264	6907	67877
1996	188.1	266	6907	69684
1997	243.0	302	6339	79046
1998	254.4	330	6989	75969
1999	259.8	357	7179	78098
2000	291.9	367	7610	75364
2001	310.0	371	8146	69807
2002	336.4	428	8555	79322
2003	406.0	429	9278	71583
2004	438.6	399	9981	82986
2005	462.6	348	9831	71600
2006	540.2	373	11899	74970
2007	556.4	391	13133	77778
2008	591.0	404	14118	80792
2009	600.0	424	14791	86881
2010	634.2	445	16144	89185
2011	644.1	473	16963	94622
2012	713.5	411	14029	93826
2013	737.4	444	14495	98178
2014	846.0	503	14994	103402
2015	885.7	506	15421	103929
2016	886.5	504	15742	108386
2017	929.0	522	16105	110587
2018	926.4	527	16448	115852
2019	873.2	598	16735	119668
2020	902.2	606	17819	112279
2021	950.4	700	18432	121312
2022	973.6	702	18998	123267
2023	993.3	709	19298	127830

注：自2012年起，自来水数据口径调整为城镇公共供水，下同。
Note: Since 2012, the statistical coverage of tap water data have been adjusted to urban public water supply, the same below.

8-4 液化石油气及天然气
LIQUEFIED PETROLEUM GAS AND NATURAL GAS

项目		Item		2023	2022
液化石油气		**Liquefied Petroleum Gas**			
供气总量	(吨)	Volume of Gas Supply	(ton)	123023	156679
销售气量	(吨)	Volume of Gas Sales	(ton)	122796	156291
#家庭用量		Household Consumption		104913	120088
家庭用户	(万户)	Household Consumers	(10000 households)	213.7	220.4
天然气		**Natural Gas**			
供气总量	(万立方米)	Volume of Gas Supply	(10000 cu.m)	2016714	1991095
销售气量	(万立方米)	Volume of Gas Sales	(10000 cu.m)	1977184	1946384
#家庭用量		Household Consumption		198309	204687
家庭用户	(万户)	Household Consumers	(10000 households)	779.6	753.2
居民燃气用户	**(万户)**	**Household Gas Users**	**(10000 households)**	**993.3**	**973.6**

注：本表液化石油气、天然气供气总量和销售气量数据均包含燕山石化数据。
资料来源：北京市城市管理委员会、中国石化集团北京燕山石化有限公司。
Note: Data on volume of liquefied petroleum gas and natural gas supply and sales in this table include the data of Yanshan Petrochemical.
Source: Beijing Municipal Commission of Urban Management, and SINOPEC Beijing Yanshan Petrochemical Co., Ltd.

8-5 自来水及城镇自建设施
TAP WATER AND URBAN SELF-BUILT FACILITIES

项目		Item		2023	2022
自来水		**Tap Water**			
综合生产能力	(万立方米/日)	Production Capacity	(10000 cu.m/day)	709.4	701.5
供水管道长度	(公里)	Length of Water Supply Pipelines	(km)	19298	18998
售水量	(万立方米)	Sales Volume of Water	(10000 cu.m)	127830	123267
生产用水		For Production Use		11257	11083
生活用水		For Daily Use		113647	109395
环卫绿化		For Environmental Sanitation and Greening Use		2927	2789
城镇自建设施		**Urban Self-built Facilities**			
供水总量	(万立方米)	Total Volume of Water Supply	(10000 cu.m)	4166	5056
生产用水		For Production Use		575	652
生活用水		For Daily Use		3540	4342
环卫绿化		For Environmental Sanitation and Greening Use		51	61

资料来源：北京市水务局。
Source: Beijing Water Authority.

8-6 市政设施情况
BASIC STATISTICS ON MUNICIPAL INFRASTRUCTURE

项 目		Item		2023	2022
境内道路总里程	（公里）	Total Length of Highways and Roads	(km)	30063	29716
高速公路里程	（公里）	Length of Expressways	(km)	1211	1196
城市道路里程	（公里）	Length of Urban Roads	(km)	6265	6209
#快速路		Rapid Roads		397	397
#主干路		Trunk Roads		1059	1040
城市道路面积	（万平方米）	Area of Urban Roads	(10000 sq.m)	11081	10892
#铺装步道		Paved Roads		1956	1908
城市道路立交桥数	（座）	Number of Overpasses in City	(unit)	441	441
城市过街天桥数	（座）	Number of Pedestrian Overpasses in City	(unit)	565	562
城市地下通道数	（座）	Number of Underpasses in City	(unit)	220	218
备案停车场个数	（个）	Number of Parking Lots Recorded	(unit)	3387	3079
备案停车场车位总数	（个）	Total Capacity of Parking Lots Recorded	(unit)	900685	822731
电视监视点位	（台）	TV Monitors	(unit)	6913	6913

注：本表统计范围为城六区。
资料来源：北京市交通委员会、北京市公安局公安交通管理局。
Note: Data in this table cover 6 urban districts.
Source: Beijing Municipal Commission of Transport, Beijing Traffic Management Bureau.

主要统计指标解释

自来水综合生产能力 指按供水设施取水、净化、送水、出厂输水干管等环节实际测定计算的综合生产能力。不包括供水高峰阶段，超负荷增加的生产能力。计算时，以四个环节中最薄弱的环节为主确定能力。

自来水供水管道长度 指从送水泵至用户水表之间所有管道的长度。不包括新安装尚未使用的管道。

生产用水 指在生产活动中取用的水量，包含农业用水量、工业用水量和建筑业用水量。

生活用水 指城乡居民家庭日常生活及商业、饮食业、宾馆业、服务业、机关团体、医院、学校、部队等服务业范围的用水。

公共交通运营车辆 指公交企业（单位）用于运营业务的全部车辆数。

运营线路长度 指全部运营线路长度之和。计算公式：

$$运营线路长度=\sum 各条运营线路长度$$

$$=\sum\left[\begin{pmatrix}上行起点至终点里程+下行起点至终点里程\\+上下行终点掉头里程\end{pmatrix}\right]$$

公路里程 指公路的长度，凡达到《公路工程技术标准（JTGB01-2003）》规定的技术等级的公路，均统计公路里程，包括大、中城市的郊区公路里程，公路通过城镇（指县城、集镇）街道的里程和公路桥梁长度、隧道长度、渡口的宽度以及分期修建的公路已验收交付使用的里程。国道、省道、县道、乡道和专用公路中新增的人工修建的、路基宽度在 4.5 米以上的等外路里程也纳入公路里程统计。按技术等级公路可分为高速公路、一级公路、二级公路、三级公路、四级公路和等外公路。

道路里程 指道路长度和与道路相通的桥梁、隧道的长度，按车行道中心线计算。城市道路由车行道和人行道两部分组成。在统计时只统计路面宽度在 3.5 米（含 3.5 米）以上的各种铺装道路，包括开放型工业区和住宅区道路在内。

道路面积 指道路面积和与道路相通的广场、桥梁、隧道的面积（统计时，将人行道面积单独统计）。人行道面积按道路两侧面积相加计算。包括步行街和广场，不含人车混行的道路。

Explanatory Notes on Main Statistical Indicators

General Production Capacity of Tap Water means the comprehensive production capacity of water facilities calculated by on-site measurement, including capacity of the water in-taking, treatment, transmission and delivery; while overloaded capacity during water supply peak hours are not included. Calculation of the capacity was mainly dependent upon the weakest link of the whole production process.

Length of Tap Water Supply Pipelines means the length of all pipes linking between the water outlet pumps and users' water meters, excluding the ones newly installed and not yet put into use.

Water for Production Use means the water used in production activities, including agricultural water, industrial water and construction water.

Water for Public Service Use means the water used in the daily life of urban and rural households and in the service industry including commerce, catering, hotels, government organizations, hospitals, schools, and troops.

Public Transport Vehicles in Operation means the number of all vehicles used for operational businesses in public transit enterprises (institutions).

Length of Public Transport Routes means the sum of all lines in operation. It is calculated with the formula:

Length of Public Transit Lines = ∑ Length of all lines in operation = ∑ [(mileage from the upward starting point to the end point + mileage from the downward starting point to the end point + mileage of double back from upward and downward end points)]

Total Length of Highways means the length of highways. Such statistics apply for any highway reaching the technical grade stated in *Highway Engineering Technical Standards* (JTGB01-2003), including the mileage of highways in suburbs of middle and large cities, mileage of highways passing through streets in towns (counties and townships), length of highway bridges, length of tunnels, width of ferries, and mileage of highways constructed in several phases and put into use. The mileage of non-graded new highways built manually onto national highways, provincial highways, county highways, township highways and special highways, with roadbed width of 4.5m and above, are also incorporated. In terms of technical grade, highways fall into expressways, first-grade highways, second-grade highways, third-grade highways, fourth-grade highways, and non-graded highways.

Length of Highways and Roads means the length of roads and bridges and tunnels connecting with roads, calculated by the central lines of carriage ways. Urban roads consist of carriageways and sidewalks. Statistics only cover paved roads with width of pavement above 3.5m (including 3.5m), roads in open industrial zones and residential zones included.

Area of Roads means the area of roads and the area of squares, bridges and tunnels connecting to the roads (the area of sidewalks is calculated separately). The area of sidewalks is the sum of area on both sides of roads, including pedestrian streets and squares, excluding roads passable for both pedestrians and vehicles.

09

固定资产投资和房地产开发

INVESTMENT IN FIXED ASSETS AND REAL ESTATE DEVELOPMENT

简要说明

一、主要内容

本章资料包括北京市固定资产投资、房地产开发情况等。

二、统计范围

1996年及以前固定资产投资统计起点为5万元及以上，1996年以后调整为50万元及以上，自2011年起调整为500万元及以上。

房地产开发的统计范围是有开发经营活动的全部房地产开发经营业法人单位。

三、有关统计标准的变化说明

（一）关于行业划分。自2018年起执行《国民经济行业分类》（GB/T 4754-2017）标准。

（二）关于三次产业划分。2003年，根据《国民经济行业分类》（GB/T 4754-2002），国家统计局印发了《国家统计局关于印发〈三次产业划分规定〉的通知》（国统字〔2003〕14号）。2012年，根据国家质检总局和国家标准委颁布的《国民经济行业分类》（GB/T 4754-2011），国家统计局对2003年《三次产业划分规定》进行了修订。主要在以下方面作出调整：一是将门类“农、林、牧、渔业”中的“农、林、牧、渔服务业”，“采矿业”中的“开采辅助活动”，“制造业”中的“金属制品、机械和设备修理业”等三个大类一并调整到第三产业。调整后，第一产业为4个大类；第二产业为2个门类和36个大类；第三产业为15个门类和3个大类。二是明确第三产业即为服务业。

本章2012年及以后三次产业的分类执行调整后的划分规定。

Brief Introduction

I. Main Content

Statistics in this chapter include figures on investment in fixed assets and real estate development in Beijing, etc.

II. Scope of Statistics

Before and in 1996, the threshold of fixed assets investment statistics was RMB 50,000 and above; after 1996, it was adjusted to RMB 500,000 and above; since 2011, the figure has been adjusted to RMB 5 million and above.

The scope of statistics on real estate development covers all legal entities in real estate exploitation management that have development and business activities.

III. Changes in Relevant Statistical Standards

(I) Classification of Sectors. The standards in the *Classification of National Economic Sectors (GB/T 4754-2017) are implemented since 2018.*

(II) Classification of Three Industries. According to the *Classification of National Economic Sectors (GB/T 4754-2002),* the National Bureau of Statistics issued the *Notice of the National Bureau of Statistics on the Issuance of the 'Regulations on Three Industries Classification'* (G.T.Z. [2003] No. 14) in 2003. According to the *Classification of National Economic Sectors (GB/T 4754-2011)* promulgated by the General Administration of Quality Supervision, Inspection and Quarantine of the People's Republic of China and the Standardization Administration of the People's Republic of China, the National Bureau of Statistics revised the *Regulations on Three Industries Classification* of 2003 version in 2012. Adjustments were mainly made in the following aspects: Firstly, the "service activities for agriculture, forestry, animal husbandry and fishing" in the category of "agriculture, forestry, animal production and hunting, fishing", the "mining support service activities" in the category of "mining and quarrying", and the "repair of fabricated metal products, machinery and equipment" in the category of "manufacturing" were adjusted to the tertiary industry. After adjustment, the primary industry fell into 4 categories; the secondary industry fell into 2 classes and 36 categories; and the tertiary industry fell into 15 classes and 3 categories. Secondly, the tertiary industry was defined as the service industry.

The classification of three industries since 2012 as mentioned in this chapter has all been subject to the classification provisions after adjustment.

9-1 全社会固定资产投资和增长速度情况(1978-2018年)
TOTAL INVESTMENT IN FIXED ASSETS AND GROWTH RATE (1978-2018)

单位：亿元 (100 million yuan)

年 份 Year	全社会固定资产投资 Total Investment in Fixed Assets		#房地产开发投资 Investment in Real Estate Development		#基础设施投资 Infrastructure Investment		#建筑安装投资 Construction and Installation Investment	
	绝对量 Value	比上年增长(%) Growth Rate over Preceding Year (%)	绝对量 Value	比上年增长(%) Growth Rate over Preceding Year (%)	绝对量 Absolute Volume	比上年增长(%) Growth Rate over Preceding Year (%)	绝对量 Absolute Volume	比上年增长(%) Growth Rate over Preceding Year (%)
1978	22.6				5.4			
1979	26.5	17.3			5.8	7.4		
1980	33.2	25.3			6.0	3.4		
1981	36.6	10.2			5.8	-3.3		
1982	38.6	5.5			6.1	5.2		
1983	51.3	32.9			6.7	9.8		
1984	66.3	29.2			8.8	31.3		
1985	94.0	41.8			13.2	50.0		
1986	106.2	13.0			14.5	9.8		
1987	136.2	28.2			22.1	52.4		
1988	163.0	19.7			23.2	5.0		
1989	139.5	-14.4			26.5	14.2		
1990	179.2	28.5	22.5		31.6	19.2		
1991	192.0	7.1	24.0	6.7	35.2	11.4	107.3	
1992	266.0	38.5	33.7	40.4	58.8	67.0	136.2	26.9
1993	410.4	54.3	58.4	73.3	91.4	55.4	232.0	70.3
1994	648.8	58.1	99.5	70.4	153.4	67.8	362.6	56.3
1995	841.5	29.7	352.8	254.6	156.1	1.8	459.0	26.6
1996	876.9	4.2	328.2	-7.0	188.8	20.9	515.8	12.4
1997	961.2	9.6	330.3	0.6	218.3	15.6	546.2	5.9
1998	1155.6	20.2	377.4	14.3	320.4	46.8	626.9	14.8
1999	1170.6	1.3	421.5	11.7	302.7	-5.5	679.1	8.3
2000	1297.4	10.8	522.1	23.9	351.9	16.3	701.5	3.3
2001	1530.5	18.0	783.8	50.1	356.4	1.3	801.6	14.3
2002	1814.3	18.5	989.4	26.2	411.9	15.6	964.9	20.4
2003	2157.1	18.9	1202.5	21.5	417.8	1.4	1151.3	19.3
2004	2528.3	17.2	1473.3	22.5	463.2	10.9	1438.9	25.0
2005	2827.2	11.8	1525.0	3.5	610.7	31.8	1569.5	9.1
2006	3371.5	19.3	1719.9	12.8	935.3	53.2	1836.0	17.0
2007	3966.6	17.6	1995.8	16.0	1175.8	25.7	2117.9	15.4
2008	3848.5	-3.0	1908.7	-4.4	1160.7	-1.3	1798.8	-15.1
2009	4858.4	26.2	2337.7	22.5	1462.0	26.0	1983.0	10.2
2010	5493.5	13.1	2901.1	24.1	1403.5	-4.0	2124.9	7.2
	(5218.3)							
2011	5910.6	13.3	3036.3	10.1	1400.2	0.3	2585.3	22.4
2012	6462.8	9.3	3153.4	3.9	1789.2	27.8	3076.6	19.0
2013	7032.2	8.8	3483.4	10.5	1785.7	-0.2	3482.2	13.2
2014	7562.3	7.5	3911.3	12.3	2018.1	13.0	3468.1	-0.4
2015	7990.9	5.7	4226.3	8.1	2174.5	7.7	2996.5	-13.6
2016	8461.7	5.9	4045.4	-4.3	2399.5	10.3	3132.8	4.5
2017	8948.1	5.7	3745.9	-7.4	2984.2	24.4	3279.1	4.7
2018		-9.9		3.4		-10.7		3.6

注：1.自2004年起，全社会固定资产投资中不包括零星购置投资，下同。
2.自2011年起，固定资产投资统计起点由50万元调整至500万元。2010年未加括号的为原口径数，括号内为调整后的数据，固定资产投资增长速度按可比口径计算。

Note: a) Since 2004, total investment in fixed assets has not included investment in acquiring minor items, the same below.
b) Since 2011, the statistical threshold of investment in fixed assets has been adjusted from RMB 500,000 to RMB 5 million. Figures for 2010 with no brackets are based on the former standard. Figures in brackets are data after adjustment. The growth rates of investment in fixed assets are calculated on a comparable basis.

9-2 按产业分全社会固定资产投资和增长速度情况(1978-2018年)
INVESTMENT IN FIXED ASSETS AND GROWTH RATE BY THREE STRATA OF INDUSTRY (1978-2018)

单位：亿元 (100 million yuan)

年 份 Year	全社会固定资产投资 Total Investment in Fixed Assets		第一产业 Primary Industry		第二产业 Secondary Industry		第三产业 Tertiary Industry	
	绝对量 Value	比上年增长(%) Growth Rate over Preceding Year (%)	绝对量 Value	比上年增长(%) Growth Rate over Preceding Year (%)	绝对量 Value	比上年增长(%) Growth Rate over Preceding Year (%)	绝对量 Value	比上年增长(%) Growth Rate over Preceding Year (%)
1978	22.6		1.4		10.8		10.4	
1979	26.5	17.3	1.0		12.0		13.5	
1980	33.2	25.3	0.7		15.7		16.8	
1981	36.6	10.2	0.6		13.6		17.2	
1982	38.6	5.5	1.2		15.4		17.9	
1983	51.3	32.9	1.2		16.4		20.9	
1984	66.3	29.2	1.3		20.3		30.6	
1985	94.0	41.8	1.6		32.4		43.8	
1986	106.2	13.0	1.5		41.4		51.6	
1987	136.2	28.2	1.6		46.9		72.9	
1988	163.0	19.7	2.0		48.8		87.9	
1989	139.5	-14.4	1.9		38.4		81.9	
1990	179.2	28.5	2.4		43.3		89.9	
1991	192.0	7.1	2.7		51.3		90.4	
1992	266.0	38.5	3.9		82.9		114.2	
1993	410.4	54.3	2.1		150.4		165.7	
1994	648.8	58.1	3.7		185.8		318.4	
1995	841.5	29.7	3.1		153.7		284.8	
1996	876.9	4.2	2.8		174.9		319.7	
1997	961.2	9.6	0.9		201.1		380.1	
1998	1155.6	20.2	1.5		201.7		479.7	
1999	1170.6	1.3	1.7		179.4		470.4	
2000	1297.4	10.8	3.0		157.2		510.3	
2001	1530.5	18.0	8.4		154.2		1367.9	
2002	1814.3	18.5	7.5		185.0		1621.8	
2003	2157.1	18.9	21.0		260.7		1875.4	
2004	2528.3	17.2	14.6		401.0		2112.7	
2005	2827.2	11.8	11.9		409.7		2405.6	
2006	3371.5	19.3	14.5	21.8	363.2	-11.4	2993.8	24.5
2007	3966.6	17.6	16.7	15.5	484.1	33.3	3465.8	15.8
2008	3848.5	-3.0	28.1	68.2	386.0	-20.3	3434.4	-0.9
2009	4858.4	26.2	57.4	104.6	411.4	6.6	4389.5	27.8
2010	5493.5	13.1	43.2	-24.8	528.1	28.4	4922.3	12.1
2011	5910.6	13.3	47.2	13.8	762.2	47.2	5101.3	9.5
2012	6462.8	9.3	145.4	208.4	719.8	-5.6	5597.5	9.7
2013	7032.2	8.8	175.5	20.6	755.0	4.9	6101.7	9.0
2014	7562.3	7.5	163.9	-6.6	716.8	-5.1	6681.6	9.5
2015	7990.9	5.7	111.0	-32.2	677.1	-5.5	7202.8	7.8
2016	8461.7	5.9	99.8	-10.1	722.9	6.8	7639.0	6.1
2017	8948.1	5.7	95.9	-3.9	893.8	23.6	7958.4	4.2
2018		-9.9		8.9		-43.2		-6.3

注：2000年及以前按产业划分中，不含房地产开发投资及农村投资。自2001年起含房地产开发投资及农村固定资产投资。

Note: Data on investment in fixed assets grouped by three strata of industry excluded investment in real estate development and rural investment in 2000 and before. Since 2001, data on investment in fixed assets have included investment in real estate development and investment in rural fixed assets.

9-3 固定资产投资增长速度情况(2019-2023年)
GROWTH RATE OF INVESTMENT IN FIXED ASSETS (2019-2023)

单位：% (%)

项目	Item	2019	2020	2021	2022	2023
固定资产投资(不含农户)	**Investment In Fixed Assets (Excluding Rural Households)**	**-2.4**	**2.2**	**4.9**	**3.6**	**4.9**
#建筑安装工程	Construction and Installation	5.9	-3.0	2.3	3.2	-0.2
设备工器具购置	Purchase of Equipment and Instruments	-24.3	-11.9	49.7	14.6	24.4
按产业分	**By Three Strata of Industry**					
第一产业	Primary Industry	20.6	-22.8	-59.5	11.6	-45.7
第二产业	Secondary Industry	-9.0	28.0	38.2	20.5	-1.1
第三产业	Tertiary Industry	-2.3	1.0	3.0	1.7	6.0
按行业分	**By Sector**					
农、林、牧、渔业	Agriculture, Forestry, Animal Husbandry and Fishery	20.9	-23.8	-59.7	14.6	-43.5
采矿业	Mining	-9.5	26.5	-21.9	0.2	-30.8
制造业	Manufacturing	0.8	66.6	68.3	18.4	-1.6
电力、热力、燃气及水生产和供应业	Production and Supply of Electricity, Heating, Gas and Water	-15.4	-10.3	-12.6	29.8	1.3
建筑业	Construction	-52.8	67.7	-36.8	-94.4	
批发和零售业	Wholesale and Retail Trades	-46.1	-40.0	3.9	9.3	1.5
交通运输、仓储和邮政业	Transport, Storage and Post	-15.4	-9.4	-3.5	-7.6	10.1
住宿和餐饮业	Hotels and Catering Services	116.2	45.0	10.5	-49.9	2.9
信息传输、软件和信息技术服务业	Information Transmission, Software and Information Technology	-13.3	0.2	20.0	36.0	47.1
金融业	Financial Intermediation	6.9	-9.1	68.2	41.3	-48.9
房地产业	Real Estate	-3.9	3.6	6.9	0.3	3.5
租赁和商务服务业	Leasing and Business Services	157.7	-22.4	-8.0	31.0	-2.3
科学研究和技术服务业	Scientific Research and Technical Services	27.0	57.0	-25.7	60.7	0.8
水利、环境和公共设施管理业	Management of Water Conservancy, Environment and Public Facilities	1.8	-10.0	-18.2	-9.5	9.6
居民服务、修理和其他服务业	Service to Households, Repair and Other Services		173.3	-93.6	212.6	245.4
教　育	Education	-13.0	34.9	17.4	13.0	-11.8
卫生和社会工作	Health and Social Service	49.0	22.7	22.8	10.9	-10.6
文化、体育和娱乐业	Culture, Sports and Entertainment	77.0	1.1	-13.7	-34.9	11.4
公共管理、社会保障和社会组织	Public Management, Social Security and Social Organizations	-27.9	8.9	29.6	-6.7	-50.5
国际组织	International Organizations					

9-4 固定资产投资资金来源情况(1978-2023年)
INVESTMENT IN FIXED ASSETS BY SOURCE OF FUNDS (1978-2023)

单位：亿元 (100 million yuan)

年份 Year	上年末结余资金 Surplus Funds by the End of the Previous Year	本年资金来源小计 Subtotal of Funds at Current Year	中央预算资金 Central Budget	国内贷款 Domestic Loans	债券 Bonds	利用外资 Foreign Investment	自筹资金 Self-raised Funds	其他资金 Other Funds
1978		22.5	16.9					
1979		26.5	19.2					
1980		33.2	18.5					
1981		31.4	15.4					
1982		34.5	14.1					
1983		38.5	16.0					
1984		52.2	22.5					
1985		77.8	30.4					
1986		94.5	33.0					
1987		126.2	43.1					
1988		149.4	37.4					
1989		123.1	35.0	12.8		18.2	44.5	12.6
1990		136.2	34.4	22.8		15.2	52.3	11.5
1991		151.1	35.5	28.2		13.9	65.5	8.0
1992		216.7	42.2	40.1		14.9	109.9	9.6
1993	54.3	425.2	47.1	79.2	1.6	28.0	205.2	64.1
1994	71.1	695.7	64.1	91.5	0.8	96.9	331.2	111.2
1995	200.8	915.8	70.3	122.7	1.1	187.3	339.8	194.6
1996	204.9	926.1	76.7	152.8	1.0	161.2	330.5	203.9
1997	183.1	1016.7	86.3	194.3		139.2	383.4	213.5
1998	207.1	1140.1	98.4	223.8	17.0	132.1	450.2	218.6
1999	212.1	1183.8	136.2	262.2	1.4	82.7	461.3	240.0
2000	293.1	1439.1	107.0	373.8	0.6	51.5	505.6	400.6
2001	325.5	1796.8	136.7	429.4	2.5	35.6	595.6	597.0
2002	433.2	2075.3	108.5	543.8	1.9	41.5	672.8	706.8
2003	542.7	2674.0	78.4	755.2		52.6	887.9	899.9
2004	654.6	3712.8	118.6	804.7		120.5	1245.7	1423.3
2005	924.4	4553.7	128.8	1055.8		70.9	1452.8	1845.4
2006	1043.8	4927.3	126.4	1347.5	32.7	76.2	1532.2	1812.3
2007	1202.2	6193.0	102.2	1513.3	22.4	82.8	2195.6	2276.7
2008	1469.5	5184.7	104.2	1394.2	35.5	80.0	2016.4	1554.5
2009	1321.7	8702.2	118.1	3038.5	17.5	39.3	2441.3	3047.4
2010	2109.1	8327.8	99.5	2218.7	4.3	43.8	3209.1	2752.4
2011	2341.4	8235.4	71.7	1853.6	85.4	29.8	3588.6	2606.3
2012	2830.7	9156.0	156.1	2186.3	12.7	24.9	3478.4	3297.6
2013	3133.1	10580.3	159.6	2554.1	0.8	23.5	4295.2	3547.2
2014	3586.5	10208.7	161.7	2841.0	8.0	33.3	4347.9	2816.8
2015	4238.6	10773.9	184.9	2390.1	10.6	13.2	4853.6	3321.5
2016	4585.2	12065.0	107.9	2677.3	9.2	13.1	5047.8	4209.6
2017	4780.5	11396.2	123.0	2729.7	29.6	21.6	4884.2	3608.1
2018	5229.3	9154.7	289.4	2116.1	27.3	24.6	3877.7	2819.6
2019	4571.7	8767.3	148.2	2021.2	12.5	3.5	2564.8	4017.1
2020	4781.3	9058.7	98.4	2010.8	…	10.0	2767.3	4172.1
2021	5013.7	10242.1	107.8	1513.8	21.9	16.3	3552.2	5030.1
2022	5667.9	9556.0	158.3	1624.0	0.9	7.5	3223.2	4542.1
2023	5527.8	9946.3	131.7	1197.1		4.8	3728.6	4884.1

注：1.本表1978—1992年不含房地产开发和农村投资，1993—2003年不含农村投资，2004—2018年为全社会口径，自2019年起为不含农户口径。
2.自2017年起，原“国家预算内资金”调整为“中央预算资金”。
3.2018—2020年固定资产投资资金来源中不含5000万元以下项目数据。

Note: a) In this table, figures from 1978 to 1992 do not include investment in real estate development and rural investment; figures from 1993 to 2003 do not include rural investment; figures from 2004 to 2018 are those of full coverage; since 2019, the figures are those that excluding rural households.
b) Since 2017, the original "state budget" has been adjusted to "central budget".
c) The data on the source of funds for investment in fixed assets from 2018 to 2020 don't cover the projects of less than RMB 50 million.

9-5 基础设施投资情况(1978-2023年)
INFRASTRUCTURE INVESTMENT (1978-2023)

单位：亿元 (100 million yuan)

年 份 Year	基础设施投资 Infrastructure Investment		#能 源 Energy		#公共服务业 Public Services		#交通运输 Transportation		#邮政电信 Post & Telecommunications		基础设施投资占固定资产投资比重(%) Infrastructure Investment as Percentage of Investment in Fixed Assets (%)
	绝对量 Value	比上年增长(%) Growth Rate over Preceding Year (%)	绝对量 Value	比上年增长(%) Growth Rate over Preceding Year (%)	绝对量 Value	比上年增长(%) Growth Rate over Preceding Year (%)	绝对量 Value	比上年增长(%) Growth Rate over Preceding Year (%)	绝对量 Value	比上年增长(%) Growth Rate over Preceding Year (%)	
1978	5.4		1.4		0.6		1.7		0.4		23.9
1979	5.8		1.1		1.3		1.7		0.4		21.9
1980	6.0		0.9		2.3		2.3		0.5		17.9
1981	5.8		1.3		2.0		1.8		0.4		15.8
1982	6.1		1.4		1.9		1.9		0.4		15.8
1983	6.7		1.5		1.9		2.6		0.6		13.1
1984	8.8		1.4		3.0		2.3		1.1		13.3
1985	13.2		3.8		2.5		2.6		2.7		14.0
1986	14.5		4.8		2.1		3.1		3.5		13.7
1987	22.1		8.0		3.1		6.6		3.2		16.2
1988	23.2		8.8		5.3		4.7		3.0		14.2
1989	26.5		9.2		6.6		5.2		5.2		19.0
1990	31.6		9.0		8.3		8.7		5.4		17.6
1991	35.2		12.4		7.5		9.3		5.8		18.3
1992	58.8		17.7		8.2		20.1		12.3		22.1
1993	91.4		19.3		4.1		29.4		24.2		22.3
1994	153.4		38.0		27.2		30.0		48.6		23.6
1995	156.1		46.7		15.9		34.2		46.4		18.6
1996	188.8		59.2		29.1		54.0		44.1		21.5
1997	218.3		75.6		24.3		51.2		60.3		22.7
1998	320.4		85.1		38.0		104.6		77.5		27.7
1999	302.7		90.3		75.0		63.0		54.0		25.9
2000	351.9		53.2		154.6		64.6		63.7		27.1
2001	356.4		40.8		114.6		104.4		84.8		23.3
2002	411.9		49.5		101.6		159.7		78.7		22.7
2003	417.8		36.1		152.8		129.2		82.2		19.4
2004	463.2		73.0		139.3		148.8		68.5		18.3
2005	610.7		102.3		160.3		224.1		69.9		21.6
2006	935.3	53.2	113.4	10.9	265.3	65.4	439.6	96.2	72.3	3.5	27.7
2007	1175.8	25.7	200.2	76.5	289.5	9.2	548.0	24.7	84.8	17.2	29.6
2008	1160.7	-1.3	144.1	-28.0	291.6	0.7	604.2	10.3	86.7	2.3	30.2
2009	1462.0	26.0	165.4	14.8	434.5	49.0	698.6	15.6	124.9	44.1	30.1
2010	1403.5	-4.0	157.2	-5.0	359.1	-17.3	720.5	3.1	94.2	-24.5	25.5
2011	1400.2	0.3	171.1	10.7	379.4	6.4	680.7	-5.4	82.3	-12.6	23.7
2012	1789.2	27.8	231.9	35.5	508.1	33.9	712.0	4.6	122.0	48.2	27.7
2013	1785.7	-0.2	270.2	16.5	451.3	-11.2	664.5	-6.7	132.9	8.9	25.4
2014	2018.1	13.0	352.7	30.5	502.5	11.3	756.5	13.9	127.3	-4.2	26.7
2015	2174.5	7.7	297.3	-15.7	494.4	-1.6	827.0	9.3	172.3	35.3	27.2
2016	2399.5	10.3	332.0	11.7	643.8	30.2	973.0	17.7	147.5	-14.3	28.4
2017	2984.2	24.4	502.5	51.4	694.5	7.9	1327.0	36.4	194.4	31.8	33.4
2018		-10.7		-45.4		-6.8		1.1		2.3	32.7
2019		-3.8		-15.4		2.4		-9.2		17.8	33.1
2020		-12.3		-10.3		-14.0		-10.2		-17.2	26.3
2021		-8.9		-12.6		-22.8		-4.0		22.6	22.9
2022		5.2		29.8		-7.6		-7.2		62.5	23.2
2023		0.9		1.3		4.4		5.4		-13.6	22.3

注：1.自2004年起基础设施投资包括农村基础设施投资。
2.2018年及以前的基础设施投资占比为占全社会固定资产投资比重，自2019年起为占固定资产投资(不含农户)的比重。

Note: a) Data on infrastructure investment since 2004 have included that of rural infrastructure investment.
b) The proportion of infrastructure investment in and before 2018 refer to the percentage of infrastructure investment in the total investment in fixed assets; since 2019, it refers to the percentage of infrastructure investment in the investment of fixed assets (excluding rural households).

9-6 房地产开发面积(1990-2023年)

单位：万平方米

年 份 Year	房 屋 施工面积 Floor Space of Buildings under Construction	#本 年 新开工 面 积 Floor Space of Buildings Started in the Year	住 宅 Residential Buildings	办公楼 Office Buildings	商业、营业用房及其他 Buildings for Business Use and Others	房 屋 竣工面积 Floor Space of Buildings Completed	住 宅 Residential Buildings
1990	774.0	249.1	643.4	17.4	41.2	271.6	226.5
1991	815.1	317.6	692.1	2.1	57.6	275.2	240.4
1992	1021.1	508.6	865.4	7.6	54.8	331.4	300.8
1993	1262.0	524.8	887.6			356.4	280.6
1994	1593.2	659.4	1107.6			445.7	385.6
1995	2810.2	1012.2	1728.7	462.7	252.6	653.0	506.3
1996	2824.6	578.7	1520.7	638.7	283.9	663.4	470.8
1997	2869.6	848.4	1541.1	637.7	260.8	682.3	478.3
1998	3499.1	1193.4	2107.2	590.7	297.7	842.8	588.7
1999	3784.0	1061.8	2447.9	484.4	281.3	1208.5	908.3
2000	4455.0	1676.9	2971.6	449.1	281.3	1365.6	1013.7
2001	5966.7	2789.8	4349.6	495.5	330.6	1707.4	1393.4
2002	7510.7	3206.0	5397.5	672.5	400.3	2384.4	1926.2
2003	9070.7	3433.8	6352.9	901.3	557.7	2593.7	2080.8
2004	9931.3	3054.3	6759.4	1122.4	641.8	3067.0	2343.9
2005	10748.5	2965.9	7283.4	1209.8	809.2	3770.9	2841.4
2006	10483.5	3179.4	6311.3	1245.8	1403.0	3193.9	2193.3
2007	10438.6	2557.4	5914.5	1364.6	1482.1	2891.7	1854.0
2008	10014.3	2337.2	5538.2	1287.2	1429.8	2558.0	1399.3
2009	9719.1	2246.6	5551.9	1132.2	1323.4	2678.6	1613.2
2010	10300.9	2974.2	6176.0	1054.8	1229.3	2386.7	1498.5
2011	12065.4	4246.1	7168.1	1422.7	1187.5	2245.2	1316.1
2012	13122.5	3224.2	7510.4	1711.9	1236.9	2390.9	1522.7
2013	13886.9	3577.5	7406.9	2114.1	4365.9	2666.4	1692.0
2014	13641.5	2502.8	6999.7	2277.1	4364.7	3054.1	1804.3
2015	13095.0	2790.2	6314.6	2426.8	4353.6	2631.5	1378.2
2016	13089.8	2813.7	5927.6	2447.3	4714.9	2383.1	1275.2
2017	12608.6	2475.7	5506.6	2428.4	4673.6	1466.7	604.0
2018	12962.6	2321.1	5877.1	2220.5	4865.0	1557.9	731.2
2019	12515.0	2073.2	5640.1	1951.0	4923.9	1343.3	583.2
2020	13918.6	3006.6	6715.3	1654.2	5549.2	1545.7	728.5
2021	14055.3	1895.9	6895.6	1461.4	5698.3	1983.9	981.1
2022	13333.1	1774.4	6713.6	1307.3	5312.3	1938.5	1096.2
2023	12531.3	1257.1	6256.8	1197.2	5077.4	2112.4	1164.9

注：1.2005年以前的商品房销售面积为竣工后的全部商品房销售面积，自2005年起为期房与现房销售面积之和。
2.自2010年起，商品房销售面积中包含定向安置房数据。
3.2012年及以前商业、营业用房及其他只包括商业及服务性等营业性用房，自2013年起统计范围包括：厂房、仓库、商业营业用房、服务业用房、教育用房、文化体育用房、医疗用房、科研用房及其他用房，下同。自2017年起，原“商业、非公益用房及其他”更名为“商业、营业用房及其他”。

STATISTICS ON FLOOR SPACE OF REAL ESTATE DEVELOPMENT (1990-2023)

(10000 sq.m)

办公楼 Office Buildings	商业、营业用房及其他 Buildings for Business Use and Others	商品房销售面积 Floor Space of Commercial Buildings Sold	住宅 Residential Buildings	办公楼 Office Buildings	商业、营业用房及其他 Buildings for Business Use and Others	年末商品房待售面积 Floor Space of Vacant Commercial Buildings at the Year End	住宅 Residential Buildings	办公楼 Office Buildings	商业、营业用房及其他 Buildings for Business Use and Others
9.7	13.3	142.2							
0.9	10.9	154.0	152.5						
2.7	8.3	159.1	153.0						
		182.0	182.0						
		168.6	149.0	17.2	1.1				
27.9	43.5	191.9	180.0	4.0	4.5	81.5			
79.0	38.3	215.3	183.1	13.7	14.4	214.8	179.6		
80.9	42.4	290.9	256.2	18.8	8.0	298.3	258.9		
92.3	69.8	409.2	377.0	23.2	7.0	334.8	262.9		
108.8	43.1	544.4	484.7	48.0	6.8	624.3	529.1		
97.2	48.7	956.9	898.2	41.2	6.1	627.4	515.1		
98.0	48.2	1205.0	1127.5	49.8	17.4	774.0	634.1		
97.4	82.9	1708.3	1604.4	44.0	32.9	919.0	763.2		
94.0	117.5	1895.8	1771.1	38.1	50.8	1123.4	896.9		
153.9	225.3	2472.0	2285.8	92.5	60.2	1044.1	723.8		
287.8	180.9	2803.2	2566.0	131.2	66.9	1374.2	799.7		
304.4	289.2	2607.6	2205.0	260.3	108.6	1039.7	494.1		
314.8	315.1	2176.6	1731.5	265.7	134.8	1136.2	411.8		
364.6	313.1	1335.4	1031.4	139.4	112.4	1438.3	522.7		
316.6	322.4	2362.3	1880.5	255.8	157.1	1351.4	426.8		
198.4	271.9	1639.5	1201.4	208.1	142.1	1482.7	511.9		
245.2	232.4	1440.0	1035.0	211.4	108.7	1792.6	699.8		
226.8	240.1	1943.7	1483.4	253.5	114.0	1911.8	789.5		
273.1	701.3	1903.1	1363.7	317.9	221.5	1861.4	829.3	180.1	852.0
387.5	862.3	1459.0	1141.3	136.8	180.9	2065.7	864.8	307.2	893.7
385.4	867.8	1554.7	1127.3	243.0	184.4	2168.1	867.7	332.5	968.0
343.7	764.2	1675.1	993.5	415.4	266.2	2160.8	845.8	320.7	994.3
321.2	541.5	875.0	612.8	108.3	153.9	2092.1	811.2	336.1	944.8
249.9	576.8	696.2	526.8	75.8	93.6	2153.3	833.7	390.6	929.0
290.3	469.8	938.9	789.0	53.4	96.5	2489.5	893.1	569.0	1027.4
242.2	575.0	970.9	733.6	73.2	164.1	2454.2	881.9	530.5	1041.8
142.9	859.9	1107.1	877.1	55.3	174.7	2396.3	830.8	555.5	1010.0
177.8	664.5	1040.0	741.9	74.8	223.3	2617.0	854.4	567.9	1194.7
166.2	781.4	1131.8	818.3	75.7	237.9	2992.6	1079.8	641.9	1270.9

Note: a) Before 2005, the floor space of commercial buildings sold referred to the total floor space of completed commercial buildings sold; since 2005, the figure refers to the sum of floor space of completed buildings sold and those under construction sold.

b) Since 2010, the floor space of commercial buildings sold has included figures of targeted resettlement buildings.

c) In and before 2012, buildings for business use and others only included business occupancies for business and service use. Since 2013,the statistical range has included: factory buildings, warehouses, buildings for business use, service industry buildings, education buildings, cultural and sports buildings, medical buildings, scientific research buildings and others, the same applies to the following table. Since 2017, the original "buildings for commercial use, non-public buildings and others "has been changed to" buildings for business use and others".

9-7 房地产开发投资情况(1990-2023年)
INVESTMENT IN REAL ESTATE DEVELOPMENT (1990-2023)

单位：亿元 (100 million yuan)

年 份 Year	房地产开发投资 Investment in Real Estate Development		#住 宅 Residential Buildings		#办公楼 Office Buildings	
	绝对量 Value	比上年增长(%) Growth Rate over Preceding Year (%)	绝对量 Value	比上年增长(%) Growth Rate over Preceding Year (%)	绝对量 Value	比上年增长(%) Growth Rate over Preceding Year (%)
1990	22.5		12.3			
1991	24.0		14.0			
1992	33.7		20.0			
1993	58.4		38.1			
1994	99.5		50.3			
1995	352.8		142.4		71.5	
1996	328.2	-7.0	124.9	-12.3	84.2	17.8
1997	330.3	0.6	132.9	6.4	91.1	8.2
1998	377.4	14.3	168.0	26.4	78.5	-13.8
1999	421.5	11.7	236.6	40.8	52.5	-33.1
2000	522.1	23.9	288.3	21.9	45.2	-13.9
2001	783.8	50.1	464.2	61.0	72.0	59.3
2002	989.4	26.2	586.7	26.4	97.3	35.1
2003	1202.5	21.5	633.0	7.9	142.7	46.7
2004	1473.3	22.5	776.0	22.6	187.9	31.7
2005	1525.0	3.5	779.5	0.5	196.2	4.4
2006	1719.9	12.8	863.6	10.8	216.7	10.4
2007	1995.8	16.0	991.7	14.8	242.2	11.8
2008	1908.7	-4.4	940.6	-5.2	170.5	-29.6
2009	2337.7	22.5	906.6	-3.6	166.7	-2.2
2010	2901.1	24.1	1509.0	66.4	259.1	55.4
2011	3036.3	10.1	1778.3	17.8	363.8	40.4
2012	3153.4	3.9	1628.0	-8.5	384.8	5.8
2013	3483.4	10.5	1724.6	5.9	611.7	59.0
2014	3911.3	12.3	1962.0	13.8	750.2	22.6
2015	4226.3	8.1	1962.7	...	906.6	20.8
2016	4045.4	-4.3	1950.9	-0.6	699.1	-22.9
2017	3745.9	-7.4	1725.5	-11.6	742.9	6.3
2018		3.4		17.4		-29.7
2019		-0.9		0.7		-27.3
2020		2.6		13.6		-17.5
2021		5.1		8.9		-7.6
2022		1.0		5.8		-22.5
2023		0.6		1.8		19.7

9−8 房地产开发企业经营情况(2023年)
OPERATING STATISTICS ON ENTERPRISES FOR REAL ESTATE DEVELOPMENT (2023)

项　　目	Item	企业单位个数(个) Number of Enterprises (unit)	实收资本合计(万元) Total Paid-in Capital (10000 yuan)	资产总计(万元) Total Assets (10000 yuan)	主营业务收入(万元) Revenue from Principal Business (10000 yuan)	利润总额(万元) Total Profits (10000 yuan)
合　　计	**Total**	**1171**	**72337385**	**523000572**	**44566181**	**933822**
按登记注册统计类别分	**By Statistical Category of Registration**					
内资企业	Domestic Invested Enterprises	1116	66670373	495638020	43864301	1230722
港澳台投资企业	Enterprises with Investment from Hong Kong, Macao and Taiwan	27	3228144	18226046	432624	-267899
外商投资企业	Foreign Invested Enterprises	28	2438869	9136506	269256	-29001
按资质等级分	**By Qualification Grade**					
一　级	First-grade	29	5008807	65599057	1233847	-212995
二　级	Second-grade	521	41566824	253583529	25012712	1165389
三　级	Third-grade	33	2138491	22355775	266144	211009
四　级	Fourth-grade	315	10273188	103755169	6255805	-406469
暂　定	Provisional	194	9353662	55107966	10472594	115259
其　他	Others	79	3996413	22599075	1325079	61628
按营业状况分	**By Operating Condition**					
营　业	Operating	1167	72337385	523000572	44566181	933822
停　业	Closed	4				
其　他	Others					

9−9 房地产开发企业开发建设情况(2023年)
DEVELOPMENT OF REAL ESTATE DEVELOPMENT ENTERPRISES (2023)

项　　目	Item	2023	2023年为2022年% 2023 as % of 2022
本年实际到位资金　（亿元）	**Actual Funds in Place in the Year (100 million yuan)**	**5849.2**	**103.9**
#国内贷款	Domestic Loans	740.8	70.8
自筹资金	Self-raised Funds	1217.6	107.1
定金及预收款	Deposit and Advance Payment	2849.2	102.9
个人按揭贷款	Individual Mortgage Loans	522.1	133.6

主要统计指标解释

全社会固定资产投资 是指以货币形式表现的在一定时期内全社会建造和购置固定资产的工作量以及与此有关的费用的总称。

固定资产投资（不含农户） 是指城镇和农村各种登记注册类型的企业、事业行政单位及城镇个体户进行的计划总投资 500 万元及以上的建设项目投资和房地产开发投资。

基础设施投资 是指能够为企业提供作为中间投入用于生产的基本需求；能够为消费者提供所需的基本消费服务；能够为社区提供用于改善不利的外部环境的服务等建设的投资，包括固定资产投资中用于市政工程、电信工程、公共设施和水利环保等建设的投资。

上年末结余资金 是指上年资金来源中没有形成固定资产投资额而结余的资金。包括尚未用到工程上去的材料价值、未开始安装的需要安装设备价值及结存的现金和银行存款等。

本年资金来源小计 是指固定资产投资单位在报告期收到的，用于固定资产投资的各种货币资金。包括中央预算内资金、国内贷款、债券、利用外资、自筹资金和其他资金。

中央预算资金 指来源于中央公共预算安排的用于项目建设的资金数额。

国内贷款 是指报告期固定资产投资项目单位向银行及非银行金融机构借入的用于固定资产投资的各种国内借款，包括银行利用自有资金及吸收存款发放的贷款、上级拨入的国内贷款、国家专项贷款，地方财政专项资金安排的贷款、国内储备贷款、周转贷款等。

利用外资 是指报告期收到的用于固定资产建造和购置投资的境外资金(包括设备、材料、技术在内)。包括外商直接投资、对外借款(外国政府贷款、国际金融组织贷款、出口信贷、外国银行商业贷款、对外发行债券和股票)及外商其他投资(包括利用外商投资收益在国内进行固定资产再投资活动的资金)。不包括我国自有外汇资金(包括国家外汇、地方外汇、留成外汇、调剂外汇和国内银行自有资金发行的外汇贷款等)。

自筹资金 指在报告期内筹集的用于项目建设和购置的资金。包括自有资金、股东投入资金和借入资金，但不包括各类财政性资金、从各类金融机构借入资金和国外资金。

其他资金来源 是指在报告期收到的除以上各种资金之外其他用于固定资产投资的资金。包括社会集资、个人资金、无偿捐赠的资金、其他单位拨入的资金、市级预算资金和区级预算资金等。

建筑安装投资 是指各种房屋、建筑物的建造工程，各种设备、装置的安装工程，又称建筑安装工作量。建筑工程投资必须经过兴工动料，通过施工活动才能实现。在安装工程中，不包括被安装设备本身价值。

房地产开发投资 指自本年 1 月 1 日起至本年最后一天止，房地产开发项目中全部用于房屋建筑物、配套的服务设施、土地开发工程和土地购置的投资；不包括单纯的土地开发和交易活动。

房屋施工面积 是指报告期内施工的全部房屋建筑面积。包括本期新开工的房屋建筑面积、上期跨入本期继续施工的房屋建筑面积、上期停缓建在本期恢复施工的房屋建筑面积、本期竣工的房屋建筑面积以及本期施工后又停缓建的房屋建筑面积。多层建筑应填各层建筑面积之和。

房屋竣工面积 是指报告期内房屋建筑按照设计要求已全部完工，达到住人和使用条件，经验收鉴定合格(或达到竣工验收标准)，可正式移交使用的各栋房屋建筑面积的总和。

待售面积 指报告期末已竣工的可供销售或出租的商品房屋建筑面积中，尚未销售或出租的商品房屋建筑面积，包括以前年度竣工和本期竣工的房屋面积，但不包括报告期已竣工的拆迁还建、统建代建、公共配套建筑、房地产公司自用及周转房等不可销售或出租的房屋面积。

Explanatory Notes on Main Statistical Indicators

Total Investment in Fixed Assets refers to the volume of activities in construction and purchases of fixed assets of the whole city and the related fees, expressed in monetary terms during the reference period.

Investment in Fixed Assets (Excluding Rural Households) refers to the investment in construction projects with a total planned investment of RMB 5 million and over by urban and rural enterprises of various registration types, public institutions and administrative units and by urban self-employed individuals as well as the real estate development investment.

Infrastructure Investment refers to the investment that can provide enterprises with the basic needs as intermediate inputs for production, the investment that can provide consumers with the basic consumer services they need, and the investment in construction that can provide communities with services to improve the unfavorable external environment, including the investment in fixed assets that are used in municipal engineering, telecommunications engineering, public facilities, water conservancy and environmental protection, etc.

Surplus Funds by the Year End of the Previous Year refers to the fund in the previous year that was not included in the investment in fixed assets, including the value of materials not yet used for projects, value of equipment to be installed, and balance of cash and bank deposits.

Subtotal of Funds at Current Year refers to various monetary funds received during the reporting period by investors that was used for investment in fixed assets, including funds from central budgetary funds, domestic loans, bonds, foreign investment, self-raised funds and other funds.

Central Budgetary Fund refers to the amount of fund that comes from the central public budget arrangement and is used for project construction.

Domestic Loans refer to loans of various forms borrowed by fixed assets investment project entities from banks and non-bank financial institutions for the purpose of investment in fixed assets during the reporting period, including loans issued by banks from their self-owned funds and deposits, domestic loans appropriated by higher authorities in charge, special loans allocated by the central government, loans arranged by local government from special funds, domestic reserve loans and revolving loans.

Foreign Investment refers to foreign funds received during the reporting period for the investment in construction and purchase of fixed assets (including equipment, materials and technologies), including foreign direct investment, foreign loans (loans from foreign governments and international financial institutions, export credit, commercial loans from foreign banks, issued bonds and stocks overseas), and other foreign investments (including funds for domestic re-investment in fixed assets by earnings from foreign investment). It does not include foreign exchanges owned by China (including foreign exchanges owned by the central and local governments, foreign exchanges retained, foreign exchange swap, loans in foreign exchanges issued by the domestic banks with their self-owned funds, etc.).

Self-raised Funds refer to non-budgetary funds received by fixed assets investors during the reporting period that are raised by different regions, departments, enterprises and public institutions for investment in fixed assets, including self-owned funds of central departments, local authorities at all levels, enterprises and public institutions.

Other Funds refer to funds for investment in fixed assets received during the reporting period from sources other than those listed above, including social funds, personal funds, donated funds and funds transferred from other institutions, municipal-level budgetary fund and district-level budgetary fund, etc.

Construction and Installation Investment refers to the investment in construction projects of various houses and buildings, and installation projects of various equipment and devices, also known as the workload of construction and installation. It can only be realized through construction work and consumption of materials. For installation projects, the value of equipment installed is not included.

Real Estate Development Investment refers to the investment in real estate development projects that is all used in houses and buildings, supporting service facilities, land development projects and land purchase from January 1st to the last day of the year, but excludes the simple land development and trading activities.

Floor Space of Buildings under Construction refers to the total floor space area of buildings under construction in the reference period. It includes buildings new started; buildings started earlier and continued during the reference period; buildings suspended earlier but restarted during the reference period; buildings completed during the reference period; and buildings under construction but suspended during the reference period. For multi-floor building, please fill in the sum of floor space of all floors.

Floor Space of Buildings Completed refers to the total floor space of all houses and buildings fully completed as required in the design plan during the reporting period, which have been examined as qualified for living and use (or have met the completion inspection standards), and can be handed over and put into use.

Floor Space for Sale refers to floor space of commercial buildings that has not been sold or rented out among the floor space of completed commercial buildings available for sale or renting by the end of the reporting period. It consists of the floor space of completed buildings in previous years and in the current year, but does not include relocated houses or buildings of unified construction or agent contract, as well as houses not for sale or renting such as public supporting buildings, owner-occupied and relocation housing of real estate companies.

10

北京统计年鉴2024　BEIJING STATISTICAL YEARBOOK 2024

对外经济贸易
FOREIGN ECONOMIC RELATIONS AND TRADE

简要说明

一、主要内容

本章资料主要反映北京市对外经济贸易的发展状况，包括对外贸易、利用外资、对外经济合作的历年概况。

二、统计范围

（一）货物进出口情况

货物进出口统计的范围是凡能引起北京市海关境内物质资源存量增加或减少的进出口货物，除制度另有规定者外，均列入该项统计，调查方法采用全面调查。主要内容包括北京地区进出口总值；主要产品进出口数量等。

（二）口岸运营情况

口岸运营的统计范围是北京首都国际机场空港口岸、北京大兴国际机场空港口岸、北京丰台货运口岸、北京朝阳口岸、北京西站铁路口岸、北京平谷国际陆港、北京天竺综合保税区。主要内容包括旅客吞吐量、货邮吞吐量、监管货物的数量、征收关税等。

（三）利用外资情况

利用外资情况统计范围为外商投资，包括外国和港澳台地区的自然人、企业或其他组织通过在中国境内设立外商投资企业，取得中国境内企业的股份、股权、财产份额或其他类似权益，设立境外银行分行、境外保险公司分公司，开发油气等方式进行的投资。

（四）对外经济合作

对外经济合作的统计范围是经各级商务部门批准的从事对外承包、劳务合作和设计咨询业务并具有法人资格的对外承包劳务企业；调查方法采用全面调查。主要内容包括对外承包工程、劳务合作和设计咨询。

Brief Introduction

I. Main Content

Data in this chapter mainly show the development of foreign economic relations and trade in Beijing, including foreign trade, use of foreign capital, and foreign economic cooperation in Beijing over the years.

II. Scope of Statistics

(I) Statistics for Imports and Exports of Goods

The scope of statistics for imports and exports of goods covers all imports and exports that lead to increase or decrease in the stock of physical resources at Beijing customs, except for those otherwise stated in regulations, and the survey was conducted with comprehensive survey method. Data mainly include: total value of imports and exports in Beijing, and quantity of imports and exports of major products, and so on.

(II) Statistics for Port Operation

The statistical scope of port operation covers the Port of Beijing Capital International Airport, the Port of Daxing International Airport, Beijing Fengtai Cargo Transport Port, Beijing Chaoyang Transport Port, Railway Port at Beijing West Railway Station, Beijing Pinggu International Land Port, and Beijing Tianzhu Comprehensive Bonded Zone. Data mainly include: passenger throughput, cargos carried, quantity of cargos under regulation and duties levied.

(III) Use of Foreign Capital

The scope of statistics for the use of foreign capital refers to foreign investment, including the investment made by natural persons, enterprises or other organizations of foreign countries or Hong Kong, Macao and Taiwan regions, in the ways such as establishing foreign invested enterprises within the territory of China, acquiring shares, equity, property shares or other similar rights and interests in Chinese domestic enterprises, establishing branches of overseas banks and overseas insurance companies, and development of oil and gas.

(IV) Foreign Economic Cooperation

Statistics cover foreign labor service enterprises with legal person statues that are engaged in foreign contracting, labor service cooperation and design consulting with approval from departments of commerce at different levels. The survey was conducted with comprehensive survey method. Data mainly include: foreign contracting projects, labor service cooperation and design consulting.

10-1 北京地区对外经济贸易(1983-2023年)
INTERNATIONAL TRADE AND ECONOMIC COOPERATION IN BEIJING (1983-2023)

年份 Year	货物进出口总值(亿美元) Total Value of Imports and Exports of Goods (USD 100 million)	出口 Exports	#高新技术产品 High and New-tech Products	#机电产品 Mechanical and Electrical Products	进口 Imports	#高新技术产品 High and New-tech Products	#机电产品 Mechanical and Electrical Products
1983	306.0	146.9			159.1		
1984	355.9	175.2			180.8		
1985	325.4	43.7			281.7		
1986	306.0	37.1			268.9		
1987	267.0	35.4			231.6		
1988	298.9	39.6			259.3		
1989	286.1	30.2			255.9		
1990	236.4	44.1			192.3		
1991	242.4	45.7			196.7		
1992	249.8	56.1		15.8	193.7	27.1	73.1
1993	279.2	67.0		15.1	212.2	30.3	88.5
1994	288.8	83.4		19.5	205.4	42.1	112.1
1995	370.4	102.5		28.2	267.9	40.7	122.5
1996	293.2	81.2		25.4	212.0	24.1	73.4
1997	303.9	96.1		27.1	207.8	34.6	76.6
1998	305.1	105.1		32.5	199.9	34.8	90.9
1999	343.6	99.0		32.1	244.6	56.8	121.4
2000	494.0	119.7	22.7	43.7	374.3	74.0	142.6
2001	515.0	117.7	26.3	47.8	397.3	99.3	188.3
2002	525.1	126.1	31.4	57.1	398.9	91.6	170.2
2003	685.0	168.9	39.6	71.5	516.1	99.0	194.9
2004	945.8	205.7	58.1	97.0	740.1	105.3	227.2
2005	1255.1	308.7	97.1	155.7	946.4	136.6	269.6
2006	1580.4	379.5	138.9	217.1	1200.8	170.5	378.7
2007	1930.0	489.3	179.8	286.2	1440.7	236.0	447.8
2008	2716.9	575.0	190.6	335.4	2141.9	241.8	498.8
2009	2147.9	483.6	175.2	308.0	1664.3	235.7	519.4
2010	3016.6	554.4	193.7	339.4	2462.2	274.9	666.1
2011	3895.8	590.0	181.2	352.3	3305.9	314.5	766.8
2012	4081.1	596.3	190.2	373.8	3484.8	298.8	721.8
2013	4299.4	631.0	203.6	389.5	3668.4	292.4	716.8
2014	4155.4	623.4	187.5	379.0	3532.0	293.7	778.5
2015	3194.2	546.7	140.3	314.4	2647.5	261.3	659.2
2016	2823.8	520.2	113.2	272.8	2303.6	255.0	655.3
2017	3237.2	585.0	112.8	284.1	2652.2	264.9	659.4
2018	4124.3	741.7	152.2	322.1	3382.6	278.3	691.1
2019	4160.8	749.8	157.5	314.5	3411.0	269.7	658.3
2020	3350.4	670.1	197.4	320.7	2680.3	279.6	666.2
2021	4710.2	946.4	403.6	416.6	3763.8	360.3	790.1
2022	5465.0	881.7	259.1	406.3	4583.3	403.1	781.0
2023	5187.5	852.7	209.0	396.3	4334.7	485.5	753.7

注：货物进出口总值为海关统计的北京地区进出口数据(包括中央单位)。
资料来源：中华人民共和国北京海关、北京市商务局。
Note: Figures of total value of imports and exports of goods are imports and exports data of Beijing counted by Beijing Customs (including central government units).
Source: Beijing Customs District P.R.China and Beijing Municipal Commerce Bureau.

10-1 续表 Continued

年份 Year	货物进出口总值(亿元) Total Value of Imports and Exports of Goods (100 million yuan)	出口 Exports	进口 Imports	新设外资企业数(个) Number of Newly Established Foreign Invested Enterprises (unit)	实际利用外商直接投资额(万美元) Amount of Foreign Direct Investment Actually Utilized (USD10000)
1983					
1984					
1985					
1986					
1987					
1988					
1989					
1990					
1991					
1992	1377.1	309.2	1067.9		
1993	1607.9	385.8	1222.1		
1994	2492.4	719.2	1773.1		
1995	3108.2	863.2	2244.9		
1996	2450.3	680.9	1769.4		
1997	2522.5	798.4	1724.0		
1998	2530.6	872.2	1658.4		
1999	2356.9	665.6	1691.3		
2000	4090.1	991.4	3098.7	1145	168368
2001	4262.2	974.3	3287.8	1146	176818
2002	4345.7	1043.9	3301.8	1370	172464
2003	5674.5	1398.6	4275.9	1539	219126
2004	7824.5	1702.1	6122.4	1806	255974
2005	10331.9	2540.4	7791.4	2138	352834
2006	12670.7	3039.9	9630.8	2110	457969
2007	14831.0	3764.7	11066.3	2177	507571
2008	19113.6	4044.2	15069.4	1896	491795
2009	14648.2	3301.9	11346.3	1422	524780
2010	20478.2	3766.1	16712.1	1629	533617
2011	25303.9	3835.4	21468.5	1638	590661
2012	25765.2	3766.8	21998.4	1361	616463
2013	26691.0	3920.1	22770.9	1190	684245
2014	25517.9	3829.4	21688.6	1318	816911
2015	19827.7	3395.0	16432.6	1386	1271540
2016	18652.2	3433.5	15218.6	1079	1258555
2017	21923.9	3962.5	17961.4	1301	2325755
2018	27182.5	4878.5	22303.9	1641	1673635
2019	28663.5	5167.8	23495.7	1636	1362385
2020	23215.9	4654.9	18561.0	1261	1339335
2021	30438.4	6118.5	24319.9	1924	1443424
2022	36445.5	5890.0	30555.5	1408	1740768
2023	36466.3	6000.1	30466.3	1729	1371411

10-2 北京地区货物进出口贸易总值(按企业性质、贸易方式分)
TOTAL VALUE OF IMPORTS AND EXPORTS OF GOODS IN BEIJING (BY ENTERPRISE TYPE AND TRADE METHOD)

项 目	Item	金 额 (万美元) Value (USD 10000)		金 额 (万元) Value (10000 yuan)	
		2023	2022	2023	2022
进出口总值	**Total Value of Imports and Exports**	**51874509**	**54649912**	**364663153**	**364455076**
出 口	**Exports**	**8527265**	**8817061**	**60000516**	**58900240**
按企业性质分	**By Enterprise Type**				
#国有企业	State-owned Enterprises	4842591	4789086	34046376	32078500
外商投资企业	Enterprises with Foreign Investment	2137252	2507669	15053428	16683359
民营企业	Private Enterprises	1467928	1439247	10341638	9589339
按贸易方式分	**By Trade method**				
#一般贸易	General Trade	6942569	7163899	48860866	47870997
来料加工装配贸易	Trade of Processing and Assembly with Supplied Materials	86591	81439	609762	542250
进料加工贸易	Trade of Processing Imported Materials	264054	303387	1860307	2019946
对外承包工程出口货物	Export of Goods for Contracted Foreign Projects	607483	478234	4272480	3218983
出料加工贸易	Trade of Processing Exported Materials	6194	871	44088	5737
进 口	**Imports**	**43347244**	**45832851**	**304662637**	**305554835**
按企业性质分	**By Enterprise Type**				
#国有企业	State-owned Enterprises	33329147	36086743	234142295	240763002
外商投资企业	Enterprises with Foreign Investment	5933806	6558929	41786885	43543047
民营企业	Private Enterprises	4052625	3113463	28510921	20744851
按贸易方式分	**By Trade method**				
#一般贸易	General Trade	37746263	40692722	265267740	271331466
来料加工装配贸易	Trade of Processing and Assembly with Supplied Materials	1724996	1651947	12152183	10988575
进料加工贸易	Trade of Processing Imported Materials	152917	154714	1075632	1030126
外商投资企业作为投资进口的设备、物品	Equipment and Goods Imported as Investment by Enterprises with Foreign Investment	76	1045	544	6765
租赁贸易	Leasing Trade	1949	17505	13736	118290

资料来源：中华人民共和国北京海关。
Source: Beijing Customs District P.R.China.

10-3 北京地区货物进出口贸易总值(按国别、地区分)
TOTAL VALUE OF IMPORTS AND EXPORTS OF GOODS IN BEIJING (BY COUNTRY AND REGION)

项目	Item	金额(万美元) Value (USD 10000)		金额(万元) Value (10000 yuan)	
		2023	2022	2023	2022
进出口总值	**Total Value of Imports and Exports**	**51874509**	**54649912**	**364663153**	**364455076**
出　口	**Exports**	**8527265**	**8817061**	**60000516**	**58900240**
按国别(地区)分	**By Country (Region)**				
#中国香港	Hong Kong, China	935071	931108	6579758	6196912
中国澳门	Macao, China	36660	22783	258022	151135
中国台湾	Taiwan, China	134156	164273	943733	1090407
日　本	Japan	386830	381896	2718969	2553866
新加坡	Singapore	757508	774920	5330728	5192796
韩　国	Republic of Korea	201537	260129	1423937	1728665
越　南	Vietnam	182280	224496	1281603	1488445
伊　朗	Iran	55945	50986	392552	342741
印　度	India	201972	159233	1423626	1064139
印度尼西亚	Indonesia	186816	191205	1316201	1271954
英　国	United Kingdom	75594	87025	531250	574918
德　国	Germany	129213	162511	908731	1076697
法　国	France	65400	87852	460331	581259
意大利	Italy	78141	106639	548068	705531
匈牙利	Hungary	10082	19236	70946	127733
俄罗斯	Russia	386537	301574	2729548	2032179
美　国	United States	526954	513497	3710923	3417566
澳大利亚	Australia	220208	240185	1549010	1627570
进　口	**Imports**	**43347244**	**45832851**	**304662637**	**305554835**
按国别(地区)分	**By Country (Region)**				
#中国香港	Hong Kong, China	519862	119299	3632369	803496
日　本	Japan	1527169	1649322	10764947	10968949
新加坡	Singapore	327645	238851	2303798	1582557
韩　国	Republic of Korea	480771	347704	3384077	2326836
沙特阿拉伯	Saudi Arabia	2141476	3179436	14991462	21151767
英　国	United Kingdom	453231	543820	3199324	3588868
德　国	Germany	2319152	2544799	16327438	16906470
法　国	France	340748	351275	2381646	2348224
意大利	Italy	262073	248367	1847858	1656578
瑞　士	Switzerland	2251448	1982120	15684574	13401589
比利时	Belgium	131646	101905	928708	670146
俄罗斯	Russia	2186923	2548910	15484940	16936496
加拿大	Canada	1862492	1863034	13157166	12739015
美　国	United States	3136219	3587006	22017844	23748428
澳大利亚	Australia	2468732	2439288	17295463	16204968
阿　曼	Oman	2113740	2411889	14831579	16095176
安哥拉	Angola	1781191	1791136	12557739	11891559

资料来源：中华人民共和国北京海关。
Source: Beijing Customs District P.R.China.

10-4 北京地区海关主要商品进口量及金额(2023年)
MAJOR IMPORTED COMMODITIES IN QUANTITY AND VALUE AT BEIJING CUSTOMS (2023)

项　目		Item		进口数量 Import Volume	进口金额(万美元) Import Value (USD 10000)
粮　食	(吨)	Grain	(ton)	37443105	1513572
食用植物油	(吨)	Edible Vegetable Oil	(ton)	1188159	130819
食　糖	(吨)	Sugar	(ton)	2124071	119430
酒类及饮料		Alcohol and Beverages			30884
天然及合成橡胶(包括胶乳)	(吨)	Natural and Synthetic Rubber (Including Latex)	(ton)	51327	7582
纸浆、纸及其制品	(吨)	Paper Pulp, Paper and Paper Products	(ton)	1448604	113230
#纸　浆	(吨)	Paper Pulp	(ton)	1174425	84326
羊毛及毛条	(吨)	Wool and Wool Tops	(ton)	5174	2027
棉　花	(吨)	Cotton	(ton)	508381	106886
纺织纱线、织物及其制品		Textile Yarn, Fabric and Its Products			36626
#合成纤维纱线	(吨)	Synthetic Fiber Yarn	(ton)	1225	2183
铁矿砂及其精矿	(吨)	Iron Ore and Concentrates	(ton)	113732071	1310239
原　油	(吨)	Crude Oil	(ton)	301454961	18439756
成品油	(吨)	Petroleum Products Refined	(ton)	7152478	470535
医药材及药品	(吨)	Pharmaceutical Materials and Drugs	(ton)	36042	1743708
肥　料	(吨)	Chemical Fertilizers	(ton)	7600567	322975
塑料制品	(吨)	Plastic Articles	(ton)	26771	63128
服装及衣着附件		Clothing and Accessories			26168
钢　材	(吨)	Rolled Steel	(ton)	118102	44797
印刷、装订机械及其零件		Printing and Binding Machinery and Its Parts			101267
自动数据处理设备及其零部件		Automatic Data Processing Equipment and Its Parts			92129
变压器	(个)	Transformer	(unit)	750085	4314
电视摄像机、数字照相机及视频摄录一体机	(台)	TV Camera, Digital Camera and Video Recorder	(set)	1222590	83394
印刷电路	(万块)	Printed Circuit	(10000 units)	135930	6927
集成电路	(万个)	Integrated Circuits	(10000 units)	1544134	892933
电线及电缆	(吨)	Wires and Cables	(ton)	3277	15072
汽车(包括底盘)		Automobile (Including Chassis)			2163489
汽车零配件		Auto Parts			483385
飞机及其他航空器	(架)	Aircraft and Others	(unit)	43	133382
船　舶		Shipping			1658
医疗仪器及器械		Medical Instruments and Appliances			288182
计量检测分析自控仪器及器具		Automatic Control Instruments and Apparatus for Measurement, Detection and Analysis			590254

资料来源：中华人民共和国北京海关。
Source: Beijing Customs District P.R.China.

10-5 北京地区海关主要商品出口量及金额(2023年)
MAJOR EXPORTED COMMODITIES IN QUANTITY AND VALUE AT BEIJING CUSTOMS (2023)

项目		Item		出口数量 Export Quantity	出口金额 Export Value (万美元) (USD 10000)
粮　食	(吨)	Grain	(ton)	1342447	74953
果蔬汁	(吨)	Fruit and Vegetable Juice	(ton)	62957	10647
肥　料	(吨)	Chemical Fertilizers	(ton)	1791820	65170
煤及褐煤	(吨)	Coal and Lignite	(ton)	1306671	35726
焦炭、半焦炭	(吨)	Coke and Semi-coke	(ton)	587886	16745
成品油	(吨)	Product Oil	(ton)	38753511	3061822
医药材及药品	(吨)	Pharmaceutical Materials and Drugs	(ton)	22668	73266
纺织纱线、织物及其制品		Textile Yarn, Fabric and Its Products			65336
铁合金	(吨)	Ferroalloy	(ton)	1701	5561
钢　材	(吨)	Rolled Steel	(ton)	2926139	284830
未锻轧铝及铝材	(吨)	Unwrought Aluminum and Aluminum Products	(ton)	42733	16458
纺织机械及其零件		Textile Machinery and Its Parts			13117
机　床	(台)	Machine Tool	(set)	34200	14474
自动数据处理设备及其零部件		Automatic Data Processing Equipment and Its Parts			71548
液晶平板显示模组	(个)	LCD Flat-panel Display Module Groups	(unit)	13316799	96709
变压器	(个)	Transformer	(unit)	599194	24725
蓄电池	(个)	Electric Accumulators	(unit)	16955561	16003
手　机	(台)	Mobile Phone	(set)	64303515	825906
二极管及类似半导体器件	(万个)	Diode and Semi Conductors	(10000 units)	487982	35364
集成电路	(万个)	Integrated Circuits	(10000 units)	950331	272993
电线及电缆	(吨)	Wires and Cables	(ton)	58855	47605
汽车(包括底盘)		Automobile (Including Chassis)			205777
汽车零配件		Auto Parts			241903
船　舶		Shipping			37301
医疗仪器及器械		Medical Instruments and Appliances			100960
家具及其零件		Furniture and Parts			15940
服装及衣着附件		Clothing and Accessories			76444
鞋　靴	(吨)	Footwear	(ton)	13466	16477
塑料制品	(吨)	Flastic Articles	(ton)	116333	55322

资料来源：中华人民共和国北京海关。
Source: Beijing Customs District P.R.China

10–6 北京口岸运营情况
STATISTICS ON PORT OPERATION IN BEIJING

项目		Item		2023	2022
北京首都国际机场空港口岸		**Port of Beijing Capital International Airport**			
旅客吞吐量	（万人次）	Passenger Throughput	(10000 person-times)	5287.9	1270.7
出入境人员	（万人次）	Inbound/Outbound Visitors	(10000 person-times)	753.2	58.4
#外籍人员出入境		Inbound/Outbound Foreign Visitors		175.8	10.0
货邮吞吐量	（万吨）	Cargos Carried	(10000 tons)	111.6	98.8
飞机起降	（架次）	Takeoff and Landing of Airplanes	(unit)	379710	157662
#出入境飞机起降		Takeoff and Landing of Airplanes Inbound/Outbound		51059	25018
海关监管货物	（万吨）	Cargos under Customs Regulation	(10000 tons)	5752.8	4466.9
北京大兴国际机场空港口岸		**Port of Daxing International Airport**			
旅客吞吐量	（万人次）	Passenger Throughput	(10000 person-times)	3940.6	1027.8
出入境人员	（万人次）	Inbound/Outbound Visitors	(10000 person-times)	209.0	...
#外籍人员出入境		Inbound/Outbound Foreign Visitors		39.2	
货邮吞吐量	（万吨）	Cargos Carried	(10000 tons)	24.4	12.7
飞机起降	（架次）	Takeoff and Landing of Airplanes	(unit)	293143	105922
#出入境飞机起降		Takeoff and Landing of Airplanes Inbound/Outbound		11805	8
海关监管货物	（万吨）	Cargos under Customs Regulation	(10000 tons)	8.3	0.2
北京丰台货运口岸		**Beijing Fengtai Cargo Transport Port**			
海关监管货物	（吨）	Cargos under Customs Regulation	(ton)	1017	940
北京朝阳口岸		**Beijing Chaoyang Transport Port**			
海关监管货物	（吨）	Cargos under Customs Regulation	(ton)	595166	669451
北京西站铁路口岸		**Railway Port at Beijing West Railway Station**			
进出境人员	（人次）	Inbound/Outbound Visitors	(person-times)		
#外籍人员进出境		Inbound/Outbound Foreign Visitors			
北京平谷国际陆港		**Beijing Pinggu International Land Port**			
海关监管货物	（吨）	Cargos under Customs Regulation	(ton)	25826	35044
北京天竺综合保税区		**Beijing Tianzhu Comprehensive Bonded Zone**			
实际进出货物	（吨）	Actual Import and Export Goods	(ton)	75634	80471
海关征收税款净入库税额	**（亿元）**	**Net Paid-in Duties Levied and Collected by Customs**	**(100 million yuan)**	**673.0**	**670.0**

资料来源：北京市人民政府口岸办公室。
Source: Port Administration Office of the People's Government of Beijing Municipality.

10-7 外商投资企业实际利用外资情况(2010-2023年)

单位：万美元

项 目	Item	2010	2011
实际利用外商直接投资额	**Amount of Foreign Direct Investment Actually Utilized**	**533617**	**590661**
按产业分	**By Three Strata of Industry**		
第一产业	Primary Industry		
第二产业	Secondary Industry		
第三产业	Tertiary Industry		
按行业分	**By Sector**		
农、林、牧、渔业	Agriculture, Forestry, Animal Husbandry and Fishery	1250	144
采矿业	Mining	85	456
制造业	Manufacturing	62774	46405
电力、热力、燃气及水生产和供应业	Production and Supply of Electricity, Heat, Gas and Water	2461	14712
建筑业	Construction	104	1920
批发和零售业	Wholesale and Retail Trades	57416	93712
交通运输、仓储和邮政业	Transport, Storage and Post	14930	13611
住宿和餐饮业	Hotels and Catering Services	2352	1074
信息传输、软件和信息技术服务业	Information Transmission, Software and Information Technology	74504	93631
金融业	Financial Intermediation	7899	23168
房地产业	Real Estate	110138	95333
租赁和商务服务业	Leasing and Business Services	153509	142154
科学研究和技术服务业	Scientific Research and Technical Services	35345	38382
水利、环境和公共设施管理业	Management of Water Conservancy, Environment and Public Facilities		3164
居民服务、修理和其他服务业	Service to Households, Repair and Other Services	5441	21390
教 育	Education	211	4
卫生和社会工作	Health and Social Service	1390	
文化、体育和娱乐业	Culture, Sports and Entertainment	3808	1401
按外商国别(地区)分	**By Country (Region) of Foreign Investors**		
#中国香港	Hong Kong, China	263620	284755
新加坡	Singapore	20331	8784
日 本	Japan	35508	56704
英属维尔京群岛	Virgin Is. (E)	69101	98505
美 国	United States	20346	28760
韩 国	Republic of Korea	12269	20406
德 国	Germany	10406	17697
瑞 典	Sweden	3150	705
瑞 士	Switzerland	1600	3915
开曼群岛	Cayman Islands	38513	33340
中国台湾	Taiwan, China	966	622
比利时	Belgium	487	62
英 国	United Kingdom	770	6247
法 国	France	3476	6139
卢森堡	Luxembourg	4780	3216

资料来源：北京市商务局。

AMOUNT OF FOREIGN INVESTMENT BY FOREIGN-INVESTED ENTERPRISES (2010-2023)

(USD 10000)

2012	2013	2014	2015	2016	2017	2018	2019	2020	2021	2022	2023
616463	**684245**	**816911**	**1271540**	**1258555**	**2325755**	**1673635**	**1362385**	**1339335**	**1443424**	**1740768**	**1371411**
						6725	63		11775	37	
						224817	56931	14919	29552	52445	72099
						1442093	1305391	1324416	1402097	1688286	1299312
632	1634	2224	7563	2303	838	6725	63		11775	37	
260		81			247						
84150	81054	67471	50535	56402	35546	90166	19502	9923	27661	43662	39143
25305	37563	12244		4347	69057	134634	36632	4957	1168	2341	26571
383	108	688	131	113	451	15	813	35	724	6442	9783
76789	69900	43601	241579	576878	167306	52009	52427	59648	61899	57485	16748
6124	22304	4962	975	88655	126718	113176	11231	48573	2810	5580	158
2648	1807	2013	548	3009	1221	29448	1873	72	43842	5500	1
130829	101372	107632	44599	111176	1303210	446614	530902	446383	390513	394366	324753
18748	14034	30570	729245	85230	20015	67749	152203	107293	37361	133554	108383
87437	139250	131627	27296	66160	205690	193193	67825	44270	70137	17795	22815
122680	155597	324028	66988	103902	202648	287787	107131	138320	177673	369097	229864
52871	56774	83140	94146	152429	188879	243834	364897	466241	591825	698192	580990
270		2635	4720	1754	490		1534		18582		
4497	390	331	83	16	176	2146	2227	964	80	5565	5165
321	73		15				253				
554		1594			397	412	1455	8734	2044		509
1965	2385	2070	3117	6181	2866	5727	11417	3922	5330	1152	6528
296511	323419	518833	981380	546756	2087813	1250642	1063860	989852	1223722	1591663	1071503
26829	18314	35268	16218	54226	8924	10743	20045	21949	40241	31718	72925
39679	42747	30706	11546	11921	18977	20290	14353	24446	33159	7544	2964
27433	45405	20661	187185	205933	26056	29388	12837	30214	29108	2895	1141
20279	14863	14421	2346	6273	12356	34892	25145	42569	25572	4230	84198
69920	13180	18236	6906	38229	24227	57825	70562	26255	16470	24384	27721
24314	68822	99654	35575	95643	11419	28588	20887	47475	16216	210	21637
840	10687	100	381	8	48	2022	8253	3465	12770	26792	20819
20271	1216	2804	313	204	68	7166	5652	474	11048	83	58
56378	37520	31535	5604	268307	34409	59455	54177	125859	8380	7599	20878
903	673	1776	288	291	134	265	220	96	7465	51	244
18	3	510	69	109	24	11	13	1649	4727	490	
3481	2216	1738	1952	1693	418	916	1430	3141	3115	9670	5100
2286	1406	6261	15154	14346	5783	7437	2424	3535	2680	134	4918
334	17139	123	250	7146		6461	860	1258	1997	62	32

Source: Beijing Municipal Commerce Bureau.

10-8 限额以上港澳台及外商投资法人企业基本情况(2022年) STATISTICS FOR HONGKONG, MACAO, TAIWAN AND FOREIGN-INVESTED CORPORATE ENTERPRISES ABOVE DESIGNATED SIZE (2022)

项 目	Item	企业单位数(个) Number of Enterprises (unit)	平均用工人数(万人) Average Number of Employees (10000 persons)	营业收入(万元) Business Income (10000 yuan)	利润总额(万元) Total Profits (10000 yuan)	应交税金合计(万元) Total Taxes Payable (10000 yuan)
合 计	**Total**	**4435**	**152.3**	**566822177**	**63103568**	**17870079**
按登记注册类型分	**By Registration Type**					
港澳台商投资企业	Hong Kong, Macao and Taiwan-invested Enterprises	1571	68.9	252819602	25320238	5518653
与港澳台商合资	Joint Ventures	378	12.7	13765826	1768428	681584
与港澳台商合作	Cooperatives	49	1.4	1011448	266758	201878
港澳台商独资	Solely-funded Enterprises	1071	46.8	220962771	25062042	3928826
港澳台商投资股份有限公司	Companies Limited by Shares	50	7.0	16233132	-1848340	674221
其他港澳台投资企业	Others	23	1.0	846425	71350	32144
外商投资企业	Foreign-invested Enterprises	2864	83.4	314002576	37783330	12351426
中外合资	Joint Ventures	768	22.7	84479326	8114167	5402438
中外合作	Cooperatives	59	1.0	900762	-30998	65904
外商独资	Solely-funded Enterprises	1924	53.4	219700776	27076156	6543039
外商投资股份有限公司	Companies Limited by Shares	101	6.1	8399577	2620873	280213
其他外商投资企业	Others	12	0.2	522136	3131	59832
按国民经济行业分	**By Sector**					
农、林、牧、渔业	Agriculture, Forestry, Animal Husbandry Fishery					
制造业	Manufacturing	624	23.4	98150508	9294805	5081578
建筑业	Construction	50	3.2	1840040	37443	44734
批发和零售业	Wholesale and Retail Trades	862	18.5	275879192	11088723	3883217
住宿和餐饮业	Accommodation and Restaurants	219	15.0	3707384	-228347	129873
交通运输、仓储和邮政业	Transport, Storage and Post	93	11.3	22180845	-1150480	871656
信息传输、软件和信息技术服务业	Information Transmission, Software and Information Technology Services	675	39.8	94591551	27345294	3579579
房地产业	Real Estate	364	9.7	9006158	431572	1054027
租赁和商务服务业	Leasing and Business Services	691	12.3	20412125	7378095	778474
其他行业	Other Sectors	857	19.1	41054375	8906463	2446943
按三次产业分	**By Industry**					
第一产业	Primary Industry					
第二产业	Secondary Industry	697	27.8	106172369	9927074	5277515
第三产业	Tertiary Industry	3738	124.5	460649808	53176493	12592563

注：1.行业划分执行《国民经济行业分类》(GB/T 4754—2017)标准。
2.应交税金合计包括应交增值税、所得税费用和税金及附加。

Note: a) Sectors in this table are classified in accordance with the Standard for Industrial Classification for National Economic Activities (GB/T 4754-2017).
b) Total tax payable includes VAT payable, income tax expense, tax and surtax.

10-9 境外投资情况(2003-2023年)
STATISTICS ON OVERSEAS INVESTMENT (2003-2023)

单位：万美元 (USD 10000)

年 份 Year	对外直接投资额 Amount of Outward Direct Investment	截至各年期末直接投资存量 Stock of Direct Investment by the Year End
2003	30054	44844
2004	15739	70086
2005	11306	92940
2006	5612	91873
2007	15295	159195
2008	47299	251019
2009	45185	375865
2010	76614	480882
2011	117503	603380
2012	168900	757800
2013	413010	1276456
2014	727353	2848870
2015	1228033	3879895
2016	1557362	5438141
2017	665126	6484394
2018	647042	6995279
2019	826601	7368891
2020	598518	8527566
2021	704790	9588300
2022	599877	10153818
2023	550807	10457776

资料来源：北京市商务局。
Source: Beijing Municipal Commerce Bureau.

10–10 对外经济合作(1984–2023年)
ECONOMIC COOPERATION WITH FOREIGN COUNTRIES OR REGIONS (1984-2023)

年份 Year	对外承包工程 Contracted Projects				对外劳务合作 Labor Services		
	新签合同数(份) Number of Newly Signed Contracts (unit)	新签合同额(万美元) Newly Signed Contract Value (USD 10000)	完成营业额(万美元) Value of Turnover Fulfilled (USD 10000)	年末在国外人数(人) Workers Staying Abroad by the End of Year (person)	新签劳务人员合同工资总额(万美元) Total Contract Wages of Newly Signed Labor Service Workers (USD 10000)	劳务人员实际收入总额(万美元) Total Actual Income of Labor Service Workers (USD 10000)	年末在国外人数(人) Workers Staying Abroad by the End of Year (person)
1984	2	2768	331	163		200	378
1985	2	736	355	18	100	1700	2383
1986	7	319	90	71	100	1400	766
1987	5	354	186	20	200	500	670
1988	5	344	281	104	500	500	715
1989	7	235	459	83	1500	500	517
1990	16	2253	625	25	1500	500	311
1991	9	1671	1469	306	1500	400	674
1992	16	7762	2543	264	1100	600	688
1993	48	27625	8871	532	1700	900	1023
1994	34	15089	17822	1694	600	1000	1026
1995	35	14014	12156	1297	1600	600	1307
1996	49	62945	38124	1559	4744	4933	957
1997	37	23374	17945	1993	12265	11684	1129
1998	48	19292	24930	2239	6233	6080	1408
1999	28	18715	19690	2199	6517	6477	1277
2000	54	9936	13543	1660	6346	6255	1545
2001	54	14758	11680	2141	6134	6591	1353
2002	42	19376	14453	1112	8779	9527	1022
2003	99	30761	17334	1270	18373	18558	827
2004	109	50788	29134	1583	30049	30389	923
2005	237	56596	35526	2854	37023	35727	1896
2006	143	158918	69227	6760	16424	13456	2202
2007	139	211493	71685	7059	25321	22350	4239
2008	190	520594	130849	6337	37741	36730	5056
2009	182	296851	184997	7057	39372	41876	5316
2010	170	251114	222514	17145	35065	37282	5354
2011	230	261088	248098	12414	1941	3805	5428
2012	344	404037	289909	12143	2434	5746	4616
2013	349	562440	335854	16549	1943	5192	4487
2014	283	429369	357432	21683	8094	7926	7774
2015	209	464840	354900	19287	7180	16012	14896
2016	229	514151	249642	13176	1519	10531	7260
2017	272	905968	402944	11806	2168	16138	12782
2018	230	730314	399820	12383	10400	19380	18744
2019	186	1173673	421872	11043	30274	66088	53899
2020	154	792162	364794	9575	15328	52136	32813
2021	181	476823	368370	8738	16080	51905	34959
2022	299	1011412	532290	8190	23054	50357	27511
2023	228	1458947	523407	9308	22113	51625	29706

注：1984–2008年，对外承包工程统计中含对外设计咨询统计数据。
资料来源：北京市商务局。
Note: Statistics for contracted projects in 1984 - 2008 include statistical data of consultation on foreign design.
Source: Beijing Municipal Commerce Bureau.

主要统计指标解释

货物进出口总值 指实际进、出我国海关并能引起我国境内物质资源增加或减少的进出口货物总金额。包括我国境内法人和其他组织以一般贸易、易货贸易、加工贸易、补偿贸易、寄售代销贸易等方式进出口的货物、租赁期一年及以上的租赁进出口货物、边境小额贸易货物、国际援助物资或捐赠品、保税区和保税仓库进出口货物等的金额合计。进出口总值用以观察一个国家在对外贸易方面的总规模。我国规定出口货物按离岸价格统计，进口货物按到岸价格统计。

一般贸易 指我国境内有进出口经营权的企业单边进口或单边出口的货物。

来料加工装配贸易 指由外商提供全部或部分原材料、辅料、零部件、元器件、配套件和包装物料，必要时提供设备，由我方按对方的要求进行加工装配，成品交对方销售，我方收取工缴费；或对方提供的作价设备价款，我方用工缴费偿还的交易形式。

进料加工贸易 指我方用外汇购买进口的原料、材料、辅料、元器件、零部件、配套件和包装物料，加工成品或半成品后再外销出口的交易形式。

旅客吞吐量 指经乘航班进出北京民用运输机场的中国公民、港澳台同胞、华侨及外国人等旅客数量的总和。

货邮吞吐量 指通过民用运输机场的航班运输的货物、邮寄物品和随身携带的行李物品重量总和。

飞机起降架次 指进出民用运输机场的正常航班架次，不包括包机和其他非正常航班。

海关征收税款净入库税额 指北京海关征收的税款合计，包含进出口关税和进口环节税。

实际利用外商直接投资额 指批准的合同外资金额的实际执行数，外国投资者根据批准外商投资企业的合同（章程）的规定实际缴付的出资额和企业投资总额内外国投资者以自己的境外自有资金实际直接向企业提供的贷款。

对外承包工程 指企业按照国际通行做法，在国（境）外承揽和实施各类工程项目的经济活动。企业承揽的我国对外经济援助项目、我国驻外使（领）馆等建设项目视同对外承包工程项目。

对外劳务合作 指企业按照与国（境）外政府有关机构、团体、企业、私人雇主所签合同规定，向国（境）外派遣各类劳务人员的经济活动。企业自带设备以提供技术服务的形式在国（境）外承揽的项目视同对外劳务合作项目。

Explanatory Notes on Main Statistical Indicators

Total Value of Imports and Exports refer to the total value of goods actually imported and exported at China's customs, which lead to increase or decrease in the physical resources in China, including goods imported/exported by China domestic legal persons and other organizations in such manners as general trade, barter trade, processing trade, compensation trade, commission-based sales trade, leasing imports/exports with a lease period of one year and more, small-sum border trade goods, international aid goods and donations, imports/exports in bonded zones and bonded warehouses. The indicator of the Total Value of Imports and Exports can be used to observe the total size of foreign trade in a country. In accordance with the stipulation of the Chinese government, imports are calculated at CIF, while exports are calculated at FOB.

General Trade means goods imported and exported unilaterally by domestic enterprises with import/export rights.

Trade of Processing and Assembling Supplied Materials is a form of transaction in which all or part of raw materials, auxiliary materials, parts and components, elements, fittings, and packaging materials, and equipment if necessary are provided by the foreign party, processed or assemble by Chinese party according to requirements of the foreign party, and the finished products are sold by the foreign party. The Chinese party charges processing fees and pays back the money of priced equipment provided by the foreign party with processing charges.

Trade of Processing Imported Materials is a form of transaction in which the Chinese party purchases raw materials, auxiliary materials, parts and components, elements, fittings, and packaging materials with foreign exchange, processing them into finished or semi-finished products and export them.

Passenger Throughput means the total number of Chinese citizens, compatriots form Hong Kong, Macao and Taiwan, oversea Chinese and foreigners that take off and land at civil airports in Beijing by flights.

Cargos Throughput means the sum of goods, mailed articles and luggage transported by flights taking off from and landing at civil airports in Beijing.

Takeoff and Landing of Airplanes means the number of regular flights taking off from and landing at civil airports in Beijing, excluding chartered flights and other non-regular flights.

Net Paid-in Duties Levied and Collected by Customs mean the sum of duties actually levied by customs in Beijing, including import and export duties and import linkage taxs.

Actual Use of Foreign Direct Investment means the value of approved contractual foreign investment actually used, the amount of actual capital contribution by foreign investors according to the contract (articles of incorporation) of the foreign-invested enterprise approved and, in the total investment of an enterprise, the amount of loans provided directly by foreign investor with its own overseas money for the enterprise.

Foreign Contracted Projects refer to economic activities in which enterprises undertake and implement various projects in foreign (overseas) countries in line with international practices. Foreign economic aid projects and construction projects of Chinese Embassies (Consulates) undertaken by enterprises are deemed as foreign contracted projects.

Foreign Labor Service Cooperation means any economic activity in which enterprises dispatch labors to foreign (overseas) countries as stated in contracts signed with foreign (overseas) government agencies, groups, enterprises, and private employers. Projects undertaken by enterprises in foreign (overseas) countries in a manner of providing technical service with their own equipment are deemed as foreign labor service cooperation projects.

11

北京统计年鉴2024　　BEIJING STATISTICAL YEARBOOK 2024

农业及农村经济
AGRICULTURE AND RURAL ECONOMY

简要说明

一、主要内容

本章资料反映北京市农业生产和农村经济基本情况，主要包括农村基本情况、农业生产条件、农林牧渔业产值及主要农产品生产情况、农作物播种面积、设施农业、农业观光园、乡村旅游等。

二、统计范围和调查方法

（一）统计范围

农林牧渔业统计范围包括辖区内全部农林牧渔业生产单位、非农行业单位附属的农林牧渔业生产活动单位以及农户的农业生产活动。军委系统的农林牧渔业生产（除军马外）也应包括在内，但不包括农业科学试验机构进行的农业生产。

1．农业：指各种农作物的种植活动。包括谷物、豆类、薯类、棉花、油料、糖料、麻类、烟叶、蔬菜、食用菌及花卉盆景园艺产品、水果、坚果、饲料和香料作物、药材及其它作物的种植。

2．林业：包括林木的栽培(不包括茶园、桑园和果园的栽培、管理和收获等活动)、木材和竹材的采运、林产品的采集。

3．牧业：包括牲畜饲养和放牧、家禽饲养以及野生动物的捕猎和饲养。

4．渔业：分为淡水养殖和海水养殖，包括水生动物和海藻类植物的养殖和捕捞。

农村社会经济统计范围包括所有乡镇辖区内的社会经济活动。

（二）调查方法

农林牧渔业生产统计采取全面调查方法，农业生产统计从行政村和农业生产单位起报。主要粮食播种面积数据通过卫星遥感测量方法取得,粮食产量数据通过抽样调查方法取得。

三、农林牧渔业总产值的核算方法

（一）核算方法

根据农业生产特点，农林牧渔业总产值的核算采用“产品法”计算，即用产品产量乘以价格求出各种产品的产值，按产品产值类别分别汇总，计算出农林牧渔各业的产值，各业相加为农林牧渔业总产值。

1．农业：包括谷物和其他作物；蔬菜、食用菌及花卉盆景园艺产品；水果、坚果、饲料、香料；中药材。

2．林业：包括林木的培育和种植；木材、竹材采运；林产品的采集。

3．牧业：包括除渔业养殖以外的一切动物饲养和放牧以及野生动物的捕猎和饲养。

4．渔业：包括水生动物和海藻类植物的养殖和捕捞。

5．农林牧渔专业及辅助性活动：产值等于农林牧渔专业及辅助性活动营业收入。

（二）核算内容的变化情况。自 1958 年起林业产值中增加了村及村以下竹木采伐产值；牧业中取消了厩肥产值；副业中取消了农民自给性手工业产值；渔业中增加了海洋捕捞水产品产值。自 1980 年起农业总产值，在副业中增加了农民家庭兼营工业商品部分的产值。自 1984 年起村及村以下办工业产值划归工业。自 1993 年起，取消副业，将野生动物的捕猎划入牧业，野生植物采集和农民家庭兼营商品性工业划归农业。自 2003 年起按照新的《国民经济行业分类》标准取消了“其他农业”；将农林牧渔服务业产值纳入农林牧渔业总产值中；从农林牧渔业总产值中取消了“家庭兼营商品性工业”；将村以上木材和竹材的采运划入了林业。

（三）核算方法变化情况。自 2003 年起，计算农林牧渔业总产值使用的价格从农产品综合平均价调整为农产品生产价格。2004 年，国家统计局报表制度规定农林牧渔业总产值增加按可比价格计算的产值及发展速度（计算方法：用现价产值的中类数据除以中类缩减指数求得各中类的可比价产值，各中类相加得大类的可比价产值，最后用大类数据相加得农业可比价总产值，可比价产值除以上年现价产值得发展速度）。自 2005 年起，取消了按 1990 年价格计算的农业产值。由于 2006 年农业普查后对农业生产历史数据进行了修订，新修订的农业产值数据只到大类，按大类缩减计算农业可比价总产值不符合国家报表制度要求，故 2005 年及以前年度没有按可比价格计算的发展速度。

四、有关统计标准的变化说明

关于行业划分标准。2003 年至 2011 年执行《国民经济行业分类》(GB/T 4754—2002) 标准；2012-2017 年执行《国民经济行业分类》(GB/T 4754-2011)标准；自 2018 年起，执行《国民经济行业分类》(GB/T 4754—2017) 标准。

五、关于历史数据调整

根据 2006 年北京市第二次全国农业普查结果，北京市统计局、国家统计局北京调查总队按照国务院农普办要求，依照国际通用做法，对 1997—2005 年的相关指标历史数据进行了修订；根据 2016 年北京市第三次全国农业普查结果，对 2016 年相关指标历史数据进行了修订。

自 2010 年起，根据新的《统计用产品分类目录》，将原林业产值中的核桃、栗子、白果、松子等干果产值调整至农业产值中，为同口径对比，将 2009 年数据也作了相应调整。

Brief Introduction

I. Main Content

Statistics in this chapter show the basic situation of agricultural production and rural economy in Beijing, mainly consisting of basic statistics on rural areas, agricultural production conditions, output of agriculture, forestry, animal production and hunting, fishing, and statistics on production of main agricultural products, sown area, facility agriculture, agricultural sightseeing gardens, and rural tourism, and so on.

II. Scope of Statistics and Method for Survey

(I) Scope of Statistics

Statistics on agriculture, forestry, animal production and hunting, fishing cover the agricultural production activities of all producing entities of agriculture, forestry, animal production and hunting, fishing within the jurisdiction, that of the production activity units of agriculture, forestry, animal production and hunting, fishing affiliated to non-agricultural industry units, and that of the farmers. Production by the military commission system shall also be included (except for army horse breeding), but the agricultural production carried out by agricultural scientific testing agencies is not included.

1. Agriculture: It refers to the growing of various agricultural crops, including grains, beans, tuber crops, cotton, oil-bearing crops, sugar plants, fiber plants, tobacco leaves, vegetables, edible fungus, flower bonsai and gardening products, fruits, nuts, feedstuff, and spice crops, herbs, and other crops.

2. Forestry: It includes tree planting (except for the cultivation, management and harvest of tea gardens, mulberry fields, and orchards), the logging of timber and bamboo, and the collection of forestry products.

3. Animal production and hunting: It includes the breeding and grazing of livestock, poultry agriculture, as well as hunting and breeding of wildlife.

4. Fishing: It falls into two parts: freshwater aquaculture and mariculture, including the cultivation and fishing for aquatic animals and algae.

Statistics for social and economic development in rural areas cover social and economic activities of all villages and towns within the jurisdiction.

(II) Method for Survey

The statistics for production of agriculture, forestry, animal production and hunting, fishing are made with the comprehensive survey method; data on agricultural production are collected from the administrative village and agricultural production unit level. Data on sown area of main grain crops are obtained by means of satellite remote sensing measurements; data on grain output are obtained by sampling survey method.

III. Accounting Method for the Gross Output Value of Agriculture, Forestry, Animal Production and Hunting, Fishing

(I) Accounting Method

Based on agricultural production characteristics, the gross output value of agriculture, forestry, animal production and hunting, fishing was calculated by the "Product Approach", that is to multiply production volume by the unit price, so as to get output value of each product, then sum it up by category, namely agriculture, forestry, animal production and hunting, fishing; and the sum total of these categories will be gross output value of the whole sector.

1. Agriculture: including cereal and other crops; vegetables, edible mushrooms, flower bonsai and gardening products; fruits, nuts, feedstuff, spices, and herbs.

2. Forestry: including the cultivation and planting of forest trees; logging of timber and bamboo; and collection of forestry products.

3. Animal production and hunting: including the breeding and grazing of animals other than fish breeding, as well as hunting and breeding of wildlife.

4. Fishing: including cultivation and catching of aquatic animals and seaweed plants.

5. Professional and supporting activities of agriculture, forestry, animal production and hunting, fishing: the output value equals the operating income of professional and supporting activities of agriculture, forestry, animal production and hunting, fishing.

(II) Changes in Accounting Content. Since 1958, output value of bamboo and timber logging by villages and units subordinated to villages has been included in the statistics of forestry; output value of barnyard manure has been excluded from animal production and hunting statistics; output value of subsistence handicrafts has been excluded from sideline products output value; and the output value of aquatic products by marine fishing has been added to fishing. Since 1980, among the gross output value of agriculture, the output value of industrial commodities operated by rural households has been included in the output value of sideline products. Since 1984, industrial output value produced by villages and units subordinated to villages has been added in the sector of industry. Since 1993, the group "sideline products" was cancelled; the hunting of wild animals has been classified as animal production and hunting, and the gathering of wild plants and commercial industrial businesses run by rural households have been included in agriculture. A new standard for the *Classification of National Economic Sectors* was introduced in 2003. According to the new *Classification*, the group "other agricultural activities" was cancelled; the output value of service activities for agriculture, forestry, animal husbandry and fishing is included in the gross output value of agriculture, forestry, animal production and hunting, fishing; the "commercial industrial businesses run by households" is excluded from the gross output value of agriculture, forestry, animal production and hunting, fishing; output value of wood and bamboo logging of units above village level is included in forestry statistics.

(III) Changes in Accounting Method. Since 2003, the price used for calculating the gross output value of agriculture, forestry, animal production and hunting, fishing has been adjusted from the overall average price of farm products into the producer price for farm products. In 2004, the Reporting System of the National Bureau of Statistics stated to add new statistical items in the gross output value of agriculture, forestry, animal production and hunting, fishing, namely the output value and the growth rate calculated at a comparable price (calculation method: use the output value of groups at present prices to divide the groups' deflator, so as to get the output value at comparable prices; then add up the groups' output value to get the whole subsector's output value at comparable prices; in the end, add up all subsectors' output value to get the gross output value at comparable prices for the agriculture sector and divide the output value at comparable prices by the output value at current prices in the previous year to get the growth rate). Since 2005, the practice of using prices of 1990 as reference numbers to calculate agricultural output value has been cancelled. As the historical data of agricultural production were revised after the Agricultural Census in 2006, revised agricultural production output value figures were presented only by subsectors; and it does not meet the requirements of the national reporting system to calculate the gross agricultural output value at comparable prices by subsectors' deflator. Therefore, there were no figures for growth rate at comparable prices in and prior to 2005.

IV. Changes in Relevant Statistical Standards

Standard for Classification of Sectors. The standards in the *Classification of National Economic Sectors (GB/T 4754-2002)* were implemented from 2003 to 2011. The standards in the *Classification of National Economic Sectors (GB/T 4754-2011)* were implemented from 2012 to 2017. The standards in the *Classification of National Economic Sectors (GB/T 4754-2017)* have been implemented since 2018.

V. Adjustments to Historical Statistics

Based on the results of the Second National Agricultural Census in 2006 in Beijing, Beijing Municipal Bureau of Statistics and Survey Office of the National Bureau of Statistics in Beijing revised the historical data of relevant indicators during 1997-2005 as required by the Agricultural Census Office of the State Council and in accordance with the international practice; and the historical data of relevant indicators for 2016 were revised based on the results of the Third National Agricultural Census in 2016 in Beijing.

Since 2010, the output value of nuts such as walnuts, chestnuts, gingkoes and pine nuts formerly included in forestry has been added in the output value of agriculture according to the new *Catalog on Statistical Product Classification*. In order to conduct same-caliber comparison, data in 2009 annual report have also been adjusted accordingly.

11-1 农村基本情况(1978-2023年)
BASIC STATISTICS ON RURAL AREAS (1978-2023)

年份 Year	乡政府 (个) Township Governments (unit)	镇政府 (个) Town Governments (unit)	村民委员会 (个) Villagers' Committees (unit)	行政村常住户数 (万户) Number of Resident Households in Administrative Villages (10000 households)	行政村常住人口 (万人) Resident Population in Administrative Villages (10000 persons)	行政村从业人员 (万人) Employed Persons in Administrative Villages (10000 persons)
1978				91.9	382.1	165.3
1979				92.9	374.7	165.1
1980				95.0	374.3	167.4
1981				98.9	377.6	172.9
1982				103.2	381.8	179.4
1983				106.6	384.0	184.6
1984				108.9	385.6	188.9
1985	350	15	4394	111.8	387.2	190.0
1986	327	15	4400	113.1	386.9	189.5
1987	324	14	4326	115.7	388.9	189.8
1988	321	13	4111	118.6	389.6	189.2
1989	322	14	4483	121.5	390.0	186.1
1990	252	77	4481	124.5	392.0	184.3
1991	209	77	4480	125.5	390.7	182.1
1992	209	77	4229	126.2	387.6	178.7
1993	192	81	4476	126.5	382.4	176.0
1994	174	92	4464	124.9	376.0	171.6
1995	166	100	4355	125.0	371.5	163.6
1996	166	100	4357	124.6	368.9	164.2
1997	132	108	4348	124.6	365.3	161.2
1998	126	105	4032	125.9	364.4	161.0
1999	125	103	4040	125.9	363.9	165.3
2000	70	142	4039	126.8	363.7	165.8
2001	52	139	4010	127.6	361.6	165.3
2002	51	141	4005	128.0	357.6	165.6
2003	45	142	3985	131.1	360.6	169.6
2004	42	142	3985	132.8	359.9	171.4
2005	43	142	3953	142.2	381.8	184.0
2006	41	142	3957	143.6	501.6	316.9
2007	41	142	3955	176.9	510.0	313.4
2008	40	142	3951	189.8	547.4	321.3
2009	40	142	3950	203.8	572.5	338.7
2010	40	142	3943	216.0	589.4	347.8
2011	38	144	3941	212.4	574.8	338.3
2012	38	144	3940	215.2	582.5	341.7
2013	38	144	3938	221.9	599.5	353.5
2014	38	144	3937	225.2	606.9	357.0
2015	38	144	3936	221.4	593.5	348.0
2016	38	143	3941	232.6	612.6	385.9
2017	38	143	3920	216.7	566.6	352.2
2018	38	143	3915	211.9	558.0	337.5
2019	38	143	3891	211.7	555.7	333.7
2020	35	143	3887	224.6	577.9	344.3
2021	35	143	3784	221.5	569.0	340.3
2022	35	143	3783	217.7	559.6	333.3
2023	35	143	3768	207.4	535.5	314.1

资料来源：乡政府、镇政府和村民委员会个数由北京市民政局提供。
Source: Data on the numbers of township governments, town governments and villagers' committees is provided by Beijing Municipal Civil Affairs Bureau

11-2 农业生产条件(1978-2023年)
CONDITIONS OF AGRICULTURAL PRODUCTION (1978-2023)

年 份 Year	农业机械 总 动 力 (万千瓦) Total Agricultural Machinery Power (10000 kW)	化 肥 施用量 (万吨) Consumption of Chemical Fertilizers (10000 tons)
1978	189.4	11.6
1979	212.2	11.3
1980	234.6	12.3
1981	244.8	11.2
1982	242.2	12.0
1983	261.8	12.0
1984	290.8	10.7
1985	320.4	8.2
1986	345.5	9.1
1987	388.4	10.0
1988	399.7	10.6
1989	423.9	11.8
1990	416.2	14.4
1991	384.8	14.4
1992	399.8	14.4
1993	450.5	14.9
1994	459.2	19.8
1995	468.1	18.8
1996	468.4	18.9
1997	433.2	19.7
1998	415.5	19.3
1999	410.4	19.0
2000	399.2	17.9
2001	394.9	15.7
2002	381.8	14.9
2003	366.9	14.3
2004	340.3	14.5
2005	337.7	14.8
2006	325.5	14.8
2007	300.5	14.0
2008	267.0	13.6
2009	271.5	13.8
2010	276.0	13.7
2011	265.2	13.8
2012	241.1	13.7
2013	207.7	12.8
2014	195.8	11.6
2015	185.9	10.5
2016	144.4	9.7
2017	133.5	8.5
2018	125.6	7.3
2019	122.8	6.2
2020	120.2	6.1
2021	121.2	6.3
2022	116.4	6.6
2023	123.9	6.7

注：1.化肥施用量为折纯量。
2.农业机械总动力数据由北京市农业农村局提供。

Note: a) Data on consumption of chemical fertilizers are net amount.
b) Figures of total agricultural machinery power are provided by Beijing Municipal Bureau of Agriculture and Rural Affairs.

11−3 农作物播种面积和造林面积(1978−2023年)
SOWN AREA OF FARM CROPS AND AREA OF AFFORESTATION (1978-2023)

单位：万公顷 (10000 hectares)

年份 Year	农作物播种面积 Sown Area of Crops	#粮食作物 Grain Crops	#玉米 Corn	#小麦 Wheat	#油料 Oil-bearing Crops	#蔬菜及食用菌 Vegetables and Edible Mushrooms	#瓜类及草莓 Melons & Strawberries	#饲料 Forage	造林面积 Area of Afforestation
1978	69.1	56.1	16.9	19.2	3.3	5.6	0.2	2.0	1.4
1979	67.7	56.0	18.2	19.7	3.0	5.4	0.3	2.0	1.6
1980	65.7	54.9	19.7	18.8	2.8	5.1	0.4	1.8	2.4
1981	64.4	53.0	19.8	18.4	2.7	5.5	0.6	1.7	2.7
1982	64.2	52.7	19.7	18.1	2.4	5.9	0.8	1.6	2.8
1983	63.8	53.0	20.1	18.7	1.9	5.7	0.5	1.5	3.3
1984	63.3	52.3	20.6	19.5	1.8	5.8	0.7	1.5	3.2
1985	61.8	51.1	21.7	19.1	2.0	5.4	0.9	1.3	3.0
1986	60.5	49.9	21.6	18.5	2.0	5.8	1.1	1.0	1.5
1987	59.8	49.5	22.3	18.3	1.6	6.0	0.9	1.1	2.0
1988	59.5	48.8	22.2	18.6	1.5	6.3	1.0	1.2	1.6
1989	58.9	48.3	21.9	18.5	1.3	6.8	0.8	1.1	0.8
1990	59.0	48.4	22.4	18.8	1.2	7.0	0.6	1.1	1.3
1991	59.0	48.3	22.3	19.2	1.2	7.3	0.5	1.0	1.5
1992	58.5	47.7	22.4	19.2	1.2	7.5	0.5	0.8	1.5
1993	56.5	45.6	21.8	17.8	1.3	7.8	0.5	0.7	4.8
1994	55.1	43.0	20.6	16.4	1.2	9.1	0.6	0.6	5.5
1995	55.3	43.4	20.8	17.2	1.2	9.1	0.5		4.7
1996	53.8	42.7	20.8	17.1	1.1	8.8	0.5	0.5	4.0
1997	53.6	42.5	20.6	17.1	1.0	8.9	0.5	0.5	3.8
1998	53.5	42.3	20.8	17.1	1.0	9.0	0.5	0.5	3.7
1999	52.6	41.0	19.8	16.8	1.0	9.2	0.5	0.5	3.0
2000	45.4	30.8	13.6	12.2	1.5	10.4	0.8	1.2	2.6
2001	38.0	21.4	10.0	7.3	1.4	11.3	0.9	1.9	3.2
2002	33.5	16.9	8.7	4.7	1.6	11.5	0.9	1.8	4.8
2003	30.1	14.1	7.5	3.6	1.4	10.8	0.9	1.9	4.7
2004	30.4	15.4	9.4	3.9	1.1	9.1	0.8	2.8	3.2
2005	30.8	19.2	12.0	5.3	0.9	7.9	0.8	1.5	1.2
2006	32.0	22.0	13.6	6.3	0.7	7.1	0.9	0.6	1.3
2007	29.5	19.7	13.9	4.1	0.7	7.0	0.9	0.4	1.1
2008	32.2	22.6	14.6	6.4	0.7	6.8	0.8	0.4	0.9
2009	32.0	22.6	15.1	6.1	0.6	6.8	0.8	0.4	1.8
2010	31.7	22.3	15.0	6.2	0.5	6.8	0.8	0.5	1.4
2011	30.3	20.9	14.1	5.8	0.5	6.7	0.8	0.5	2.1
2012	28.3	19.4	13.2	5.2	0.5	6.4	0.8	0.3	3.6
2013	24.2	15.9	11.4	3.6	0.3	6.2	0.7	0.2	4.4
2014	20.0	12.0	8.9	2.4	0.3	5.7	0.6	0.3	2.3
2015	17.7	10.4	7.6	2.1	0.2	5.4	0.5	0.2	0.8
2016	15.0	8.6	6.4	1.6	0.2	4.7	0.4	0.3	1.0
2017	12.6	6.7	5.0	1.1	0.2	4.2	0.4	0.3	0.9
2018	10.6	5.6	4.0	1.0	0.2	3.6	0.4	0.2	2.0
2019	9.2	4.7	3.4	0.8	0.1	3.1	0.3	0.3	2.2
2020	10.2	4.9	3.6	0.8	0.1	3.8	0.3	0.4	1.8
2021	12.2	6.1	4.3	1.3	0.1	4.6	0.3	0.4	1.3
2022	14.7	7.7	5.1	1.8	0.3	5.3	0.3	0.6	1.0
2023	16.2	8.9	5.6	2.5	0.4	5.3	0.3	0.8	0.1

注：1.2016年粮食作物、玉米播种面积为农业普查衔接数据。
2.造林面积2009年以前为人工造林面积，自2009年起调整为人工造林、无林地和疏林地新封面积之和。造林面积数据由北京市园林绿化局提供。

Note: a) The data on sown area of grain crops and corn for 2016 are linked up with the agricultural census.
b) Area of afforestation before 2009 was manual planting area, and since 2009 it has been the sum of the area of manual planting, non-forest land and newly closed forest land. The data on area of afforestation are provided by Beijing Municipal Forestry and Parks Bureau.

11-4 农、林、牧、渔业总产值(1978-2023年)
GROSS OUTPUT VALUE OF AGRICULTURE, FORESTRY, ANIMAL HUSBANDRT AND FISHERY (1978-2023)

年份 Year	农林牧渔业总产值(亿元) Gross Output Value of Agriculture, Forestry, Animal Husbandry and Fishery (100 million yuan)	农业 Agriculture	林业 Forestry	牧业 Animal Husbandry	渔业 Fishery	农林牧渔专业及辅助性活动 Professional and Support Services of Agriculture, Forestry, Animal Husbandry and Fishery	农林牧渔业总产值比上年增长(%) Growth Rate over Preceding Year (%) 按当年价格计算 Calculated at Current Price	按可比价格计算 Calculate at Comparable Price
1978	11.5	8.9	0.2	2.4	0.01			
1979	12.3	8.8	0.2	3.3	0.02		7.0	
1980	14.3	9.8	0.5	3.9	0.05		16.3	
1981	14.9	10.1	0.7	4.1	0.05		4.2	
1982	16.8	11.3	0.7	4.7	0.05		12.8	
1983	19.6	12.7	0.8	6.0	0.1		16.7	
1984	22.2	14.4	0.9	6.7	0.2		13.3	
1985	25.9	16.1	0.8	8.6	0.4		16.7	
1986	28.1	17.2	0.8	9.4	0.7		8.5	
1987	34.4	20.3	0.8	12.3	1.0		22.4	
1988	52.6	31.4	0.9	18.6	1.7		52.9	
1989	60.4	34.2	0.7	23.3	2.2		14.8	
1990	70.2	39.0	0.9	28.0	2.3		16.2	
1991	76.5	39.6	1.5	32.8	2.6		9.0	
1992	84.5	43.2	1.6	36.3	3.4		10.5	
1993	100.4	51.1	2.3	42.7	4.3		18.8	
1994	144.3	72.5	3.1	64.0	4.7		43.7	
1995	164.4	86.8	2.7	68.8	6.1		13.9	
1996	168.9	89.2	2.8	71.1	5.8		2.7	
1997	170.5	86.8	2.9	74.6	6.2		0.9	
1998	174.8	88.3	3.2	75.8	7.5		2.5	
1999	180.6	89.4	4.1	79.5	7.6		3.3	
2000	188.6	88.1	5.2	87.5	7.8		4.4	
2001	202.2	84.7	9.0	99.3	9.2		7.2	
2002	213.5	83.5	11.9	108.6	9.5		5.6	
2003	224.7	80.9	12.3	114.3	9.3	7.9	5.2	
2004	234.9	83.1	11.4	124.3	8.9	7.2	4.5	
2005	239.3	91.0	12.4	120.8	8.7	6.4	1.9	
2006	240.2	104.5	14.8	105.1	9.8	6.0	0.4	0.9
2007	272.3	115.5	17.8	122.4	10.1	6.5	13.4	0.8
2008	303.9	128.1	20.5	140.5	9.8	5.0	11.6	0.8
2009	315.0	146.1	17.2	136.1	10.3	5.3	3.6	5.5
2010	328.0	154.2	16.8	139.6	11.5	5.9	4.1	-1.7
2011	363.1	163.4	18.9	162.7	11.5	6.6	10.7	0.9
2012	395.7	166.3	54.8	154.2	13.0	7.5	9.0	2.9
2013	421.8	170.4	75.9	154.8	12.8	8.0	6.6	2.1
2014	420.1	155.1	90.7	152.7	13.2	8.4	-0.4	…
2015	368.2	154.5	57.3	135.9	11.9	8.7	-12.3	-11.7
2016	338.1	145.2	52.2	122.7	9.2	8.7	-8.2	-9.9
2017	308.3	129.8	58.8	101.4	9.6	8.7	-8.8	-6.9
2018	296.8	114.7	95.1	72.0	6.1	8.8	-3.7	-6.0
2019	281.7	102.3	115.6	49.3	5.3	9.1	-5.1	-6.3
2020	263.4	107.6	97.7	45.2	4.1	8.8	-6.5	-6.7
2021	269.5	123.0	88.8	46.3	4.4	7.1	2.3	2.8
2022	268.2	129.8	86.5	42.3	3.9	5.8	-0.5	-2.0
2023	252.6	135.6	65.9	42.0	4.0	5.1	-5.8	-4.6

11-5 主要农业产品产量(1978-2023年)
OUTPUT OF MAJOR FARM PRODUCTS (1978-2023)

单位：万吨 (10000 tons)

年 份 Year	粮 食 Grain	油 料 Oil-bearing Crops	蔬菜及食用菌 Vegetables and Edible Mushroom	干鲜果品 Nuts and Fresh Fruits	牛 奶 Milk	肉 类 Meat	#猪牛羊肉 Pork, Beef and Mutton	禽蛋产量 Poultry and Eggs	水产品 Aquatic Products
1978	186.0	2.6	164.5	17.5	5.4	11.9	11.9	2.1	0.2
1979	172.8	2.6	181.3	15.8	6.0	13.1	13.1	3.1	0.3
1980	186.0	3.1	175.9	15.9	6.8	15.1	15.1	3.4	0.4
1981	180.7	2.2	172.8	15.6	7.6	13.2	13.2	3.7	0.4
1982	185.5	2.3	208.3	13.8	8.9	13.9	13.9	5.4	0.4
1983	201.5	2.1	199.1	18.2	10.6	14.9	14.9	8.9	0.6
1984	217.4	2.6	218.0	20.2	12.6	13.4	13.4	12.2	1.0
1985	219.7	3.9	204.0	18.9	13.5	13.6	13.6	14.1	1.6
1986	216.5	3.0	222.7	18.7	14.6	13.3	13.3	14.7	2.2
1987	227.0	3.3	241.1	22.5	15.5	12.9	12.9	16.8	3.0
1988	234.6	3.0	271.3	23.8	18.0	14.5	14.5	21.8	3.9
1989	239.2	2.8	331.0	26.7	19.9	23.3	17.2	24.7	4.6
1990	264.6	3.1	356.1	27.6	21.7	26.8	20.4	25.8	5.1
1991	279.7	3.3	368.4	29.3	23.9	33.9	24.8	27.9	5.6
1992	281.9	3.4	381.4	34.0	24.5	35.9	27.3	30.0	6.4
1993	284.1	3.8	418.8	39.6	22.5	36.7	28.2	31.4	7.0
1994	249.2	3.8	350.0	48.8	22.2	34.4	24.8	31.2	7.6
1995	259.8	3.3	397.3	46.8	20.6	39.8	28.9	28.5	8.1
1996	237.4	2.9	403.2	51.3	21.0	38.2	27.3	24.7	7.8
1997	237.5	2.7	408.8	54.8	22.2	39.9	27.8	23.8	7.7
1998	239.3	2.8	403.8	59.5	22.7	43.4	30.3	17.9	7.6
1999	201.0	2.8	419.8	60.2	24.0	46.1	30.2	15.8	7.6
2000	144.2	3.8	466.3	66.0	30.3	50.5	30.9	16.0	7.5
2001	104.9	4.3	491.0	71.9	42.9	55.9	33.0	15.6	7.4
2002	82.3	4.6	507.4	78.7	55.1	60.9	35.2	15.2	7.4
2003	58.0	3.3	486.7	84.1	63.3	60.6	35.2	16.2	7.1
2004	70.2	2.9	444.1	90.9	70.0	57.4	34.0	15.9	6.7
2005	94.9	2.5	373.1	93.9	64.2	53.3	31.7	16.0	6.4
2006	109.2	2.2	341.2	88.7	61.9	45.3	26.9	15.2	5.4
2007	102.1	2.2	340.1	91.1	62.2	47.9	27.1	15.6	6.0
2008	125.5	2.2	321.3	89.8	66.4	45.1	25.9	15.2	6.1
2009	124.8	1.8	317.1	90.3	67.4	47.2	27.6	15.4	5.8
2010	115.7	1.6	303.0	85.4	64.1	46.3	27.5	15.1	6.3
2011	121.8	1.4	296.9	87.8	64.0	44.4	27.6	15.1	6.1
2012	113.8	1.3	279.9	84.3	65.1	43.2	27.3	15.2	6.4
2013	96.1	1.0	266.9	79.5	61.5	41.8	27.9	17.5	6.4
2014	63.9	0.7	236.2	74.5	59.5	39.3	26.9	19.6	6.8
2015	62.6	0.6	205.1	71.4	57.2	36.4	25.2	19.6	6.6
2016	52.8	0.6	183.6	66.1	45.7	30.4	24.4	18.3	5.4
2017	41.1	0.5	156.8	61.1	37.4	26.4	21.7	15.7	4.5
2018	34.1	0.4	130.6	49.9	31.1	17.5	15.1	11.2	3.0
2019	28.8	0.3	111.5	48.9	26.4	5.1	3.4	9.6	3.0
2020	30.5	0.3	137.9	43.0	24.2	3.5	2.1	9.7	2.3
2021	37.8	0.5	165.6	38.5	25.8	4.4	3.3	9.4	2.3
2022	45.4	0.9	198.9	29.4	26.2	4.3	3.4	8.7	1.7
2023	47.8	1.0	207.5	30.9	26.5	4.2	3.4	9.1	1.9

注：1.1988年及以前肉类产量为猪牛羊肉产量。
2.2006年及以前水产品产量为淡水鱼产量，自2007年起含远洋捕捞量。水产品数据由北京市农业农村局提供。

Note: a) Output of meat in and before 1988 referred to the output of pork, beef and mutton.
b) Output of aquatic products referred to output of fresh water fish in and before 2006, and long-range fishing has been included since 2007. Figures of aquatic products are provided by Beijing Municipal Bureau of Agriculture and Rural Affairs.

11-6 农业观光园、乡村旅游、种业和设施农业(2005-2023年)

项目	Item	2005	2006	2007
农业观光园	**Agricultural Sightseeing Gardens**			
农业观光园个数（个）	Number of Agricultural Sightseeing Gardens (unit)	1012	1230	1302
高峰期从业人员（人）	Employed Persons in Peak Production Period (person)	40729	52828	51392
接待人次（万人次）	Visits Received (10000 person-times)	892.5	1210.6	1446.8
经营总收入（亿元）	Total Operating Income (100 million yuan)	7.9	10.5	13.1
乡村旅游	**Rural Tourism**			
实际经营的乡村旅游接待户和单位（户、个）	Number of Actual Operating Households and Units in Rural Tourism Reception (household, unit)	7268	8726	10323
高峰期从业人员（人）	Employed Persons in Peak Production Period (person)	14070	18253	20750
乡村旅游接待人次（万人次）	Number of Visits Received by Rural Tourism (10000 person-times)	758.9	982.5	1167.6
乡村旅游总收入（亿元）	Total Income of Rural Tourism (100 million yuan)	3.1	3.7	5.0
种业	**Seed Industry**			
种业收入（亿元）	Income (100 million yuan)	5.9	7.7	9.9
#销往外埠收入	Income from Sales to Other Areas			4.0
#牧业收入	Income from Animal Production and Hunting			8.3
设施农业	**Facility Agriculture**			
设施农业实际利用占地面积（公顷）	Actual Area Utilized by Facility Agriculture (hectare)	15645	17832	18022
设施农业播种面积（公顷）	Sown Area of Facility Agriculture (hectare)			30331
设施农业产值（亿元）	Output Value of Facility Agriculture (100 million yuan)	18.6	21.1	28.1

注：2018年及以前乡村旅游为民俗旅游口径；自2019年起，乡村旅游统计范围除包括民俗旅游农户外，还包括乡镇及乡镇以下范围内为乡村旅游服务的宾馆、饭店、旅游商品专卖店等。

AGRICULTURAL SIGHTSEEING GARDENS, RURAL TOURISM, SEED INDUSTRY AND FACILITY AGRICULTURE (2005-2023)

2008	2009	2010	2011	2012	2013	2014	2015	2016	2017	2018	2019	2020	2021	2022	2023
1332	1294	1303	1300	1283	1299	1301	1328	1258	1216	1172	948	925	1009	1027	1044
49366	49504	42561	46038	48906	50406	47088	42617	40349	39624	39726	33815	28706	29451	29441	30190
1498.2	1597.4	1774.9	1842.9	1939.9	1944.4	1911.2	1903.3	2250.5	2105.3	1897.6	1538.0	867.2	1154.5	707.0	936.2
13.6	15.2	17.8	21.7	26.9	27.4	24.9	26.3	28.0	29.9	27.3	23.2	15.5	18.4	18.4	21.2
9151	8705	7979	8396	8367	8530	8863	8941	9026	8363	7783	7354	5832	6793	7105	7738
19421	19790	16856	18232	18705	19578	21493	22313	22215	22455	21203	23720	19626	21607	21463	23571
1205.6	1393.1	1553.6	1668.9	1695.8	1806.5	1914.2	2139.7	2297.4	2232.1	2042.3	1920.1	1010.3	1365.7	1080.9	1273.9
5.3	6.1	7.3	8.7	9.1	10.2	11.3	12.9	14.4	14.2	13.0	14.4	9.5	14.1	13.7	15.0
10.9	12.8	14.6	18.1	16.1	14.0	14.0	12.7	14.0	12.7	12.4	15.1	12.1	11.9	8.9	11.5
5.8	7.3	8.1	11.7	9.7	8.2	8.0	6.6	7.7	6.7	7.4	10.6	8.5	8.4	5.5	8.7
9.3	10.6	12.1	15.1	13.6	12.6	12.5	11.2	12.9	11.1	10.8	13.3	10.7	10.1	7.1	9.7
17051	18762	18323	18616	19059	18852	18232	17397	15404	14941	13880	12900	13252	13026	13370	13678
33889	36203	36811	38006	37797	38763	38115	41088	37666	35740	32324	27068	29010	31172	32496	31766
28.2	33.9	40.7	45.6	52.0	57.3	51.3	55.5	54.4	54.5	51.7	47.1	50.1	57.9	59.8	60.4

Note: In and before 2018, rural tourism was uniformly called folk-custom tourism; since 2019, the scope of statistics of rural tourism has covered not only the rural households engaging in folk-custom tourism, but also the hotels, restaurants and tourists commodities stores, etc. at or below township level that serve the rural tourism.

11-7 农业生产条件
CONDITIONS OF AGRICULTURAL PRODUCTION

项　　目		Item		2023	2022
主要农业机械拥有量		**Possession of Major Agricultural Machinery**			
农业机械总动力	(万千瓦)	Total Agricultural Machinery Power	(10000 kW)	123.9	116.4
大中型拖拉机	(混合台)	Large and Medium-sized Tractors	(unit)	4528	4069
小型拖拉机	(台)	Small Tractors	(unit)	1769	1816
机引农具	(台)	Tractor-propelled Farm Tools	(unit)	14532	13039
机动喷雾器	(部)	Motorized Sprayers	(unit)	11616	11597
联合收割机	(台)	Combine Harvesters	(unit)	713	679
机动脱粒机	(台)	Motorized Shellers	(unit)	3471	3545
米面加工机	(台)	Processing Machines of Rice and Flour	(unit)	3044	3154
机动挤奶器	(台)	Motorized Milkers	(unit)	1382	755
饲料粉碎机	(台)	Fodder Grinders	(unit)	1959	1925
农业机械作业面积		**Operation Area of Agricultural Machinery**			
机耕面积	(公顷)	Cultivated Area by Machinery	(hectare)	93432	90404
占应机耕面积比重	(%)	Share in the Area Supposed to be Cultivated by Machinery	(%)	96.5	97.2
机播面积	(公顷)	Sown Area by Machinery	(hectare)	105887	95943
占播种面积比重	(%)	Share in the Total Sown Area	(%)	71.6	71.2
机收面积	(公顷)	Harvest Area by Machinery	(hectare)	82004	71069
占收获面积比重	(%)	Share in the Total Harvest Area	(%)	55.7	52.8
农田水利		**Irrigation and Water Conservancy**			
排灌用动力机械	(台)	Power Machinery for Drainage and Irrigation	(unit)	30381	30456
排灌用动力机械动力	(万千瓦)	Power of the Power Machinery for Drainage and Irrigation	(10000 kW)	37.4	37.5
机(电)井	(眼)	Motor-pumped (Electric) Wells	(unit)	33470	38024
化肥施用量(折纯)		**Consumption of Chemical Fertilizers (converted into net amount)**			
化肥施用量	(吨)	Consumption of Chemical Fertilizers	(ton)	67497.1	66087.5
#氮　肥	(吨)	Nitrogenous Fertilizer	(ton)	19003.7	20413.0
磷　肥	(吨)	Phosphate Fertilizer	(ton)	2995.8	3271.9
钾　肥	(吨)	Potash Fertilizer	(ton)	3167.4	3274.8

注：1.主要农业机械拥有量、农业机械作业面积及排灌动力机械数据由北京市农业农村局提供。
2.机(电)井数据由北京市水务局提供。

Note: a) Figures of possession of major agricultural machinery, operation area of agricultural machinery, and power machinery for drainage and and irrigationare provided by Beijing Municipal Bureau of Agriculture and Rural Affairs.
b) Figures of motor-pumped (electric) wells are provided by Beijing Water Authority.

11-8 农、林、牧、渔业总产值
GROSS OUTPUT VALUE OF AGRICULTURE, FORESTRY, ANIMAL HUSBANDRY AND FISHERY

单位：万元 (10000 yuan)

项目	Item	总产值 Gross Output Value 2023	2022	2023年为2022年% 2023 as % of 2022
合计	**Total**	**2526231.9**	**2681755.8**	**94.2**
农业	**Agriculture**	**1356002.2**	**1297652.4**	**104.5**
#谷物	Cereals	124599.6	121423.8	102.6
豆类	Beans	7064.4	6357.7	111.1
油料	Oil-bearing	8168.8	7021.5	116.3
蔬菜、食用菌	Vegetables and Edible Mushrooms	719979.4	723650.3	99.5
水果（含瓜果类）	Fruits (including melons)	399829.3	344062.1	116.2
林业	**Forestry**	**658742.8**	**865169.3**	**76.1**
牧业	**Animal Husbandry**	**419922.5**	**422891.8**	**99.3**
牲畜饲养	Livestock	183975.3	182685.2	100.7
养猪	Hogs	61355.2	71327.8	86.0
家禽饲养	Poultry	169276.1	165116.0	102.5
#禽蛋	Poultry Eggs	119644.8	122583.4	97.6
其他	Others	5315.9	3762.8	141.3
渔业	**Fishery**	**40409.4**	**38531.3**	**104.9**
农林牧渔专业及辅助性活动	**Professional and Support Services for Agricultare, Forestry, Animal Husbandry and Fishery**	**51155.0**	**57511.0**	**88.9**

11-9 主要农作物播种面积及产量
SOWN AREA AND OUTPUT OF MAJOR FARM CROPS

项目	Item	2023			2022		
		播种面积（公顷） Sown Area (hectare)	单产（公斤／公顷） Output Per Hectare (kg/hectare)	总产量（吨） Total Output (ton)	播种面积（公顷） Sown Area (hectare)	单产（公斤／公顷） Output Per Hectare (kg/hectare)	总产量（吨） Total Output (ton)
粮食	**Grain**	**89465.0**	**5340.6**	**477797.8**	**76734.4**	**5910.9**	**453565.9**
按季节分	By Season						
夏粮	Summer Grain	24997.2	5359.5	133972.7	18222.6	5251.9	95702.7
秋粮	Autumn Grain	64467.8	5333.3	343825.1	58511.7	6116.1	357863.1
按品种分	By Variety						
#稻谷	Rice	334.9	5345.2	1790.4	416.6	5062.1	2108.9
冬小麦	Winter Wheat	24563.2	5378.3	132108.2	17631.5	5292.6	93316.4
玉米	Corn	56135.9	5632.1	316161.7	51149.4	6556.6	335368.5
薯类	Tubers	2068.1	5716.3	11822.1	1251.2	5348.5	6691.9
大豆	Soybeans	4257.2	2231.6	9500.5	3774.7	2289.7	8642.8
棉花	**Cotton**	**2.3**	**1071.4**	**2.5**	**4.4**	**1120.4**	**4.9**
油料	**Oil-bearing Crops**	**3544.8**	**2892.4**	**10252.9**	**3179.7**	**2795.1**	**8887.8**
#花生	Peanuts	2710.9	3320.8	9002.5	2762.6	3020.0	8343.1
中草药材	**Chinese Medicine Herbs**	**1551.7**	**616.5**	**956.6**	**1537.7**	**502.0**	**771.9**
蔬菜及食用菌	**Vegetables and Edible Mushrooms**	**53019.3**	**39133.3**	**2074820.7**	**53166.0**	**37404.4**	**1988641.1**
瓜类及草莓	**Melons & Strawberries**	**3153.1**	**40834.4**	**128754.4**	**3001.8**	**38591.2**	**115842.4**
#西瓜	Watermelons	2223.0	47396.4	105362.9	2086.5	45076.8	94051.5
饲料	**Forage**	**7681.1**	**40795.3**	**313354.5**	**5507.3**	**38420.6**	**211591.8**
#牧草	Forage Grass	5.7	37500.0	212.5	14.8	31385.1	464.5
花卉	**Flowers**	**1608.8**			**1724.9**		

11-10 林业及干鲜果品生产
FORESTRY, NUTS AND FRESH FRUIT PRODUCTION

项　　目	Item	2023	2022	2023年为2022年% 2023 as % of 2022
林业生产	**Forestry**			
营造林面积　(公顷)	Sulviculture and Afforestation Area　(hectare)	57147	100600	56.8
#人工造林面积	Artificial Afforestation Area	890	10120	8.8
育苗面积　(公顷)	Seedling Growing Area　(hectare)	8077	10542	76.6
果类生产	**Fruits**			
干鲜果总产量　(吨)	Output of Nuts and Fresh Fruits　(ton)	309195	293514	105.3
干　果	Nuts	20294	26021	78.0
#核　桃	Walnuts	5389	6284	85.7
板　栗	Chinese Chestnuts	14369	18475	77.8
鲜　果	Fresh Fruits	288901	267493	108.0
#苹　果	Apples	29810	28832	103.4
梨	Pears	34748	43290	80.3
葡　萄	Grapes	9226	10111	91.3
柿　子	Persimmons	4329	4854	89.2
桃	Peaches	184150	149443	123.2
年末实有果园面积　(公顷)	**Area of Orchards (year-end)　(hectare)**	**28407**	**32588**	**87.2**

注：本表中营造林面积为人工造林、飞播造林、封山育林、退化林修复、人工更新、森林抚育面积之和。
资料来源：林业生产数据由北京市园林绿化局提供。
Note: The data on sulviculture and afforestation area in this table refer to the sum of the area of afforestation by approach of manual planting, airplane planting, closed hillsides for afforestation, restoration of degraded forest, artificial regeneration and forest tending.
Source: Figures of forestry are provided by Beijing Municipal Forestry and Parks Bureau.

11-11 牲畜饲养及畜产品产量
NUMBER OF LIVESTOCK AND OUTPUT OF LIVESTOCK PRODUCTS

项 目		Item		2023	2022	2023年为2022年% 2023 as % of 2022
畜禽存栏		**Amount of Livestock and Poultry on Hand**				
大牲畜	(万头)	Large Animals	(10000 heads)	8.4	8.4	100.1
#牛		Cattle and Buffaloes		8.3	8.2	101.3
猪	(万头)	Hogs	(10000 heads)	26.7	36.8	72.6
羊	(万只)	Sheep and Goats	(10000 units)	22.0	19.5	113.0
山 羊		Goats		7.5	6.1	122.4
绵 羊		Sheep		14.5	13.3	108.7
家 禽	(万只)	Poultry	(10000 units)	744.5	774.0	96.2
#产蛋鸡		Hens		728.5	765.8	95.1
肉 鸡		Chickens		1.5	1.8	81.3
鸭		Ducks		13.6	5.7	238.6
兔	(万只)	Rabbits	(10000 units)	0.2	0.2	132.3
畜禽出栏		**Amount of Livestock and Poultry Marketed**				
牛	(万头)	Cattle and Buffaloes	(10000 heads)	2.8	2.3	121.4
猪	(万头)	Hogs	(10000 heads)	32.9	32.2	102.3
羊	(万只)	Sheep and Goats	(10000 units)	12.1	10.9	111.0
畜禽产品产量		**Output of Livestock and Poultry Products**				
肉类产量	(万吨)	Output of Meat	(10000 tons)	4.2	4.3	96.8
#猪 肉		Pork		2.7	2.8	97.1
牛 肉		Beef		0.5	0.4	115.6
羊 肉		Mutton		0.2	0.2	107.4
牛奶产量	(万吨)	Output of Milk	(10000 tons)	26.5	26.2	101.1
禽 蛋	(万吨)	Poultry Eggs	(10000 tons)	9.1	8.7	104.2
#鸡 蛋		Eggs		9.1	8.7	104.6
蜂 蜜	(吨)	Honey	(ton)	1101.4	882.1	124.9

11-12 水产品生产
PRODUCTION OF AQUATIC PRODUCTS

项目	Item	2023	2022
渔业水域面积（公顷）	**Area of Fishery Waters (hectare)**	**24805**	**24832**
#淡水养殖面积	Freshwater Aquaculture Area	1360	1387
#池塘	Puddles and Ponds	1359	1381
水产品产量（吨）	**Output of Aquatic Products (ton)**	**18554**	**17492**
#淡水鱼产量	Output of Freshwater Fish	11262	13240
#大水库	Large Reservoirs	1357	2801
池塘	Puddles and Ponds	9473	10439

资料来源：北京市农业农村局。
Source: Beijing Municipal Bureau of Agriculture and Rural Affairs.

11-13 种业生产
PRODUCTION OF SEED INDUSTRY

项目	Item	产量 Output			收入(万元) Income (10000 yuan)		
		2023	2022	2023年为2022年% 2023 as % of 2022	2023	2022	2023年为2022年% 2023 as % of 2022
合计	**Total**				**115036.0**	**89448.2**	**128.6**
农业	**Agriculture**				**15300.6**	**13080.5**	**117.0**
#小麦种（公斤）	Wheat Seeds (kg)	1438000	500000	287.6	373.8	140.0	267.0
玉米种（公斤）	Corn Seeds (kg)	52700	68000	77.5	49.7	54.9	90.5
蔬菜种（公斤）	Vegetable Seeds (kg)	10672	9337	114.3	649.0	688.0	94.3
林业	**Forestry**				**718.1**	**3598.3**	**20.0**
#树苗（百株）	Saplings (100 units)	734.4	2028.1	36.2	718.1	3598.3	20.0
牧业	**Animal Husbandry**				**96963.7**	**71225.2**	**136.1**
#种猪（头）	Breeding Pig (head)	48537	34123	142.2	8842.1	8931.7	99.0
种雏禽（万只）	Brood Bird (10000 units)	1646.0	1433.2	114.8	40894.2	25709	159.1
种蛋（万枚）	Breeding Eggs (10000 units)	19834.4	19203.7	103.3	28870.0	22424.4	128.7
渔业	**Fishery**				**2053.6**	**1544.2**	**133.0**
#种鱼苗（万尾）	Breeding Fish Fry (10000 units)	6198.3	6431.8	96.4	2053.6	1544.2	133.0

11-14 设施农业(2023年)
FACILITY AGRICULTURE (2023)

项　　目	Item	设施农业播种面积 (公顷) Sown Area of Facility Agriculture (hectare)	设施农业产量 (吨) Output of Facility Agriculture (ton)	设施农业产值 (万元) Output Value of Facility Agriculture (10000 yuan)
合　计	**Total**	**31765.8**		**603949.8**
温　室	**Greenhouse**	**13906.1**		**384807.9**
蔬菜及食用菌	Vegetables and Edible Mushrooms	12207.8	564637.5	260752.5
花卉苗木	Flowers and Saplings	495.1		19093.9
#切　花	Cut Flowers	28.6	34294.2	1201.7
盆　花	Potted Flowers	462.3	469775.2	17839.7
瓜果类	Melons	1007.9	27149.0	94562.3
园林水果	Fruits	152.9	1248.7	6211.8
其　他	Others	42.5		4187.4
大　棚	**Greenhouse Garden**	**17065.2**		**210100.7**
蔬菜及食用菌	Vegetables and Edible Mushrooms	14818.7	536824.9	150674.3
花卉苗木	Flowers and Sapling	178.7		4725.1
#切　花	Cut Flowers	42.1	86442.0	689.2
盆　花	Potted Flowers	136.6	211176.0	4035.9
瓜果类	Melons	1873.8	88964.6	49734.0
园林水果	Fruits	142.3	997.4	2688.7
其　他	Other	51.7		2278.6
中小棚	**Medium and Small Shed**	**794.5**		**9041.2**
蔬菜及食用菌	Vegetables and Edible Mushrooms	663.7	19047.4	6178.2
花卉苗木	Flowers and Sapling	5.3		292.2
#切　花	Cut Flowers			
盆　花	Potted Flowers	5.3	5727.0	291.9
瓜果类	Melons	124.8	5654.0	2570.8
园林水果	Fruits	0.7		
其　他	Other			

注：切花产量的计量单位是百枝，盆花产量的计量单位是百盆。
Note: Cut flowers output is measured in 100 ones; and potted flowers output is measured in 100 pots.

11−15 农村双层经营主要指标情况(2023年)
MAIN INDICATORS OF RURAL DOUBLE-LAYER MANAGEMENT SYSTEM (2023)

项目		Item		2023
集体经济组织情况		**Organizations of Collective Economy**		
乡镇级集体经济组织数	(个)	Number of Township-level Collective Economic Organizations	(unit)	188
村级集体经济组织数	(个)	Number of Village-level Collective Economic Organizations	(unit)	4000
汇总农户数	(户)	Total Number of Rural Households	(household)	1332806
汇总人口数	(人)	Total Number of Population	(person)	3134727
劳动力总人数	(人)	Total Number of Labor Force	(person)	1806523
就业率	(%)	Employment Rate	(%)	93.4
集体经济经营情况		**Operation of Collective Economy**		
集体经济总收入	(亿元)	Gross Income of Collective Economy	(100 million yuan)	740.7
#主营业务收入		Revenue from Principal Business		443.9
利润总额	(亿元)	Total Profits	(100 million yuan)	13.5
净利润	(亿元)	Net Profit	(100 million yuan)	4.4
可供分配的利润	(亿元)	Profit Available for Distribution	(100 million yuan)	-175.1
未分配利润	(亿元)	Undistributed Profit	(100 million yuan)	-214.4
资产总计	(亿元)	Total Assets	(100 million yuan)	9965.0
乡镇级		Township Level		3507.3
村　级		Village Level		6457.6
所有者权益合计	(亿元)	Total Owner's Equity	(100 million yuan)	3368.7
乡镇级		Township Level		653.6
村　级		Village Level		2715.2
人均所有者权益	(元)	Per Capita Owner's Equity	(yuan)	107465
农户收入情况		**Income of Rural Households**		
农户总收入	(亿元)	Total Income	(100 million yuan)	1472.5
农户所得总额	(亿元)	Total Earnings	(100 million yuan)	988.2
人均所得	(元)	Per Capita Earnings	(yuan)	31526
农户从集体经济获取的所得总额	(亿元)	Total Earnings of Rural Household from Collective Economy	(100 million yuan)	219.3

注：双层经营指农民家庭分散经营和集体统一经营相结合。
资料来源：北京市农业农村局。
Note: Double-layer management system refers to a system with integration of decentralized management of rural households and collective unified management.
Source: Beijing Municipal Bureau of Agriculture and Rural Affairs.

主要统计指标解释

农林牧渔业总产值 是以货币表现的农林牧渔业的全部产品总量和对农林牧渔业生产活动进行的各种支持性服务活动的价值。

农作物播种面积 指本年度内收获农作物在全部土地（耕地或非耕地）上的播种或移植面积。凡是本年内收获的农作物，无论是本年还是上年播种，都算为播种面积，但不包括本年播种、下年收获的农作物面积。在播种季节基本结束后，因遭灾而重新改种和补种的农作物面积，也包括在内。

设施农业 指以工厂化生产方式，建造人工设施，改变气候条件，提高农作物抵御自然灾害的能力，改良生物特性，使作物实现错季或反季节生产，达到农作物均衡生产的目的。

农业机械总动力 指主要用于农、林、牧、渔业的各种动力机械的动力总和。包括耕作机械、排灌机械、收获机械、农用运输机械、植物保护机械、牧业机械、渔业机械和其他农用机械[内燃机按引擎马力折成瓦（特）计算，电动机按功率折成瓦（特）计算]。不包括专门用于乡、镇、村、组办工业、基本建设、非农业运输、科学实验和教学等非农业生产方面用的动力机械与作业机械。

农用化肥施用量 指本年度内实际用于农业生产的化学肥料数量，包括氮肥、磷肥、钾肥和复合肥。施用量要求按折纯量计算数量，即各类化学肥料的实际施用数量按其含氮、含五氧化二磷、含氧化钾的百分比进行计算。

折纯量＝实物量×某种化肥有效成份含量的百分比

行政村常住户数 指长期（一年以上）居住在行政村管理区域内的住户，户口不在本地而在本地居住一年及以上的住户也包括在本地农村住户内；有本地户口，但举家外出谋生一年以上的住户，无论是否保留承包耕地都不包括在本地农村住户范围内。不包括乡村地区内的国有经济的机关、团体、学校、企业、事业单位的集体户。

行政村常住人口 指行政村常住居民户数中的常住人口数，即经常在家或在家居住6个月以上，而且经济和生活与本户连成一体的人口。外出从业人员在外居住时间虽然在6个月以上，但收入主要带回家中，经济与本户连为一体，仍视为家庭常住人口；在家居住，生活和本户连成一体的国家职工、退休人员也为家庭常住人口。但是现役军人、中专及以上（走读生除外）的在校学生、以及常年在外（不包括探亲、看病等）且已有稳定的职业与居住场所的外出从业人员，不应当作家庭常住人口。

行政村从业人员 指全部行政村人口中16周岁以上实际参加生产经营活动并取得实物或货币收入的人员，既包括劳动年龄内经常参加劳动的人员，也包括超过劳动年龄但经常参加劳动的人员。但不包括户口在家的在外学生、现役军人和丧失劳动能力的人，也不包括待业人员和家务劳动者。从业人员按从事主业时间最长（时间相同按收入）分为农业从业人员，工业从业人员，建筑业从业人员，交通运输仓储及邮政业从业人员，信息传输、计算机服务和软件业从业人员，批发与零售业从业人员，住宿和餐饮业从业人员，其他从业人员。

Explanatory Notes on Main Statistical Indicators

Gross Output Value of Agriculture, Forestry, Animal Production and Hunting, Fishing refers to the monetary value of all products of agriculture, forestry, animal production and hunting, fishing, as well as the monetary value of services provided in support of all the above-mentioned sectors.

Sown Area refers to the area of all lands actually sown or transplanted with crops, including both the cultivated and non-cultivated land. Area of lands re-planted after seedtime has passed due to natural disasters is also included.

Facility Agriculture means to produce in an industrialized manner, put in place facilities of manual intervention, change climate conditions, increase the crops' capability to resist natural disasters, and improve the crops' biological property, so as to stagger harvest seasons, create anti-season production, and achieve balanced production of crops.

Total Power of Agricultural Machinery refers to the total power of motive power machines used in agriculture, forestry, animal production and hunting, fishing sectors, including machinery for ploughing, irrigation and drainage, harvesting, agricultural transport, plant protection, animal production and hunting, fishing and other farm machinery (The horsepower of internal combustion engines is converted into watts, and the output of electric motors is also converted into watts). Motive power machines and operating machines exclusively used for non-agricultural production activities, such as industrial operations run by counties, towns, villages and teams, capital construction, non-agricultural transport, scientific experiments and teaching, are not included.

Consumption of Chemical Fertilizers refers to the total quantity of chemical fertilizers applied in agricultural production within the year, including nitrogenous fertilizer, phosphate fertilizer, potash fertilizer, and compound fertilizer. The amount of chemical fertilizers applied is calculated in terms of net amount, that is, to use the gross weight of the respective fertilizers in calculating the quantity of effective ingredients (e.g. nitrogen content in nitrogenous fertilizer, phosphorous pent oxide content in phosphate fertilizer, and potassium oxide content in potash fertilizer).

Net Amount = Physical Quantity × Content (%) of Effective Ingredients in Certain Chemical Fertilizer

Number of Resident Households in Towns and Administrative Villages refers to households living in the administrative areas of towns and villages (excluding township government premises) on a long-term basis (more than one year), including those living in administrative villages within township government premises. Households with non-local household registration but having been living locally for more than one year are also counted as local rural households; while households with local household registration but left to make a living elsewhere for more than one year, with or without contract lands, are not counted as local rural households. Collective households of state-owned government agencies, organizations, schools, enterprises, and public institutions of the state-owned economy in rural areas are not included.

Permanent Population in Towns and Administrative Villages refers to the population of permanent households in rural areas, namely those who stay home regularly or live at home for more than 6 months with their economic life and livelihood incorporated into the household. Migrant workers who live away from home for more than 6 months but taking most of their earnings back home, with their economic life still incorporated into the household, are also counted as permanent population of the household; state employees and retirees who live locally with their life incorporated into the household are also considered permanent population. But soldiers in active service, enrolled students (externs excluded) in technical secondary schools or above, as well as migrant workers who lived away from home for years (excluding those who travel to visit their families or to seek medical care) with a stable job and residence elsewhere, are not regarded as permanent population.

Employed Persons in Towns and Administrative Villages refer to persons aged above 16 in all towns and administrative villages, who actually participate in productive and operating activities and earn incomes in kind or cash, including persons within the range of labor age and regularly participating in labor, and persons beyond the range of labor age but regularly participating in labor; while local registered students who left home for education, soldiers in active service, and people who lost the ability to work are not included, neither are the people waiting for employment or domestic workers. In terms of the length of employment period (or in terms of income if the employment periods are identical), employment falls into the following categories: agriculture, industry, construction, transportation, storage and post, information transmission, computer services and software industry, wholesale and retail trade, accommodation and restaurants, and other sectors.

12

工 业
INDUSTRY

简要说明

一、主要内容

本章资料反映北京市工业基本情况，主要包括按登记注册类型、轻重工业、企业规模、行业大类等分组的主要经济指标数据。

具体指标包括单位数、工业总产值、资产总计、负债合计、营业收入、营业成本、税金及附加、利润总额、应交增值税、总资产贡献率、资产负债率、主要工业产品产量等。

二、统计范围

1984年以前农村的村及村以下办工业归属农业，自1984年起划归工业。

1999年及以前，工业的统计范围按隶属关系划分为乡及乡以上独立核算工业企业和非独立核算生产单位、村办工业、城镇合作工业、农村合作工业、城镇个体工业、农村个体工业六大部分（1984年以前村办工业不在工业统计范围内）。

自2000年起，工业统计调查范围由按隶属关系划分，改变为按企业规模划分。其中，2000-2006年规模以上工业统计范围为全部国有及年主营业务收入在500万元及以上非国有工业企业；2007-2010年为年主营业务收入在500万元及以上法人工业企业；自2011年起为年主营业务收入在2000万元及以上法人工业企业。

三、有关统计标准的变化说明

（一）关于行业划分。2002年及以前，工业行业分类执行《国民经济行业分类及代码》(GB/T 4754- 94)标准，2003-2011年执行《国民经济行业分类标准》(GB/T 4754- 2002)标准，2012-2017年执行《国民经济行业分类》(GB/T 4754-2011)标准，自2018年起执行《国民经济行业分类》(GB/T 4754-2017)标准。

与2002版相比，2011版《国民经济行业分类》标准中，将原“交通运输设备制造业”调整为“汽车制造业”，将原“通信设备、计算机及其他电子设备制造业”调整为“计算机、通信和其他电子设备制造业”，将原“石油加工业”与“炼焦、煤气及煤制品业”合并为“石油加工、炼焦和核燃料加工业”。

（二）关于企业标准划分。2010年以前企业大中小型划分执行2003年《统计上大中小型企业划分办法（暂行）》。2011年至2017年大中小微型企业划分标准执行国家统计局《关于统计上大中小微型企业划分办法》（国统字〔2011〕75号）；自2018年起，执行《统计上大中小微型企业划分办法（2017）》（国统字〔2017〕213号）。

四、关于历史数据调整

1993-2003年规模以上工业总产值历史资料根据北京市第一次全国经济普查的结果采用“趋势离差法”进行了修订，2004年为北京市第一次全国经济普查数据，2008年为北京市第二次全国经济普查数据，2013年为北京市第三次全国经济普查数据，2018年为北京市第四次全国经济普查数据。

Brief Introduction

I. Main Content

Data in this chapter show the basic situation of industry in Beijing, mainly including major economic indicators grouped by type of registration, light or heavy industry, enterprise scale, and industries.

Specific indicators include unit number, gross industrial output value, total assets, total liabilities, business income, business cost, business tax and surtax, total profits, payable VAT, contribution rate to total assets, asset-liability ratio, and output of main industrial products, etc.

II. Scope of Statistics

Prior to 1984, the rural industrial production run by villages and units subordinated to villages was classified as agriculture. Since 1984, it has been grouped into industry.

Before 1999, industrial statistics coverage was divided into six parts by administrative relationship, i.e. independent accounting industrial enterprises and non-independent accounting production units at the township-level and above, village-run industry, urban cooperative industry, rural cooperative industry, urban individual operated industry, and rural individual operated industry (village-run industry was not included in the industrial statistics before 1984).

Since 2000, the scope of industrial statistics was grouped by enterprise scale instead of administrative relationship. Specifically, from 2000 to 2006, the scope of statistics of industry above designated size covers all state-owned enterprises and non-state-owned industrial enterprises with annual main business income of RMB 5 million and above; from 2007 to 2010, the scope of statistics covers the corporate industrial enterprises with annual main business income of RMB 5 million and above; since 2011, the scope of statistics covers the corporate industrial enterprises with annual main business income of RMB 20 million and above.

III. Changes in Relevant Statistical Standards

(I) Classification of Sectors: The standards in the *Classification and Codes of National Economic Sectors (GB/T 4754-94)* were implemented in the classification of industrial sectors before 2002. The standards in the *Standard for Classification of National Economic Sectors (GB/T 4754-2002)* were implemented from 2003 to 2011. The standards in the *Classification of National Economic Sectors (GB/T 4754-2011)* were implemented from 2012 to 2017. The standards in the *Classification of National Economic Sectors (GB/T 4754-2017)* are implemented since 2018.

Contrary to the 2002 version, in the standards in the *Classification of National Economic Sectors* (2011), the original "manufacture of transport equipment" was adjusted to "manufacture of motor vehicles", the original "manufacture of communication equipment, computer and electronic equipment" was adjusted to "manufacture of computer, communication equipment and other electronic equipment", and the original "petroleum processing and coking, gas and coal products"were combined into"processing of petroleum, coking, processing of nucleus fuel".

(II) Before 2010, the classification of small, medium and large-sized enterprises should comply with the standards in the *Measures for Statistical Classification of Small, Medium and Large-sized Enterprises (Temporary)* (2003). The classification of micro, small, medium and large-sized enterprises should comply with the standards in the *Measures for Statistical Classification of Micro, Small, Medium and Large-sized Enterprises* (G.T.Z. [2011] No. 75) of the National Bureau of Statistics from 2011 to 2017. Since 2018, the classification has been in line with the standards in the *Measures for Statistical Classification of Micro, Small, Medium and Large-sized Enterprises (2017)* (G.T.Z. [2017] No. 213).

IV. Adjustment to Historical Data

The historical data on gross output value of industry above designated size for the period between 1993 and 2003 had been revised based on results from the first national economic census in Beijing by the trend deviation method. The data for 2004 were collected from the first national economic census in Beijing, the data for 2008 were collected from the second national economic census in Beijing, the data for 2013 were collected from the third national economic census in Beijing, and the data for 2018 were collected from the fourth national economic census in Beijing.

12-1 规模以上工业总产值(1984-2023年)

单位：亿元

年 份 Year	合 计 Total	轻工业 Light Industry	重工业 Heavy Industry	#大中型工业 Large and Medium-sized Industry	#制造业 Manufacturing	#计算机、通信和其他电子设备制造业 Manufacture of Computers, Communication and Other Electronic Equipment	#汽车制造业 Manufacture of Automobiles	#电力、热力生产和供应业 Production and Supply of Electric Power and Heat Power
1984	276.2	118.0	158.2	178.7				
1985	324.2	135.8	188.4	213.7				
1986	336.5	140.8	195.7	231.6		14.5	23.1	9.2
1987	387.6	160.1	227.5	272.1		19.5	28.6	9.4
1988	495.6	212.5	283.1	345.4		28.9	39.2	11.0
1989	602.7	264.1	338.6	408.3		33.6	44.0	13.7
1990	625.9	262.2	363.7	433.8		37.3	48.7	16.1
1991	730.2	298.1	432.1	507.4		45.7	69.6	18.7
1992	860.0	306.5	553.5	587.4		47.8	100.9	22.5
1993	1166.6	361.9	804.7	747.6		71.4	126.6	28.9
1994	1576.6	497.9	1078.7	990.7		120.3	162.1	39.9
1995	1493.3	472.2	1021.1	937.7		154.8	173.8	41.1
1996	1590.6	509.1	1081.5	962.3		199.2	166.6	17.5
1997	1819.7	577.8	1241.9	999.6		300.9	158.5	75.5
1998	1947.0	598.2	1348.8	1059.8		467.1	112.9	71.1
1999	2183.5	621.8	1561.7	1090.9		611.8	121.6	74.8
2000	2842.0	719.3	2122.7	1653.1		934.1	109.7	83.2
2001	3270.1	842.4	2427.7	2298.4		1066.0	180.9	83.8
2002	3620.2	882.4	2737.8	2434.7		1018.9	269.4	99.9
2003	4410.8	936.7	3474.1	3183.9		1091.1	528.0	118.3
2004	5733.3	1084.7	4648.6	3699.3		1235.6	748.9	492.8
2005	6946.2	1164.9	5781.3	5242.1	6159.3	1775.5	817.7	600.0
2006	8210.0	1258.2	6951.8	6237.9	7130.2	2234.2	1003.6	847.6
2007	9648.4	1505.5	8142.9	7365.9	8273.0	2663.1	1057.4	1068.0
2008	10413.1	1674.3	8738.8	7898.9	8654.5	2385.9	1153.3	1242.4
2009	11039.1	1766.7	9272.4	8349.3	8897.3	2095.5	1663.8	1435.6
2010	13699.8	2000.0	11699.8	10505.3	10793.4	2229.1	2177.7	2120.2
2011	14513.6	2227.2	12286.4	11289.3	10925.1	2026.2	2495.6	2283.4
2012	15596.2	2402.1	13194.1	12239.6	11103.1	2054.9	2521.5	3018.1
2013	17370.9	2541.5	14829.4	13941.3	12259.0	2217.0	3269.2	3739.1
2014	18452.9	2568.0	15884.9	15039.5	13103.8	2424.5	3647.6	4087.0
2015	17449.6	2610.8	14838.8	14250.3	12591.5	2110.2	3882.9	4085.6
2016	18087.3	2731.6	15355.7	15053.2	13291.9	2019.9	4771.6	4105.5
2017	18901.1	2924.1	15977.0	15747.2	13640.9	2199.5	4492.5	4496.7
2018	19669.0	2975.7	16693.3	16224.5	13769.2	2492.0	3945.3	5032.2
2019	20386.1	2964.1	17422.0	16541.0	13997.4	2600.5	3964.5	5474.9
2020	20879.3	2945.5	17933.8	17211.4	14394.4	2881.8	4139.4	5585.7
2021	24988.1	5649.6	19338.5	20896.4	17869.1	3744.4	3433.2	6176.7
2022	23870.0	3388.4	20481.7	19649.6	15597.0	3517.0	3398.6	7317.4
2023	24652.2	3326.8	21325.4	20375.5	15682.9	3342.5	3574.1	8089.3

注：工业总产值按当年价格计算。

GROSS OUTPUT VALUE OF INDUSTRY ABOVE DESIGNATED SIZE (1984-2023)

(100 million yuan)

#铁路、船舶、航空航天和其他运输设备制造业 Manufacture of Railway, Ship, Aerospace and Other Transport Equipments	#化学原料和化学制品制造业 Manufacture of Raw Chemical Materials and Chemical Products	#通用设备制造业 Manufacture of General Purpose Machinery	#专用设备制造业 Manufacture of Special Purpose Machinery	#电气机械和器材制造业 Manufacture of Electrical Machinery and Apparatus	#仪器仪表制造业 Manufacture of Measuring Instruments and Machinery	#医药制造业 Manufacture of Medicines	#非金属矿物制品业 Manufacture of Non-metallic Mineral Products	#石油、煤炭及其他燃料加工业 Processing of Petroleum, Coal and Other Fuels
	48.1			15.7	3.7	5.4	15.9	4.8
	57.2			17.0	4.0	7.1	17.6	5.6
	69.4			22.2	5.3	9.8	20.1	7.0
	83.4			27.0	5.5	10.8	24.7	8.2
	87.1			22.1	4.9	11.4	24.1	9.7
	42.8			25.7	5.7	14.0	27.1	65.6
	62.0			30.5	7.4	15.8	31.8	67.4
	70.1	64.8	33.8	40.9	12.2	18.2	50.3	92.4
	90.6	76.1	62.1	53.4	15.4	21.8	81.1	117.3
	101.4	55.3	40.4	37.0	24.3	21.9	54.5	133.9
	104.3	54.3	41.4	44.8	32.1	26.4	71.4	133.3
	100.1	49.9	53.1	52.2	30.6	32.3	73.7	148.4
	100.1	53.5	81.0	69.2	33.2	38.9	92.6	111.8
	116.6	43.4	100.0	87.5	37.0	47.1	95.0	156.7
	144.2	49.1	123.4	97.7	42.4	58.5	102.8	289.2
	145.6	71.9	98.0	111.5	49.7	71.5	102.8	269.8
	168.0	81.4	130.2	119.1	74.8	98.6	132.9	318.0
	312.7	128.1	151.0	169.2	97.8	123.0	143.4	241.9
	399.0	186.7	189.8	197.5	124.4	119.7	184.5	274.6
	236.9	237.1	232.0	222.3	158.2	131.1	193.8	592.5
	257.5	292.5	300.9	260.7	183.9	150.1	234.6	540.4
	318.0	347.8	331.9	333.7	215.7	202.3	258.5	601.7
	306.7	409.2	434.4	387.2	211.4	263.9	296.5	753.2
	255.9	377.9	423.1	596.4	205.4	313.1	344.4	682.1
	358.3	547.7	502.4	699.1	227.9	372.8	392.5	825.2
	371.2	597.9	565.6	775.1	242.3	452.9	445.2	902.5
200.2	345.9	524.7	510.3	669.7	224.3	543.3	461.1	886.3
262.0	349.6	516.9	614.7	714.1	245.8	599.1	491.1	767.2
381.5	352.1	550.6	590.3	737.6	257.3	669.0	488.0	845.4
384.5	319.3	488.0	543.7	786.2	257.7	733.0	392.2	591.1
391.5	302.3	490.0	512.1	678.6	254.9	814.4	432.1	494.4
423.7	333.9	537.3	557.2	665.8	269.1	981.6	432.1	580.0
434.8	303.4	532.0	694.8	665.1	241.9	1142.7	464.5	638.5
457.3	270.1	507.7	789.0	686.0	294.0	1221.6	482.1	579.8
446.7	255.0	524.4	805.6	848.3	268.3	1313.9	471.0	455.9
497.1	290.4	596.9	872.3	794.6	307.3	3930.3	522.0	616.8
509.0	279.7	666.8	1010.4	795.6	323.1	1748.8	481.2	732.3
702.8	221.4	623.3	1127.2	1038.6	324.6	1459.0	449.1	669.1

Note: Gross output value of industry is calculated at current prices.

12-2 规模以上工业企业主要经济指标(1978-2023年)
MAIN ECONOMIC INDICATORS OF INDUSTRIAL ENTERPRISES ABOVE DESIGNATED SIZE (1978-2023)

单位：亿元 (100 million yuan)

年份 Year	企业单位个数(个) Number of Enterprises (unit)	平均用工人数(万人) Average Number of Employed Persons (10000 persons)	资产总计 Total Assets	负债合计 Total Liabilities	固定资产原价 Original Value of Fixed Assets	营业收入 Business Revenue	营业成本 Business Cost	利润总额 Total Profits	利税总额 Total Taxes & Profits
1978	4225	114.8			130.5	109.8		37.1	50.2
1979	3746	116.8	141.7		137.1	118.6		41.4	55.5
1980	3733	140.9	154.7		149.5	198.8		45.3	60.4
1981	3778	152.9	165.1		162.2	205.5		44.1	59.9
1982	3867	158.7	174.9		175.1	218.3		44.0	60.4
1983	4011	162.0	184.7		188.7	240.9		46.9	64.2
1984	4291	165.5	200.4		204.5	272.9		50.5	70.7
1985	4458	165.6	233.8		233.7	317.6		54.9	82.9
1986	5461	169.9	272.0		262.7	338.5		52.4	81.4
1987	5746	170.5	314.7		300.9	393.5		57.1	88.5
1988	5932	170.5	360.7		341.3	503.2		70.2	108.1
1989	6175		434.3		389.0	559.8		63.8	108.7
1990	6272	173.5	498.3		438.2	610.5		48.9	95.7
1991	6344	172.4	567.3		505.2	727.2		58.3	110.6
1992	6205	175.5	640.9		575.4	852.7		74.8	134.7
1993	10320	167.9	1521.0		998.7	1282.2		109.5	181.2
1994	10889	179.5	1969.2		964.8	1320.7		96.2	185.7
1995	10712	176.2	2582.6	1528.8	1390.0	1590.4		85.3	193.0
1996	16905	166.6	2875.6	1722.1	1632.0	1580.1		33.1	122.5
1997	19387	157.5	3408.3	2049.7	1850.3	1707.1	1409.1	40.5	140.5
1998	18089	167.1	4012.9	2483.9	2221.3	2034.5	1669.7	48.4	161.7
1999	19682	161.1	4254.1	2586.3	2312.1	2218.6	1824.7	69.8	184.6
2000	16027	145.6	4612.7	2676.4	2531.6	2821.4	2338.0	127.1	256.1
2001	4356	108.0	4448.2	2459.6	2503.7	3006.9	2533.4	137.0	279.5
2002	4551	107.6	4742.9	2527.8	2655.4	3182.8	2612.9	165.5	322.0
2003	4019	100.8	5178.0	2751.2	2756.0	3885.7	3203.2	235.3	419.0
2004	6872	113.6	12049.5	4143.1	3922.2	5992.7	4288.5	397.4	641.8
2005	6301	117.1	12829.8	4706.7	4434.0	7279.1	6309.6	413.5	683.1
2006	6400	117.4	14244.4	5542.3	5030.6	8914.2	7779.9	531.1	847.9
2007	6398	119.3	16215.5	6508.3	5814.8	10440.2	9034.1	695.6	1055.2
2008	7206	123.4	16802.4	8085.0	6574.6	11275.8	9866.7	557.0	937.9
2009	6891	120.4	19540.7	9874.6	7083.6	12173.1	10406.4	742.9	1269.9
2010	6885	124.2	22750.6	11548.1	7936.1	14807.1	12611.2	1028.3	1649.0
2011	3740	117.9	25321.7	12648.6	8620.8	16105.8	13681.9	1129.5	1806.2
2012	3692	120.2	28613.2	14837.2	10277.2	17277.1	14595.8	1267.9	2010.4
2013	3641	116.1	30800.7	16208.0	10788.6	19058.7	16124.8	1282.9	2125.2
2014	3686	116.6	33557.0	17137.6	11532.9	20179.4	17012.1	1515.8	2407.9
2015	3548	110.4	38609.8	18102.4	12265.5	19256.1	15998.5	1597.7	2528.0
2016	3340	104.4	43093.7	19798.1	12978.0	20213.8	16750.7	1608.3	2521.6
2017	3231	99.5	45985.8	20671.0	13964.0	21181.0	17481.1	2023.7	2937.0
2018	3108	92.7	49321.5	22270.2	14651.0	22348.1	18482.2	1647.0	2594.9
2019	3121	86.8	52222.0	21974.5	15448.8	23419.1	19364.2	1710.3	2544.7
2020	3028	83.1	55167.0	24193.8	17105.1	23849.0	19709.9	1729.5	2429.7
2021	3073	81.0	61056.0	26371.6	18044.1	28745.1	22261.5	3684.4	4583.8
2022	3141	81.7	66052.5	29327.9	19093.5	27713.6	23090.6	1998.7	2970.5
2023	3145	80.6	72994.0	32590.1	20086.9	28950.6	24419.1	1684.1	2518.5

注：2010年及以前，营业收入为主营业务收入数据，营业成本为主营业务成本数据。

Note: In and before 2010, the data on business revenue referred to the data on revenue from principal business, and the data on business cost referred to the data on cost of principal business.

12-3 规模以上工业产品产量(1978-2023年)
OUTPUT OF INDUSTRIAL PRODUCTS ABOVE DESIGNATED SIZE (1978-2023)

年 份 Year	布 (万米) Cloth (10000 m)	机制纸及纸板 (万吨) Machine-made Paper and Paperboard (10000 tons)	饮料酒 (万千升) Alcoholic Beverage (10000 kL)	乳制品 (万吨) Dairy Products (10000 tons)	家用电冰箱 (万台) Household Refrigerators (10000 units)	照相机 (万台) Cameras (10000 units)	家具 (万件) Furniture (10000 pieces)	原煤 (万吨) Coal (10000 tons)
1978	25436	12.1	8.4			0.5	137.8	818.7
1979	27297	13.9	9.9		2.0	0.7	171.3	711.1
1980	28940	14.0	11.6		2.6	1.0	200.2	791.0
1981	28635	14.5	13.4		3.1	4.2	217.7	788.7
1982	29758	15.8	14.9	0.2	4.5	0.9	243.5	811.3
1983	30068	17.1	17.4	0.3	6.4	2.8	254.2	840.5
1984	27621	18.9	20.3	0.6	10.3	5.3	297.9	884.3
1985	25998	20.6	21.3	0.9	17.3	12.5	335.1	944.3
1986	27503	21.9	21.5	0.7	18.1	15.9	303.8	917.2
1987	29738	24.1	22.7	0.8	19.4	16.5	283.0	899.8
1988	32262	23.3	23.9	1.0	23.6	15.8	347.1	906.0
1989	32271	25.8	28.7	1.0	24.7	13.5	572.1	1016.8
1990	31258	25.4	34.6	1.2	10.7	12.9	590.6	1005.5
1991	31497	27.2	43.8	1.3	7.1	5.4	602.0	996.5
1992	29717	22.6	56.6	1.2	9.1	4.2	570.0	1015.2
1993	26816	19.1	72.6	1.6	4.2	39.3	729.0	835.4
1994	21440	21.0	83.1	0.3	6.6	158.8	605.0	1008.5
1995	24524	26.6	91.2	1.5		243.1	755.0	995.4
1996	22585	15.3	102.2	1.2	6.3	234.3	510.6	1013.7
1997	25185	18.1	…	1.7	…	157.7	469.4	1011.7
1998	21299	13.1		0.9	0.3	177.7	348.5	989.5
1999	14753	13.0	148.8	1.4	5.8	81.6	386.2	792.1
2000	12183	10.6	185.6	2.1	3.6	55.2	272.1	553.0
2001	11353	8.8	135.8	3.7	5.9	61.3	370.6	690.2
2002	10314	6.2	138.7	1.4	16.2	220.7	368.3	880.9
2003	8393	7.9	132.8	1.3	22.8	238.3	323.8	822.6
2004	4081	19.6	148.0	56.4	63.1	116.8	567.7	1067.9
2005	4270	17.0	145.6	56.9	81.7	47.9	406.5	897.9
2006	930	14.0	170.8	63.5	74.1	49.2	893.4	629.2
2007	536	10.4	189.1	57.9	73.1	34.7	638.8	633.3
2008	1583	14.9	180.0	44.9	79.0	49.0	690.9	567.7
2009	965	14.1	181.1	52.2	128.7	27.1	719.4	641.3
2010	495	10.6	185.8	52.3	92.1	29.2	822.8	500.0
2011	339	10.0	187.0	58.6	73.5	26.6	750.2	500.1
2012	351	11.3	191.7	56.6	80.4	18.2	720.1	493.1
2013	361	10.0	198.0	58.5	83.7	17.9	995.9	500.1
2014	361	6.6	187.4	60.6		6.6	674.7	457.5
2015	174	5.0	167.1	62.1		1.6	700.5	450.1
2016		6.1	167.5	62.2		0.1	776.2	317.6
2017		5.9	164.9	59.7		0.1	686.3	255.0
2018		4.4	148.5	53.2			626.1	176.2
2019		4.2	128.2	55.4			463.1	36.1
2020		3.9	115.1	53.7			389.9	
2021		3.4	121.9	54.2			402.0	
2022		3.2	129.1	48.9			333.5	
2023		3.1	139.5	49.6			374.6	

12-3 续表 1 Continued 1

年 份 Year	原 油 加工量 (万吨) Crude Oil Processed (10000 tons)	乙 烯 (万吨) Ethylene (10000 tons)	发电量 (万千瓦时) Electricity Generation (10000 kW·h)	粗 钢 (万吨) Crude Steel (10000 tons)	钢 材 (万吨) Rolled Steel (10000 tons)	水 泥 (万吨) Cement (10000 tons)	交 流 电动机 (万千瓦) Alternator (10000 kW)
1978			990750	191.0	116.8	191.5	152.5
1979			1042870	196.5	137.5	196.9	179.7
1980	591.1		1065060	200.9	152.1	217.4	142.7
1981	533.5	24.7	993071	190.3	149.5	225.7	104.0
1982	533.5	25.6	1003446	200.4	159.4	249.1	123.3
1983	563.8	27.3	1028826	214.1	177.9	270.8	148.3
1984	589.4	26.9	1038842	241.7	200.1	291.6	165.4
1985	591.1	27.8	1037171	267.7	221.0	318.5	172.0
1986	619.0	25.3	1043208	303.6	255.5	310.5	178.4
1987	640.2	27.0	1057493	335.5	283.4	319.6	196.4
1988	645.0	30.3	1110758	369.0	314.9	334.3	199.5
1989	651.9	29.1	1191269	386.0	327.9	345.9	163.8
1990	654.4	30.1	1253554	443.7	375.0	339.0	151.6
1991	653.4	31.1	1318000	499.7	402.9	377.6	156.7
1992	662.5	32.8	1423000	575.0	438.3	403.0	174.9
1993	664.0	27.2	1410900	702.7	525.3	477.9	162.3
1994	642.0	28.1	1298718	828.7	617.6	531.7	165.0
1995	648.0	53.0	1322114	804.9	629.8	574.2	165.4
1996	633.6	57.5	1415555	794.7	654.3	666.0	151.9
1997	657.0	58.0	1464302	801.7	652.4	700.9	148.7
1998	602.3	57.0	1566621	803.2	676.1	762.0	149.7
1999	701.9	68.0	1431772	734.5	663.8	803.0	142.0
2000	741.7	65.5	1452564	803.4	696.7	827.0	161.0
2001	647.9	54.3	1326588	824.9	727.3	809.0	175.1
2002	695.2	90.4	1419754	816.9	750.0	884.0	199.3
2003	701.1	88.8	1451197	816.4	785.0	882.0	253.1
2004	783.4	98.2	2038933	827.5	868.3	1204.5	279.4
2005	796.9	99.0	2133451	827.6	966.3	1183.8	262.9
2006	828.9	99.1	2136918	818.1	1016.3	1269.4	269.0
2007	915.0	90.9	2278658	810.8	1030.4	1167.3	281.9
2008	1114.6	85.4	2431255	466.8	656.8	880.8	259.7
2009	1161.3	84.1	2424839	464.9	769.6	1077.4	159.0
2010	1123.4	96.2	2688350	427.5	794.0	1049.0	191.1
2011	1103.1	89.6	2628331	2.9	287.0	911.5	146.0
2012	1075.0	84.0	2908214	2.6	253.8	874.5	117.1
2013	881.6	72.3	3312116	2.3	221.8	868.4	145.4
2014	1051.1	77.6	3385699	2.1	195.0	703.1	115.0
2015	1000.1	78.6	4173847	1.5	175.0	553.5	40.3
2016	844.8	69.6	4336690		162.8	510.3	46.1
2017	898.9	79.3	3878163		179.0	374.4	48.2
2018	911.3	79.4	4372998		179.1	397.0	35.4
2019	936.5	81.5	4311921		170.7	318.7	20.7
2020	779.6	81.7	4413422		184.4	286.9	7.4
2021	775.5	71.2	4589948		203.4	258.1	12.3
2022	774.0	71.1	4499192		184.3	203.4	13.0
2023	790.4	69.8	4548755		183.2	200.0	2.7

12-3 续表 2 Continued 2

年 份 Year	汽 车 (万辆) Motor Vehicles (10000 units)	#轿 车 Cars	移动通信手持机 (万台) Mobile Phones (10000 units)	微型计算机设 备 (万台) Micro Computer Equipment (10000 units)	数控金属切削机床 (台) Metal-cutting Machine Tools (unit)	显示器 (万台) Display (10000 units)	集 成 电 路 (亿块) Integrated Circuits (100 million units)
1978	1.8						
1979	2.4						
1980	2.8						
1981	2.7						
1982	2.8						
1983	3.1			0.3			
1984	3.6			1.2			
1985	5.0			0.5			
1986	5.8			0.5			
1987	7.4			0.9			
1988	9.0			3.0			
1989	8.5			1.3			
1990	8.8			1.2			
1991	11.0			1.7			
1992	13.8			3.0			
1993	13.4			4.1			
1994	14.7			4.3			
1995	17.9			19.2			
1996	13.4			28.1	326		0.5
1997	11.0			59.8	433		0.6
1998	8.5			160.9	430		0.6
1999	12.3	1.0		180.0	481		1.3
2000	12.5	0.5	1549.6	257.8	568		2.4
2001	14.3	0.5	2163.4	339.7	1004		2.1
2002	18.1	0.7	2280.1	415.7	912		2.5
2003	34.7	7.3	3334.5	469.3	1188		4.7
2004	53.9	15.0	4172.1	532.7	1024		11.1
2005	58.6	22.2	9131.1	649.6	1655		12.6
2006	68.3	27.0	14068.0	736.1	1875	680.7	11.8
2007	70.7	20.3	22719.9	843.3	2382	513.6	15.7
2008	76.6	28.3	20725.5	691.7	3108	478.1	19.1
2009	127.1	53.8	21355.3	842.7	6125	655.6	18.3
2010	150.3	62.2	27388.0	938.6	9766	877.8	25.3
2011	150.5	67.1	25962.3	1083.7	12537	851.4	32.0
2012	167.0	78.5	19949.3	1074.5	13332	796.9	31.9
2013	203.8	94.5	18783.4	1106.9	6983	305.3	38.4
2014	216.7	118.6	17983.6	1015.6	13890	548.1	54.3
2015	221.9	118.9	9540.8	885.6	12471	519.0	62.7
2016	260.4	120.7	6923.9	684.1	12420	503.5	80.5
2017	225.0	107.6	7483.1	742.4	14877	360.8	93.1
2018	163.2	78.8	8448.0	555.5	11862	406.3	149.5
2019	164.0	77.8	8373.3	513.2	7611	470.1	154.5
2020	166.0	65.3	9928.5	552.4	8188	577.8	170.7
2021	135.5	52.2	11624.5	647.3	6184	518.2	207.7
2022	87.1	46.5	9429.5	858.6	5072	233.6	217.9
2023	100.3	49.6	10286.8	615.8	5421	213.9	219.1

注：根据统计制度规定，自2022年起，汽车整车制造行业产业活动单位视同法人单位按经营地在地原则进行统计，北京在京外设立的汽车整车制造分厂按照制度规定在当地纳统。

Note: According to the statistical system, since 2022, the industrial activity units in the sector of manufacture of finished automobiles shall be deemed as corporate units and shall be subject to statistics in accordance with the principle of regional statistics of the business place, the finished automobile manufacturing branches set up outside of Beijing shall be included in local statistics according to the rules and regulations.

12-4 规模以上工业企业主要经济指标(2023年)

单位：万元

项　目	Item	企业单位个数(个) Number of Enterprises (unit)	#亏损企业 Loss-Suffering Enterprises	工业总产值(当年价格) Gross Output Value of Industry (at current prices)	平均用工人数(人) Average Number of Employed Persons (person)
合　计	**Total**	**3145**	**734**	**246522293**	**806310**
按行业分	**By Sector**				
采矿业	Mining	7	2	2259152	23896
制造业	Manufacturing	2967	705	156828757	692825
电力、热力、燃气及水生产和供应业	Production and Supply of Electricity, Heating, Gas and Water	171	27	87434384	89589
按轻重工业分	**By Light and Heavy Industries**				
轻工业	Light Industry	1024	267	33268133	254177
重工业	Heavy Industry	2121	467	213254160	552133
按规模分	**By Size**				
大　型	Large	111	20	164442174	327491
中　型	Medium-sized	423	91	39312621	220509
小　型	Small	2376	548	40672529	252857
微　型	Micro	235	75	2094969	5453
按登记注册统计类别分	**By Statistical Category of Registration**				
内资企业	Domestic Invested Enterprises	2565	583	166612877	577129
#有限责任公司	Limited Liability Corporations	2127	459	140730967	425735
股份有限公司	Corporations Limited by Shares	382	109	25549940	145660
非公司企业法人	Unincorporated Business Entity	55	15	329318	5706
港澳台投资企业	Enterprises with Investment from Hong Kong, Macao and Taiwan	138	41	26909384	55759
#港澳台投资有限责任公司	Limited Liability Corporations with Investment from Hong Kong, Macao and Taiwan	119	36	24261808	48865
港澳台投资股份有限公司	Companies Limited by Shares with Investment from Hong Kong, Macao and Taiwan	18	5	2291726	6280
外商投资企业	Foreign Invested Enterprises	442	110	53000033	173422
#外商投资有限责任公司	Limited Liability Corporations with Foreign Investment	410	105	48920197	152798
外商投资股份有限公司	Companies Limited by Shares with Foreign Investment	30	5	2314952	19229
按控股类型分	**By Holding Types**				
#国有控股	State-holding	688	144	156768185	342575
集体控股	Collective-holding	49	16	457005	5819
私人控股	Private-holding	1932	452	37859021	287400
港澳台控股	Hong Kong, Macao, and Taiwan-holding	104	29	24436812	50123
外商控股	Holding by Foreign Investors	370	93	26990450	119740

注：应交税金合计包括应交增值税、所得税费用、税金及附加，下同。

MAIN ECONOMIC INDICATORS OF INDUSTRIAL ENTERPRISES ABOVE DESIGNATED SIZE (2023)

(10000 yuan)

资产负债 Assets and Liabilities							
资产总计 Total Assets	#流动资产合计 Total Current Assets	#存货 Inventories	#产成品 Finished Products	#应收账款 Accounts Receivable	#固定资产原价 Original Value of Fixed Assets	负债合计 Total Liabilities	#流动负债合计 Total Current Liabilities
729939536	**303862612**	**40119846**	**14087409**	**70830455**	**200869276**	**325900955**	**235463364**
39557038	8180957	78749	13253	1572677	9896351	25133419	11970974
346285834	228525819	39613070	13977443	57523373	68409523	181411089	159837030
344096665	67155837	428028	96713	11734405	122563402	119356448	63655360
74288139	47752022	8586886	4215916	8540807	15582462	28042207	23661257
655651397	256110590	31532960	9871493	62289648	185286815	297858748	211802107
530782039	179339957	18333719	7108488	38307013	162466060	240146173	163368025
108967140	65822971	10676356	2914691	13693430	19747364	43865648	35277518
86180237	55669231	10797126	3970920	17169637	17108803	40418781	35709280
4010121	3030453	312644	93311	1660375	1547049	1470354	1108541
580090796	199830390	25847534	7853371	43204212	163575967	239628787	157347730
485365870	150461522	19308642	5591306	32835989	149959675	204634891	127484909
94159143	48908648	6483061	2238235	10247222	13437708	34675124	29609647
560944	457253	53476	23830	120426	178331	315752	250154
56845714	39426447	5108366	2232719	7939272	10128288	28397179	24338864
49264568	34716727	4657278	2136231	6860203	9119192	25605575	22230806
7236269	4648615	448870	96488	1021935	479305	2486782	2150275
93003026	64605774	9163946	4001320	19686971	27165021	57874989	53776770
78182351	54873484	8227462	3597012	14071963	25052318	49602168	46111572
8311769	4193054	502679	119449	512630	986901	1846802	1240850
513230879	160769111	18690822	5784274	40034712	162073062	216904349	140885362
1223888	964037	120652	68580	337878	289419	584242	526556
104561834	65581495	10545440	3578928	17262275	15008674	47847156	39374048
49653069	35447722	4684855	2068909	6969408	7747028	26415860	22860036
58673259	40749376	6070102	2584718	6225271	15689314	33737539	31477488

Note: Total tax payable includes VAT payable, income tax expense, tax and surtax, the same below.

12-4 续表

单位：万元

项目	Item	资产负债 Assets and Liabilities #应付账款 Accounts Payable	所有者权益合计 Total Owners' Equity	#实收资本 Paid-in Capital
合计	**Total**	**74275827**	**404038561**	**263989940**
按行业分	**By Sector**			
采矿业	Mining	953089	14423619	6350032
制造业	Manufacturing	60858768	164874726	58539869
电力、热力、燃气及水生产和供应业	Production and Supply of Electricity, Heating, Gas and Water	12463969	224740215	199100039
按轻重工业分	**By Light and Heavy Industries**			
轻工业	Light Industry	6615963	46245927	10692500
重工业	Heavy Industry	67659864	357792634	253297440
按规模分	**By Size**			
大型	Large	47514104	290635865	222853125
中型	Medium-sized	11822318	65101491	20631953
小型	Small	14405404	45761440	18740451
微型	Micro	534001	2539766	1764411
按登记注册统计类别分	**By Statistical Category of Registration**			
内资企业	Domestic Invested Enterprises	41039548	340461991	240719070
#有限责任公司	Limited Liability Corporations	33164902	280730965	227179210
股份有限公司	Corporations Limited by Shares	7780377	59484017	13453642
非公司企业法人	Unincorporated Business Entity	94270	245191	85418
港澳台投资企业	Enterprises with Investment from Hong Kong, Macao and Taiwan	11286649	28448535	5600446
#港澳台投资有限责任公司	Limited Liability Corporations with Investment from Hong Kong, Macao and Taiwan	10727027	23658993	4565868
港澳台投资股份有限公司	Companies Limited by Shares with Investment from Hong Kong, Macao and Taiwan	530188	4749487	1034578
外商投资企业	Foreign Invested Enterprises	21949630	35128034	17670425
#外商投资有限责任公司	Limited Liability Corporations with Foreign Investment	15346170	28580180	16377005
外商投资股份有限公司	Companies Limited by Shares with Foreign Investment	316590	6464967	1293419
按控股类型分	**By Holding Types**			
#国有控股	State-holding	44243510	296326525	229939680
集体控股	Collective-holding	189890	639645	202885
私人控股	Private-holding	12942089	56714665	18144829
港澳台控股	Hong Kong, Macao, and Taiwan-holding	10690128	23237209	3485613
外商控股	Holding by Foreign Investors	6155809	24935718	11910925

12-4 Continued

(10000 yuan)

损益 Profits and Losses							应交税金合计 Total Tax Payable	#税金及附加 Tax and Surtax	#应交增值税 Value Added Tax Payable
营业收入 Business Revenue	营业成本 Business Cost	销售费用 Selling Expenses	管理费用 Management Expenses	研发费用 R&D Expenses	财务费用 Financial Expenses	利润总额 Total Profits			
289506253	**244190701**	**12771736**	**9818238**	**8444527**	**2096513**	**16840812**	**11216140**	**3571770**	**4772804**
5475068	4936589	4626	216656	89123	519012	384258	136148	45046	63280
194810739	154007849	12657399	8617769	8006023	-226042	10936738	9060568	3096373	3824639
89220446	85246263	109710	983813	349382	1803543	5519816	2019424	430350	884885
40374194	25739053	6526955	2769432	1931999	-58118	3548888	2819587	821964	1404742
249132059	218451648	6244781	7048806	6512528	2154631	13291925	8396553	2749805	3368062
192673853	169798549	7080316	3728463	3232978	2013717	9990339	6917057	2649171	2529780
44933345	33184762	3085660	2872579	3026792	-115953	4111629	2351127	638624	1031462
49494354	39115303	2537585	3093891	2143863	176048	2698689	1883776	272970	1172046
2404701	2092087	68175	123305	40895	22701	40155	64180	11005	39516
183571536	158829918	5616312	6542804	5928490	2424722	9523627	6403684	2278342	2826343
152287727	135075140	3215234	4567438	3968552	2389231	7739707	4414464	1159736	2128253
30895501	23432963	2379535	1943598	1951718	34941	1772094	1973064	1116717	686811
385326	319560	21397	31487	7991	539	11783	16094	1883	11233
44754257	39464482	2086845	958793	1407615	-277049	1206797	519983	113109	172206
41946986	37471666	1962138	826211	1246373	-271602	850144	422609	97847	140194
2448950	1658661	124707	132582	161242	-11540	334349	76547	11549	14897
61180460	45896301	5068579	2316641	1108423	-51160	6110388	4292474	1180318	1774255
56511332	42747286	4536280	2137860	809688	-44146	5561398	3979614	1082404	1606885
2463869	1165122	487053	156365	298736	-15437	507055	139417	18537	84089
171087180	151319976	3250525	4335240	2662849	2329668	10798934	7625285	3077072	2706135
560176	447789	28464	56901	18164	4837	-12567	19267	3845	18840
41969009	29614384	4217311	2905930	3683454	97300	2198118	1580804	232791	1047836
42316651	37615386	2085631	828900	1263512	-266094	812912	420880	95237	134774
33472483	25094357	3188883	1677413	763983	-69451	3034409	1564350	162307	857523

12-5 分行业规模以上工业企业主要经济指标(2023年)

单位：万元

项目	Item	企业单位个数(个) Number of Enterprises (unit)	#亏损企业 Loss-Suffering Enterprises	工业总产值(当年价格) Gross Output Value of Industry (at current prices)
合计	**Total**	**3145**	**734**	**246522293**
采矿业	**Mining**	**7**	**2**	**2259152**
石油和天然气开采业	Extraction of Petroleum and Natural Gas	1	1	***
黑色金属矿采选业	Mining and Processing of Ferrous Metal Ores	1		***
开采专业及辅助性活动	Professional and Support Activities for Mining	5	1	1806955
制造业	**Manufacturing**	**2967**	**705**	**156828757**
农副食品加工业	Processing of Food from Agricultural Products	101	32	2711244
食品制造业	Manufacture of Foods	113	27	2974685
酒、饮料和精制茶制造业	Manufacture of Liquor, Beverages and Refined Tea	36	14	2151735
烟草制品业	Manufacture of Tobacco	1		***
纺织业	Manufacture of Textile	9	3	188225
纺织服装、服饰业	Manufacture of Textile, Wearing Apparel and Accessories	64	26	675275
皮革、毛皮、羽毛及其制品和制鞋业	Manufacture of Leather, Fur, Feather and Related Products, and Footwear	1		***
木材加工和木、竹、藤、棕、草制品业	Processing of Timber, Manufacture of Wood, Bamboo, Rattan, Palm and Straw Products	7	1	65173
家具制造业	Manufacture of Furniture	35	10	717339
造纸和纸制品业	Manufacture of Paper and Paper Products	26	4	608178
印刷和记录媒介复制业	Printing and Reproduction of Recording Media	88	22	1209630
文教、工美、体育和娱乐用品制造业	Manufacture of Articles for Culture, Education, Arts and Crafts, Sport and Entertainment Activities	20	5	206137
石油、煤炭及其他燃料加工业	Processing of Petroleum, Coal and Other Fuels	13	4	6691116
化学原料和化学制品制造业	Manufacture of Raw Chemical Materials and Chemical Products	126	32	2214286
医药制造业	Manufacture of Medicines	274	59	14590330
化学纤维制造业	Manufacture of Chemical Fibres	1		***
橡胶和塑料制品业	Manufacture of Rubber and Plastics Products	46	8	421549
非金属矿物制品业	Manufacture of Non-metallic Mineral Products	161	41	4491397
黑色金属冶炼和压延加工业	Smelting and Pressing of Ferrous Metals	5		1136633
有色金属冶炼和压延加工业	Smelting and Pressing of Non-ferrous Metals	21	5	1330387
金属制品业	Manufacture of Metal Products	136	31	1985289
通用设备制造业	Manufacture of General Purpose Machinery	212	43	6232960
专用设备制造业	Manufacture of Special Purpose Machinery	378	78	11271530
汽车制造业	Manufacture of Automobiles	182	63	35741013
铁路、船舶、航空航天和其他运输设备制造业	Manufacture of Railway, Ship, Aerospace and Other Transport Equipments	104	21	7027538
电气机械和器材制造业	Manufacture of Electrical Machinery and Apparatus	227	43	10386009
计算机、通信和其他电子设备制造业	Manufacture of Computers, Communication and Other Electronic Equipment	334	98	33425127
仪器仪表制造业	Manufacture of Measuring Instruments and Machinery	199	31	3246365
其他制造业	Other Manufacture	12	2	2962666
废弃资源综合利用业	Utilization of Waste Resources	13		162561
金属制品、机械和设备修理业	Repair Service of Metal Products, Machinery and Equipment	22	2	1301890
电力、热力、燃气及水生产和供应业	**Production and Supply of Electricity, Heating, Gas and Water**	**171**	**27**	**87434384**
电力、热力生产和供应业	Production and Supply of Electric Power and Heat Power	110	17	80892815
燃气生产和供应业	Production and Supply of Gas	24	5	5155218
水的生产和供应业	Production and Supply of Water	37	5	1386351

MAIN ECONOMIC INDICATORS OF INDUSTRIAL ENTERPRISES ABOVE DESIGNATED SIZE BY INDUSTRIAL SECTOR (2023)

(10000 yuan)

平均用工人数(人) Average Number of Employed Persons (person)	资产负债 Assets and Liabilities							
	资产总计 Total Assets	#流动资产合计 Total Current Assets	#存货 Inventories	#产成品 Finished Products	#应收账款 Accounts Receivable	#固定资产原价 Original Value of Fixed Assets	负债合计 Total Liabilities	#流动负债合计 Total Current Liabilities
806310	**729939536**	**303862612**	**40119846**	**14087409**	**70830455**	**200869276**	**325900955**	**235463364**
23896	**39557038**	**8180957**	**78749**	**13253**	**1572677**	**9896351**	**25133419**	**11970974**
***	***	***	***	***	***	***	***	***
***	***	***	***	***	***	***	***	***
13927	4695794	1962087	57831	2493	716098	2946733	1952670	1412153
692825	**346285834**	**228525819**	**39613070**	**13977443**	**57523373**	**68409523**	**181411089**	**159837030**
19735	5249541	2571904	630595	454891	325470	1083326	2828114	2210447
33541	5110132	3216493	335130	150552	756290	1599521	2561143	1952885
17185	6199006	3645504	446421	157722	337078	1919061	2731151	2553641
***	***	***	***	***	***	***	***	***
1573	288038	257428	99494	77946	39082	35456	154829	150448
16574	1457347	1139752	337960	207626	169214	321768	710851	658816
***	***	***	***	***	***	***	***	***
239	49814	45310	4561	1727	17472	5839	36220	34552
5355	1429182	936696	257927	206290	186191	289966	974459	742591
2810	485869	319172	99175	33852	108022	285578	226472	211303
15254	2308637	1501304	276822	98125	224450	1587191	783320	654122
2323	610939	405713	249879	133726	49333	138888	463176	366751
9317	7862340	4343076	1562067	158936	217698	4558091	5164896	3160057
14285	5047110	3330289	422250	192256	784646	1142746	1709281	1611703
95014	36445712	23434753	4378897	2162474	3992055	6528364	10730268	8987493
***	***	***	***	***	***	***	***	***
4609	552535	422119	88562	35248	139038	203988	217738	208587
26371	10854745	7531044	663536	300525	3576265	1576737	6375430	5976151
974	595832	208496	94855	31098	56170	713784	650169	247316
2747	1072669	689080	171583	59585	193899	212093	495808	426704
15166	6254947	3980550	695869	150551	772685	1050518	3318392	2966858
40491	13051628	9880635	2365292	888021	2166659	2055570	5750305	5362572
69313	33070336	20710372	3937998	1403990	4803073	2434118	16200498	13644391
68798	50236449	34421836	4151846	2096454	18202492	15431564	37011644	33617746
37692	16834293	12974321	3823150	640785	2979253	2724148	8262034	7677016
37324	18136792	14401349	1666576	510047	4671082	1345801	11463324	10703647
108193	105512800	67242132	10276981	3489622	10346900	18877843	55218489	49023351
26683	7852559	5632357	1157511	284510	1565188	746299	2900795	2789171
4047	3680807	3162115	927007	5003	492576	513075	2820262	2674276
1064	380060	263881	21045	4938	82555	52909	107896	102358
14396	5024664	1375476	355048	16343	258300	646633	1407809	996474
89589	**344096665**	**67155837**	**428028**	**96713**	**11734405**	**122563402**	**119356448**	**63655360**
65611	319767507	61112922	354617	92519	9978261	107062457	108342444	57986410
9953	10641065	2852988	49769	3254	195386	5138789	4161722	2523683
14025	13688092	3189927	23643	940	1560757	10362156	6852283	3145267

12-5 续表

单位：万元

项　目	Item	资产负债 Assets and Liabilities #应付账款 Accounts Payable	所有者权益合计 Total Owners' Equity	#实收资本 Paid-in Capital
合　计	**Total**	**74275827**	**404038561**	**263989940**
采矿业	**Mining**	**953089**	**14423619**	**6350032**
石油和天然气开采业	Extraction of Petroleum and Natural Gas	***	***	***
黑色金属矿采选业	Mining and Processing of Ferrous Metal Ores	***	***	***
开采专业及辅助性活动	Professional and Support Activities for Mining	740511	2743124	3124949
制造业	**Manufacturing**	**60858768**	**164874726**	**58539869**
农副食品加工业	Processing of Food from Agricultural Products	277043	2421426	1244107
食品制造业	Manufacture of Foods	703893	2548989	883603
酒、饮料和精制茶制造业	Manufacture of Liquor, Beverages and Refined Tea	333710	3467855	1128169
烟草制品业	Manufacture of Tobacco	***	***	***
纺织业	Manufacture of Textile	50972	133209	38146
纺织服装、服饰业	Manufacture of Textile, Wearing Apparel and Accessories	113192	746496	284052
皮革、毛皮、羽毛及其制品和制鞋业	Manufacture of Leather, Fur, Feather and Related Products, and Footwear	***	***	***
木材加工和木、竹、藤、棕、草制品业	Processing of Timber, Manufacture of Wood, Bamboo, Rattan, Palm and Straw Products	15735	13595	9500
家具制造业	Manufacture of Furniture	167623	454723	250198
造纸和纸制品业	Manufacture of Paper and Paper Products	76835	259396	99541
印刷和记录媒介复制业	Printing and Reproduction of Recording Media	244281	1525317	836450
文教、工美、体育和娱乐用品制造业	Manufacture of Articles for Culture, Education, Arts and Crafts, Sport and Entertainment Activities	142620	147763	184269
石油、煤炭及其他燃料加工业	Processing of Petroleum, Coal and Other Fuels	597634	2697444	1251130
化学原料和化学制品制造业	Manufacture of Raw Chemical Materials and Chemical Products	553492	3337828	1170520
医药制造业	Manufacture of Medicines	2688064	25715441	3899002
化学纤维制造业	Manufacture of Chemical Fibres	***	***	***
橡胶和塑料制品业	Manufacture of Rubber and Plastics Products	83179	334797	221873
非金属矿物制品业	Manufacture of Non-metallic Mineral Products	3076232	4479314	1669398
黑色金属冶炼和压延加工业	Smelting and Pressing of Ferrous Metals	191252	-54337	275429
有色金属冶炼和压延加工业	Smelting and Pressing of Non-ferrous Metals	167181	576860	149641
金属制品业	Manufacture of Metal Products	801897	2936554	1208751
通用设备制造业	Manufacture of General Purpose Machinery	1979109	7301323	2048555
专用设备制造业	Manufacture of Special Purpose Machinery	3960419	16869836	4213650
汽车制造业	Manufacture of Automobiles	20931569	13224804	9757219
铁路、船舶、航空航天和其他运输设备制造业	Manufacture of Railway, Ship, Aerospace and Other Transport Equipments	3253819	8572258	2325440
电气机械和器材制造业	Manufacture of Electrical Machinery and Apparatus	4053697	6673467	2641887
计算机、通信和其他电子设备制造业	Manufacture of Computers, Communication and Other Electronic Equipment	13926759	50294309	19960931
仪器仪表制造业	Manufacture of Measuring Instruments and Machinery	1029677	4951762	1271536
其他制造业	Other Manufacture	1068349	860544	346849
废弃资源综合利用业	Utilization of Waste Resources	66999	272164	72906
金属制品、机械和设备修理业	Repair Service of Metal Products, Machinery and Equipment	288616	3616855	979677
电力、热力、燃气及水生产和供应业	**Production and Supply of Electricity, Heating, Gas and Water**	**12463969**	**224740215**	**199100039**
电力、热力生产和供应业	Production and Supply of Electric Power and Heat Power	11470694	211425063	192510863
燃气生产和供应业	Production and Supply of Gas	442325	6479343	1512915
水的生产和供应业	Production and Supply of Water	550951	6835809	5076261

12-5 Continued

(10000 yuan)

损 益 Profits and Losses							应交税金合计 Total Tax Payable	#税金及附加 Tax and Surtax	#应交增值税 Value Added Tax Payable
营业收入 Business Revenue	营业成本 Business Cost	销售费用 Selling Expenses	管理费用 Management Expenses	研发费用 R&D Expenses	财务费用 Financial Expenses	利润总额 Total Profits			
289506253	**244190701**	**12771736**	**9818238**	**8444527**	**2096513**	**16840812**	**11216140**	**3571770**	**4772804**
5475068	**4936589**	**4626**	**216656**	**89123**	**519012**	**384258**	**136148**	**45046**	**63280**
***	***	***	***	***	***	***	***	***	***
***	***	***	***	***	***	***	***	***	***
1887340	1710481	3867	60684	53725	-986	53320	38003	7682	19238
194810739	**154007849**	**12657399**	**8617769**	**8006023**	**-226042**	**10936738**	**9060568**	**3096373**	**3824639**
4472629	4060799	201592	169569	43632	22906	22912	35607	10943	14826
5471275	3860707	930615	296847	58215	-3438	389550	329072	32240	201409
2604804	1920256	277816	215492	28905	12872	-119377	315143	220089	81882
***	***	***	***	***	***	***	***	***	***
185588	131620	4498	10161	7451	-350	30729	15230	1349	9302
940354	601527	197560	82724	24884	3337	27155	52395	7617	39898
***	***	***	***	***	***	***	***	***	***
69490	60977	3408	3688		298	1048	1342	119	984
909391	741380	43430	57340	23254	15502	30303	25943	3556	20212
687505	539430	21921	52526	6164	1481	57839	38753	4047	21316
1435924	1105093	36393	157326	33406	-9736	112546	91588	13387	55436
301124	238659	23665	26902	5396	4910	5718	11007	2831	5904
7004015	6047021	20225	206604	21714	24530	-72627	911982	761469	93127
3097895	2359608	252964	221997	104879	-661	196291	124709	14182	82787
15755457	7896802	4053753	1172515	1270011	-74162	1997103	1111461	123860	720635
***	***	***	***	***	***	***	***	***	***
491278	395007	19826	37598	13049	1652	23873	18296	2376	12279
4981888	4213031	135956	282970	162277	34222	457837	164648	24310	128821
1219826	1182078	1691	10269	4708	6009	6550	11119	3289	7838
1390067	1270936	7586	32807	29881	570	52775	23112	2993	16295
2461122	2086335	74387	174291	92320	5774	79363	61701	13403	45640
7016583	5204477	382602	416398	336268	7226	961742	331773	39279	183189
11806697	8348200	852329	831295	799225	2940	1046469	426684	72359	234674
41371296	33953095	1786205	1135868	905204	78169	2407287	3023939	1131288	1040182
7394126	5974958	111134	442900	411026	10863	470520	281766	31799	171828
11640768	9468097	590278	493856	431941	-1186	821512	319446	40119	158135
53054397	45517217	2299757	1509420	2829532	-383783	1080869	597248	136198	252052
3931971	2712435	294331	325254	271023	-2713	451996	182314	25336	112972
2835926	2639944	3622	60324	53510	-1973	105034	54634	4509	30744
197110	151309	2056	21877	8084	-872	18279	10165	1009	6471
1379368	1139050	15823	130005	22643	29347	188578	43837	7689	15205
89220446	**85246263**	**109710**	**983813**	**349382**	**1803543**	**5519816**	**2019424**	**430350**	**884885**
82322354	79212483	22670	730385	152763	1677611	5109017	1713339	180884	853622
5226526	4771646	16547	145046	181024	-1434	349349	33958	6581	8287
1671567	1262135	70493	108382	15595	127365	61450	272128	242886	22976

12-6 分行业规模以上国有控股工业企业主要经济指标(2023年)

单位：万元

项目	Item	企业单位个数(个) Number of Enterprises (unit)	#亏损企业 Loss-Suffering Enterprises	工业总产值(当年价格) Gross Output Value of Industry (at current prices)
合计	**Total**	**688**	**144**	**156768185**
采矿业	**Mining**	**5**	**1**	**2132062**
石油和天然气开采业	Extraction of Petroleum and Natural Gas	1	1	***
黑色金属矿采选业	Mining and Processing of Ferrous Metal Ores	1		***
开采专业及辅助性活动	Professional and Support Activities for Mining	3		***
制造业	**Manufacturing**	**567**	**127**	**72013353**
农副食品加工业	Processing of Food from Agricultural Products	17	8	1085456
食品制造业	Manufacture of Foods	13	3	645493
酒、饮料和精制茶制造业	Manufacture of Liquor, Beverages and Refined Tea	11	5	1300779
烟草制品业	Manufacture of Tobacco	1		***
纺织业	Manufacture of Textile	2	1	***
纺织服装、服饰业	Manufacture of Textile, Wearing Apparel and Accessories	4	2	36959
家具制造业	Manufacture of Furniture	2	1	***
造纸和纸制品业	Manufacture of Paper and Paper Products	3	1	***
印刷和记录媒介复制业	Printing and Reproduction of Recording Media	29	7	716974
文教、工美、体育和娱乐用品制造业	Manufacture of Articles for Culture, Education, Arts and Crafts, Sport and Entertainment Activities	5	2	63409
石油、煤炭及其他燃料加工业	Processing of Petroleum, Coal and Other Fuels	8	2	6669292
化学原料和化学制品制造业	Manufacture of Raw Chemical Materials and Chemical Products	22	5	738241
医药制造业	Manufacture of Medicines	36	5	2594202
化学纤维制造业	Manufacture of Chemical Fibres	1		***
橡胶和塑料制品业	Manufacture of Rubber and Plastics Products	4		23426
非金属矿物制品业	Manufacture of Non-metallic Mineral Products	44	7	1636440
黑色金属冶炼和压延加工业	Smelting and Pressing of Ferrous Metals	3		***
有色金属冶炼和压延加工业	Smelting and Pressing of Non-ferrous Metals	6	1	1032267
金属制品业	Manufacture of Metal Products	19	5	975707
通用设备制造业	Manufacture of General Purpose Machinery	41	10	1173982
专用设备制造业	Manufacture of Special Purpose Machinery	55	8	3535414
汽车制造业	Manufacture of Automobiles	40	12	26310809
铁路、船舶、航空航天和其他运输设备制造业	Manufacture of Railway, Ship, Aerospace and Other Transport Equipments	45	6	6110699
电气机械和器材制造业	Manufacture of Electrical Machinery and Apparatus	22	7	1169570
计算机、通信和其他电子设备制造业	Manufacture of Computers, Communication and Other Electronic Equipment	84	20	9099057
仪器仪表制造业	Manufacture of Measuring Instruments and Machinery	32	7	1107553
其他制造业	Other Manufacture	5		2870945
废弃资源综合利用业	Utilization of Waste Resources	6		92146
金属制品、机械和设备修理业	Repair Service of Metal Products, Machinery and Equipment	7	2	1158469
电力、热力、燃气及水生产和供应业	**Production and Supply of Electricity, Heating, Gas and Water**	**116**	**16**	**82622770**
电力、热力生产和供应业	Production and Supply of Electric Power and Heat Power	77	11	80531297
燃气生产和供应业	Production and Supply of Gas	12	1	842393
水的生产和供应业	Production and Supply of Water	27	4	1249080

MAIN ECONOMIC INDICATORS OF STATE-HOLDING INDUSTRIAL ENTERPRISES ABOVE DESIGNATED SIZE BY INDUSTRIAL SECTOR (2023)

(10000 yuan)

平均用工人数(人) Average Number of Employed Persons (person)	资产负债 Assets and Liabilities							
	资产总计 Total Assets	#流动资产合计 Total Current Assets	#存货 Inventories	#产成品 Finished Products	#应收账款 Accounts Receivable	#固定资产原价 Original Value of Fixed Assets	负债合计 Total Liabilities	#流动负债合计 Total Current Liabilities
342575	**513230879**	**160769111**	**18690822**	**5784274**	**40034712**	**162073062**	**216904349**	**140885362**
23324	**38623109**	**7766359**	**59181**	**11023**	**1246983**	**9857978**	**24567609**	**11745420**
***	***	***	***	***	***	***	***	***
***	***	***	***	***	***	***	***	***
***	***	***	***	***	***	***	***	***
242994	**141338245**	**89104811**	**18288543**	**5688261**	**27372659**	**34762944**	**77399421**	**68031762**
8038	2097910	1274426	426280	381893	98361	424639	1159548	728908
5832	1170996	386835	66326	38946	136850	282634	393525	343304
11616	4341286	2519493	345893	115079	31128	1210967	1431010	1278680
***	***	***	***	***	***	***	***	***
***	***	***	***	***	***	***	***	***
389	42714	31849	13047	7581	10777	13001	30391	26297
***	***	***	***	***	***	***	***	***
***	***	***	***	***	***	***	***	***
8649	1435352	969817	184942	71729	88984	1053540	416228	343675
598	252289	138799	68318	50349	14817	44094	165828	87419
9142	7790113	4289660	1549111	154812	200537	4549880	5151668	3146940
2844	1599646	818739	173248	98955	168067	389806	702264	664354
16483	10188645	5788186	1201626	380260	816738	2024906	2451856	2013169
***	***	***	***	***	***	***	***	***
499	78900	63482	5238	3332	5305	10872	12874	11311
10989	5756766	3379115	334259	187588	1333218	874352	2837129	2561036
***	***	***	***	***	***	***	***	***
1365	803030	496891	129923	43882	153873	105091	342069	303625
5927	2785428	1896978	415417	52256	169164	599968	1686656	1459045
9514	3036317	2187454	456366	83839	500327	478106	1854809	1709699
16842	11247698	6758004	1774527	723973	1864493	794760	6153819	5474337
38666	39209753	26685061	2943505	1584434	14807432	12487217	28985487	27097865
29098	13244796	10297551	3403944	537216	2204561	2322423	6933244	6499308
2981	2410911	1758967	213633	66370	663877	134731	1515517	1426693
36708	21690276	12529643	2789485	958922	2861759	4601269	9116940	7820000
6419	2575410	1899776	349851	88669	504008	191640	1094096	1033626
3647	3543029	3038579	919018	15	478652	472014	2796406	2651267
563	139220	109495	2769	1078	50031	22468	76073	74535
12961	4610835	1066032	313530	625	135046	603621	1278004	874076
76257	**333269525**	**63897941**	**343099**	**84990**	**11415069**	**117452140**	**114937320**	**61108181**
61310	318740100	60520615	333110	83304	9865191	106619152	107868108	57639959
1842	1365329	346248	2525	1308	37134	516132	521861	425659
13105	13164096	3031078	7464	379	1512745	10316856	6547350	3042563

12-6 续表

单位：万元

项目	Item	资产负债 Assets and Liabilities #应付账款 Accounts Payable	所有者权益合计 Total Owners' Equity	#实收资本 Paid-in Capital
合计	**Total**	**44243510**	**296326525**	**229939680**
采矿业	**Mining**	**899596**	**14055500**	**6174528**
石油和天然气开采业	Extraction of Petroleum and Natural Gas	***	***	***
黑色金属矿采选业	Mining and Processing of Ferrous Metal Ores	***	***	***
开采专业及辅助性活动	Professional and Support Activities for Mining	***	***	***
制造业	**Manufacturing**	**31325678**	**63938821**	**25661425**
农副食品加工业	Processing of Food from Agricultural Products	79139	938362	473106
食品制造业	Manufacture of Foods	138045	777471	303638
酒、饮料和精制茶制造业	Manufacture of Liquor, Beverages and Refined Tea	116414	2910276	590302
烟草制品业	Manufacture of Tobacco	***	***	***
纺织业	Manufacture of Textile	***	***	***
纺织服装、服饰业	Manufacture of Textile, Wearing Apparel and Accessories	8632	12323	49115
家具制造业	Manufacture of Furniture	***	***	***
造纸和纸制品业	Manufacture of Paper and Paper Products	***	***	***
印刷和记录媒介复制业	Printing and Reproduction of Recording Media	130567	1019124	554495
文教、工美、体育和娱乐用品制造业	Manufacture of Articles for Culture, Education, Arts and Crafts, Sport and Entertainment Activities	58744	86461	144005
石油、煤炭及其他燃料加工业	Processing of Petroleum, Coal and Other Fuels	595831	2638444	1226281
化学原料和化学制品制造业	Manufacture of Raw Chemical Materials and Chemical Products	158090	897382	519465
医药制造业	Manufacture of Medicines	440159	7736789	1038953
化学纤维制造业	Manufacture of Chemical Fibres	***	***	***
橡胶和塑料制品业	Manufacture of Rubber and Plastics Products	2756	66026	52146
非金属矿物制品业	Manufacture of Non-metallic Mineral Products	1041765	2919636	1037881
黑色金属冶炼和压延加工业	Smelting and Pressing of Ferrous Metals	***	***	***
有色金属冶炼和压延加工业	Smelting and Pressing of Non-ferrous Metals	131765	460960	117654
金属制品业	Manufacture of Metal Products	399260	1098771	469818
通用设备制造业	Manufacture of General Purpose Machinery	606209	1181509	667427
专用设备制造业	Manufacture of Special Purpose Machinery	1767651	5093878	1390802
汽车制造业	Manufacture of Automobiles	17126499	10224265	7921533
铁路、船舶、航空航天和其他运输设备制造业	Manufacture of Railway, Ship, Aerospace and Other Transport Equipments	2757772	6311552	1744718
电气机械和器材制造业	Manufacture of Electrical Machinery and Apparatus	581595	895394	434126
计算机、通信和其他电子设备制造业	Manufacture of Computers, Communication and Other Electronic Equipment	3234883	12573336	4917147
仪器仪表制造业	Manufacture of Measuring Instruments and Machinery	403498	1481313	353137
其他制造业	Other Manufacture	1063253	746623	328604
废弃资源综合利用业	Utilization of Waste Resources	43360	63147	24632
金属制品、机械和设备修理业	Repair Service of Metal Products, Machinery and Equipment	226722	3332831	883873
电力、热力、燃气及水生产和供应业	**Production and Supply of Electricity, Heating, Gas and Water**	**12018237**	**218332204**	**198103726**
电力、热力生产和供应业	Production and Supply of Electric Power and Heat Power	11400846	210871991	192318759
燃气生产和供应业	Production and Supply of Gas	98229	843468	870497
水的生产和供应业	Production and Supply of Water	519162	6616746	4914471

12-6 Continued

(10000 yuan)

损 益 Profits and Losses							应交税金合计 Total Tax Payable		
营业收入 Business Revenue	营业成本 Business Cost	销售费用 Selling Expenses	管理费用 Manage-ment Expenses	研发费用 R&D Expenses	财务费用 Financial Expenses	利润总额 Total Profits		#税金及附加 Tax and Surtax	#应交增值税 Value Added Tax Payable
171087180	**151319976**	**3250525**	**4335240**	**2662849**	**2329668**	**10798934**	**7625285**	**3077072**	**2706135**
5284082	**4769234**	**760**	**210086**	**85245**	**512747**	**381721**	**134738**	**44850**	**62379**
***	***	***	***	***	***	***	***	***	***
***	***	***	***	***	***	***	***	***	***
***	***	***	***	***	***	***	***	***	***
81510103	**65742435**	**3156803**	**3296687**	**2404622**	**24500**	**5281009**	**5512709**	**2611816**	**1769276**
2472091	2341252	104823	51719	8433	10889	-18100	11992	4787	-220
964518	785952	124641	40170	15431	1848	34599	24880	3984	15425
1339756	935830	103073	153848	20605	5044	-182852	247185	196898	46299
***	***	***	***	***	***	***	***	***	***
***	***	***	***	***	***	***	***	***	***
56535	52186	1330	3888	597	630	-2373	1301	226	1065
***	***	***	***	***	***	***	***	***	***
***	***	***	***	***	***	***	***	***	***
833854	604721	11822	110757	22360	-11830	92032	71294	10625	41589
114030	87289	10565	10820	2347	1671	5542	5804	1568	2958
6966881	6015534	18884	203719	20302	24206	-72739	910864	761296	92558
1043856	838360	35394	90495	41577	-1365	22589	24387	4165	27297
2484793	1292580	441291	197462	173573	-35932	693679	215484	31288	131702
***	***	***	***	***	***	***	***	***	***
49175	32293	3112	7221	2280	-575	4648	3424	602	2396
1911618	1612150	45202	141549	77509	13149	370210	60781	12506	44927
***	***	***	***	***	***	***	***	***	***
1062557	997448	4629	17854	15787	21	30746	12584	1538	9355
1131321	1001117	11316	70557	56456	-1704	-13696	21778	7800	14489
1437849	1189767	47430	106193	79324	7722	14495	47129	9771	33797
3674924	2847406	165717	213426	203367	13015	264941	58755	27123	22670
30931858	24615838	1560107	728581	359706	49796	2553082	2811625	1069183	955157
6418206	5372576	63909	317917	259013	3558	414829	223442	26145	140175
1310187	1133411	35312	51675	47412	2480	62736	24825	3577	11855
10039605	7939489	285116	439798	839540	-80181	601764	148531	50968	28834
1247807	922239	58627	99064	76179	-2142	95349	59047	8691	42064
2748061	2608429	2166	57295	48710	-2381	65019	34152	3585	23281
117344	87120	1476	16177	3884	232	10377	6094	577	3505
1194353	1028199	5198	111503	16920	29956	147524	28991	6639	8422
84292996	**80808306**	**92963**	**828467**	**172983**	**1792421**	**5136203**	**1977838**	**420407**	**874480**
81881900	78836870	16682	692972	146796	1673526	5071977	1701316	179219	849162
875229	796930	7602	36471	13570	69	23795	13476	1190	6510
1535867	1174507	68679	99023	12617	118826	40432	263046	239998	18808

12-7 分行业规模以上港澳台及外商投资工业企业主要经济指标(2023年)

单位：万元

项　目	Item	企业单位个数(个) Number of Enterprises (unit)	#亏损企业 Loss-Suffering Enterprises	工业总产值(当年价格) Gross Output Value of Industry (at current prices)
合　计	**Total**	**580**	**151**	**79909417**
采矿业	**Mining**	**1**		*******
开采专业及辅助性活动	Professional and Support Activities for Mining	1		***
制造业	**Manufacturing**	**564**	**151**	**74107541**
农副食品加工业	Processing of Food from Agricultural Products	18	5	489681
食品制造业	Manufacture of Foods	42	11	2055914
酒、饮料和精制茶制造业	Manufacture of Liquor, Beverages and Refined Tea	17	5	585204
纺织业	Manufacture of Textile	1	1	***
纺织服装、服饰业	Manufacture of Textile, Wearing Apparel and Accessories	13	3	131287
家具制造业	Manufacture of Furniture	8	2	342793
造纸和纸制品业	Manufacture of Paper and Paper Products	8	2	505610
印刷和记录媒介复制业	Printing, Reproduction of Recording Media	10	4	152087
文教、工美、体育和娱乐用品制造业	Manufacture of Articles for Culture, Education, Arts and Crafts, Sport and Entertainment Activities	2		***
石油、煤炭及其他燃料加工业	Processing of Petroleum, Coal and Other Fuels	1	1	***
化学原料和化学制品制造业	Manufacture of Raw Chemical Materials and Chemical Products	26	6	851486
医药制造业	Manufacture of Medicines	41	9	6140592
橡胶和塑料制品业	Manufacture of Rubber and Plastics Products	10	3	142540
非金属矿物制品业	Manufacture of Non-metallic Mineral Products	6	2	106061
有色金属冶炼和压延加工业	Manufacture and Pressing of Non-ferrous Metals	2		***
金属制品业	Manufacture of Metal Products	19	6	188396
通用设备制造业	Manufacture of General Purpose Machinery	50	10	3722140
专用设备制造业	Manufacture of Special Purpose Machinery	76	18	2989270
汽车制造业	Manufacture of Automobiles	88	34	31241314
铁路、船舶、航空航天和其他运输设备制造业	Manufacture of Railway, Ship, Aerospace and Other Transport Equipments	1		***
电气机械和器材制造业	Manufacture of Electrical Machinery and Apparatus	32	7	2949432
计算机、通信和其他电子设备制造业	Manufacture of Computers, Communication and Other Electronic Equipment	56	19	19424439
仪器仪表制造业	Manufacture of Measuring Instruments and Machinery	29	2	711813
其他制造业	Other Manufacture	2	1	***
废弃资源综合利用业	Utilization of Waste Resources			
金属制品、机械和设备修理业	Repair Service of Metal Products, Machinery and Equipment	6		1152449
电力、热力、燃气及水生产和供应业	**Production and Supply of Electricity, Heating, Gas and Water**	**15**		**5690073**
电力、热力生产和供应业	Production and Supply of Electric Power and Heat Power	7		1348380
燃气生产和供应业	Production and Supply of Gas	3		***
水的生产和供应业	Production and Supply of Water	5		134041

MAIN ECONOMIC INDICATORS OF INDUSTRIAL ENTERPRISES WITH HONGKONG, MACAO, TAIWAN AND FOREIGN FUNDS ABOVE DESIGNATED SIZE BY SECTOR (2023)

(10000 yuan)

平均用工人数(人) Average Number of Employed Persons (person)	资产负债 Assets and Liabilities							
	资产总计 Total Assets	#流动资产合计 Total Current Assets	#存货 Inventories	#产成品 Finished Products	#应收账款 Accounts Receivable	#固定资产原价 Original Value of Fixed Assets	负债合计 Total Liabilities	#流动负债合计 Total Current Liabilities
229181	**149848740**	**104032222**	**14272311**	**6234038**	**27626243**	**37293310**	**86272168**	**78115634**
***	***	***	***	***	***	***	***	***
***	***	***	***	***	***	***	***	***
218580	**137679344**	**100338490**	**14083876**	**6151884**	**26740485**	**30508543**	**81073843**	**75284553**
3463	507766	342968	70394	13995	86724	221808	264078	201383
20502	3497467	2110506	157583	85306	562275	1144036	1712405	1436346
4272	755194	546062	69829	37024	224030	401347	674549	656616
***	***	***	***	***	***	***	***	***
3410	210459	177301	59138	15900	32992	41936	173278	168458
1458	643489	580189	185044	170205	79405	127251	652059	522177
1650	355563	234716	68547	14652	87080	236027	140068	136100
1986	222010	168076	21516	7226	38710	171514	72823	58197
***	***	***	***	***	***	***	***	***
***	***	***	***	***	***	***	***	***
5518	1818420	1356315	150218	50140	156422	534858	352873	332706
34191	14972992	11244879	2142466	1268394	1651495	1859603	4385324	3378644
942	128331	102585	31907	8681	38904	57170	40194	40144
1730	143154	112863	20595	8360	42541	103527	74355	72967
***	***	***	***	***	***	***	***	***
1822	478691	309707	71728	17639	125787	89109	266161	189684
17748	5027803	4372842	1157145	509758	841548	1194590	1810101	1722776
16241	7374288	4491573	533236	155046	872178	628493	3343161	2756293
42074	35615482	26185679	3380173	1708567	15698649	12535228	27384800	25578820
***	***	***	***	***	***	***	***	***
7978	3162477	2636100	419241	75760	721663	375363	1846127	1697585
36774	60456229	43711349	5000032	1965160	5005302	10102976	36675141	35256911
4219	1243336	898203	213248	22586	300058	138185	488073	482432
***	***	***	***	***	***	***	***	***
11513	814151	530474	298286	6510	123106	469690	647114	537257
10304	**11269894**	**3302552**	**170886**	**79924**	**576063**	**6765343**	**4638127**	**2611081**
1683	1779899	799839	125277	78962	413727	2132602	897242	530820
***	***	***	***	***	***	***	***	***
832	360210	70187	688		23622	93044	192820	74068

12-7 续表

单位：万元

项目	Item	资产负债 Assets and Liabilities		
		#应付账款 Accounts Payable	所有者权益合计 Total Owners' Equity	#实收资本 Paid-in Capital
合 计	**Total**	**33236279**	**63576569**	**23270870**
采矿业	**Mining**	***	***	***
开采专业及辅助性活动	Professional and Support Activities for Mining	***	***	***
制造业	**Manufacturing**	**32471778**	**56605498**	**21851026**
农副食品加工业	Processing of Food from Agricultural Products	50849	243688	146673
食品制造业	Manufacture of Foods	516568	1785063	623417
酒、饮料和精制茶制造业	Manufacture of Liquor, Beverages and Refined Tea	122484	80645	293062
纺织业	Manufacture of Textile	***	***	***
纺织服装、服饰业	Manufacture of Textile, Wearing Apparel and Accessories	15335	37182	30129
家具制造业	Manufacture of Furniture	94856	-8570	40205
造纸和纸制品业	Manufacture of Paper and Paper Products	60695	215495	72921
印刷和记录媒介复制业	Printing and Reproduction of Recording Media	27107	149187	96071
文教、工美、体育和娱乐用品制造业	Manufacture of Articles for Culture, Education, Arts and Crafts, Sport and Entertainment Activities	***	***	***
石油、煤炭及其他燃料加工业	Processing of Petroleum, Coal and Other Fuels	***	***	***
化学原料和化学制品制造业	Manufacture of Raw Chemical Materials and Chemical Products	101192	1465546	315087
医药制造业	Manufacture of Medicines	1088859	10587667	1005803
橡胶和塑料制品业	Manufacture of Rubber and Plastics Products	23540	88136	41792
非金属矿物制品业	Manufacture of Non-metallic Mineral Products	35142	68799	46345
有色金属冶炼和压延加工业	Smelting and Pressing of Non-ferrous Metals	***	***	***
金属制品业	Manufacture of Metal Products	66856	212530	112180
通用设备制造业	Manufacture of General Purpose Machinery	860249	3217703	779996
专用设备制造业	Manufacture of Special Purpose Machinery	610861	4031126	765596
汽车制造业	Manufacture of Automobiles	18533389	8230681	6182199
铁路、船舶、航空航天和其他运输设备制造业	Manufacture of Railway, Ship, Aerospace and Other Transport Equipments	***	***	***
电气机械和器材制造业	Manufacture of Electrical Machinery and Apparatus	790580	1316350	814859
计算机、通信和其他电子设备制造业	Manufacture of Computers, Communication and Other Electronic Equipment	8994670	23781087	10040728
仪器仪表制造业	Manufacture of Measuring Instruments and Machinery	215374	755263	181331
其他制造业	Other Manufacture	***	***	***
废弃资源综合利用业	Utilization of Waste Resources			
金属制品、机械和设备修理业	Repair Service of Metal Products, Machinery and Equipment	231284	167038	223849
电力、热力、燃气及水生产和供应业	**Production and Supply of Electricity, Heating, Gas and Water**	**713987**	**6631767**	**1250980**
电力、热力生产和供应业	Production and Supply of Electric Power and Heat Power	369895	882657	509992
燃气生产和供应业	Production and Supply of Gas	***	***	***
水的生产和供应业	Production and Supply of Water	25379	167390	143171

12-7 Continued

(10000 yuan)

损益 Profits and Losses							应交税金合计 Total Tax Payable	#税金及附加 Tax and Surtax	#应交增值税 Value Added Tax Payable
营业收入 Business Revenue	营业成本 Business Cost	销售费用 Selling Expenses	管理费用 Management Expenses	研发费用 R&D Expenses	财务费用 Financial Expenses	利润总额 Total Profits			
105934717	**85360783**	**7155424**	**3275434**	**2516038**	**-328209**	**7317185**	**4812456**	**1293427**	**1946461**
***	***	***	***	***	***	***	***	***	***
***	***	***	***	***	***	***	***	***	***
100058891	**80081229**	**7143201**	**3135055**	**2327295**	**-348266**	**6846584**	**4717328**	**1276852**	**1903871**
648363	566194	39541	28519	2106	2082	9298	11553	1958	6089
4295917	3014404	796796	220096	24958	-5499	303946	265368	25179	158084
822002	594774	101997	43192	6136	-652	68454	51081	9470	29315
***	***	***	***	***	***	***	***	***	***
203149	160837	21473	10687	3411	2091	4579	6730	1191	4335
393605	304530	13882	26247	10337	8052	29967	12592	1376	9258
565715	438748	17668	40849	3418	103	55818	35404	3397	18784
173309	137147	5963	17405	4348	-693	9922	9140	1054	6327
***	***	***	***	***	***	***	***	***	***
***	***	***	***	***	***	***	***	***	***
1162832	837842	153312	72495	22786	-5069	136958	69243	5761	32218
7765625	4454941	2022068	570690	423201	-21157	552901	520077	49793	328494
158141	131536	5513	12339	2640	-144	6214	4957	641	2530
118690	87910	6140	6494	2381	306	12051	11437	1269	7068
***	***	***	***	***	***	***	***	***	***
334529	269476	26445	19911	4931	1602	13145	8833	1220	6626
4072499	2929154	210511	192577	151189	-17415	597442	244642	22767	114691
3348463	2207703	216453	216370	170764	7436	489987	176177	18436	71333
33420215	26757435	1624616	730269	261403	29944	2863666	2758692	1054457	904597
***	***	***	***	***	***	***	***	***	***
3129548	2260566	176032	155453	84012	-11	452865	142669	13861	51118
37092659	33121954	1630930	599497	1110023	-361771	970643	284171	53576	117908
931476	673067	63247	68168	24892	-114	124659	42623	4496	18629
***	***	***	***	***	***	***	***	***	***
1189352	994680	9214	93656	13215	11152	64624	30457	5473	5582
5700128	**5123579**	**9975**	**135454**	**186319**	**13863**	**466629**	**94214**	**16456**	**42183**
1322269	1149676	2937	15383	18390	9144	131688	69625	9422	38147
***	***	***	***	***	***	***	***	***	***
137049	103226		16462		6350	9680	7153	1998	4275

12-8 分行业规模以上大中型工业企业主要经济指标(2023年)

单位：万元

项目	Item	企业单位个数(个) Number of Enterprises (unit)	#亏损企业 Loss-Suffering Enterprises	工业总产值(当年价格) Gross Output Value of Industry (at current prices)
合计	**Total**	**534**	**111**	**203754795**
采矿业	**Mining**	**5**	**1**	**2132062**
石油和天然气开采业	Extraction of Petroleum and Natural Gas	1	1	***
黑色金属矿采选业	Mining and Processing of Ferrous Metal Ores	1		***
开采专业及辅助性活动	Professional and Support Activities for Mining	3		***
制造业	**Manufacturing**	**494**	**108**	**117859427**
农副食品加工业	Processing of Food from Agricultural Products	16	5	1301558
食品制造业	Manufacture of Foods	29	4	2066382
酒、饮料和精制茶制造业	Manufacture of Liquor, Beverages and Refined Tea	8	2	1746970
烟草制品业	Manufacture of Tobacco	1		***
纺织业	Manufacture of Textile	2		***
纺织服装、服饰业	Manufacture of Textile, Wearing Apparel and Accessories	10	3	384578
家具制造业	Manufacture of Furniture	3	1	***
造纸和纸制品业	Manufacture of Paper and Paper Products	3		***
印刷和记录媒介复制业	Printing and Reproduction of Recording Media	11	3	599997
文教、工美、体育和娱乐用品制造业	Manufacture of Articles for Culture, Education, Arts and Crafts, Sport and Entertainment Activities	1		***
石油、煤炭及其他燃料加工业	Processing of Petroleum, Coal and Other Fuels	3	1	***
化学原料和化学制品制造业	Manufacture of Raw Chemical Materials and Chemical Products	6	1	473699
医药制造业	Manufacture of Medicines	69	14	11264217
化学纤维制造业	Manufacture of Chemical Fibres	1		***
橡胶和塑料制品业	Manufacture of Rubber and Plastics Products	1		***
非金属矿物制品业	Manufacture of Non-metallic Mineral Products	21	5	2013496
黑色金属冶炼和压延加工业	Smelting and Pressing of Ferrous Metals	1		***
有色金属冶炼和压延加工业	Smelting and Pressing of Non-ferrous Metals	3		***
金属制品业	Manufacture of Metal Products	6	1	874907
通用设备制造业	Manufacture of General Purpose Machinery	29	4	4237149
专用设备制造业	Manufacture of Special Purpose Machinery	49	7	6695570
汽车制造业	Manufacture of Automobiles	37	12	31844719
铁路、船舶、航空航天和其他运输设备制造业	Manufacture of Railway, Ship, Aerospace and Other Transport Equipments	31	4	5764452
电气机械和器材制造业	Manufacture of Electrical Machinery and Apparatus	34	9	6507169
计算机、通信和其他电子设备制造业	Manufacture of Computers, Communication and Other Electronic Equipment	90	29	27429047
仪器仪表制造业	Manufacture of Measuring Instruments and Machinery	21	3	1333876
其他制造业	Other Manufacture	5		2870945
金属制品、机械和设备修理业	Repair Service of Metal Products, Machinery and Equipment	3		***
电力、热力、燃气及水生产和供应业	**Production and Supply of Electricity, Heating, Gas and Water**	**35**	**2**	**83763306**
电力、热力生产和供应业	Production and Supply of Electric Power and Heat Power	25	2	78232985
燃气生产和供应业	Production and Supply of Gas	3		***
水的生产和供应业	Production and Supply of Water	7		1015632

MAIN ECONOMIC INDICATORS OF LARGE AND MEDIUM -SIZED INDUSTRIAL ENTERPRISES ABOVE DESIGNATED SIZE BY INDUSTRIAL SECTOR (2023)

(10000 yuan)

平均用工人数（人） Average Number of Employed Persons (person)	资产负债 Assets and Liabilities: 资产总计 Total Assets	#流动资产合计 Total Current Assets	#存货 Inventories	#产成品 Finished Products	#应收账款 Accounts Receivable	#固定资产原价 Original Value of Fixed Assets	负债合计 Total Liabilities	#流动负债合计 Total Current Liabilities
548000	**639749179**	**245162928**	**29010076**	**10023178**	**52000443**	**182213424**	**284011821**	**198645543**
23324	**38623109**	**7766359**	**59181**	**11023**	**1246983**	**9857978**	**24567609**	**11745420**
***	***	***	***	***	***	***	***	***
***	***	***	***	***	***	***	***	***
***	***	***	***	***	***	***	***	***
447771	**265773208**	**173518302**	**28711280**	**10009741**	**40260259**	**55288547**	**144272174**	**125781773**
11144	3702766	1565638	429375	365169	109897	616257	1868323	1337261
24621	3302714	1938851	179857	90356	591353	1097636	1731509	1499915
14479	5181218	2925219	336900	126028	113376	1483274	2011828	1848659
***	***	***	***	***	***	***	***	***
***	***	***	***	***	***	***	***	***
11037	921396	762626	195507	134505	91028	142796	369724	342648
***	***	***	***	***	***	***	***	***
***	***	***	***	***	***	***	***	***
7111	1294714	810281	145313	47148	108735	918086	369359	324366
***	***	***	***	***	***	***	***	***
***	***	***	***	***	***	***	***	***
5052	1967842	1129589	86872	55124	148909	231236	661036	613912
70489	30835837	19709114	3506812	1710139	2974983	5219398	8307593	6742897
***	***	***	***	***	***	***	***	***
***	***	***	***	***	***	***	***	***
13319	6254514	3659378	249351	98998	1292871	881358	3113879	2810527
***	***	***	***	***	***	***	***	***
***	***	***	***	***	***	***	***	***
5193	3291838	1991482	368813	16116	135251	497042	1772201	1568752
23562	8622332	6308711	1475710	647273	1133474	1469007	3474865	3189379
33453	21206155	12301036	2143875	837525	2731270	1195305	10485775	8497265
54616	45459099	31131943	3619328	1931528	16758644	13743780	34422241	31173622
28753	12650474	9976595	3313774	515096	2172506	2218669	6423206	6058830
21754	11531936	9102219	865964	277072	2562679	830480	7484569	6919493
80408	87896996	58164601	8259311	2780042	7653132	17498169	50042432	44251915
8988	3290303	2234263	425277	104030	587555	246596	1089496	1060051
3647	3543029	3038579	919018	15	478652	472014	2796406	2651267
***	***	***	***	***	***	***	***	***
76905	**335352862**	**63878268**	**239615**	**2415**	**10493201**	**117066900**	**115172038**	**61118350**
57526	314830504	59137552	189110	982	9434874	103285588	105403311	56110655
***	***	***	***	***	***	***	***	***
10955	11146875	2159407	5622	365	895942	9168500	6010774	2791926

12-8 续表

单位：万元

项 目	Item	资产负债 Assets and Liabilities		
		#应付账款 Accounts Payable	所有者权益合计 Total Owners' Equity	#实收资本 Paid-in Capital
合 计	**Total**	**59336422**	**355737355**	**243485078**
采矿业	**Mining**	**899596**	**14055500**	**6174528**
石油和天然气开采业	Extraction of Petroleum and Natural Gas	***	***	***
黑色金属矿采选业	Mining and Processing of Ferrous Metal Ores	***	***	***
开采专业及辅助性活动	Professional and Support Activities for Mining	***	***	***
制造业	**Manufacturing**	**46933639**	**121501031**	**41816560**
农副食品加工业	Processing of Food from Agricultural Products	110489	1834443	817263
食品制造业	Manufacture of Foods	566953	1571205	558531
酒、饮料和精制茶制造业	Manufacture of Liquor, Beverages and Refined Tea	207658	3169390	609815
烟草制品业	Manufacture of Tobacco	***	***	***
纺织业	Manufacture of Textile	***	***	***
纺织服装、服饰业	Manufacture of Textile, Wearing Apparel and Accessories	47632	551672	76099
家具制造业	Manufacture of Furniture	***	***	***
造纸和纸制品业	Manufacture of Paper and Paper Products	***	***	***
印刷和记录媒介复制业	Printing and Reproduction of Recording Media	119599	925355	463403
文教、工美、体育和娱乐用品制造业	Manufacture of Articles for Culture, Education, Arts and Crafts, Sport and Entertainment Activities	***	***	***
石油、煤炭及其他燃料加工业	Processing of Petroleum, Coal and Other Fuels	***	***	***
化学原料和化学制品制造业	Manufacture of Raw Chemical Materials and Chemical Products	147827	1306806	344020
医药制造业	Manufacture of Medicines	1833162	22528243	2749661
化学纤维制造业	Manufacture of Chemical Fibres	***	***	***
橡胶和塑料制品业	Manufacture of Rubber and Plastics Products	***	***	***
非金属矿物制品业	Manufacture of Non-metallic Mineral Products	1309652	3140635	895030
黑色金属冶炼和压延加工业	Manufacture and Pressing of Ferrous Metals	***	***	***
有色金属冶炼和压延加工业	Manufacture and Pressing of Non-ferrous Metals	***	***	***
金属制品业	Manufacture of Metal Products	342707	1519637	523447
通用设备制造业	Manufacture of General Purpose Machinery	1133980	5147467	1194070
专用设备制造业	Manufacture of Special Purpose Machinery	2286967	10720380	2385349
汽车制造业	Manufacture of Automobiles	19667769	11036857	8521253
铁路、船舶、航空航天和其他运输设备制造业	Manufacture of Railway, Ship, Aerospace and Other Transport Equipments	2536849	6227267	1459220
电气机械和器材制造业	Manufacture of Electrical Machinery and Apparatus	2282003	4047367	1529846
计算机、通信和其他电子设备制造业	Manufacture of Computers, Communication and Other Electronic Equipment	11667075	37854564	16361775
仪器仪表制造业	Manufacture of Measuring Instruments and Machinery	372890	2200806	507041
其他制造业	Other Manufacture	1063253	746623	328604
金属制品、机械和设备修理业	Repair Service of Metal Products, Machinery and Equipment	***	***	***
电力、热力、燃气及水生产和供应业	**Production and Supply of Electricity, Heating, Gas and Water**	**11503188**	**220180824**	**195493990**
电力、热力生产和供应业	Production and Supply of Electric Power and Heat Power	10731055	209427193	191194460
燃气生产和供应业	Production and Supply of Gas	***	***	***
水的生产和供应业	Production and Supply of Water	413351	5136101	3665211

12-8 Continued

(10000 yuan)

损益 Profits and Losses							应交税金合计 Total Tax Payable	#税金及附加 Tax and Surtax	#应交增值税 Value Added Tax Payable
营业收入 Business Revenue	营业成本 Business Cost	销售费用 Selling Expenses	管理费用 Management Expenses	研发费用 R&D Expenses	财务费用 Financial Expenses	利润总额 Total Profits			
237607198	**202983311**	**10165976**	**6601042**	**6259770**	**1897764**	**14101968**	**9268185**	**3287795**	**3561242**
5284082	**4769234**	**760**	**210086**	**85245**	**512747**	**381721**	**134738**	**44850**	**62379**
***	***	***	***	***	***	***	***	***	***
***	***	***	***	***	***	***	***	***	***
***	***	***	***	***	***	***	***	***	***
146932026	**116318287**	**10084655**	**5571239**	**5854004**	**-360213**	**8554455**	**7314475**	**2848306**	**2705432**
2609663	2374746	136339	99723	26825	13604	13491	16906	6943	4833
4351702	3085601	774529	198938	34081	-6033	299173	264082	24627	158206
2037552	1516850	246542	163540	24134	13694	-179602	258111	194152	60974
***	***	***	***	***	***	***	***	***	***
***	***	***	***	***	***	***	***	***	***
551959	294202	157778	42525	20528	-452	37398	41158	4981	29992
***	***	***	***	***	***	***	***	***	***
***	***	***	***	***	***	***	***	***	***
714194	549650	13170	83105	17694	-9238	57330	51591	8691	30263
***	***	***	***	***	***	***	***	***	***
***	***	***	***	***	***	***	***	***	***
621804	357728	115641	76346	31623	-5282	55039	27530	4085	16915
12356174	5987152	3473749	877686	1040894	-80874	1603206	902656	100863	577312
***	***	***	***	***	***	***	***	***	***
***	***	***	***	***	***	***	***	***	***
2189611	1808294	48286	156423	82211	15637	406617	69611	12868	53846
***	***	***	***	***	***	***	***	***	***
***	***	***	***	***	***	***	***	***	***
1089053	944619	22973	76205	44829	-4362	68586	24198	7463	15435
4557530	3340691	222559	210819	204762	-537	858755	246159	27563	123497
6495064	4637125	443726	366082	392746	-6632	759150	220573	37466	96136
36785488	29926870	1711665	896192	820450	61637	2296903	2880618	1115406	954208
6021992	5026062	57028	306694	295732	3797	353116	206059	24431	125957
7434239	6054268	431911	290286	245787	-11552	577282	206141	25647	93943
43993534	37815059	2048514	1124783	2351237	-391755	784420	341936	99423	91694
1607390	1157091	114706	116357	84048	-4473	200505	69405	10183	43841
2748061	2608429	2166	57295	48710	-2381	65019	34152	3585	23281
***	***	***	***	***	***	***	***	***	***
85391089	**81895790**	**80561**	**819718**	**320521**	**1745231**	**5165792**	**1818971**	**394639**	**793431**
79564874	76790392	7935	622764	135567	1637396	4805238	1553542	160835	777711
***	***	***	***	***	***	***	***	***	***
1273648	943359	65667	83459	9169	110512	31660	246458	228522	15152

12–9 规模以上工业企业主要效益指标(2023年)

单位：%

项　　目	Item	总资产贡献率 Contribution Rate of Total Assets
合　计	**Total**	**3.74**
按行业分	**By Sector**	
采矿业	Mining	2.56
制造业	Manufacturing	5.11
电力、热力、燃气及水生产和供应业	Production and Supply of Electricity, Heating, Gas and Water	2.49
按轻重工业分	**By light and heavy industries**	
轻工业	Light Industry	7.73
重工业	Heavy Industry	3.29
按规模分	**By Size**	
大　型	Large	3.24
中　型	Medium-sized	5.23
小　型	Small	4.97
微　型	Micro	2.75
按登记注册统计类别分	**By Statistical Category of Registration**	
内资企业	Domestic Invested Enterprises	2.93
有限责任公司	Limited Liability Corporations	2.76
股份有限公司	Corporations Limited by Shares	3.82
非公司企业法人	Unincorporated Business Entity	4.48
个人独资企业	Sole Proprietorship Enterprises	2.23
港澳台投资企业	Enterprises with Investment from Hong Kong, Macao and Taiwan	2.37
#港澳台投资有限责任公司	Limited Liability Corporations with Investment from Hong Kong, Macao and Taiwan	1.92
港澳台投资股份有限公司	Companies Limited by Shares with Investment from Hong Kong, Macao and Taiwan	4.84
外商投资企业	Foreign Invested Enterprises	9.59
#外商投资有限责任公司	Limited Liability Corporations with Foreign Investment	10.39
外商投资股份有限公司	Companies Limited by Shares with Foreign Investment	7.16
按控股类型分	**By Holding Types**	
#国有控股	State-holding Enterprises	3.67

INDUSTRIAL ENTERPRISES ABOVE DESIGNATED SIZE (2023)

(%)

资 产 负债率 Assets- Liabilities Ratio	流动资产 周 转 率 (次) Turnover of Current Assets (times)	收 入 利润率 Revenue-Profit Margin	每百元营业 收入成本费用 (元) Cost Expense of Per 100 Yuan of Business Revenue (yuan)	人均营业 收 入 (元) Per Capita Business Revenue (yuan)
44.65	**0.95**	**5.82**	**95.79**	**3590508**
63.54	0.67	7.02	105.31	2291207
52.39	0.85	5.61	93.97	2811832
34.69	1.33	6.19	99.18	9958862
37.75	0.85	8.79	91.42	1588428
45.43	0.97	5.34	96.50	4512175
45.24	1.07	5.19	96.46	5883333
40.26	0.68	9.15	93.59	2037710
46.90	0.89	5.45	95.10	1957405
36.67	0.79	1.67	97.61	4409868
41.31	0.92	5.19	97.70	3180771
42.16	1.01	5.08	97.98	3577054
36.83	0.63	5.74	96.27	2121070
56.29	0.84	3.06	98.87	675300
62.41	1.00	1.44	98.02	1064643
49.95	1.14	2.70	97.51	8026374
51.98	1.21	2.03	98.30	8584260
34.37	0.53	13.65	84.35	3899602
62.23	0.95	9.99	88.82	3527837
63.44	1.03	9.84	88.81	3698434
22.22	0.59	20.58	84.90	1281330
42.26	1.06	6.31	95.80	4994153

12-10 规模以上工业企业主要工业产品生产能力
PRODUCTION CAPACITY OF MAIN INDUSTRIAL PRODUCTS OF INDUSTRIAL ENTERPRISES ABOVE DESIGNATED SIZE

主要工业产品名称		Name of Main Industrial Products		2023	2022
原油加工能力	(万吨)	Crude Oil Processing Capacity	(10000 tons)	1100.0	1100.0
硅酸盐水泥熟料	(万吨)	Portland Cement Chamotte	(10000 tons)	305.0	305.0
发电设备容量总计	(万千瓦)	Installed Capacity of Power Generation Equipment	(10000 kW)	1231.2	1223.3
#火电设备容量		Capacity of Thermal Power Equipment		1117.1	1106.6
水电设备容量		Capacity of Hydropower Equipment		80.1	80.0
风电设备容量		Capacity of Wind Power Equipment		6.2	0.4
卷　烟	(亿支)	Cigarettes	(100 million pieces)	284.1	286.0
水　泥	(万吨)	Cement	(10000 tons)	400.0	400.0
钢　材	(万吨)	Rolled Steel	(10000 tons)	170.3	170.3
金属切削机床	(台)	Metal-Cutting Machine Tools	(unit)	15062	12082
汽　车	(万辆)	Motor Vehicles	(10000 units)	192.4	207.2
#基本型乘用车(轿车)		Basic-type Passenger Vehicles (Cars)		175.2	190.2
移动通信手持机(手机)	(万台)	Mobile Communication Handsets (Mobile Phones)	(10000 units)	129.3	192.8
微型计算机设备	(万台)	Micro Computer Equipment	(10000 units)	1120.0	1150.0

12-11 规模以上工业主要产品产量
OUTPUT OF MAIN INDUSTRIAL PRODUCTS ABOVE DESIGNATED SIZE

工业产品名称		Name of Main Industrial Product		2023	2022
鲜、冷藏肉	(万吨)	Fresh, Chilled Meat	(10000 tons)	47.5	46.2
乳制品	(万吨)	Dairy Products	(10000 tons)	49.6	48.9
饮料酒	(万千升)	Alcoholic Beverage	(10000 kL)	139.5	129.1
中成药	(万吨)	Traditional Chinese Medicines	(10000 tons)	4.7	4.4
家　具	(万件)	Furniture	(10000 units)	374.6	333.5
耐火材料制品	(万吨)	Products Made from Fire-resistant Materials	(10000 tons)	25.3	25.8
钢　材	(万吨)	Rolled Steel	(10000 tons)	183.2	184.3
发动机	(万千瓦)	Engines	(10000 kW)	15355.1	14261.5
气动元件	(万件)	Pneumatic Components	(10000 units)	37305.7	50403.4
数控金属切削机床	(台)	CNC Metal-cutting Machine Tools	(unit)	5421	5072
汽　车	(万辆)	Motor Vehicles	(10000 sets)	100.3	87.1
#基本型成用车(轿车)		Basic-type Passenger Vehicles (Cars)		49.6	46.5
运动型多用途乘用车(SUV)		Sport Utility Vehicles (SUV)		43.5	35.1
改装汽车	(万辆)	Refitted Automobiles	(10000 units)	1.4	1.2
风力发电机组	(万千瓦)	Wind Power Generator Units	(10000 kW)	1085.9	643.3
移动通信手持机(手机)	(万台)	Mobile Phones	(10000 units)	10286.8	9429.5
液晶显示模组	(万套)	Liquid Crystal Display Modules	(10000 sets)	20747.8	14680.2
显示器	(万台)	Display	(10000 units)	213.9	233.6
集成电路	(亿块)	Integrated Circuits	(100 million pieces)	219.1	217.9
矿山专用设备	(万吨)	Special Equipment for Mining	(10000 tons)	25.9	19.5
炼油、化工生产专用设备	(万吨)	Specialized Equipment for Oil Refining and Chemical Production	(10000 tons)	3.3	2.6

注：根据统计制度规定，自2022年起，汽车整车制造行业产业活动单位视同法人单位按经营地在地原则进行统计，北京在京外设立的汽车整车制造分厂按照制度规定在当地纳统。

Note: According to the statistical system, since 2022, the industrial activity units in the sector of manufacture of finished automobiles shall be deemed as corporate units and shall be subject to statistics in accordance with the principle of regional statistics of the business place, the finished automobile manufacturing branches set up outside of Beijing shall be included in local statistics according to the rules and regulations.

12-12 规模以上高技术制造业主要经济指标(2023年)
MAIN ECONOMIC INDICATORS OF HIGH TECHNOLOGY MANUFACTURING ENTERPRISES ABOVE DESIGNATED SIZE (2023)

单位：亿元 (100 million yuan)

项目	Item	工业总产值 Gross Output Value of Industry	营业收入 Business Revenue	利润总额 Total Profits	应交税金 Tax Payable
合计	**Total**	**6315.6**	**8475.4**	**462.7**	**230.5**
按登记注册统计类别分	**By Statistical Category of Registration**				
内资企业	Domestic Invested Enterprises	3308.3	3509.0	235.8	129.0
有限责任公司	Limited Liability Corporations	2490.8	2587.2	135.7	80.2
股份有限公司	Corporations Limited by Shares	813.2	916.9	99.6	48.5
非公司企业法人	Unincorporated Business Entity	4.3	4.9	0.4	0.2
港澳台商投资企业	Enterprises with Investment from Hong Kong, Macao and Taiwan	1803.3	3530.1	63.3	28.2
外商投资企业	Foreign Invested Enterprises	1204.0	1436.3	163.6	73.3
按高技术领域分	**By Field of High Technology**				
医药制造业	Manufacture of Medicines	1459.0	1575.5	199.7	111.1
航空、航天器及设备制造业	Manufacture of Aircrafts and Spacecrafts	626.0	649.5	24.6	19.4
电子及通信设备制造业	Manufacture of Electronic Equipment and Communication Equipment	3292.9	5014.6	100.1	51.1
计算机及办公设备制造业	Manufacture of Computers and Office Equipment	263.5	470.3	20.8	5.9
医疗仪器设备及仪器仪表制造业	Manufacture of Medical Equipments and Meters	674.3	765.4	117.5	42.9
信息化学品制造业	Manufacture of Information Chemicals				

12-13 规模以上工业战略性新兴产业总产值
GROSS OUTPUT VALUE OF STRATEGIC EMERGING INDUSTRIES AMONG INDUSTRIAL ABOVE DESIGNATED SIZE

单位：亿元 (100 million yuan)

项目	Item	2023	2022
合计	**Total**	**7635.6**	**7656.7**
新一代信息技术产业	New Generation IT Industry	3129.0	3149.2
高端装备制造业	High-end Equipment Manufacturing	756.7	761.3
新材料产业	New Material Industry	458.1	497.5
生物产业	Bioindustry	1787.4	2025.8
新能源汽车产业	New Energy Automobiles	271.1	185.9
新能源产业	New Energy Industry	417.4	341.5
绿色节能环保产业	Green Energy Conservation and Environmental Protection Industry	457.0	442.1
航空航天产业	Aerospace Industry	354.9	248.6
海洋装备产业	Marine Equipment Industry	4.1	4.8

注：2023年，国家统计局联合相关部门对工业战略性新兴产业分类目录进行了修订，本表是依据《工业战略性新兴产业分类目录(2023)》汇总形成，2022年数据为可比口径数据。

Note: In 2023, the National Bureau of Statistics worked with relevant authorities to modify the Classification Catalogue of Strategic Emerging Industries of Industry. This table is summarized on the basis of the Classification Catalogue of Strategic Emerging Industries of Industry (2023), and the data for 2022 are comparable ones.

主要统计指标解释

工业 指从事自然资源的开采，对采掘品和农产品进行加工和再加工的物质生产部门。具体包括：(1) 对自然资源的开采，如采矿、晒盐、森林采伐等（但不包括禽兽捕猎和水产捕捞）；(2) 对农副产品的加工、再加工，如粮油加工、食品加工、扎花、纺织、制革等；(3) 对采掘品的加工、再加工，如炼铁、炼钢、化工生产、石油加工、机器制造、木材加工等，以及电力、自来水、煤气的生产和供应等；(4) 对工业品的修理、翻新，如机器设备的修理。

轻工业 指主要提供生活消费品和制作手工工具的工业。按其所使用的原料不同，可分为两大类：(1) 以农业为原料的轻工业，是指直接或间接以农产品为基本原料的轻工业。主要包括食品制造、饮料制造、烟草加工、纺织、缝纫、皮革和毛皮制作、造纸以及印刷等工业；(2) 以非农产品为原料的轻工业，是指以工业品为原料的轻工业。主要包括文教体育用品、化学药品制造、合成纤维制造、日用化学制品、日用玻璃制品、日用金属制品、手工工具制造、医疗器械制造、文化和办公用机械制造等工业。

重工业 是指为国民经济各部门提供物质技术基础的主要生产资料的工业。按其生产性质和产品用途，可以分为下列三类：(1) 采掘（伐）工业，是指对自然资源的开采，包括石油开采、煤炭开采、金属矿开采、非金属矿开采和木材采伐等工业；(2) 原材料工业，指向国民经济各部门提供基本材料、动力和燃料的工业。包括金属冶炼及加工、炼焦及焦炭化学、化工原料、水泥、人造板以及电力、石油和煤炭加工等工业；(3) 加工工业，是指对工业原材料进行再加工制造的工业。包括装备国民经济各部门的机械设备制造工业、金属结构、水泥制品等工业，以及为农业提供的生产资料如化肥、农药等工业。

根据上述划分原则，修理业中以重工业产品为修理作业对象的划为重工业，反之划为轻工业。

工业总产值 指工业企业在报告期内生产的以货币形式表现的工业最终产品和提供工业劳务活动的总价值量。它包括：在本企业内不再进行加工，经检验、包装入库已经销售和准备销售的全部工业成品（包括半成品）价值，对外加工费收入，自制半成品、在制品期末期初差额价值。工业总产值采用“工厂法”计算，即以工业企业作为一个整体，按企业生产活动的最终成果来计算。

资产总计 指企业过去的交易或者事项形成的、由企业拥有或者控制的、预期会给企业带来经济利益的资源。资产一般按流动性分为流动资产和非流动资产。其中流动资产可分为货币资金、交易性金融资产、应收票据、应收账款、预付款项、其他应收款、存货等；非流动资产可分为长期股权投资、固定资产、无形资产及其他非流动资产等。

(1) 流动资产合计 资产满足以下条件之一应归为流动资产：①预计在一个正常营业周期中变现、出售或耗用，主要包括存货、应收账款等；②主要为交易目的而持有；③预计在资产负债表日起一年内（含一年）变现；④自资产负债表日起一年内，交换其他资产或清偿负债的能力不受限制的现金或现金等价物。包括货币资金、应收票据、应收账款、存货等项目。

(2) 固定资产原价 指固定资产的成本，包括企业在购置、自行建造、安装、改建、扩建、技术改造某项固定资产时所发生的全部支出总额。

负债合计 指企业过去的交易或者事项形成的，预期会导致经济利益流出企业的现时义务。负债一般按偿还期长短分为流动负债和非流动负债。

流动负债合计 负债满足下列条件之一的应归为流动负债：①预计在一个正常营业周期中清偿；②主要为交易目的而持有；③自资产负债表日起一年内到期应予清偿；④企业无权自主地将清偿推迟至资产负债表日后一年以上。包括短期借款、应付票据、应付账款、应付职工薪酬、应交税费等项目。

所有者权益合计 指企业资产扣除负债后由所有者享有的剩余权益。公司的所有者权益又称股东权益。包括实收资本、资本公积、盈余公积、未分配利润等。

实收资本 指企业各投资者实际投入的资本（或股本）总额，包括货币、实物、无形资产等各种形式的投入。实收资本按投资主体可分为国家资本、集体资本、法人资本、个人资本、港澳台资本和外商资本。

营业收入 指企业从事销售商品、提供劳务和让渡资产使用权等生产经营活动形成的经济利益流入。

营业成本 指企业从事销售商品、提供劳务和让渡资产使用权等生产经营活动发生的实际成本。

税金及附加 指企业因从事生产经营活动按税法规定应缴纳的消费税、城市维护建设税、资源税、环境保护税、教育费附加及房产税、土地使用税、车船使用税、印花税等相关税费。

利润总额 指企业在一定会计期间的经营成果，是生产经营过程中各种收入扣除各种耗费后的盈余，反映企业在报告期内实现的亏盈总额。

应交增值税 指企业按税法规定，以销售货物、服务、无形资产或提供加工、修理修配劳务的增值额和货物进口金额为计税依据而课征的一种流转税。

应交增值税=销项税额-（进项税额-进项税额转出）-

出口抵减内销产品应纳税额−减免税款+出口退税+简易计税

平均用工人数 指报告期企业平均实际拥有的、参与本企业生产经营活动的人员数。

流动资产周转率 指在一定时期内流动资产完成的周转次数，反映流动资产的周转速度。计算公式：

$$流动资产周转率(次)=\frac{营业收入}{流动资产平均余额}$$

资产负债率 反映在企业资产总额中有多少资产是通过借债而得的，也可以用于衡量企业利用债权人提供资金进行经营活动的能力以及企业在清算时保护债权人利益的程度。计算公式：

$$资产负债率=\frac{负债总额}{资产总额}\times 100\%$$

总资产贡献率 反映企业全部资产的获利能力，是企业经营业绩和管理水平的集中体现，是评价和考核企业盈利能力的核心指标。计算公式为：

总资产贡献率=（利润总额+税金总额+利息支出）÷平均资产总额×100%

其中：税金总额为税金及附加与应交增值税之和；平均资产总额为期初期末资产总计的算术平均值。

高技术制造业 是指国民经济行业中 R&D 投入强度相对较高的制造业行业，根据国家统计局《高技术产业（制造业）分类（2017)》标准界定。

Explanatory Notes on Main Statistical Indicators

Industry refers to the material production sector which is engaged in extraction of natural resources and processing and reprocessing of mining products and agricultural products, including (1) extraction of natural resources, such as mining, salt production, logging (but not including animal hunting and fishing); (2) processing and reprocessing of agricultural products, such as grain and oil processing, food processing, embroidery, textile manufacturing and leather making; (3) processing and reprocessing of mining products, such as iron making, steel making, chemical production, petroleum processing, machine building, timber processing; and production and supply of electric power, tap water and gas; (4) repair and refurbishment of industrial products, such as the repair of machinery equipment.

Light Industry refers to the industries that produce consumer goods and hand tools. It falls into two categories, based on different raw materials: (1) Light industries basing the raw materials on agriculture, which directly or indirectly use farm products as basic raw materials, mainly include the manufacture of foods and beverages, tobacco processing, textile manufacturing, tailoring, fur and leather manufacturing, paper making, printing, etc. (2) Light industries using non-agricultural products as raw materials, which means the manufactured goods are used as raw materials, mainly include the manufacture of cultural, educational articles and sports goods, chemical medicines, synthetic fiber, daily chemical products, glass products for daily use, metal products for daily use, hand tools, medical appliances and instruments, as well as stationery and office machinery.

Heavy Industry refers to the industries that provide material and technical foundation as key means of production for various sectors of the national economy. It falls into the following three categories according to the nature of its production and the use of its products: (1) Mining, quarrying and logging industry refers to the industry that extracts natural resources, including the extraction of petroleum, coal, metal and non-metal ores and logging. (2) Raw material industry refers to the industry that provides various sectors of the national economy with basic materials, power and fuels. It includes smelting and processing of metals, coking and coke chemistry, chemical materials, cement, artificial boards, as well as power generation, petroleum refining and coal processing. (3) Processing industry refers to the industry that reprocesses the industrial raw materials. It includes machine manufacturing, which equips various sectors of the national economy, metal structure, cement products, and chemical fertilizer and pesticide industry that provide means of production for agriculture.

According to the above principle of classification, the repair services for products of heavy industry are classified as heavy industry, while the repair services for products of light industry are classified as light industry.

Gross Output Value of Industry is the total value in monetary terms for final industrial products and industrial labor service provided by industrial enterprises during the reporting period. It includes the value of all the finished industrial products (including semi-finished products), which will not be further processed in the enterprises and have been sold or have been prepared for sales upon being inspected, packed and put in storage, the revenue from processing products for others, the difference value of self-made semi-finished products and the articles in process at the end and beginning of the period. The gross industrial output value is calculated with factory method; that is, to take an industrial enterprise as a whole. It calculates the final products created by the enterprise.

Total Assets refer to resources formed by previous transactions or matters of an enterprise, owned or controlled by the enterprise, and expected to bring economic benefits to the enterprise. Classified by the liquidity, assets fall into current assets and non-current assets. Current assets include monetary capital, tradable financial assets, notes receivable, accounts receivable, prepayment, other receivables, and inventory, etc.; while non-current assets include long-term equity investment, fixed assets, intangible assets, and other non-current assets, etc.

(1) Total Current Assets Assets that meet any of the following requirements are considered current assets: ①assets expected to be cashed in, sold or consumed in a normal operating cycle, which mainly includes inventory and accounts receivable, etc.; ②assets held mainly for transaction; ③assets expected to be cashed in within one year (including one year) from the balance sheet date; ④ cash or cash equivalents with unrestricted capacity of exchanging for other assets or paying off debts within one year from the balance sheet date, which include monetary capital, notes receivable, accounts receivable, inventory, etc.

(2) Original Value Fixed Assets refers to the cost of fixed assets, including the total amount of expenditure incurred to an enterprise in its acquisition, self-construction, installation, reconstruction, expansion or technological transformation of a certain fixed asset.

Total Liabilities refer to the present obligations formed by previous transactions or matters of an enterprise, expected to lead the flow of economic benefits out of the enterprise. By the term of payment, liabilities generally include current liabilities and non-current liabilities.

Total Current liabilities Liabilities that meet any of the following requirements are considered current liabilities: ① assets expected to be paid off within one normal operating cycle; ② assets held mostly for the purpose of transaction; ③ assets expected to be due and paid off within one year from the balance sheet date; ④ liabilities for which the enterprise has no right to delay the payment to more than one year after the balance sheet date on its own. They include short-term loans, notes payable, accounts payable, wages payable, taxes and fees payable, etc.

Total Owner's Equity refers to the remaining equity of assets in an enterprise held by owners after deducting the liabilities. Owner's equity of a company is also called shareholders' equity, including paid-up capital, capital reserves, operating surplus reserves and non-distributed profits, etc.

Paid-up Capital refers to the total capital (or equity) actually contributed by investors to an enterprise, including input in various forms, such as monetary investment, physical investment and intangible assets. Categorized by investors, paid-up capital includes state capital, collective capital, legal person's capital, personal capital, capital from Hong Kong, Macao and Taiwan, and foreign capital.

Business Income refers to the inflow of economic benefits formed in an enterprise's production and operating activities such as sales of commodities, rendering of labor services and assignment of the right to use assets, etc.

Business Cost refers to the actual cost incurred by an enterprise in its production and operating activities such as sales of commodities, rendering of labor services and assignment of the right to use assets, etc.

Tax and Surtax refers to the consumption tax, urban maintenance and construction tax, resource tax, environmental protection tax, educational surcharge as well as the house property tax, land use tax, vehicle and vessel use tax, stamp tax and other relevant taxes and fees that are payable by an enterprise for engaging in production and operating activities in accordance with the tax law.

Total Profits refer to the operating results of an enterprise during certain accounting period, representing the surplus of various incomes from production and operation deducting various expenses, reflecting the total gains and losses realized by the enterprise during the reporting period.

VAT Payable refer to a kind of turnover tax that should be levied on an enterprise according to the provisions tax law, with the value added and the import amount of goods in its sales of goods, services, intangible assets or in its offering of processing, repair and replacement labor services.

VAT Payable = Output Tax – (Input Tax – Transfer-out of Input Tax) – Tax Payable Deducted by Export from Output Tax of Domestically Sold Products – Tax Concession + Export Rebate+Simple Taxation.

Average Number of Employees refers to the average number of employees actually in the enterprise and engaged in its production and operation activities during the reporting period.

Turnover of Current Assets refers to the number of times for current assets turnover within a period of time. It reflects the turnover velocity of current assets. Calculation formula is listed below:

Turnover of Current Assets (No. of times) = Business Income / Average Balance of Current Assets

Assets-liabilities Ratio reflects how many assets—out of the total assets of the enterprise, are obtained by borrowing. It can be used to evaluate the enterprise's capability of operating by using the funds provided by creditors, and to what extent the enterprise will be able to protect the creditors' interests in the case of liquidation. The following formula is used:

Assets-liabilities Ratio = Total Liabilities / Total Assets × 100%

Contribution Rate of Total Assets indicates the profitability of all assets in an enterprise, reflecting the operating performance and management of the enterprise. It serves as a core indicator evaluating the enterprise's profitability. The following formula is used:

Contribution Rate of Total Assets = (Total Profit + Total Tax + Total Interest Expenses) / Average Total Assets × 100%

Specifically, the total tax is the sum of tax and surtax, and VAT payable; average total assets are represented by the arithmetic average of total assets at the beginning and the end of the period.

High-tech Manufacturing Sector refers to the manufacturing industry with relatively high R&D input intensity in national economic sectors, and is defined in accordance with the standards in the *High Technology Industry (Manufacturing Industry) Classification 2017* of the National Bureau of Statistics.

13

建筑业
CONSTRUCTION

简要说明

一、主要内容

本章资料主要反映北京市建筑业企业基本情况和生产经营情况。主要指标包括企业个数、建筑业总产值、建筑业企业房屋建筑面积、利润、税金等。

二、统计范围

建筑业统计范围从 2004 年起，由原具有建筑业资质等级四级及四级以上的独立核算的建筑业企业调整为具有施工总承包、专业承包资质的所有法人建筑业企业。

三、调查方法

本章建筑业企业统计数据根据国家统计局制定的《建筑业统计报表制度》整理汇总。建筑业统计数据采取全面调查的方法。

四、有关统计标准的变化说明

2002-2011 年建筑业行业分类执行《国民经济行业分类》(GB/T 4754-2002)标准，2012-2017 年执行《国民经济行业分类》(GB/T 4754-2011)标准。自 2018 年起，执行《国民经济行业分类》(GB/T 4754-2017) 标准。

五、关于历史数据调整

2004 年开展了北京市第一次全国经济普查，按照国家统计局统一要求和统一方法，1993-2003 年建筑业总产值根据普查结果采用“趋势离差法”进行了修订，2004 年为北京市第一次全国经济普查数据，2008 年为北京市第二次全国经济普查数据，2013 年为北京市第三次全国经济普查数据，2018 年为北京市第四次全国经济普查数据。

Brief Introduction

I. Main Content

Statistics in this chapter mainly show the basic situation and operation of construction enterprises in Beijing. Main indicators include number of enterprises, gross output value of the construction sector, as well as floor space, profits, and tax of construction enterprises.

II. Scope of Statistics

Since 2004, data on construction sector, which previously covered construction enterprises with independent accounting at or above Level-4 in construction qualifications, have been adjusted to cover all construction enterprises with qualifications of general and specialized contracting.

III. Methods of Survey

Data on construction enterprises in this chapter were gathered based on *Statistical Statement System for Construction Sector* developed by the National Bureau of Statistics. The figures were gained through complete survey.

IV. Changes in Relevant Statistical Standards

Classification of construction sectors during 2002-2011 was based on the standards in the *Classification of National Economic Sectors* (GB/T 4754-2002). The standards in the *Classification of National Economic Sectors* (GB/T 4754-2011) were implemented from 2012 to 2017. The standards in the *Classification of National Economic Sectors* (GB/T 4754-2017) are implemented since 2018.

V. Adjustment to Historical Data

As “the first national economic census in Beijing” was conducted in 2004, in accordance with the unified requirements and methods of the National Bureau of Statistics, the data on gross output value of construction sector during 1993-2003 were adjusted by “trend deviation method” based on the census results. The data for 2004 were collected from the first national economic census in Beijing, the data for 2008 were collected from the second national economic census in Beijing, the data for 2013 were collected from the third national economic census in Beijing, and the data for 2018 were collected from the fourth national economic census in Beijing.

13-1 建筑业企业基本情况(1978-2023年)
BASIC STATISTICS ON CONSTRUCTION ENTERPRISES (1978-2023)

年份 Year	企业单位数(个) Number of Construction Enterprises (unit)	建筑业总产值(亿元) Gross Output Value of Construction (100 million yuan)	企业利润总额(亿元) Total Profits (100 million yuan)	房屋建筑面积(万平方米) Floor Space of Buildings (10000 sq.m)	
				施工面积 Floor Space under Construction	竣工面积 Floor Space Completed
1978	64	10.5	0.7		
1979	70	12.7	0.9		
1980	71	14.7	1.5		
1981	71	14.5	1.6		
1982	91	17.3	1.7		
1983	116	22.6	2.5		
1984	2765	33.4	3.2		
1985	2549	43.9	3.9		
1986	2361	51.3	3.3		
1987	2292	67.0	4.1		
1988	1659	81.6	3.9		
1989	1545	89.0	3.8		
1990	994	94.7	3.4		
1991	922	99.6	2.8	2495	1172
1992	976	122.6	3.1	2774	1227
1993	1098	215.5	6.1	3499	1428
1994	1259	336.0	9.4	4035	1437
1995	1332	426.6	7.8	4602	1593
1996	1292	494.7	8.9	5328	1967
1997	1297	556.4	10.4	5801	2117
1998	1482	678.6	12.4	6525	2225
1999	1588	750.6	13.6	6824	2632
2000	1697	812.5	16.4	7247	2809
2001	1811	1055.4	18.7	8919	3198
2002	2122	1211.3	24.7	10241	3827
2003	2419	1521.2	31.5	12160	4486
2004	2623	1659.8	40.0	14424	5258
2005	2752	1894.0	67.3	15418	4862
2006	2800	2167.9	112.8	16202	4786
2007	2845	2576.8	115.7	18225	4946
2008	3527	3066.2	84.5	19537	4803
2009	3556	4059.7	217.4	22721	5225
2010	3594	5196.0	265.2	29440	5933
2011	3667	6046.3	219.6	36507	6456
2012	3572	6588.3	293.0	41660	8414
2013	3522	7459.6	385.8	49259	8950
2014	3426	8209.8	473.2	56477	9275
2015	3369	8436.7	520.1	59777	9886
2016	3218	8841.2	725.7	61098	10703
2017	2888	9736.7	773.5	65290	9844
2018	2854	10939.8	498.5	71969	9771
2019	2877	11999.4	822.7	80557	10937
2020	2625	12905.9	1072.1	88594	9592
2021	2658	13987.7	1011.9	91155	13255
2022	2768	13726.8	924.2	83834	13815
2023	2868	14318.5	877.0	88153	13836

注：1.建筑业企业房屋建筑面积包括在本市和外省完成的施工、竣工面积。
　　2.按照国家统计局统一要求，本表2022年数据进行了修订。

Note: a) Data on floor space of Buildings of construction enterprises cover the area of buildings under construction and completed in Beijing and other provinces.
b) In accordance with the unified requirements of the National Bureau of Statistics, the data for 2022 in this table have been revised.

13-2 建筑业企业基本情况(2023年)
BASIC STATISTICS ON CONSTRUCTION ENTERPRISES (2023)

项目	Item	建筑业总产值(亿元) Gross Output Value of Construction (100 million yuan)	签订合同额(亿元) Value of Contracts Signed (100 million yuan)	竣工产值(亿元) Output Value of Completion (100 million yuan)
合计	**Total**	**14318.5**	**51209.4**	**7498.4**
按登记注册统计类别分	**By Statistical Category of Registration**			
内资企业	Domestic Invested Enterprises	14204.9	50821.6	7402.8
港澳台投资企业	Enterprises with Investment from Hong Kong, Macao and Taiwan	63.5	146.6	45.7
外商投资企业	Enterprises with Foreign Investment	50.0	241.2	49.9
按行业分	**By Sector**			
房屋建筑业	Construction of Buildings	7565.5	28362.9	4500.3
土木工程建筑业	Civil Engineering	4718.2	19584.8	1888.8
建筑安装业	Building Installation	974.4	1880.8	505.7
建筑装饰、装修和其他建筑业	Building Decoration and Other Constructions	1060.4	1380.9	603.6

注：统计范围为施工总承包、专业承包的法人建筑业企业（下表同）。
Note: Statistics covers general contracting and specialized contracting corporate construction enterprises (the same applies to the following table).

13-3　建筑业企业主要财务指标(2023年)

单位：亿元

项　　目	Item	企业单位数(个) Number of Enterprises (unit)	资产负债 Assets and Liabilities					
			资产总计 Total Assets	流动资产合计 Total Current Assets	固定资产原价 Original Value of Fixed Assets	负债合计 Total Liabilities	#流动负债合计 Total Current Liabilities	#应付账款 Accounts Payable
合　计	**Total**	**2868**	**41611.1**	**24098.5**	**1175.8**	**27929.4**	**24862.3**	**9790.8**
按登记注册统计类别分	**By Statistical Category of Registration**							
内资企业	Domestic Invested Enterprises	2821	41398.8	23904.8	1169.6	27759.5	24747.5	9734.4
港澳台投资企业	Enterprises with Investment from Hong Kong, Macao and Taiwan	24	89.7	85.9	2.8	62.6	47.2	24.9
外商投资企业	Enterprises with Foreign Investment	23	122.6	107.8	3.4	107.3	67.7	31.4
按国民经济行业分	**By Sector**							
房屋建筑业	Construction of Buildings	508	15708.6	10642.9	431.2	11619.0	10210.7	4499.9
土木工程建筑业	Civil Engineering	618	21995.5	10402.7	558.5	13624.9	12127.4	4001.7
建筑安装业	Building Installation	614	2074.7	1504.0	87.7	1225.1	1171.1	667.9
建筑装饰、装修和其他建筑业	Building Decoration and Other Constructions	1128	1832.1	1548.9	98.5	1460.5	1353.1	621.2

MAIN FINANCIAL INDICATORS OF CONSTRUCTION ENTERPRISES (2023)

(100 million yuan)

		损益 Profits and Losses						应交			
所有者权益合计 Total Owners' Equity	#实收资本 Paid-in Capital	营业收入 Business Revenue	营业成本 Business Cost	管理费用 Manage-ment Expenses	研发费用 R&D Expenses	财务费用 Financial Expenses	利润总额 Total Profits	税金合计 Total Taxes Payable	税金及附加 Tax and Surtax	所得税费用 Income Tax Expense	应交增值税(本期累计发生额) Value Added Tax Payable (Cumulative Amount Incurred in Current Period)
13676.9	**4145.4**	**18160.9**	**16602.6**	**531.5**	**442.0**	**98.1**	**877.0**	**324.6**	**44.5**	**58.7**	**221.4**
13634.6	4121.9	17992.2	16451.8	523.0	440.3	97.6	871.4	320.9	44.1	57.6	219.1
27.0	11.3	76.7	68.0	3.4	0.9	0.1	5.2	2.0	0.2	0.7	1.1
15.4	12.2	91.9	82.9	5.1	0.9	0.5	0.4	1.8	0.2	0.4	1.2
4089.6	1577.3	8473.8	7858.3	188.3	199.5	40.5	306.0	133.6	20.1	26.1	87.4
8370.6	2041.3	7094.8	6424.3	195.5	205.2	54.9	501.1	125.2	16.1	24.5	84.6
843.8	262.4	1335.5	1204.6	70.0	22.2	-2.3	60.9	31.3	3.6	5.9	21.8
372.9	264.4	1256.7	1115.4	77.8	15.1	5.0	9.0	34.5	4.6	2.3	27.6

13-3 续表 Continued

项 目	Item	流动比率(倍) Current Ratio (times)	速动比率(倍) Quick Ratio (times)	资产负债率(%) Assets-Liabilities Ratio (%)	资本金利润率(%) Capital-Profit Ratio (%)
合 计	**Total**	**0.97**	**0.94**	**67.1**	**21.2**
按登记注册统计类别分	**By Statistical Category of Registration**				
内资企业	Domestic Invested Enterprises	0.97	0.94	67.1	21.1
港澳台投资企业	Enterprises with Investment from Hong Kong, Macao and Taiwan	1.82	1.72	69.9	46.0
外商投资企业	Enterprises with Foreign Investment	1.59	1.28	87.5	3.2
按国民经济行业分	**By Sector**				
房屋建筑业	Construction of Buildings	1.04	1.01	74.0	19.4
土木工程建筑业	Civil Engineering	0.86	0.84	61.9	24.5
建筑安装业	Building Installation	1.28	1.21	59.0	23.2
建筑装饰、装修和其他建筑业	Building Decoration and Other Constructions	1.14	1.08	79.7	3.4

13-4 建筑业企业竣工率
PROJECT COMPLETION RATE OF CONSTRUCTION ENTERPRISES

单位：% (%)

项目	Item	产值竣工率 Completion Rate by Output Value	面积竣工率 Completion Rate by Floor Space
合计	**Total**	**52.4**	**15.7**
按登记注册统计类别分	**By Statistical Category of Registration**		
内资企业	Domestic Invested Enterprises	52.1	15.6
港澳台投资企业	Enterprises with Investment from Hong Kong, Macao and Taiwan	71.9	24.0
外商投资企业	Enterprises with Foreign Investment	99.7	23.2
按国民经济行业分	**By Sector**		
房屋建筑业	Construction of Buildings	59.5	15.7
土木工程建筑业	Civil Engineering	40.0	15.7
建筑安装业	Building Installation	51.9	11.5
建筑装饰、装修和其他建筑业	Building Decoration and Other Constructions	56.9	15.4

主要统计指标解释

建筑业总产值 指以货币表现的建筑业企业在一定时期内生产的建筑产品和服务的总和。它包括建筑工程产值、安装工程产值、其他产值三部分内容。

（1）**建筑工程产值** 指列入建筑工程预（概）算内的各种工程价值。

（2）**安装工程产值** 指为设备安装而发生的安装工程费用，在设备安装产值中，不得包括被安装设备本身价值。

（3）**其他产值** 建筑业总产值中除建筑工程、安装工程以外的产值，包括房屋构筑物修理产值、非标准设备制造产值、总包企业向分包企业收取的管理费，以及不能明确划分的施工活动所完成的产值。

房屋施工面积 指报告期内施工的全部房屋建筑面积，包括：本期新开工的房屋面积、上期施工跨入本期继续施工的房屋面积、上期停缓建本期复工的房屋面积、本期施工又停缓建和本期竣工的房屋面积。

房屋竣工面积 指在报告期内房屋建筑按照设计要求已全部完工，达到了住人和使用条件，经验收鉴定合格或达到竣工验收标准，可正式移交使用的各栋房屋建筑面积的总和。

签订合同额 指建筑业企业在报告期直接同建设单位签订的各种国内工程合同的总价款和以前年度同建设单位签订的各种国内工程合同的未完工程跨入本年度继续施工工程合同的总价款余额。

营业收入 指企业经营主要业务和其他业务所确认的收入总额。

营业成本 指企业从事销售商品、提供劳务和让渡资产使用权等生产经营活动发生的实际成本。

应交增值税（本期累计发生额） 指按照税法规定，以销售货物、服务、无形资产、不动产或提供加工、修理修配劳务的增值额和货物进口金额为计税依据而课征的一种流转税。

利润总额 指企业在一定会计期间的经营成果，是生产经营过程中各种收入扣除各种耗费后的盈余，反映企业在报告期内实现的亏盈总额。

Explanatory Notes on Main Statistical Indicators

Gross Output Value of Construction refers to total of construction products and services, expressed in money terms, completed by construction enterprises during a given period of time. It includes: output value of construction works, output value of installation works and other output value.

(1) Output Value of Construction Works means the value of works involved in project budgets.

(2) Output Value of Installation Works means the costs of installation works incurred for equipment installation. Output value of equipment installation does not include the value of installed equipment itself.

(3) Other Output Value means the total output value of construction other than that of construction and installations works. It includes the repair output value of houses and structures, manufacturing output value of non-standard equipment, management charges collected by general contracting enterprises from subcontracting enterprises, as well as the output value of construction activities falling in no specific categories.

House Construction Area means the building area of all houses in the reporting period, including: the area of houses newly started in current period, area of houses built in the previous period and continued in current period, area of houses suspended in the previous period and restarted in current period, area of houses built and suspended in current period, and area of houses completed in current period.

Area of Houses Completed means the total area of all houses and buildings entirely completed in line with requirements of design, meeting conditions of living and use, being checked and accepted as qualified or reaching the acceptance standards of completed projects and officially delivered for use in the reporting period.

Value of Signed Contracts means total price of all kinds of domestic engineering contracts signed directly between construction enterprises and builders in the reporting period and the balance of total price of domestic engineering contracts signed with builders in previous year and continued for implementation in the current year.

Business Income means the income recognized by an enterprise from main business such as sale of commodities and rendering of service.

Business Cost means the total cost incurred in an enterprise for the operation of main business.

VAT Payable means a kind of turnover tax levied on the basis of the appreciation amount and amount of goods imported for sale of goods, services, intangible assets, real estate or for rendering of processing, repair and replacement services in accordance with the tax laws.

Total Profits mean the operating result of an enterprise in certain accounting period. It is the surplus of all revenues deducting all costs in its production and operation, reflecting its total profit and loss realized in the reporting period.

14

第三产业
TERTIARY INDUSTRY

简要说明

一、主要内容

本章资料包括第三产业主要指标及占全市比重、规模以上第三产业主要指标、规模以上第三产业企业财务状况以及会展活动情况等。

二、统计范围

（一）年主营业务收入 2000 万元及以上的批发业企业。年主营业务收入 500 万元及以上的零售业企业。年主营业务收入 200 万元及以上的住宿业和餐饮业企业。年营业收入 2000 万元及以上的交通运输、仓储和邮政业，信息传输、软件和信息技术服务业，水利、环境和公共设施管理业，卫生行业服务业企业法人单位。年营业收入 1000 万元及以上的租赁和商务服务业，科学研究和技术服务业，教育，以及物业管理、房地产中介服务、房地产租赁经营和其他房地产业服务业企业法人单位。年营业收入 500 万元及以上的居民服务、修理和其他服务业，文化、体育和娱乐业，社会工作行业服务业企业法人单位。年收入合计 1000 万元及以上的交通运输、仓储和邮政业，信息传输、软件和信息技术服务业，租赁和商务服务业，科学研究和技术服务业，水利、环境和公共设施管理业，居民服务、修理和其他服务业，教育，文化、体育和娱乐业，以及社会工作、物业管理、房地产中介服务、房地产租赁经营和其他房地产业事业、民间非营利组织服务业法人单位。年收入合计 2000 万元及以上的卫生行业事业、民间非营利组织服务业法人单位。金融业包括：属于人民银行、金融监管总局、证监会及其下属分支机构监管范围的金融业法人单位、视同法人单位及产业活动单位；属于市金融监管局审批、备案范围的金融业法人单位；年营业收入（或收入合计）2000 万元及以上或资产总计 5 亿元及以上的非金融监管的金融业法人单位；从事互联网金融业务的其他法人单位。重点房地产开发经营法人单位。

（二）会展业统计对象涉及会展活动的举办服务单位和接待单位。具体包括限额以上住宿业法人单位和产业活动单位、全市重点场馆、大型会展活动的举办单位（名单主要由北京市公安局提供）以及为会展活动提供各类专业服务的规模以上单位和旅行社。

三、有关统计标准的变化说明

（一）关于行业划分。行业划分执行《国民经济行业分类》（GB/T 4754-2017）标准。

（二）关于三次产业划分。2003 年，根据《国民经济行业分类》（GB/T 4754-2002），国家统计局印发了《国家统计局关于印发〈三次产业划分规定〉的通知》（国统字〔2003〕14 号）。2012 年，根据国家质检总局和国家标准委颁布的《国民经济行业分类》（GB/T 4754-2011），国家统计局对 2003 年《三次产业划分规定》进行了修订。主要在以下方面作出调整：一是将门类“农、林、牧、渔业”中的“农、林、牧、渔服务业”，“采矿业”中的“开采辅助活动”，“制造业”中的“金属制品、机械和设备修理业”等三个大类一并调整到第三产业。调整后，第一产业为 4 个大类；第二产业为 2 个门类和 36 个大类；第三产业为 15 个门类和 3 个大类。二是明确第三产业即为服务业。

自 2012 年起，本章三次产业的分类执行调整后的划分规定。

Brief Introduction

I. Main Content

Statistics in this chapter include: main indicators for the tertiary industry and their percentages of Beijing's total, main indicators for tertiary industry above designated size, financial status of tertiary industry enterprises above designated size and exhibition activities.

II. Scope of Statistics

(I) Enterprises in wholesale with annual main business income of RMB 20 million and above, enterprises in retail trade with annual main business income of RMB 5 million and above. Enterprises with annual main business income of RMB 2 million and above in accommodation and restaurants. Enterprises with annual business income of RMB 20 million and above in transport, storage and post, in information transmission, software and information technology services, in management of water conservancy, environment and public facilities, and in health care services. Enterprises with annual business income of RMB 10 million and above in renting and leasing activities and business services, in scientific research and development, technical services, in education, and in realty management, real estate agency service, real estate leasing operation and other real estate services. Enterprises with annual business income of RMB 5 million and above in resident services, repair and other services, and in culture, sports and entertainment as well as in social works services. Enterprises with total annual income of RMB 10 million and above in transport, storage and post, in information transmission, software and information technology services, in renting and leasing activities and business services, in scientific research and development, technical services, in management of water conservancy, environment and public facilities, in education, in culture, sports and entertainment as well as in social works, in realty management, real estate agency service, real estate leasing operation and other real estate public institutions and non-government non-profit organizations services. Legal entities in public institutions and non-government non-profit organizations services in health care sector with total annual income of RMB 20 million and above. In finance, it includes legal entities, deemed legal entities and industrial activity units in finance that are under the supervision of The People's Bank of China, National Financial Regulatory Administration, China Securities Regulatory Commission and its subordinate branches; legal entities in finance that are subject to approval and filing by NFRA Beijing Office; legal entities in finance that are not subject to financial regulation and with annual business income (or total income) of RMB 20 million and above or with total assets of RMB 500 million and above; other legal entities engaged in Internet finance business. Key real estate development and operation legal entities.

(II) Statistical scope of MICE industry covers service companies and reception companies holding the exhibitions, in details, including: legal entities and industrial activity units in accommodation sector above designated size, key venues in Beijing, venues for exhibitions and sponsors of large exhibitions (with the list provided by Beijing Municipal Public Security Bureau), together with the above-designated-size units and travel agencies providing various professional services for exhibition activities.

III. Changes in Relevant Statistical Standards

(I) Classification of Sectors. The standards in the *Classification of National Economic Sectors (GB/T 4754-2017)* have been implemented in the classification of sectors.

(II) Classification of Three Industries. According to the *Classification of National Economic Sectors (GB/T 4754-2002),* the National Bureau of Statistics issued the *Notice of the National Bureau of Statistics on the Issuance of the 'Regulations on Three Industries Classification'* (G.T.Z. [2003] No. 14) in 2003. According to the *Classification of National Economic Sectors (GB/T 4754-2011)* promulgated by the General Administration of Quality Supervision, Inspection and Quarantine of the People's Republic of China and the Standardization Administration of the People's Republic of China, the National Bureau of Statistics revised the *Regulations on Three Industries Classification* of 2003 version. Adjustments were mainly made in the following aspects: Firstly, the "service activities for agriculture, forestry, animal husbandry and fishing" in the category of "agriculture, forestry, animal production and hunting, fishing", the "mining support service activities" in the category of "mining and quarrying", and the "repair of fabricated metal products, machinery and equipment" in the category of "manufacturing" were adjusted to the tertiary industry. After adjustment, the primary industry fell into 4 categories; the secondary industry fell into 2 classes and 36 categories; and the tertiary industry fell into 15 classes and 3 categories. Secondly, the tertiary industry was defined as the service industry.

The classification of three industries since 2012 as mentioned in this chapter has all been subject to the classification provisions after adjustment.

14-1 第三产业主要指标及占全市比重(2000-2023年)

项 目		Item		2000	2001	2002
增加值	(亿元)	Value Added	(100 million yuan)	2174.9	2653.6	3208.2
占全市比重	(%)	Proportion to the Total	(%)	66.4	68.7	70.9
劳动生产率	(元/人)	Labor Productivity	(yuan/person)	65302	78046	89352
相当于全市比例	(%)	Proportion to the Total	(%)	123.3	126.1	129.1
常住就业人口	(万人)	Resident Employed Population	(10000 persons)			
占全市比重	(%)	Proportion to the Total	(%)			
固定资产投资	(亿元)	Investment in Fixed Assets	(100 million yuan)	510.3	1367.9	1621.8
占全市比重	(%)	Proportion to the Total	(%)	39.3	89.3	89.4
实际利用外商直接投资金额	(亿美元)	Actual Use of Foreign Direct Investment	(USD 100 million)			
占全市比重	(%)	Proportion to the Total	(%)			
能源消费总量	(万吨标准煤)	Total Energy Consumption	(10000 tce)	1080.9	1196.2	1334.5
占全市比重	(%)	Proportion to the Total	(%)	26.1	28.3	30.1

14-1 续表

项 目		Item		2012	2013	2014
增加值	(亿元)	Value Added	(100 million yuan)	15020.3	16806.5	18333.9
占全市比重	(%)	Proportion to the Total	(%)	79.0	79.5	80.0
劳动生产率	(元/人)	Labor Productivity	(yuan/person)	186426	199247	212038
相当于全市比例	(%)	Proportion to the Total	(%)	108.1	106.2	105.4
常住就业人口	(万人)	Resident Employed Population	(10000 persons)	828.2	858.8	870.5
占全市比重	(%)	Proportion to the Total	(%)	74.3	75.5	76.2
固定资产投资	(亿元)	Investment in Fixed Assets	(100 million yuan)	5597.5	6101.7	6681.6
占全市比重	(%)	Proportion to the Total	(%)	86.6	86.8	88.4
实际利用外商直接投资金额	(亿美元)	Actual Use of Foreign Direct Investment	(USD 100 million)			
占全市比重	(%)	Proportion to the Total	(%)			
能源消费总量	(万吨标准煤)	Total Energy Consumption	(10000 tce)	2967.0	3109.1	3236.5
占全市比重	(%)	Proportion to the Total	(%)	45.2	46.2	47.4

MAIN INDICATORS OF THE TERTIARY INDUSTRY AND THEIR PROPORTION OF BEIJING'S TOTAL (2000-2023)

2003	2004	2005	2006	2007	2008	2009	2010	2011
3726.7	4393.4	5155.5	6227.7	7912.8	9175.1	10047.7	11608.1	13491.0
70.8	70.3	72.1	74.3	75.9	77.7	77.9	77.6	78.5
94215	90158	90091	102203	122898	134512	138876	154363	175197
123.6	112.3	109.1	109.5	109.8	109.5	106.5	104.7	109.9
							756.9	783.2
							70.9	71.9
1875.4	2112.7	2405.6	2993.8	3465.8	3434.4	4389.5	4922.3	5101.3
86.9	83.6	85.1	88.8	87.4	89.2	90.3	89.6	86.3
1391.0	1638.0	1771.7	1962.8	2198.4	2394.3	2527.3	2654.4	2818.9
29.9	31.9	35.1	36.4	38.2	41.4	42.1	41.7	44.1

14—1 Continued

2015	2016	2017	2018	2019	2020	2021	2022	2023
20218.9	22245.7	24711.7	27508.1	29663.4	30095.9	33545.2	34793.7	37129.6
81.6	82.3	82.7	83.1	83.7	83.7	81.7	83.8	84.8
228231	243228	264934	292888	315216	319642	356902	374328	402926
106.2	105.8	105.5	105.3	105.5	104.4	100.9	103.2	104.1
901.3	927.9	937.6	940.8	941.3	941.8	938.0	921.0	922.0
77.4	78.1	78.7	79.1	79.5	80.9	81.0	81.4	81.7
7202.8	7639.0	7958.4						
90.1	90.3	88.9	92.4	92.3	91.3	89.5	87.9	88.8
			144.2	130.5	132.4	140.2	168.8	129.9
			86.2	95.8	98.9	97.1	97.0	94.7
3312.6	3414.4	3519.3	3681.4	3762.5	3246.9	3534.2	3314.8	3941.9
48.7	49.4	49.6	50.6	51.1	48.0	49.8	48.1	52.1

14-2 规模以上第三产业法人单位主要经济指标(2004-2023年)
MAIN ECONOMIC INDICATORS OF TERTIARY INDUSTRY CORPORATE UNITS ABOVE DESIGNATED SIZE (2004-2023)

年 份 Year	单位数 (个) Number of Units (unit)	平均用工人数 (万人) Average Number of Employed Persons (10000 persons)	资产总计 (亿元) Total Assets (100 million yuan)	收入合计 (亿元) Total Income (100 million yuan)	应交税金合计 (亿元) Total Tax Payable (100 million yuan)	企业利润总额 (亿元) Total Profits (100 million yuan)
2004	25725	301.4	184985.5	21467.2	908.1	1544.8
2005	23661	323.3	274180.3	24444.6	1004.0	2696.1
2006	24921	340.4	336485.9	29468.7	1376.0	2967.2
2007	25651	373.5	422458.7	38361.8	2360.9	4511.2
2008	34820	443.6	579095.5	47524.3	1855.2	4577.6
2009	36177	472.1	712313.4	55390.3	2560.8	10540.8
2010	36064	487.9	798485.4	69106.8	3122.4	10236.3
2011	36102	509.9	909953.5	79246.0	4018.9	11413.1
2012	36616	545.0	1022849.7	92138.2	4652.8	14248.4
2013	36504	565.2	1093973.1	103398.8	5415.4	18410.6
2014	36361	586.6	1242344.8	110308.2	5998.0	20601.7
2015	32698	616.9	1397969.4	110154.4	6725.2	24752.9
2016	33308	635.5	1583118.8	116751.1	5928.1	23973.9
2017	34055	665.6	1716653.2	131866.5	6239.9	26742.6
2018	32747	664.4	1781671.1	134677.6		23006.8
2019	39736	680.3	1859323.9	151615.5	6211.7	28815.1
2020	39640	673.9	2094323.2	151919.5	5978.4	26152.4
2021	40322	680.6	2234249.5	178861.8	6513.9	30015.1
2022	41042	664.8	2414790.1	179653.5	5902.1	30420.9
2023	40001	645.8	2579745.5	181124.0	3294.6	32160.9

注：1.自2020年起，表中数据不包括公共管理、社会保障和社会组织，下同。
2.应交税金合计主要包括应交增值税、所得税费用、税金及附加等，下同。
3.2018年金融业相关指标数据为北京市第四次全国经济普查数据，统计范围和方法与年度调查有所差异，平均用工人数、企业利润总额、应交税金合计汇总数据不可比。
4.2021-2022年，平均用工人数中，除批发和零售业、住宿和餐饮业、金融业、房地产开发以外行业为期末用工人数。
5.表中2023年数据均为2023年1-12月定报数据，下同。

Note: a) Since 2020, the data in this table have excluded that of public management, social security and social organization, the same below.
b) Total tax payable mainly includes VAT payable, income tax expense, tax and surtax, etc, the same below.
c) The relevant indicators and data of financial intermediation for 2018 are collected from the Fourth National Economic Census in Beijing, with the statistical coverage and method being different from that of the annual survey, so the aggregate data of average number of employed persons, total profits, total tax payable are not comparable.
d) From 2021 to 2022, the average number of employed persons in the sectors other than wholesale and retail trades, hotels and catering services, financial intermediation and real estate development have referred to the period-end number of employed persons.
e)The data for 2023 in this table are all the regularly submitted data for January to December 2023, the same below.

14−3 规模以上第三产业法人单位主要经济指标(2023年)
MAIN ECONOMIC INDICATORS OF TERTIARY INDUSTRY CORPORATE UNITS ABOVE DESIGNATED SIZE (2023)

项　目	Item	单位数 (个) Number of Units (unit)	平均用工人数 (万人) Average Number of Employed Persons (10000 persons)	资产总计 (亿元) Total Assets (100 million yuan)	收入合计 (亿元) Total Income (100 million yuan)	应交税金合计 (亿元) Total Tax payable (100 million yuan)	利润总额 (亿元) Total Profits (100 million yuan)
合　计	**Total**	**40001**	**645.8**	**2579745.5**	**181124.0**	**3294.6**	**32160.9**
按行业分	**By Sector**						
批发和零售业	Wholesale and Retail Trade	10778	61.3	63396.4	77693.8	933.9	2665.9
交通运输、仓储和邮政业	Transport, Storage and Post	821	50.9	31179.8	9461.6	303.1	655.9
住宿和餐饮业	Hotels and Catering Services	3320	35.0	2835.7	1362.4	40.2	66.5
信息传输、软件和信息技术服务业	Information Transmission, Software and Information Technology	4231	112.4	82907.8	29285.8	1032.3	5811.1
金融业	Financial Intermediation	2698	58.2	2152344.3	29473.9	1543.9	14548.3
房地产业	Real Estate	3259	44.7	48782.1	5206.3	580.1	536.3
租赁和商务服务业	Leasing and Business Services	5201	102.4	142441.5	9722.2	418.7	6727.0
科学研究和技术服务业	Scientific Research and Technical Services	3745	62.9	31195.7	9005.9	-1709.9	905.8
水利、环境和公共设施管理业	Management of Water Conservancy, Environment and Public Facilities	500	10.7	6648.5	773.8	22.7	22.1
居民服务、修理和其他服务业	Service to Households, Repair and Other Services	672	11.0	398.0	278.3	11.5	13.3
教　育	Education	1877	45.6	6000.5	3164.7	23.9	44.1
卫生和社会工作	Health and Social Service	891	32.3	3360.6	3367.5	7.5	22.7
文化、体育和娱乐业	Culture, Sports and Entertainment	2008	18.4	8254.4	2327.9	86.6	141.9
按登记注册类型分	**By Status of Registration**						
内　资	Domestic Invested Units	36337	524.5	2454009.2	129631.0	1783.8	24903.1
国　有	State-owned Units	3384	95.9	300907.5	9112.8	136.6	2620.2
集　体	Collective-owned Units	278	2.6	2071.0	185.1	15.0	17.2
股份合作	Cooperative Units	267	2.0	1071.7	154.3	7.3	-3.7
联　营	Joint Ownership Units	14	0.1	30.0	5.7	0.7	0.2
有限责任公司	Limited Liability Corporations	14336	220.4	833588.5	82970.8	639.9	17800.9
股份有限公司	Share-holding Corporations Ltd.	882	65.5	1288342.5	20358.1	574.3	3830.1
私　营	Private Units	16917	132.7	26895.2	16388.5	402.4	618.4
其　他	Others	259	5.3	1102.7	455.7	7.6	19.8
港澳台商投资	Units with Investment from Hong Kong, Macao and Taiwan	1393	59.3	53510.7	24327.6	806.3	3658.4
外商投资	Units with Foreign Investment	2271	62.0	72225.5	27165.4	704.5	3599.4

14-4 按登记注册类型分规模以上第三产业企业财务状况(2023年)

单位：亿元

项 目	Item	企业单位个数(个) Number of Enterprises (unit)	资产总计 Total Assets
合 计	**Total**	**36711**	**2291464.9**
按登记注册类型分	**By Status of Registration**		
内资企业	Domestic Invested Enterprises	33049	2165730.3
国有企业	State-owned Enterprises	329	13082.5
集体企业	Collective-owned Enterprises	256	2028.0
股份合作企业	Cooperative Enterprises	267	1071.7
联营企业	Joint Ownership Enterprises	14	30.0
有限责任公司	Limited Liability Corporations	14334	833588.1
股份有限公司	Share-holding Corporations Ltd.	882	1288342.5
私营企业	Private Enterprises	16905	26891.6
其他企业	Others	62	695.9
港澳台商投资企业	Enterprises with investment from Hong Kong, Macao and Taiwan	1393	53510.7
外商投资企业	Enterprises with Foreign Investment	2269	72223.8

14-4 续表

单位：亿元

项 目	Item	营业收入 Business Revenue	营业成本 Business Cost	销售费用 Sales Expenses
合 计	**Total**	**173202.1**	**118804.9**	**8274.4**
按登记注册类型分	**By Status of Registration**			
内资企业	Domestic Invested Enterprises	121710.4	81583.1	4113.3
国有企业	State-owned Enterprises	1564.4	1302.4	46.7
集体企业	Collective-owned Enterprises	158.4	96.0	12.4
股份合作企业	Cooperative Enterprises	154.3	101.9	14.6
联营企业	Joint Ownership Enterprises	5.7	3.9	0.5
有限责任公司	Limited Liability Corporations	82969.8	60683.9	2534.7
股份有限公司	Share-holding Corporations Ltd.	20358.1	6523.9	298.2
私营企业	Private Enterprises	16381.1	12825.0	1198.9
其他企业	Others	118.4	46.0	7.4
港澳台商投资企业	Enterprises with Investment from Hong Kong, Macao and Taiwan	24327.6	15641.2	2721.7
外商投资企业	Enterprises with Foreign Investment	27164.1	21580.5	1439.4

FINANCIAL STATUS OF TERTIARY INDUSTRY ENTERPRISES ABOVE DESIGNATED SIZE BY STATUS OF REGISTRATION (2023)

(100 million yuan)

资产负债 Assets and Liabilities			
#应收账款 Accounts Receivable	固定资产原价 Original Value of Fixed Assets	负债合计 Total Liabilities	所有者权益合计 Total Owner's Equity
31382.0	**42725.0**	**1722247.0**	**562167.6**
22907.7	30679.1	1650871.6	508039.0
119.0	758.7	1229.3	11853.0
45.7	372.4	1322.2	702.3
18.6	265.1	643.2	408.3
0.7	9.2	14.0	16.0
11974.4	20613.8	545523.2	282220.6
7678.2	7064.1	1085375.9	202173.4
3052.1	1582.4	16294.7	10438.6
18.9	13.5	469.1	226.8
3847.1	8188.0	31891.3	21514.6
4627.2	3857.9	39484.1	32614.0

14-4 Continued

(100 million yuan)

损益及分配 Profits and Losses				应交税金合计 Total Tax Payable		
管理费用 Management Expenses	研发费用 R&D Expenses	财务费用 Financial Expenses	利润总额 Total Profits		#税金及附加 Tax and Surtax	#所得税费用 Income Tax Expense
8013.3	**4010.5**	**1606.1**	**32160.9**	**3280.1**	**807.5**	**1782.5**
5144.4	2314.4	1553.8	24903.1	1769.3	641.4	1124.5
164.9	1.2	-77.2	2620.2	122.8	48.4	43.7
40.2	0.2	8.7	17.2	14.8	7.0	3.1
42.1	1.1	1.9	-3.7	7.3	3.7	1.3
1.9	0.1	-0.1	0.2	0.7	0.3	0.1
3166.6	1425.8	1223.9	17800.9	639.9	413.1	1130.1
442.5	423.8	302.2	3830.1	574.3	120.8	-148.5
1271.7	462.2	97.1	618.4	402.4	47.7	91.4
14.5	0.02	-2.7	19.8	7.0	0.4	3.2
1549.4	1371.1	-5.7	3658.4	806.3	93.0	320.9
1319.5	325.0	58.0	3599.4	704.5	73.1	337.2

14-5 分行业规模以上第三产业企业财务状况(2023年)

单位：亿元

项目	Item	企业单位个数(个) Number of Enterprises (unit)	资产负债 资产总计 Total Assets
合计	**Total**	**36711**	**2291464.9**
批发和零售业	**Wholesale and Retail Trades**	**10778**	**63396.4**
批发业	Wholesale Trade	8178	58224.3
零售业	Retail Trade	2600	5172.1
交通运输、仓储和邮政业	**Transport, Storage and Post**	**821**	**31179.8**
铁路运输业	Railway Transport	17	8850.3
道路运输业	Road Transport	330	4878.6
水上运输业	Water Transport	4	6.6
航空运输业	Air Transport	34	3521.6
管道运输业	Pipeline Transport	3	10912.4
多式联运和运输代理业	Multimodal and Forwarding Agencies	288	1421.8
装卸搬运和仓储业	Loading, Unloading and Storage	108	771.2
邮政业	Post	37	817.3
住宿和餐饮业	**Hotels and Catering Services**	**3320**	**2835.7**
住宿业	Hotels	1141	2232.6
餐饮业	Catering Services	2179	603.0
信息传输、软件和信息技术服务业	**Information Transmission, Software and Information Technology**	**4184**	**82583.8**
电信、广播电视和卫星传输服务	Telecommunications, Radio and Television and Satellite Transmission Service	234	32391.2
互联网和相关服务	Internet and Related Service	757	13106.8
软件和信息技术服务业	Software and Information Technology	3193	37085.7
金融业	**Financial Intermediation**	**2680**	**1879559.4**
货币金融服务	Monetary and Financial Service	796	1534753.1
资本市场服务	Capital Market Service	1027	95818.5
保险业	Insurance	586	100679.0
其他金融业	Other Financial Activities	271	148308.8

FINANCIAL STATUS OF TERTIARY INDUSTRY ENTERPRISES ABOVE DESIGNATED SIZE BY SECTOR (2023)

(100 million yuan)

Assets and Liabilites			
#应收账款 Accounts Receivable	固定资产原价 Original Value of Fixed Assets	负债合计 Total Liabilities	所有者权益合计 Total Owners' Equity
31382.0	**42725.0**	**1722247.0**	**562167.6**
7181.9	**2280.7**	**41940.5**	**21463.2**
6589.3	1729.2	38002.7	20221.3
592.6	551.4	3937.9	1241.9
831.3	**14201.5**	**14426.4**	**16753.5**
170.7	6540.0	3019.8	5830.5
161.8	2344.8	2822.0	2056.6
0.9	10.3	4.1	2.5
127.0	2330.3	2716.0	805.6
10.8	2568.4	3830.9	7081.4
195.4	60.6	795.4	626.4
22.7	140.4	580.6	190.6
142.0	206.6	657.4	159.9
56.8	**1054.9**	**1798.3**	**1035.6**
21.1	928.7	1278.5	952.4
35.7	126.2	519.8	83.2
8597.4	**7760.4**	**41197.5**	**41386.2**
749.6	2948.4	11922.7	20468.6
1418.7	1554.3	8473.0	4633.9
6429.1	3257.7	20801.9	16283.8
8262.9	**4389.8**	**1503499.0**	**376060.3**
5496.6	3330.0	1363730.1	171023.0
426.0	283.9	37767.3	58051.2
1493.5	551.3	65542.9	35136.1
846.9	224.7	36458.6	111850.1

14-5 续表 1

单位：亿元

项目	Item	损益及分配 营业收入 Business Revenue	营业成本 Business Cost	销售费用 Sales Expenses
合计	**Total**	**173202.1**	**118804.9**	**8274.4**
批发和零售业	**Wholesale and Retail Trades**	**77693.8**	**72222.6**	**2668.3**
批发业	Wholesale Trade	67908.0	63600.1	1843.6
零售业	Retail Trade	9785.8	8622.5	824.7
交通运输、仓储和邮政业	**Transport, Storage and Post**	**9461.6**	**8466.9**	**136.6**
铁路运输业	Railway Transport	1972.6	1588.7	0.5
道路运输业	Road Transport	2414.1	2400.7	32.2
水上运输业	Water Transport	6.5	5.3	0.1
航空运输业	Air Transport	1356.0	1302.8	49.8
管道运输业	Pipeline Transport	640.5	369.5	1.1
多式联运和运输代理业	Multimodal and Forwarding Agencies	1556.7	1437.6	26.9
装卸搬运和仓储业	Loading, Unloading and Storage	181.3	154.7	3.0
邮政业	Post	1333.8	1207.5	23.0
住宿和餐饮业	**Hotels and Catering Services**	**1362.4**	**625.0**	**440.8**
住宿业	Hotels	403.3	155.5	94.8
餐饮业	Catering Services	959.1	469.4	345.9
信息传输、软件和信息技术服务业	**Information Transmission, Software and Information Technology**	**29205.5**	**17170.4**	**3595.5**
电信、广播电视和卫星传输服务	Telecommunications, Radio and Television and Satellite Transmission Service	1608.8	1165.5	126.9
互联网和相关服务	Internet and Related Service	8410.7	5647.3	1131.6
软件和信息技术服务业	Software and Information Technology	19186.0	10357.6	2337.0
金融业	**Financial Intermediation**	**29380.9**	**820.7**	**147.0**
货币金融服务	Monetary Financial Service	9724.6	123.1	8.5
资本市场服务	Capital Market Service	4341.1	75.3	24.1
保险业	Insurance	9030.0	241.4	36.7
其他金融业	Other Financial Activities	6285.3	380.9	77.7

14-5 Continued 1

(100 million yuan)

Profits and Losses and Distribution				应交税金合计 Total Tax Payable	#税金及附加 Tax and Surtax	#所得税费用 Income Tax Expense
管理费用 Management Expenses	研发费用 R&D Expenses	财务费用 Financial Expenses	利润总额 Total Profits			
8013.3	**4010.5**	**1606.1**	**32160.9**	**3280.1**	**807.5**	**1782.5**
1623.8	**154.6**	**188.2**	**2665.9**	**933.9**	**159.9**	**299.4**
1391.7	142.8	160.7	2585.9	777.6	127.2	265.9
232.1	11.9	27.5	80.0	156.3	32.7	33.5
414.4	**30.2**	**164.5**	**655.9**	**303.1**	**24.2**	**170.3**
48.3	7.1	49.8	281.5	103.9	5.3	60.6
151.9	9.8	17.6	37.0	50.9	5.9	8.2
0.5		0.03	0.2	0.2	0.01	0.2
41.9	1.5	65.6	-55.5	12.4	5.1	2.2
24.9	7.3	26.3	267.9	90.7	3.4	69.5
66.8	3.3	1.6	79.0	16.8	1.0	11.2
13.1	0.7	0.03	11.6	5.9	1.3	2.8
67.0	0.6	3.5	34.2	22.2	2.1	15.6
220.9	**0.1**	**23.5**	**66.5**	**40.2**	**12.9**	**10.0**
111.8	0.03	17.7	33.2	25.0	11.7	3.6
109.1	0.1	5.8	33.2	15.2	1.2	6.3
2213.5	**2952.1**	**-78.5**	**5811.1**	**1032.1**	**106.9**	**356.5**
171.7	141.6	-17.9	2236.7	46.4	8.5	18.9
440.7	693.6	-5.3	596.0	167.9	27.4	51.4
1601.2	2116.8	-55.2	2978.4	817.9	71.1	286.2
389.4	**160.3**	**36.0**	**14548.3**	**1543.9**	**137.9**	**495.2**
35.3	72.1	2.4	3080.4	981.0	92.7	283.4
182.9	12.3	15.0	3709.6	402.5	14.3	263.7
73.1	9.5	-1.5	1948.1	5.5	18.6	-116.2
98.0	66.4	20.0	5810.2	154.9	12.3	64.3

14-5 续表 2

单位：亿元

项 目	Item	企业单位个数(个) Number of Enterprises (unit)	资产负债 资产总计 Total Assets
房地产业	**Real Estate**	**3254**	**48735.1**
租赁和商务服务业	**Leasing and Business Services**	**4991**	**141544.8**
租赁业	Leasing	195	1260.2
商务服务业	Business Services	4796	140284.6
科学研究和技术服务业	**Scientific Research and Technical Services**	**3280**	**27292.5**
研究和试验发展	Research and Experimental Development	364	5774.1
专业技术服务业	Professional Technical Services	1772	16245.4
科技推广和应用服务业	Science and Technology Popularization and Application Services	1144	5272.9
水利、环境和公共设施管理业	**Management of Water Conservancy, Environment and Public Facilities**	**329**	**5347.9**
水利管理业	Management of Water Conservancy	10	1772.5
生态保护和环境治理业	Ecological Protection and Environmental Treatment	92	752.3
公共设施管理业	Management of Public Facilities	218	2015.3
土地管理业	Management of Land	9	807.8
居民服务、修理和其他服务业	**Service to Households, Repair and Other Services**	**655**	**368.6**
居民服务业	Service to Households	170	187.2
机动车、电子产品和日用产品修理业	Repair of Motor Vehicles, Electronics and Household Products	195	95.4
其他服务业	Other Services	290	86.0
教 育	**Education**	**337**	**1033.3**
卫生和社会工作	**Health and Social Service**	**333**	**652.7**
卫 生	Health	305	558.4
社会工作	Social Service	28	94.4
文化、体育和娱乐业	**Culture, Sports and Entertainment**	**1749**	**6934.9**
新闻和出版业	Journalism and Publishing Activities	443	2151.5
广播、电视、电影和影视录音制作业	Radio, Television, Motion Pictures and Audio-visual Programme Production Services	620	3192.5
文化艺术业	Culture and Art Activities	168	254.5
体 育	Sports Activities	146	428.0
娱乐业	Entertainment	372	908.5

14-5 Continued 2

(100 million yuan)

Assets and Liabilites			
#应收账款 Accounts Receivable	固定资产原价 Original Value of Fixed Assets	负债合计 Total Liabilities	所有者权益合计 Total Owners' Equity
455.1	**3283.6**	**33084.0**	**8595.4**
2552.8	**3950.2**	**64673.2**	**76871.5**
114.5	922.4	699.7	560.5
2438.3	3027.8	63973.6	76311.0
2636.8	**2128.8**	**14234.5**	**13057.9**
253.3	561.4	2956.9	2817.2
1795.4	1044.6	8758.1	7487.3
588.1	522.8	2519.5	2753.4
362.1	**2046.3**	**2754.2**	**2593.7**
100.1	1417.6	361.0	1411.5
135.3	68.8	408.0	344.3
119.9	545.6	1341.2	674.1
6.8	14.3	644.0	163.8
43.1	**55.5**	**295.6**	**73.0**
9.5	27.6	168.4	18.8
13.4	16.1	75.8	19.6
20.1	11.8	51.4	34.5
42.4	**82.0**	**1040.9**	**-7.6**
65.9	**158.1**	**583.5**	**69.2**
59.5	143.1	510.3	48.0
6.4	15.0	73.2	21.2
293.5	**1333.1**	**2719.3**	**4215.6**
98.4	265.9	600.9	1550.6
121.8	413.1	845.6	2346.9
13.3	54.6	126.3	128.1
22.0	146.2	374.4	53.6
38.0	453.3	772.2	136.3

14-5 续表 3

单位：亿元

项目	Item	损益及分配 营业收入 Business Revenue	 营业成本 Business Cost
房地产业	**Real Estate**	**5200.7**	**3699.0**
租赁和商务服务业	**Leasing and Business Services**	**9505.1**	**7412.7**
租赁业	Leasing	328.4	242.7
商务服务业	Business Services	9176.7	7169.9
科学研究和技术服务业	**Scientific Research and Technical Services**	**7512.1**	**5692.8**
研究和试验发展	Research and Experimental Development	1235.9	794.7
专业技术服务业	Professional Technical Services	4843.5	3888.5
科技推广和应用服务业	Science and Technology Popularization and Application Services	1432.7	1009.6
水利、环境和公共设施管理业	**Management of Water Conservancy, Environment and Public Facilities**	**581.7**	**469.6**
水利管理业	Management of Water Conservancy	87.4	76.7
生态保护和环境治理业	Ecological Protection and Environmental Treatment	153.1	116.2
公共设施管理业	Management of Public Facilities	298.5	243.7
土地管理业	Management of Land	42.6	33.0
居民服务、修理和其他服务业	**Service to Households, Repair and Other Services**	**259.7**	**170.9**
居民服务业	Service to Households	87.7	46.8
机动车、电子产品和日用产品修理业	Repair of Motor Vehicles, Electronics and Household Products	69.9	50.8
其他服务业	Other Services	102.1	73.3
教　育	**Education**	**578.1**	**277.7**
卫生和社会工作	**Health and Social Service**	**507.0**	**360.8**
卫　生	Health	495.2	352.2
社会工作	Social Service	11.9	8.6
文化、体育和娱乐业	**Culture, Sports and Entertainment**	**1953.5**	**1415.9**
新闻和出版业	Journalism and Publishing Activities	741.2	444.6
广播、电视、电影和影视录音制作业	Radio, Television, Motion Picture and Audio-visual Programme Production Services	709.6	602.8
文化艺术业	Culture and Art Activities	68.6	51.8
体　育	Sports Activities	111.4	86.7
娱乐业	Entertainment	322.7	229.9

14-5 Continued 3

(100 million yuan)

Profits and Losses					应交税金合计 Total Tax Payable	#税金及附加 Tax and Surtax	#所得税费用 Income Tax Expense
销售费用 Sales Expenses	管理费用 Manage-ment Expenses	研发费用 R&D Expenses	财务费用 Financial Expenses	利润总额 Total Profits			
184.1	**534.9**	**4.1**	**345.2**	**536.3**	**580.0**	**237.1**	**160.4**
469.8	**1299.1**	**190.9**	**892.6**	**6727.0**	**416.8**	**70.2**	**155.6**
12.3	21.3	7.3	8.9	36.7	18.0	1.7	9.2
457.4	1277.8	183.7	883.8	6690.3	398.7	68.5	146.4
264.2	**721.3**	**450.3**	**27.3**	**905.8**	**-1714.1**	**35.9**	**92.7**
67.1	138.0	180.8	-11.1	300.1	54.5	7.6	21.4
113.8	408.0	163.0	23.7	484.8	172.7	21.6	56.8
83.2	175.3	106.6	14.7	120.9	-1941.4	6.7	14.5
15.2	**64.3**	**11.3**	**18.1**	**22.1**	**22.0**	**3.4**	**5.5**
0.2	7.5	0.5	7.0	-8.9	3.3	0.4	0.2
5.1	15.9	7.2	2.7	8.8	5.4	0.6	1.4
9.6	35.8	3.5	2.8	18.1	11.8	2.2	3.1
0.2	5.1		5.6	4.1	1.4	0.1	0.8
32.1	**43.4**	**1.1**	**1.0**	**13.3**	**11.4**	**1.0**	**3.3**
13.2	14.9	0.5	0.5	12.8	4.6	0.4	2.6
8.3	10.3	0.4	0.3	-0.5	2.6	0.3	0.3
10.6	18.2	0.2	0.2	1.0	4.3	0.4	0.4
120.4	**93.7**	**38.0**	**-1.3**	**44.1**	**19.2**	**1.8**	**5.2**
53.7	**74.0**	**5.3**	**3.5**	**22.7**	**6.6**	**0.4**	**4.8**
53.0	71.2	5.3	3.0	23.1	6.2	0.2	4.6
0.8	2.8	0.01	0.5	-0.5	0.5	0.1	0.2
146.7	**320.6**	**12.1**	**-14.0**	**141.9**	**85.0**	**15.8**	**23.7**
78.2	133.5	2.1	-15.7	152.6	40.6	5.9	10.6
25.8	103.7	6.0	-19.7	6.8	21.7	5.3	5.7
4.4	12.8	0.7	-0.3	4.9	3.6	1.0	0.7
13.0	21.4	0.4	2.3	-13.1	3.8	1.5	0.7
25.3	49.1	2.9	19.5	-9.3	15.3	2.2	6.1

14-6 会议、展览及相关服务活动情况(2023年)
STATISTICS FOR MEETINGS, EXHIBITIONS AND RELATED ACTIVITIES (2023)

项　　目		Item		2023	2023年为2022年% 2023 as % of 2022
会议情况		**Meetings**			
接待会议个数	(万个)	Number of Meetings Held in Beijing	(10000 units)	21.0	235.0
接待会议人数	(万人次)	Number of Meeting Participants	(10000 person-times)	1349.9	339.3
展览情况		**Exhibitions**			
接待展览个数	(个)	Number of Exhibitions Held in Beijing	(unit)	259	719.4
接待展览观众人数	(万人次)	Number of Exhibition Visitors	(10000 person-times)	536.2	870.0
收入情况		**Revenues**			
会展收入	(亿元)	Total Revenues from MICE Industry	(100 million yuan)	291.7	195.4
#会议收入	(亿元)	Revenues from Meetings	(100 million yuan)	143.9	187.3
展览收入	(亿元)	Revenues from Exhibitions	(100 million yuan)	145.1	205.0

注：1.收入情况包括规模以上会议、展览及相关服务业和旅行社及相关服务业法人单位以及其他会展举办单位，重点会展场馆，限额以上住宿业单位。
2.会议情况和展览情况包括重点会展场馆、限额以上住宿业单位。
3.表中发展速度按可比口径计算。

Note: a) Data on revenues cover the legal entities above designated size in meetings, exhibitions and related service industries and in travel agency and related service industries as well as other organizers of MICE, key MICE venues, and units above designed size in accommodation industry.
b) Data on meetings and exhibitions cover the key MICE venues and the units above designated size in accommodation industry.
c) Indicators of development rate in the table are calculated in terms of comparable caliber.

主要统计指标解释

接待会议个数 指报告期内，接待的各种类型会议的个数。

接待展览个数 指报告期内，接待的各种类型展览的个数。

Explanatory Notes on Main Statistical Indicators

Number of Meeting Held in Beijing refers to the number of various types of conference held in Beijing in the reporting period.

Number of Exhibitions Held in Beijing refers to the number of various types of exhibitions held in Beijing in the reporting period.

15

交通运输邮电业

TRANSPORT, POST AND TELECOMMUNICATION SERVICES

简要说明

一、主要内容

本章资料主要反映北京市交通运输业和邮政电信业发展的基本情况。包括客货运输、机动车保有量、邮政电信业务等数据。

二、统计调查范围和口径说明

铁路数据统计范围为国家铁路运营情况，不含地方铁路、合资铁路和军用铁路及由厂矿企事业单位自建的铁路专用线和专用铁道；公路里程口径为年末通车里程数，不含在建和未正式投入使用的公路里程；公路运输统计范围包括在北京市注册从事公路货运的全部企事业单位和私人(包括个体联户)的车辆；管道运输资料包括输送原油、成品油、天然气以及其他气体的管线长度、输送能力及完成的运输量；民航运输资料统计范围为各航空公司从事国内运输、港澳台运输、国际运输的定期航班航线条数及里程、运输量，不包括在京运输飞行的外省市及外国航空公司。

邮政电信资料包括邮政和基础电信运营企业为社会公众提供的各类邮政和电信服务，不含专用网业务资料；民用汽车包括在公安交通管理部门已注册登记领有民用车辆牌照的全部汽车。

Brief Introduction

I. Main Content

Statistics in this chapter mainly show the basic situation of development of transport, post and telecommunication in Beijing, including passenger and freight traffic, number of motor vehicles possessed, and business volume of post and telecommunication services, and so on.

II. Scope of Statistics and Survey and Explanations on Statistical Standards

Scope of statistics for data on railways covers the operation of national railways, excluding local railways, railways built by joint ventures, military railways, and dedicated lines and railways built by factories, mines, enterprises and public institutions. Data on the length of highways refer to the length open to traffic at the year end, excluding those under construction and not put into use. Highway transport statistics cover the vehicles of all enterprises and public institutions as well as individuals (including self-employed) registered in Beijing for highway freight transport. Data on pipeline transport include the length, capacity and completed traffic of pipelines for transport of crude oil, refined oil, natural gas, and other gases. Scope of statistics for data on civil aviation covers the number, mileage, and traffic volume of regular flight lines for domestic transport, transport from and to Hong Kong, Macao and Taiwan, and international transport of different airline companies, excluding non-local and foreign airlines which operate flights in Beijing.

Data on post and telecommunication include those on postal and telecom services offered by post and basic telecom operators to the public, excluding data on services of dedicated networks. Data on civil automobiles include all vehicles registered with public security traffic administration and granted with the license plates for civil automobiles.

15-1 交通运输邮电业基本情况(1978-2023年)
BASIC STATISTICS ON TRANSPORT, POSTAL AND TELECOMMUNICATION SERVICES (1978-2023)

年 份 Year	铁路里程(公里) Length of Railways (km)	公路里程(公里) Length of Highways (km)	客运量(万人) Passenger Traffic (10000 persons)	铁 路 Railways	公 路 Highways	民 航 Civil Aviation	货运量(万吨) Freight Traffic (10000 tons)	铁 路 Railways	公 路 Highways	民 航 Civil Aviation	管 道 Petroleum and Gas Pipelines
1978	699	6562	4431	2264	2120	47	7394	3370	4023	1	
1979	700	7278	4777	2504	2220	53	7764	3485	4277	2	
1980	707	7487	5285	2762	2465	58	7571	3356	4213	2	
1981	858	7566	5877	2982	2824	71	8546	3046	5498	2	
1982	858	7683	6215	3205	2931	79	9097	3065	5812	2	218
1983	860	8058	6662	3546	3038	78	9403	3152	6016	3	232
1984	864	8271	7273	3877	3287	109	9671	3133	6301	3	234
1985	876	8482	7203	4078	2978	147	8739	3029	5436	4	270
1986	876	8995	7337	4106	3059	172	22121	3030	18794	6	291
1987	876	9103	7763	4418	3117	228	23068	3125	19734	8	201
1988	876	9124	8491	4782	3460	249	24749	3168	21308	9	264
1989	876	9371	7434	4214	3034	186	25184	3144	21767	8	265
1990	876	9648	7480	3770	3490	220	26648	3051	23326	10	262
1991	876	10259	7704	4036	3378	289	26804	2983	23739	11	71
1992	875	10827	8158	4196	3593	369	27707	2912	24700	14	80
1993	875	11260	7607	4374	2781	452	29865	3048	26730	17	70
1994	875	11532	8537	3992	4008	537	30825	3006	27700	19	99
1995	875	11811	8913	4017	4250	646	32184	2974	29087	17	106
1996	922	12084	8801	3650	4395	756	32907	2851	29960	18	78
1997	924	12306	9263	3613	4902	748	32351	2883	29360	20	87
1998	924	12498	11228	3762	6704	762	30127	2563	27490	22	52
1999	997	12825	14866	4201	9878	788	28275	2583	25635	30	27
2000	997	13600	18396	4458	13009	929	30717	2612	28010	35	60
2001	987	13891	22469	4750	16630	1090	30607	2505	28007	38	57
2002	987	14359	28384	5032	22103	1249	30961	2348	28375	44	194
2003	964	14453	30520	4352	24940	1228	30925	2265	28361	45	254
2004	964	14630	49750	5437	41463	2850	31700	1959	29256	73	412
2005	966	14696	60841	5779	51925	3137	32509	1976	30050	77	406
2006	962	20503	12276	6269	2482	3525	33547	1956	30953	89	549
2007	962	20754	20040	6915	9275	3850	20770	1925	17872	98	875
2008	956	20340	128525	7644	117118	3763	21885	1733	18689	93	1369
2009	956	20755	133872	8161	121373	4339	22017	1635	18753	98	1531
2010	956	21114	140663	8903	126130	5630	23712	1572	20184	130	1827
2011	1067	21347	145773	9755	129918	6100	26849	1380	23276	132	2061
2012	1115	21492	149037	10315	132333	6389	28650	1232	24925	134	2359
2013	1116	21673	71056	11588	52481	6988	28294	1078	24651	136	2429
2014	1124	21849	71715	12609	52354	6752	29518	1132	25416	149	2821
2015	1124	21885	69924	12821	49931	7172	23236	1004	19044	158	3030
2016	1103	22026	69292	13380	48040	7872	24099	725	19972	163	3239
2017	1103	22226	67420	13873	44940	8607	23879	704	19374	175	3627
2018	1103	22256	67571	14273	44175	9123	25244	569	20278	177	4221
2019	1205	22366	72148	14755	48151	9241	27338	449	22325	166	4398
2020	1242	22264	36270	6383	24548	5339	26346	360	21789	147	4049
2021	1340	22320	42308	8550	28059	5699	28127	311	23075	162	4580
2022	1354	22363	28010	3907	21105	2998	24030	346	18549	128	5008
2023	1372	22433	49771	15055	25720	8995	25730	278	19399	135	5917

注：1.铁路数据为北京市市辖范围，2005年以前来源于北京铁路分局，自2005年起来源于北京铁路局(现中国铁路北京局集团有限公司)，公路里程数据来源于北京市交通委员会。

2.自2006年起，公路里程包括村道数据。

3.2006—2007年公路客运量为持有道路运输经营许可证的客运车辆发生的旅客运输量；自2008年起，调整为旅游客运、省际客运企业、郊区客运和市郊公交的运输量。2013年公路客运量、公路旅客周转量范围调整为省际客运、旅游客运和郊区客运，市郊公交不再纳入客运量统计。

4.自2007年起，公路货物运输为营业性运量。2019年开展了道路货物运输量专项调查，公路货运量和公路货物周转量为当年调查数据，下同。

5.民航统计范围为北京地区的民航运输法人单位，不包括在京运输飞行的外省市及外国航空公司。

Note: a) Railway figures are statistics within Beijing's jurisdiction. Figures for years before 2005 are from Beijing Railway Branch, those in and after 2005 are from Beijing Railway Administration (currently known as China Railway Beijing Group Co., Ltd.). Highway mileage figures are from Beijing Municipal Commission of Transport.

b) Since 2006, figures on highway mileage have included figures of rural roads.

c) In 2006 and 2007, the passenger traffic of highways referred to passenger traffic of passenger vehicles with road transport operation permit; since 2008, passenger traffic of highways has been adjusted to refer to the transportation volume of tourist passenger transport, inter-provincial passenger transport enterprises, suburban passenger transport and suburban public transport. In 2013, the statistical scope of passenger traffic of highways and total passenger of highways was adjusted to inter-provincial, tourist and suburban passenger transport, and suburban public transport was no longer included in the statistics on passenger traffic.

d) Since 2007, freight transport of highways has referred to freight for operational purpose. Specific survey of road freight transport volume was carried out in 2019; data on freight transport volume of highways and total freight of highways in the table refer to the survey data of the year, the same below.

e) Civil aviation covers corporate units of civil aviation registered in Beijing, excluding airlines of other provinces and other countries with transport and flight in Beijing.

15-1 续表 1 Continued 1

年份 Year	旅客周转量(万人公里) Total Passenger (10000 passenger-km)	铁路 Railways	公路 Highways	民航 Civil Aviation	货物周转量(万吨公里) Total Freight (10000 ton-km)	铁路 Railways	公路 Highways	民航 Civil Aviation	管道 Petroleum and Gas Pipelines
1978			59367				92247		
1979			64033				97616		
1980			73692				93899		
1981			81879				93254		
1982	755815	641550	90092	24173	3451037	3329450	106767	13530	1290
1983	853655	723200	103742	26713	3794223	3666600	110118	16099	1406
1984	968481	821431	113871	33179	4309798	4171789	115740	20896	1373
1985	1089919	936300	109184	44435	4719663	4576400	114156	27437	1670
1986	1133620	496288	119065	518267	2569579	2133836	405645	28281	1817
1987	1281763	534720	133735	613308	2792589	2282106	471393	37966	1124
1988	1503508	588947	141625	772936	2887270	2344684	498391	42612	1583
1989	1216981	521263	122435	573283	2765660	2179878	546022	38194	1566
1990	1198022	467332	132350	598339	2688246	2067402	574635	44662	1547
1991	1383465	506431	139041	737993	2799731	2153176	591187	54929	439
1992	1666810	531574	161735	973501	2938746	2230406	642200	65614	527
1993	1656130	551392	127461	977277	3143512	2301941	767790	73216	565
1994	1906718	547488	180030	1179200	3107722	2303265	725740	78142	575
1995	2076879	508995	234540	1333344	3231034	2393403	762027	74940	663
1996	2219196	459514	250488	1509194	3176234	2311011	784888	79983	352
1997	2272177	477538	261204	1533435	3129097	2263274	769190	96202	431
1998	2419787	505554	304592	1609641	2846652	1952602	783237	110470	343
1999	2701471	579759	400597	1721115	2838857	1929269	754264	155171	153
2000	3139918	627222	527645	1985051	2996414	2001875	826438	167691	410
2001	3462571	677146	529776	2255649	3159848	2167201	826437	165832	378
2002	3961623	642676	603510	2715437	3405498	2213728	835873	195792	160105
2003	3933077	619631	693100	2620346	3620777	2409620	789952	208058	213147
2004	7580057	738956	1582441	5258660	4022791	2571459	822992	270182	358158
2005	8380778	776028	1873754	5730996	4577370	3108137	854944	281672	332617
2006	8254536	890691	791947	6571898	4231243	2625719	885991	335693	383840
2007	9603464	908438	1474249	7220776	4490390	2684862	792883	376074	636572
2008	10419977	902281	2409604	7108091	4542168	2535249	840878	356744	809297
2009	11464758	935596	2677144	7852018	4412317	2293902	878887	355257	884271
2010	13995404	995507	2906492	10093405	5136580	2574567	1015944	482467	1063602
2011	15286501	1086609	3036655	11163237	6169272	3113203	1323259	474856	1257955
2012	15957877	1163833	3047757	11746287	6383052	3076143	1397736	489845	1419328
2013	14987719	1179555	1360831	12447333	6809063	3231824	1561929	491861	1523448
2014	16027249	1356313	1382967	13287969	6728238	2843623	1651938	553661	1679016
2015	17476775	1493106	1301210	14682459	6236947	2247538	1563562	637018	1788829
2016	18893132	1508200	1176740	16208192	6713288	2290438	1613192	671413	2138246
2017	20558450	1537625	993965	18026860	7000530	2464289	1592419	743891	2199932
2018	22199810	1545658	993699	19660453	7806542	2668681	1674068	784179	2679614
2019	22918448	1589007	1047823	20281618	9007714	2575184	2756801	727190	2948539
2020	10149918	706947	436697	9006274	8427606	2443443	2656831	660195	2667136
2021	10471705	954820	541106	8975779	8803872	2488089	2744131	756980	2814673
2022	5733035	435780	450311	4846944	8812490	2745242	2254273	668125	3144850
2023	18861523	1631829	734912	16494782	9103902	2555457	2569263	644742	3334440

15-1 续表 2 Continued 2

年份 Year	机动车保有量(万辆) Possession of Motor Vehicles (10000 units)	#民用汽车 Civil Motor Vehicles	#私人汽车 Private Vehicles	邮政行业业务总量(亿标准量) Business Volume of Post Services (volume in 100 million)	电信业务总量(亿元) Business Volume of Telecommunication Services (100 million yuan)
1978		6.1			
1979		7.0			
1980		8.1			
1981		8.9			
1982		9.3			
1983		9.8			
1984		12.1			
1985		16.0			
1986		18.6			
1987		19.3	0.7		
1988		22.2	1.3		
1989		24.8	2.4		
1990		27.1	2.8		
1991		29.7	3.5	3.4	12.3
1992		34.1	4.9	4.2	17.3
1993		41.6	6.7	5.4	25.8
1994		48.1	8.5	5.9	35.9
1995		58.9	12.8	7.0	49.2
1996		62.2	17.4	8.1	64.8
1997		78.4	29.8	9.0	84.0
1998		89.8	40.7	11.0	118.1
1999		95.1	44.7	13.2	152.7
2000	157.8	104.1	49.4	15.2	199.5
2001	169.9	114.5	62.4	30.1	188.2
2002	189.9	133.9	81.1	29.8	224.3
2003	212.4	163.1	107.1	31.3	272.7
2004	229.6	187.1	129.8	31.1	312.7
2005	258.3	214.6	154.0	33.5	379.4
2006	287.6	244.1	181.0	35.1	469.5
2007	312.8	277.8	212.1	70.1	634.9
2008	350.4	318.1	248.3	87.8	753.8
2009	401.9	372.1	300.3	88.9	866.7
2010	480.9	452.9	374.4	107.3	1066.8
2011	498.3	473.2	389.7	130.2	436.3
2012	520.0	495.7	407.5	142.3	488.0
2013	543.7	518.9	426.5	163.0	594.0
2014	559.1	532.4	437.2	203.2	687.4
2015	561.9	535.0	440.3	258.5	923.4
2016	571.7	548.4	452.8	386.0	1396.4
2017	590.9	563.8	467.2	419.3	875.5
2018	608.4	574.6	479.0	397.9	1771.0
2019	636.5	590.8	497.4	460.1	2682.0
2020	657.0	600.3	507.9	480.2	3247.6
2021	685.0	614.3	521.1	283.0	513.0
2022	712.8	625.6	532.6	281.4	558.6
2023	758.9	637.6	543.1	324.3	633.3

注：1.邮政行业业务总量与电信业务总量2000年及以前按1990年不变价格计算，2001—2010年按2000年不变价格计算，2011—2016年按2010年不变价格计算。2017—2020年，邮政行业业务总量按2010年不变价格计算，电信业务总量按2015年不变价格计算。自2021年起，邮政行业业务总量按2020年不变价格计算，电信业务总量按上年不变价格计算。

2.2006年及以前邮政行业业务总量统计范围为中国邮政集团公司北京分公司和中国邮政快递物流股份有限公司北京分公司。自2007年起，邮政行业业务总量统计范围为邮政企业、取得快递业务经营许可的企业及其备案分支机构，下同。

Note: a)The business volume of post and telecommunication services in and before 2000 was calculated at 1990's constant prices; that of 2001-2010 was calculated at 2000's constant prices; that of 2011-2016 was calculated at 2010's constant prices; since 2017 until 2020, the business volume of post services was calculated at 2010's constant prices, and that of telecommunication services was calculated at 2015's constant prices. Since 2021, The business volume of post service was calculated at 2020's constant prices, and that of telecommunication services was calculated at constant prices of last year.

b) Among the "business volume of post and telecommunication services" in this table, the statistical range of the business volume of post services in and before 2006 was China Post Group Beijing Branch and China Postal Express & Logistics Co., Ltd. Beijing Branch.Since 2007, the statistical range of the business volume of post services covered the post enterprises, the enterprises permitted to conduct express delivery businesses and their filed branches, the same below.

15-1 续表 3 Continued 3

年 份 Year	年末固定电话用户数(万户) Year-end Number of Fixed Telephone Subscribers (10000 subscribers)	年末移动电话用户数(万户) Year-end Number of Mobile Phone Subscribers (10000 subscribers)	固定电话主线普及率(线/百人) Popularization Rate of Main Line of Fixed Line Telephones (line/100 persons)	移动电话普及率(户/百人) Popularization Rate of Mobile Phones (subscriber/100 persons)	固定互联网宽带接入用户数(万户) Subscribers of Broadband Subscribers of Internet (10000 subscribers)
1978	7.3		0.8		
1979	7.8		0.9		
1980	8.4		0.9		
1981	9.2		1.0		
1982	9.8		1.1		
1983	10.9		1.2		
1984	12.1		1.3		
1985	13.6		1.4		
1986	16.5		1.6		
1987	19.5		1.9		
1988	23.8		2.2		
1989	27.8		2.6		
1990	33.3	0.3	3.1	0.03	
1991	39.5	0.7	3.6	0.1	
1992	48.0	1.2	4.4	0.1	
1993	66.5	3.2	6.0	0.3	
1994	100.4	7.7	8.9	0.7	
1995	150.5	16.9	12.0	1.4	
1996	195.7	31.0	15.5	2.5	
1997	251.2	62.0	20.3	5.0	
1998	313.3	104.2	25.1	8.4	
1999	376.3	186.2	29.9	14.8	
2000	451.2	347.2	33.1	25.5	
2001	525.7	629.4	38.0	45.4	
2002	585.5	919.5	41.1	64.6	
2003	682.7	1109.0	46.9	76.1	
2004	847.8	1340.9	56.8	89.8	
2005	943.5	1459.8	61.3	94.9	228.9
2006	905.2	1571.1	56.5	98.1	281.2
2007	914.5	1598.3	54.6	95.4	347.2
2008	884.9	1616.2	50.0	91.3	382.7
2009	893.1	1825.4	48.0	98.1	451.7
2010	885.6	2129.8	45.1	108.6	545.6
2011	883.9	2575.9	43.7	127.3	523.4
2012	883.1	3168.0	42.5	152.5	572.0
2013	867.6	3373.8	40.8	158.7	534.7
2014	831.1	4076.2	38.3	187.7	552.7
2015	784.7	4051.6	35.9	185.1	491.7
2016	694.4	3868.7	31.6	176.2	475.5
2017	649.0	3752.1	29.6	171.0	541.6
2018	614.5	4008.8	28.0	182.9	634.7
2019	555.4	4019.7	25.4	183.5	688.5
2020	480.6	3906.4	22.5	178.5	747.8
2021	485.2	3972.0	22.2	181.5	806.3
2022	474.2	3926.9	21.7	179.8	877.3
2023	467.4	4021.1	21.4	184.0	933.4

注：表中固定电话主线普及率和移动电话普及率2006—2009年数据根据北京市第六次全国人口普查结果进行了修订，2011—2019年数据根据北京市第七次全国人口普查结果进行了修订。

Note: Data on popularization rate of main line of fixed line telephones for 2006-2009 in this table have been adjusted according to the results of the Sixth National Population Census in Beijing, and the results for 2011-2019 have been adjusted on the basis of the Seventh National Population Census in Beijing.

15-2 社会客货运总量(换算周转量)
TOTAL PASSENGER AND FREIGHT TRAFFIC (CONVERTED TOTAL PASSENGER AND FREIGHT)

单位：万吨公里 (10000 ton-km)

项　　目	Item	2023	2022	2023年为2022年% 2023 as % of 2022	构　成(%) Composition(%)	
					2023	2022
运输总量	**Total**	**12254560.5**	**9720041.3**	**126.1**	**100.0**	**100.0**
铁　路	Railway	4187286.7	3181022.1	131.6	34.2	32.7
公　路	Highway	2642754.4	2299304.3	114.9	21.6	23.7
民　航	Civil Aviation	2090079.3	1094865.2	190.9	17.1	11.3
管　道	Petroleum and Gas Pipelines	3334440.1	3144849.7	106.0	27.2	32.4

15-3 运输线路
TRANSPORT ROUTES

项　　目	Item	条　数 (条) Number (line)		长　度 (公里) Length (km)	
		2023	2022	2023	2022
铁　路	Railway	76	72	1372.4	1353.7
公　路	Highway	10276	10191	22433.3	22362.8
民　航	Civil Aviation				
#中国国际航空公司	Air China	440	403		
中国新华航空有限责任公司	China Xinhua Airlines	561	408		
管　道	Pipeline	18	18	5715.4	5715.4

注：铁路长度为营业里程，管道长度为管输里程。

Note: Length of railway refers to the lengths of railway in operation, and length of petroleum and gas pipelines refers to the length of transportation via petroleum and gas pipelines.

15－4 铁路、民航主要技术经济指标
MAIN TECHNICAL AND ECONOMIC INDICATORS OF RAILWAY AND CIVIL AVIATION

项　　目	Item	2023	2022	2023年为2022年% 2023 as % of 2022
铁　路	**Railways**			
内燃机车每万吨公里耗柴油　（千克）	Diesel Consumption of Diesel Locomotives per 10000 Ton-km (kg)	34.7	34.7	100.0
电力机车每万吨公里耗电　（千瓦时）	Electricity Consumption of Electric Locomotives per 10000 Ton-km (kW·h)	140.9	96.5	146.0
民　航	**Civil Aviation**			
每吨公里耗航空油　（千克）	Aviation-oil Consumption per Ton-km (kg)	0.30	0.33	90.9

15－5 机动车保有量
POSSESSION OF MOTOR VEHICLES

单位：万辆　　(10000 units)

项　　目	Item	2023	2022
机动车	**Motor Vehicles**	**758.9**	**712.8**
#民用汽车	Civil Vehicles	637.6	625.6
#载货汽车	Trucks	55.4	54.7
载客汽车	Passenger Vehicles	570.9	561.2
#私人汽车	Private Vehicles	543.1	532.6
#轿　车	Cars	285.4	290.6

资料来源：北京市公安局公安交通管理局。
Source: Beijing Traffic Management Bureau.

15-6 邮电业务主要指标(2023年)
MAIN INDICATORS OF POSTAL AND TELECOMMUNICATION SERVICES(2023)

项目		Item		2023	2023年为2022年% 2023 as % of 2022
邮政行业业务总量	(亿标准量)	Business Volume of Post Services	(volume in 100 million)	324.3	115.2
电信业务总量	(亿元)	Business Volume of Telecommunication Services	(100 million yuan)	633.3	114.7
邮电业务		**Postal and Telecommunication Services**			
函件	(万件)	Letters	(10000 pcs)	10615.5	98.4
包裹	(万件)	Packages	(10000 pcs)	132.2	121.2
特快专递业务量	(万件)	Express Deliveries	(10000 pcs)	227115.2	116.1
汇兑	(万笔)	Postal Remittance Transactions	(10000 pcs)	18.0	98.4
订销报纸(累计)	(万份)	Number of Newspapers Subscribed and Sold (Cumulative)	(10000 copies)	60572.7	97.4
订销杂志(累计)	(万份)	Number of Magazines Subscribed and Sold (Cumulative)	(10000 copies)	2294.2	103.7
邮政代理储蓄期末余额	(亿元)	Ending Balance of Postal Agency Savings	(100 million yuan)	1645.3	112.4
移动电话通话量	(亿分钟)	Calls of Mobile Phones	(100 million minutes)	792.7	91.4
移动短信业务量	(亿条)	Short Message Services	(100 million messages)	2601.1	159.4
年末移动电话用户	(万户)	Year-end Number of Mobile Phone Subscribers	(10000 subscribers)	4021.1	102.4
年末固定电话用户	(万户)	Year-end Number of Fixed Telephone Subscribers	(10000 subscribers)	467.4	98.6
移动电话交换机容量	(万户)	Capacity of Mobile Phone Exchanges	(10000 subscribers)	10750	100.0
固定电话主线普及率	(线/百人)	Popularization Rate of Main Line of Fixed Line Telephones	(line/100 persons)	21.4	98.5
移动电话普及率	(户/百人)	Popularization Rate of Mobile Phones	(subscriber/100 persons)	184.0	102.3
固定互联网宽带接入用户数	(万户)	Subscribers of Broadband Subscribers of Internet	(10000 subscribers)	933.4	106.4

注：1.邮政行业业务总量按2020年不变价格计算，电信业务总量按上年不变价格计算。
2.特快专递业务量范围为取得快递业务经营许可企业及其备案分支机构。
3.表中发展速度按可比口径计算。

Note: a) Business volume of postal services are calculated at 2020 constant prices, and that of telecommunication services are calculated at the same price in the previous year.
b) Data on business volume of express deliveries cover enterprises permitted to conduct express delivery businesses and their filed branches.
c) Data on development rate in the table are calculated in terms of comparable caliber.

主要统计指标解释

货（客）运量 指在一定时期内，各种运输工具实际运送的货物重量（旅客数量）。是反映运输业为国民经济和人民生活服务的数量指标，也是制定和检查运输生产计划，研究运输发展规模和速度的重要指标。货运按吨计算，客运按人计算。货物不论运输距离长短，货物类别，均按实际重量统计；旅客不论行程远近或票价多少，均按一人一次作为客运量统计。半价票、小孩票也按一人统计。

货物（旅客）周转量 指在一定时期内，由各种运输工具运送的货物（旅客）数量与其相应运输距离的乘积之总和，是反映运输业生产总成果的重要指标，也是编制和检查运输生产计划、计算运输效率、劳动生产率以及核算运输单位的主要基础资料。计算货物周转量通常按发出站与到达站之间的最短距离，也就是计费距离计算。

函件 是指邮政部门为用户传递以书面信息为主的邮件，包括信件、印刷品和邮送广告。

包裹 指符合包裹准寄范围，通过邮政渠道寄递的物品。包括国内普通包裹、国内快递包裹、国际及港澳台包裹。

移动电话用户 指报告期末通过移动电话交换机进入移动电话网的全部电话用户。包括各类签约用户、智能网预付费用户、无线上网卡用户等。

固定电话用户 指在电信企业登记注册，且在报告期末实际已经接入电信企业固定电话网上的全部电话用户（包括局用电话交换机、接入网设备、软交换用户接入设备、无线市话设备）上的全部电话用户。

移动电话交换机容量 指移动电话交换机根据一定话务模型和交换机处理能力计算出来的最大同时服务用户的数量。

固定电话主线普及率 是指报告期行政区域常住人口中，平均每百人拥有的固定电话主线数。计算公式为：

$$固定电话主线普及率=\frac{电话主线数(本地电话用户)}{行政区域常住人口数}$$

移动电话普及率 是指报告期行政区域常住人口中，平均每百人拥有的移动电话的用户数。计算公式为：

$$移动电话普及率=\frac{移动电话用户总数}{行政区域常住人口数}$$

固定互联网宽带接入用户数 指报告期末在电信企业登记注册，通过 xDSL、FTTx+LAN 以及其他宽带接入方式和普通专线接入公众互联网的用户。

Explanatory Notes on Main Statistical Indicators

Freight (Passenger) Traffic refers to the weight of freight (number of passenger) transported with various means within a specific period of time. It is a quantitative measure to show how the transport industry serves the national economy and people's life, and is also an important indicator for preparing and reviewing transport plan and studying the development scale and speed of the transport industry. Freight transport is calculated in tons and passenger traffic is calculated in the number of persons. Regardless of the types or traveling distance of freight, freight transport is calculated in terms of the actual weight of goods; and regardless of the traveling distance or ticket price, passenger traffic is calculated following the principle that one person can be counted only once in one trip. The passenger who travels with a half-price ticket or a child ticket is also calculated as one person.

Freight (Passenger) Turnover refers to the sum of the product of the volume of transported cargo (passengers) multiplied by the transport distance during a certain period of time. This is an important indicator to show the total results of the transport industry, and also serves as main basic data for preparing and reviewing transport plans and measuring transport efficiency, labor productivity and the transport unit. Freight turnover is usually calculated by the shortest distance between the departure station and the arrival station, namely the charging distance.

Letters mean mails mainly in the form of written information delivered by postal authorities, including letters, prints and delivered advertisements.

Package means articles permitted for mailing, and mailed through postal channels, including domestic regular parcels, domestic express parcels, international parcels, and parcels from and to Hong Kong, Macao and Taiwan.

Mobile Phone Subscribers refer to all users who have been connected with the mobile telephone communication network through the mobile telephone switchboards at the end of the reporting period. Included are various types of subscriber, prepaid users for intelligent network and wireless network card users.

Fixed-line Telephone Subscribers refer to all subscribers who have gone through registration procedures in the telecom companies and have actually been connected to the fixed-line telephone network of telecom companies at the end of the reporting period. Included are all subscribers of office telephone exchanges, access network equipment, soft switch user access equipment, and wireless local telephone equipment.

Capacity of Mobile Phone Exchanges means the maximum number of users receiving services simultaneously from mobile phone exchangers, calculated from certain traffic model and exchanger processing capacity.

Popularization Rate of Fixed-line Telephones means the average number of main lines of fixed-line telephones owned per one hundred persons of permanent population in administrative areas in the reporting period. It is calculated with the following formula:

Popularization Rate of Fixed-line Telephones = Number of Main Lines of Telephone (Local Phone Users) / Number of Permanent Population in Administrative Areas

Popularization Rate of Mobile Phones means the average number of mobile phones owned per 100 persons among permanent population in administrative areas in the reporting period. It is calculated with the following formula:

Popularization Rate of Mobile Phones = Total Number of Mobile Phone Users / Permanent Population in Administrative Areas

Subscribers of Broadband Internet means subscribers registered at telecom companies to connect with public Internet through xDSL, FTTx+LAN as well as other broadband connections and general special lines at the end of reporting period.

16

批发和零售业、住宿和餐饮业

WHOLESALE AND RETAIL TRADE, ACCOMMODATION AND CATERING

简要说明

一、主要内容

本章资料反映北京市商品流通市场发展及批发和零售业、住宿和餐饮业经营情况。包括社会消费品零售总额，批发和零售业商品购进、销售、库存、商品分类销售情况，住宿和餐饮业经营情况，限额以上批发和零售业、住宿和餐饮业财务状况，连锁企业基本情况，商品交易市场基本情况、成交额，北京消费者信心指数。

二、统计范围

社会消费品零售总额指标于1993年、1997年和2003年进行了调整。1993年起不再包括对农民的农业生产资料；1997年起不再包括居民购买住房；2003年起不再包括由各种经济类型的制造业法人企业、产业活动单位直接售给城乡居民（包括本企业职工）和社会集团的商品以及农民对非农业居民的零售额。

限额以上批发和零售业、住宿和餐饮业统计限额标准：2008 年以前，批发业为年销售额 2000 万元及以上；零售业为年销售额 500 万元及以上；住宿业为星级饭店和星级以外年营业收入 500 万元及以上；餐饮业为年营业额 200 万元及以上。自 2008 年起，批发业为年主营业务收入 2000 万元及以上；零售业为年主营收入 500 万元及以上；住宿业为星级饭店和星级以外年主营业务收入 200 万元及以上；餐饮业为年主营业务收入 200 万元及以上。2020 年调整后，住宿业为年主营业务收入 200 万元及以上。

北京消费者信心指数调查范围覆盖全市 16 个区。

三、调查方法

限额以上批发和零售业、住宿和餐饮业单位采用全面调查；连锁企业、商品交易市场采取全数调查。

北京消费者信心指数调查采用计算机辅助电话方式调查，调查对象为居住在北京市半年以上 19-64 周岁的城乡居民。

四、有关统计标准的变化说明

2010 年及以前，企业大中小型划分执行 2003 年《统计上大中小型企业划分办法（暂行）》。2011 年至 2017 年大中小微型企业划分标准执行国家统计局《关于统计上大中小微型企业划分办法》（国统字〔2011〕75 号）；自 2018 年起，执行《统计上大中小微型企业划分办法（2017）》（国统字〔2017〕213 号）。

五、本章中关于历史数据调整的问题

按照国家统计局统一要求和统一方法，本章中 1978 年至 2003 年的社会消费品零售总额数据，根据北京市第一次全国经济普查结果，采用“速度推算法”进行了修订，2004 年数据为北京市第一次全国经济普查数据；2005-2007 年数据根据北京市第二次全国经济普查结果，采用“趋势离差法”进行了修订，2008 年数据为北京市第二次全国经济普查数据；2009-2012 年数据根据北京市第三次全国经济普查结果进行了修订，2013 年数据为北京市第三次全国经济普查数据；在前三次普查数据修订基础上，1992-2019 年社会消费品零售总额数据根据北京市第四次全国经济普查结果，采用“趋势离差法”进行了修订，2018 年数据为北京市第四次全国经济普查数据。

Brief Introduction

I. Main Content

Statistics in this chapter show the development of commodity circulation market and the operations of wholesale and retail trades, hotels and catering services. Including: total retail sales of consumer goods, commodity purchase, sales and inventory in wholesale and retail trades, and sales of commodities by category, operation situation of hotels and catering services, financial status of wholesale, retail, accommodation and restaurants enterprises above designated size, basic situation of chain businesses, basic situation and turnover of commodity transaction markets, and Beijing consumer confidence index.

II. Scope of Statistics

Adjustments were made to the indicators of total retail sales of consumer goods in 1993, 1997 and 2003. From 1993, the indicator did not cover agricultural means of production for farmers any longer; from 1997, it did not cover houses bought by residents any longer; from 2003, it did not cover goods sold by corporate manufacturing enterprises and industrial activity entities of various economic types to urban and rural residents (including enterprises' own employees) and social groups as well as retail sales by farmers to non-agricultural residents any longer.

As for standards for wholesale and retail trades, hotels and catering services above designated size, before 2008, for wholesale trades, the standard was annual sales of RMB 20 million and above; for retail trades, annual sales of RMB 5 million and above; for accommodation, star-rated hotels and non-star-rated hotels with annual business income of RMB 5 million and above; for restaurants, annual turnover of RMB 2 million and above. Since 2008, the designated size is, for wholesale trades, annual main business income of RMB 20 million and above; for retail trades, annual main business income of RMB 5 million and above; for accommodation, star-rated hotels and non-star-rated hotels with annual main business income of RMB 2 million and above; for restaurants, annual main business income of RMB 2 million and above. After adjustments were made in 2020, for accommodation, annual main business income of RMB 2 million and above.

Survey of Beijing consumer confidence index covers 16 districts in the City.

III. Methods of Survey

The method of comprehensive survey was used for statistics of wholesale and retail trades, hotels and catering services enterprises above designated size; complete enumeration was used for chain businesses, and commodity transaction markets.

Statistics on Beijing consumer confidence index were obtained through computer-aided phone calls to urban and rural residents aged 19-64 who have been living in Beijing for more than half a year.

IV. Changes in Relevant Statistical Standards

2010 and before, the classification of small, medium and large-sized enterprises should comply with the standards in the *Measures for Statistical Classification of Small, Medium and Large-sized Enterprises (Temporary)* 2003. The classification of micro, small, medium and large-sized enterprises should comply with the standards in the *Measures for Statistical Classification of Micro, Small, Medium and Large-sized Enterprises* (G.T.Z. [2011] No. 75) of the National Bureau of Statistics from 2011 to 2017. Since 2018, the classification has been in line with the standards in the *Measures for Statistical Classification of Micro, Small, Medium and Large-sized Enterprises (2017)* (G.T.Z. [2017] No. 213).

V. Adjustment to Historical Data

In accordance with the unified requirements and methods put forward by the National Bureau of Statistics, data for 1978-2003 on total retail sales of consumer goods were revised with the "speed calculation method" according to the results of the first national economic census in Beijing. Data for 2004 were gathered from the first national economic census in Beijing. Data for 2005-2007 were revised with the "trend deviation method" in accordance with the second national economic census in Beijing results in Beijing Data for 2008 were gathered from the second national economic census. Data for 2009-2012 were revised in accordance with the third national economic census in Beijing results. Data for 2013 were gathered from the third national economic census in Beijing. On the basis of the previous three revisions of the census data, data for 1992-2019 on total retail sales of consumer goods were revised with the "trend deviation method" in accordance with the fourth national economic census in Beijing results; and data for 2018 were gathered from the fourth national economic census in Beijing.

16−1 社会消费品零售总额(1978−2023年)
TOTAL RETAIL SALES OF CONSUMER GOODS (1978-2023)

单位：亿元 (100 million yuan)

年 份 Year	社会消费品零售总额 Total Retail Sales of Consumer Goods	#限额以上批发和零售业、住宿和餐饮业网上零售额 Online Retail Sales of Wholesale and Retail Trades, Hotels and Catering Services above Designated Size	按商品类别分 By Category of Goods 吃类商品 Food	穿类商品 Clothing	用类商品 Daily use Articles	烧类商品 Fuels
1978	44.2		18.0	8.9	16.0	1.3
1979	53.3		20.8	11.3	19.7	1.5
1980	62.8		24.9	13.4	22.9	1.6
1981	70.7		28.0	14.5	26.5	1.7
1982	75.4		29.7	13.7	30.3	1.7
1983	86.4		34.0	15.7	34.8	1.9
1984	105.8		39.6	18.7	45.2	2.3
1985	134.4		49.6	22.5	59.4	2.9
1986	155.0		60.7	22.8	68.0	3.5
1987	188.9		77.4	27.4	80.2	3.9
1988	256.0		100.6	36.0	114.9	4.5
1989	294.8		119.4	34.9	134.1	6.4
1990	345.1		136.8	45.6	154.6	8.1
1991	408.3		158.2	53.7	187.6	8.8
1992	503.0		193.6	66.9	230.5	12.0
1993	615.8		220.8	96.6	281.8	16.5
1994	778.1		283.5	125.6	349.3	19.7
1995	971.8		406.4	139.4	407.9	18.2
1996	1093.6		428.4	153.2	491.8	20.2
1997	1254.3		449.1	162.5	608.3	34.3
1998	1436.2		401.1	168.4	823.1	43.7
1999	1589.9		419.4	145.4	951.7	73.4
2000	1760.3		459.6	161.8	1050.5	88.4
2001	1958.1		515.7	180.8	1161.1	100.5
2002	2159.9		527.3	179.4	1330.2	123.0
2003	2492.6		563.0	200.8	1587.2	141.7
2004	2883.6		691.1	231.2	1748.7	212.6
2005	3221.4		802.8	269.1	1901.1	248.3
2006	3673.3		873.2	299.4	2172.8	328.0
2007	4307.4		1000.3	341.1	2614.9	351.1
2008	5257.5		1223.0	413.2	3233.4	387.8
2009	6140.0		1344.9	476.9	3928.0	390.2
2010	7273.0		1517.8	552.7	4718.9	483.5
2011	8334.8		1781.6	671.2	5262.8	619.3
2012	9440.2		1916.9	725.3	6140.2	657.8
2013	10382.5		1965.9	733.4	7039.2	644.0
2014	11354.0	1456.9	2027.7	740.1	7937.2	649.0
2015	12271.9	2016.9	2215.5	747.6	8758.8	549.9
2016	13134.9	2049.0	2336.4	764.2	9457.2	577.1
2017	13933.7	2458.0	2468.6	794.9	10069.9	600.4
2018	14422.3	2757.2	2623.1	817.3	10339.9	642.1
2019	15063.7	3507.6	2822.8	811.2	10829.1	600.6
2020	13716.4	4423.3	2795.7	697.7	9766.2	456.9
2021	14867.7	5392.7	2966.3	827.3	10472.5	601.7
2022	13794.2	5485.6	2832.4	657.0	9723.6	581.2
2023	14462.7	5458.2	3153.3	780.9	9910.2	618.3

注：2014−2016年，限额以上批发和零售业、住宿和餐饮业网上零售额不含住宿和餐饮业。

Note: The data on the online retail sales of wholesale and retail trades, hotels and catering services above designated size from 2014 to 2016 didn't cover the hotels and catering services.

16-2 社会消费品零售总额(2023年)
TOTAL RETAIL SALES OF CONSUMER GOODS (2023)

单位：亿元 (100 million yuan)

项　目	Item	2023	2023年为2022年% 2023 as % of 2022
社会消费品零售总额	**Total Retail Sales of Consumer Goods**	**14462.7**	**104.8**
按商品类别分	**By Category of Goods**		
吃类商品	Food	3153.3	109.4
穿类商品	Clothing	780.9	118.2
用类商品	Daily Use Articles	9910.2	102.3
烧类商品	Fuels	618.3	109.1
按消费品形态分	**By Form of Consumer Goods**		
餐饮收入	Food and Beverage Income	1314.6	132.5
商品零售	Retail Sales of Goods	13148.1	102.7

注：表中发展速度按可比口径计算。
Note: Indicators of development rate in the table are calculated in terms of comparable caliber.

16-3 按登记注册统计类别分限额以上批发和零售业商品零售额(2023年) RETAIL SALES OF CONSUMER GOODS IN WHOLESALE AND RETAIL TRADES ABOVE DESIGNATED SIZE BY STATUS OF REGISTRATION (2023)

单位：亿元 (100 million yuan)

项 目	Item	商品零售额 Retail Sales of Goods	批发业 Wholesale Trade	零售业 Retail Trade
合 计	**Total**	**9591.5**	**979.6**	**8611.9**
#内资企业	Domestic Invested Enterprises	7297.3	838.4	6458.9
#有限责任公司	Limited Liability Corporations	6835.5	725.2	6110.2
股份有限公司	Corporations Limited by Shares	391.3	107.2	284.1
非公司企业法人	Unincorporated Business Entity	69.0	5.8	63.2
港澳台投资企业	Enterprises with Investment from Hong Kong, Macao and Taiwan	548.2	41.6	506.6
外商投资企业	Foreign Invested Enterprises	1744.6	99.5	1645.1

注：本表统计范围为限额以上批发和零售业法人单位(16—4至16—5表同)。
Note: This table covers corporate units in wholesale and retail trades above designated size (the same applies to table 16-4 to table 16-5).

16-4 限额以上批发和零售业商品购进、销售、库存情况(2023年) TOTAL PURCHASES, TOTAL SALES AND TOTAL STOCK IN WHOLESALE AND RETAIL TRADES ABOVE DESIGNATED SIZE (2023)

单位：亿元 (100 million yuan)

项 目	Item	合计 Total	批发业 Wholesale Trade	零售业 Retail Trade
商品购进额	**Total Purchases Value**	**90367.7**	**80392.3**	**9975.5**
商品销售额	**Total Sales Value**	**94599.1**	**83648.4**	**10950.7**
批发额	Wholesale Sales	85007.5	82668.8	2338.8
零售额	Retail Sales	9591.5	979.6	8611.9
期末商品库存额	**Total Stock at Year-end**	**7613.1**	**6751.1**	**862.0**

16-5 限额以上批发和零售业商品销售类值(2023年)
SALES BY CATEGORY FOR WHOLESALE AND RETAIL TRADES ABOVE DESIGNATED SIZE (2023)

单位：亿元 (100 million yuan)

项 目	Item	商品销售额 Total Sales Value	批发额 Wholesale Sales	零售额 Retail Sales
合 计	**Total**	**94599.1**	**85007.5**	**9591.5**
粮油、食品类	Grain and Oil, Food	6055.4	5184.4	871.0
#粮油类	Grain and Oil	3238.3	3154.5	83.8
肉禽蛋类	Meat, Poultry and Eggs	725.2	605.1	120.0
饮料类	Beverages	689.5	463.4	226.2
烟酒类	Tobacco and Liquor	1585.7	1323.3	262.4
服装、鞋帽、针纺织品类	Clothing, Shoes, Hats and Textiles	1095.8	510.4	585.4
#服装类	Clothing	725.9	265.2	460.8
鞋帽类	Footwear and Hats	243.5	149.8	93.8
针纺织品类	Knitwear and Textiles	126.3	95.5	30.9
化妆品类	Cosmetics	373.4	160.6	212.8
金银珠宝类	Gold, Silver and Jewellery	1406.5	918.0	488.6
日用品类	Articles for Daily Use	2307.2	1669.5	637.7
#儿童玩具类	Children's Toys	40.6	24.7	15.9
五金、电料类	Hardware & Electrical Materials	377.1	363.4	13.7
体育、娱乐用品类	Sports & Recreational Articles	1702.7	1468.7	234.0
书报杂志类	Newspapers and Magazines	366.7	220.2	146.5
电子出版物及音像制品类	E-book and Video Products	91.4	50.2	41.2
家用电器和音像器材类	Household Appliances and Audio-visual Equipment	3442.2	3080.1	362.1
中西药品类	Traditional Chinese and Western Medicine	2754.6	2628.5	126.2
#西药类	Western Medicine	1715.7	1638.9	76.8
中草药及中成药类	Traditional Chinese Medicine	391.2	360.9	30.3
文化办公用品类	Cultural and Office Goods	6608.1	5679.7	928.5
家具类	Furniture	152.2	55.7	96.5
通讯器材类	Communication Appliances	9892.7	8253.9	1638.8
煤炭及制品类	Coal and Related Products	5615.3	5613.8	1.5
木材及制品类	Wood and Wooden Products	681.1	681.1	
石油及制品类	Petroleum and Related Products	11446.9	10949.3	497.6
化工材料及制品类	Raw Chemical Materials and Related Products	8137.2	8137.2	
#化肥类	Fertilizer	1256.0	1256.0	
金属材料类	Metal Materials	10188.6	10188.6	
建筑及装潢材料类	Building and Decoration Materials	726.2	645.2	80.9
机电产品及设备类	Mechanical & Electrical Products	3880.9	3774.1	106.8
#农机类	Agricultural Machinery	123.9	123.9	
汽车类	Automobile	9734.4	7899.2	1835.3
种子饲料类	Seed and Feedstuff	1065.7	1065.7	
棉麻类	Cotton and Hemp	642.3	642.3	
其他类	Others	3579.1	3381.1	198.0

16−6 限额以上住宿和餐饮业经营情况(2023年)

OPERATING STATISTICS ON HOTELS AND CATERING SERVICES ABOVE DESIGNATED SIZE (2023)

项　目	Item	合　计 Total	住宿业 Hotels	餐饮业 Catering Services
客房数　（间）	**Number of Rooms　(room)**	**227672**	**223169**	**4503**
床位数　（个）	**Number of Beds　(bed)**	**347450**	**339573**	**7877**
餐位数　（位）	**Number of Dining-seats　(unit)**	**1684554**	**233541**	**1451013**
营业额　（万元）	**Business Revenue　(10000 yuan)**	**15493859**	**4557928**	**10935931**
客房收入	From Hotel Rooms	2710558	2674682	35876
餐费收入	From Meals	10966657	880332	10086325
商品销售额	Total Sales Value	367200	44131	323070
其他收入	Other Revenues	1449443	958783	490660

注：本表统计范围为限额以上住宿和餐饮业法人单位。
Note: This table covers corporate units in hotels and catering services above designated size.

16-7 限额以上批发和零售业企业财务状况(2023年)

单位：亿元

项 目	Item	企业单位个数(个) Number of Enterprises (unit)	资产总计 Total Assets	流动资产合计 Total Current Assets
合 计	**Total**	**12026**	**65080.9**	**44240.7**
按登记注册统计类别分	**By Statistical Category of Registration**			
内资企业	Domestic Invested Enterprises	11262	48765.1	32447.5
#有限责任公司	Limited Liability Corporations	10863	42599.2	29065.3
股份有限公司	Corporations Limited by Shares	213	5760.5	3024.0
非公司企业法人	Unincorporated Business Entity	172	399.4	352.8
港澳台投资企业	Enterprises with Investment from Hong Kong, Macao and Taiwan	277	7417.1	5768.6
外商投资企业	Foreign Invested Enterprises	478	8897.0	6023.4
农民专业合作社(联合社)	Farmers Specialized Cooperatives	9	1.7	1.2
按国民经济行业分	**By Sector**			
批发业	Wholesale Trade	9223	59767.4	40243.8
农、林、牧、渔产品批发	Wholesale of Agriculture, Forestry, Animal Husbandry and Fishery Products	213	4418.3	2983.2
食品、饮料及烟草制品批发	Wholesale of Foods, Beverages and Tobaccos	1307	4470.8	3618.9
纺织、服装及家庭用品批发	Wholesale of Textiles, Garments and Household Commodities	723	5180.3	3936.4
文化、体育用品及器材批发	Wholesale of Culture, Sports Appliances and Equipments	500	1643.5	1150.5
医药及医疗器材批发	Wholesale of Medicines and Medical Appliances	1121	3605.6	2873.8
矿产品、建材及化工产品批发	Wholesale of Mineral Products, Building Materials, and Chemical Products	2069	24055.9	12956.2
机械设备、五金交电及电子产品批发	Wholesale of Mechanical Equipment, Hardware and Electronic Products	3078	13669.7	10503.7
贸易经纪与代理	Trade Broker and Agent	49	1732.4	1508.3
其他批发业	Others	163	991.0	712.8
零售业	Retail Trade	2803	5313.5	3996.9
综合零售	General Retail	261	1511.3	886.3
食品、饮料及烟草制品专门零售	Special Retail of Foods, Beverages and Tobaccos	310	308.8	269.6
纺织、服装及日用品专门零售	Special Retail of Textiles, Garments and Daily Consumer Articles	261	251.4	202.3
文化、体育用品及器材专门零售	Special Retail of Culture, Sports Appliances and Equipments	246	479.3	390.9
医药及医疗器材专门零售	Special Retail of Medicines and Medical Appliances	138	69.8	59.7
汽车、摩托车、零配件和燃料及其他动力销售	Sales of Motor Vehicles, Motorcycles, Parts and Fuels and Other Power	941	1108.4	850.3
家用电器及电子产品专门零售	Special Retail of Household Electric Appliances and Electronic Products	232	567.7	432.3
五金、家具及室内装饰材料专门零售	Special Retail of Hardware, Furniture and Interior Decoration Material	98	101.3	61.6
货摊、无店铺及其他零售业	Stalls, Non-Shop and Other Retails	316	915.5	843.8
按规模划分	**By Size**			
#大中型企业	Large and Medium-sized Enterprises	3826	53866.0	35170.7

FINANCIAL STATUS OF ENTERPRISES ABOVE DESIGNATED SIZE OF WHOLESALE AND RETAIL TRADE (2023)

(100 million yuan)

资产负债 Assets and Liabilities						
#应收账款 Accounts Receivable	固定资产原价 Original Value of Fixed Assets	负债合计 Total Liabilities	#流动负债合计 Total Current Liabilities	#应付账款 Accounts Payable	所有者权益合计 Total Owners' Equity	#实收资本 Paid-in Capital
7293.0	**2265.8**	**42935.1**	**37667.7**	**10490.6**	**22147.7**	**10656.2**
5937.2	1800.5	32440.5	28065.5	7480.9	16326.4	9073.3
5622.7	1618.5	29456.1	25627.6	7185.6	13144.8	8349.2
303.2	139.0	2798.3	2253.7	275.3	2962.1	702.9
10.3	42.1	181.3	179.5	18.3	218.2	20.7
387.6	157.7	5637.3	5458.6	1554.8	1779.9	613.4
967.4	306.9	4856.2	4142.6	1454.5	4040.7	969.3
0.7	0.6	1.0	1.0	0.3	0.7	0.1
6674.4	1711.9	38864.6	34180.0	9265.0	20904.5	9713.3
424.6	52.9	3029.6	2730.0	324.1	1388.7	500.8
286.2	139.1	3451.8	3266.8	393.4	1019.0	643.0
179.0	88.0	3617.5	3573.2	962.3	1562.7	481.7
102.8	78.5	934.4	717.1	151.2	709.1	396.0
758.6	102.8	2310.9	2163.6	901.7	1294.6	492.7
2145.3	898.8	14351.6	11495.4	2574.9	9704.4	5235.4
1941.2	307.1	8953.4	8213.3	2774.2	4718.0	1692.7
735.8	23.8	1401.1	1356.5	1024.0	331.2	180.1
100.8	20.9	814.3	664.1	159.1	176.7	90.8
618.6	553.8	4070.4	3487.7	1225.6	1243.2	942.9
53.5	209.0	1025.3	803.9	252.8	486.1	241.0
34.7	30.7	206.3	164.3	48.6	102.5	35.9
64.6	31.1	232.5	218.2	92.6	18.9	95.9
42.0	39.3	292.4	270.1	72.5	186.9	65.5
11.2	2.8	61.4	57.2	22.4	8.4	13.8
90.4	183.3	922.4	840.6	142.0	186.0	317.6
234.7	15.6	356.9	327.4	184.0	210.7	45.6
10.1	13.4	81.0	65.3	15.8	20.3	24.5
77.5	28.7	892.2	740.8	394.8	23.4	103.0
5310.4	1660.6	34082.9	29647.3	7430.0	19783.1	8371.4

16-7 续表

单位：亿元

项　　目	Item	损益 营业收入 Business Revenue	营业成本 Business Cost	销售费用 Selling Expenses
合　　计	**Total**	**81090.0**	**75449.9**	**2770.8**
按登记注册统计类别分	**By Statistical Category of Registration**			
内资企业	Domestic Invested Enterprises	59223.6	55980.1	1629.4
#有限责任公司	Limited Liability Corporations	54647.2	51724.0	1499.0
股份有限公司	Corporations Limited by Shares	3646.2	3436.6	110.8
非公司企业法人	Unincorporated Business Entity	903.9	794.4	19.0
港澳台投资企业	Enterprises with Investment from Hong Kong, Macao and Taiwan	10984.9	9965.4	499.6
外商投资企业	Foreign Invested Enterprises	10878.2	9501.3	641.8
农民专业合作社(联合社)	Farmers Specialized Cooperatives	3.3	3.1	0.03
按国民经济行业分	**By Sector**			
批发业	Wholesale Trade	71072.3	66646.0	1914.9
农、林、牧、渔产品批发	Wholesale of Agriculture, Forestry,Animal Husbandry and Fishery Products	3399.0	3236.5	22.0
食品、饮料及烟草制品批发	Wholesale of Foods, Beverages and Tobaccos	4277.8	3803.7	258.8
纺织、服装及家庭用品批发	Wholesale of Textiles, Garments and Household Commodities	8873.8	8051.4	360.9
文化、体育用品及器材批发	Wholesale of Culture, Sports Appliances and Equipments	1680.9	1496.5	81.6
医药及医疗器材批发	Wholesale of Medicines and Medical Appliances	3842.9	3264.7	278.5
矿产品、建材及化工产品批发	Wholesale of Mineral Products, Building Materials, and Chemical Products	29803.3	29147.5	238.3
机械设备、五金交电及电子产品批发	Wholesale of Mechanical Equipment, Hardware and Electronic Products	17500.6	16068.4	630.2
贸易经纪与代理	Trade Broker and Agent	179.2	148.4	7.5
其他批发业	Others	1514.6	1429.0	37.2
零售业	Retail Trade	10017.6	8803.9	855.9
综合零售	General Retail	1250.3	977.4	188.4
食品、饮料及烟草制品专门零售	Special Retail of Foods, Beverages and Tobaccos	294.1	218.6	44.4
纺织、服装及日用品专门零售	Special Retail of Textiles, Garments and Daily Consumer Articles	311.7	177.1	109.8
文化、体育用品及器材专门零售	Special Retail of Culture, Sports Appliances and Equipments	603.7	475.2	60.2
医药及医疗器材专门零售	Special Retail of Medicines and Medical Appliances	125.5	93.8	23.6
汽车、摩托车、零配件和燃料及其他动力销售	Sales of Motor Vehicles, Motorcycles, Parts and Fuels and Other Power	2473.1	2296.9	116.8
家用电器及电子产品专门零售	Special Retail of Household Electric Appliances and Electronic Products	1050.6	942.0	73.5
五金、家具及室内装修材料专门零售	Special Retail of Hardware, Furniture and Interior Decoration Material	97.2	62.1	23.6
货摊、无店铺及其他零售业	Stalls, Non-Shop and Other Retail	3811.4	3560.9	215.7
按规模划分	**By Size**			
#大中型企业	Large and Medium-sized Enterprises	66109.7	61364.3	2269.4

16-7 Continued

(100 million yuan)

Profits and Losses				应交税金合计 Total Tax Payable			
管理费用 Management Expenses	研发费用 R&D Expenses	财务费用 Financial Expenses	利润总额 Total Profits		税金及附加 Tax and Surtax	所得税费用 Income Tax Expense	应交增值税 Value Added Tax Payable
1664.6	**156.4**	**186.8**	**2731.2**	**968.7**	**162.1**	**305.4**	**501.2**
931.8	121.9	206.0	1412.8	623.3	125.1	168.6	329.6
847.5	106.2	190.8	1220.7	515.0	77.2	142.9	294.9
68.8	15.3	22.0	135.4	43.3	9.3	13.3	20.6
15.1	0.3	-6.8	56.6	64.8	38.5	12.3	14.0
448.7	23.1	-24.1	589.8	92.9	14.1	19.7	59.1
284.0	11.4	4.9	728.6	252.5	22.9	117.1	112.5
0.1		...	0.1	...	...	...	...
1417.8	139.2	158.0	2658.6	808.1	128.6	270.3	409.3
37.7	7.5	19.4	170.4	44.5	4.4	20.8	19.3
91.4	3.5	14.5	114.4	119.6	45.2	26.2	48.1
380.4	10.7	-33.2	571.5	86.6	9.9	23.3	53.4
54.0	11.1	3.4	56.0	22.5	2.6	10.3	9.6
158.6	5.3	2.4	179.6	106.6	8.9	34.6	63.1
286.9	21.7	151.7	866.5	150.4	30.3	36.5	83.6
358.9	74.5	5.4	665.3	258.0	25.2	107.7	125.2
14.9	0.1	-6.7	37.8	8.7	0.8	5.8	2.0
35.2	4.8	1.1	-2.9	11.3	1.3	5.0	5.0
246.7	17.2	28.8	72.7	160.6	33.5	35.2	91.9
59.5	0.2	11.2	28.2	32.8	7.3	7.9	17.6
15.6	0.8	0.2	16.6	11.7	0.8	3.9	6.9
25.2	2.0	1.5	0.4	12.3	1.2	1.7	9.4
29.6	2.1	2.7	26.9	24.8	7.3	7.9	9.6
5.6	0.3	0.7	1.0	3.3	0.3	0.5	2.5
59.0	1.7	10.8	-16.8	31.2	11.4	3.5	16.3
14.1	6.4	0.6	13.3	18.4	1.4	6.5	10.4
11.2	0.7	0.7	-4.1	3.0	0.6	-0.03	2.4
26.9	3.0	0.4	7.3	23.0	3.2	3.2	16.6
1388.5	136.8	144.8	2617.4	824.5	142.6	274.0	407.8

16−8 限额以上住宿和餐饮业企业财务状况(2023年)

单位：万元

项目	Item	企业单位个数(个) Number of Enterprises (unit)	资产总计 Total Assets	流动资产合计 Total Current Assets
合计	**Total**	**3793**	**23076031.3**	**9684122.1**
按登记注册统计类别分	**By Statistical Category of Registration**			
#内资企业	Domestic Invested Enterprises	3616	14790310.3	7028014.7
有限责任公司	Limited Liability Corporations	3389	13249474.0	6427098.2
股份有限公司	Corporations Limited by Shares	7	232230.3	69576.3
非公司企业法人	Unincorporated Business Entity	154	1275013.8	500846.7
个人独资企业	Sole Proprietorship Enterprises	30	18331.1	17463.4
合伙企业	Partnership Enterprises	36	15261.1	13030.1
港澳台投资企业	Enterprises with Investment from Hong Kong, Macao and Taiwan	99	4261486.4	1668844.4
外商投资企业	Foreign Invested Enterprises	77	4024234.6	987263.0
按行业类别分	**By Sector Category**			
住宿业	Hotels	1262	16676124.3	5843596.9
#旅游饭店	Tourist Hotel	539	13807256.2	4290503.5
一般旅馆	General Hotel	665	2612614.5	1453658.4
餐饮业	Catering Services	2531	6399907.0	3840525.2
正餐服务	Restaurant	2031	3341514.7	2147931.1
快餐服务	Fast Food	141	1562714.2	592891.1
饮料及冷饮服务	Beverages and Cold Drinks	53	583392.3	319291.3
餐饮配送及外卖送餐服务	Catering Distribution and Delivery Service	107	314917.2	270763.9
其他餐饮业	Others	199	597368.6	509647.8

FINANCIAL STATUS OF ENTERPRISES ABOVE DESIGNATED SIZE OF HOTELS AND CATERING SERVICES (2023)

(10000 yuan)

资产负债 Assets and Liabilities						
#应收账款 Accounts Receivable	固定资产原价 Original Value of Fixed Assets	负债合计 Total Liabilities	#流动负债合计 Total Current Liabilities	#应付账款 Accounts Payable	所有者权益合计 Total Owners' Equity	#实收资本 Paid-in Capital
627684.5	**10603192.6**	**17487180.8**	**13132023.0**	**1570160.6**	**5594523.8**	**5969318.0**
541259.2	7703814.4	12897084.2	10269107.7	1347077.7	1896902.6	4172745.9
517631.5	6342897.0	12014761.2	9616807.8	1293637.8	1235751.0	3769856.1
5916.1	72953.1	101102.0	94427.0	11749.3	131128.3	42187.9
16469.5	1282826.6	749965.4	527890.4	34625.1	527686.7	358717.1
280.1	3796.0	18911.1	18788.1	2737.1	-580.0	647.1
962.0	1341.7	12344.5	11194.4	4328.4	2916.6	1337.7
42247.2	2019001.1	2629225.8	1323818.2	123772.2	1632260.6	1195467.6
44178.1	880377.1	1960870.8	1539097.1	99310.7	2065360.6	601104.5
223804.9	9309250.9	11897875.6	8582039.9	543079.0	4778477.3	4759444.9
142207.8	8226942.1	9678829.2	6791483.3	378390.6	4128655.6	3806570.2
75679.2	1005409.6	2004894.5	1601272.2	151550.9	607720.0	912047.1
403879.6	1293941.7	5589305.2	4549983.1	1027081.6	816046.5	1209873.1
194632.0	699142.7	3298077.5	2815774.2	543834.3	46648.9	699009.8
44236.3	407171.3	1056892.9	608726.1	123579.2	505879.1	157175.9
10607.7	106784.1	558777.2	464338.9	92077.0	26554.1	196471.0
62099.4	29773.1	197705.7	195143.5	94290.3	117211.5	63385.4
92304.2	51070.5	477851.9	466000.4	173300.8	119752.9	93831.0

16-8 续表

单位：万元

项目	Item	损益			
		营业收入 Business Revenue	营业成本 Business Cost	销售费用 Selling Expenses	管理费用 Management Expenses
合　计	**Total**	**14589262.0**	**6721825.8**	**4739053.4**	**2376656.3**
按登记注册统计类别分	**By Statistical Category of Registration**				
#内资企业	Domestic Invested Enterprises	10523736.5	5138844.4	3084021.7	1920442.6
有限责任公司	Limited Liability Corporations	9849585.4	4927943.9	2869424.8	1723009.3
股份有限公司	Corporations Limited by Shares	109246.2	59630.6	27410.5	16106.6
非公司企业法人	Unincorporated Business Entity	503731.6	125555.3	165576.0	170326.9
个人独资企业	Sole Proprietorship Enterprises	25712.6	11952.1	9283.2	4721.5
合伙企业	Partnership Enterprises	35460.7	13762.5	12327.2	6278.3
港澳台投资企业	Enterprises with Investment from Hong Kong, Macao and Taiwan	2553509.0	818481.9	1201021.7	263156.7
外商投资企业	Foreign Invested Enterprises	1512016.5	764499.5	454010.0	193057.0
按行业类别分	**By Sector Category**				
住宿业	Hotels	4321614.2	1693442.5	1015387.2	1187826.0
#旅游饭店	Tourist Hotel	3004084.8	1120600.1	682035.9	891934.3
一般旅馆	General Hotel	1222824.0	515327.7	318702.8	276308.7
餐饮业	Catering Services	10267647.8	5028383.3	3723666.2	1188830.3
正餐服务	Restaurant	5377934.4	2465243.9	2034014.9	726343.3
快餐服务	Fast Food	2238483.7	944914.7	1025109.1	148510.6
饮料及冷饮服务	Beverages and Cold Drinks	867137.6	336106.8	394390.2	88676.4
餐饮配送及外卖送餐服务	Catering Distribution and Delivery Service	586449.4	464388.4	61639.3	61493.2
其他餐饮业	Others	1197642.7	817729.5	208512.7	163806.8

16–8 Continued

(10000 yuan)

Profits and Losses			应交税金合计 Total Tax Payable			
研发费用 R&D Expenses	财务费用 Financial Expenses	利润总额 Total Profits		税金及附加 Tax and Surtax	所得税费用 Income Tax Expenses	应交增值税 Value Added Tax Payable
2200.6	**233636.4**	**604534.6**	**440874.5**	**124750.2**	**133221.4**	**182902.9**
1907.3	160165.7	250535.1	310949.3	87935.3	78809.9	144204.1
1661.2	161007.2	206232.1	265783.9	69666.2	69915.3	126202.4
246.1	101.4	9256.5	2016.3	744.5	53.2	1218.6
	-2032.6	33208.4	42328.9	17417.1	8809.0	16102.8
	520.5	-800.5	419.9	65.2	24.1	330.6
	569.2	2638.6	400.3	42.3	8.3	349.7
281.6	46248.6	274616.2	95824.1	25265.8	38173.2	32385.1
11.7	27222.1	79383.3	34101.1	11549.1	16238.3	6313.7
219.3	173352.1	294857.9	282879.0	112724.4	68416.3	101738.3
151.6	147232.7	182371.6	219591.7	100849.6	44325.5	74416.6
67.7	22494.7	107499.0	60152.6	10689.3	23345.1	26118.2
1981.3	60284.3	309676.7	157995.5	12025.8	64805.1	81164.6
376.7	36091.8	132651.2	84298.8	7684.4	26956.4	49658.0
740.0	20812.6	115846.8	30050.6	1285.6	22876.6	5888.4
746.3	948.5	49923.7	11950.1	665.3	8042.5	3242.3
0.3	-17.1	792.3	6415.0	528.3	1717.1	4169.6
118.0	2448.5	10462.7	25281.0	1862.2	5212.5	18206.3

16-9 连锁企业基本情况(2001-2023年)
BASIC STATISTICS ON CHAIN ENTERPRISES (2001-2023)

年份 Year	连锁总店(个) Number of Head Stores (unit)	门店总数(个) Number of Stores (unit)	从业人员年末人数(人) Year-end Number of Employed Persons (person)	营业面积(平方米) Operating Area (sq.m)	商品销售额(营业额)(万元) Total Sales of Value (Turnover) (10000 yuan)	#零售额 Retail Sales
2001	129	2123	139470	1605808	4831168	2186540
2002	146	3523	109089	2356266	6621975	6487185
2003	153	4519	132030	3405562	8404232	7601221
2004	196	5432	153942	3783507	8603560	8337829
2005	188	5973	166598	4376383	10612658	9507168
2006	205	6730	170007	5546003	11229026	9514297
2007	210	7645	185114	6677266	13890913	11573838
2008	240	8611	223954	6745802	15720473	12954839
2009	240	8928	218024	6995047	17366414	13816796
2010	234	9299	228292	7268786	21329783	16255496
2011	233	9845	280798	7953891	25742536	19507890
2012	220	10014	287975	8339674	26758403	20140433
2013	241	11111	299445	9026207	27834646	21495798
2014	243	11433	279567	9252645	28173728	21100845
2015	238	11942	279596	9238023	30453838	24508274
2016	245	12604	303319	11519137	32375249	27797369
2017	252	13450	316141	11121572	35574270	29557163
2018	277	15603	331018	11394589	38230004	31093369
2019	291	16126	326133	11183441	38223984	32566351
2020	295	16560	288096	11012622	36839402	32666424
2021	292	17974	290447	10059135	40485087	35526775
2022	288	17706	252537	9805062	38849911	33548258
2023	302	18369	272211	9731342	36522301	31096488

16-10 连锁企业基本情况(按登记注册统计类别、经营业态分)(2023年)
BASIC STATISTICS ON CHAIN ENTERPRISES (BY STATUS OF REGISTRATION AND BUSINESS CATEGORIES) (2023)

项目	Item	门店总数(个) Number of Stores (unit)	从业人员年末人数(人) Year-end Number of Employed Persons (person)	营业面积(平方米) Operating Area (sq.m)	商品销售额(营业额)(万元) Total Sales of Value (Turnover) (10000 yuan)	#零售额 Retail Sales
合计	**Total**	**18369**	**272211**	**9731342**	**36522301**	**31096488**
按登记注册统计类别分	**By Statistical Category of Registration**					
内资企业	Domestic Invested Enterprises	10119	120047	7360577	17975132	14862163
有限责任公司	Limited Liability Corporations	8721	92218	3603152	10113407	8473983
股份有限公司	Corporations Limited by Shares	1372	27388	3706841	7816144	6346906
非公司企业法人	Unincorporated Business Entity	15	405	49614	44233	39926
个人独资企业	Sole Proprietorship Enterprises	11	36	970	1348	1348
港澳台投资企业	Enterprises with Investment from Hong Kong, Macao and Taiwan	4439	71578	1208910	3327790	2909780
外商投资企业	Foreign Invested Enterprises	3811	80586	1161855	15219379	13324545
按经营业态分	**By Business Categories**					
零售业态	Retail	9545	100037	7438605	31120285	26129250
便利店	Convenience Store	2204	3122	191212	562702	447340
折扣店	Discount Store	1355	37874	2386171	7000857	6051867
超市	Supermarket	202	699	98495	229493	228180
仓储会员店	Warehouse Club	4	1002	33848	354356	354356
百货店	Department Store	91	11308	3179566	3655029	3648276
专业店	Specialty Store	2910	21880	1127984	8750446	6086280
#加油站	Gas Station	618	5546	301691	5024853	3129229
专卖店	Exclusive Store	2779	24152	421329	10567401	9312951
餐饮业态	Catering Services	8680	169378	2286706	5201107	4962994
正餐服务	Restaurant	2203	75874	1018096	2211941	2093856
快餐服务	Fast Food	3787	75687	911520	2197650	2086785
咖啡馆服务	Cafés	2319	15751	303720	635150	626060
其他饮料及冷饮服务	Other Beverages and Cold Drinks	363	1994	52670	151868	151793
小吃服务	Snacks	8	72	700	4499	4499
住宿业态	Accommodation Enterprises	144	2796	6031	200909	4244
旅游饭店	Tourist Hotel	20	445		35377	45
经济型连锁酒店	Economical Chain Hotel	124	2351	6031	165532	4199

16－11 商品交易市场基本情况(2023年)
BASIC STATISTICS ON COMMODITY EXCHANGE MARKETS (2023)

项　　目	Item	市场数量 (个) Number of Markets (unit)	总摊位数 (个) Number of Booths (unit)	成交额 (亿元) Turnover (100 million yuan)
合　　计	**Total**	**413**	**123894**	**3262.1**
按经营方式分	**By Business Practice**			
批发市场	Wholesale Market	44	37602	2476.7
零售市场	Retail Market	369	86292	785.5
按经营环境分	**By Business Environment**			
露天式	Open-air	79	33807	1903.4
封闭式	Closed	318	82823	1296.3
其　他	Others	16	7264	62.4

16－12 亿元及以上商品交易市场基本情况(2023年)
BASIC STATISTICS ON COMMODITY EXCHANGE MARKETS WITH TRANSACTION VALUE OVER 100 MILLION YUAN (2023)

项　　目	Item	市场数量 (个) Number of Markets (unit)	总摊位数 (个) Total Number of Booths (unit)	#出租摊位数 Number of Booths on Lease	成交额 (亿元) Turnover (100 million yuan)
合　　计	**Total**	**73**	**59316**	**48069**	**3200.9**
按经营方式分	**By Business Practice**				
批发市场	Wholesale Market	25	31644	23983	2471.3
零售市场	Retail Market	48	27672	24086	729.5
按经营环境分	**By Business Environment**				
露天式	Open-air	10	11684	8285	1895.9
封闭式	Closed	59	42610	35236	1246.3
其　他	Others	4	5022	4548	58.6

16-13 商品交易市场经营情况(2023年)
OPERATING STATISTICS ON COMMODITY EXCHANGE MARKETS (2023)

项目	Item	市场数量(个) Number of Markets (unit)	出租摊位数(个) Number of Booths on Lease (unit)	营业面积(万平方米) Operating Area (10000 sq.m)	成交额(亿元) Turnover (100 million yuan)
合计	**Total**	**413**	**88648**	**845.3**	**3262.1**
综合市场	**General Markets**	**224**	**42982**	**389.4**	**2084.0**
生产资料综合市场	Production Comprehensive Market				
工业消费品综合市场	Industrial Consumable Comprehensive Markets	18	2993	16.7	10.0
农产品综合市场	Farm Produce Comprehensive Markets	141	30206	297.9	2059.6
其他综合市场	Other Comprehensive Markets	65	9783	74.8	14.5
专业市场	**Specialized Markets**	**189**	**45666**	**455.9**	**1178.1**
生产资料市场	**Markets for Means of Production**	**22**	**4528**	**42.7**	**22.0**
木材市场	Wood Markets				
建材市场	Building Material Markets	20	3956	38.6	20.9
化工材料及制品市场	Chemical Materials and Products Markets				
金属材料市场	Metal Materials Markets	1	278	2.4	0.2
机械设备市场	Mechanical Equipment Markets				
其他生产资料市场	Others	1	294	1.7	0.9
农产品市场	**Farm Produce Markets**	**34**	**6107**	**76.3**	**409.0**
粮油市场	Grain and Oil Markets	1	42	0.1	0.1
肉禽蛋市场	Meat, Poultry and Eggs Markets	6	1296	3.3	7.3
水产品市场	Aquatic Products Markets	5	1552	15.5	163.6
蔬菜市场	Vegetables Markets	14	2514	37.7	231.3
干鲜果品市场	Dried and Fresh Melons and Fruits Markets	2	144	18.1	5.9
其他农产品市场	Others	6	559	1.6	0.8
食品、饮料及烟酒市场	**Markets for Food, Beverages, Tobacco and Liquor**	**10**	**1051**	**6.9**	**3.5**
食品饮料市场	Food and Beverages Markets				
茶叶市场	Tea Markets	8	989	6.5	3.3
其他食品饮料及烟酒市场	Others	2	62	0.5	0.3
纺织、服装、鞋帽市场	**Markets for Textiles, Clothing, Shoes and Hats**	**22**	**7322**	**39.1**	**29.3**
布料及纺织品市场	Cloth and Textiles Markets	1	115	0.4	0.3
服装市场	Clothing Markets	15	1340	12.5	3.6
鞋帽市场	Shoes and Hats Markets				
其他纺织服装鞋帽市场	Others	6	5867	26.3	25.4
日用品及文化用品市场	**Markets for Daily Use Articles and Cultural Goods**	**12**	**2000**	**9.3**	**3.6**
小商品市场	Small Merchandise Markets				

16-13 续表 Continued

项目	Item	市场数量(个) Number of Markets (unit)	出租摊位数(个) Number of Booths on Lease (unit)	营业面积(万平方米) Operating Area (10000 sq.m)	成交额(亿元) Turnover (100 million yuan)
箱包市场	Luggage Markets				
玩具市场	Toys Markets				
文具市场	Stationary Markets				
图书、报刊杂志市场	Markets for Books, Newspapers and Magazines	2	164	1.6	1.2
音像制品及电子出版物市场	Markets for Video and E-book Products				
体育用品市场	Sports Article Markets				
其他日用品及文化用品市场	Others	10	1836	7.7	2.4
黄金、珠宝、玉器等首饰市场	**Gold, Jewelry, Jade Markets**	**13**	**2152**	**11.1**	**6.4**
电器、通讯器材、电子设备市场	**Markets for Electrical Appliances, Communication Appliances and Electronic Appliances**	**6**	**2130**	**7.4**	**32.4**
家电市场	Household Appliances Markets	1	54	0.6	0.1
通讯器材市场	Communication Appliances Markets	1	195	0.8	1.2
照相、摄像器材市场	Cameras and Video Equipments Markets	1	162	0.9	1.1
计算机及辅助设备市场	Computer and Auxiliary Equipments Markets	2	1213	2.9	19.5
其他电器、通讯器材、电子设备市场	Others	1	506	2.2	10.7
医药、医疗用品及器材市场	**Markets for Medicine, Medical Materials and Medical Instruments**				
中药材市场	Chinese Medicine Markets				
其他医药、医疗用品及器材市场	Others				
家具、五金及装饰材料市场	**Markets for Furniture, Hardware and Decoration Materials**	**40**	**10634**	**169.8**	**198.4**
家具市场	Furniture Markets	17	4161	96.0	47.6
装饰材料市场	Decoration Materials Markets	13	4154	46.4	129.0
灯具市场	Lamps Markets	3	623	8.3	2.7
厨具、盥洗设备市场	Markets for Kitchen Utensils and Washing Equipment				
五金材料市场	Hardware Materials Markets	1	25	0.3	0.2
其他装修市场	Others	6	1671	18.9	18.9
汽车、摩托车及零配件市场	**Markets for Cars, Motocycles and Spare Parts**	**13**	**3169**	**72.7**	**466.6**
汽车市场	Cars Markets	8	1043	45.4	428.3
摩托车市场	Motocycles Markets				
机动车零配件市场	Vehicle Spare Parts Markets	5	2126	27.4	38.3
花、鸟、鱼、虫市场	**Markets for Flower, Bird, Fish and Insects**	**6**	**1163**	**2.9**	**0.7**
花卉市场	Flower Markets	5	733	1.7	0.4
鸟市场	Bird Markets				
观赏鱼市场	Markets for Fish for Display				
其他花鸟鱼虫市场	Others	1	430	1.1	0.2
旧货市场	**Second-hand Articles Markets**	**8**	**5347**	**10.4**	**4.6**
古玩、古董、字画市场	Markets for Antiques, Calligraphy and Painting	5	1090	5.6	0.6
邮票、硬币市场	Stamps and Coins Markets	1	887	0.8	0.5
其他旧货市场	Markets for Others Second-hand Articles	2	3370	4.1	3.5
其他专业市场	**Other Specialized Markets**	**3**	**63**	**7.2**	**1.7**

主要统计指标解释

社会消费品零售总额 指企业（单位、个体户）通过交易直接售给个人、社会集团用于非生产、非经营用的实物商品金额，以及提供餐饮服务所取得的收入金额。个人包括城乡居民和入境人员，社会集团包括机关、社会团体、部队、学校、企事业单位、居委会或村委会等。

批发和零售业单位 指在流通环节主要从事商品批发活动和零售活动的单位（含法人单位、产业活动单位、个体经营户）。

商品购进额 指从企业以外的单位和个人购进（包括从国外直接进口）作为转卖或加工后转卖的商品金额（含增值税）。本指标反映批发和零售业从国内外市场上购进商品的总价。

商品销售额 指对本单位以外的单位和个人出售的商品金额（包括售给本单位消费用的商品，含增值税）。本指标反映批发和零售业在国内市场上销售商品以及出口商品的总价。

期末商品库存额 对于批发和零售业法人单位和个体经营户，是指报告期末取得所有权的全部商品金额（含增值税）；对于批发和零售业产业活动单位，是指报告期末实际在库且归属法人具有所有权的全部商品金额（含增值税）。本指标反映批发和零售业的商品库存情况，以及对市场商品供应的保证程度。

连锁总店（总部） 负责连锁企业资源（商号、商誉、经营模式、服务标准、管理模式等）的开发、配置、控制或使用等功能的企业核心管理机构。连锁经营是指经营同类商品或服务，使用统一商号的若干店铺，在同一总店（总部）的管理下，采取统一采购或特许经营等方式，实现规模效益的组织形式，包括直营连锁、特许连锁和自愿连锁三种形式。直营连锁是指连锁店铺由连锁公司全资或控股开设，在总部的直接控制下，开展统一经营的连锁经营形式；特许连锁是指拥有注册商标、企业标志、专利、专有技术等经营资源的企业（特许人），以合同形式将其拥有的经营资源许可其他经营者（被特许人）使用，被特许人按合同约定在统一的经营模式下开展经营，并向特许人支付特许经营费用的连锁经营形式；自愿连锁是指若干个店铺或企业自愿组合起来，在不改变各自资产所有权关系的情况下，以同一个品牌形象面对消费者，以共同进货为纽带开展的连锁经营形式。

连锁门店 在连锁企业经营管理的基础上，按照总店（总部）的指示和服务规范要求，承担日常销售业务的店铺，称连锁门店，包括直营店（控股店）和加盟店。

（1）直营店（控股店）是指由连锁企业总部投资开设，按连锁经营管理模式，由总部统一管理的店铺。

（2）加盟店是指在特许连锁中，被特许人获得特许人授权后，使用其商标、商号、经营模式、专利和专有技术等经营资源建立的店铺，也包括自愿连锁的成员店。

门店总数 指该连锁企业所拥有的全部门店（包括直营店和加盟店）数量。其中，总店（如果总公司有门店的话）作为一个直营店处理。此外，有的地区分出控股店，控股店按直营店统计。

餐饮业单位 指在一定场所，专门从事对食物进行现场烹饪、调制，并出售给顾客主要供现场消费服务活动的单位（含法人单位、产业活动单位、个体经营户）。如各种饭馆、中西餐厅、酒馆、茶馆和火车餐车、车站食堂、飞机场餐厅等。

住宿业单位 指有偿为顾客提供临时住宿服务活动的单位（含法人单位、产业活动单位、个体经营户）。如旅游饭店、宾馆、酒店和旅馆、旅店等。

商品交易市场 指经有关部门和组织批准设立，有固定场所、设施，有经营管理部门和监管人员，若干市场经营者入内，常年或实际开业三个月以上，集中、公开、独立地进行生活消费品、生产资料等现货商品交易以及提供相关服务的交易场所，包括各类消费品市场、生产资料市场等。

Explanatory Notes on Main Statistical Indicators

Total Retail Sales of Consumer Goods refer to the total prices of physical commodities sold by enterprises (entities or self-employed businesses) through transaction directly to individuals and social groups to be used for non-productive and non-operating purposes, combined with the amount of income from provision of food and beverage services. Individuals include urban and rural residents and persons entering China. Social groups include government agencies, social organizations, armies, schools, enterprises and public institutions, residents' committee or villagers' committee, and so on.

Wholesale and Retail Entities refer to entities engaged in commodity wholesale and retail activities in circulation (including legal entities, activity entities and individual entities).

Total Purchases of Commodities refer to the total value (VAT included) of purchases (including direct imports from foreign countries) of commodities by the enterprises from other entities or individuals for the purpose of re-selling, either with or without further processing of the commodities purchased. This indicator is used to show the total price of purchases of retail and wholesale commodities from domestic and overseas markets.

Total Sales of Commodities refer to value of commodities sold by the entities to other entities and individuals (including the commodities consumed by the enterprises themselves, VAT included). This indicator is used to show the total price of wholesale and retail commodities sold in domestic markets and exported.

Inventory (year-end) refers to, for legal entities and self-employed businesses in wholesale and retail trades, the value of all commodities with ownership gained (VAT included) at the end of the reference period; for industrial activity entities in wholesale and retail trades, it refers to the value of all commodities actually in storage and owned by their legal person at the end of the reference period (VAT included). This indicator shows the commodity inventory in wholesale and retail trades, and to what extent the commodities will be supplied to the market.

General Chain Store (Headquarters) means the core management organization in an enterprise, responsible for the development, deployment, control or use of resources (trade name, goodwill, operating model, service standards and management model, etc.) of the chain enterprise. Chain operation means an organization form in which several stores using unified trade name dealing in the same commodities or providing the same services through uniform purchase or franchise operation under the management of the same general store (headquarters) to achieve benefits of scale. Chain operation falls into direct-sale chain, franchised chain and voluntary chain. Direct-sale chain is a form of chain operation that chain stores are wholly funded or controlled by chain companies, carrying out uniform operation under the direct control of headquarters; franchised chain is a form of chain operation that any enterprise (the franchiser) owning operating resources, such as trademarks, logos, patents and proprietary technologies, authorize such operating resources to any other operator (the franchisee) by contract, and the franchisee operates under uniform operating model as stated in the contract, and pays franchise fees to the franchiser; voluntary chain is a form of chain operation that several stores or enterprises combine together voluntarily to face consumers with the same brand image without changing their own asset ownership relations, and link together through joint purchase.

Chain Stores Based on the operation and management of chain enterprises, stores carrying out daily sales business by following the general store's (headquarters') instruction and required service standards are called chained stores. They include direct-sale stores (controlled stores) and franchised stores.

(1) Direct-sale Stores (Controlled Stores) refer to stores opened with funds from the headquarters of chain enterprises, using the chain operation and management model, and under the uniform management of the headquarters.

(2) Franchised Stores refer to, in franchise chains, stores established after the franchisee is authorized by the franchiser to use its trademark, trade name, operating model, patent and proprietary technologies and other operating resources. Voluntary chain members are also included.

Total Number of Stores refers to the number of all stores owned by the chain enterprises (including direct-sale stores and franchised stores). The general store (if the parent company has stores) is regarded as a direct-sale store. In addition, controlled stores are considered separately in some areas, which are regarded as direct-sale stores.

Restaurants Entities refer to entities (including legal entities, industrial activity entities and self-employed businesses) specialized in cooking and seasoning food which is sold to clients for on-site consumption at a specific site, such as various restaurants, Chinese food and Western food restaurants, pubs, teahouses, dining compartments on trains, canteens at railway stations, and restaurants at airports.

Accommodation Entities refer to entities (including legal entities, industrial activity entities and self-employed businesses) providing clients with temporary accommodation services, such as tourist hotels, guesthouses, hotels, rest houses and inns, for a fee.

Commodity Transaction Markets refer to transaction sites approved by competent authorities and organizations, with fixed places and facilities. There are operation management departments and regulating personnel in the markets, where several operators stay over years or open for over three months, conducting transactions of on-hand commodities such as living consumables and capital goods, and offering relevant services in a concentrated, open and independent manner. Commodity transaction markets include various markets of consumer goods and capital goods markets, etc.

17

旅游业
TOURISM

简要说明

一、主要内容

本章资料主要反映北京市国际旅游和国内旅游情况。包括旅游人数及其在京花费情况、重点住宿业经营及接待住宿者情况、旅行社接待及出境旅游情况、旅游区（点）活动情况等。

二、调查方法

重点住宿业、旅行社、旅游区（点）有关数据通过全面调查取得。

三、调查范围

重点住宿业统计范围为有经营活动的星级及非星级重点住宿业法人单位、产业活动单位和个体经营户。

旅行社统计范围为有经营活动的全部旅行社（其中出境旅游情况统计范围为有特许经营出境旅游业务权的旅行社）。

旅游区（点）统计范围为有经营活动的A级及以上旅游区（点）和其他主要旅游区（点）。

Brief Introduction

I. Main Content

Statistics in this chapter mainly show the situation of tourism and international tourism in Beijing. Including: statistics for the number and spending of tourists to Beijing, operation and reception of key accommodation services, reception and outbound tourism made through travel agencies, activities of tourist attractions (sightseeing spots), and so on.

II. Methods of Survey

Data concerning key accommodation services, travel agencies, tourist attractions (sightseeing spots) were obtained through comprehensive survey.

III. Scope of Survey

The scope of statistics on key accommodation services covers the star-rated and non-star-rated key accommodation industry legal person units, industrial activity units and self-employed households that engage in business activities.

The scope of statistics on travel agencies covers all travel agencies that engage in business activities (of which, the scope of statistics for outbound tourism covers the travel agencies that have the franchise to engage in outbound tourism business).

The scope of statistics on tourist attractions (sightseeing spots) covers the Level A-or-above tourist attractions (sightseeing spots) and other major tourist attractions (sightseeing spots) that engage in business activities.

17−1 国际、国内旅游情况(1978−2023年)
STATISTICS ON INTERNATIONAL AND DOMESTIC TOURISM (1978-2023)

年 份 Year	来京游客人数 (万人次) Number of Visitors to Beijing (10000 person-times)	入境游客 Number of Overseas Visitor Arrivals	国内游客 Number of Domestic Visitors	国际旅游收入 (亿美元) Earnings from International Tourism (100 million USD)	国内旅游收入 (亿元) Earnings from Domestic Tourism (100 million yuan)
1978		18.7		1.0	
1979		25.2		0.9	
1980		28.6		1.2	
1981		39.4		1.2	
1982		45.7		1.3	
1983		50.9		1.4	
1984		65.7		2.3	
1985		93.7		3.2	
1986		99.0		4.6	
1987		108.1		5.5	
1988		120.4		6.7	
1989		64.5		4.7	
1990		100.0		6.6	
1991		132.0		8.5	
1992		174.8		10.7	
1993		202.8		12.4	
1994	6913.0	203.0	6710.0	20.1	298.0
1995	6527.0	207.0	6320.0	21.8	352.6
1996	7901.9	218.9	7683.0	22.5	359.6
1997	8450.8	229.8	8221.0	22.5	391.3
1998	8951.5	220.1	8731.4	23.8	424.5
1999	9512.4	252.4	9260.0	25.0	530.0
2000	10468.1	282.1	10186.0	27.7	683.0
2001	11292.8	285.8	11007.0	29.5	887.7
2002	11810.4	310.4	11500.0	31.1	930.0
2003	8885.1	185.1	8700.0	19.0	706.0
2004	12265.5	315.5	11950.0	31.7	1145.0
2005	12862.9	362.9	12500.0	36.2	1300.0
2006	13590.3	390.3	13200.0	40.3	1482.7
2007	14715.5	435.5	14280.0	45.8	1753.6
2008	14560.0	379.0	14181.0	44.6	1907.0
2009	16669.5	412.5	16257.0	43.6	2144.5
2010	18390.1	490.1	17900.0	50.4	2425.1
2011	21404.4	520.4	20884.0	54.2	2864.3
2012	23134.6	500.9	22633.7	51.5	3301.3
2013	25189.0	450.1	24738.8	47.9	3666.3
2014	26149.7	427.5	25722.2	46.1	3997.0
2015	27279.0	420.0	26859.0	46.1	4320.0
2016	28531.5	416.5	28115.0	50.7	4683.0
2017	29746.2	392.6	29353.6	51.3	5122.4
2018	31093.6	400.4	30693.2	55.2	5556.2
2019	32209.9	376.9	31833.0	51.9	5866.2
2020	18386.5	34.1	18352.4	4.8	2880.9
2021	25512.8	24.5	25488.3	4.3	4138.5
2022	18230.8	24.1	18206.7	4.4	2490.9
2023	32853.7	116.8	32736.9	16.6	5731.2

资料来源：本表除2019年以前入境游客数据外，其他数据均来源于北京市文化和旅游局。
Source: Except for the data on the number of overseas visitor arrivals before 2019, all other data in this table are provided by Beijing Municipal Bureau of Culture and Tourism.

17−2 按客源地分入境游客人数(1978−2023年)
NUMBER OF VISITOR ARRIVALS BY COUNTRY/REGION (1978-2023)

单位：万人次 (10000 person-times)

年 份 Year	入境游客人数 Number of Overseas Visitor Arrivals	港澳台同胞 Chinese Compatriots from Hong Kong, Macao and Taiwan Province	#中国香港 Hong Kong, China	外国人 Foreigner	#日本 Japan	#韩国 Korea	#美国 United States	#英国 United Kingdom	#法国 France	#德国 Germany	#俄罗斯 Russia
1978	18.7	3.3		15.4							
1979	25.2	4.1		21.1							
1980	28.6	5.8		21.7	6.0		3.7	1.3	0.9	0.9	
1981	39.4	6.8		31.3	5.3		3.8	1.1	1.1	1.0	
1982	45.7	8.2		35.9	8.2		6.6	1.3	1.3	1.4	
1983	50.9	8.9		39.7	10.0		9.4	1.5	1.5	1.7	0.1
1984	65.7	10.0		52.1	17.2		12.5	2.3	2.1	2.5	0.1
1985	93.7	13.6		74.0	27.6		14.8	3.9	3.2	4.0	0.2
1986	99.0	15.8		79.0	25.5		14.7	4.1	3.1	4.6	0.3
1987	108.1	21.8		81.7	26.3		16.5	4.5	4.3	5.1	0.3
1988	120.4	28.8		86.5	27.8		16.7	4.2	4.2	5.4	0.7
1989	64.5	16.6		46.0	12.2		7.3	2.4	2.1	3.3	1.0
1990	100.0	34.7	11.4	63.8	18.2		8.6	2.9	2.0	4.0	1.5
1991	132.0	38.2	17.6	91.4	27.6	4.3	9.5	4.3	3.7	6.0	3.5
1992	174.8	51.2	24.6	120.5	37.6	5.6	12.3	4.4	6.6	9.4	5.1
1993	202.8	52.8	29.4	145.0	39.3	7.3	14.3	5.3	6.9	12.0	7.7
1994	203.0	39.4	25.7	160.0	41.1	12.7	15.4	5.4	6.7	9.7	4.9
1995	207.0	36.3	25.4	166.5	42.4	17.3	17.4	5.8	6.2	8.8	6.2
1996	218.9	38.6	25.5	176.2	43.0	18.0	18.5	7.5	6.6	10.0	6.9
1997	229.8	40.3	26.3	186.9	43.0	19.4	21.7	9.0	6.5	9.1	6.5
1998	220.1	39.1	25.0	178.2	43.5	8.2	23.2	8.8	6.9	11.3	6.2
1999	252.4	44.1	26.5	205.0	45.6	19.2	24.1	8.8	7.9	10.5	4.6
2000	282.1	44.1	25.0	238.0	54.3	27.8	31.1	9.7	9.6	12.1	3.9
2001	285.8	45.9	26.9	239.9	50.7	32.7	33.1	11.1	10.2	12.3	4.9
2002	310.4	43.9	25.5	266.5	56.5	38.0	37.4	12.9	11.3	12.2	5.2
2003	185.1	32.4	21.7	152.7	29.2	24.5	19.4	8.1	5.5	6.3	5.2
2004	315.5	47.4	27.7	268.1	52.3	42.4	37.4	11.8	11.1	11.5	8.2
2005	362.9	51.3	31.4	311.6	45.0	45.3	46.5	13.9	13.6	14.6	9.7
2006	390.3	52.0	30.3	338.3	50.6	42.4	49.8	14.8	14.2	15.3	15.0
2007	435.5	52.9	31.3	382.6	58.8	44.4	60.3	17.0	16.4	17.5	18.3
2008	379.0	43.3	28.1	335.7	40.0	35.3	53.8	17.5	14.5	16.0	17.9
2009	412.5	69.6	44.4	342.9	46.2	35.2	57.9	16.3	12.9	16.8	15.0
2010	490.1	68.4	40.3	421.6	52.6	50.6	70.0	16.8	14.3	20.1	19.0
2011	520.4	73.0	43.4	447.4	51.0	53.4	78.9	18.8	15.0	22.2	20.5
2012	500.9	66.5	37.6	434.4	43.7	44.2	75.1	18.5	15.1	24.5	20.0
2013	450.1	62.5	35.4	387.6	24.9	37.7	74.7	17.5	13.4	23.0	16.7
2014	427.5	62.0	34.2	365.5	24.9	38.7	71.5	16.9	13.4	22.6	13.7
2015	420.0	62.4	34.9	357.6	25.8	41.6	69.4	17.2	15.3	21.2	10.3
2016	416.5	61.8	35.3	354.8	24.8	37.9	70.3	18.3	13.2	20.6	9.5
2017	392.6	60.6	34.4	332.0	24.2	23.5	67.3	16.5	12.3	19.4	9.3
2018	400.4	60.6	34.8	339.8	24.9	24.8	72.0	15.9	12.7	19.4	8.7
2019	376.9	56.2	32.2	320.7	24.7	24.2	62.9	15.3	12.0	19.8	9.6
2020	34.1	7.7	4.8	26.4	1.9	2.5	5.8	1.1	0.9	1.7	0.9
2021	24.5	7.0	4.4	17.5	1.5	2.3	3.4	0.7	0.5	1.2	0.7
2022	24.1	5.2	3.2	18.9	3.2	1.6	3.0	0.9	0.4	1.2	0.6
2023	116.8	21.9	14.4	95.0	7.9	4.2	12.9	4.1	2.8	5.4	6.8

注：1.1980—1999年的入境游客人数由外国游客、港澳台游客、华侨三部分组成，自2000年起华侨包括在外国游客内。
2.1990—1999年香港游客人数为香港、澳门合计。

资料来源：自2019年起，本表数据来源于北京市文化和旅游局。

Note: a) Number of overseas visitor arrivals in 1980-1999 consists of foreign visitors, visitors from Hong Kong, Macao and Taiwan, and overseas Chinese. Overseas Chinese have been included in the number of foreign visitors since 2000.

b) Visitors from Hong Kong in 1990-1999 refer to the total number of visitors from Hong Kong and Macao.

Source: Since 2019, all data in this table have been from Beijing Municipal Bureau of Culture and Tourism.

17-3 来京游客人数
NUMBER OF VISITORS TO BEIJING

单位：万人次 (10000 person-times)

项 目	Item	2023	2022
合 计	**Total**	**32853.7**	**18230.8**
国内游客人数	**Number of Domestic Visitors**	**32736.9**	**18206.7**
外地来京游客	Visitors to Beijing from Outside Beijing	18119.2	8295.0
本市游客	Local Visitors	14617.7	9911.7
入境游客人数	**Number of Overseas Visitor Arrivals**	**116.8**	**24.1**
港澳台同胞	Chinese Compatriots from Hong Kong, Macao and Taiwan Province	21.9	5.2
中国香港	Hong Kong, China	14.4	3.2
中国澳门	Macao, China	1.1	0.2
中国台湾	Taiwan, China	6.4	1.7
外国人	Foreigners	95.0	18.9
亚 洲	Asia	38.8	7.8
#日 本	Japan	7.9	3.2
韩 国	Korea	4.2	1.6
菲律宾	Philippines	0.6	…
印度尼西亚	Indonesia	1.8	0.1
马来西亚	Malaysia	3.0	0.2
新加坡	Singapore	4.9	0.5
泰 国	Thailand	2.5	0.7
印 度	India	1.6	0.2
蒙 古	Mongolia	3.6	…
美 洲	America	15.6	3.7
#美 国	United States	12.9	3.0
加拿大	Canada	2.7	0.7
欧 洲	Europe	28.2	5.6
#英 国	United Kingdom	4.1	0.9
法 国	France	2.8	0.4
德 国	Germany	5.4	1.2
意大利	Italy	1.6	0.4
西班牙	Spain	0.9	0.2
瑞 典	Sweden	0.6	0.1
瑞 士	Switzerland	0.6	0.3
俄罗斯	Russia	6.8	0.6
大洋洲	Oceania	3.6	0.5
#澳大利亚	Australia	2.7	0.4
新西兰	New Zealand	0.7	0.1
非 洲	Africa	5.3	0.9
其 他	Others	3.5	0.4

资料来源：北京市文化和旅游局。
Source: Beijing Municipal Bureau of Culture and Tourism.

17-4 在京旅游花费构成情况(2005-2023年)

单位：%

项　　目	Item	2005	2006	2007	2008	2009	2010
入境游客	**Composition of Expenditures for**	**100.0**	**100.0**	**100.0**	**100.0**	**100.0**	**100.0**
花费构成	**Overseas Visitor Arrivals**						
长途交通费	Long Distance Transportation Expenses	35.3	30.0	29.0	31.1	37.4	28.1
民　航	Civil Aviation	30.9	29.6	24.4	25.3	27.1	19.8
铁　路	Railway	1.1	0.3	3.0	3.6	5.5	5.3
公　路	Highway	3.3	0.1	1.6	2.2	4.8	3.0
市内交通费	Local Transportation Expenses	1.1	1.7	2.6	2.4	2.7	3.4
住　宿	Accommodation	17.3	32.0	16.9	16.4	14.5	14.4
餐　饮	Food and Beverage	9.2	11.7	8.7	8.7	7.5	8.7
购　物	Shopping	19.9	15.9	22.5	19.1	20.4	25.1
邮电通讯	Postal and Communication Services	3.4	0.8	2.7	3.8	2.7	3.2
景区游览	Scenic Spot Sightseeing	4.7	2.3	4.2	4.8	3.9	4.7
文化娱乐	Culture and Entertainment	4.6	3.2	5.0	4.5	4.6	5.0
其　他	Others	4.5	2.4	8.4	9.2	6.3	7.4
外地来京游客	**Composition of Expenditures for**	**100.0**	**100.0**	**100.0**	**100.0**	**100.0**	**100.0**
花费构成	**Visitors from Outside Beijing**						
长途交通费	Long Distance Transportation Expenses	12.8	15.1	16.3	15.4	12.9	12.8
民　航	Civil Aviation		8.0	9.2	9.1	6.6	6.0
铁　路	Railway		6.1	6.4	4.5	1.3	5.8
公　路	Highway		1.1	0.7	1.8	5.0	1.0
市内交通费	Local Transportation Expenses	5.7	5.1	5.5	5.6	4.9	5.0
住　宿	Accommodation	17.2	14.9	17.3	15.1	17.7	19.6
餐　饮	Food and Beverage	19.8	18.7	20.5	23.2	21.8	20.2
购　物	Shopping	24.1	22.2	25.8	32.7	34.5	34.5
邮电通讯	Postal and Communication Services	1.0	1.2	1.8	1.0	0.6	0.5
景区游览	Scenic Spot Sightseeing	9.1	9.5	7.2	4.5	6.1	6.2
文化娱乐	Culture and Entertainment	3.1	2.5	1.9	1.6	1.2	1.0
其　他	Others	7.1	10.8	3.7	0.9	0.3	0.2

资料来源：北京市文化和旅游局。

COMPOSITION OF TOURISM EXPENDITURES IN BEIJING (2005-2023)

(%)

2011	2012	2013	2014	2015	2016	2017	2018	2019	2020	2021	2022	2023
100.0	**100.0**	**100.0**	**100.0**	**100.0**	**100.0**	**100.0**	**100.0**	**100.0**	**100.0**	**100.0**	**100.0**	**100.0**
26.4	28.0	26.9	27.0	36.8	38.3	37.7	27.2	28.4	31.5	32.6	32.6	35.1
20.5	22.3	21.2	21.4	30.8	38.0	37.1	26.2	27.6	30.5	31.6	31.6	34.3
3.4	3.3	3.7	3.6	3.2	0.2	0.4	0.6	0.6	0.7	0.7	0.7	0.6
2.5	2.4	2.0	2.0	2.7	0.1	0.2	0.3	0.2	0.3	0.3	0.3	0.2
3.5	3.5	2.5	2.6	2.4	2.5	1.4	3.0	4.0	1.8	4.3	4.3	4.7
15.5	16.5	16.9	16.7	12.8	18.3	14.4	19.0	19.0	34.6	27.1	27.1	27.0
6.8	7.4	7.3	7.4	6.2	11.4	6.8	8.2	9.4	17.1	13.4	13.4	12.5
25.3	23.5	27.6	26.7	19.9	18.5	27.6	26.0	24.5	5.4	13.0	13.0	11.3
2.0	2.2	1.7	1.7	2.4	0.2	0.6	0.7	0.4	0.8	0.6	0.6	0.6
4.2	5.0	4.2	4.3	3.3	4.2	2.4	3.9	4.5	1.0	2.4	2.4	2.4
6.0	5.4	3.8	4.0	4.2	4.6	2.1	2.3	1.4	0.3	0.7	0.7	4.5
10.3	8.5	9.1	9.6	12.1	2.0	7.0	9.7	8.3	7.6	6.0	5.9	1.9
100.0	**100.0**	**100.0**	**100.0**	**100.0**	**100.0**	**100.0**	**100.0**	**100.0**	**100.0**	**100.0**	**100.0**	**100.0**
13.5	15.5	17.0	17.6	17.0	15.8	14.3	12.4	11.8	14.6	17.9	16.1	12.6
6.2	7.7	7.5	7.1	7.4	7.5	6.2	4.7	4.8	6.9	10.0	8.5	4.5
6.9	7.5	9.1	10.2	9.3	8.0	7.3	6.4	5.8	6.3	6.4	6.1	6.4
0.3	0.3	0.4	0.3	0.3	0.3	0.8	1.4	1.2	1.4	1.6	1.6	1.7
4.5	4.0	3.8	3.8	4.0	3.9	4.1	3.9	4.2	4.3	2.4	2.4	1.3
20.0	19.8	19.5	20.2	18.7	17.8	19.0	18.8	19.1	20.1	17.3	17.4	15.9
20.9	21.4	21.4	22.1	22.1	22.8	22.2	21.6	21.1	20.0	18.7	19.7	16.3
34.3	32.1	30.9	28.2	30.2	31.3	31.2	32.4	31.8	25.6	24.5	23.6	31.1
0.3	0.2	0.2	0.3	0.3	0.2	0.2	0.2	0.2	0.2	0.1	0.1	0.2
5.7	6.1	6.6	6.5	6.2	6.6	7.3	8.0	9.2	10.0	10.8	13.2	10.6
0.8	0.7	0.5	0.6	0.7	0.9	1.2	1.9	2.0	2.4	6.7	6.2	9.9
0.1	0.1	0.1	0.7	0.8	0.7	0.6	0.8	0.8	2.8	1.6	1.3	2.1

Source: Beijing Municipal Bureau of Culture and Tourism.

17-5 重点住宿业单位出租率和平均房价
RENTING RATE AND AVERAGE PRICES OF KEY ENTITIES IN ACCOMMODATION INDUSTRY

项 目	Item	出租率(%) Renting Rate (%)		平均房价(元/间夜) Average Prices (yuan/room.day)	
		2023	2022	2023	2022
合 计	**Total**	**64.4**	**38.7**	**534**	**442**
按住宿业等级分	**By the Rating of Hotels**				
五 星	5-Star	64.1	28.9	793	712
四 星	4-Star	62.1	33.2	567	504
三 星	3-Star	58.0	36.8	390	372
二星及一星级	2-Star and 1-Star	61.9	42.7	313	307
非星级	Non-star-rated	66.2	42.3	500	409

注：本表统计范围为全市范围内的星级及非星级重点住宿业法人单位、产业活动单位和个体经营户，下同。
This table covers star-rated and non-star-rated key legal entities, industrial activity units and the self-employed in accommodation industry throughout Beijing., the same below.

资料来源：北京市文化和旅游局。
Source: Beijing Municipal Bureau of Culture and Tourism.

17-6 重点住宿业单位经营情况
OPERATING STATISTICS ON KEY ENTITIES IN ACCOMMODATION INDUSTRY

项 目	Item	企业个数(个) Number of Enterprises (unit)		营业收入(万元) Business Revenue (10000 yuan)		利润总额(万元) Total Profits (10000 yuan)		从业人员平均人数(人) Average Number of Employed Persons (person)	
		2023	2022	2023	2022	2023	2022	2023	2022
合 计	**Total**	**1159**	**1177**	**4514545**	**2683764**	**345303**	**-655298**	**96525**	**92398**
按住宿业等级分	**By the Rating of Hotels**								
五星级	5-Star	60	64	952952	532913	101930	-188045	18989	19135
四星级	4-Star	98	100	748949	470845	33020	-121782	18176	18427
三星级	3-Star	128	132	413078	292419	7168	-52745	10511	10408
二星及一星级	2-Star and 1-Star	51	54	53870	40537	8136	-179	1425	1486
非星级	Non-star-rated	822	827	2345695	1347050	195049	-292547	47424	42942

资料来源：北京市文化和旅游局。
Source: Beijing Municipal Bureau of Culture and Tourism.

17-7 重点住宿业单位接待情况
RECEPTION OF KEY ENTITIES IN ACCOMMODATION INDUSTRY

项　目	Item	接待住宿者人数（万人次）Guests Received (10000 person-times)		接待住宿者人天数（万人天）Person-days of Guests Received (10000 person-days)	
		2023	2022	2023	2022
合　计	**Total**	**3970.2**	**1833.3**	**6919.1**	**3772.4**
按住宿业等级分	**By the Rating of Hotels**				
五星级	5-Star	482.7	188.7	825.2	369.0
四星级	4-Star	448.4	143.9	876.9	442.7
三星级	3-Star	316.7	147.0	675.3	415.2
二星及一星级	2-Star and 1-Star	67.7	44.8	129.0	117.4
非星级	Non-star-rated	2654.7	1308.9	4412.6	2428.0
按住宿者类别分	**By the Category of Guests**				
国内过夜游客	Overnight Domestic Visitors	3863.6	1811.6	6711.5	3702.2
入境过夜游客	Overnight Inbound Visitors	106.6	21.7	207.5	70.2
外国人	Foreigners	86.8	17.1	168.1	53.5
中国香港	Hong Kong, China	13.0	2.9	25.4	10.8
中国澳门	Macao, China	1.0	0.2	2.2	0.4
中国台湾	Taiwan, China	5.8	1.6	11.8	5.5

资料来源：北京市文化和旅游局。
Source: Beijing Municipal Bureau of Culture and Tourism.

17-8 旅行社接待及经营情况(1990—2023年)
RECEPTION AND OPERATION OF TRAVEL AGENCIES (1990-2023)

年份 Year	企业个数(个) Number of Enterprises (unit)	外联(组团)人数(万人次) Number of Visitors Grouped (Organized) (10000 person-times)	接待人数(万人次) Visitors Received (10000 person-times)	国内居民出境人数(万人次) Number of Chinese Outbound Visitors (10000 person-times)	营业收入(万元) Business Revenue (10000 yuan)	利润总额(万元) Total Profits (10000 yuan)	从业人员平均人数(人) Average Number of Employed Persons (person)
1990		32.5	54.7				
1991		53.3	69.1				
1992		61.2	100.7				
1993		71.3	103.6				
1994		84.1	91.0	1.0			
1995	100	85.7	87.4	1.2	290987.9	107654.6	
1996	105	88.0	78.6	2.7	351634.7	13520.8	
1997	110	87.3	76.0	3.8	386254.1	16009.6	
1998	131	85.0	69.0	6.6	387562.7	21319.9	
1999	120	103.1	92.9	11.1	485678.8	26572.0	
2000	127	123.7	101.0	13.7	576244.6	28744.7	6280
2001	140	143.4	130.1	21.9	700529.0	18682.5	8259
2002	151	179.4	176.3	28.5	823551.0	23362.0	9350
2003	147	80.2	82.4	31.9	553787.0	-11829.0	8382
2004	147	274.8	252.6	51.4	1059989.0	11444.0	7760
2005	147	308.4	278.2	51.7	1316063.0	10240.0	8752
2006	147	343.9	315.7	79.2	1610265.0	7012.0	8659
2007	189	424.1	377.9	100.2	2101874.5	28409.2	11597
2008	245	359.6	310.1	102.0	2166898.1	18121.6	14369
2009	265	370.6	306.6	84.9	2134058.8	5904.6	15262
2010	819	538.1	542.2	149.6	3517099.4	22636.2	21454
2011	919	593.9	552.3	184.3	4436713.3	20879.2	23871
2012	1021	684.5	519.1	272.5	5415692.9	35274.4	28022
2013	1147	661.3	441.6	331.0	6103603.4	64177.5	31694
2014	1243	628.0	427.0	410.2	6989125.4	27881.7	33591
2015	1238	655.5	468.0	533.1	8355826.3	-17132.1	37780
2016	1162	667.9	466.8	571.3	8788779.0	-29589.9	40812
2017	1139	573.0	422.3	511.5	8819738.7	122815.9	37952
2018	1192	544.5	377.8	510.9	9439120.6	590.2	37660
2019	1440	635.8	455.7	484.5	10394925.9	-6714.6	39779
2020	1413	168.1	91.1	47.2	1994239.0	-289717.0	26155
2021	1239	300.0	153.2		2265107.1	-147166.4	17125
2022	1225	177.9	31.8		2007777.4	-116756.9	13852
2023	1450	455.8	470.9	36.3	5478800.3	466519.8	18529

注：本表2009年及以前为国际旅行社口径，自2010年起调整为全部旅行社口径。
资料来源：自2020年起，表中数据均来自北京市文化和旅游局。
Note: Figures in this table refer to international travel agencies in and before 2009, and all travel agencies since 2010.
Source: Since 2020, the data in the table have been provided by Beijing Municipal Bureau of Culture and Tourism.

17-9 旅行社外联(组团)及接待情况
VISITORS GROUPED (ORGANIZED) AND RECEIVED BY TRAVEL AGENCIES

项　　目	Item	2023	2022
外联(组团)人数　(万人次)	**Number of Visitors Grouped (Organized)　(10000 person-times)**	**455.8**	**177.9**
国内旅游者	Domestic Visitors	451.6	177.9
港澳同胞	Chinese Compatriots from Hong Kong and Macao	1.2	
台湾同胞	Chinese Compatriots from Taiwan Province	0.4	…
外国人	Foreigners	2.6	
接待人数　(万人次)	**Visitors Received　(10000 person-times)**	**470.9**	**31.8**
国内旅游者	Domestic Visitors	462.5	31.8
港澳同胞	Chinese Compatriots from Hong Kong and Macao	1.4	
台湾同胞	Chinese Compatriots from Taiwan Province	0.4	…
外国人	Foreigners	6.6	
外联(组团)人天数(万人天)	**Persons-day of Visitors Grouped (Organized)　(10000 persons-day)**	**1338.5**	**534.6**
国内旅游者	Domestic Visitors	1313.5	534.5
港澳同胞	Chinese Compatriots from Hong Kong and Macao	6.6	
台湾同胞	Chinese Compatriots from Taiwan Province	1.9	…
外国人	Foreigners	16.6	
接待人天数　(万人天)	**Persons-day of Visitors Received　(10000 persons-day)**	**1167.2**	**64.8**
国内旅游者	Domestic Visitors	1123.3	64.8
港澳同胞	Chinese Compatriots from Hong Kong and Macao	6.5	
台湾同胞	Chinese Compatriots from Taiwan Province	1.5	…
外国人	Foreigners	35.8	

资料来源：北京市文化和旅游局。
Source: Beijing Municipal Bureau of Culture and Tourism.

17–10 旅行社经营情况
OPERATING STATISTICS ON TRAVEL AGENCIES

单位：万元 (10000 yuan)

项　　目		Item		2023	2022
企业个数	（个）	Number of Enterprises	(unit)	1450	1225
营业收入		Business Revenue		5478800	2007777
营业成本		Business Cost		5309066	2023566
营业利润		Business Profits		828	-152663
利润总额		Total Profits		466520	-116757
从业人员平均人数	（人）	Average Number of Employed Persons	(person)	18529	13852

资料来源：北京市文化和旅游局。
Source: Beijing Municipal Bureau of Culture and Tourism.

17–11 旅游区(点)活动情况
STATISTICS ON ACTIVITIES OF TOURIST ATTRACTIONS (SIGHT SPOTS)

项　　目		Item		2023	2022
旅游区(点)个数	（个）	Number of Tourist Attractions (Sight Spots)	(unit)	258	240
收入合计	（万元）	Total Earnings	(10000 yuan)	1328311	673984
门票收入		Earnings from Ticket		500909	244295
商品销售收入		Earnings from Shopping		345749	53728
其他收入		Other Earnings		481653	375960
接待人数	（万人次）	Number of Visitors Received	(10000 person-times)	41437	19064

资料来源：北京市文化和旅游局。
Source: Beijing Municipal Bureau of Culture and Tourism.

主要统计指标解释

入境游客 指来中国（大陆）观光、度假、探亲访友、就医疗养、购物、参加会议或从事经济、文化、体育、宗教活动，且在中国（大陆）的旅游住宿设施内至少停留一夜的外国人、港澳台同胞等游客。入境游客不包括以下人员：(1) 应邀来华访问的政府部长以上官员及其随行人员；(2) 外国驻华使领馆官员、外交人员以及随行的家庭服务人员和受赡养者；(3) 常住中国（大陆）一年以上的外国专家、留学生、记者、商务机构人员等；(4) 乘坐国际航班过境不需要通过护照检查进入中国（大陆）口岸的中转旅客；(5) 边境地区往来的边民；(6) 回大陆定居的港澳台同胞；(7) 已在中国（大陆）定居的外国人和原已出境又返回在中国（大陆）定居的外国侨民；(8) 归国的中国（大陆）出国人员。

国内游客 指中国（大陆）居民离开惯常居住地在境内其他地方的旅游住宿设施内至少停留一夜，最长不超过 12 个月的国内游客。

国际旅游收入 指入境游客在中国（大陆）境内旅行、游览过程中用于交通、参观游览、住宿、餐饮、购物、娱乐等全部花费。

国内旅游收入 指国内游客在国内旅行、游览过程中用于交通、参观游览、住宿、餐饮、购物、娱乐等全部花费。

外联（组团）入境旅游者人数 指报告期内旅行社自组外联的入境旅游者人数，反映旅行社对外招徕的能力。旅行社按以下要求统计外联人数：入境游客不论其停留时间多少、旅游线路长短，只统计一次；旅行社只统计本社自组外联团的实到人数，不包括非本社外联，仅由本社接受委托办理签证的人数。

接待入境旅游者人数 指报告期内本旅行社派地陪接待的入境人数。

国内居民出境人数 指旅行社组织的中国（大陆）公民因公或因私出境前往其他国家、中国香港特别行政区、澳门特别行政区和台湾省观光、度假、探亲访友、就医疗养、购物、参加会议或从事经济、文化、体育、宗教活动的人数。统计时，出境游客按每出境一次统计 1 人次。

Explanatory Notes on Main Statistical Indicators

Inbound Tourists refer to tourists from foreign countries, Hong Kong, Macao and Taiwan to (mainland of) China for sightseeing, holidays, visiting relatives and friends, medical service and rehabilitation, shopping, conferences, or economic, cultural, sports and religious activities, and staying in a tour accommodation facility in (the mainland of) China for at least one night. They do not include: (1) officials above the rank of governmental ministers, and their accompanying persons who visit China upon invitation; (2) officials in foreign embassies and consulates in China, diplomatic personnel, and their accompanying family service personnel and dependents; (3) foreign experts, students, reporters, and personnel in business institutions who have been in (the mainland of) China for more than one year; (4) transit passengers via (the mainland of) China by international flights without passport checking; (5) people living on the frontiers who pass through borders; (6) compatriots from Hong Kong, Macao and Taiwan who settle down in the mainland of China; (7) Foreigners that have settled down in China and foreign nationals that have left the country and then come back to settle down in (the mainland of) China; (8) Chinese (mainland) people who have gone abroad and returned to China.

Domestic Tourists refer to domestic visitors as residents in (the mainland of) China who leave their regular dwelling places to stay at least one night and at most 12 months in a travel accommodation facility of other domestic places.

Revenue from Inbound Tourism means the total spending of inbound tourists on traffic, tour, accommodation, restaurants, shopping, entertainment and so on during their tour and travel in (the mainland of) China.

Revenue from Domestic Tourism means the total spending of domestic tourists on traffic, tour, accommodation, restaurants, shopping and entertainment, and so on during their tour and travel in China.

Number of Inbound Tourists Organized by Travel Agencies means the number of inbound tourists organized by travel agencies in the reporting period. It shows the capacity of travel agencies in attracting inbound tourists; travel agencies shall count the tourists organized as follows: an inbound tourist is regarded as one visit regardless of the duration and distance of the tour; only the actual tourists organized by travel agencies are included. Those organized by other travel agencies or those who have visa submitted by the travel agencies are not included.

Number of Inbound Tourists Received means the number of inbound tourists received by local guides dispatched by travel agencies in the reporting period.

Number of Chinese Residents Going Abroad means the number of citizens from (the mainland of) China who are organized by travel agencies to visit other countries, Hong Kong Special Administrative Region of PRC, Macao Special Administrative Region of PRC, and Taiwan for sightseeing, holiday, visiting relatives and friends, medical service and rehabilitation, shopping, conferences, or economic, cultural, sport and religious activities for official or private purpose. In compiling statistics, each time of leaving is counted as one person-time.

18

金融业
FINANCE

简 要 说 明

主要内容

本章资料主要包括北京市金融机构信贷收支情况、证券市场交易情况、保险业务情况、上市公司基本情况。

Brief Introduction

Main Content

Statistics in this chapter mainly consist of the balance of credit for financial institutions, transactions in securities market, insurance business, and basic information of listed companies in Beijing.

18−1 金融机构(含外资)存贷款余额(1978−2023年)
DEPOSIT AND LOAN BALANCE OF FINANCIAL INSTITUTIONS (INCLUDING FOREIGN-FUNDED BANKS) (1978-2023)

单位：亿元 (100 million yuan)

年份 Year	金融机构本外币存款余额 Balance of Deposits in Domestic and Foreign Currencies in Financial Institutions		金融机构本外币存款 Deposits in Domestic and Foreign Currencies in Financial Institutions					
		#人民币存款 RMB Deposits	中资金融机构存款合计 Total Deposits in Chinese Financial Institutions	#人民币存款 RMB Deposits	#外汇(亿美元) Foreign Exchange (USD 100 million)	外资银行存款合计 Total Deposits in Foreign-funded Banks	#人民币存款 RMB Deposits	#外汇(亿美元) Foreign Exchange (USD 100 million)
1978				114.7				
1979				139.1				
1980				168.0				
1981				220.5				
1982				279.2				
1983				321.3				
1984				375.5				
1985				411.0				
1986				508.8				
1987				610.8				
1988				609.9				
1989				717.6				
1990				893.9				
1991				1244.1				
1992				1528.3				
1993				1873.1				
1994				2677.3				
1995				3527.2				
1996				4378.9				
1997				5228.0				
1998				6666.8				
1999				8267.2				
2000	11526.0		11461.8	9759.8	205.6			
2001	14109.2		14042.1	12223.4	219.8			7.3
2002	17438.4		17369.9	15392.7	238.9			8.3
2003	20476.0		20398.2	18321.9	250.9			9.4
2004	23781.3	21625.9	23679.3	21625.9	248.1			12.3
2005	28969.9	26785.9	28800.9	26731.3	256.4		54.6	14.2
2006	33793.3	31313.8	33484.1	31179.2	295.2		134.5	22.4
2007	37700.3	35369.7	37087.5	35014.1	283.8		355.6	35.2
2008	43980.7	42107.6	43094.4	41500.0	233.3	886.3	607.5	40.8
2009	56960.1	54275.5	55804.8	53428.8	348.0	1155.3	846.6	45.2
2010	66584.6	64453.9	64897.6	63025.2	282.7	1687.0	1428.7	39.0
2011	75001.9	72655.4	73018.9	70985.1	322.8	1983.1	1670.3	49.6
2012	84837.3	81389.6	82615.9	79620.6	476.5	2221.4	1769.1	72.0
2013	91660.5	87990.6	89187.4	85897.2	539.6	2473.1	2093.4	62.3
2014	100095.5	95370.5	97645.9	93326.0	706.0	2449.6	2044.5	66.2
2015	128573.0	123767.4	126164.8	121878.9	660.0	2461.0	1941.3	80.0
2016	138408.9	132791.9	135510.3	130648.0	700.9	2933.1	2178.5	108.8
2017	144086.0	137952.1	141013.6	135501.4	843.6	3155.7	2534.0	95.1
2018	157092.2	150430.4	154237.3	148136.3	888.9	2960.6	2399.8	81.7
2019	171062.3	164349.5	168238.8	162063.9	885.1	2931.3	2393.4	77.1
2020	188081.6	181105.6	185026.8	178754.8	961.2	3069.8	2365.8	107.9
2021	199741.5	192104.3	196670.8	189717.8	1090.5	3112.7	2428.5	107.3
2022	218628.8	212446.7	215708.2	210025.3	816.0	2954.1	2454.9	71.7
2023	246430.0	240438.6	243638.2	238218.1	765.3	2859.8	2288.5	80.7

资料来源：中国人民银行北京市分行。
Source: The People's Bank of China Beijing Municipal Branch.

18−1 续表 Continued

单位：亿元 (100 million yuan)

年 份 Year	金融机构本外币贷款余额 Balance of Loans in Domestic and Foreign Currencies in Financial Institutions	#人民币贷款 RMB Loans	#中长期贷款 Medium-term &Long-term Loans	金融机构本外币贷款 Loans in Domestic and Foreign Currencies in Financial Institutions					
				中资金融机构贷款合计 Total Loans in Chinese Financial Institutions	#人民币贷款 RMB Loans	#外汇(亿美元) Foreign Exchange (USD 100 million)	外资银行贷款合计 Total Loans in Foreign-funded Banks	#人民币贷款 RMB Loans	#外汇(亿美元) Foreign Exchange (USD 100 million)
1978					53.9				
1979					74.2				
1980					87.3				
1981					91.3				
1982					109.1				
1983					149.5				
1984					174.3				
1985					249.8				
1986					299.2				
1987					346.1				
1988					415.7				
1989					487.1				
1990					573.1				
1991					735.8				
1992					894.7				
1993					1128.1				
1994					1429.0				
1995					1779.1				
1996					2082.8				
1997					2720.7				
1998					3326.6				
1999					4007.8				
2000	6407.9		3106.7	6306.3	6008.2	27.7			9.0
2001	7612.2		3797.3	7514.9	7202.9	37.4			10.8
2002	9704.3		5026.9	9602.6	9230.8	44.9			12.1
2003	12057.7		6352.0	11884.4	11314.7	68.8			20.9
2004	13577.7		7506.4	13312.3	12600.2	86.0			32.0
2005	15335.5		8632.4	14996.6	13792.2	149.2		42.3	36.8
2006	18131.6	15632.7	11142.8	17631.7	15486.9	274.7		145.8	45.4
2007	19861.5	17812.5	12217.6	19053.9	17360.2	231.9	807.5	452.3	48.6
2008	23010.7	19985.0	14688.9	22160.5	19431.1	399.4	850.2	554.0	43.3
2009	31052.9	25421.8	21163.8	30151.6	24805.1	783.0	901.3	616.7	41.7
2010	36479.6	29563.8	26180.2	35352.0	28748.1	997.2	1127.6	815.6	47.1
2011	39660.5	33367.0	24886.3	38410.3	32434.6	948.4	1250.2	932.5	50.4
2012	43189.5	36441.3	26333.5	41839.8	35441.7	1017.9	1349.7	999.6	55.7
2013	47880.9	40506.7	28171.7	46539.5	39557.5	1145.2	1341.4	949.2	64.3
2014	53650.6	45458.7	30882.3	52254.3	44438.8	1277.3	1396.2	1019.9	61.5
2015	58559.4	50559.5	33671.3	57281.2	49530.8	1193.6	1994.3	1676.9	48.9
2016	63739.4	56618.9	37471.3	62492.2	55553.2	1000.3	2005.9	1725.8	40.4
2017	69556.2	63382.5	42001.7	68091.3	62132.4	911.9	2275.3	1945.2	50.5
2018	70483.7	66767.0	42948.9	69071.1	65520.3	517.4	1865.9	1641.2	32.7
2019	76875.6	73575.9	42861.7	75336.5	72177.0	452.9	1744.6	1589.7	22.2
2020	84308.8	81035.2	47507.1	82942.0	79808.6	480.2	1548.0	1402.7	22.3
2021	89032.9	86077.5	56189.6	87559.1	84741.4	441.9	1560.3	1414.7	22.8
2022	97819.9	95496.9	61514.6	96416.0	94201.9	317.9	1514.4	1388.9	18.0
2023	110835.5	108601.2	69622.2	109457.0	107296.3	305.1	1465.7	1374.9	12.8

18-2 金融机构(含外资)本外币信贷收支情况(2023年) BALANCE OF CREDIT FUNDS IN DOMESTIC AND FOREIGN CURRENCIES OF FINANCIAL INSTITUTIONS (INCLUDING FOREIGN-FUNDED BANKS)(2023)

单位：亿元，汇率：7.0827　　(100 million yuan ,at an exchange rate of 7.0827)

项　目	Item	余　额 Balance	比年初增减额(+、-) Increase or Decrease than the Beginning of the Year
各项存款	**Total Deposits**	**246430.0**	**27968.8**
#人民币存款	RMB Deposits	240438.6	28159.5
境内存款	Domestic Deposits	244476.4	28151.7
住户存款	Deposits of Households	65809.3	7190.7
非金融企业存款	Deposits of Non-financial Enterprises	75984.9	5125.4
机关团体存款	Deposits of Government Departments & Organizations	55591.3	9135.0
财政性存款	Fiscal Deposits	2206.5	580.8
非银行业金融机构存款	Deposits of Non-banking Financial Institutions	44884.4	6119.8
境外存款	Overseas Deposits	1953.6	-182.9
各项贷款	**Total Loans**	**110835.5**	**12711.6**
#人民币贷款	RMB Loans	108601.2	12800.2
境内贷款	Domestic Loans	108934.2	12443.1
住户贷款	Loans to Households	25320.5	1262.7
企(事)业单位贷款	Loans to Non-financial Enterprises and Government Departments & Organizations	82960.0	11081.8
非银行业金融机构贷款	Loans to Non-banking Financial Institutions	653.7	98.7
境外贷款	Overseas Loans	1901.3	268.5

资料来源：中国人民银行北京市分行。
Source: The People's Bank of China Beijing Municipal Branch.

18-3 中资金融机构本外币信贷收支情况(2023年)
BALANCE OF CREDIT IN DOMESTIC AND FOREIGN CURRENCIES OF CHINESE FINANCIAL INSTITUTIONS(2023)

单位：亿元，汇率：7.0827 (100 million yuan ,at an exchange rate of 7.0827)

项　　目	Item	余　　额 Balance	比年初增减额(+、-) Increase or Decrease than Year-beginning
各项存款	**Total Deposits**	**243638.2**	**28097.6**
#人民币存款	RMB Deposits	238218.1	28360.4
境内存款	Domestic Deposits	241919.4	28237.3
住户存款	Deposits of Households	65323.4	7040.0
非金融企业存款	Deposits of Non-financial Enterprises	73988.1	5370.4
机关团体存款	Deposits of Government Departments & Organizations	55591.2	9135.1
财政性存款	Fiscal Deposits	2206.5	580.8
非银行业金融机构存款	Deposits of Non-banking Financial Institutions	44810.2	6111.1
境外存款	Overseas Deposits	1718.8	-139.7
各项贷款	**Total Loans**	**109457.0**	**12736.9**
#人民币贷款	RMB Loans	107296.3	12790.3
境内贷款	Domestic Loans	107639.9	12472.0
住户贷款	Loans to Households	25176.0	1312.5
企(事)业单位贷款	Loans to Non-financial Enterprises and Government Departments & Organizations	81812.1	11062.8
非银行业金融机构贷款	Loans to Non-banking Financial Institutions	651.7	96.7
境外贷款	Overseas Loans	1817.1	264.9

资料来源：中国人民银行北京市分行。
Source: The People's Bank of China Beijing Municipal Branch.

18-4 银行、保险系统机构及人员(2023年) INSTITUTIONS AND PERSONNEL OF BANKING AND INSURANCE SYSTEMS (2023)

项目	Item	银行系统 Banking System		保险系统 Insurance System	
		机构(个) Institutions (unit)	人员(人) Personnel (person)	机构(个) Institutions (unit)	人员(人) Personnel (person)
合计	**Total**	**3694**	**220133**	**704**	**130070**
东城区	Dongcheng District	263	15888	66	16851
西城区	Xicheng District	384	88167	88	24068
朝阳区	Chaoyang District	806	32433	173	50681
丰台区	Fengtai District	300	7457	39	8073
石景山区	Shijingshan District	94	7665	25	2039
海淀区	Haidian District	638	35726	56	6842
门头沟区	Mentougou District	51	1024	11	182
房山区	Fangshan District	116	2258	30	2727
通州区	Tongzhou District	172	3725	40	3444
顺义区	Shunyi District	165	12474	32	2298
昌平区	Changping District	170	3279	35	6518
大兴区	Daxing District	159	3095	22	1704
怀柔区	Huairou District	83	1361	18	801
平谷区	Pinggu District	84	1314	26	1754
密云区	Miyun District	83	1463	22	1178
延庆区	Yanqing District	51	1016	15	553
北京经济技术开发区	Beijing Economic-Technological Development Area	75	1788	6	357

注：1.本表口径为在北京地区经营的银行、保险公司的总行(总公司)、分行(分公司)及所属分支机构。
2.保险系统人员构成中含营销员。

Note: a) Figures in this table cover the headquarters (head offices), branches (branch companies) and subsidiaries of banks and insurance companies operating in Beijing.
b) Personnel of insurance system includes marketing personnel.

18-5 上市公司基本情况(1993-2023年)
BASIC STATISTICS ON LISTED COMPANIES (1993-2023)

年 份 Year	年 末 上市公司 (家) Number of Listed Companies at Year-end (unit)	上市公司 总 股 本 (万股) Total Equity of Listed Companies (10000 Shares)	股 票 首发数量 (万股) Initial Public Offering Shares (10000 Shares)	首 发 募集资金 (亿元) Funds Raised Through IPO (100 million yuan)	增 发 募集资金 (亿元) Funds Raised Through Additional Issue (100 million yuan)	配 股 募集资金 (亿元) Funds Raised Through Allotment of Shares (100 million yuan)
1993	3	24592	3924	58.0		28.8
1994	7	124038	20300	11.7		0.5
1995	7	133309				3.8
1996	13	198956	29763	12.8		1.9
1997	26	470026	80200	52.2		7.0
1998	33	723561	52750	32.9		20.2
1999	43	1439894	121242	63.0	10.8	10.7
2000	54	2015049	156000	143.5	22.2	46.0
2001	63	9764783	345500	191.6		17.0
2002	68	11929954	23800	16.8	14.9	
2003	74	11493598	373600	188.7	2.8	2.2
2004	83	12553074	21300	16.7	28.4	7.1
2005	83	13159721			3.1	
2006	92	58156652	2667911	1073.4	79.4	
2007	104	86151941	2428976	2433.3	304.7	12.1
2008	109	90486962	698853	546.9	502.0	63.8
2009	126	97911881	2179290	1154.2	430.7	
2010	165	137726461	3481552	1298.3	348.7	777.0
2011	194	143088054	420483	462.0	661.7	175.6
2012	217	146788089	211752	191.4	436.2	69.1
2013	219	151694399			183.9	32.5
2014	235	214359521	67787	74.9	1319.0	4.9
2015	264	225020500	532142	312.5	1423.3	
2016	281	232028500	149046	130.3	1859.3	49.4
2017	306	240045300	224743	127.0	1281.4	7.7
2018	316	255999835	266223	127.3	1963.8	10.7
2019	346	269765900	1222741	686.7	924.0	
2020	381	276090100	804755	969.1	624.6	37.9
2021	424	295643400	1955335	988.0	1712.1	
2022	460	306071824	650555	1434.4	692.8	51.8
2023	475	313895543	151486	267.1	1417.4	

注：1.本表数据按注册地统计。
2.1995年、2005年和2013年无新股发行。
资料来源：中国证券监督管理委员会北京监管局。
Note: a) Statistics in this table are counted in terms of registered area.
b) There were no shares issued in 1995, 2005 and 2013.
Source: Beijing Office of China Securities Regulatory Commission.

18-6 证券市场交易情况(2000-2023年)
STATISTICS ON TRADING IN SECURITIES MARKETS (2000-2023)

单位：亿元 (100 million yuan)

年 份 Year	证券市场交易额 Trading Volume of Securities Market	#股 票 交 易 Stock Trading	#基 金 交 易 Fund Trading
2000	14727.2	9546.2	376.2
2001	12734.2	6473.1	401.2
2002	12827.0	4504.4	269.4
2003	24703.7	5492.9	152.3
2004	22169.4	7290.1	100.2
2005	12930.0	5352.1	69.1
2006	22639.7	15233.3	353.4
2007	92468.8	76476.3	1512.4
2008	71281.5	49581.7	734.0
2009	119975.9	95815.6	1229.3
2010	129495.2	100366.0	1649.5
2011	148956.4	80737.8	2188.2
2012	190779.0	62644.5	2413.6
2013	318274.3	92020.5	3732.5
2014	450773.4	138493.4	10557.4
2015	918064.8	453359.2	32363.6
2016	859649.2	208613.3	31085.7
2017	1000257.0	194744.7	22105.7
2018	911465.7	149887.0	25144.4
2019	946425.6	185027.5	25041.5
2020	1259914.7	318941.8	35120.9
2021	1800772.3	429319.5	46239.9
2022	1846185.7	402066.4	69664.1
2023	2114284.5	392308.0	100295.6

注：2021年及以前，数据来源于上海证券交易所和深圳证券交易所；自2022年起，数据来源于北京证券交易所、上海证券交易所和深圳证券交易所。

Note: Data for 2021 and before were derived from Shanghai Stock Exchange and Shenzhen Stock Exchange; since 2022, data are derived from Beijing Stock Exchange,shanghai Stock Exchange and Shenzhen Stock Exchange.

18−7 保险业务情况(1997−2023年)
STATISTICS ON INSURANCE BUSINESS (1997-2023)

单位：亿元 (100 million yuan)

年 份 Year	原保险 保费收入 Premium of Primary Insurance	人身险 Life Insurance	财产险 Property Insurance	赔付 支出 Compensation Expenses	人身险 Life Insurance	财产险 Property Insurance
1997	102.5					
1998	88.6					
1999	91.8			29.9		
2000	93.4			28.4		
2001	141.3			32.0		
2002	234.1			46.9		
2003	282.5			48.0		
2004	279.3			55.3		
2005	498.2			75.4		
2006	411.5	327.2	84.4	84.0	45.1	38.9
2007	498.1	386.3	111.8	135.4	85.7	49.7
2008	585.9	451.8	134.1	188.9	121.0	67.9
2009	697.6	533.2	164.4	196.0	110.6	85.4
2010	966.5	754.2	212.3	199.7	105.9	93.7
2011	820.9	588.4	232.6	232.8	113.8	119.0
2012	923.1	656.1	267.0	286.2	133.9	152.3
2013	994.4	706.4	288.0	318.2	152.9	165.3
2014	1207.2	892.5	314.8	407.2	224.6	182.7
2015	1403.9	1059.2	344.7	506.6	300.0	206.6
2016	1839.0	1469.7	369.2	596.6	367.3	229.3
2017	1973.2	1568.8	404.4	577.7	365.3	212.5
2018	1793.3	1370.7	422.7	629.4	383.5	245.9
2019	2076.5	1621.6	454.8	719.0	449.6	269.3
2020	2302.9	1861.6	441.4	750.6	488.1	262.5
2021	2526.9	2083.4	443.5	838.5	567.8	270.7
2022	2758.5	2279.4	479.1	776.0	495.9	280.1
2023	3204.7	2686.8	517.9	878.4	533.2	345.2

资料来源：国家金融监督管理总局北京监管局。
Source: Beijing Office of National Financial Regulatory Administration.

18-8 保险业务情况
STATISTICS ON INSURANCE BUSINESS

单位：亿元 (100 million yuan)

项　　目	Item	原保险保费收入 Premium of Primary Insurance		赔付支出 Compensation Expenses	
		2023	2022	2023	2022
合　　计	**Total**	**3204.7**	**2758.5**	**878.4**	**776.0**
人身险业务小计	**Subtotal of Life Insurance**	**2686.8**	**2279.4**	**533.2**	**495.9**
人寿保险	Life Insurance	2079.7	1724.2	325.9	283.6
非分红产品	Non-participating Products	1606.1	1202.1	65.6	91.5
分红产品	Participating Products	467.6	516.6	259.0	190.8
投资连接产品	Investment-linked Products	0.4	0.4	0.1	0.4
万能产品	Universal Products	5.5	5.1	1.1	0.9
意外伤害保险	Accident Insurance	48.2	48.5	21.7	22.1
健康保险	Health Insurance	558.9	506.7	185.7	190.3
财产险业务小计	**Subtotal of Property Insurance**	**517.9**	**479.1**	**345.2**	**280.1**
#企业财产保险	Enterprise Property Insurance	56.6	51.0	32.0	21.5
家庭财产保险	Family Property Insurance	6.6	4.8	2.0	1.0
机动车辆及第三者责任保险	Motor Vehicle and Third Party Liability Insurance	237.9	231.9	171.4	142.7
货物运输保险	Freight Transport Insurance	25.4	20.0	13.0	7.9
责任保险	Liability Insurance	89.7	79.0	55.5	45.0
工程险	Engineering Insurance	20.6	13.3	6.7	6.2

资料来源：国家金融监督管理总局北京监管局。
Source: Beijing Office of National Financial Regulatory Administration.

主要统计指标解释

存款 企业、机关、团体或居民根据可以收回的原则，把货币资金存入银行或其他信用机构保管并取得一定利息的一种信用活动形式。根据存款对象的不同可划分为非金融企业存款、财政性存款、机关团体存款、住户存款、非银行金融机构存款等科目。它是银行信贷资金的主要来源。

贷款 银行或其他信用机构根据必须归还的原则，按一定利率，为企业、个人等提供资金的一种信用活动形式。我国银行贷款分为短期贷款、中长期贷款、委托及信托类贷款、其他类贷款等。

原保险保费收入 是指保险企业确认的原保险合同保费收入。是投保人根据保险合同的有关规定，为被保险人取得因约定危险事故发生所造成的经济损失补偿（或给付）权利，付给保险人的代价。包括财产险和人身险收入。

保险赔付支出 公司按保险合同约定支付给被保险人（或受益人）的赔款、保险金、给付等。包括赔款支出、死伤医疗给付、满期给付和年金给付。

股票交易额 统计期末北京地区证券营业部在北京证券交易所、上海证券交易所和深圳证券交易所的股票交易金额。

基金交易额 统计期末北京地区证券营业部在北京证券交易所、上海证券交易所和深圳证券交易所的基金交易金额。

Explanatory Notes on Main Statistical Indicators

Deposit is a form of credit activity that enterprises, public institutions, groups or residents save their money, on a reclaimable basis, in banks or other credit institutions and receive certain interest. In terms of depositors, there are non-financial enterprise deposit, fiscal deposit, government agency deposit, household deposit, non-bank financial institution deposit and so on, which constitute a main source of bank funds for extending credit.

Loan is a form of credit activity that banks or other credit institutions provide funds which must be repaid for enterprise and individuals at a given interest rate. In China, bank loans are classified as short-, medium-, and long-term loans, entrusted and trust loans, and others.

Premium Income means the income of insurance premium of original insurance contracts confirmed by insurance companies. It is the price paid by policy holders to the insurer for the right to receive compensation (claim settlement) for any economic loss caused by agreed dangerous accidents pursuant to relevant provisions in the insurance contract. There are property insurance and life insurance incomes.

Insurance Indemnity Payments refer to indemnity, insurance money, and claim settlement, etc. paid by the insurance company to the insurant (or beneficiary) as agreed in the insurance contract, including indemnity payment, claim settlement for medical costs of death and injury, maturity payment and annuity payment.

Stock Market Turnover means the transaction amount of stocks traded by Beijing securities sales departments in Beijing Stock Exchange, Shanghai Stock Exchange and Shenzhen Stock Exchange, by the end of the statistical period.

Funds Turnover means the transaction amount of funds traded by Beijing securities sales departments in Beijing Stock Exchange, Shanghai Stock Exchange and Shenzhen Stock Exchange, by the end of the statistical period.

19

科 技
SCIENCE AND TECHNOLOGY

简 要 说 明

一、主要内容

本章资料主要包括研究与试验发展（R&D）人员情况，研究与试验发展（R&D）经费情况，研究与试验发展（R&D）项目（课题）情况，研究机构情况，规模以上工业企业 R&D 活动基本情况，限额以上信息传输、软件和信息技术服务业企业研究与试验发展(R&D)活动基本情况，规模以上高技术制造业主要科技指标，高等学校科技活动情况，研究与开发机构研发活动、专利申请及授权情况等。

二、统计范围

国民经济中研究与试验发展（R&D）活动相对密集行业的法人单位，主要数据包括：农、林、牧、渔业，采矿业，制造业，电力、热力、燃气及水的生产和供应业，建筑业，交通运输、仓储和邮政业，信息传输、软件和信息技术服务业，金融业，租赁和商务服务业，科学研究和技术服务业，水利、环境和公共设施管理业，教育，卫生和社会工作，文化、体育和娱乐业，公共管理、社会保障和社会组织等。

三、有关统计标准的变化说明

（一）关于行业划分。2017 年及以前执行《国民经济行业分类》（GB/T 4754-2011）标准，自 2018 年起执行《国民经济行业分类》（GB/T 4754-2017）标准。

（二）关于三次产业划分。2003 年，根据《国民经济行业分类》（GB/T 4754-2002），国家统计局印发了《国家统计局关于印发〈三次产业划分规定〉的通知》（国统字〔2003〕14 号）。2012 年，根据《国民经济行业分类》（GB/T 4754-2011），国家统计局对 2003 年《三次产业划分规定》进行了修订。主要在以下方面作出调整：一是将门类“农、林、牧、渔业”中的“农、林、牧、渔服务业”，“采矿业”中的“开采辅助活动”，“制造业”中的“金属制品、机械和设备修理业”等三个大类一并调整到第三产业。调整后，第一产业为 4 个大类；第二产业为 2 个门类和 36 个大类；第三产业为 15 个门类和 3 个大类。二是明确第三产业即为服务业。

本章自 2012 年起三次产业的分类执行调整后的划分规定。

（三）关于高技术制造业。根据国家统计局《关于印发高技术产业（制造业）分类（2017）的通知》（国统字〔2017〕200 号），自 2018 年开始执行此标准。

Brief Introduction

I. Main Content

Statistics in this chapter mainly consist of the situation of R&D personnel, R&D funds, R&D projects (tasks), research institutions, basic information on R&D activities of industrial enterprises above designated size, basic information on R&D activities of information transmission, software and information technology service enterprises above designated size, major science and technology indicators of high-tech manufacturing above designated size, scientific and technological activities of colleges and universities, R&D activities of research and development institutions, patent application and licensing, etc.

II. Scope of Statistics

Included in this chapter are the corporate entities in sectors with relatively intensive R&D activities in national economy, such as agriculture, forestry, animal production and hunting, fishing, mining, manufacturing, generation and distribution of electricity, heating, gas and water, construction, transport, storage and post, scientific research and development, technology services, information transmission, software and information technology services, finance, renting and leasing activities and business services, management of water conservancy, environment and public facilities, education, health and social works, culture, sports and entertainment, public administration, social security and social organizations, etc.

III. Changes in Relevant Statistical Standards

(I) Classification of Sectors. The standards in the *Classification of National Economic Sectors (GB/T 4754-2011)* were implemented before 2017. The standards in the *Classification of National Economic Sectors (GB/T 4754-2017) are implemented since 2018.*

(II) Classification of Three Industries. According to the *Classification of National Economic Sectors (GB/T 4754-2002),* the National Bureau of Statistics issued the *Notice of the National Bureau of Statistics on the Issuance of the 'Regulations on Three Industries Classification'* (G.T.Z. [2003] No. 14) in 2003. According to the *Classification of National Economic Sectors (GB/T 4754-2011)* the National Bureau of Statistics revised the *Regulations on Three Industries Classification* of 2003 version in 2012. Adjustments were mainly made in the following aspects: Firstly, the "service activities for agriculture, forestry, animal husbandry and fishing" in the category of "agriculture, forestry, animal production and hunting, fishing", the "mining support service activities" in the category of "mining and quarrying", and the "repair of fabricated metal products, machinery and equipment" in the category of "manufacturing" were adjusted to the tertiary industry. After adjustment, the primary industry fell into 4 categories; the secondary industry fell into 2 classes and 36 categories; and the tertiary industry fell into 15 classes and 3 categories. Secondly, the tertiary industry was defined as the service industry.

The classification of three industries since 2012 as mentioned in this chapter has all been subject to the classification provisions after adjustment.

(III) High-tech Manufacturing. According to the *Circular of National Bureau of Statistics on Printing and Issuing the Classification of High-tech Industry (Manufacturing) 2017* (G.T.Z. [2017] No.200). The standard has been put in place since 2018.

19-1 科技活动及专利情况(1986-2023年)
STATISTICS ON SCIENTIFIC AND TECHNOLOGICAL ACTIVITIES AND PATENTS (1986-2023)

年份 Year	科技活动人员(人) Personnel Engaged in Scientific and Technological Activities (person)	研究与试验发展(R&D)人员折合全时当量(人年) Full-time Equivalent of R&D Personnel (man-year)	研究与试验发展(R&D)经费内部支出(万元) Internal Expenditure on R&D (10000 yuan)	研究与试验发展(R&D)经费内部支出相当于地区生产总值比例(%) Ratio of Internal Expenditure on R&D to GDP (%)
1986				
1987				
1988				
1989				
1990				
1991	228167			
1992	247525			
1993	252811			
1994	240386			
1995	252232			
1996	265552	84793	418614	2.32
1997	273161	84913	532257	2.54
1998	237127	86602	861138	3.58
1999	229584	85740	938437	3.46
2000	261113	98723	1557011	4.85
2001	240609	95255	1711696	4.54
2002	257326	114919	2195402	4.99
2003	270921	110358	2562518	5.02
2004	301202	152132	3169064	5.14
2005	383153	177765	3795450	5.31
2006	382756	168875	4329878	5.21
2007	450331	204668	5270591	5.23
2008	450147	200080	6200983	5.44
2009	529985	191779	6686351	5.38
2010	529811	193718	8218234	5.69
2011	605980	217255	9366440	5.63
2012	651003	235493	10633640	5.59
2013	681346	242175	11850469	5.61
2014	726792	245384	12687953	5.53
2015	747461	245728	13840231	5.59
2016	810195	253337	14845762	5.49
2017		269835	15796512	5.29
2018		267338	18707701	5.65
2019		313986	22335870	6.30
2020		336280	23265793	6.47
2021		338297	26293208	6.41
2022		373235	28433394	6.84
2023		402152	29470733	6.73

资料来源：北京市统计局、北京市科学技术委员会、中关村科技园区管理委员会、北京市教育委员会、北京市经济和信息化局、北京市知识产权局。

Source: Beijing Municipal Bureau of Statistics, Beijing Municipal Science & Technology Commission, Administrative Commission of Zhongguancun Science Park, Beijing Municipal Education Commission, Beijing Municipal Bureau of Economy and Information Technology, Beijing Municipal Intellectual Property Office.

19-1 续表 Continued

年 份 Year	PCT国际专利申请量(件) PCT International Patent Applications (piece)	专利授权量(件) Patents Granted (piece)	发明 Inventions	实用新型 Utility Models	外观设计 Designs	国内专利有效量(件) Domestic Patents in Force (piece)	#发明专利 Invention Patents	万人发明专利拥有量(件) Invention Patent Ownership per 10000 Persons (piece)	万人高价值发明专利拥有量(件) High-value Invention Patent Ownership per 10000 Persons (piece)
1986		491	43	408	40				
1987		776	102	630	44				
1988		1376	169	1147	60				
1989		1789	207	1497	85				
1990		2268	216	1932	120				
1991		2369	263	1917	189				
1992		3265	312	2724	229				
1993		5806	530	4780	496				
1994		3914	368	3245	301				
1995		4025	328	3169	528				
1996		3295	246	2563	486				
1997		3327	281	2340	706				
1998		3800	309	2522	969				
1999		5829	573	3948	1308				
2000		5905	1074	3463	1368				
2001		6246	946	3600	1700				
2002		6345	1061	3721	1563				
2003		8248	2261	4244	1743				
2004		9005	3216	3956	1833				
2005		10100	3476	4498	2126		12102	8.0	
2006		11238	3864	5490	1884	36645	13319	8.5	
2007		14954	4824	7364	2766	43584	18421	11.2	
2008		17747	6478	8776	2493	55771	20329	11.8	
2009		22921	9157	10141	3623	71076	28774	15.8	
2010	1272	33511	11209	16579	5723	100623	38996	20.4	
2011	1862	40888	15880	19628	5380	131255	52522	26.4	
2012	2705	50511	20140	24672	5699	170516	69554	34.0	
2013	2981	62671	20695	36301	5675	219243	85434	40.8	
2014	3606	74661	23237	44071	7353	274667	103638	48.6	23.6
2015	4490	94031	35308	45773	12950	344916	133040	61.6	29.4
2016	6651	102323	41425	45376	15522	417666	166722	76.8	36.6
2017	5069	106948	46091	46011	14846	494941	205320	94.5	47.5
2018	6527	123496	46978	59219	17299	569929	241282	112.0	57.2
2019	7165	131716	53127	58393	20196	653053	284288	132.0	67.4
2020	8283	162824	63266	75336	24222	768090	335575	155.8	79.3
2021	10358	198778	79210	96078	23490	913616	405037	185.0	94.2
2022	11463	202722	88127	91947	22648	1046715	477790	218.0	112.0
2023	11438	193973	107875	68901	17197	1181142	574323	262.9	137.0

注：自2016年起，对专利相关数据的统计范围进行了调整，下同。

Note: The statistical range of patent-related data has been adjusted since 2016, the same below.

19-2 研究与试验发展(R&D)人员情况

项　目	Item	研究与试验发展(R&D)人员(人) R&D Personnel (person) 2023	2022
合　计	**Total**	**571650**	**546747**
按执行部门分	**By Executive Department**		
企　业	Enterprises	224929	237479
工业企业	Industrial Enterprises	82701	79152
非工业企业	Non-industrial Enterprises	142228	158327
科研机构	Scientific Research Institutions	156930	150908
高等学校	Institutions of Higher Education	177088	146363
事业单位	Public Institutions	12703	11997
按行业门类分	**By Sector**		
#制造业	Manufacturing	77956	73478
信息传输、软件和信息技术服务业	Information Transmission, Software and Information Technology Services	83307	78603
科学研究和技术服务业	Scientific Research and Technical Services	206043	212556
教　育	Education	177088	146363

资料来源：北京市统计局，北京市科学技术委员会、中关村科技园区管理委员会，北京市教育委员会，北京市经济和信息化局。

STATISTICS ON RESEARCH AND R&D PERSONNEL

研究与试验发展(R&D)人员折合全时当量(人年) Full-time Equivalent of R&D Personnel (man-year)		基础研究 Basic Research		应用研究 Applied Research		试验发展 Experimental Development	
2023	2022	2023	2022	2023	2022	2023	2022
402152	**373235**	**91950**	**84525**	**115836**	**110283**	**194367**	**178429**
167325	154507	965	1751	11280	14249	155081	138508
59993	53459	203	256	3053	3875	56737	49328
107332	101048	762	1495	8227	10374	98344	89180
132323	127513	49556	46540	51663	47763	31104	33210
93481	83037	39569	34031	48859	44034	5053	4973
9023	8178	1860	2203	4034	4237	3129	1738
57292	49707	203	256	2264	3082	54825	46370
65997	51730	69	122	1761	3007	64167	48600
167373	167132	51905	49492	60862	58160	54606	59480
93481	83037	39569	34031	48859	44034	5053	4973

Source: Beijing Municipal Bureau of Statistics, Beijing Municipal Science & Technology Commission, Administrative Commission of Zhongguancun Science Park, Beijing Municipal Education Commission, Beijing Municipal Bureau of Economy and Information Technology.

19-3 研究与试验发展(R&D)经费情况

单位：万元

项目	Item	研究与试验发展(R&D)经费内部支出 Internal Expenditure on R&D		基础研究 Basic Research	
		2023	2022	2023	2022
合计	**Total**	**29470733**	**28433394**	**4723226**	**4706662**
按执行部门分	**By Executive Department**				
企业	Enterprises	13729278	12400254	83780	124982
工业企业	Industrial Enterprises	4410019	3489973	18042	32863
非工业企业	Non-industrial Enterprises	9319259	8910281	65738	92120
科研机构	Scientific Research Institutions	11174596	12332269	3339302	3470484
高等学校	Institutions of Higher Education	3658596	3116342	1243165	1035284
事业单位	Public Institutions	908263	584530	56979	75912
按行业门类分	**By Sector**				
#制造业	Manufacturing	4283405	3341972	18042	32817
信息传输、软件和信息技术服务业	Information Transmission, Software and Information Technology	6916104	6067299	13159	14732
科学研究和技术服务业	Scientific Research and Technical Services	13882623	14769399	3443293	3592153
教育	Education	3658596	3116342	1243165	1035284

资料来源：北京市统计局，北京市科学技术委员会、中关村科技园区管理委员会，北京市教育委员会，北京市经济和信息化局。

RESEARCH AND EXPERIMENTAL DEVELOPMENT FUNDS

(10000 yuan)

按活动类型分 Group by Type of Activity				按支出用途分 Group by Purpose of Payment			
应用研究 Applied Research		试验发展 Experimental Development		日常性支出 Routine Expenses		#人员劳务费 Labor Cost	
2023	2022	2023	2022	2023	2022	2023	2022
7526219	**7311006**	**17221288**	**16415727**	**26240361**	**25324198**	**12202462**	**10582789**
695939	802923	12949558	11472349	12936937	11345318	7823316	6521372
149809	141996	4242168	3315114	4076430	3313750	1908095	1394239
546130	660927	8707390	8157234	8860507	8031568	5915221	5127132
4236006	4281885	3599288	4579901	9700189	10915229	3377917	3184248
2073095	1833435	342336	247623	3182892	2731135	787339	697238
521178	392764	330106	115855	420343	332515	213890	179931
118403	112256	4146960	3196900	3954316	3180728	1851775	1330927
201496	330509	6701449	5722057	6588285	5223312	4612379	4183735
5032966	4918904	5406364	6258341	11807966	12980677	4620962	4304700
2073095	1833435	342336	247623	3182892	2731135	787339	697238

Source: Beijing Municipal Bureau of Statistics, Beijing Municipal Science & Technology Commission, Administrative Commission of Zhongguancun Science Park, Beijing Municipal Education Commission, Beijing Municipal Bureau of Economy and Information Technology.

19−3 续表

单位：万元

项 目	Item	资产性支出 Expenditures for Assets		#仪器和设备 Instruments and Equipment	
		2023	2022	2023	2022
合 计	**Total**	**3230372**	**3109196**	**2648280**	**2510375**
按执行部门分	**By Executive Department**				
企 业	Enterprises	792340	1054935	782385	1048934
工业企业	Industrial Enterprises	333589	176223	327721	172896
非工业企业	Non-industrial Enterprises	458752	878713	454664	876037
科研机构	Scientific Research Institutions	1474407	1417040	992506	904831
高等学校	Institutions of Higher Education	475705	385206	412751	336989
事业单位	Public Institutions	487920	252015	460637	219621
按行业门类分	**By Sector**				
#制造业	Manufacturing	329089	161244	323919	158602
信息传输、软件和信息技术服务业	Information Transmission, Software and Information Technology Services	327818	843987	325439	842703
科学研究和技术服务业	Scientific Research and Technical Services	2074657	1788721	1564646	1244129
教 育	Education	475705	385206	412751	336989

19—3　Continued

(10000 yuan)

按资金来源分 Grouped by Fund Source							
政府资金 Governmental Funds		企业资金 Enterprise Funds		国外资金 Foreign Funds		其他资金 Others	
2023	2022	2023	2022	2023	2022	2023	2022
12442443	**12896678**	**14670143**	**13422113**	**268966**	**146522**	**2089182**	**1968082**
482255	409771	13048281	11917787	179835	61742	18906	10954
316660	262553	4020640	3208071	58238	12093	14481	7256
165596	147217	9027641	8709716	121597	49649	4425	3699
8915846	10109344	633487	647991	31583	40472	1593680	1534463
2228367	1889977	978023	844654	49692	43655	402514	338055
815974	487586	10352	11682	7855	652	74082	84610
316115	262137	3894571	3060486	58238	12093	14481	7256
39471	64867	6866054	5996720	8481	3655	2097	2056
9825759	10656765	2257556	2417899	131284	74443	1668024	1620292
2228367	1889977	978023	844654	49692	43655	402514	338055

19-4 规模以上工业企业研究与试验发展(R&D)活动基本情况 (2023年)

项　目	Item	有研究与试验发展(R&D)活动的企业数(个) Enterprises with R&D Activities (unit)	研究与试验发展(R&D)人员(人) R&D Personnel (person)	研究与试验发展(R&D)人员折合全时当量(人年) Full-time Equivalent of R&D Personnel (man-year)	研究与试验发展(R&D)经费内部支出(万元) Internal Expenditure on R&D (10000 yuan)
合　计	**Total**	**1167**	**82701**	**59993**	**4410019**
#大中型企业	Large and Medium-sized Enterprises	317	60968	44165	3538501
按登记注册统计类别分	**By Statistical Category of Registration**				
内资企业	Domestic Invested Enterprises	992	62560	43640	3062922
港澳台投资企业	Enterprises with Investment from Hong Kong, Macao and Taiwan	53	8966	7431	733565
外商投资企业	Foreign Invested Enterprises	122	11175	8923	613531

BASIC STATISTICS ON R&D ACTIVITIES OF INDUSTRIAL ENTERPRISES ABOVE DESIGNATED SIZE (2023)

政府资金 Governmental Funds	企业资金 Enterprise Funds	国外资金 Foreign Funds	其他资金 Others	专利申请数(件) Number of Patent Applications (piece)	#发明专利 Invention Patents	新产品销售收入(万元) Sales Income of New Products (10000 yuan)	#出口 Exports
316660	**4020640**	**58238**	**14481**	**31980**	**20643**	**56484637**	**8982306**
289145	3184360	52509	12488	21069	15452	43836813	8090634
302090	2714219	32478	14136	24582	15843	26742492	1436216
5364	726328	1528	345	4531	3284	19577815	6803372
9205	580094	24233		2867	1516	10164331	742718

19-5 规模以上工业企业研究与试验发展(R&D)及相关活动情况(按行业分)(2023年)

项目	Item	有研究与试验发展(R&D)活动的企业数(个) Enterprises with R&D Activities (unit)	研究与试验发展(R&D)人员(人) R&D Personnel (person)
合计	**Total**	**1167**	**82701**
采矿业	**Mining**	**6**	**3058**
煤炭开采和洗选业	Mining and Washing of Coal		
石油和天然气开采业	Extraction of Petroleum and Natural Gas	1	***
黑色金属矿采选业	Mining and Processing of Ferrous Metal Ores	1	***
有色金属矿采选业	Mining and Processing of Non-Ferrous Metal Ores		
非金属矿采选业	Mining and Processing of Nonmetal Ores		
开采专业及辅助性活动	Professional and Support Activities for Mining	4	2539
其他采矿业	Mining of Other Ores		
制造业	**Manufacturing**	**1140**	**77956**
农副食品加工业	Processing of Food from Agricultural Products	14	668
食品制造业	Manufacture of Foods	23	904
酒、饮料和精制茶制造业	Manufacture of Liquor, Beverages and Refined Tea	6	788
烟草制品业	Manufacture of Tobacco	1	***
纺织业	Manufacture of Textile	4	81
纺织服装、服饰业	Manufacture of Textile, Wearing Apparel and Accessories	3	***
皮革、毛皮、羽毛及其制品和制鞋业	Manufacture of Leather, Fur, Feather and Related Products and Footwear		
木材加工和木、竹、藤、棕、草制品业	Processing of Timbers, Manufacture of Wood, Bamboo, Rattan, Palm, and Straw Products		
家具制造业	Manufacture of Furniture	5	172
造纸和纸制品业	Manufacture of Paper and Paper Products	5	159
印刷和记录媒介复制业	Printing, Reproduction of Recording Media	16	437
文教、工美、体育和娱乐用品制造业	Manufacture of Articles for Culture, Education, Artwork, Sport and Entertainment Activities	5	117
石油、煤炭及其他燃料加工业	Processing of Petroleum, Coal and Other Fuels	7	268
化学原料和化学制品制造业	Manufacture of Raw Chemical Materials and Chemical Products	41	1433
医药制造业	Manufacture of Medicines	133	10557
化学纤维制造业	Manufacture of Chemical Fibers	1	***
橡胶和塑料制品业	Manufacture of Rubber and Plastics Products	8	173
非金属矿物制品业	Manufacture of Non-Metallic Mineral Products	44	1615
黑色金属冶炼和压延加工业	Smelting and Pressing of Ferrous Metals	1	***
有色金属冶炼和压延加工业	Smelting and Pressing of Non-ferrous Metals	9	368
金属制品业	Manufacture of Metal Products	35	1292
通用设备制造业	Manufacture of General Purpose Machinery	82	3885
专用设备制造业	Manufacture of Special Purpose Machinery	204	8569
汽车制造业	Manufacture of Automobiles	44	8145
铁路、船舶、航空航天和其他运输设备制造业	Manufacture of Railway, Ship, Aerospace and Other Transport Equipments	55	5963
电气机械和器材制造业	Manufacture of Electrical Machinery and Equipment	98	4470
计算机、通信和其他电子设备制造业	Manufacture of Computers, Communication and Other Electronic Equipment	188	23408
仪器仪表制造业	Manufacture of Measuring Instruments and Machinery	94	3253
其他制造业	Other Manufacture	6	531
废弃资源综合利用业	Utilization of Waste Resources	2	***
金属制品、机械和设备修理业	Repair Service of Metal Products, Machinery and Equipment	6	423
电力、热力、燃气及水的生产和供应业	**Production and Supply of Electricity, Heat, Gas and Water**	**21**	**1687**
电力、热力生产和供应业	Production and Supply of Electric Power and Heat Power	12	569
燃气生产和供应业	Production and Supply of Gas	3	***
水的生产和供应业	Production and Supply of Water	6	187

STATISTICS ON RESEARCH AND EXPERIMENTAL DEVELOPMENT AND RELATED ACTIVITIES OF INDUSTRIAL ENTERPRISES ABOVE DESIGNATED SIZE (BY SECTOR) (2023)

研究与试验发展(R&D)人员折合全时当量(人年) Full-time Equivalent of R&D Personnel (man-year)	研究与试验发展(R&D)经费内部支出(万元) Internal Expenditure on R&D (10000 yuan)	政府资金 Governmental Funds	企业资金 Enterprise Funds	国外资金 Foreign Funds	其他资金 Others	专利申请数(件) Number of Patent Applications (piece)	#发明专利 Invention Patents	新产品销售收入(万元) Sales Income of New Products (10000 yuan)	#出口 Exports
59993	**4410019**	**316660**	**4020640**	**58238**	**14481**	**31980**	**20643**	**56484637**	**8982306**
1210	**67291**	**237**	**67054**			**298**	**265**	**111857**	
***	***	***	***	***	***	***	***	***	***
***	***	***	***	***	***	***	***	***	***
802	42374	171	42203			15	3	111857	
57292	**4283405**	**316115**	**3894571**	**58238**	**14481**	**29397**	**18500**	**51972163**	**8982306**
501	17644	4311	13333			207	75	411467	7325
679	18278	406	17872			182	43	389856	7640
374	14705		14705			128	25	463546	2281
***	***	***	***	***	***	***	***	***	***
56	3803		3803			19	5	86441	5503
***	***	***	***	***	***	***	***	***	***
150	3122		3122			122	13	179435	351
112	1870		1870			31	9	48743	29700
289	12911		12911			185	75	450573	6571
89	1805		1805			89	1	39917	1497
55	6378	154	6224			41	25	229878	
1221	40254	563	39691			494	319	555766	22384
8127	838315	22694	815045		576	1267	869	2821356	26821
***	***	***	***	***	***	***	***	***	***
137	6683		6683			86	20	91907	313
1161	56989	1991	54998			848	507	1672390	55673
***	***	***	***	***	***	***	***	***	***
216	8984	5144	3840			203	178	511140	84834
781	61959	12798	49161			416	161	371512	52171
2871	169885	7434	162451			1250	559	1907681	304976
5637	395275	8930	349668	35931	746	4464	2579	4532043	583435
6170	360561	2975	356058	1528		3200	1542	8461489	132167
3720	178424	58466	115564	231	4163	669	369	1088265	5319
2905	207364	2824	202184	2357		2290	1159	6609925	67549
19065	1716308	175922	1513198	18192	8996	11408	9079	19282352	7493241
2289	108350	8854	99496			1493	781	1226041	40128
280	41996	2639	39357			8	6	726	
***	***	***	***	***	***	***	***	***	***
183	3852		3852			83	11	42229	292
1491	**59323**	**308**	**59015**			**2285**	**1878**	**4400617**	
421	8085		8085			2084	1753	222002	
***	***	***	***	***	***	***	***	***	***
173	6710	308	6402			96	63	9121	

19-6 规模以上高技术制造业研究与试验发展(R&D)及相关活动情况

项　目	Item	R&D人员折合全时当量(人年) Full-time Equivalent of R&D Personnel (man-year)	
		2023	2022
高技术制造业	**High-tech Manufacturing**	**35879**	**30279**
医药制造业	**Manufacture of Medicines**	**8127**	**5981**
#化学药品制造	Manufacture of Chemical Medicine	2047	1610
生物药品制品制造	Manufacture of Biopharmaceutical Products	5089	3528
航空、航天器及设备制造业	**Manufacture of Aircrafts and Spacecrafts**	**3230**	**1754**
#航空航天器修理	Repair of Aircrafts and Spacecrafts	89	87
电子及通信设备制造业	**Manufacture of Electronic Equipment and Communication Equipment**	**17309**	**15148**
#通信设备制造、雷达及配套设备制造	Manufacture of Communication Equipment, Manufacture of Radar and Matching Equipment	5513	6260
电子器件制造	Manufacture of Electronic Appliances	5368	3856
电子元件及电子专用设备制造	Manufacture of Electronic Components and Electronic Specialized Equipment	1038	1219
其他电子设备制造	Other Electronic Equipment	3393	2179
计算机及办公设备制造业	**Manufacture of Computers and Office Equipment**	**2287**	**2336**
#计算机整机制造	Manufacture of Entired Computer	289	239
医疗仪器设备及仪器仪表制造业	**Manufacture of Medical Equipments and Meters**	**4927**	**5059**
#医疗仪器设备及器械制造	Manufacture of Medical Equipment and Appliances	2638	2619
通用仪器仪表制造	Manufacture of General Instruments	1657	1610

STATISTICS ON RESEARCH AND EXPERIMENTAL DEVELOPMENT AND RELATED ACTIVITIES OF HIGH-TECH MANUFACTURING ABOVE DESIGNATED SIZE

R&D经费支出 (万元) Expenditure on R&D (10000 yuan)		新产品销售收入 (万元) Sales Income of New Products (10000 yuan)		专利申请数 (件) Number of Patent Applications (piece)		#发明专利 Inventions Patents	
2023	2022	2023	2022	2023	2022	2023	2022
3036250	**2209862**	**25712804**	**29261987**	**17038**	**17170**	**12380**	**12039**
838315	**577976**	**2821356**	**3995466**	**1267**	**1474**	**869**	**1039**
181485	113573	845846	1227820	401	454	314	268
601966	418838	1002743	1729488	505	713	398	622
150318	**95628**	**223587**	**771596**	**337**	**770**	**171**	**472**
2089	3550	21057	2934	51	54	2	3
1634633	**1144715**	**18968579**	**19897283**	**8705**	**8825**	**6909**	**7100**
420803	367567	11963149	13738552	2560	2538	2224	2314
591732	355259	2018102	2258690	2845	3351	2384	2779
74227	56929	912286	1185967	648	774	385	581
426519	274239	1584077	1073627	1183	914	921	696
141406	**126655**	**1379548**	**2419032**	**3482**	**2287**	**2737**	**1697**
23198	18514	908457	1608441	2980	1855	2443	1484
271579	**264887**	**2319734**	**2178611**	**3247**	**3814**	**1694**	**1731**
163229	143723	1109541	785572	1754	1929	913	831
76781	78681	1002084	1021489	1154	1154	609	489

19-7 限额以上信息传输、软件和信息技术服务业企业研究与试验发展(R&D)及相关活动情况(2023年)

项　目	Item	有研究与试验发展(R&D)活动的企业数(个) Enterprises with R&D Activities (unit)	研究与试验发展(R&D)人员(人) R&D Personnel (person)	研究与试验发展(R&D)人员折合全时当量(人年) Full-time Equivalent of R&D Personnel (person-year)
合　计	**Total**	**657**	**83307**	**65997**
按登记注册统计类别分	**By Statistical Category of Registration**			
内资企业	Domestic Invested Enterprises	578	51775	43094
港澳台投资企业	Enterprises with Investment from Hong Kong, Macao and Taiwan	53	20095	14414
外商投资企业	Foreign Invested Enterprises	26	11437	8489
按行业分	**By Sector**			
电信、广播电视和卫星传输服务	Telecommunication, Radio and Television and Satellite Transmission Service	38	6049	3849
互联网和相关服务	Internet and Related Service	111	22572	20469
软件和信息技术服务业	Software and Information Technology	508	54686	41679

STATISTICS ON RESEARCH AND EXPERIMENTAL DEVELOPMENT AND RELATED ACTIVITIES OF ENTERPRISES ABOVE DESIGNATED SIZE OF INFORMATION TRANSMISSIOM, SOFTWARE AND INFORMATION TECHNICIAL (2023)

研究与试验发展(R&D)经费内部支出(万元) Internal Expenditure on R&D (10000 yuan)					专利申请数(件) Number of Patent Applications (piece)	
	政府资金 Govern-mental Funds	企业资金 Enterprise Funds	境外资金 Overseas Funds	其他资金 Others		#发明专利 Inventions Patents
6916104	**39471**	**6866054**	**8481**	**2097**	**75409**	**62545**
3979237	36693	3939053	1395	2097	56309	46241
2102363	1742	2098898	1723		15020	12492
834503	1036	828104	5363		4080	3812
368317	2122	365942		253	10098	9063
2260808	1150	2259501		157	10405	8758
4286978	36199	4240612	8481	1686	54906	44724

19-8 研究与开发机构研究与试验发展(R&D)及相关活动情况(2007-2023年)

项　目	Item	2007
研究与开发机构基本情况	**Basic Statistics on R&D Institutions**	
机构数 (个)	Number of Institutions (unit)	265
中　央	Central	221
地　方	Local	44
研究与试验发展(R&D)投入情况	**Statistics on R&D Input**	
R&D人员 (万人)	R&D Personnel (10000 persons)	4.6
按隶属关系分	By Affiliation	
中　央	Central	4.4
地　方	Local	0.2
R&D人员折合全时当量 (万人年)	Full-time Equivalent of R&D Personnel (10000 man-years)	3.8
基础研究	Basic Research	1.2
应用研究	Applied Research	1.6
试验发展	Experimental Development	1.0
R&D经费内部支出 (亿元)	Internal Expenditure on R&D (100 million yuan)	103.1
按隶属关系分	By Affiliation	
中　央	Central	99.0
地　方	Local	4.1
按活动类型分	By Type of Activity	
基础研究	Basic Research	26.4
应用研究	Applied Research	45.2
试验发展	Experimental Development	31.5
按资金来源分	By Source of Funds	
政府资金	Governmental Funds	88.6
企业资金	Enterprise Funds	3.2
境外资金	Foreign Funds	1.3
其他资金	Others	10.0
研究与试验发展(R&D)项目(课题)情况	**Statistics on R&D Projects**	
R&D项目(课题)数 (项)	Number of R&D Projects (item)	15079
R&D项目(课题)人员折合全时当量 (万人年)	Participants (Full-time Equivalent) (10000 man-years)	2.2
R&D项目(课题)经费内部支出 (亿元)	Internal Expenditure on R&D Projects (100 million yuan)	57.1
科技产出及成果情况	**Statistics on S&T Outputs and Results**	
发表科技论文 (篇)	Scientific Papers Issued (piece)	37232
#国外发表	Published in Foreign Periodicals	9005
出版科技著作 (种)	Publications on Science and Technology (kind)	1489
专利申请数 (件)	Number of Patent Applications (piece)	1993
#发明专利	Inventions	1784
专利授权数 (件)	Number of Patent Grants (piece)	985
#发明专利	Inventions	752

注：表中2018年及以前研究与开发机构统计范围为北京市政府部门所属的科学研究与技术开发机构、科技信息与文献机构，自2019年起，调整为北京市科学研究和技术服务业事业单位。

资料来源：北京市科学技术委员会、中关村科技园区管理委员会。

STATISTICS ON RESEARCH AND EXPERIMENTAL DEVELOPMENT AND RELATED ACTIVITIES OF RESEARCH AND DEVELOPMENT INSTITUTIONS (2007-2023)

2008	2009	2010	2011	2012	2013	2014	2015	2016	2017	2018	2019	2020	2021	2022	2023
266	275	281	280	288	287	299	296	303	300	292	432	445	417	405	411
225	228	231	231	238	237	248	245	254	250	242	334	345	344	328	334
41	47	50	49	50	50	51	51	49	50	50	98	100	73	77	77
4.8	5.2	5.7	5.9	6.3	6.6	6.6	6.8	6.9	7.4	7.3	8.7	9.6	9.9	10.7	11.1
4.5	4.9	5.4	5.6	5.9	6.2	6.2	6.3	6.4	6.9	6.8	8.1	9.0	9.2	9.0	10.1
0.3	0.3	0.3	0.3	0.4	0.4	0.4	0.5	0.5	0.5	0.5	0.6	0.6	0.7	1.7	0.9
3.9	4.2	4.6	4.7	5.3	5.5	5.5	5.6	5.6	5.9	6.0	6.8	7.6	7.8	8.2	8.5
1.3	1.4	1.5	1.6	1.8	1.9	2.0	2.1	2.5	2.4	2.6	2.8	3.4	3.4	3.8	4.0
1.6	1.7	2.0	2.1	2.2	2.3	2.3	2.2	2.2	2.7	2.6	2.9	3.1	3.1	3.4	3.3
1.0	1.1	1.1	1.0	1.3	1.3	1.2	1.3	0.9	0.8	0.8	1.1	1.1	1.3	1.0	1.2
123.8	150.3	187.0	195.1	222.0	246.8	271.2	295.6	301.5	329.1	373.0	505.2	509.2	572.6	597.1	659.4
117.4	143.9	178.9	185.1	211.5	236.3	253.6	277.0	280.4	309.2	351.3	480.7	481.3	543.2	551.0	605.5
6.4	6.4	8.1	10.0	10.5	10.5	17.6	18.6	21.1	19.9	21.7	24.5	27.9	29.4	46.1	53.9
28.3	39.2	49.9	58.5	65.1	73.6	86.5	96.8	109.1	130.2	156.9	200.4	206.1	226.9	252.3	268.8
49.0	61.5	78.0	84.0	92.0	102.2	108.9	120.5	131.3	146.4	157.8	222.6	228.1	259.5	282.7	302.4
46.5	49.6	59.1	52.6	64.9	71.0	75.8	78.3	61.1	52.5	58.3	82.2	75.0	86.2	62.1	88.3
106.6	126.3	164.4	168.0	192.6	220.0	244.6	266.3	262.1	289.6	317.9	440.5	442.5	496.2	507.0	561.8
4.0	4.4	3.6	6.6	6.5	8.2	8.2	12.1	16.1	16.7	22.7	24.6	34.0	45.2	47.1	46.2
1.8	2.0	1.5	2.5	1.5	1.9	1.8	2.0	1.7	2.2	2.1	2.6	1.7	2.6	4.1	3.9
11.4	17.6	17.5	18.0	21.4	16.7	16.6	15.2	21.6	20.6	30.3	37.5	30.9	28.6	38.9	47.5
16383	17816	19545	20333	22842	23949	25550	26762	26998	31749	32133	36994	40066	41018	43320	45937
2.3	3.8	4.1	4.3	4.9	5.0	5.0	5.0	4.7	5.0	5.1	5.7	6.0	6.4	6.7	7.1
70.9	87.1	107.2	115.0	142.7	156.8	161.0	173.5	162.0	189.3	215.3	250.1	269.7	256.1	279.4	299.0
37149	39380	39384	41442	44218	45509	48040	48734	49517	49346	50178	59406	64425	65200	68417	65448
9184	12011	11696	13361	14003	17216	17905	18915	19800	21687	23176	27628	31316	29902	36740	34735
1636	1873	1601	1828	1670	1921	2058	2261	2453	2164	2461	2410	2445	2372	2273	2248
2488	3182	3879	4880	5456	6192	6004	6464	6657	7141	7574	9693	10630	11716	12344	14447
2119	2772	3450	4373	4798	5144	5115	5164	5543	5779	6059	7561	8436	9487	10055	11868
1146	1574	1879	2260	3251	3646	3932	4702	5522	5449	5319	6733	8922	9995	10794	11572
922	1299	1455	1756	2635	2763	3001	3529	4184	4246	3767	4670	6350	7115	7964	8835

Note: The scope of statistics of R&D institutions in and before 2018 covered the scientific research and technological development institutions, and the scientific and technological information and literature institutions subordinate to government authorities of Beijing. Since 2019, the scope of statistics has been adjusted to the public institutions of scientific research and technical services of Beijing.

Source: Beijing Municipal Science & Technology Commission, Administrative Commission of Zhongguancun Science Park.

19-9 高等学校研究与试验发展(R&D)及相关活动情况
STATISTICS ON RESEARCH AND EXPERIMENTAL DEVELOPMENT AND RELATED ACTIVITIES BY HIGHER EDUCATION INSTITUTIONS

项目	Item	2023	2022
高等学校基本情况	**Basic Statistics on Higher Education Institutions**		
学校数 (个)	Number of Institutions (unit)	170	168
研究与试验发展(R&D)机构数 (个)	Number of R&D Institutions (unit)	1612	1475
研究与试验发展(R&D)投入情况	**Statistics on R&D Input**		
R&D人员 (万人)	R&D Personnel (10000 person)	17.48	14.64
R&D人员折合全时当量 (万人年)	Full-time Equivalent of R&D Personnel (10000 man-years)	9.18	8.30
基础研究	Basic Research	3.73	3.40
应用研究	Applied Research	4.91	4.40
试验发展	Experimental Development	0.54	0.50
R&D经费内部支出 (亿元)	Internal Expenditure on R&D (100 million yuan)	365.86	311.63
按活动类型分	By Type of Activity		
基础研究	Basic Research	124.32	103.53
应用研究	Applied Research	207.31	183.34
试验发展	Experimental Development	34.23	24.76
按资金来源分	By Source of Funds		
#政府资金	Governmental Funds	222.84	189.00
企业资金	Enterprise Funds	97.80	84.47
研究与试验发展(R&D)项目(课题)情况	**Statistics on R&D Projects**		
R&D项目(课题)数 (项)	Number of R&D Projects (Tasks) (item)	148260	133210
R&D项目(课题)人员折合全时当量 (万人年)	Participants (Full-time Equivalent) (10000 man-years)	9.19	8.30
R&D项目(课题)经费内部支出 (亿元)	Internal Expenditure on R&D (100 million yuan)	288.31	242.13
科技产出及成果情况	**Statistics on S&T Outputs and Results**		
发表科技论文 (篇)	Scientific Papers Issued (piece)	147332	140824
#国外发表	Published in Foreign Periodicals	85568	76330
出版科技著作 (种)	Publications on Science and Technology (kind)	4596	4345
专利申请数 (件)	Number of Patent Applications (piece)	27712	23874
#发明专利	Inventions	24694	20926
专利授权数 (件)	Number of Patent Grants (piece)	21174	22278
#发明专利	Inventions	16988	17205

资料来源：北京市教育委员会。
Source: Beijing Municipal Education Commission.

19-10　技术合同成交情况(1990-2023年)
STATISTICS ON CONCLUSION OF TECHNOLOGICAL CONTRACTS (1990-2023)

年　份 Year	合同数(项) Number of Contracts (unit)	技术合同成交总额(亿元) Total Volume of Transaction of Technological Contracts (100 million yuan)	#技术交易额 Total Volume of Transaction of Technology	#流向外省市 Flowing to Other Provinces and Municipalities	#流向天津和河北 Flowing to Tianjin and Hebei	实现合同总金额(亿元) Total Volume of Transaction Achieved in Contracts (100 million yuan)	#技术交易实现金额 Amount of Technological Transactions Achieved
1990	18588	20.3	10.5			15.4	8.4
1991	18547	22.4	13.1			15.3	9.1
1992	23395	31.3	22.2			20.0	14.4
1993	20461	35.6	25.6			24.9	17.6
1994	15220	37.2	26.9			26.9	20.4
1995	16347	41.2	32.2			28.4	22.3
1996	14850	45.8	39.2			29.6	25.4
1997	13866	54.3	48.1			31.1	27.8
1998	20724	81.6	73.9			42.1	37.6
1999	20711	92.2	88.5			43.6	41.0
2000	21270	140.3	126.3	65.5		60.3	56.3
2001	23921	191.0	164.8	85.4		97.6	93.0
2002	27037	221.1	181.0	100.4		101.9	97.2
2003	32173	265.5	226.8	132.4		119.9	113.9
2004	35478	331.8	294.3	165.8		148.7	143.4
2005	37505	434.4	350.4	204.9		201.4	180.6
2006	51575	697.3	572.6	325.3		349.5	319.7
2007	50972	882.6	660.3	407.4		418.1	353.5
2008	52742	1027.2	778.1	487.0		406.2	375.0
2009	49938	1236.2	906.9	498.2		516.8	452.9
2010	50847	1579.5	1066.7	654.8		536.0	505.6
2011	53552	1890.3	1268.3	635.9		580.4	563.3
2012	59969	2458.5	2048.6	1385.0		739.8	707.0
2013	62743	2851.2	2252.4	1615.9		684.0	659.3
2014	67278	3136.0	2531.5	1722.0		708.2	675.1
2015	72272	3452.6	2767.8	1878.7	111.5	1229.7	1206.9
2016	74965	3940.8	2919.3	1997.2	154.7	749.2	717.0
2017	81266	4485.3	3703.9	2327.3	203.5	889.0	853.0
2018	82486	4957.8	4069.5	3014.9	227.4	986.2	889.5
2019	83171	5695.3	4389.0	2866.9	282.8	1075.7	1006.1
2020	84451	6316.2	4816.3	3718.5	347.0	938.6	898.5
2021	93563	7005.7	5347.8	4347.7	350.4	788.5	760.1
2022	95061	7947.5	6135.3	4555.7	356.9	942.4	910.8
2023	106552	8536.9	6410.7	4948.9	748.7	997.1	982.2

资料来源：北京市科学技术委员会、中关村科技园区管理委员会。
Source: Beijing Municipal Science & Technology Commission, Administrative Commission of Zhongguancun Science Park.

19-11 技术合同成交情况
STATISTICS ON CONCLUSION OF TECHNICAL CONTRACTS

项目	Item	合同数(项) Number of Contracts (unit)		成交额(亿元) Volume of Transaction (100 million yuan)	
		2023	2022	2023	2022
合计	**Total**	**106552**	**95061**	**8536.9**	**7947.5**
按合同类别分类	**By Type of Contract**				
技术开发合同	Technological Development	31713	26669	2179.8	1661.1
技术转让合同	Technology Transfer	3173	2422	147.3	411.4
技术咨询合同	Technical Consultation	9874	10096	155.0	101.3
技术服务合同	Technical Service	61792	55874	6054.8	5773.7
按合同卖方类别分类	**By Type of Seller**				
机关法人	Government Organizations				
事业法人	Public Institutions	32013	23308	710.4	493.7
社团法人	Mass Organizations	57	37	0.4	0.4
企业法人	Enterprises	74180	71457	7796.5	7438.6
自然人	Natural Persons	44	44	3.0	0.9
其他组织	Other Organizations	258	215	26.7	13.9
按合同买方类别分类	**By Type of Buyer**				
机关法人	Government Organizations	6885	7181	239.5	223.4
事业法人	Public Institutions	18511	16720	623.8	413.7
社团法人	Mass Organizations	272	246	1.9	2.5
企业法人	Enterprises	79431	69711	6887.8	6668.6
自然人	Natural Persons	140	147	1.7	1.2
其他组织	Other Organizations	1313	1056	782.3	638.1
按服务社会经济目标分类	**By Social and Economic Objectives Served**				
环境保护、生态建设及污染防治	Environmental Protection, Ecological Building and Pollution Prevention	5501	4358	206.3	357.9
能源生产、分配和合理利用	Energy Production, Distribution and Application	9922	8656	1031.3	864.4
卫生事业发展	Sanitation Services	5951	3401	222.9	289.7
教育事业发展	Education Development	4624	4537	33.4	30.2
基础设施以及城市和农村规划	Infrastructure and Rural and Urban Planning	4224	5602	1662.2	2071.1
社会发展和社会服务	Social Development and Social Service	40420	33655	3335.7	2553.1
地球和大气层的探索与利用	Earth and Atmosphere Exploration and Utility	346	175	1.9	1.8
民用空间探测及开发	Civil Aerospace Exploration	282	167	7.3	7.9
农林牧渔业发展	Farming, Forestry and Fishery	6182	3921	50.7	31.8
工商业发展	Industry Promotion	5460	5012	353.3	499.0
非定向研究	Non-directive Research	3898	2866	129.1	167.1
其他民用目标	Other Civilian Purpose	16480	19436	1069.8	874.3
国防	Defense	3262	3275	433.0	199.0
按技术流向分类	**By Spread Area of Technology**				
流向本市	To Beijing	35361	33049	2333.1	1931.5
流向外省市	To Other Provinces and Municipalities	70096	60968	4948.9	4555.7
#流向天津	To Tianjin	2324	2256	151.6	82.1
流向河北	To Hebei	4434	3625	597.1	274.8
技术出口	Exports	1095	1044	1254.9	1460.3

资料来源：北京市科学技术委员会、中关村科技园区管理委员会。
Source: Beijing Municipal Science & Technology Commission, Administrative Commission of Zhongguancun Science Park.

19−12　科技成果及获奖情况(2001−2023年)
STATISTICS ON SCIENTIFIC AND TECHNOLOGICAL ACHIEVEMENTS AND AWARDS (2001-2023)

单位：项　(unit)

年　份 Year	科技成果登记数 Registered Number of Scientific and Technological Achievements	#国家技术发明奖 National Awards of Technical Invention	#国家科学技术进步奖 National Awards of Scientific and Technological Advancement
2001	326	1	38
2002	275	5	48
2003	468	5	52
2004	976	6	43
2005	1018	8	52
2006	1002	12	64
2007	1010	9	44
2008	1016	13	42
2009	1023	11	54
2010	1030	11	53
2011	1035	5	56
2012	1040	22	53
2013	1043	19	38
2014	1042	15	49
2015	1045	17	42
2016	728	10	47
2017	844	23	40
2018	863	16	40
2019	766	11	42
2020	801	10	39
2021	196		
2022	1139		
2023	1560	16	24

注：2020年10月7日，国务院公布修订后的《国家科学技术奖励条例》(国务院令第731号)，自2020年12月1日起施行。新修订的《国家科学技术奖励条例》不再规定国家科学技术奖每年评审一次。2021年度与2022年度的国家科学技术奖提名工作均未启动，故没有相关获奖信息及数据统计。

资料来源：北京市科学技术委员会、中关村科技园区管理委员会。

Note: On October 7, 2020, the State Council promulgated the revised Regulations on National Awards for Science and Technology (Decree No. 731 of the State Council) which took effect as of December 1, 2020. In the revised Regulations on National Awards for Science and Technology, it is no longer required that the National Awards for Science and Technology should be reviewed once every year. Neither the nomination for the National Awards for Science and Technology for 2021 nor that for 2022 was launched; therefore, there is no related awards information or data statistics.

Source: Beijing Municipal Science & Technology Commission, Administrative Commission of Zhongguancun Science Park.

19-13 专利授权情况
STATISTICS ON GRANTING OF PATENTS

单位：件 (piece)

项 目	Item	2023	2022
合 计	**Total**	**193973**	**202722**
按种类分	**By Type**		
发 明	Inventions	107875	88127
实用新型	Utility Models	68901	91947
外观设计	Industrial Designs	17197	22648
按对象分	**By Applicant**		
工矿企业	Industrial and Mining Enterprises	147371	151168
大专院校	Universities & Colleges	17249	20962
科研单位	Scientific Research Institutes	14321	17392
机关团体	Government Agencies and Organizations	10074	6014
个 人	Individuals	4958	7186

资料来源：北京市知识产权局。
Source: Beijing Municipal Intellectual Property Office.

19-14 有效发明和高价值发明专利情况
STATISTICS ON EFFECTIVE INVENTIONS AND HIGH-VALUE INVENTION PATENTS

单位：件 (piece)

项 目	Item	有效发明 Effective Inventions		高价值发明专利拥有量 High-value Invention Patent Ownership	
		2023	2022	2023	2022
合 计	**Total**	**574323**	**477790**	**299142**	**245074**
按对象分	**By Applicant**				
工矿企业	Industrial and Mining Enterprises	391814	315792		
大专院校	Universities & Colleges	90263	78439		
科研单位	Scientific Research Institutes	73525	70521		
机关团体	Government Agencies and Organizations	10961	5474		
个 人	Individuals	7760	7564		

资料来源：北京市知识产权局。
Source: Beijing Municipal Intellectual Property Office.

19-15　科学技术协会及所属学会工作情况(2022年)
STATISTICS ON SCIENCE AND TECHNOLOGY ASSOCIATION AND SUBORDINATE INSTITUTES (2022)

项　目		Item		合计 Total	市科协 Municipal Science and Technology Association	市级学会 Institutes at Municipal Level
基本情况		**Basic Information**				
机构数	(个)	Number of Institutions	(unit)	218	9	209
机关从业人员	(人)	Number of Employed Persons in the Institutions	(person)	1370	61	1309
学术交流活动		**Academic Exchange Activities**				
国内学术会议	(次)	Domestic Academic Meetings	(time)	978	22	956
参加人数	(人次)	Number of Participants	(person-time)	24264336	7355451	16908885
交流论文	(篇)	Number of Papers Exchagned	(unit)	19834	92	19742
境内国际学术会议	(次)	Domestically-held International Academic Meetings	(time)	39	3	36
参加人数	(人次)	Number of Participants	(person-time)	395071	2285	392786
交流论文	(篇)	Number of Papers Exchagned	(unit)	1253	41	1212
港澳台地区学术会议	(次)	Academic Meetings Held in Hong Kong,Macao and Taiwan	(time)	27	18	9
参加人数	(人次)	Number of Participants	(person-time)	38211	5220	32991
交流论文	(篇)	Number of Papers Exchagned	(unit)	187	130	57
科技期刊		**Science and Technology Journals**				
主办科技期刊种数	(种)	Types of Science and Technology Journals Sponsored	(sort)	22	1	21
科技期刊总印数	(册)	Number of Total Printings of Science and Technology Journals	(copy)	926140	499800	426340
科技期刊发表论文数	(篇)	Papers Published on Science and Technology Journals	(unit)	6040	798	5242
科普基础设施		**Infrastructure for Popularizing Scientific Knowledge**				
科技馆	(个)	Science and Technology Museum	(unit)	6	5	1
科技馆全年参观数	(人次)	Annual Visitors of Science and Technology Museum	(person-time)	146730	144730	2000
科普活动		**Activities to Popularize Scientific Knowledge**				
举办科普宣讲活动	(次)	Scientific Knowledge Lectures	(time)	4073	690	3383
青少年科普活动受众人次	(人次)	Audiences to activities to Popularize Scientific Knowledge to Teenagers	(person-time)	3846701	21390	3825311
播放科技广播、影视节目	(分钟)	Playing Radio, Films and TV Programs on Science and Technology	(minute)	8355	1490	6865
举办实用技术培训	(次)	Holding Practical Technology Trainings	(time)	1049	598	451
推广新技术、新品种	(项)	Promoting New Technologies and New Varieties	(unit)	259	210	49
参加活动科技人员总数	(人次)	Participating in Science and Technology Personnel	(person-time)	19248	631	18617
参加活动的学会、协会、研究会	(个次)	Participating in Socieities, Associations and Research Institutes	(unit-time)	156	41	115
科技传播		**Science and Technology Dissemination**				
主办科技报纸种数	(种)	Types of Science and Technology Newspaper Sponsored	(sort)	2	1	1
制作科普挂图种数	(种)	Types of Scientific Knowledge Flip Charts Produced	(sort)	30		30
制作科技广播、影视节目套数	(套)	Science and Technology Raido, Films and TV Programs Produced	(unit)	551	53	498
主办科技网站	(个)	Science and Technology Websites Sponsored	(unit)	55	4	51
科技开放与交流		**Science and Technology Opening-up and Exchange**				
加入国际民间科技组织	(个)	International Cilvilian Science and Technology Organizations Joined	(unit)	1	1	
参加国际科学计划	(项)	International Science Programs Participated	(unit)	2		2
参加国外科技活动人数	(人次)	Number of Persons Participating in Foreign Science and Technology Activities	(person-time)	40		40
参加港澳台地区科技活动人数	(人次)	Number of Persons Participating in Science and Technology Activities in Hong Kong, Macao and Taiwan	(person-time)	15120	5000	10120
接待国外专家学者	(人次)	Foreign Experts and Scholars Received	(person-time)	68		68
科技服务		**Science and Technology Service**				
举办决策咨询活动	(次)	Holding Policy-making Consulting Activities	(time)	631	9	622

注：本表统计范围为北京市科学技术协会所属学会、研究会。

资料来源：北京市科学技术协会。

Note: Figures in this table cover societies and research institutes affiliated with Beijing Association for Science & Technology.

Source: Beijing Association for Science & Technology.

主要统计指标解释

科技活动人员 指报告年度调查单位直接从事科技活动、以及从事科技活动管理和为科技活动提供直接服务的人员。直接从事科技活动人员包括：在单位办的研究室、实验室、技术开发中心及中试车间（基地）等机构中从事科技活动的人员；虽不在上述机构工作，但编入科技活动项目（课题）组的人员等。从事科技活动管理和为科技活动提供直接服务的人员，包括：与科技活动相关的行政管理人员，以及直接为科技活动提供资料文献、材料供应、设备维护等服务的人员。

研究与试验发展（R&D） 指在科学技术领域，为增加知识总量、以及运用这些知识去创造新的应用而进行的系统的创造性的活动，包括基础研究、应用研究、试验发展三类活动。

研究与试验发展（R&D）人员 指单位内部从事基础研究、应用研究和试验发展三类活动的人员。包括直接参加上述三类项目活动的人员以及这三类项目的管理人员和直接服务人员。为研发活动提供直接服务的人员包括直接为研发活动提供资料文献、材料供应、设备维护等服务的人员。

研究与试验发展（R&D）人员折合全时当量 是国际上通用的、用于比较科技人力投入的指标。指 R&D 全时人员（全年从事 R&D 活动累积工作时间占全部工作时间的 90% 及以上人员）工作量与非全时人员按实际工作时间折算的工作量之和。

研究与试验发展（R&D）内部支出 指调查单位在报告年度用于内部开展 R&D 活动（基础研究、应用研究和试验发展）的实际支出。包括用于 R&D 项目（课题）活动的直接支出，以及间接用于 R&D 活动的管理费、服务费、与 R&D 有关的基本建设支出以及外协加工费等，不包括生产性活动支出、归还贷款支出以及与外单位合作或委托外单位进行 R&D 活动而转拨给对方的经费支出。

专利 是专利权的简称，是对发明人的发明创造经审查合格后，由专利局依据专利法授予发明人和设计人对该项发明创造享有的专有权。包括发明、实用新型和外观设计。

发明专利 指专利法及其实施细则所称的发明，指对产品、方法或者改进所提出的新的技术方案。

实用新型专利 指专利法及其实施细则所称的实用新型，指对产品的形状、构造或者其结合所提出的适于实用的新的技术方案。

外观设计专利 指专利法及其实施细则所称的外观设计，指对产品的形状、图案、色彩或者其结合所做出的富有美感并适于工业上应用的新设计。

Explanatory Notes on Main Statistical Indicators

Personnel Engaged in Science and Technology Activities refer to persons directly engaged in science and technology activities as well as persons engaged in science and technology management and persons offering direct services to science and technology activities in the surveyed entities in the reporting year. Persons directly engaged in science and technology activities include: persons engaged in science and technology activities in such institutions as research labs of entities, laboratories, technical development centers and middle-stage test workshops (bases); persons not working in the above-mentioned institutions but included in the science and technology activity project (task) team, etc. Persons engaged in science and technology management and persons offering direct services for science and technology activities include administrative staff related to science and technology activities, as well as persons directly providing information and literature, supply of materials, equipment maintenance and other services.

R&D refers to systematic and creative activities in the field of science and technology to increase the total knowledge, and apply such knowledge to create new applications, including three kinds of activities, i.e. basic research, applied research, and experimental development.

R&D Personnel refer to persons in the surveyed entities who are engaged in three kinds of activities, i.e. basic research, applied research and experimental development. They include those who participate in the above-mentioned three kinds of activities directly, research management personnel and persons directly serving these activities. Persons providing direct services include those who provide information and literature, supply of materials, equipment maintenance and other services.

Full-Time Equivalent of R&D Personnel is an indicator globally used to compare input of scientific talents. It refers to the sum of workload of full-time R&D personnel (the personnel whose accumulative annual working time involved in R&D activities takes 90% and above of the whole working time) plus the workload of non-full time personnel that is equivalent of the actual working time.

Internal R&D Expenditure means the actual disbursement of investigated entities on internal R&D activities (basic research, applied research, and experimental development) in the reporting year, including direct spending on R&D project (task) activities, and management expenses and service fees indirectly spent on R&D activities, R&D related basic construction expense and external assisting processing charges, etc., excluding production-based activity expense, loan repayment expense and fund transferred to external institution cooperated or entrusted to conduct R&D activities.

Patent is the abbreviation of patent right, referring to the exclusive right granted by patent authorities upon examination and approval of inventions and creations to the inventors and designers with regard to the invention, including inventions, utility models and industrial designs.

Invention Patents means the invention mentioned in the Patent Law and its detailed rules for implementation, i.e. the new technological solutions presented for the product, methodology, or improvement.

Utility Model means the utility model mentioned in the Patent Law and its detailed rules for implementation, i.e. the new practical technological solutions presented for the product shape, structure, color or combination.

Industrial Design means the industrial design mentioned in the Patent Law and its detailed rules for implementation, i.e. new designs of product shape, pattern, color or combination which are aesthetic and suitable for industrial applications.

20

教育
EDUCATION

简要说明

主要内容

本章资料包括高等教育（研究生教育、普通本专科教育、成人本专科教育、其他各类高等学历教育）、中等教育(高中阶段、初中阶段)、小学教育、学前教育、特殊教育、专门学校等资料。主要指标包括学校数、在校生数、招生数、毕业生数、教职工数、专任教师数等内容。

Brief Introduction

Main Content

Statistics in this chapter include those for higher education (postgraduate education, undergraduate and junior college education, undergraduate and junior college education for adults, and other kinds of higher education for diplomas); secondary education (senior high school, junior high school); primary education; preschool education; special education; special schools for delinquent children. Main indicators include the number of schools, number of student enrollment, number of new enrollment, number of graduates, number of teachers and staff, and number of full-time teachers, etc.

20-1 教育基本情况(1978-2023年)

年份 Year	全市各类学校数(个) Total Number of Various Schools (unit)	#普通高等学校 Regular Higher Education Institutions	#中等教育 Secondary Education	#普通高中 Regular Senior Secondary Schools	#小学教育 Primary Schools	全市各类学校在校生数(人) Enrolment of Various Schools (person)	#普通本专科 Undergraduates in Regular Higher Education Institutions
1978		35			4666		48618
1979		48			4534		55073
1980		50			4485		83032
1981		51			4445		98044
1982		51			4381		93878
1983		54			4269		90894
1984		57			4168		102962
1985		61			4059		122791
1986		66			3995		129647
1987		67			3875		136694
1988		67			3793		145134
1989		67			3703		141625
1990		67			3611		139646
1991	8496	67	1168	282	3482	2142085	136940
1992	8052	67	1150	279	3306	2194268	139978
1993	7789	66	1145	280	3190	2266932	158906
1994	7574	67	1150	280	3035	2348406	175203
1995	7158	65	1170	286	2867	2380096	182173
1996	7121	65	1189	296	2780	2388002	189953
1997	6858	65	1181	288	2696	2361438	195842
1998	6456	63	1190	282	2511	2325043	212984
1999	5807	64	1182	275	2352	2297673	234033
2000	5458	59	1159	302	2169	2299433	282585
2001	4873	61	1111	289	1960	2297107	340284
2002	4447	62	998	325	1824	2294947	398573
2003	4158	74	977	329	1652	2299416	458898
2004	3971	77	945	338	1504	2291594	500245
2005	3782	79	917	335	1403	2264004	536724
2006	3751	82	888	335	1310	2910228	554702
2007	3593	83	863	328	1235	3195763	567875
2008	3508	82	838	325	1202	3208704	575639
2009	3425	88	804	305	1160	3214354	577154
2010	3330	89	779	289	1104	3299555	577828
2011	3367	89	769	290	1090	3426025	578633
2012	3314	91	760	289	1081	3568273	581844
2013	3439	89	757	291	1093	3736003	589234
2014	3437	89	766	306	1040	3774868	594614
2015	3454	90	768	306	996	3734245	593448
2016	3524	91	767	305	984	3733544	588389
2017	3556	92	766	304	984	3861492	580663
2018	3585	92	757	309	970	4083211	581133
2019	3640	93	765	318	941	4124862	585971
2020	3799	92	766	321	934	4038504	590335
2021	3723	92	750	332	837	3970617	595776
2022	3605	92	761	351	719	4023949	602512
2023	3605	92	763	363	714	3953472	618348

注：1.自2007年起，小学、中学、特殊教育和学前教育在校生数、招生数、毕业生数包括非本市户籍学生数。

2.小学、初中在校生数包括小学、初中附设特教班、随班就读和送教上门学生数，高中包括随班就读特教学生数。

3.1991—2005年，中等教育为普通中等学校口径，包括普通中学、普通中专、职业中学、技工学校和专门学校；2006—2020年，中等教育包括普通中学、普通中专、成人中专、职业高中和技工学校，其中，技工学校数据由市人力资源和社会保障局提供；自2021年起，中等教育不包括技工学校。

4.自2021年起，全市各类学校数不含民办的其他高等教育机构，在校生数不含在职人员攻读硕士学位人数。

5.全市各类学校在校生数、全市各类学校招生数和全市各类学校毕业生数不包括国家开放大学附设中职班北京校区在校生数、招生数和毕业生数。

6.在校生数、招生数、毕业生数不含国际学生数。

资料来源：北京市教育委员会、北京市人力资源和社会保障局。

BASIC STATISTICS ON EDUCATION (1978-2023)

#中等教育 Secondary Education	#普通高中 Regular Senior Secondary Schools	#小学教育 Primary Schools	全市各类学校招生数（人） Entrants of Various Schools (person)	#普通本专科 Undergraduates in Regular Higher Education Institutions	#中等教育 Secondary Education	#普通高中 Regular Senior Secondary Schools	#小学教育 Primary Schools
	415612	937336		17445		161288	199076
	299974	968723		15848		160340	154809
	312188	951763		17972		131961	138751
	175180	900350		17921		54296	121744
	92401	854516		21936		35212	104357
	88657	838078		27988		40282	96028
	110916	763204		31805		47068	103482
	119876	733605		40670		35265	135048
	109862	749101		35390		27863	160513
	109023	777982		41163		41186	156954
	108106	850577		42187		35429	184516
	110745	934696		33557		33254	184609
	100669	995831		36275		30596	161742
565357	93728	1013268	571685	37700	205107	28589	148300
617847	82894	1001762	622142	41517	232765	25790	157145
679821	78261	1022166	651729	52205	242274	26275	175853
758310	86584	1024503	704933	51884	287642	34704	186315
834903	102522	1007301	691972	52868	308786	40803	168903
881912	118476	999740	628772	55269	289612	42603	156898
887644	133461	977323	581091	56884	289719	49566	124231
895042	145966	919531	581786	62264	308157	52956	100415
931029	161473	836655	603332	78354	320731	56998	94358
972930	179002	743109	635328	99397	324862	65890	92002
988985	194283	664443	641432	116344	313257	69195	91230
984117	220667	594241	671956	128320	326835	84679	86406
968035	250959	546530	662877	143483	302071	94894	82631
919178	274803	516042	635842	147298	271396	93519	73577
859132	278358	494482	630515	156124	259133	88605	71020
799074	259414	473275	851808	154969	234524	76375	73138
839038	243818	666617	927144	156222	252709	71590	109203
782866	219163	659500	938891	157238	236714	68397	110440
740396	203477	647101	962648	158992	240937	65983	102414
727741	198415	653255	1002141	155228	238954	65649	113728
711130	195072	680457	1050131	157543	243754	64146	132719
732224	193505	718655	1108574	162042	254790	63381	141738
706713	187586	789276	1182301	163081	239010	59983	165807
651443	177554	821152	1113688	160056	202434	55184	153249
587112	169412	850321	1091756	152741	186517	56743	145876
552468	163130	868417	1115515	154715	180881	53544	145274
522658	163977	875849	1248003	153028	181936	53755	157559
525434	155478	913216	1286509	155784	172981	47355	184339
538096	152857	941614	1196902	156820	190366	51403	182873
563743	160152	995046	1169955	159301	209327	61071	202157
573734	176095	1036584	1091101	160417	199189	62263	186440
609344	198928	1083813	1175320	165860	215522	74681	189935
646320	216891	1161797	1045932	175835	235335	79716	235253

Note: a) Since 2007, the number of enrolment, entrants and graduates in primary schools, secondary schools, schools for special education and pre-school education has included the number of students from other provinces, municipalities and autonomous regions.

b) The number of enrolment in primary schools and junior secondary schools includes the number of students in special education classes attached to primary schools and special education classes attached to junior secondary schools, students of regular classes in primary schools and junior secondary schools, and students receiving 'home delivery' teaching for primary school and junior secondary education; the number of enrolment in senior secondary schools includes the number of students of regular classes for special education in senior secondary schools.

c) Since 1991 until 2005, secondary education covered the regular schools for secondary education, including regular secondary schools, regular technical secondary schools, vocational secondary schools, skilled workers schools, and specialized schools. Since 2006 until 2020, secondary education covered regular secondary schools, regular technical secondary schools, technical secondary schools for adults, senior secondary vocational schools, and skilled workers schools. Specifically, the data on skilled workers schools are provided by Beijing Municipal Human Resources and Social Security Bureau. Since 2021, secondary education has not covered skilled workers schools.

d) Since 2021, the total number of various schools has not included the number of other non-government higher education institutions, and the number of enrolment has not included the number of on-the-job students for master's degree.

e) The number of enrolment in various schools, the number of entrants in various schools and the number of graduates in various schools do not include the number of enrolment, entrants and graduates in Beijing campus for secondary vocational education classes attached to the National Open University.

f) The number of enrolment, entrants and graduates do not include the number of international students.

Source: Beijing Municipal Education Commission, Beijing Municipal Human Resources and Social Security Bureau.

20-1 续表 Continued

年份 Year	全市各类学校毕业生数（人） Number of Graduates in Various Schools (person)	#普通本专科 Undergraduates in Regular Higher Education Institutions	#中等教育 Secondary Education	#普通高中 Regular Senior Secondary Schools	#小学教育 Primary Schools	专任教师数（人） Full-time Teachers (person)	平均每一专任教师负担学生数（人） Average Number of Students Instructed by a Full-time Teacher (person)：普通中学 Regular Secondary Schools	小学 Primary Schools
1978		10881		174899	151950		19.9	20.7
1979		8585		239813	114047		16.1	21.3
1980		8233		145501	144025		14.8	21.7
1981		2289		170992	162306		13.4	19.7
1982		25753		111153	135562		12.3	19.5
1983		31009			95919		11.5	19.6
1984		20110		24498	169251		13.2	18.2
1985		21442		24720	156035		13.9	17.4
1986		26953		36942	138350		14.1	17.3
1987		34894		43589	121599		12.8	16.8
1988		33066		36127	105948		11.4	17.6
1989		35863		29267	97208		11.0	19.1
1990		36171		40369	102782		10.1	18.6
1991	487740	37702		34428	132544	168485	10.5	18.0
1992	520787	37075		32471	156306	169249	11.3	17.4
1993	526982	32888		27428	157838	170361	12.1	17.4
1994	528199	34855		24112	184566	175025	13.1	16.9
1995	554690	45094		23353	183894	176591	13.6	16.5
1996	575969	46471		25170	162030	178006	13.7	16.1
1997	584120	49973		33010	146023	179080	13.2	15.7
1998	600662	49322		39683	156194	178210	12.8	14.9
1999	603027	49936		40660	175656	175496	13.2	13.7
2000	604900	51556		47569	185059	167040	14.1	12.8
2001	617889	55831		51263	167076	168080	14.3	12.1
2002	624329	67621		51180	156683	166490	14.2	11.2
2003	610826	83816		56601	123580	166510	13.7	11.0
2004	614137	99637		66556	100139	172055	12.9	10.6
2005	622974	117367		73260	93486	174589	11.8	10.3
2006	787596	132488	290047	78037	90799	191365	10.8	9.8
2007	851126	138834	272651	78408	112332	195568	11.5	13.8
2008	832585	149459	262871	78468	112268	199114	10.9	13.5
2009	865025	152336	253067	70132	110730	203825	10.0	13.0
2010	834340	150156	233837	62305	102971	206602	10.2	13.2
2011	838521	151277	223955	58275	101678	199789	9.8	13.4
2012	881804	152980	224938	55657	109492	204812	9.7	13.7
2013	923050	148689	240225	58072	111839	216463	9.5	14.4
2014	937209	147023	229640	57773	112819	225165	9.0	14.4
2015	961180	152118	205795	57738	103893	226043	8.4	14.3
2016	924267	153005	182511	52841	111481	231251	7.9	14.0
2017	939184	152990	168125	49685	125938	236346	7.7	13.6
2018	940336	146654	158863	51065	124610	241719	7.9	13.9
2019	1018835	144645	157545	50390	138968	248239	8.2	13.8
2020	1082842	147556	167817	52094	136671	256594	8.3	14.0
2021	1028294	147346	147102	45077	134051	264551	8.6	13.9
2022	1033042	154382	165804	49775	133331	272543	8.8	14.1
2023	1047009	153749	185085	59193	146245	275506	9.2	14.7

20-2 幼儿园基本情况(1978-2023年)
BASIC STATISTICS ON KINDERGARTENS (1978-2023)

单位：人

(person)

年 份 Year	园数(所) Number of Kindergartens (unit)	班数(个) Number of Classes (unit)	离园人数 Children Leaving	入园人数 Children Entering	在园人数 Children Enrolment	教职工数 Educational Personnel	#专任教师 Full-time Teachers
1978	5074				235923	39982	8369
1979	4623				237037	40424	8777
1980	3991				219407	38475	7765
1981	3888				233089	38832	8814
1982	3849				254458	42663	9271
1983	1999				306975	48666	8234
1984	3682				295427	47721	9499
1985	2955				316024	47033	10523
1986	3503				342824	52654	12690
1987	3732				364011	54211	14449
1988	3563				354367	52105	14705
1989	3509				344394	50280	17208
1990	3798				372555	49587	17972
1991	3761		133788	172884	402699	49472	18788
1992	3510		158740	181299	404779	48007	18513
1993	3369		165963	170580	372368	44741	18114
1994	3301		113652	167267	352979	42118	17413
1995	3024		103355	148272	315277	38549	16084
1996	3056		135376	112449	271752	33586	14792
1997	2892		110345	95140	253478	32811	14596
1998	2662		99279	93819	245046	30362	13841
1999	2180		91996	89463	237055	29367	13216
2000	2047		85301	91724	229012	27257	12595
2001	1719	8259	85842	87892	217521	26106	12479
2002	1540	8494	79447	91092	213794	25402	12127
2003	1430	7733	76879	86465	199390	26324	13056
2004	1422	8087	71677	86672	205532	28326	14208
2005	1358	8148	71926	83485	202301	28026	14813
2006	1361	8051	70400	68299	197546	28958	15632
2007	1306	8132	70681	83969	214423	30465	17013
2008	1266	8382	72119	85938	226681	32535	18176
2009	1253	9036	65684	89761	247778	34973	17952
2010	1245	9883	68135	105048	276994	37227	21677
2011	1305	11213	76790	115539	311417	44458	24170
2012	1266	11882	79131	115248	331524	48080	26330
2013	1384	12580	88322	128106	348681	53049	28806
2014	1426	13245	96478	133977	364954	57950	31692
2015	1487	14098	101928	149042	394121	61903	34040
2016	1570	14913	99626	152769	416982	65806	36071
2017	1604	15810	105651	177354	445535	69100	37903
2018	1657	16176	117102	165130	450645	71686	38867
2019	1733	16934	118178	168166	467595	79777	41187
2020	1899	18770	132884	221767	525878	88467	44740
2021	2000	20067	136077	190211	566735	98322	47973
2022	1989	20662	162717	178620	574235	99987	48774
2023	1991	19753	208037	164082	515267	96381	47125

资料来源：北京市教育委员会。
Source: Beijing Municipal Education Commission.

20-3 各类学校基本情况
BASIC STATISTICS ON VARIOUS SCHOOLS

单位：人　(person)

项目	Item	校数(所) Number of Schools (unit) 2023	2022	教职工数 Educational Personnel 2023	2022	#专任教师 Full-time Teachers 2023	2022
合计	**Total**	**3605**	**3605**	**437665**	**437816**	**275506**	**272543**
高等教育	**Higher Education**	**110**	**110**	**161545**	**161304**	**77710**	**76730**
研究生培养机构(不计校数)	Institutions Providing Postgraduate Programs (Number of Schools Not Counted)	(146)	(146)			(87328)	(75067)
高等学校(不计校数)	Higher Education Schools (Number of Schools Not Counted)	(59)	(59)			(72456)	(61309)
科研机构(不计校数)	Scientific Research Institutions (Number of Schools Not Counted)	(87)	(87)			(14872)	(13758)
普通高等学校	Regular Higher Education Institutions	92	92	158418	158136	76327	75381
成人高等学校	Adult Higher Education Institutions	18	18	3127	3168	1383	1349
中等教育	**Secondary Education**	**763**	**761**	**110188**	**108169**	**87713**	**85230**
高中阶段教育	High School Level Education	439	428	110188	108169	62535	59773
普通高中	Regular Senior Secondary Schools	363	351	102060	99779	57277	54382
中等职业教育	Secondary Vocational Education	76	77	8128	8390	5258	5391
普通中专	Regular Technical Secondary Schools	28	28	3190	3193	1661	1630
成人中专	Technical Secondary Schools for Adults	9	10	316	357	178	193
职业高中	Senior Secondary Vocational Schools	39	39	4622	4840	3419	3568
初中阶段教育	Junior Secondary Education	324	333			25178	25457
小学教育	**Primary Education**	**714**	**719**	**67888**	**66748**	**61546**	**60484**
专门学校	**Specialized Schools**	**7**	**6**	**279**	**253**	**239**	**204**
特殊教育	**Special Education**	**20**	**20**	**1384**	**1355**	**1173**	**1121**
学前教育	**Pre-school Education**	**1991**	**1989**	**96381**	**99987**	**47125**	**48774**

注：1.小学、初中在校生数包括小学、初中附设特教班、随班就读和送教上门学生数，高中包括随班就读特教学生数。
2.自2021年起，中等教育不包括技工学校。
3.自2021年起，全市各类学校数不含民办的其他高等教育机构，在校生数不含在职人员攻读硕士学位人数。
4.毕业生数、招生数和在校生数不包括国家开放大学附设中职班北京校区毕业生数、招生数和在校生数。
5.毕业生数、招生数和在校生数不含国际学生数。
6.表中带( )数据不计入“校数”的合计数据中。

资料来源：北京市教育委员会。

Note: a) The number of enrolment in primary schools and junior secondary schools includes the number of students in special education classes attached to primary schools and special education classes attached to junior secondary schools, students of regular classes in primary schools and junior secondary schools, and students receiving 'home delivery' teaching for primary school and junior secondary education; the number of enrolment in senior secondary schools includes the number of students of regular classes for special education in senior secondary schools.
b) Since 2021, secondary education has not covered skilled workers schools.
c) Since 2021, the total number of various schools has not included the number of other non-government higher education institutions, and the number of enrolment has not included the number of on-the-job students for master's degree.
d) The number of graduates, entrants and enrolment do not include the number of graduates, entrants and enrolment in Beijing campus for secondary vocational education classes attached to the National Open University.
e) The number of graduates, entrants and enrolment do not include the number of international students.
f) The data with ( ) in this table are not included in the total number of schools.

Source: Beijing Municipal Education Commission.

20-3 续表 Continued

单位：人 (person)

项 目	Item	毕业生数 Graduates 2023	2022	招生数 Entrants 2023	2022	在校生数 Enrolment 2023	2022
合 计	**Total**	**1047009**	**1033042**	**1045932**	**1175320**	**3953472**	**4023949**
高等教育	**Higher Education**	**505655**	**569297**	**409771**	**589955**	**1621820**	**1748388**
研究生	Postgraduates	121447	114422	151932	145894	454631	435035
高等学校	Higher Education Schools	115238	108694	143716	138245	429949	412030
科研机构	Scientific Research Institutions	6209	5728	8216	7649	24682	23005
普通本专科	Regular Higher Education Institutions Offering Degree Programs and Short-cycle Courses	153749	154382	175835	165860	618348	602512
中央部委属高校	Under Central Ministries and Commissions	79254	78131	86591	87348	341999	338754
市属高校	Under Municipal Government	74495	76251	89244	78512	276349	263758
公办高校	Public Colleges and Universities	59222	61667	71420	63240	220499	210493
民办高校	Non-government Colleges and Universities	15273	14584	17824	15272	55850	53265
成人本专科	Adult Higher Education Institutions Offering Degree Programs and Short-cycle Courses	29659	39448	30029	29620	75956	78225
成人高等学校	Adult Higher Education Institutions	1525	3437	2040	1613	3833	3652
普通高等学校	Regular Higher Education Institutions	28134	36011	27989	28007	72123	74573
网络本专科生	Students Enrolled in Internet-based Courses	200800	261045	51975	248581	472885	632616
中等教育	**Secondary Education**	**185085**	**165804**	**235335**	**215522**	**646320**	**609344**
高中阶段教育	High School Level Education	74720	62290	100350	94252	275400	253524
普通高中	Regular Senior Secondary Schools	59193	49775	79716	74681	216891	198928
中等职业教育	Secondary Vocational Schools	15527	12515	20634	19571	58509	54596
普通中专	Regular Technical Secondary Schools	9751	8166	12939	11822	37081	34471
成人中专	Technical Secondary Schools for Adults	1369	1483	1088	1404	3858	4152
职业高中	Senior Secondary Vocational Schools	4407	2866	6607	6345	17570	15973
初中阶段教育	Junior Secondary Education	110365	103514	134985	121270	370920	355820
小学教育	**Primary Education**	**146245**	**133331**	**235253**	**189935**	**1161797**	**1083813**
专门学校	**Specialized Schools**	**199**	**227**	**195**	**178**	**443**	**447**
特殊教育	**Special Education**	**1788**	**1666**	**1296**	**1110**	**7825**	**7722**
学前教育	**Pre-school Education**	**208037**	**162717**	**164082**	**178620**	**515267**	**574235**

20−4 高等教育学生情况(2023年)
STATISTICS ON STUDENTS OF HIGHER EDUCATION (2023)

单位：人 (person)

项 目	Item	毕(结)业生人数 Graduates (Students Completing Courses)	招生数 Entrants	在校学生数 Enrolment
普通本科、专科生	Undergraduates in Regular Higher Education Institutions	153749	175835	618348
专 科	Bachelor Degree	23332	32527	76237
本 科	Short-cycle Courses	130417	143308	542111
成人本科、专科生	Adult Undergraduates in Regular Higher Education Institutions	29659	30029	75956
专 科	Bachelor Degree	3714	3834	8404
本 科	Short-cycle Courses	25945	26195	67552
网络本科、专科生	Internet-based Undergraduates in Regular Higher Education Institutions	200800	51975	472885
专 科	Bachelor Degree	59448	28060	165816
本 科	Short-cycle Courses	141352	23915	307069
研究生	Postgraduates	121447	151932	454631
硕 士	Master's Degree	100126	118131	319428
博 士	Doctor's Degree	21321	33801	135203
国际学生	International Students	13137	15403	31785

资料来源：北京市教育委员会。
Source: Beijing Municipal Education Commission.

20−5 普通高等学校本专科基本情况(2023年)
BASIC STATISTICS ON UNDERGRADUATES IN REGULAR HIGHER EDUCATION INSTITUTIONS (2023)

单位：人 (person)

项 目	Item	校 数(所) Number of Schools (unit)	毕业生数 Graduates	招生数 Entrants	在校生数 Enrolment	教职工数 Educational Personnel	#专任教师 Full-time Teachers
合 计	**Total**	**92**	**153749**	**175835**	**618348**	**158418**	**76327**
#女 生	Females		77562	84549	300763	83364	35598
按性质类别分	**By Nature and Category**						
综合大学	Comprehensive Universities	5	19370	21465	73226	25903	12015
理工院校	Science and Engineering	30	60298	70355	246745	62040	30587
农业院校	Agriculture	3	6456	8137	27685	4562	2933
林业院校	Forestry	1	3270	3444	13779	2202	1470
医药院校	Medicine	4	5239	5910	21980	19139	3673
师范院校	Teacher Training	2	5545	5659	22099	8620	3814
语文院校	Literature	10	11706	11995	44689	9992	6081
财经院校	Finance and Economics	16	20775	24382	79382	11366	6811
政法院校	Politics and Law	8	9267	11203	38021	5348	3201
体育院校	Physical Culture	3	3398	3414	13709	1859	1288
艺术院校	Art	9	5414	5334	21946	5478	3339
民族院校	Minorities Colleges	1	3011	4537	15087	1909	1115

资料来源：北京市教育委员会。
Source: Beijing Municipal Education Commission.

20–6 全市分学科研究生情况(2023年)
STATISTICS ON POSTGRADUATES BY SUBJECT OF STUDY OF THE WHOLE CITY (2023)

单位：人 (person)

项　目	Item	毕业生数 Graduates			招生数 Entrants			在校生数 Enrolment		
		合计 Total	硕士 Master's Degree	博士 Doctor's Degree	合计 Total	硕士 Master's Degree	博士 Doctor's Degree	合计 Total	硕士 Master's Degree	博士 Doctor's Degree
合　计	**Total**	**121447**	**100126**	**21321**	**151932**	**118131**	**33801**	**454631**	**319428**	**135203**
#女　生	Females	63922	54500	9422	75292	61248	14044	221335	165576	55759
按学科分	**By Subject of Study**									
哲　学	Philosophy	618	403	215	740	449	291	2766	1426	1340
经济学	Economics	8378	7488	890	9016	7832	1184	23377	17759	5618
法　学	Law	10281	8923	1358	11365	9531	1834	33847	25900	7947
教育学	Education	5682	5148	534	6227	5429	798	18961	15433	3528
文　学	Literature	6437	5740	697	7099	6101	998	19953	15476	4477
历史学	History	848	649	199	1038	733	305	3518	2153	1365
理　学	Science	9106	4545	4561	12808	6743	6065	44379	18837	25542
工　学	Engineering	42820	34996	7824	57946	43693	14253	179239	121798	57441
农　学	Agriculture	4195	3335	860	5512	4317	1195	15645	11209	4436
医　学	Medicine	7006	4411	2595	10361	5988	4373	30515	17036	13479
军事学	Military	4	4		1	1		10	10	
管理学	Management	21078	19958	1120	23803	22339	1464	65259	58343	6916
艺术学	Art	4517	4118	399	4900	4285	615	14496	12395	2101
交叉学科	Interdiscipline	477	408	69	1116	690	426	2666	1653	1013
按学位类型分	**By Degree Type**									
学术型学位	Academic Degree	59906	40008	19898	75550	47170	28380	254643	134066	120577
专业学位	Professional Degree	61541	60118	1423	76382	70961	5421	199988	185362	14626

资料来源：北京市教育委员会。
Source: Beijing Municipal Education Commission.

20-7 高等教育国际学生情况(2023年)
STATISTICS FOR INTERNATIONAL STUDENTS FOR HIGHER EDUCATION (2023)

单位：人 (person)

项 目	Item	毕(结)业生数 Graduates (Students Completing Courses)	授予学位人数 Number of Students Conferred with Degree	招生数 Entrants	在校生数 Enrolment
合 计	**Total**	**13137**	**5597**	**15403**	**31785**
学历教育	**Academic-degree Education**	**6113**	**5597**	**6231**	**25795**
按学历划分	**By Educational Background**				
专 科	Short-cycle Courses	120		210	571
本 科	Bachelor Degree	3089	2938	2433	12101
硕 士	Master's Degree	2394	2243	2791	8215
博 士	Doctor's Degree	510	416	797	4908
按地区划分	**By Region**				
亚 洲	Asia	3592	3311	3603	16194
非 洲	Africa	1109	959	1294	4566
欧 洲	Europe	659	632	658	2377
北美洲	North America	481	447	411	1598
南美洲	South America	158	147	163	630
大洋洲	Oceania	114	101	102	430
非学历教育(培训)	**Non-academic-degree Education (Training)**	**7024**		**9172**	**5990**

资料来源：北京市教育委员会。
Source: Beijing Municipal Education Commission.

20-8 幼儿园基本情况(2023年)
BASIC STATISTICS ON KINDERGARTENS (2023)

项　目	Item	总　计 Total	#女 Females	城　区 In City	镇　区 In Counties and Towns	乡　村 In Villages
园　数　(所)	Number of Kindergartens (unit)	1991		1600	165	226
班　数　(个)	Number of Classes (unit)	19753		16638	1578	1537
在园幼儿数 (人)	Children Enrolment (person)	515267	248560	438121	39972	37174
教职工数　(人)	Educational Personnel (person)	96381	86401	83185	6889	6307
#园　长	Headmasters	3139	2956	2607	259	273
专任教师	Full-time Teachers	47125	46184	40635	3472	3018
卫生保健人员	Health Workers	5184	5118	4514	365	305

资料来源：北京市教育委员会。
Source: Beijing Municipal Education Commission.

20-9　高等教育自学考试情况
STATISTICS ON HIGHER EDUCATION SELF-STUDY EXAMINATION

项　　目		Item		2023	2022
报考人次	(人次)	Number of Registered Person-times	(person-time)	74834	42028
报考科次	(科次)	Number of Registered Subject-times	(subject-time)	209163	111059
发出专科毕业证书	(个)	Number of Junior College Diplomas Issued	(unit)	1662	1828
发出本科毕业证书	(个)	Number of Undergraduate Diplomas Issued	(unit)	2159	2685
开考专业	(个)	Number of Majors Examined	(unit)	52	48

资料来源：北京教育考试院。
Source: Beijing Education Examinations Authority.

20-10　特殊教育情况(2023年)
STATISTICS ON SPECIAL EDUCATION (2023)

单位：人　　(person)

项　　目	Item	毕业生数 Graduates	招生数 Entrants	在校生数 Enrolment
合　计	**Total**	**1788**	**1296**	**7825**
#女　生	Females	619	451	2620
#特殊教育学校	Schools for Special Education	603	613	3435
小学附设特教班	Special Education Classes Attached to Primary Schools	6	3	91
小学随班就读	Regular Classes in Primary Schools	485	205	2650
普通(职业)初中随班就读	Regular Classes in Regular Junior Secondary (Vocational) Schools	689	474	1632

资料来源：北京市教育委员会。
Source: Beijing Municipal Education Commission.

20−11 职业技术培训机构基本情况(2023年) BASIC STATISTICS ON VOCATIONAL AND TECHNICAL TRAINING INSTITUTIONS(2023)

项　目	Item	学校数(所) Number of Schools (unit)	教学班(点、个) Teaching Classes (sites, units)	结业生数(人次) Students Completing Courses (person-time)	#女性 Females
合　计	**Total**	**1270**	**15814**	**684322**	**391964**
#少数民族	National Minorities			3515	2467
按培训机构分	**By Training Institution**				
职工技术培训学校(机构)	**Technical Training Schools (Institutions) for Employees**	**22**	**308**	**32820**	**17545**
#教育部门和集体办	Run by Education Authorities and Collectively-run	3	170	22599	14368
其他部门办	Run by Other Authorities				
民　办	Civilian-run	19	138	10221	3177
农村成人文化技术培训学校(机构)	**Cultural and Technical Training Schools (Institutions) for Rural Adults**	**705**	**5979**	**336549**	**224109**
#教育部门和集体办	Run by Education Authorities and Collectively-run	705	5979	336549	224109
县　办	Run by Counties	11	128	86852	60865
乡　办	Run by Townships	76	3840	174440	115771
村　办	Run by Villages	618	2011	75257	47473
其他培训机构(含社会培训机构)	**Other Training Institutions (Including Social Training Institutions)**	**543**	**9527**	**314953**	**150310**
教育部门和集体办	Run by Education Authorities and Collectively-run	5	427	30844	10639
其他部门办	Run by Other Authorities	53	134	2689	1435
民　办	Civilian-run	485	8966	281420	138236
中外合作办	Jointly Run with Sino-foreign Investment				
按培训形式分	**By Form of Training**				
#资格证书培训	Qualification Certificate Training			107975	60983
岗位证书培训	Job Post Certificate Training			71733	46002

资料来源：北京市教育委员会。
Source: Beijing Municipal Education Commission.

20-11 续表 Continued

单位：人 (person)

项 目	Item	注册学生数 Student Enrolment	#女性 Females	教职工数 Educational Personnel	#专任教师 Full-time Teachers	聘请校外教师 External Teachers Retained
合 计	**Total**	**659045**	**370488**	**7532**	**4984**	**4308**
#少数民族	National Minorities	2619	1952	79	44	18
按培训机构分	**By Training Institution**					
职工技术培训学校(机构)	**Technical Training Schools (Institutions) for Employees**	**16841**	**7952**	**434**	**320**	**212**
#教育部门和集体办	Run by Education Authorities and Collectively-run	6620	4775	234	177	128
其他部门办	Run by Other Authorities					
民 办	Civilian-run	10221	3177	200	143	84
农村成人文化技术培训学校(机构)	**Cultural and Technical Training Schools (Institutions) for Rural Adults**	**304110**	**204715**	**602**	**340**	**704**
#教育部门和集体办	Run by Education Authorities and Collectively-run	304110	204715	602	340	704
县 办	Run by Counties	83266	56792	196	171	178
乡 办	Run by Townships	154774	105642	235	132	289
村 办	Run by Villages	66070	42281	171	37	237
其他培训机构(含社会培训机构)	**Other Training Institutions (Including Social Training Institutions)**	**338094**	**157821**	**6496**	**4324**	**3392**
教育部门和集体办	Run by Education Authorities and Collectively-run			82	29	106
其他部门办	Run by Other Authorities	3192	1608	566	391	183
民 办	Civilian-run	334902	156213	5848	3904	3103
中外合作办	Jointly Run with Sino-foreign Investment					
按培训形式分	**By Form of Training**					
#资格证书培训	Qualification Certificate Training					
岗位证书培训	Job Post Certificate Training					

20-12 民办教育基本情况(2023年)
BASIC STATSTICS ON NON-GOVERNMENT EDUCATION (2023)

单位：人 (person)

项目	Item	校数(所) Number of Schools (unit)	毕业生数 Graduates	招生数 Entrants	在校生数 Enrolment	教职工数 Educational Personnel	#专任教师 Full-time Teachers	校外教师数 Number of External Teachers
合计	**Total**	**1223**	**119505**	**101796**	**337219**	**65471**	**30500**	**1038**
民办高等教育	**Civilian-run Higher Education**	**15**	**15526**	**18094**	**56529**	**5501**	**3055**	**977**
普通高校	Regular Higher Education Institutions	15	15526	18094	56529	5501	3055	977
民办中等教育	**Civilian-run Secondary Education**	**125**	**6930**	**11510**	**29360**	**15086**	**8640**	**38**
高中阶段教育	High School Level Education	103	2160	5100	12271	15086	8640	38
民办普通高中	Civilian-run Regular Senior Secondary School	86	1903	4604	10932	14598	8414	38
民办中等职业教育	Civilian-run Secondary Vocational Education	17	257	496	1339	488	226	
初中阶段教育	Junior Secondary Education	22	4770	6410	17089			
民办小学	**Civilian-run Primary Schools**	**38**	**5688**	**6772**	**38109**	**1022**	**633**	**3**
民办幼儿园	**Civilian-run Kindergartens**	**1045**	**91361**	**65420**	**213221**	**43862**	**18172**	**20**

注：民办普通高中的教职工数、专任教师数、校外教师数中包含初中阶段教育的教职工数、专任教师数、校外教师数。
资料来源：北京市教育委员会。
Note: The number of educational personnel, full-time teachers, and external teachers in civilian-run regular senior secondary schools includes the number of educational personnel, full-time teachers, and external teachers for junior secondary education.
Source: Beijing Municipal Education Commission.

20-13　高校办学条件(2023年)
SCHOOL CONDITIONS OF HIGHER EDUCATION INSTITUTIONS (2023)

项　　目	Item	合 计 Total	中 央 Central	市属市管 Municipal
普通高校	**Regular Higher Education Institutions**			
校舍建筑面积 (平方米)	Building Area (sq.m)	43851420	31342969	12508451
占地面积 (平方米)	Floor Space (sq.m)	56815898	40621784	16194115
图　书 (万册)	Books (10000 volumes)	12638	8224	4415
固定资产总值 (万元)	Total Value of Fixed Assets (10000 yuan)	25503811	18794615	6709196
#科学科研仪器设备值	Value of Scientific Research Instruments and Equipment	8070096	5662858	2407237
成人高校	**Adult Higher Education Institutions**			
校舍建筑面积 (平方米)	Building Area (sq.m)	**647380**	**354301**	**293080**
占地面积 (平方米)	Floor Space (sq.m)	712997	516405	196592
图　书 (万册)	Books (10000 volumes)	201	61	141
固定资产总值 (万元)	Total Value of Fixed Assets (10000 yuan)	383878	282481	101397
#科学科研仪器设备值	Value of Scientific Research Instruments and Equipment	41087	18360	22727

资料来源：北京市教育委员会。
Source: Beijing Municipal Education Commission.

20−14 基础教育办学条件(2023年)
SCHOOL CONDITIONS OF BASIC EDUCATION (2023)

单位：平方米 (sq.m)

项　　目	Item	普通中学 Regular Secondary Schools	小　学 Primary Schools
学校占地面积	Floor Space	28806311	14356640
校舍建筑面积	Building Area	19145968	8476840
#当年新增	Newly Added in the Year	1254327	880581
#危房面积	Area of Dangerous Buildings		7944
教学及辅助用房面积	Area of Teaching and Auxiliary Houses	8772258	4870580
普通教室	Regular Classrooms	3152967	2328547
专用教室	Classrooms for Special Purposes	2336029	1022873
理化生实验室	Physics, Chemistry, Biology Laboratories	841247	269
其他	Others	1494782	1022604
公共教学用房	Public Teaching Houses	3283262	1519160
图书室	Libraries	503891	201170
室内体育用房	Indoor Sports Houses	1006359	318068
心理辅导室	Psychological Counseling Room	72862	53310
其他	Others	1700151	946612
行政办公用房	Administrative Houses	2324483	1185721
生活用房	Houses for Life	7467121	2299804
其他用房	Houses for Other Purposes	582106	120735
数字终端数(台)	Number of Digital Terminals (set)	404757	263220
图书藏量(册)	Books Collections (volume)	33566836	28028175

资料来源：北京市教育委员会。
Source: Beijing Municipal Education Commission.

20-15　基础教育国际学生情况(2023年)
STATISTICS ON INTERNATIONAL STUDENTS FOR BASIC EDUCATION(2023)

单位：人　　(person)

项　目	Item	国际学生数 International Students	#民办学校 Civilian-run Schools
合　计	**Total**	**3036**	**1040**
普通中学	Regular Secondary Schools	724	167
初　中	Junior Secondary Schools	460	150
高　中	Senior Secondary Schools	264	17
中等职业教育	Secondary Vocational Education	79	
小　学	Primary Schools	1577	386
幼儿园	Kindergartens	656	487

资料来源：北京市教育委员会。
Source: Beijing Municipal Education Commission.

20-16　教育经费情况(2014-2022年)
STATISTICS ON EDUCATIONAL FINANCE (2014-2022)

单位：万元　　(10000 yuan)

年份 Year	合计 Total	国家财政性教育经费 Government Appropriation for Education	#一般公共预算教育经费 General Public Budget for Education	民办学校中举办者投入 Funds from Sponsors of Non-public Schools	社会捐赠经费 Funds from Social Donations	事业收入 Income from Teaching Research and Other Auxiliary Activities	#学费 Tuition	其他教育经费 Other Educational Funds
2014	10937374	9683641	7584873	10529	10431	1048953	833849	183820
2015	11171250	9810774	8474342	10685	9624	1177133	925848	163034
2016	11934724	10491718	8822890	9261	10879	1299205	1034188	123662
2017	12512746	10863394	9557007	6368	9341	1478756	1201615	154888
2018	13525400	11661674	10207229	8711	6503	1651516	1331358	196996
2019	14794780	12791460	11253649	8906	5505	1876698	1536289	112212
2020	15085043	13130881	11279953	11903	5732	1531203	1251681	405325
2021	15325981	13130243	11351611	13689	5027	2056343	1689286	120679
2022	15854348	13736713	11609960	9662	5577	1966234	1636322	136162

资料来源：北京市教育委员会。
Source: Beijing Municipal Education Commission.

20−17　生均一般公共预算教育事业费支出和公用经费支出情况
AVERAGE GENERAL PUBLIC BUDGET FOR EDUCATIONAL EXPENSES AND PUBLIC EXPENDITURE

单位：元　(yuan)

项　　目	Item	2022	2021	2022年为2021年% 2022 as % of 2021
生均一般公共预算	**Average General Public Budget**			
教育事业费支出	**Educational Expenses**			
幼儿园	Kindergartens	37880.85	38540.98	98.3
普通小学	Regular Primary Schools	35265.13	33633.65	104.9
普通初中	Regular Junior Secondary Schools	58564.07	57156.75	102.5
普通高中	Regular Senior Secondary Schools	63467.48	66433.98	95.5
中等职业学校	Secondary Vocational Schools	70456.50	70514.69	99.9
普通高等学校	Regular Higher Education Institutions	60731.14	65957.02	92.1
生均一般公共预算	**Average General Public Budget**			
公用经费支出	**Public Expenditure**			
幼儿园	Kindergartens	13451.46	14642.97	91.9
普通小学	Regular Primary Schools	10055.04	9791.18	102.7
普通初中	Regular Junior Secondary Schools	18312.17	17717.04	103.4
普通高中	Regular Senior Secondary Schools	17484.75	19545.35	89.5
中等职业学校	Secondary Vocational Schools	24353.64	24652.56	98.8
普通高等学校	Regular Higher Education Institutions	21684.64	29133.45	74.4

资料来源：北京市教育委员会。
Source: Beijing Municipal Education Commission.

主要统计指标解释

研究生培养机构　指经国家批准按国家计划招收和培养硕士、博士和其他研究生的高等学校和科学研究机构。

普通高等学校　指按国家规定的设置标准和审批程序批准举办的，通过国家统一招生考试，招收高中毕业生为主要培养对象，实施高等教育的全日制大学、独立设置的学院和高等专科学校、短期职业大学。

成人高等学校　指按国家规定的设置标准和审批程序批准举办的，通过全国成人高等教育统一招生考试，招收具有高中毕业或同等学历的人员为主要培养对象，利用函授、业余、脱产等多种形式对其实施高等学历教育的学校。包括：职工高等学校、农民高等学校、管理干部学院、教育学院、独立函授学院、广播电视大学和其他机构。

高等教育机构　指经省、自治区、直辖市教育行政部门审批并颁发办学许可证，不具有颁发学历文凭资格的实施高等教育的单位。

民办学校　指经有关主管部门批准，公民个人、社会团体及其他社会组织等利用非国家财政性教育经费，面向社会举办的学校及其他教育机构。

专科教育　应当使学生掌握本专业必备的基础理论、专门应用技术知识，具有从事本专业实际工作的基本技能和技术应用能力。全日制专科教育的基本修业年限为二至三年。

本科教育　应当使学生比较系统地掌握本学科、专业必需的基础理论、基本知识，掌握本专业必要的基本技能、方法和相关知识，具有从事本专业实际工作和研究工作的初步能力。全日制本科教育的基本修业年限为四至五年。

硕士研究生教育　应当使学生掌握本学科坚实的基础理论、系统的专业知识，掌握相应的技能、方法和相关知识，具有从事本专业实际工作和科学研究工作的能力。硕士研究生教育的基本修业年限为二至三年。

博士研究生教育　应当使学生掌握本学科坚实宽广的基础理论、系统深入的专业知识、相应的技能和方法，具有独立从事本学科创造性科学研究工作和实际工作的能力。博士研究生教育的基本修业年限为三至四年。

网络学生　指经教育部批准的现代远程教育试点学校设立的网络教育学院，基于互联网上实施高等学历教育所招收的普通和成人本科、专科学生。

国际学生　指根据《学校招收和培养国际学生管理办法》，不具有中国国籍在学校接受教育的外国学生。

毕业生数　指上学年度内具有学籍的学生完成教学计划规定课程，考试合格并且取得毕业证书的学生数。

招生数　是指实际招收入学并完成学籍注册的新生数。

在校生数　是指有学籍并在本学年初进行学籍注册的学生数。

结业生数　指具有学籍的学生学习期满，有一门以上主要课程（包括毕业论文或毕业设计）不及格或其他方面不合格，未予毕业而发给结业证书的学生数。不包括短训班和单科结业学生。

教职工数　指各级各类学校（机构）根据岗位聘用的全职为学校工作的人员（含在编人员和签订一年以上聘用合同人员）。

专任教师　指具有《中华人民共和国教师法》《教师资格条例》规定的教师资格，学校根据相关岗位设置管理指导意见，聘用的专职从事教学工作的教师岗位人员。

特殊教育学校　指具备适应残疾儿童少年学习、康复、生活特点的场所和设施，招收盲聋哑、智力残疾及其他有特殊需要的儿童少年实施普通初等、普通中等或中等职业教育的独立设置学校。包括盲人学校、聋人学校、弱智学校、其他特殊教育学校。

学校占地面积　指学校校园内的土地面积，不包括校园外学校拥有的农场、林场及校办工厂等的土地面积。

校舍建筑面积　指学校用于办学并可长期（一年以上）占有使用或拥有产权校舍的建筑面积。

危房面积　指年久失修、结构构件受到严重损坏，有倒塌危险，经房管部门鉴定属于危房的面积。

Explanatory Notes on Main Statistical Indicators

Institutions Providing Postgraduate Programs refer to institutions of higher education and scientific research institutions recruiting and educating postgraduates of master's degree, doctor's degree and other degree upon approval by the State and under the State plan.

Regular Institutions of Higher Education refer to full-time universities, independent colleges and higher professional schools, short-term vocational colleges that are set up according to the State's establishment standards and examination and approval procedures, recruiting graduates from senior secondary schools as the main target through national unified entrance examination, and providing higher education.

Adult Institutions of Higher Education refer to educational establishments, set up in line with the State's establishment standards and examination and approval procedures, recruiting personnel with senior high school or equivalent educational diploma as the main target through national unified entrance examination for adult higher education, and providing higher education courses in many forms including correspondence, spare-time, or full-time teaching for adults. Adult institutions of higher education include schools of higher education for staff and workers, schools of higher education for farmers, colleges for management cadres, pedagogical colleges, independent correspondence colleges, Radio and TV universities and other educational establishments.

Higher Education Institutions refer to institutions offering higher education upon examination and approval by administrative departments in charge of education in provinces, autonomous regions and municipalities, with an education license, which are not eligible for conferring diploma.

Privately-funded Schools refer to schools and other educational institutions run by individuals, social groups and other social organizations upon approval by relevant competent authorities, by using educational funds not from state revenues.

Secondary Technical Education shall enable students to understand necessary basic theories and special knowledge on applied technologies of a specialty, have basic skills and technical application ability for practice of the specialty. Full-time secondary technical education offers a basic study term of 2-3 years.

Undergraduate Education shall enable students to understand necessary basic theories and knowledge of a subject or specialty, have necessary basic skills, methodology and relevant knowledge of the specialty, and have preliminary skills for practical work and research of the specialty. Full-time undergraduate education offers a basic study term of 4-5 years.

Master's-degree Postgraduate Education shall enable students to understand solid basic theories, systematic professional knowledge of a subject, have relevant skills, methodology and relevant knowledge of the specialty, and have the ability for practical work and research of the specialty. Master's-degree postgraduate education offers a basic study term of 2-3 years.

Doctor's-degree Postgraduate Education shall enable students to understand solid and extensive basic theories, systematic and in-depth professional knowledge, relevant skills and methodology of a subject, have the ability for independent creative scientific research and practical work of the specialty. Doctor's-degree postgraduate education offers a basic study term of 3-4 years.

Online Students refer to students for Internet-based higher education for diplomas for general undergraduate courses, undergraduate courses for adults, and secondary technical courses, recruited in online education colleges opened in schools as modern remote education pilots approved by the Ministry of Education.

International Students refers to foreign students without Chinese nationality who are educated in schools in accordance with the *Administrative Measures for Schools in Recruiting and Educating International Students*.

Number of Graduates means the number of enrolled students who have completed all courses stated in the teaching plan within the last academic year, passed all exams and obtained a diploma.

Number of New Enrollments refers to the number of new students who have actually been recruited and completed their student status registration.

Number of Enrolled Students means the number of enrolled students who registered their student status at the beginning of this academic year.

Number of Students Completing Courses means the number of enrolled students completing their schooling with one and more courses not passed (including the graduation paper or graduation design) or other aspects not passed, who are not granted for graduation and awarded a certificate of completion, excluding the number of students completing short-term training courses and single-subject programs.

Number of Teachers and Staff means the number of full-time staff (including the permanent staff and those who have signed the employment contract for one year or more) employed by schools (institutions) of all levels and all kinds according to the position.

Full-time Teachers refer to the staff in teacher position engaged in full-time teaching work who have the teaching qualification under the *Teachers Law of the People's Republic of China* and the *Regulations on the Qualification of Teachers* and have been employed by schools according to the guidance on the management of setting of relevant positions.

Schools for Special Education refer to the independently set up schools with places and facilities with such characteristics as being suitable for learning, rehabilitation and life of disabled children and adolescents that enroll the blind, deaf and mute children and adolescents as well as those with mentally disabilities or other special needs to offer general primary, general secondary or secondary vocational education. They include schools for the blind, schools for the deaf, schools for the mentally disabled and other special education schools.

Area of Land Occupied by School means the area of land within campus, excluding the area of land occupied by farms, forest farms and school-run factories that are owned by the school but are outside the schoolyard.

Floor Space of Schoolhouse refers to the floor space of schoolhouses that are used by the school for school running and can be occupied and used for a long time (more than one year) or in which the school has property right.

Area of Dilapidated Houses refers to the area of those houses that have not been repaired for many years, have seriously damaged components, are at the risk of collapse, and are identified by the house administration authority as dilapidated houses.

21

卫生及社会服务
HEALTH AND SOCIAL SERVICES

简要说明

主要内容

本章资料主要反映卫生、社会服务、残疾人事业的发展情况。

卫生部分统计资料主要包括卫生事业基本情况、卫生总费用、医疗卫生机构、卫生技术人员、床位数、医院工作情况、全市主要健康指标等情况。

社会服务部分统计资料主要包括基层社会工作、收养性单位、社会救助、婚姻登记情况。

残疾人统计资料主要包括残疾人康复、培训、就业、社会保障和维权援助情况。

Brief Introduction

Main Content

Statistics in this chapter mainly show the development of health, social services and undertakings for disabled persons.

Statistics for health mainly include basic statistics on health, the total health expenditures, the number of medical and health institutions, number of medical technical personnel, number of ward beds, works of hospitals, main health indicators of Beijing, and so on.

Statistics for social services mainly consist of grass-roots social work, adoption institutions, social relief, and marriage registration.

Statistics for disabled persons mainly include information on rehabilitation, training, employment, social security and aid for right protection of disabled persons.

21-1 卫生事业基本情况(1978—2023年)

年 份 Year	医疗卫生机构(个) Health Care Institutions (unit)	#医 院 Hospitals	#疾病预防控制中心 Centers for Disease Control	#妇幼保健机构 Maternity and Child Care Institutions	#社区卫生服务中心(站) Community Health Services Centers (Stations)
1978	3263	125	22	15	
1979	3614	124	22	17	
1980	3818	129	22	19	
1981	4135	139	22	19	
1982	4389	149	22	18	
1983	4312	149	22	19	
1984	4173	160	22	18	
1985	4248	188	22	18	
1986	4483	198	22	20	
1987	4744	222	22	19	
1988	4342	266	22	17	
1989	4398	284	22	17	
1990	4953	325	22	17	
1991	4970	337	22	17	
1992	4868	345	22	16	
1993	4962	364	32	16	
1994	4958	387	33	16	
1995	4955	387	33	15	
1996	6470	405	33	13	
1997	6577	435	33	13	
1998	5723	449	32	11	
1999	5990	460	32	8	
2000	6176	458	30	8	
2001	5969	458	30	9	
2002	4998	461	24	19	35
2003	5075	459	29	19	36
2004	7236	503	29	19	43
2005	7536	519	28	18	93
2006	7640	541	28	18	90
2007	9023	535	31	18	1126
2008	9647	537	31	19	1282
2009	9717	522	31	19	1395
2010	9511	550	31	19	1587
2011	9599	569	32	19	1744
2012	9974	608	32	19	1897
2013	10141	647	32	19	1926
2014	10265	672	32	19	1958
2015	10425	701	30	19	1979
2016	10637	713	29	20	1997
2017	10986	732	28	20	2066
2018	11100	736	29	21	2079
2019	11340	745	29	19	2075
2020	11211	733	29	19	2069
2021	11727	733	25	19	2111
2022	12211	741	27	18	2123
2023	12518	765	27	18	2143

注：1.2010年及以前，本表中所有数据都不包含村卫生室及驻京部队医院情况。自2011年起，包含村卫生室情况。自2012年起，除床位数外均包含驻京部队医院数据，下同。

2.自2010年起，原卫生院数据并入到社区卫生服务中心(站)等其他卫生机构。

资料来源：北京市卫生健康委员会。

BASIC STATISTICS ON PUBLIC HEALTH (1978-2023)

医疗卫生机构人员(人) Personnel in Health Care Institutions (person)	#卫生技术人员 Health Technical Personnel	#执业(助理)医师 Licensed Physicians & Physician Assistants	#注册护士 Registered Nurses
90174	65943	28435	16085
97942	72131	31842	17398
102601	74753	34365	17492
110774	81183	37886	20025
114420	83843	39385	20389
119222	86593	41216	21181
124664	89362	42112	22286
127771	90831	42216	23782
132865	94433	43403	25383
142556	101829	46007	27786
145362	105237	48216	30250
150062	108108	49361	32056
156304	111614	50934	34565
161103	114342	52309	35714
164213	115825	53254	36768
165170	116173	53906	36687
164867	116818	53865	36608
164436	115967	54114	36719
164981	116849	54091	37712
167090	119256	54909	38630
162609	115976	51902	38883
161823	116597	52646	39625
160258	115510	51570	39900
158185	115935	52100	40537
144021	109564	47236	38879
148406	112212	47887	39912
157157	116905	49283	41547
161432	120170	50913	42897
170586	127193	53084	45647
186290	139478	55156	50926
197765	150134	58904	55348
212086	160695	62578	61634
223694	171328	66165	67308
235708	181938	69749	72812
276654	219714	82192	95202
294012	229720	85819	100652
304990	242923	89590	106167
321151	256531	96445	114294
330777	264850	100878	117760
346255	276969	105732	123158
351765	281686	109376	123589
369139	297259	115771	131314
375673	303699	118541	134656
389779	317659	123503	141685
395381	322187	124916	142711
419029	342767	133685	152548

Note: a) In and before 2010, figures in this table did not cover village clinics and hospitals of troops stationed in Beijing. Since 2011, figures covered village clinics. Since 2012, figures in this table have included data on troops stationed in Beijing with the bed number excluded, the same below.

b) From 2010, data on health centers have been incorporated into other health care institutions such as community health service centers (stations).

Source: Beijing Municipal Health Commission.

21-1 续表 Continued

年 份 Year	医疗机构实有床位数(张) Beds in Health Care Institutions (bed)	#医 院 Hospitals	每千户籍人口执业(助理)医师数(人) Licensed Physicians & Physician Assistants per 1000 Registered Population (person)	每千户籍人口注册护士数(人) Registered Nurses per 1000 Registered Population (person)	每千户籍人口医院床位数(张) Hospital Beds per 1000 Registered Population (unit)	每千常住人口执业(助理)医师数(人) Licensed Physicians & Physician Assistants per 1000 Resident Population (person)	每千常住人口注册护士数(人) Registered Nurses per 1000 Resident Population (person)	每千常住人口医院床位数(张) Hospital Beds per 1000 Resident Population (unit)
1978	29767	23668	3.35	1.89	2.79			
1979	30231	24092	3.66	1.87	2.77			
1980	32453	25770	3.88	1.97	2.91			
1981	33666	26934	4.20	2.20	2.99			
1982	34574	28209	4.30	2.23	3.07			
1983	35987	29612	4.40	2.26	3.17			
1984	38580	31933	4.40	2.33	3.38			
1985	41603	35166	4.44	2.48	3.67			
1986	43956	38133	4.47	3.72	3.93			
1987	47538	41178	4.66	2.81	4.17			
1988	53078	45334	4.82	3.02	4.53			
1989	55623	48558	4.83	3.14	4.76			
1990	59036	51860	4.93	3.35	5.02			
1991	61744	54888	5.03	3.44	5.28			
1992	63230	55858	5.10	3.52	5.35			
1993	65621	58605	5.13	3.49	5.58			
1994	67112	60661	5.07	3.45	5.71			
1995	66925	60337	5.06	3.43	5.64			
1996	66760	60997	5.02	3.50	5.66			
1997	67946	61865	5.06	3.56	5.70			
1998	69095	63144	4.76	3.56	5.79			
1999	69465	63660	4.79	3.60	5.79			
2000	71245	65138	4.66	3.60	5.88			
2001	73053	66537	4.64	3.61	5.93			
2002	75188	67750	4.18	3.44	5.96			
2003	74298	66990	4.21	3.51	5.83			
2004	77359	69850	4.25	3.60	6.01	3.30	2.78	
2005	79067	72329	4.32	3.66	6.13	3.31	2.79	
2006	81440	74762	4.41	3.84	6.24	3.36	2.89	6.77
2007	83736	76915	4.53	4.19	6.34	3.38	3.12	4.71
2008	86196	79089	4.78	4.50	6.43	3.48	3.27	4.67
2009	90100	82471	5.00	4.94	6.62	3.57	3.51	4.70
2010	92871	85935	5.24	5.35	6.83	3.37	3.43	4.38
2011	94735	87596	5.46	5.70	6.85	3.46	3.61	4.34
2012	100167	92610	6.33	7.34	7.14	3.97	4.60	4.48
2013	104034	96558	6.52	7.65	7.34	4.06	4.76	4.57
2014	109789	102851	6.72	7.96	7.71	4.16	4.93	4.78
2015	111555	104644	7.17	8.50	7.78	4.44	5.27	4.82
2016	116963	110021	7.40	8.64	8.07	4.64	5.42	5.06
2017	120530	113576	7.78	9.06	8.36	4.87	5.67	5.23
2018	123508	116279	7.95	8.98	8.45	5.08	5.74	5.40
2019	127111	119574	8.28	9.40	8.56	5.38	6.10	5.55
2020	127143	119310	8.46	9.61	8.52	5.41	6.15	5.45
2021	130259	122287	8.74	10.02	8.65	5.64	6.47	5.59
2022	133932	126309	8.75	10.00	8.85	5.72	6.53	5.78
2023	138823	130831	9.34	10.66	9.14	6.12	6.98	5.99

21-2 卫生总费用(2000-2022年)
TOTAL HEALTH EXPENDITURE (2000-2022)

年 份 Year	卫 生 总费用 (亿元) Total Health Expenditure (100 million yuan)	政府卫生支出 Government Health Expenditure		社会卫生支出 Social Health Expenditure		个人现金卫生支出 Personal Health Expenditure in Cash	
		绝对数 (亿元) Value (100 million yuan)	占卫生总费用比重(%) As Percentage of Health Expenditure (%)	绝对数 (亿元) Value (100 million yuan)	占卫生总费用比重(%) As Percentage of Health Expenditure (%)	绝对数 (亿元) Value (100 million yuan)	占卫生总费用比重(%) As Percentage of Health Expenditure (%)
2000	166.7	34.7	20.8	61.8	37.1	70.3	42.1
2001	201.1	45.3	22.5	73.2	36.4	82.7	41.1
2002	262.4	48.5	18.5	99.6	38.0	114.2	43.5
2003	314.2	65.8	20.9	132.0	42.0	116.3	37.0
2004	357.2	69.4	19.4	150.7	42.2	137.1	38.4
2005	432.8	85.7	19.8	187.8	43.4	159.2	36.8
2006	497.4	115.9	23.3	208.0	41.8	173.5	34.9
2007	523.2	142.0	27.2	212.0	40.5	169.2	32.3
2008	668.5	180.0	26.9	271.3	40.6	217.3	32.5
2009	689.6	201.1	29.2	296.3	43.0	192.2	27.9
2010	814.7	226.8	27.8	385.1	47.3	202.8	24.9
2011	977.3	275.5	28.2	453.2	46.4	248.6	25.4
2012	1190.0	320.4	26.9	601.0	50.5	268.7	22.6
2013	1349.6	356.4	26.4	717.8	53.2	275.5	20.4
2014	1594.6	394.4	24.7	890.6	55.9	309.7	19.4
2015	1834.8	445.8	24.3	1069.9	58.3	319.1	17.4
2016	2049.0	468.0	22.8	1247.2	60.9	333.8	16.3
2017	2193.8	507.4	23.1	1327.4	60.5	359.0	16.4
2018	2500.8	580.0	23.2	1530.0	61.2	390.9	15.6
2019	2964.8	703.2	23.7	1850.5	62.4	411.1	13.9
2020	3028.3	809.8	26.7	1812.8	59.9	405.6	13.4
2021	3351.9	784.0	23.4	2127.2	63.5	440.7	13.2
2022	3649.4	940.0	25.8	2214.6	60.7	494.8	13.6

资料来源：北京市卫生健康委员会。
Source: Beijing Municipal Health Commission.

21-3 医疗卫生机构基本情况
BASIC STATISTICS ON HEALTH CARE INSTITUTIONS

项 目	Item	2023	2022	构 成 (%) Composition (%)	
				2023	2022
机构数 （个）	**Number of Institutions (unit)**	**12518**	**12211**	**100.0**	**100.0**
#医 院	Hospitals	765	741	6.1	6.1
社区卫生服务中心(站)	Community Health Service Centers (Stations)	2143	2123	17.1	17.4
门诊部	Outpatient Departments	1632	1568	13.0	12.8
妇幼保健机构	Maternity and Child Care Institutions	18	18	0.1	0.1
疾病预防控制中心	Disease Prevention and Control Centers	27	27	0.2	0.2
专科疾病防治机构	Specific Disease Prevention and Cure Institutions	20	21	0.2	0.2
诊所、卫生所、医务室、护理站	Clinics, Health Centers, Infirmaries, Nursing Stations	4742	4565	37.9	37.4
床位数 （张）	**Number of Beds (bed)**	**138823**	**133932**	**100.0**	**100.0**
#医 院	Hospitals	130831	126309	94.2	94.3
社区卫生服务中心(站)	Community Health Service Centers (Stations)	5487	5229	4.0	3.9
妇幼保健机构	Maternity and Child Care Institutions	1921	1830	1.4	1.4
专科疾病防治机构	Disease Prevention and Control Centers	584	564	0.4	0.4
卫生技术人员数 （人）	**Number of Health Technical Personnel (person)**	**342767**	**322187**	**100.0**	**100.0**
#医 院	Hospitals	242677	230090	70.8	71.4
社区卫生服务中心(站)	Community Health Service Centers (Stations)	38265	35885	11.2	11.1
妇幼保健机构	Maternity and Child Care Institutions	6187	5991	1.8	1.9
专科疾病防治机构	Disease Prevention and Control Centers	723	641	0.2	0.2
#执业(助理)医师	Licensed Physicians & Physician Assistants	133685	124916	39.0	38.8
注册护士	Registered Nurses	152548	142711	44.5	44.3

注：本表数据除床位数外均包含驻京部队医院数据。
资料来源：北京市卫生健康委员会。
Note: Figures in this table include that of troops stationed in Beijing with the bed number excluded.
Source: Beijing Municipal Health Commission.

21－4 医院基本情况(2023年)
BASIC STATISTICS ON HOSPITALS (2023)

项目	Item	医院数 (个) Hospitals (unit)	床位数 (张) Beds (bed)	职工人数 (人) Employed Persons (person)	#卫生技术人员 Health Technical Personnel	#执业医师 Licensed Physicians	#中医 Doctors of Traditional Chinese Medicine
合计	Total	765	130831	291166	242677	87130	14954
按隶属关系分	By Affiliation						
#市属	Municipal	29	26065	58911	49684	16808	968
区属	Districts	92	34291	59505	50010	18344	4588
按专业分	By Specialty						
#综合医院	General Hospitals	242	68760	172765	148165	53164	2390
中医医院	Hospitals Specialized in Traditional Chinese Medicine	210	17414	36025	29611	12322	8709
中西医结合医院	Hospitals Combining Western Medicine with Traditional Chinese Medicine	61	12900	20801	17073	6438	2895
民族医医院	Nationality Hospitals	5	258	394	283	126	95
口腔医院	Stomatology Hospitals	49	930	6657	5183	2058	19
眼科医院	Ophthalmology Hospitals	18	667	1446	933	290	20
肿瘤医院	Tumor Hospitals	12	4494	7879	6342	1859	43
心血管病医院	Hospitals for Cardiovascular Diseases	2	1411	3998	3485	916	16
胸科医院	Thorax Hospitals	1	625	971	798	235	6
妇(产)科医院	Hospitals for Gynecology and Obstetrics	18	1502	4779	3381	1135	45
儿童医院	Children's Hospitals	11	2498	6925	5739	1909	92
精神病医院	Psychiatric Hospital	25	8379	6499	4943	1229	75
传染病医院	Infectious Disease Hospitals	3	1634	3389	2841	942	54
骨科医院	Hospitals of Orthopedics	7	779	1220	952	343	81
整形外科医院	Orthopaedics Hospitals	1	474	1145	791	353	1
其他类型专科医院	Other Specialized Hospitals	91	7358	15508	11715	3690	389
护理院	Nursing Hospitals	9	748	765	442	121	24

注：本表数据除床位数外均包括驻京部队数据。
资料来源：北京市卫生健康委员会。
Note: Figures in this table include that of troops stationed in Beijing with the bed number excluded.
Source: Beijing Municipal Health Commission.

21-4 续表 Continued

单位：人 (person)

项　目	Item	#执业助理医师 Licensed Physician Assistants	#中医 Doctors of Traditional Chinese Medicine	#注册护士 Registered Nurses	#药师(士) Pharmacists	#影像技师(士) Image Technicians (Assistant Technicians)	#检验师(士) Laboratorians (Assistant Laboratorians)
合　计	**Total**	**1757**	**623**	**118198**	**10381**	**4191**	**6859**
按隶属关系分	**By Affiliation**						
#市　级	Municipal	111	2	24420	2086	987	1509
区　级	Districts	244	34	23536	2717	949	1841
按专业分	**By Specialty**						
#综合医院	General Hospitals	478	104	75637	4944	2483	3724
中医医院	Hospitals Specialized in Traditional Chinese Medicine	482	347	11121	2650	549	1011
中西医结合医院	Hospitals Combining Western Medicine with Traditional Chinese Medicine	215	110	7725	1009	262	571
民族医医院	Nationality Hospitals	16	14	95	19	9	9
口腔医院	Stomatology Hospitals	147	1	2302	73	88	53
眼科医院	Ophthalmology Hospitals	18	2	460	43	26	27
肿瘤医院	Tumor Hospitals	19	2	3082	257	281	174
心血管病医院	Hospitals for Cardiovascular Diseases			1947	64	56	58
胸科医院	Thorax Hospitals			443	32	28	26
妇(产)科医院	Hospitals for Gynecology and Obstetrics	26		1712	127	29	205
儿童医院	Children's Hospitals	19	3	2668	275	97	292
精神病医院	Psychiatric Hospitals	48	4	2819	246	39	145
传染病医院	Infectious Disease Hospitals	1		1385	151	51	135
骨科医院	Hospitals of Orthopedics	23	9	427	43	25	35
整形外科医院	Orthopaedics Hospitals			328	17	6	15
其他类型专科医院	Other Specialized Hospitals	255	26	5791	418	158	368
护理院	Nursing Hospitals	10	1	256	13	4	11

21-5 医院工作情况(2023年)
STATISTICS ON WORKS OF HOSPITALS (2023)

项 目	Item	诊疗人次数(千人次) Visits (1000 person-times)	#门诊 Out-patients	健康检查人数(千人次) Health Examinations (1000 person-times)	平均开放病床数(张) Average Beds Opened (bed)	入院人数(千人次) Inpatients (1000 person-times)	出院人数(千人次) Discharged Patients (1000 person-times)
合 计	**Total**	**179710.2**	**164902.4**	**4595.3**	**124732**	**4342.4**	**4927.4**
#综合医院	General Hospitals	109599.6	98277.3	3327.7	66735	2852.2	3439.8
中医医院	Hospitals Specialized in Traditional Chinese Medicine	32716.8	31516.2	518.1	15875	366.7	355.3
中西医结合医院	Hospitals Combining Western Medicine with Traditional Chinese Medicine	12097.1	11250.4	365.7	12644	255.8	256.4
民族医医院	Nationality Hospitals	94.7	94.7		186	1.7	1.8
口腔医院	Stomatology Hospitals	4161.2	4026.5	8.3	573	12.1	12.1
眼科医院	Ophthalmology Hospitals	518.3	517.1		510	14.2	14.2
肿瘤医院	Tumor Hospitals	2155.4	2112.9	108.6	4069	288.6	287.5
心血管病医院	Hospitals for Cardiovascular Diseases	1004.0	957.5	4.6	1411	88.3	87.9
胸科医院	Thorax Hospitals	270.8	262.1		622	27.2	27.2
妇(产)科医院	Hospitals for Gynecology and Obstetrics	2210.3	2152.2	5.7	1249	63.3	63.1
儿童医院	Children's Hospitals	6847.9	6054.3	6.1	2277	135.4	132.8
精神病医院	Psychiatric Hospitals	2001.5	1966.3	8.3	8415	37.0	36.2
传染病医院	Infectious Disease Hospitals	1358.3	1248.7	1.9	1664	53.4	52.9
骨科医院	Hospitals of Orthopedics	597.9	564.7	17.4	779	15.9	16.1
整形外科医院	Orthopaedics Hospitals	334.3	318.1		464	14.2	14.2
其他类型专科医院	Other Specialized Hospitals	3720.2	3561.9	223.0	6608	113.1	126.8
护理院	Nursing Hospitals	21.9	21.6		652	3.2	3.2

资料来源：北京市卫生健康委员会。
Source: Beijing Municipal Health Commission.

21-5 续表 Continued

项 目	Item	病死率 (%) Fatality Rate (%)	病床周转次数 (次) Turnover of Hospital Beds (time)	病床使用率 (%) Occupancy Rate of Hospital Beds (%)	出院者平均住院日 (日) Average Length of Stay in Hospital (day)
合 计	**Total**	**1.2**	**34.8**	**80.3**	**7.8**
#综合医院	General Hospitals	1.1	42.9	83.9	7.1
中医医院	Hospitals Specialized in Traditional Chinese Medicine	1.5	22.4	66.3	10.6
中西医结合医院	Hospitals Combining Western Medicine with Traditional Chinese Medicine	3.1	20.3	76.9	14.1
民族医医院	Nationality Hospitals	0.3	9.4	40.2	14.6
口腔医院	Stomatology Hospitals	0.0	21.1	34.3	5.9
眼科医院	Ophthalmology Hospitals		27.9	28.2	3.7
肿瘤医院	Tumor Hospitals	0.2	70.6	83.9	4.3
心血管病医院	Hospitals for Cardiovascular Diseases	0.2	62.3	92.6	5.4
胸科医院	Thorax Hospitals	0.5	43.8	90.4	7.6
妇(产)科医院	Hospitals for Gynecology and Obstetrics	0.0	50.5	57.6	4.1
儿童医院	Children's Hospitals	0.1	58.3	93.0	5.7
精神病医院	Psychiatric Hospitals	0.5	4.3	94.9	106.2
传染病医院	Infectious Disease Hospitals	1.6	31.8	75.9	8.7
骨科医院	Hospitals of Orthopedics	2.8	20.7	70.6	11.9
整形外科医院	Orthopaedics Hospitals		30.6	55.8	6.5
其他类型专科医院	Other Specialized Hospitals	2.3	17.1	73.8	14.9
护理院	Nursing Hospitals	3.4	4.9	76.1	51.9

21-6 主要健康指标情况(1978-2023年)
STATISTICS ON MAJOR HEALTH INDICATORS (1978-2023)

年 份 Year	婴 儿 死亡率 (‰) Infant Mortality (‰)	新生儿 死亡率 (‰) Newborn Baby Mortality (‰)	孕产妇 死亡率 (1/10万) Pregnant & Lying-in Women Mortality (1/100 thousand)	甲乙类传染 病发病率 (1/10万) Morbidity Rate of Class A and B Infectious Diseases (1/100000)
1978	17.11	12.21	31.00	
1979	16.97	10.08	34.70	1584.25
1980	14.79	10.24	26.30	2165.23
1981	13.84	9.22	48.50	2225.71
1982	12.97	8.02	24.50	2193.16
1983	13.79	8.78	28.10	1904.55
1984	10.98	7.78	16.80	1666.68
1985	13.94	10.41	22.90	1335.23
1986	16.05	12.13	30.50	1120.19
1987	15.56	11.08	26.60	826.51
1988	14.98	10.48	24.80	640.98
1989	14.96	10.53	34.50	547.61
1990	11.66	8.49	25.00	509.55
1991	12.46	8.56	24.00	448.23
1992	12.12	8.93	30.10	385.98
1993	10.38	7.21	16.50	356.66
1994	10.93	7.29	18.94	374.31
1995	11.45	7.52	22.27	309.99
1996	10.05	6.97	15.32	340.24
1997	9.45	6.36	23.69	294.41
1998	7.58	5.53	10.46	306.37
1999	7.95	5.94	17.53	308.10
2000	5.36	3.70	9.70	301.19
2001	6.01	4.05	11.71	276.85
2002	5.56	3.70	15.12	282.95
2003	5.89	3.83	15.60	228.00
2004	4.61	3.49	15.19	408.03
2005	4.35	3.29	15.91	445.91
2006	4.66	3.42	7.87	448.70
2007	3.89	2.65	16.74	421.02
2008	3.70	2.45	18.52	312.99
2009	3.49	2.47	14.55	339.89
2010	3.29	2.06	12.14	268.99
2011	2.84	1.88	9.09	226.76
2012	2.87	1.91	6.05	174.45
2013	2.33	1.52	9.45	155.87
2014	2.33	1.46	7.19	165.49
2015	2.42	1.52	8.69	150.86
2016	2.21	1.48	10.83	138.00
2017	2.29	1.45	8.17	139.60
2018	2.15	1.26	10.64	131.50
2019	1.99	1.21	2.96	139.80
2020	1.98	1.06	4.98	80.80
2021	1.44	0.90	2.22	94.57
2022	1.26	0.67	3.73	265.40
2023	1.50	0.91	1.56	1191.76

注：自2023年起，孕产妇死亡率由户籍人口口径调整为常住人口口径。
资料来源：北京市卫生健康委员会。
Note: Since 2023, data on the pregnant & lying-in women mortality was adjusted from the statistical caliber of registered population into the statistical caliber of resident population.
Source: Beijing Municipal Health Commission.

21-7 基层社会工作情况
STATISTICS ON GRASSROOT SOCIAL WORK

单位：个 (unit)

项　目	Item	2023	2022	2023年为2022年% 2023 as % of 2022
社区服务机构数	Number of Service Facilities in Urban Communities	9243	10062	91.9
#社区服务中心	Community Service Centers	204	131	155.7

21-8 提供住宿机构情况(2023年)
STATISTICS ON INSTITUTIONS WITH ACCOMMODATIONS (2023)

项　目	Item	合　计 Total	社　会福利院 Social Welfare Institutions	儿　童福利院 Child Welfare Institutions	福利类精神病院和医院 Welfare Mental Illness Service Institutions and Hospitals	其他各类养老机构 Other Elderly Care Agencies	其他收养服务机构 Other Adopting Service Institutions
单位数 (个)	Institutions (unit)	628	9	12	1	581	25
职工人数 (人)	Employed Persons (person)	21696	863	506	96	19598	633
床位数 (张)	Beds (bed)	118537	3644	2518	52	110034	2289
年末在院人数 (人)	Persons Received (person)	48679	1675	1090	10	45570	334
#自　费	Self-supported	41286	867		10	40409	

资料来源：北京市民政局。
Source: Beijing Municipal Civil Affairs Bureau.

21-9 婚姻登记(1981-2023年) MARRIAGE REGISTRATION (1981-2023)

年份 Year	结婚对数(对) Total Number of Marriage Registration (couple)	#涉外及华侨、港澳台居民登记结婚对数 Total Number of Marriage Registration Involving Foreigners, Overseas Chinese or Residents of Hong Kong, Macao, Taiwan	初婚人数(人) Number of First Marriages (person)	离婚对数(对) Total Number of Divorces (couple)	#民政部门登记离婚对数 Total Number of Divorces Registered in Civil Affairs Department
1981	200352		389936	5170	1780
1982	141253		261851	5359	1581
1983	117976		227676	5322	1465
1984	113362		217649	5654	1387
1985	134462		258255	5874	1746
1986	143105		274634	7541	2474
1987	149952		267424	8916	3218
1988	113333		212544	10664	4198
1989	103829		188287	12515	5174
1990	92988		169510	14748	5791
1991	91979		165752	15287	6483
1992	89095		158241	15567	6477
1993	89938		160127	17829	7589
1994	90379		160793	19928	8327
1995	85511		148722	20160	8096
1996	86803		146666	20716	8225
1997	84208		144040	22257	8628
1998	85534		146750	23708	9381
1999	83312		141740	23922	8502
2000	80212		136500	26616	6384
2001	79385	873	133259	27683	5425
2002	76136	606	126371	27691	5810
2003	93526	761	158729	30637	10142
2004	126436	974	214443	32657	21013
2005	96956	937	158736	34244	23991
2006	171286	1172	294223	35505	24954
2007	117926	991	193387	36622	26432
2008	147516	1165	246309	37619	27277
2009	181771	1176	305803	41299	29998
2010	138104	1085	222269	43970	32595
2011	173238	1260	288406	43521	32999
2012	174114	1242	287436	48575	38243
2013	163676	1070	251636	65018	54536
2014	170027	1149	253774	65627	56192
2015	166018	1018	229546	82195	73000
2016	166207	1012	200750	105806	97583
2017	151454	916	179316	80697	72964
2018	137818	847	169157	74349	66616
2019	128959	754	141528	83792	76358
2020	113790	376	124281	81949	76134
2021	103360	430	136303	52664	44582
2022	91300	435	118125	44320	36858
2023	137335	685	195159	55058	45933

注：离婚对数包括在民政部门登记的对数以及经法院调离和判离的对数。
资料来源：北京市民政局、北京市高级人民法院。
Note: Total number of divorces includes those registered in civil affairs department and those mediated and judged by courts.
Source: Social Work Commission of Beijing Municipal Committee of the Communist Party of China Beijing Municipal Civil Affairs Bureau, and The High People's Court of Beijing Municipality.

21－10 婚姻登记情况
STATISTICS ON MARRIAGE REGISTRATION

项目	Item	2023	2022	2023年为2022年% 2023 as % of 2022
登记结婚对数（对）	**Total Number of Marriage Registration (couple)**	**137335**	**91300**	**150.4**
按婚前状况分	**By Pre-marriage Status**			
初婚人数（人）	First Marriages (person)	195159	118125	165.2
再婚人数（人）	Remarriages (person)	79511	64475	123.3
#女　性	Females	38538	31161	123.7
按居住地分	**By Place of Residence**			
内地居民登记结婚对数（对）	Total Number of Marriage Registration of Mainland Residents (couple)	136650	90865	150.4
涉外及华侨、港澳台居民登记结婚对数（对）	Total Number of Marriage Registration Involving Foreigners, Overseas Chinese or Residents of Hong Kong, Macao, Taiwan (couple)	685	435	157.5
内地居民（人）	Mainland Residents (person)	685	435	157.5
#女　性	Females	418	281	148.8
香港居民（人）	Hong Kong Residents (person)	114	48	237.5
澳门居民（人）	Macao Residents (person)	7	9	77.8
台湾居民（人）	Taiwan Residents (person)	115	70	164.3
华　侨（人）	Overseas Chinese (person)		1	
外国人（人）	Foreigners (person)	449	307	146.3
离婚登记对数（对）	**Total Number of Divorces Registered (couple)**	**45933**	**36858**	**124.6**
内地居民登记离婚对数（对）	Total Number of Divorces Registered of Mainland Residents (couple)	45764	36758	124.5
涉外及华侨、港澳台居民登记离婚对数（对）	Total Number of Divorces Registered Involving Foreigners, Overseas Chinese or Residents of Hong Kong, Macao, Taiwan (couple)	169	100	169.0

注：离婚登记对数不含法院调离和判离数。
资料来源：北京市民政局。
Note: Total number of divorces registered excludes the number of divorces mediated and ruled by courts.
Source: Beijing Municipal Civil Affairs Bureau.

21-11 残疾人事业基本情况
BASIC STATISTICS ON THE WORK FOR PERSONS WITH DISABILITY

项　　目		Item		2023	2022
康　复		**Rehabilitation**			
0-6岁残疾儿童享受康复		Number of Disabled Children of 0 to 6 Years Old Enjoying		2931	3077
政策人数	(人)	Rehabilitation Policies	(person)		
7-15岁残疾儿童少年享受康复		Number of Disabled Children and Teenagers of 7 to15		2148	1646
政策人数	(人)	Years Old Enjoying Rehabilitation Policies	(person)		
残疾人接受辅助器具服务人数	(人)	Number of Disabled Persons With Assistive Devices	(person)	95052	82568
精神残疾人接受免费服药人数	(人)	Number of Mentally Disabled Persons Receiving Free	(person)	41404	34352
培　训		**Training**			
职业教育与培训机构数(残联认定)	(个)	Number of Vocational Education and Training Institutions		94	93
		(recognized by China Disabled Persons' Federation)	(unit)		
职业技能培训人数	(人次)	Number of Persons Receiving Vocational Skill Training	(person-time)	6362	4123
就　业		**Employment**			
盲人按摩		Massage by Persons with Visual Disability			
医疗按摩机构	(家)	Medical Massage Institutions	(unit)	3	3
医疗按摩员培训人次	(人次)	Medical Massager Training	(person-time)	62	200
社会保障		**Social Security**			
已纳入最低生活保障范围人数	(人)	Covered by the Minimum Living Allowance	(person)	32412	33322
参加城乡居民养老保险残疾人数	(人)	Number of Disabled Persons Covered by Endowment		42383	45455
		Insurance for Urban and Rural Residents	(person)		
参加城乡居民医疗保险残疾人数	(人)	Number of Disabled Persons Covered by Medical Insurance for		218626	216000
		Urban and Rural Residents	(person)		
残联组织建设		**Organization Building of Disabled Persons' Federation**			
残疾人工作者数	(人)	Workers for Disabled Persons	(person)	1204	1229
维权援助		**Aid for Rights Protection**			
维权信访咨询件数	(件)	Rights Protection Letters, Visits and Consulting	(case)	9765	8086
维权法律服务件数	(件)	Rights Protection Legal Aid	(case)	1048	2024

资料来源：北京市残疾人联合会。
Source: Beijing Disabled Persons' Federation.

21-12 救助情况
STATISTICS ON ASSISTANCE

单位：人 (person)

项目	Item	人数 Number of Persons		2023年为2022年% 2023 as % of 2022
		2023	2022	
社会救助对象总人数	**Total Number of Persons Receiving Social Assistance**	**111027**	**113169**	**98.1**
城市居民最低生活保障人数	Number of Urban Residents Entitled to Minimum Living Allowance	69136	69899	98.9
农村居民最低生活保障人数	Number of Rural Residents Entitled to Minimum Living Allowance	35347	36696	96.3
农村特困供养人数	Rural Households in Extreme Difficulty with Living Arrangement	5012	5140	97.5
#农村特困集中供养人数	Rural Households in Extreme Difficulty with Centralized Living Arrangement	1538	1611	95.5
城市特困供养人数	Urban Households in Extreme Difficulty with Living Arrangement	1532	1434	106.8
#城市特困集中供养人数	Urban Households in Extreme Difficulty with Centralized Living Arrangement	719	759	94.7

资料来源：北京市民政局。
Source:Beijing Municipal Civil Affairs Bureau.

主要统计指标解释

卫 生

医疗卫生机构 指从卫生（卫生健康）行政部门取得《医疗机构执业许可证》《中医诊所备案证》《计划生育技术服务许可证》或从民政、工商行政、机构编制管理部门取得法人单位登记证书，为社会提供医疗服务、公共卫生服务或从事医学科研和在职培训等工作的单位。

卫生技术人员 包括执业医师、执业助理医师、注册护士、药师（士）、检验及影像技师（士）、卫生监督员和见习医（药、护、技）师（士）等卫生专业人员，包括从事临床或监督工作并同时从事管理工作的人员（如院长、书记等）。

执业（助理）医师和注册护士 指取得医师、护士执业证书且实际从事临床工作的人员，包括从事临床工作并同时从事管理工作的人员（如院长、书记等）。

死亡率 是指在一定时期内，在一定人群中，死于某病（或死于所有原因）的频率。是表示人群死亡危险最常用的指标。其分子为死亡人数，分母通常为年中人口数或平均人口数，单位常以 1/10 万或千分率表示。

婴儿死亡率 指某地区一年内每 1000 名活产婴儿与未满 1 岁的婴儿死亡人数之比。婴儿死亡率可以衡量一个国家或地区经济文化、居民健康状况和卫生保健事业发展情况，同时也是人口平均期望寿命研究的重要内容。

新生儿死亡率 指年内新生儿死亡数与活产数之比，一般以千分率表示。新生儿死亡指出生至 28 天以内（即 0-27 天）死亡人数。

孕产妇死亡率 指某年某地每十万活产中的孕产妇死亡比例。孕产妇死亡率是评价某一地区社会发展状况的重要指标，它的高低与社会经济状况、孕产妇社会环境及卫生保健服务有直接的联系。

社会服务

社会救助对象总人数 指在报告期末生活在当地规定的最低生活保障线以下的家庭人员及国家规定由民政部门救济的特殊人员和 60 年代精简退职老职工救济人员等。

社区服务机构数 指报告期末社区服务站、社区服务中心、其它社区服务设施的总和。

Explanatory Notes on Main Statistical Indicators

Health

Medical and Health Institutions refer to units which have been granted with the *Practice License of Medical Institution*, the *TCM Clinic Registration Certificate* or the *License for Family Planning Technology Services* by the health administration authority, or granted with certificate of corporate unit by the civil affair, administration for industry and commerce, management authority of institutional organization, providing medical service and public health service for the society or engaging in medical research and on-job training, and so on.

Medical Technical Personnel include certified doctors, certified assistant doctors, registered nurses, pharmacists, laboratory and imaging technicians, health care supervisors and intern doctors (pharmacists, nurses, and technical personnel) as well as other professional staff engaged in health care, including personnel engaged in clinical or supervisory work and simultaneously engaged in management (e.g. president and secretary of the party committee, etc).

Certified（Assistant） Doctors and Registered Nurses refer to personnel who have received a physician practicing certificate or certified nurse certificate and actually engaged in clinical work, including personnel engaged in clinical work and simultaneously engaged in management (e.g. president and secretary of the party committee, etc).

Mortality means the frequency of death from certain disease (or death from all causes) in a given population during a given period of time. It is the most commonly used indicator of the risk of death of the population. The numerator is the number of deaths and the denominator is usually the mid-year population or the average population, and its unit is often expressed in 1/100,000 or in permillage.

Infant Mortality means the rate of dead infants under 1 year old to 1,000 live infants in an area in a year. Infant mortality can measure the development of economy, culture, citizen health and health care in a country or region. It is also an important component of study on average life expectancy of population.

Neonatal Mortality Rate refers to the rate of dead newborn babies to live births in a year, generally expressed in permillage. Death of newborns refers to the number of newborns that died within 28 days after birth (i.e. 0-27 days).

Pregnant and Lying-in Women Mortality refers to the rate of dead pregnant and lying-in women to 100,000 live births in an area in a year. This is an important indicator to evaluate the social development status in an area. The figure of this indicator is directly related to the social and economic status, social environment and health care service for pregnant and lying-in women.

Social Services

Total Number of Persons Receiving Social Relief refers to the number of family members living under the minimum living standard provided by local governments, special persons receiving relief by civil affair authorities in line with national regulations, as well as employed persons retired because of streamlining in the 1960s, at the end of the reporting period.

Number of Service Facilities in Urban Communities refers to the total number of community service stations, service centers, and other service facilities, by the end of reporting period.

22

北京统计年鉴2024　　BEIJING STATISTICAL YEARBOOK 2024

文化和体育
CULTURE AND SPORTS

简要说明

一、主要内容

本章资料主要反映文化、体育发展情况。

文化部分主要包括公共图书馆、文化馆、档案馆、博物馆、广播、电影、电视、新闻出版以及文化产业发展等情况。

体育部分主要包括体育场地情况、运动员和裁判员情况、运动员获奖情况以及体育彩票等。

二、有关统计标准的变化说明

关于文化产业。执行国家统计局印发的《文化及相关产业分类（2018)》。

关于体育产业。执行国家统计局印发的《体育产业统计分类（2019)》。

Brief Introduction

I. Main Content

Statistics in this chapter mainly show the development of culture and sports.

Cultural statistics mainly include the situation of public libraries, cultural centers, archives, museums, broadcast, films, television and press, and the development of cultural industry, etc.

Sports statistics mainly include sports venues, athletes and referees, awards received by athletes and sports lottery tickets, etc.

II. Changes in Relevant Statistical Standards

Cultural Industry. The *Classification of Cultural and Related Industries (2018)* issued by the National Bureau of Statistics is implemented.

Sports Industry. The *Classification of Sports Industry (2019)* issued by the National Bureau of Statistics is implemented.

22-1 图书馆、文化馆、档案馆情况(1978-2023年) STATISTICS ON LIBRARIES, CULTURAL CENTERS AND ARCHIVES (1978-2023)

Year	公共图书馆 Public Libraries				文化馆 Cultural Centers		档案馆 Archiving Institutions			
	个数 (个) Number (unit)	总藏数 (万册、万件) Total Collections (10000 copies)	建筑面积 (万平方米) Floor Space (10000 sq.m)	书刊文献外借人次 (万人次) Borrowing from Libraries of Books and Periodicals Lent (10000 person-times)	个数 (个) Number (unit)	组织文艺活动 (次) Art Performances and Story-telling Sessions (time)	个数 (个) Number (unit)	建筑面积 (平方米) Floor Space (sq.m)	馆藏纸质档案 (万卷件) Number of Paper Archives (10000 volumes, 10000 pieces)	利用档案资料人次 (万人次) Person-times of Utilized Archives (10000 piece-times)
1978	18	1423		169	19	516				
1979	21	1502		174	19	1033				
1980	20	1606	1.8	210	19	778				
1981	21	1614	1.9	211	19	1131				
1982	21	1676	2.0	228	20	1334				
1983	21	1733	1.9	243	20	1015				
1984	22	1824	2.3	224	22	489				
1985	22	1860	3.0	220	23	469				
1986	23	1874	6.0	220	23	883				
1987	23	1959	20.6	170	23	1067	20	10695	86.1	1.30
1988	23	2050	23.4	300	23	647	20	21472	116.0	1.46
1989	23	2128	24.5		23	1411	20	31280	156.3	1.48
1990	23	2205	25.0		23	1429	20	23618	167.4	2.51
1991	23	2281	25.3		23	1128	20	33491	177.5	3.24
1992	23	2397	25.4	147	23	978	20	35950	181.3	2.64
1993	23	2461	25.5	212	23	764	20	37650	192.4	1.73
1994	23	2548	23.8	384	23	1034	20	42641	192.4	1.50
1995	23	2629	24.1	139	23	1127	20	65489	204.1	1.42
1996	22	2652	25.3	146	23	2277	20	62994	223.7	3.03
1997	23	2789	25.7	188	23	1875	20	64147	227.4	2.69
1998	24	2848	25.6	189	23	2554	20	67759	240.8	2.71
1999	24	2934	26.4	607	23	1490	20	72597	259.5	2.52
2000	26	3020	27.0	283	23	1809	20	72596	278.3	3.01
2001	26	3133	31.4	288	23	1822	20	72730	297.0	4.17
2002	26	3248	30.7	338	20	1817	20	72946	328.4	4.53
2003	26	3355	30.9	335	20	2023	20	81519	359.0	6.27
2004	26	3451	30.9	405	22	1826	20	83162	379.1	7.03
2005	26	3626	31.7	480	22	3697	20	84656	404.7	6.97
2006	25	3776	31.0	515	21	2200	20	93773	436.7	10.59
2007	25	3940	31.5	479	21	4752	20	93463	461.7	9.51
2008	25	4100	33.4	450	20	3007	20	97605	495.7	9.00
2009	25	4368	41.9	471	20	3470	20	97605	523.8	9.88
2010	25	4613	42.4	441	20	3564	18	97611	558.0	13.45
2011	25	5049	42.1	333	20	3401	18	97976	582.9	12.30
2012	25	5556	47.6	317	20	3848	18	98879	602.5	12.37
2013	25	5316	48.4	325	20	4769	18	101896	636.1	23.85
2014	25	5601	52.7	407	20	2158	18	98220	697.9	22.18
2015	25	5943	52.4	438	20	2587	18	96256	733.2	14.90
2016	25	6229	55.3	549	21	3417	18	119930	764.7	21.95
2017	24	6528	57.8	431	20	3431	18	123401	827.7	19.99
2018	24	6777	57.6	503	20	3278	18	122722	867.5	15.04
2019	24	7048	57.6	480	20	3182	18	212864	910.0	14.83
2020	24	7241	57.7	88	20	1210	18	212864	980.3	11.53
2021	21	7548	62.1	171	19	2942	18	210076	1049.5	13.83
2022	21	7819	62.2	143	18	1774	18	227658	1093.8	10.13
2023	20	8099	70.0	237	18	3003	18	286698	1162.4	11.66

注：1978—1981年，文化馆数据不包括群众艺术馆。

资料来源：北京市文化和旅游局、国家图书馆、中共北京市委办公厅(北京市档案局)。

Note: In 1978-1981, the data on cultural centers didn't include those of mass art centers.

Source: Beijing Municipal Bureau of Culture and Tourism, National Library of China, General Office of Beijing Municipal Committee of the Communist Party of China (Beijing Municipal Archives Bureau).

22-2 博物馆情况(1982-2023年)
STATISTICS ON MUSEUMS (1982-2023)

年 份 Year	全市按行业管理登记的博物馆 Museums Registered by Industry Administration		文物局系统内博物馆及文物保护机构 Museums and Other Cultural Relics Preservation Agencies under the Municipal Cultural Heritage Bureau				
	个 数 (个) Number (unit)	文 物 藏品数 (万件) Cultural Relic Collections (10000 pieces)	个 数 (个) Number (unit)	#博物馆 Museums	文物藏品数 (万件) Cultural Relic Collections (10000 pieces)	#一级品 (件) Grade I Collection (piece)	参观人次 (万人次) Visitors (10000 person-times)
1982			28		8.4	294	9.7
1983			29		4.0		58.0
1984							
1985			32		9.0		20.0
1986			39	7	21.0		905.0
1987							
1988			42	11	21.0		1098.0
1989			46	12	14.0		992.0
1990							
1991			46	12	11.7	2901	6629.1
1992							
1993			50	16	17.4	479	2423.4
1994			51	17	16.7	447	955.0
1995			51	17	16.7	447	2100.3
1996			51	17	18.0	443	2009.3
1997			54	24	18.2	443	935.8
1998			56	26	18.3	387	697.8
1999			54	26	18.5	374	5641.8
2000			53	25	18.2	367	702.7
2001			58	26	17.3	366	99.1
2002			48	27	20.1	716	170.8
2003			55	27	112.4	716	119.2
2004			66	31	370.4	656	599.9
2005			73	34	115.1	620	1370.9
2006			70	33	115.5	643	1416.7
2007			69	34	113.5	439	1493.0
2008	148	331	71	37	116.0	678	1368.4
2009	151	331	76	40	117.0	722	1647.9
2010	156	332	79	41	117.0	725	1712.1
2011	162	430	78	41	117.0	852	1373.4
2012	165	430	78	41	117.0	903	1887.9
2013	167	430	78	41	117.0	903	1760.0
2014	171	430	78	41	128.0	891	1848.0
2015	173	430	77	40	126.0	931	2069.1
2016	178	430	79	43	128.0	960	1994.3
2017	179	430	78	43	128.0	1160	2362.7
2018	179	463	78	43	128.0	1144	2383.5
2019	183	463	78	43	129.0	1167	2530.8
2020	197	1625	80	45	130.0	1139	562.9
2021	204	1629	80	45	131.0	1093	1019.0
2022	215	1784	58	33	130.0	1098	413.3
2023	226	832	50	26	130.0	904	1829.0

注：1.自2020年起，全市按行业管理登记的博物馆包含中央属及非国有博物馆。
2.自2023年起，全市按行业管理登记的博物馆文物藏品数统计范围不包括参考品、标本等，下同。
资料来源：北京市文物局。

Note: 1.Since 2020, the data on museums registered by industry administration have included the data of museums directly under the CPC Central Committee and the data of non-state-owned museums.
2.Since 2023, the statistical coverage of cultural relic collections of the museums registered by industry administration has excluded the reference works and specimens, etc., the same below.

Source: Beijing Municipal Cultural Heritage Bureau.

22-3 博物馆及其他文物保护管理机构情况(2023年)
STATISTICS ON MUSEUMS AND OTHER CULTURAL RELICS PRESERVATION AND MANAGEMENT AGENCIES (2023)

项目		Item		合计 Total	市属 Under the Jurisdiction of the City	区属 Under the Jurisdiction of the District
全市按行业管理登记的博物馆		**Museums Registered by Industry Administration**				
博物馆数	(个)	Museums	(unit)	226	54	50
#正常开放的博物馆数		Museums Normally Open		186	47	47
#免费开放的博物馆数		Museums Open for Free		107	29	29
文物藏品数	(万件)	Cultural Relic Collections	(10000 pieces)	831.8		
参观人次	(万人次)	Visitors	(10000 person-times)	8704.8		
文物古迹个数	(处)	Cultural Relics and Historical Sites	(unit)	3840		
文物拍卖机构数	(个)	Organizations of Cultural Relic Auctions	(unit)	359		
举办文物艺术品拍卖场次	(场)	Cultural Relic Auctions	(time)	3995		
文物拍卖标的数	(件、套)	Auction Targets	(piece, set)	244536		
文物拍卖标的成交金额	(亿元)	Turnover of Cultural Relic Auctions	(100 million yuan)	225.1		
文物局系统内博物馆及文物保护管理机构		**Museums and Cultural Relics Preservation and Management Agencies under the Municipal Cultural Heritage Bureau**				
个数	(个)	Number	(unit)	50	15	35
#博物馆		Museums		26	10	16
博物馆按类别分		By Category				
综合性		Comprehensive		12	3	9
历史性		Historical		9	5	4
艺术性		Art		2	2	
自然科技类		Natural Science		2		2
其他类		Others		1		1
从业人员	(人)	Number of Employed Persons	(person)	3052	1406	1646
文物藏品数	(万件)	Cultural Relic Collections	(10000 pieces)	130	118	12
#一级品	(件)	Grade I Collection	(piece)	904	652	252
参观人次	(万人次)	Visitors	(10000 person-times)	1829.0	306.2	1522.8
本年收入	(万元)	Revenue in the Year	(10000 yuan)	323519	144117	179402
#财政收入		Fiscal Revenue		278689	118095	160594
门票收入		Revenue from Entrance Tickets		6579	3263	3316
本年支出	(万元)	Expenditure in the Year	(10000 yuan)	330892	152330	178562

注：全市按行业管理登记的博物馆合计数中包含中央属及非国有博物馆数据。
资料来源：北京市文物局。
Note: The total number of museums registered by industry administration includes the data on museums directly under the CPC Central Committee and the non-state-owned museums.
Source: Beijing Municipal Cultural Heritage Bureau.

22-4 公共图书馆情况(2023年)
STATISTICS ON PUBLIC LIBRARIES (2023)

项目		Item		合计 Total	中央属 Under Central Jurisdiction	市属 Under the Jurisdiction of the City	区属 Under the Jurisdiction of the District
个　数	（个）	Number	(unit)	20	1	1	18
从业人员	（人）	Number of Employed Persons	(person)	2662	1361	372	929
总藏数	（万册、万件）	Total Collections	(10000 copies)	8099	4424	994	2680
#图　书		Books		5223	1794	838	2591
建筑面积	（万平方米）	Floor Space	(10000 sq.m)	70.0	28.0	17.0	25.0
阅览座席	（个）	Seating Capacity of Reading Roo	(unit)	26374	5339	5721	15314
总流通人次	（万人次）	Total Number of Circulation	(10000 person-times)	1883	410	489	984
#书刊文献外借人次		Borrowing from Libraries of Books and Periodicals		237	28	24	186
书刊文献外借册次	（万册次）	Number of Books and Periodicals Lent to Readers	(10000 copies-times)	1064	49	118	897

资料来源：北京市文化和旅游局、国家图书馆。
Source: Beijing Municipal Bureau of Culture and Tourism, and National Library of China.

22-5 文化馆和文化站情况(2023年)
STATISTICS ON CULTURAL CENTERS AND CULTURAL STATIONS (2023)

项目		Item		合计 Total	市级文化馆 Cultural Centers at Municipal Level	区级文化馆 Cultural Centers at District Level	文化站 Cultural Stations
个　数	（个）	Number	(unit)	357	1	17	339
从业人员	（人）	Number of Employed Persons	(person)	3857	77	828	2952
举办展览个数	（个）	Number of Exhibitions	(unit)	1646	12	261	1373
组织文艺活动	（次）	Art Performances and Story-telling Sessions	(time)	35697	71	2932	32694

资料来源：北京市文化和旅游局。
Source: Beijing Municipal Bureau of Culture and Tourism.

22-6 档案事业基本情况(2023年)
STATISTICS ON ARCHIVE INSTITUTIONS (2023)

项目		Item		合计 Total	市属 Under the Jurisdiction of the City	区属 Under the Jurisdiction of the District
档案馆个数	**（个）**	**Number of Archives**	**(unit)**	**18**	**2**	**16**
建筑面积	**（平方米）**	**Floor Space**	**(sq.m)**	**286698**	**125650**	**161048**
馆藏档案情况		**Number of Archives**				
全　宗	（个）	Full Archives	(unit)	3783	1078	2705
纸质档案	（万卷件）	Paper Archives	(10000 volumes, 10000 pieces)	1162.4	402.8	759.6
新中国成立前档案		Archives Prior to the Foundation of PRC		100.8	98.8	1.9
新中国成立后档案		Archives After the Foundation of PRC		1061.6	303.9	757.7
录音、录像、影片档案	（盘）	Tape, Video, and Film Archives	(piece)	50266	35903	14363
照片档案	（张）	Photo Archives	(sheet)	798522	358787	439735
缩微胶片	（万幅）	Microfiches	(10000 rolls)	5652.1	5602.0	50.1
馆藏电子档案	（GB）	Electronic archives in collections	(GB)	145297.4	111027.1	34270.3
#文书类电子档案		Administrative instruments electronic archives		11307.0	42.8	11264.2
数码照片		Digital photo		5492.2	3148.8	2343.4
数字录音录像		Digital audio and video recording		122362.9	107835.5	14527.4
档案利用情况		**File Utilization**				
本年利用档案人次	（人次）	Person-times Utilizing Archives in the Year	(person-time)	116369	7158	109211
本年利用档案卷件次	（万卷件次）	Utilized Archives in the Year	(10000 piece-times)	50.3	27.8	22.5
本年利用现行文件和资料人次	（人次）	Person-times Utilizing Existing Documents and Data in the Year	(person-time)	203	61	142
本年利用现行文件和资料册次	（件册次）	Existing Documents and Data Books Utilized in the Year	(piece/copy-times)	649	173	476

资料来源：中共北京市委办公厅(北京市档案局)。
Source: General Office of Beijing Municipal Committee of the Communist Party of China (Beijing Municipal Archives Bureau).

22-7 电影、电视、广播电台情况(1978-2023年)

年份 Year	电影 Films 放映场次 (万场次) Show Times (10000 times)	观影人次 (万人次) Person-times Watching Film (10000 person-times)	票房收入 (亿元) Box Office Revenue (100 million yuan)	电视 Television 公共电视节目套数 (套) Number of Public TV Programs (set)	平均每日电视节目播出时间 (小时) Average Daily Hours of Broadcasting of TV Programs (hour)	电视综合覆盖率 (%) Comprehensive Coverage Rate of TVs (%)
1978	31.9	29924.1				
1979	35.5	34626.0				
1980	33.1	31189.5		1	4.3	
1981	31.9	30067.0		1	5.5	100.00
1982	32.8	28743.5		1	6.9	91.00
1983	30.1	27345.5		1	7.1	90.00
1984	27.8	23966.7		1	7.2	98.00
1985	23.0	18875.0		1	7.5	98.00
1986	20.6	15904.4		2	19.1	98.00
1987	19.0	13517.7		2	13.6	98.00
1988	19.2	13269.4		2	19.4	98.00
1989	21.5	14492.6		4	25.4	98.00
1990	20.7	12771.2		4	29.4	98.00
1991	21.3	12558.3		4	27.8	98.00
1992	22.1	11587.4		6	45.0	98.00
1993	11.9	5369.8		7	58.2	98.00
1994	10.6	2166.5	0.5	9	77.8	98.30
1995	9.2	1598.6	0.9	12	98.4	98.30
1996	11.5	1644.1	1.1	12	101.0	98.81
1997	12.6	1742.3	1.2	12	111.0	99.12
1998	12.3	1443.5	1.3	12	110.7	99.60
1999	11.7	964.7		12	118.4	99.80
2000	12.2	873.2		12	122.5	99.80
2001	12.6	804.7	0.9	16	200.2	99.91
2002	12.3	827.4	1.1	18	329.4	99.82
2003	11.8	683.0	1.4	19	259.3	99.90
2004	18.1	814.4	1.9	24	244.2	99.50
2005	22.6	873.8	2.3	25	329.8	99.99
2006	28.0	1221.0	3.0	25	294.2	99.99
2007	38.0	1711.0	3.7	25	309.1	99.99
2008	46.8	1767.3	5.4	24	309.1	99.99
2009	62.4	2451.5	8.2	26	319.1	99.99
2010	74.3	2923.3	11.8	26	319.2	99.99
2011	97.4	3235.9	13.5	25	334.2	100.00
2012	120.0	3954.6	16.2	26	343.7	100.00
2013	137.8	4288.5	18.6	26	347.9	100.00
2014	162.8	5281.3	22.9	26	344.0	100.00
2015	198.1	7212.7	31.6	26	351.1	100.00
2016	228.5	6926.7	30.3	26	360.3	100.00
2017	273.9	7701.7	34.0	26	360.5	100.00
2018	309.6	7645.3	35.0	26	375.7	100.00
2019	356.2	7634.1	36.1	26	353.5	100.00
2020	146.0	2117.5	10.3	26	370.2	100.00
2021	335.4	4224.3	22.3	26	446.4	100.00
2022	262.9	2575.4	14.2	27	482.9	100.00
2023	338.0	5040.9	27.7	26	471.6	100.00

注：1.自2019年起，原"电视节目套数"更名为"公共电视节目套数"，原"广播节目套数"更名为"公共广播节目套数"。
2.自2020年起，原"有线电视用户数"更名为"有线电视实际用户数"。

资料来源：北京市电影局、北京市广播电视局。

STATISTICS ON FILMS, TELEVISION, AND BROADCASTING STATIONS (1978-2023)

电视 TVs			广播电台 Broadcasting Stations		
无线电视综合覆盖率 (%) Comprehensive Coverage Rate of Wireless TVs (%)	有线电视实际用户数 (万户) Actual Users of Cable TV (10000 households)	有线电视入户率 (%) Access Rate of Cable TV (%)	公共广播节目套数 (套) Number of Public Radio Programs (set)	平均每日广播节目播出时间 (小时) Average Daily Hours of Broadcasting of Radio Programs (hour)	广播综合覆盖率 (%) Comprehensive Coverage Rate of Broadcasts (%)
			4	56.1	
			4	57.2	100.00
			4	59.4	98.00
			5	62.0	98.00
			5	73.7	98.00
			5	65.9	98.00
			5	66.2	98.00
			6	68.8	98.00
			6	76.3	98.00
			7	78.7	98.00
			7	77.9	98.00
			7	77.9	98.00
			10	94.8	98.00
			12	134.8	98.00
	52.71		12	134.9	98.00
	82.21		13	148.3	91.00
	182.97		13	150.3	96.97
	202.75		15	156.1	98.44
	230.97		16	174.7	99.98
	165.78	43.24	16	178.2	99.96
	175.71	45.80	16	188.9	97.70
	205.95	51.76	16	192.4	99.91
	231.24	57.05	16	197.4	99.88
	243.00	58.39	16	197.9	99.91
97.57	265.50	62.09	16	229.6	100.00
99.99	282.00	64.12	17	281.9	100.00
94.90	319.58	70.75	17	282.9	100.00
93.13	345.06	74.43	17	288.9	99.98
93.19	383.13	81.00	17	297.4	99.98
94.38	413.50	85.90	18	316.6	99.99
98.72	448.12	91.68	18	324.8	99.99
99.74	475.92	95.90	18	329.6	100.00
99.75	495.70	99.13	25	471.7	100.00
99.75	524.59	103.00	25	473.6	100.00
99.75	551.57	106.85	25	472.6	100.00
99.75	569.13	108.88	25	470.4	100.00
99.75	580.42	109.66	26	493.6	100.00
99.81	586.83	109.04	26	496.3	100.00
99.81	594.55	109.48	26	496.2	100.00
100.00	598.92	109.12	26	499.6	100.00
100.00	606.24	109.35	26	476.7	100.00
100.00	614.67	110.24	19	339.0	100.00
100.00	612.54	109.24	19	340.0	100.00
100.00	617.52	117.68	16	293.8	100.00

Note: a) Since 2019, the original "number of TV programs" has been changed to "number of public TV programs", and the original "number of radio programs" has been changed to "number of public radio programs".

b) Since 2020, the original "users of Cable TV" has been changed to "actual users of Cable TV".

Source: Beijing Municipal Film Administration, Beijing Municipal Radio and Television Bureau.

22−8　电影、电视剧制作情况
STATISTICS ON PRODUCTION OF FILMS AND TV DRAMAS

项　　目		Item		2023			2022		
				全国 National Total	北京 Beijing	占全国比重(%) As % of National Total	全国 National Total	北京 Beijing	占全国比重(%) As % of National Total
生产电影	(部)	Production of Films	(reel)	971	144	14.8	485	135	27.8
制作电视剧	(部)	Production of	(series)	156	28	18.0	160	38	23.8
	(集)	TV Dramas	(episode)	4632	872	18.8	5283	1326	25.1

资料来源：北京市电影局、北京市广播电视局。
Source: Beijing Municipal Film Administration, Beijing Municipal Radio and Television Bureau.

22−9　电影放映单位情况
STATISTICS ON MOVIE PROJECTION ORGANIZATIONS

项　　目		Item		2023	2022
放映单位数	(个)	Number of Projection Organizations	(unit)	309	292
总银幕数	(块)	Total Film Screens	(piece)	2245	2118
放映场次	(万场次)	Show Times	(10000 times)	338.0	262.9
观影人次	(万人次)	Audience	(10000 person-times)	5040.9	2575.4
票房收入	(亿元)	Box Office Revenues	(100 million yuan)	27.7	14.2

资料来源：北京市电影局。
Source: Beijing Municipal Film Administration.

22-10 电视台情况
STATISTICS ON TELEVISION STATIONS

项目		Item		2023 中央 Central	2023 地方 Local	2022 中央 Central	2022 地方 Local
基本情况		**Basic Statistics**					
公共电视节目套数	(套)	Number of Public TV Programs	(set)	36	26	36	27
全年公共电视节目播出时间	(小时)	Annual Broadcasting Hours of Public TV Programs	(hour)	299648	172419	299369	176266
播放节目情况		**Broadcasting of TV Programs**					
新闻资讯类节目	(小时)	News Programs	(hour)	77294	29450	80985	26783
专题服务类节目	(小时)	Special Subject Programs	(hour)	88225	41600	86589	48233
综艺益智类节目	(小时)	General Entertainment Programs	(hour)	51341	9181	49338	7831
影视剧类节目	(小时)	TV Drama Programs	(hour)	62813	45805	62710	44211
广告类节目	(小时)	Advertising Programs	(hour)	11153	12227	11131	16857
其他类节目	(小时)	Others	(hour)	8823	34157	8615	32351

资料来源：北京市广播电视局、国家广播电视总局。
Source: Beijing Municipal Radio and Television Bureau, National Radio and Television Administration.

22-11 广播电台情况
STATISTICS ON BROADCASTING STATIONS

项目		Item		2023 中央 Central	2023 地方 Local	2022 中央 Central	2022 地方 Local
基本情况		**Basic Statistics**					
公共广播节目套数	(套)	Number of Public Radio Programs	(set)	22	16	23	19
全年公共广播节目播出时间	(小时)	Annual Broadcasting Hours of Public Radio Programs	(hour)	171095	107246	172127	124049
播放节目情况		**Broadcasting of Radio Programs**					
新闻资讯类节目	(小时)	News Programs	(hour)	36729	15309	36331	17673
专题服务类节目	(小时)	Special Subject Programs	(hour)	56430	42137	56512	41092
综艺类节目	(小时)	General Entertainment Programs	(hour)	67009	30996	68070	37748
广播剧类节目	(小时)	Radio Play Programs	(hour)	3123	5203	3329	5017
广告类节目	(小时)	Advertising Programs	(hour)	7152	5998	7238	10613
其他类节目	(小时)	Others	(hour)	654	7602	647	11906

注：公共节目套数中含区级广播电视台的广播节目套数。
资料来源：北京市广播电视局、国家广播电视总局。
Note: The number of public programs includes the number of radio programs of broadcasting and TV stations at district levels.
Source: Beijing Municipal Radio and Television Bureau, National Radio and Television Administration.

22-12 广播电视综合覆盖率(2023年)
COMPREHENSIVE COVERAGE RATE OF BROADCASTS AND TELEVISIONS (2023)

项　目		Item		2023
广播综合覆盖率	(%)	Comprehensive Coverage Rate of Broadcasts	(%)	100.00
无线广播综合覆盖率	(%)	Comprehensive Coverage Rate of Radios	(%)	100.00
电视综合覆盖率	(%)	Comprehensive Coverage Rate of Televisions	(%)	100.00
无线电视综合覆盖率	(%)	Comprehensive Coverage Rate of Wireless Televisions	(%)	100.00
有线电视入户率	(%)	Access Rate of Cable TV	(%)	117.68
有线电视实际用户数	(万户)	Actual Users of Cable TV	(10000 households)	617.52
#高清电视实际用户数		Actual Users of High-definition Interactive Digital Television		324.54
#农村有线广播电视实际用户数		Actual Users of Wire Broadcasting and Cable TV in Rural Areas		98.37
增值业务用户数	(万户)	Users of Value-Added Service	(10000 households)	62.13

资料来源：北京市广播电视局。
Source: Beijing Municipal Radio and Television Bureau.

22-13 报纸、期刊、图书出版情况(1978-2022年)
STATISTICS ON NEWSPAPERS, PERIODICALS AND BOOKS (1978-2022)

年 份 Year	报纸出版 Newspapers Published 种 数(种) Number of Publications (kind)	平均期印数(万份) Average Printed Copies Per Issue (10000 copies)	总印数(亿份) Total Printed Copies (100 million copies)	总印张(亿印张) Total Printed Sheets (100 million sheets)	期刊出版 Periodicals Published 种 数(种) Number of Publications (kind)	平均期印数(万册) Average Printed Copies Per Issue (10000 copies)	总印数(亿册) Total Printed Copies (100 million copies)	总印张(亿印张) Total Printed Sheets (100 million sheets)	图书出版 Books Published 种 数(种) Number of Publications (kind)	总印数(亿册、亿张) Total Printed Copies (100 million copies)	总印张(亿印张) Total Printed Sheets (100 million sheets)
1978	11		68.5		468		4.5		5253	5.1	
1979	16		81.6		697		5.9		6723	5.9	
1980	41		84.5		839		5.8		9534	6.3	
1981	55		83.1		886		6.7		11139	7.8	
1982	57		78.3		882		6.7		13862	8.7	
1983	61		79.9		940		6.8		14384	8.5	
1984	73		83.0		987		7.9		15636	8.4	
1985	99		86.0		1098		8.2		17178	9.0	
1986	126		82.0		1206		8.0		19362	5.8	
1987	129		86.0		1409		8.2		21843	6.9	
1988	151		87.0		1514		8.2		23689	7.3	
1989	161		66.0		1580		6.2		25980	6.3	
1990	148		68.0		1415		5.9		27345	6.2	
1991	157		76.7		1499		6.8		29609	7.1	
1992	164	3886	81.4	88.4	1594	6043	7.8	22.3	31320	7.8	58.7
1993	170	3965	81.7	87.7	1597	6037	7.8	22.4	34393	8.6	71.0
1994	233	3759	70.0	92.6	1854	5328	6.3	19.1	38498	8.3	71.7
1995	240	3823	72.9	108.3	1884	5018	6.4	19.6	38819	8.3	70.2
1996	242		70.5		2129		6.1		41572	9.5	
1997	242	3624	71.8	122.2	2162	5396	6.6	22.9	45775	9.9	78.6
1998	247	3561	71.7	130.0	2274	5797	7.3	26.5	50155	11.0	86.1
1999	247	3520	71.7	144.7	2273	6116	8.0	35.2	54783	11.3	93.4
2000	240	3343	68.7	149.6	2352	5909	7.9	33.0	57821	9.6	93.0
2001	243	3339	69.4	153.2	2374	5761	8.1	32.6	63928	10.3	105.1
2002	247	3364	71.0	169.9	2377	5708	8.2	34.3	73836	12.2	127.5
2003	250	3393	72.5	190.4	2382	5702	8.2	34.3	85244	13.8	140.8
2004	253	3405	70.4	206.5	2791	5233	8.0	35.5	98312	15.2	157.2
2005	255	3169	66.2	227.2	2809	4957	7.7	40.8	108152	17.1	180.5
2006	256	3651	74.0	240.4	2809	5077	8.3	47.4	113232	17.2	186.1
2007	256	3454	73.1	218.6	2809	5340	9.2	54.2	125412	18.7	195.3
2008	259	3328	73.2	241.3	2898	5392	9.4	55.4	136284	20.8	220.0
2009	260	3232	71.6	232.5	3030	5373	9.7	59.4	144211	21.0	220.2
2010	262	3406	77.5	275.6	3063	5519	10.0	69.6	155209	21.5	251.2
2011	254	3453	83.1	293.7	3044	5991	10.2	76.7	167942	22.6	243.1
2012	257	3725	89.5	300.2	3064	5940	10.3	76.7	179634	22.5	250.7
2013	254	3737	91.7	298.2	3053	6094	10.4	78.0	192137	24.0	269.5
2014	256	3550	89.9	289.3	3123	5867	10.0	74.0	194259	23.6	258.7
2015	253	3389	87.4	267.5	3168	5539	9.3	68.0	205992	24.5	271.0
2016	252	3297	86.0	259.3	3221	5471	9.1	63.2	213413	26.9	292.0
2017	249	3215	83.9	249.7	3242	5325	8.6	57.1	217765	26.7	294.3
2018	247	3120	83.1	239.9	3244	5299	8.1	55.1	220632	29.7	327.1
2019	246	2981	81.3	219.7	3266	5326	7.9	53.7	216994	31.2	342.2
2020	241	2857	77.7	196.8	3279	5143	7.5	54.3	211863	30.0	327.0
2021	30	111	2.7	8.4	171	129	0.2	1.5	14775	4.0	33.3
2022	30	105	2.6	6.5	171	117	0.2	1.1	12354	2.7	24.0

注：1.1991年及以前，报纸、期刊、图书为出版数；自1992年起均为总印数。

2.自2021年起，本表统计范围不含中央在京单位，下同。

资料来源：北京市新闻出版局。

Note: a) Figures on newspaper, periodicals and books in and before 1991 were figures of publications; since 1992, they have referred to the total printed copies.

b) Since 2021, the statistical scope of this table has excluded central units in Beijing, the same below.

Source: Beijing Municipal Bureau of Press and Publication.

22-14 报纸出版情况(2022年)
STATISTICS ON PUBLICATION OF NEWSPAPERS (2022)

项　目	Item	种　数 (种) Number of Publications (kind)	平均期印数 (万册) Average Printed Copies Per Issue (10000 copies)	总 印 数 (万册) Total Printed Copies (10000 copies)	总 印 张 (万印张) Total Printed Sheets (10000 sheets)
合　计	**Total**	**30**	**105.3**	**25887**	**65278.2**
#综合报	Comprehensive	12	65.8	22109	57790.9
专业报	Professional	11	26.0	3133	6648.0

资料来源：北京市新闻出版局。
Source: Beijing Municipal Bureau of Press and Publication.

22-15 期刊出版情况(2022年)
STATISTICS ON PUBLICATION OF PERIODICALS (2022)

项　目	Item	种　数 (种) Number of Publications (kind)	平均期印数 (万册) Average Printed Copies Per Issue (10000 copies)	总 印 数 (万册) Total Printed Copies (10000 copies)	总 印 张 (万印张) Total Printed Sheets (10000 sheets)
合　计	**Total**	**171**	**116.7**	**1680**	**11464.6**
综　合	Comprehensive	2	0.1	0.2	6.2
哲学、社会科学	Philosophy and Social Sciences	49	46.9	709	4105.7
自然科学技术	Natural Sciences and Technology	75	19.0	249	1927.6
文化、教育	Culture and Education	33	31.1	477	3121.1
文学、艺术	Literature and Arts	12	19.6	245	2304.0

资料来源：北京市新闻出版局。
Source: Beijing Municipal Bureau of Press and Publication.

22-16 图书出版情况(2022年)
STATISTICS ON PUBLICATION OF BOOKS (2022)

项目	Item	出版图书种数合计(种) Total Number of Publications of Books (kind)	#新书 New Books	总印数(万册、万张) Total Printed Copies (10000 copies)	总印张(万印张) Total Printed Sheets (10000 sheets)
合计	**Total**	**12354**	**5256**	**26653**	**239608.2**
使用"中国标准书号"部分合计	**Publications with "China Standard Book Numbering"**	**12352**	**5254**	**26651**	**239603.5**
马列主义、毛泽东思想	Marxism-Leninism, Mao Zedong Thought	17	8	7	143.1
哲学	Philosophy	259	124	528	6660.0
社会科学总论	General Social Sciences	91	47	82	917.4
政治、法律	Politics and Law	141	86	168	1874.2
军事	Military Affairs	23	6	55	422.3
经济	Economics	616	358	672	10800.4
文化、科学、教育、体育	Culture, Science, Education and Sports	5977	1938	15048	123406.1
语言、文字	Languages	288	131	548	4681.8
文学	Literature	2488	1045	6387	59500.2
艺术	Arts	608	413	946	8310.3
历史、地理	History and Geography	509	285	738	7961.3
自然科学总论	General Natural Sciences	32	15	88	430.1
数学科学、化学	Mathematics and Chemistry	112	60	310	2066.7
天文学、物理科学	Astronomy and Physics	97	55	182	1544.1
生物科学	Biology	123	65	187	1712.6
医药、卫生	Medicine and Health Care	355	244	252	3697.9
农业科学	Agricultural Science	27	12	30	384.9
工业技术	Industrial Technology	354	246	175	2702.9
交通运输	Transportation	67	41	41	364.6
航空、航天	Aeronautics and Aerospace	30	6	34	171.3
环境科学	Environmental Science	18	11	23	241.5
综合性图书	General Books	120	58	150	1609.9
不使用"中国标准书号"部分合计	**Publications without "China Standard Book Numbering"**	**2**	**2**	**2**	**4.7**

资料来源：北京市新闻出版局。
Source: Beijing Municipal Bureau of Press and Publication.

22-17 录音制品出版情况(2022年)
STATISTICS ON PUBLICATION OF AUDIO PRODUCTS (2022)

项 目 Item	录音带 Audio-tapes		激光唱盘 CDs		高密度激光唱盘及其他 DVDs-A and Others	
	种数(种) Number of Publications (kind)	数量(万盒) Volume (10000 cassettes)	种数(种) Number of Publications (kind)	数量(万张) Volume (10000 pieces)	种数(种) Number of Publications (kind)	数量(万张) Volume (10000 pieces)
合 计 Total	**220**	**465.5**	**1151**	**4346.3**	**248**	**141.2**
#市 属 Municipal	6	2.55	138	91.7	100	42.0

资料来源：北京市新闻出版局。
Source: Beijing Municipal Bureau of Press and Publication.

22-18 录像制品出版情况(2022年)
STATISTICS ON PUBLICATION OF VIDEO PRODUCTS (2022)

项 目 Item	录像带 Videotapes		激光视盘 VCDs		高密度激光视盘 DVD-Vs	
	种数(种) Number of Publications (kind)	数量(万盒) Volume (10000 cassettes)	种数(种) Number of Publications (kind)	数量(万张) Volume (10000 discs)	种数(种) Number of Publications (kind)	数量(万张) Volume (10000 discs)
合 计 Total			**37**	**45.9**	**844**	**1579.9**
#市 属 Municipal					43	9.7

资料来源：北京市新闻出版局。
Source: Beijing Municipal Bureau of Press and Publication.

22-19 电子出版物出版情况(2022年)
STATISTICS ON PUBLICATION OF ELECTRONIC PUBLICATIONS (2022)

项 目 Item	只读光盘 CD-ROMs		高密度只读光盘 DVD-ROMs		交互式光盘及其他 CD-Is and Others	
	种数(种) Number of Publications (kind)	数量(万盒) Volume (10000 discs)	种数(种) Number of Publications (kind)	数量(万盒) Volume (10000 discs)	种数(种) Number of Publications (kind)	数量(万盒) Volume (10000 discs)
合 计 Total	**1683**	**4386.0**	**675**	**1460.8**	**458**	**448.7**
#市 属 Municipal	44	2.2	7	8.2		

资料来源：北京市新闻出版局。
Source: Beijing Municipal Bureau of Press and Publication.

22-20 引进版权量情况
STATISTICS ON IMPORT OF COPYRIGHT

单位：件 (item)

项　目	Item	2022	2021
引进版权量	**Number of Imported Copyright**	**6390**	**7526**
软件和电子出版物	Software and Electronic Publications	10	15
图　书	Books	6377	7499

资料来源：北京市新闻出版局。
Source: Beijing Municipal Bureau of Press and Publication.

22-21 主要年份文化产业增加值情况
STATISTICS ON ADDED VALUE OF CULTURAL INDUSTRY IN MAIN YEARS

年　份 Year	增加值 (亿元) Added Value (100 million yuan)	占地区生产总值比重 (%) Proportion to GDP (%)
2004	398.3	6.4
2008	681.6	5.8
2011	1358.7	7.9
2012	1569.4	8.2
2013	1754.2	8.3
2014	1937.2	8.5
2015	2081.4	8.4
2016	2217.4	8.2
2017	2723.5	9.1
2018	3075.1	9.3
2019	3318.4	9.4
2020	3770.2	10.5
2021	4509.2	11.0
2022	4700.3	11.3

注：2004—2012年文化产业增加值仅包括法人单位数据，自2013年起为包括个体经营户在内的全口径数据。
Note: The figures on the added value of cultural industry for 2004 to 2012 included the data of corporate units only; and figures for and after 2013 have been those of full coverage including data of self-employed businesses.

22−22 规模以上文化产业企业经营情况(2013−2023年)
OPERATING STATISTICS ON CULTURAL INDUSTRY ENTERPRISES ABOVE DESIGNATED SIZE (2013-2023)

年 份 Year	企业单位数 (个) Number of Enterprises (unit)	年末从业人员 (万人) Employed Persons at Year-end (10000 persons)	资产总计 (亿元) Total Assets (100 million yuan)	营业收入 (亿元) Business Revenue (100 million yuan)	利润总额 (亿元) Total Profits (100 million yuan)
2013	3981	41.6	5731.0	5155.2	390.2
2014	3820	47.8	7937.9	6876.9	495.6
2015	3418	47.4	9419.6	7548.1	550.8
2016	3539	48.1	10870.2	8195.4	530.5
2017	3994	54.1	13887.9	9586.0	802.9
2018	3887	53.7	16579.0	10963.0	852.7
2019	4831	54.2	19020.3	12997.3	739.1
2020	5119	56.0	23738.4	14944.0	1324.4
2021	5309	59.9	28067.4	17628.6	1458.0
2022	5450	54.9	29934.9	17797.3	1949.1
2023	5304	50.8	32701.1	20140.1	2614.3

注:表中2023年数据均为2023年1−12月定报数据。
Note: The data for 2023 in this table are all the regularly submitted data for January to December 2023.

22−23 规模以上文化产业法人单位基本情况(2023年)
BASIC STATISTICS ON CORPORATE UNITS OF CULTURAL INDUSTRY ABOVE DESIGNATED SIZE (2023)

项 目	Item	资产总计 (亿元) Total Assets (100 million yuan)	收入合计 (亿元) Total Revenue (100 million yuan)	年末从业人员 (万人) Employed Persons at Year-end (10000 persons)
合 计	**Total**	**33933.7**	**20638.3**	**57.5**
文化核心领域	**Core Fields of Culture**	**31916.7**	**18721.9**	**48.6**
新闻信息服务	News and Information Service	8901.0	5508.6	11.5
内容创作生产	Content Creation and Production	12273.2	6445.3	17.1
创意设计服务	Creative Design Service	3318.8	3563.4	9.7
文化传播渠道	Culture Transmission Channel	4634.1	2955.4	7.0
文化投资运营	Cultural Investment and Operation	1862.3	54.6	0.3
文化娱乐休闲服务	Cultural, Entertainment and Recreational Service	927.4	194.6	3.0
文化相关领域	**Culture-related Fields**	**2017.0**	**1916.3**	**8.8**
文化辅助生产和中介服务	Cultural Auxiliary Production and Intermediary Service	1272.7	863.7	7.2
文化装备生产	Cultural Equipment Production	203.3	82.7	0.6
文化消费终端生产	Cultural Consumption Terminal Production	541.1	969.9	1.0

注:1.规模以上文化产业法人单位包括企业法人单位和事业单位。
2.表中数据均为2023年1−12月定报数据。
Note: a) Corporate units of cultural industry above designated size include the corporate enterprises and the public institutions.
b)The data in this table are all the regularly submitted data for January to December 2023.

22-24 体育场地情况(2018-2023年) STATISTICS ON GYMNASIUMS AND STADIUMS (2018-2023)

项　目	Item	2018	2019	2020	2021	2022	2023
综合指标	**Comprehensive Indicators**						
人均体育场地面积（平方米）	Per Capita Area of Gymnasiums and Stadiums (sq.m)	2.32	2.45	2.57	2.69	2.90	2.95
体育场地数量 （万个）	Number of Gymnasiums and Stadiums (10000 units)	3.16	3.57	3.86	4.24	4.28	4.43
基础运动场地 （个）	**Gymnasiums and Stadiums for Basic Sports (unit)**						
田径场地	Track-and-Field Ground	1771	1772	1878	1914	2015	1771
游泳场地	Natatorium	904	912	925	903	941	907
球类运动场地 （个）	**Gymnasiums and Stadiums for Ball Games (unit)**						
足球场地	Football Pitch	1785	1915	2356	2467	2518	2538
篮球场地	Basketball Court	6087	6150	7033	7273	7447	7370
排球场地	Volleyball Court	280	296	401	415	431	402
乒乓球场地	Table Tennis Court	4358	6199	6295	6536	6587	7368
羽毛球场地	Badminton Court	949	1152	1242	1448	1403	1482
冰雪运动场地 （个）	**Gymnasiums and Stadiums for Ice & Snow Sports (unit)**						
滑冰场地	Skating Ground	65	72	82	112	124	123
滑雪场地	Skiing Field	22	28	35	35	33	26
体育健身场地	**Gymnasiums and Stadiums for Physical Fitness and Exercise**						
全民健身路径 （个）	Public Fitness Path (unit)	9064	9984	11382	12626	12306	12778
健身房 （个）	Gym (unit)	2773	2789	2886	4067	4112	4135
健身步道 （公里）	Fitness Footpath (km)	635.0	1001.9	1106.9	1289.6	2517.8	3320.9

注：本表为北京市全国体育场地统计调查数据。
资料来源：北京市体育局。
Note: Data in this table are the statistical survey data of the national gymnasiums and stadiums of Beijing.
Source: Beijing Municipal Bureau of Sports.

22-25 运动员、裁判员情况
STATISTICS ON ATHLETES AND REFEREES

单位：人 (person)

项　　目	Item	2023	#女　性 Females	2022	#女　性 Females
分等级运动员发展人数	**Number of Graded Athletes**	**3242**	**1425**	**2524**	**1045**
一　级	First Grade Athletes	1096	535	764	342
二　级	Second Grade Athletes	2146	890	1760	703
分等级裁判员发展人数	**Number of Graded Referees**	**2453**	**983**	**933**	**301**
一　级	First Grade Referees	561	241	183	76
二　级	Second Grade Referees	1892	742	750	225

资料来源：北京市体育局。
Source: Beijing Municipal Bureau of Sports.

22-26 运动员获奖牌情况(2023年)
STATISTICS ON MEDALS WON BY ATHLETES (2023)

单位：块 (piece)

项　　目	Item	金　牌 Gold	银　牌 Silver	铜　牌 Copper
合　　计	**Total**	**96**	**68**	**74**
国际比赛	International Competitions	34	12	12
国内比赛	Domestic Competitions	62	56	62

资料来源：北京市体育局。
Source: Beijing Municipal Bureau of Sports.

22-27　体育彩票
SPORTS LOTTERY

项　　目	Item	2023	2022
电脑体育彩票销售点数　（个）	Number of Computer Sports Lottery Tickets Sold　(unit)	3782	3016
体育彩票发行额　（万元）	Circulation of Sports Lottery　(10000 yuan)	1082446	728816
体育彩票公益金提取额　（万元）	Withdrawal of Public Welfare Fund from Sports Lottery　(10000 yuan)	257482	180139

资料来源：北京市体育局。
Source: Beijing Municipal Bureau of Sports.

22-28　体育产业增加值情况(2015-2022年)
STATISTICS ON ADDED VALUE OF SPORT INDUSTRY(2015-2022)

年　份 Year	增加值 (亿元) Added Value (100 million yuan)	占地区生产总值比重 (%) Proportion to GDP (%)
2015	225.2	0.91
2016	251.3	0.93
2017	289.7	0.97
2018	326.3	0.99
2019	345.4	0.97
2020	309.3	0.86
2021	340.1	0.83
2022	330.5	0.80

主要统计指标解释

文　化

文化及相关产业（文化产业）　是指为社会公众提供文化产品和文化相关产品的生产活动的集合。

公共图书馆藏书　指各级文化部门举办的面向社会服务的独立的图书馆（不包括文化馆的图书室，也不包括文化系统以外的图书馆）藏书数量。

广播综合覆盖率　根据国家广电总局制定的《广播电视人口覆盖率统计技术标准和方法》进行统计调查的，在对象区内能接收到广播节目的覆盖人口数占本行政区域内人口总数的比率。

无线广播综合覆盖率　根据国家广电总局制定的《广播电视人口覆盖率统计技术标准和方法》进行统计调查的，在对象区内能接收到用中、短波、调频等无线传输技术发射转播的广播节目的人口数占本行政区域内人口总数的比率。包括中央、省、地市、县四级无线广播综合覆盖人口。

电视综合覆盖率　根据国家广电总局制定的《广播电视人口覆盖率统计技术标准和方法》进行统计调查的，在对象区内能接收到电视节目的人口数占本行政区域内人口总数的比率，包括中央、省、地市、县电视节目综合覆盖人口。

无线电视综合覆盖率　根据国家广电总局制定的《广播电视人口覆盖率统计技术标准和方法》进行统计调查的，在对象区内能接收到用中、短波、调频等无线传输技术发射转播的电视节目的人口数占本行政区域内人口总数的比率。包括中央、省、地市、县四级无线电视综合覆盖人口。

有线电视入户率　指通过广播电视有线传输网收看电视节目的家庭用户数（包括接收模拟信号和接收数字信号的有线电视用户数，不包括宾馆、单位、写字楼等集体用户）与本行政区域内总户数的比率。

有线电视实际用户数　指通过广播电视有线传输网收看电视节目的用户数。

体　育

体育产业　是指为社会提供各种体育产品（货物和服务）和体育相关产品的生产活动的集合。

体育场地　指专门用于体育训练、比赛和健身活动的，有一定投资的公益性或经营性体育建筑设施，包括必要的附属功能用房。

等级运动员人数　指经考核正式批准授予等级运动员称号的人数。运动员等级分为国际级运动健将、国家级运动健将、一级运动员、二级运动员、三级运动员、少年级运动员。

等级裁判员人数　指经考核正式批准授予等级裁判员称号的人数。裁判员等级分为国际级裁判、国家级裁判、一级裁判、二级裁判、三级裁判。

运动员获奖牌情况　指当年北京市运动员在世界比赛、亚洲比赛、全国比赛中获得金、银、铜牌的数量。

Explanatory Notes on Main Statistical Indicators

Culture

Cultural and Related Industries (Cultural Industry) means the collection of production activities that provide the public with cultural products and culture related products.

Collection of Books in Public Libraries means the number of books collected in independent libraries open to the public and run by all-level cultural bodies (excluding book rooms in cultural centers, and libraries not included in the cultural system).

Comprehensive Coverage Rate of Broadcast means the share of population who can receive broadcasting programs in the target area, calculated in line with the *Statistical Standard and Method on Television and Radio Coverage of Population* established by the National Radio and Television Administration, of the total population in the administrative area.

Comprehensive Coverage Rate of Radio means the share of population who can receive broadcasting programs transmitted with short-wave, medium-wave, FM and other radio transmission technologies in the target area, calculated in line with the *Statistical Standard and Method on Television and Radio Coverage of Population* established by the National Radio and Television Administration, of the total population in the administrative area, including the population covered by broadcasting programs from central, provincial, prefectural cities and county radio stations.

Comprehensive Coverage Rate of TV means the share of population who can receive TV programs in the target area, calculated in line with the *Statistical Standard and Method on Television and Radio Coverage of Population* established by the National Radio and Television Administration, of the total population in the administrative area, including the population covered by TV programs from central, provincial, prefectural cities and county TV stations.

Comprehensive Coverage Rate of Wireless TV means the share of population who can receive TV programs transmitted with short-wave, medium-wave, FM and other radio transmission technologies in the target area, calculated in line with the *Statistical Standard and Method on Television and Radio Coverage of Population* established by the National Radio and Television Administration, of the total population in the administrative area, including the population covered by wireless television programs from central, provincial, prefectural cities and county TV stations.

Access Rate of Cable TVs refers to the percentage of households which can watch television programs through the cable broadcasting and television transmission network (including cable TV households receiving analog signals and digital signals, excluding collective subscribers such as hotels, companies and entities, office buildings), to the total households in the administrative area.

Actual Number of Cable TV Subscribers means the number of subscribers watching television programs through the cable broadcasting and television transmission network.

Sports

Sports Industry refers to the collection of production activities that provide the society with various sports products (goods and services) and sports related products.

Sports Venues refer to sports building facilities, including necessary ancillary functional rooms, for public welfare or operating purpose, specially used for sports training, games and fitness activities, and with certain investment.

Number of Graded Athletes means the number of athletes formally granted with the title of graded athlete upon examination. Grades of athletes include international master sportsman, national maser sportsman, grade-I athlete, grade-II athlete, grade-III athlete and juvenile athlete.

Number of Graded Referees means the number of referees formally granted with the title of graded referees upon examination. Grades of referees include international referee, national referee, grade-I referee, grade-II referee and grade-III referee.

Medals Won by Athletes mean the number of gold, silver and copper medals won by athletes of Beijing in world games, Asian games and national games.

23

北京统计年鉴2024　　BEIJING STATISTICAL YEARBOOK 2024

公共管理、社会保障和社会组织

PUBLIC MANAGEMENT, SOCIAL SECURITY AND SOCIAL ORGANIZATION

简要说明

主要内容

本章资料主要包括社会活动参与、公检法司、社会保障、妇女及儿童发展规划监测情况等。

1.社会活动参与部分主要包括历届北京市人大代表和政协委员人数及议案情况、妇联组织和工会组织等情况。

2.公检法司部分主要包括公安机关、法院、检察院的收案、结案情况，交通事故、安全生产情况，以及司法局提供的律师、公证、调解工作等情况。

3.社会保障部分主要包括社会保障相关待遇标准和参加社会保障情况。

4.妇女与儿童发展规划监测资料主要包括妇女的社会保障、妇女参与决策和管理、教育、健康、家庭建设、法律保护等情况及儿童的健康、教育、环境、法律保护等情况。

Brief Introduction

Main Content

Statistics in this chapter mainly consist of statistics for social activity participation, public security institutions, procuratorates, courts, judicial authorities, social security, women and children development planning and monitoring.

1. Statistics for social activity participation mainly consist of the numbers of deputies and proposals at people's congress and political consulting conferences of Beijing in previous years, women's federation organizations and labor unions.

2. Statistics for public security institutions, procuratorates, courts, and judicial authorities cover the cases accepted and settled by public security organs, courts and procuratorates, the statistics on traffic accidents, safe production, and the information on lawyers, notary, mediation provided by juridical bureaus.

3. Statistics for social security mainly consist of the social security benefits level and the social security participation.

4. Supervisory data on women and children development programs are mainly composed of women's social security, participation in decision making and management, education, health, family building, and legal protection etc. as well as children's health, education, environment, legal protection, and so on.

23-1 历届北京市人代会代表人数性别构成及议案、建议数
NUMBER AND SEX COMPOSITION OF DEPUTIES, NUMBER OF PROPOSALS AND SUGGESTIONS OF PREVIOUS BEIJING MUNICIPAL PEOPLE'S CONGRESSES

项目 Item	代表人数(人) Number of Deputies (person)	女性 Females	男性 Males	性别比例(%) Sex Percentage (%) 女性 Females	男性 Males	议案立案数(件) Number of Proposals on Record (proposal)	建议数(件) Number of Suggestions (suggestion)
第一届 First Congress	564	106	458	18.8	81.2		
第二届 Second Congress	619	142	477	22.9	77.1		
第三届 Third Congress	618	162	456	26.2	73.8		
第四届 Fourth Congress	745	202	543	27.1	72.9		
第五届 Fifth Congress	751	203	548	27.0	73.0		
第七届 Seventh Congress	1195	325	870	27.1	72.9		
第八届 Eighth Congress	973	252	721	25.9	74.1	55	6644
第九届 Ninth Congress	880	217	663	24.7	75.3	86	7921
第十届 Tenth Congress	885	224	661	25.3	74.7	156	7281
第十一届 Eleventh Congress	763	197	566	25.8	74.2	166	9717
第十二届 Twelfth Congress	762	235	527	30.8	69.2	276	9859
第十三届 Thirteenth Congress	771	236	535	30.6	69.4	153	7576
第十四届 Fourteenth Congress	771	257	514	33.3	66.7	157	6136
第十五届 Fifteenth Congress	771	296	475	38.4	61.6	262	4018
第十六届 Sixteenth Congress	774	309	465	39.9	60.1	106	1779

注：1.北京市人大常委会是经北京市七届三次人民代表大会选举成立的，故一至七届人代会无议案及建议数。
2.代表人数为届首选举数，议案立案数及建议数均为本届五年会上及平时议案立案及建议的合计数。
资料来源：北京市人民代表大会常务委员会。

Note: a) The Standing Committee of Beijing Municipal People's Congress was established upon election at the third Session of Beijing Seventh People's Congress. Therefore, there were no data on the number of proposals and suggestions at the first to the Seventh People's Congresses.
b) Number of deputies refers to those first elected for that term. Number of proposals on record and number of suggestions include those at the meeting of the term and at ordinary times.

Source: The Standing Committee of Beijing Municipal People's Congress.

23-2 历届北京市政协会委员人数及提案立案数
NUMBER OF MEMBERS AND PROPOSALS OF PREVIOUS BEIJING CPPCC

届别 Term		起止年月 Beginning-ending Month	委员人数（人） Number of Members (person)	女性 Females	男性 Males	提案立案数（件） Number of Proposals on Record (proposal)
第一届	First Conference	1955.04-1959.09	270	40	230	37
第二届	Second Conference	1959.09-1962.12	463	84	379	13
第三届	Third Conference	1962.12-1965.09	519	92	427	884
第四届	Fourth Conference	1965.09-1977.11	529	88	441	23
第五届	Fifth Conference	1977.11-1983.03	779	161	618	1610
第六届	Sixth Conference	1983.03-1988.01	766	168	598	3122
第七届	Seventh Conference	1988.01-1993.01	703	179	524	4276
第八届	Eighth Conference	1993.01-1998.01	740	185	555	4975
第九届	Ninth Conference	1998.01-2003.01	782	203	579	6240
第十届	Tenth Conference	2003.01-2008.01	824	226	598	6871
第十一届	Eleventh Conference	2008.01-2013.01	737	233	504	5354
第十二届	Twelfth Conference	2013.01-2018.01	758	237	521	5410
第十三届	Thirteenth Conference	2018.01-2023.01	761	261	500	6514
第十四届	Fourteenth Conference	2023.01-2023.12	759	235	524	1248

资料来源：中国人民政治协商会议北京市委员会。
Source: Beijing Municipal Committee of the Chinese People's Political Consultative Conference.

23-3 公安、法院、检察院收案、结案情况(2005-2023年)

项 目		Item		2005	2006	2007	2008	2009
公安机关办理案件		Cases Handled by Public Security Organs						
刑事案件立案情况		Registration Status of Criminal Cases						
立 案	(起)	Number of Cases Registered	(case)	107988	120554	127446	90045	98750
法院办理案件		Cases Handled by Courts						
刑事案件收、结案情况		Criminal Cases Accepted and Settled						
收 案	(件)	Cases Accepted	(case)	17488	17725	19592	20024	18819
结 案	(件)	Cases Settled	(case)	17624	17701	19536	20004	18773
婚姻家庭、继承纠纷案件收、结案情况		Cases on Disputes of Marriage, Family and Inheritance Cases Accepted and Settled						
收 案	(件)	Cases Accepted	(case)	26739	27860	28089	30402	33056
结 案	(件)	Cases Settled	(case)	27002	27845	27916	29499	32902
合同纠纷案件收、结案情况		Cases on Contract Dispute Cases Accepted and Settled						
收 案	(件)	Cases Accepted	(case)	133534	141485	135099	144948	153766
结 案	(件)	Cases Settled	(case)	135612	141439	134829	140512	152128
权属、侵权纠纷及其他民事案件收、结案情况		Ownership, Infringement Dispute and Other Civil Cases Accepted and Settled						
收 案	(件)	Cases Accepted	(case)	42690	44890	46892	53864	58057
结 案	(件)	Cases Settled	(case)	43166	45005	46372	51668	57135
检察机关办理案件		Cases Handled by Procuratorial Organs						
审查逮捕案件		Cases of Arrests Approved						
收 案	(件)	Cases Accepted	(case)	17441	18137	19126	16584	17593
结 案	(件)	Cases Settled	(case)	16398	16795	17210	16562	17606
审查起诉案件		Cases of Prosecution Approved						
收 案	(件)	Cases Accepted	(case)	19672	19869	21462	20137	20453
结 案	(件)	Cases Settled	(case)	17899	18517	20394	19047	19989

资料来源：北京市公安局、北京市人民检察院、北京市高级人民法院。

STATISTICS ON CASES ACCEPTED AND SETTLED BY PUBLIC SECURITY ORGANS,COURTS AND PROCURATORATES (2005-2023)

2010	2011	2012	2013	2014	2015	2016	2017	2018	2019	2020	2021	2022	2023
104327	142835	145724	140498	153334	174374	150312	140250	138696	138291	137728	144711	116575	119117
19824	19574	22168	19109	20556	19980	16737	18584	17091	20320	16440	21513	12082	16073
19870	19423	22084	19012	20357	19667	16905	18628	17062	19582	15796	20837	12468	16599
36799	35251	35418	37347	39390	43869	43141	50467	52675	49077	35187	48507	33101	41699
37160	35149	35201	35296	38565	40436	43606	51800	52950	49402	34753	43256	32411	42301
148655	144433	145017	149237	162893	237850	253456	279287	347240	343861	261610	334410	259513	261235
153130	144766	143153	141642	155472	207012	255852	285872	346884	338714	261681	296185	268087	269435
64379	65972	62736	64747	69541	85554	100574	114284	109296	119759	119735	173375	134058	130831
65763	66405	62235	61688	67444	76644	100399	115125	110443	118326	119037	148058	135679	137163
18060	18279	18563	16861	16594	14880	14307	16651	17359	19995	14525	20195	13920	20230
17946	18208	18644	16860	16606	14840	14265	16663	17318	19992	14507	20347	13932	19962
20982	20986	23553	21798	22251	20181	18786	21039	20311	24023	17850	25164	17491	24257
19825	20293	21980	20684	22455	19935	18361	20807	19688	22825	18297	25276	17149	22342

Source: Beijing Municipal Public Security Bureau, People's Procuratorate of Beijing Municipality, and The High People's Court of Beijing Municipality.

23-4 公安机关刑事案件立案情况
STATISTICS ON CRIMINAL CASES REGISTERED IN PUBLIC SECURITY ORGANS

单位：起 (case)

项 目	Item	立 案 Cased Registered	
		2023	2022
刑事案件	**Criminal Cases**	**119117**	**116575**
杀 人	Homicide	139	142
伤 害	Injury	1351	1433
抢 劫	Robbery	67	63
强 奸	Rape	430	514
盗 窃	Larceny	12463	13424
诈 骗	Fraud	77308	78660
其 他	Others	27359	22339

资料来源：北京市公安局。
Source: Beijing Municipal Public Security Bureau.

23-5 公安机关治安案件查处情况
STATISTICS ON CASES OF OFFENCE AGAINST PUBLIC ORDER INVESTIGATED AND TREATED BY PUBLIC SECURITY ORGANS

单位：起 (case)

项 目	Item	查 处 Cases Investigated and Treated	
		2023	2022
治安案件	**Cases of Offence Against Public Order**	**788541**	**709385**
扰乱公共场所秩序	Disturbing Orders in Public Venues	25424	15089
寻衅滋事	Causing Quarrels and Making Troubles	25207	20579
阻碍执行职务	Obstructing Government Officials in Performing Their Duties	1837	1602
殴打他人	Battering Other Persons	114438	113789
盗 窃	Larceny	176543	152525
抢 夺	Robbery and Snatch	209	216
伪造、变造、倒卖有价票证、凭证	Forge, Alter, Scalp Valuable Coupons or Certificates	224	63
诈 骗	Swindling	112539	100426
卖淫、嫖娼	Prostitution or Soliciting Prostitutes	12991	7291
赌 博	Gambling	11056	8807
其 他	Others	308073	288998

资料来源：北京市公安局。
Source: Beijing Municipal Public Security Bureau.

23-6 检察机关办理各类案件情况(2023年)
STATISTICS ON CASES HANDLED BY PROCURATORIAL ORGANS (2023)

项　　目	Item	受案(受理) Cases Accepted		审结案合计 Total Cases Concluded	
		件 Case	人 Person	件 Case	人 Person
审查逮捕案件	**Cases of Arrests Approved**	**20230**	**27655**	**19962**	**27266**
批准逮捕	Approved			10094	12898
不批准逮捕	Disapproved			9868	14368
审查起诉案件	**Cases of Prosecution Approved**	**24257**	**29676**	**22342**	**26965**
起　诉	Prosecuted			15655	18734
不起诉	Non-prosecution			6593	8104
附条件不起诉	Conditional Non-prosecution			94	127
举报案件	**Reported Cases**				
控告案件	**Complaints**	**154**		**154**	
申诉案件	**Appeal Cases**	**6168**		**6108**	
民事检察案件	**Civil Cases**	**17932**		**17800**	
行政检察案件	**Administrative Cases**	**13712**		**12971**	

资料来源：北京市人民检察院。
Source: People's Procuratorate of Beijing Municipality.

23-7 法院行政案件收、结案情况(2023年)
STATISTICS ON ADMINISTRATIVE CASES ACCEPTED AND SETTLED BY COURTS (2023)

单位：件 (case)

项　　目	Item	收　案 Cases Accepted	结　案 Cases Settled	#判　决 Judgment	#裁　定 Mediation
合　　计	**Total**	**33184**	**34387**	**25725**	**8002**
公　安	Public Security	2134	1974	921	970
资　源	Resources	689	726	258	439
城　建	Urban Construction	1542	1454	559	842
工　商	Industry and Commerce	902	847	237	488
专　利	Patents	1859	2108	1892	210
劳动和社会保障	Labor and Social Security	607	533	340	188
教　育	Education	130	136	30	105
商　标	Trademarks	18439	19967	18897	1043
乡政府	Township Governments	2300	1986	957	999
其　他	Others	4582	4656	1634	2718

注：法院行政案件收结案为一审审结数。
资料来源：北京市高级人民法院。
Note: The statistics on administrative cases accepted and settled by courts refer to the number of concluded cases at the first trial.
Source: The High People's Court of Beijing Municipality.

23-8 法院刑事案件收、结案情况(2023年)
STATISTICS ON CRIMINAL CASES ACCEPTED AND SETTLED BY COURTS (2023)

项　目	Item	收　案（件）Cases Accepted (case)	结　案（件）Cases Settled (case)	判决发生法律效力 Judgment with Legal Forces	
				件　数（件）Number of Cases (case)	人　数（人）Number of Persons (person)
合　计	**Total**	**16073**	**16599**	**16002**	**20352**
#危害公共安全罪	Offences against Public Security	4641	4653	1239	1296
破坏社会主义市场经济秩序罪	Offences against Socialist Market Economic Order	1521	1661	4963	6632
侵犯公民人身权利、民主权利罪	Offences against Citizens' Personal and Democratic Rights	1945	2087	1964	2118
侵犯财产罪	Offences against Properties	4350	4502	4307	5265
妨害社会管理秩序罪	Offences against Social Management of Order	3276	3392	2776	3829
贪污贿赂罪	Offences on Corruption and Bribery	313	264	246	286
渎职罪	Offences on Dereliction of Duty	9	17	22	23

注：法院刑事案件收结案为一审审结数。
资料来源：北京市高级人民法院。
Note: The statistics on criminal cases accepted and settled by courts refer to the number of concluded cases at the first trial.
Source: The High People's Court of Beijing Municipality.

23–9 法院婚姻家庭、继承纠纷案件收、结案情况(2023年)
STATISTICS ON CASES OF DISPUTES OF MARRIAGE, FAMILY AND INHERITANCE ACCEPTED AND SETTLED BY COURTS (2023)

单位：件 (case)

项目	Item	收案 Cases Accepted	结案 Cases Settled	#判决 Judgment	#调解 Mediation
合计	**Total**	**41699**	**42301**	**13164**	**17890**
婚姻家庭纠纷	**Disputes of Marriage and Family**	**25024**	**26019**	**9142**	**9402**
离婚	Divorces	15153	15950	5352	6375
同居关系	Cohabitation	175	205	87	49
抚养纠纷	Upbringing Disputes	2560	2494	1077	801
扶养纠纷	Maintenance Disputes	57	47	22	6
赡养纠纷	Support Disputes	779	823	409	154
分家析产	Family Property Division	3068	3205	916	1229
其他	Others	3232	3295	1279	788
继承纠纷	**Inheritance Disputes**	**15812**	**15055**	**3726**	**7807**
继承	Inheritance	4610	4287	1094	2248
法定继承	Legal Inheritance	8504	8183	1585	4677
遗嘱继承	Testamentary Inheritance	1870	1767	688	696
其他	Others	828	818	359	186
婚姻家庭、继承纠纷	**Marriage and Family, and Inheritance Disputes**	**863**	**1227**	**296**	**681**

注：法院婚姻家庭、继承纠纷案件收、结案为一审审结案数。
资料来源：北京市高级人民法院。
Note: The statistics on cases of disputes of marriage, family and inheritance accepted and settled by courts refer to the number of concluded cases at the first trial.
Source: The High People's Court of Beijing Municipality.

23-10 法院合同纠纷案件收、结案情况(2023年)
STATISTICS ON CASES OF CONTRACT DISPUTES ACCEPTED AND SETTLED BY COURTS (2023)

单位：件 (case)

项　　目	Item	收　案 Cases Accepted	结　案 Cases Settled	#判　决 Judgment	#调　解 Mediation
合　　计	**Total**	**261235**	**269435**	**127530**	**43858**
买卖合同纠纷	Trade Contracts	36692	36056	14301	7658
房地产开发经营合同纠纷	Real Estate Development & Operation Contracts	39	33	15	2
供电、水、气、热力合同纠纷	Electricity, Water, Gas, Heat Supply Contracts	4618	5122	1251	525
借款合同纠纷	Loan Contracts	53354	54917	32737	9060
租赁合同纠纷	Lease Contracts	26309	26752	12596	4656
建设工程合同纠纷	Construction Contracts	10943	11178	5026	2217
承揽合同纠纷	Contracts for Hire of Work	3882	3740	1583	819
运输合同纠纷	Transportation Contracts	1094	1124	508	186
土地承包经营权合同纠纷	Contracts for the Right to Land Contracting and Management	610	664	330	62
劳务合同纠纷	Labor Contracts	9448	9626	3700	2277
服务合同纠纷	Service Contracts	36523	36488	14530	5277
其　他	Others	77723	83735	40953	11119

注：法院合同纠纷案件收结案为一审审结数。
资料来源：北京市高级人民法院。
Note: The statistics on cases of contract disputes accepted and settled by courts refer to the number of concluded cases at the first trial.
Source: The High People's Court of Beijing Municipality.

23-11 法院权属、侵权纠纷及其他民事案件收、结案情况(2023年)
STATISTICS ON CASES OF OWNERSHIP, TORTIOUS DISPUTES AND OTHER CIVIL CASES ACCEPTED AND SETTLED BY COURTS (2023)

单位：件 (case)

项目	Item	收案 Cases Accepted	结案 Cases Settled	#判决 Judgment	#调解 Mediation
合计	**Total**	**130831**	**137163**	**64287**	**18110**
所有权纠纷	Ownership Disputes	3349	3471	1392	680
票据纠纷	Disputes on Bills	1920	2610	1577	289
证券纠纷	Disputes on Securities	1993	2188	83	7
与公司有关的纠纷	Disputes Relating to Companies	5879	5510	2821	417
不正当竞争纠纷	Unfair Competition Disputes	721	847	317	90
人格权纠纷	Personality Disputes	5343	5723	3260	801
侵权责任纠纷	Tort Liability Disputes	27315	28188	14843	4794
适用特别程序案件(一级案由)	Special-proceeding Cases (Primary Cause of Action)	6857	6266	3658	63
其他	Others	77454	82360	36336	10969

注：法院权属、侵权纠纷及其他民事案件收、结案为一审审结数。
资料来源：北京市高级人民法院。
Note: The statistics on cases of ownership, tort disputes and other civil cases accepted and settled by courts refer to the number of concluded cases at the first trial.
Source: The High People's Court of Beijing Municipality.

23-12 离婚、青少年刑事案犯情况
STATISTICS ON DIVORCE CASES AND JUVENILE CRIMINAL OFFENDERS

项目	Item	2023	2022
婚姻家庭纠纷案件数(结案) (件)	Cases of Marriage and Family Disputes(Settled) (case)	26019	22341
#离婚案件数	Divorce Cases	15950	14042
#调离案件数	Cases of Divorce Reconciled	6375	5101
判离案件数	Cases of Divorce Judged	2750	2361
青少年罪犯人数 (人)	Number of Juvenile Offenders (person)	1931	1765
14周岁以上不满16周岁罪犯人数	Juvenile Offenders Between 14 and 16	11	8
16周岁以上不满18周岁罪犯人数	Juvenile Offenders Between 16 and 18	94	76
18周岁以上不满25周岁罪犯人数	Juvenile Offenders Between 18 and 25	1826	1681
青少年刑事案犯占全部刑事案犯的比重 (%)	Proportion of Juvenile Criminal Offenders in the Total Number of Criminal Offenders (%)	9.5	10.9

注：婚姻家庭纠纷案件数为一审审结数。
资料来源：北京市高级人民法院。
Note: The statistics on cases of marriage and family disputes refer to the number of concluded cases at the first trial.
Source: The High People's Court of Beijing Municipality.

23－13 律师工作
LAWYERS

项　目		Item		2023	2022	2023年为2022年% 2023 as % of 2022
律师事务所	（个）	Number of Law Firms	(unit)	3391	3297	102.9
执业律师	（人）	Number of Practicing Lawyers	(person)	52859	46971	112.5
专职律师		Full-time Lawyers		45458	42057	108.1
兼职律师		Part-time Lawyers		958	2132	44.9
公司律师		Company Lawyers		2857	1049	272.4
公职律师		Government Lawyers		2964	1733	171.0
法律援助律师		Legal Aid Lawyers		622		
担任法律顾问	（家）	Number of Units with Legal Advisors	(unit)	34530	33217	104.0
民事诉讼代理	（件）	Agent of Civil Litigations	(case)	200657	142721	140.6
行政诉讼代理	（件）	Agent of Administrative Litigations	(case)	35911	27956	128.5
刑事诉讼辩护及代理	（件）	Agent and Defender of Criminal Litigations	(case)	24942	21994	113.4
非诉讼法律事务	（件）	Non-litigious Legal Affairs	(case)	152805	133671	114.3

资料来源：北京市司法局。
Source: Beijing Municipal Justice Bureau.

23－14 调解工作
MEDIATION

项　目		Item		2023	2022	2023年为2022年% 2023 as % of 2022
人民调解委员会个数	（个）	Number of People's Mediation Committees	(unit)	7869	7849	100.3
调解员人数	（万人）	Number of Mediators	(10000 persons)	4.1	4.2	97.8
调解各类纠纷件数	（万件）	Number of Disputes Mediated	(10000 cases)	25.1	20.7	121.1
#调解各类纠纷成功件数		Number of Disputes Mediated Successfully		15.0	10.7	139.6
人民调解组织排查纠纷	（次）	Disputes Investigated by People's Mediation Organization	(time)	314455	394195	79.8
预防纠纷	（件）	Disputes Prevented	(case)	8235	8648	95.2

资料来源：北京市司法局。
Source: Beijing Municipal Justice Bureau.

23-15 公证工作
NOTARIZATIONS

项　　目	Item	2023	2022	2023年为2022年% 2023 as % of 2022
公证机构个数 (个)	Number of Notary Offices (unit)	24	24	100.0
执业公证员人数 (人)	Number of Practicing Notaries (person)	444	429	103.5
总办证数 (件)	Number of Notarized Documents (case)	646620	526650	122.8
国内公证业务	Domestic Notarial Services	382028	351612	108.7
涉外公证业务	Foreign-Related Notarial Services	257718	170462	151.2
涉港澳公证业务	Hong Kong and Macao Affairs Related Notarial Services	4185	2731	153.2
涉台公证业务	Taiwan Affairs Related Notarial Services	2689	1845	145.7

资料来源：北京市司法局。
Source: Beijing Municipal Justice Bureau.

23-16 法律援助工作情况
STATISTICS ON LEGAL AID

项　　目	Item	2023	2022	2023年为2022年% 2023 as % of 2022
法律援助机构个数 (个)	Number of Legal Aid Agencies (unit)	17	17	100.0
法律援助机构人员数 (人)	Number of Personnel of Legal Aid Agencies (person)	104	110	94.5
承办民事法律援助案件数 (件)	Civil Cases Aided (case)	29963	23436	127.9
承办刑事法律援助案件数 (件)	Criminal Cases Aided (case)	6658	5359	124.2
承办行政法律援助案件数 (件)	Administrative Cases Aided (case)	144	56	257.1
法律援助机构接待咨询人次 (万人次)	Consultations Received by Legal Aid Agencies (10000 person-times)	240.8	189.5	127.1
得到法律援助机构援助的妇女人数 (人次)	Females Receiving Aids from Legal Aid Agencies (person-times)	11987	11820	101.4
得到法律援助机构援助的未成年人数 (人次)	Juveniles Receiving Aids from Legal Aid Agencies (person-times)	866	570	151.9

资料来源：北京市司法局。
Source: Beijing Municipal Justice Bureau.

23-17 司法鉴定工作情况
STATISTICS ON JUDICIAL APPRAISAL

项目	Item	2023	2022
司法鉴定机构个数 (个)	Number of Judicial Appraisal Organizations (unit)	93	90
司法鉴定人员数 (人)	Number of Judicial Appraisal Personnel (person)	1360	1172
司法鉴定业务量 (件)	Judicial Appraisal Cases Proceeded (case)	125597	104900

注：本表中司法鉴定机构数为北京市司法局审核登记的全部司法鉴定机构个数。
资料来源：北京市司法局。
Note: In the table, the number of judicial appraisal organizations is the number of all judicial appraisal organizations approved by and registered with Beijing Municipal Justice Bureau.
Source: Beijing Municipal Justice Bureau.

23-18 生产安全情况
STATISTICS ON PRODUCTION SAFETY

项目	Item	2023	2022
单位地区生产总值	Per Unit GDP	1.01	0.97
生产安全事故死亡率 (人/百亿元)	Death Rate of Production Safety Accidents (person/10 billion yuan)		
道路交通万车死亡率 (人/万辆)	Road Traffic Death Rate per 10 000 Vehicles (person/10000 vehicles)	1.32	1.48
食品安全	Food Safety	99.14	98.52
抽检合格率 (%)	Up-to-standard Rate of Spot Checks (%)		
药品抽验合格率 (%)	Up-to-standard Rate of Drug Spot Checks (%)	99.96	99.96

资料来源：北京市应急管理局、北京市公安局公安交通管理局、北京市市场监督管理局、北京市药品监督管理局。
Source: Beijing Emergency Management Bureau, Beijing Traffic Management Bureau, Beijing Municipal Market Regulation Administration, Beijing Municipal Medical Products Administration.

23-19 消防建设情况(1996-2023年)
STATISTICS ON FIRE PROTECTION CONSTRUCTION (1996-2023)

年 份 Year	消防站数 (支) Number of Fire Stations (unit)	消防站消防车辆数 (辆) Number of Fire-fighting Vehicles of Fire Station (unit)	企业专职消防队队数 (支) Number of Full-time Fire Brigades in Enterprises (unit)	企业专职消防队人数 (人) Number of Full-time Fire-fighters in Enterprises (person)
1996	36	180	101	1865
1997	38	190	104	1885
1998	41	210	108	1993
1999	44	236	120	2447
2000	47	259	120	2447
2001	50	266	120	2447
2002	52	296	112	2228
2003	56	303	112	2147
2004	57	381	120	2477
2005	57	342	120	2477
2006	64	357	109	2269
2007	69	401	109	2269
2008	77	558	109	2269
2009	86	572	109	2269
2010	91	664	109	2269
2011	98	604	87	1766
2012	107	670	76	1405
2013	122	735	76	1405
2014	125	799	76	1405
2015	134	858	78	1410
2016	143	916	65	1307
2017	145	924	65	1307
2018	211	1066	65	1307
2019	250	1177	65	1307
2020	270	1198	66	1040
2021	304	1272	66	1040
2022	377	1332	66	1040
2023	394	1353	67	1048

资料来源：2017年及以前数据来源于北京市公安局消防局，自2018年起数据来源于北京市消防救援总队。
Source: Data for and before 2017 were from Fire Department of Beijing Municipal Public Security Bureau. Data since 2018 are from Beijing Fire Rescue Corps.

23-20 火灾及损失
FIRE ACCIDENTS AND LOSSES

项目	Item	火灾起数(起) Fire Accidents (case)		直接经济损失(万元) Direct Economic Losses (10000 yuan)	
		2023	2022	2023	2022
火灾起数 (起)	**Fire Accidents (case)**	**5856**	**6846**	**13165.1**	**8290.7**
特别重大火灾	Extraordinarily Serious				
重大火灾	Serious	1		3841.4	
较大火灾	Big Fire	1	3	10.0	1748.1
一般火灾	Relatively Big Fire	5854	6843	9313.7	6542.6
起火原因	**Cause of Fire**				
电　气	Electricity and Gas	2411	2634	5704.7	3999.7
生产作业	Production Operation	165	171	4927.1	280.0
生活用火不慎	Carelessness in Fire Use	838	1071	489.7	2081.0
吸　烟	Smoking	589	667	234.8	245.5
玩　火	Fire Playing	34	34	17.3	4.9
自　燃	Spontaneous Combustion	49	68	92.1	83.9
雷　击	Thunderstroke	1	2	0.6	0.2
静　电	Static	2	2	0.9	0.3
放　火	Incendiarism	72	69	157.8	177.2
其　他	Others	1695	2128	1540.2	1418.0
受伤人数 (人)	**Number of Injuries (person)**	**155**	**106**		
死亡人数 (人)	**Number of Deaths (person)**	**89**	**62**		

资料来源：北京市消防救援总队。
Source: Beijing Fire Rescue Corps.

23-21 交通事故及损失
TRAFFIC ACCIDENTS AND LOSSES

项目	Item	2023	2022	2023年为2022年% 2023 as % of 2022
交通事故	**Traffic Accidents**			
交通事故发生数 (起)	Number of Traffic Accidents (case)	6468	5249	123.2
受伤人数 (人)	Number of Injuries (person)	5413	4087	132.4
死亡人数 (人)	Number of Deaths (person)	1001	1052	95.2
机动车事故	**Motor Vehicle Accidents**			
机动车事故发生数 (起)	Number of Motor Vehicle Accidents (case)	4884	3768	129.6
受伤人数 (人)	Number of Injuries (person)	3743	2698	138.7
死亡人数 (人)	Number of Deaths (person)	766	728	105.2
直接经济损失 (万元)	**Direct Economic Losses (10000 yuan)**	**3541.1**	**3171.6**	**111.6**
每万辆机动车死亡人数 (人)	**Number of Deaths Per 10000 Motor Vehicles (person)**	**1.32**	**1.48**	**89.2**

资料来源：北京市公安局公安交通管理局。
Source: Beijing Traffic Management Bureau.

23-22 社会保障相关待遇标准(1994-2023年)
LEVEL OF SOCIAL SECURITY BENEFITS (1994-2023)

单位：元/月 (yuan/month)

年份	Year	职工最低工资 Minimum Wages of Employed Persons	失业保险金最低标准 Minimum Unemployment Insurance	城乡最低生活保障标准 Minimum Living Allowance for Urban and Rural Residents
1994		210		
1995		240	174	
1996		270	189	170
1997		290	203	190
1998		310	217	200
1999年第一次	First-time in 1999	320	224	210
1999年第二次	Second-time in 1999	400	291	273
2000		412	300	280
2001		435	305	285
2002		465	326	290
2003		465	326	290
2004年第一次	First-time in 2004	495		
2004年第二次	Second-time in 2004	545	347	290
2005		580	382	300
2006		640	392	310
2007		730	422	330
2008		800	502	390
2009		800	562	410
2010		960	632	430
2011年第一次	First-time in 2011		752	
2011年第二次	Second-time in 2011	1160	782	500
2012		1260	842	520
2013		1400	892	580
2014		1560	1012	650
2015		1720	1122	710
2016		1890	1212	800
2017		2000	1292	900
2018		2120	1536	1000
2019		2200	1706	1100
2020		2200	1816	1170
2021		2320	2034	1245
2022		2320	2034	1320
2023		2420	2124	1395

注：表中2017年及以前"城乡最低生活保障标准"为"城市居民最低生活保障标准"数据。

资料来源：城乡最低生活保障标准由北京市民政局提供，其他资料由北京市人力资源和社会保障局提供。

Note: Data on minimum living allowance for urban and rural residents in and before 2017 in this table refer to the data of minimum living allowance for urban residents.

Source: Data on minimum living allowance for urban and rural residents are provided by Beijing Municipal Civil Affairs Bureau. the other data are provided by Beijing Municipal Human Resources and Social Security Bureau.

23-23 参加社会保障情况(1995-2023年)

单位：万人

年　份 Year	参加企业职工基本养老保险人数 Participants of Basic Endowment Insurance for Enterprise Employed Persons	参加职工基本医疗保险人数 Participants of Basic Medical Insurance for Employed Persons	参加失业保险人数 Participants of Unemployment Insurance	参加工伤保险人数 Participants of Work-related Injury Insurance	参加生育保险人数 Participants of Birth Insurance
1995	261.1		219.8		
1996	252.0		214.5		
1997	264.3		214.0		
1998	359.2		222.9		
1999	379.0		289.0		
2000	391.6		287.8	212.0	
2001	425.9	210.2	287.2	212.7	
2002	436.2	353.8	299.5	221.0	
2003	448.5	436.1	306.6	242.9	
2004	460.0	484.0	308.0	259.0	
2005	520.0	574.8	394.6	328.9	226.1
2006	604.1	679.5	482.2	465.3	263.3
2007	671.7	783.0	535.3	609.2	290.6
2008	758.1	871.0	614.3	666.5	324.1
2009	827.7	938.4	675.7	747.1	346.8
2010	982.5	1063.7	774.2	823.8	372.2
2011	1091.9	1188.0	881.0	862.4	395.3
2012	1206.4	1279.7	1006.7	897.2	844.7
2013	1311.3	1354.8	1025.1	920.3	883.2
2014	1392.6	1431.3	1057.1	961.0	915.6
2015	1424.2	1475.7	1082.3	1020.1	941.6
2016	1459.1	1517.6	1117.5	1060.2	981.0
2017	1514.3	1569.2	1170.2	1117.9	1035.2
2018	1591.5	1628.9	1240.7	1187.0	1104.0
2019	1651.6	1682.5	1294.8	1242.2	1164.4
2020	1679.9	1741.6	1318.4	1267.2	1341.1
2021	1725.1	1486.0	1359.0	1307.2	1082.7
2022	1764.7	1499.4	1391.4	1337.0	1077.5
2023	1801.5	1504.7	1418.4	1363.9	1070.8

注：1.自2001年起设置基本医疗保险指标，以前年份为大病统筹，2000年参加大病统筹人数为232.6万人。
　　2.参加城乡居民基本医疗保险人数2017年及以前数据为参加城镇居民基本医疗保险人数。
　　3.自2006年起，农村居民最低生活保障人数不含农村五保供养人员。
　　4.自2021年9月起，"参加职工基本医疗保险人数"统计口径进行调整，去除6个月及以上未缴费人员，按调整后口径计算，2020年参加职工基本医疗保险人数为1450.7万人。历史年份数据未按新口径进行调整。

资料来源：城市居民最低生活保障人数和农村居民最低生活保障人数来源于北京市民政局，其他资料来源于北京市人力资源和社会保障局、北京市医疗保障局。

STATISTICS ON SOCIAL SECURITY PARTICIPATION (1995-2023)

(10000 persons)

参加城乡居民基本养老保障人数 Participants of Basic Endowment Security for Urban and Rural Residents	参加城乡居民基本医疗保险人数 Participants of Basic Medical Insurance for Urban and Rural Residents	参加新型农村合作医疗人数 Participants of New-type Rural Cooperative Medical Care	城市居民最低生活保障人数 Number of Residents Receiving Minimum Living Allowance in Urban Areas	农村居民最低生活保障人数 Number of Residents Receiving Minimum Living Allowance in Rural Areas
			0.9	
			0.9	
			2.8	
			4.3	1.2
			6.7	1.6
			7.8	1.8
			12.0	5.4
			16.1	6.7
		234.0	16.1	7.5
		250.4	15.5	7.8
		261.0	15.2	7.1
		268.5	14.8	7.8
		272.5	14.5	7.9
		274.9	14.7	8.0
	143.7	278.5	13.7	7.7
	159.8	276.8	11.7	7.0
	151.9	267.5	11.0	6.3
	160.1	254.4	10.4	6.0
	173.0	242.6	8.9	5.1
	181.0	223.9	8.5	4.9
215.7	191.2	211.9	8.2	4.7
213.1	202.2	186.9	7.8	4.4
209.0	392.2		6.7	3.8
204.7	400.1		6.5	3.8
200.4	398.3		7.0	4.0
192.4	400.8		7.1	3.9
187.5	404.3		7.0	3.7
180.3	403.9		6.9	3.5

Note: a) The basic medical insurance indicator was set from 2001. Before that it was called general healthcare program for major diseases which cover 2.326 million people in 2000.

b) Figures on participants of basic medical insurance for urban and rural residents in and before 2017 referred to that of participants of basic medical insurance for urban residents, the same below.

c) Figures on residents receiving minimum living allowance in rural areas have excluded the rural persons enjoying five guarantees since 2006.

d) Since September 2021, the statistical coverage of the "participants of basic medical insurance for employed persons" has been adjusted and those who failed to make payment for 6 months or more have been excluded. Calculated according to the adjusted coverage, the participants of basic medical insurance for employed persons totaled 14.507 million in 2020. Data for the previous years have not been adjusted according to the new caliber.

Source: Figures on residents receiving minimum living allowance in urban areas and residents receiving minimum living allowance in rural areas are from Beijing Municipal Civil Affairs Bureau; the other data are from Beijing Municipal Human Resources and Social Security Bureau and Beijing Municipal Medical Insurance Bureau.

23-24 城镇职工参加社会保险情况(2023年)
STATISTICS ON PARTICIPATION OF SOCIAL INSURANCE BY URBAN WORKERS (2023)

项目	Item	参加企业职工基本养老保险 Participation of Basic Endowment Insurance for Enterprise Employed Persons		参加职工基本医疗保险 Participation of Basic Medical Insurance for Employed Persons	
		单位个数(个) Number of Entities (unit)	人数(人) Number of Persons (person)	单位个数(个) Number of Entities (unit)	人数(人) Number of Persons (person)
合　计	**Total**	**874088**	**18014990**	**816388**	**15046774**
按登记注册统计类别分	**By Statistical Category of Registration**				
国　有	State-owned	5879	1145441	5855	991499
集　体	Collective-owned	5105	178781	4185	150925
其　他	Others	863104	16690768	806348	13904350
按隶属关系划分	**By Affiliation**				
中央单位	Central	6992	1577823	6865	1289393
地方单位	Local	867096	16437167	809523	13757381

资料来源：北京市人力资源和社会保障局、北京市医疗保障局。
Source: Beijing Municipal Human Resources and Social Security Bureau, Beijing Municipal Medical Insurance Bureau.

23-24 续表 Continued

项目	Item	参加失业保险 Unemployment Insurance		参加工伤保险 Industrial Injury Insurance		参加生育保险 Maternity Insurance	
		单位个数(个) Number of Entities (unit)	人数(人) Number of Persons (person)	单位个数(个) Number of Entities (unit)	人数(人) Number of Persons (person)	单位个数(个) Number of Entities (unit)	人数(人) Number of Persons (person)
合　计	**Total**	**864862**	**14183684**	**864730**	**13638687**	**799890**	**10707719**
按登记注册统计类别分	**By Statistical Category of Registration**						
国　有	State-owned	17023	2011543	17973	2079000	5134	819865
集　体	Collectively-owned	4106	92087	4252	91451	3281	82266
其　他	Others	843733	12080054	842505	11468236	791475	9805588
按隶属关系划分	**By Affiliation**						
中央单位	Central	6575	1460337	6707	1409882	6288	1087355
地方单位	Local	858287	12723347	858023	12228805	793602	9620364

资料来源：北京市人力资源和社会保障局、北京市医疗保障局。
Source: Beijing Municipal Human Resources and Social Security Bureau, Beijing Municipal Medical Insurance Bureau.

23−25 城乡居民参加社会保险情况(2010−2023年)

STATISTICS ON PARTICIPATION OF SOCIAL INSURANCE BY URBAN AND RURAL RESIDENTS (2010-2023)

单位：万人 (10000 persons)

年 份 Year	参加城乡居民基本养老保障人数 Participants of Basic Endowment Security for Urban and Rural Residents	参加城乡居民基本医疗保险人数 Participants of Basic Medical Insurance for Urban and Rural Residents	学生儿童 Students and Children	城乡老年人 Urban and Rural Senior Citizens	劳动年龄内居民 Residents of Labor Age
2010		143.7	121.3	17.7	4.7
2011		159.8	135.5	19.1	5.3
2012		151.9	128.6	18.5	4.8
2013		160.1	137.5	18.8	3.7
2014		173.0	149.8	19.7	3.6
2015		181.0	157.7	19.8	3.4
2016	215.7	191.2	168.0	19.9	3.3
2017	213.1	202.2	179.2	19.9	3.2
2018	209.0	392.2	221.9	111.8	58.6
2019	204.7	400.1	232.5	114.3	53.3
2020	200.4	398.3	239.2	112.3	46.8
2021	192.4	400.8	246.1	110.3	44.4
2022	187.5	404.3	254.6	111.5	38.2
2023	180.3	403.9	259.7	111.0	33.2

注：2017年及以前“参加城乡居民基本医疗保险人数”为“参加城镇居民基本医疗保险人数”数据。

资料来源：北京市人力资源和社会保障局、北京市医疗保障局。

Note: Figures on "participants of basic medical insurance for urban and rural residents" in and before 2017 referred to "participants of basic medical insurance for urban residents".

Source: Beijing Municipal Human Resources and Social Security Bureau, Beijing Municipal Medical Insurance Bureau.

23−26 妇联组织状况

STATISTICS ON WOMEN'S FEDERATION AND ORGANIZATIONS

项 目	Item	2023	2022	2023年为2022年% 2023 as % of 2022
妇联组织数 （个）	**Number of Women's Federations and Organizations (unit)**			
区妇联数	Number of Women's Federations in Districts	16	16	100.0
乡、镇妇联组织数	Number of Women's Federations in Townships and Towns	177	177	100.0
街道妇联组织数	Number of Women's Federations in Sub-districts	163	163	100.0
社区妇联组织数	Number of Women's Federations in Communities	3482	3404	102.3
村妇联组织数	Number of Women's Federations in Villages	3602	3602	100.0
妇联干部人数 （人）	**Number of Cadres in Women's Federation (person)**			
区妇联干部数	Cadres in Women's Federations in Districts	325	317	102.5
乡、镇、街道妇联干部数	Cadres in Women's Federations in Townships, Towns and Sub-districts	680	680	100.0
各类妇女联谊组织数（个）	**Number of Women's Sodalities (unit)**	**38**	**38**	**100.0**

资料来源：北京市妇女联合会。

Source: Beijing Women's Federation.

23-27 工会组织建设情况(2023年)
STATISTICS ON TRADE UNIONS (2023)

项　　目	Item	基层工会组织(个) Grassroot Trade Unions (unit)	职工人数(人) Staff and Workers (person)	会员人数(人) Membership (person)
合　　计	**Total**	**32266**	**7215898**	**5607045**
按单位类别划分	**By Unit Category**			
国有企业	State-owned Enterprises	940	453350	406673
集体企业	Collective-owned Enterprises	1245	146901	129016
股份合作企业	Cooperative Enterprises	322	34791	32813
联营企业	Joint Ownership Enterprises	31	5980	5893
国有独资公司	State Sole-proprietorship Enterprises	784	311742	301751
其他有限责任公司	Other Limited-Liability Corporations	12270	1957164	1298155
国有控股公司	State-holding Companies	343	253203	244942
其他股份有限公司	Other Share-holing Corporations Ltd.	990	215590	189927
私营企业	Private Enterprises	4643	785884	545205
其他内资企业	Other Domestic Invested Enterprises	60	19228	10620
港澳台商投资企业	Enterprises with Investment from Hong Kong, Macao and Taiwan	456	128052	96504
外商投资企业	Foreign Invested Enterprises	863	303584	270894
事业单位	Public Institutions	682	526176	299922
机关	Governmental Agencies	1623	601953	580448
其他	Other	7014	1472300	1194282
按系统分	**By System**			
工业国防工会	Trade Unions for Industry and National Defence	693	264788	254522
工　业	Industry	679	257975	247744
国　防	National Defence	14	6813	6778
建筑工会	Trade Unions for Construction	476	509195	397021
服务业工会	Trade Unions for Services	647	250247	224701
交通运输工会	Trade Unions for Transportation	225	226233	225920
政法卫文工会	Trade Unions for Politics, Law, Health Care and Culture	255	132094	131144
教育工会	Trade Unions for Education	80	190728	183225
金融工会	Trade Unions for Finance	71	160693	159881
市直机关工会	Trade Unions for Institutions under Direct Municipal Leadership	386	57216	56749
区工会	Trade Unions in Districts	29433	5424704	3973882

资料来源：北京市总工会。
Source: Beijing Federation of Trade Unions.

23-28 北京市妇女发展规划监测统计资料
SUPERVISORY STATISTICS ON WOMEN DEVELOPMENT PROGRAMS OF BEIJING

项目	Item	2023	2022
参加职工基本养老保险人数 （万人）	Participants of Basic Endowment Insurance for Workers (10000 persons)	1906.9	1867.8
#女性	Females	871.5	855.6
参加职工基本医疗保险人数 （万人）	Participants of Basic Medical Insurance for Workers (10000 persons)	1504.7	1499.4
#女性	Females	708.4	712.5
参加失业保险人数 （万人）	Participants of Unemployment Insurance (10000 persons)	1418.4	1391.4
#女性	Females	621.0	610.0
参加工伤保险人数 （万人）	Participants of Work-related Injury Insurance (10000 persons)	1363.9	1337.0
#女性	Females	590.6	571.5
参加生育保险人数 （万人）	Participants of Birth Insurance (10000 persons)	1070.8	1077.5
#女性	Females	471.3	480.0
参加城乡居民养老保障人数 （万人）	Participants of Endowment Security for Urban and Rural Residents (10000 persons)	180.3	187.5
#女性	Females	100.0	103.7
市人大代表中女性比例 (%)	Percentage of Females in Deputies to Municipal People's Congress (%)	40.0	39.5
普通高中在校生中女生所占比例 (%)	Percentage of Female Students in Total Enrolment in Regular Senior Secondary Schools (%)	49.6	49.9
中等职业教育在校生中女生所占比例 (%)	Percentage of Female Students in Total Enrolment in Schools for Secondary Vocational Education (%)	42.9	42.5
高等职业本专科在校生中女生所占比例 (%)	Percentage of Female Students in Total Enrolment in Normal and Short-cycle Courses in Higher Vocational Education Institutions (%)	47.2	47.5
高等学校在校生中女生所占比例 (%)	Percentage of Female Students in Total Enrolment in Higher Education Institutions (%)	47.3	47.2
孕产妇系统服务率 (%)	Rate of Systematic Service for Pregnant and Lying-in Women (%)	99.5	99.4
宫颈癌人群筛查率 (%)	Screening Rate of Cervical Cancer Population (%)	59.5	51.5
乳腺癌人群筛查率 (%)	Screening Rate of Breast Cancer Population (%)	73.1	65.9
艾滋病母婴传播率 (%)	Mother-to-Child Transmission Rate of AIDS (%)		
开展婚姻家庭服务指导的婚姻登记机构比例 (%)	Proportion of Marriage Registration Agencies Providing Guidance on Marriage and Family Services (%)	100.0	100.0
法律援助妇女人数 （人）	Number of Women Receiving Legal Aid (person)	11987	10580

资料来源：北京市人力资源和社会保障局、北京市医疗保障局、北京市人民代表大会常务委员会、北京市教育委员会、北京市卫生健康委员会、北京市民政局、北京市司法局。

Source: Beijing Municipal Human Resources and Social Security Bureau, Beijing Municipal Medical Insurance Bureau, The Standing Committee of Beijing Municipal People's Congress, Beijing Municipal Education Commission, Beijing Municipal Health Commission, Beijing Municipal Civil Affairs Bureau, Beijing Municipal Justice Bureau.

23-29 北京市儿童发展规划监测统计资料
SUPERVISORY STATISTICS ON CHILDREN DEVELOPMENT PROGRAMS OF BEIJING

项　　目	Item	2023	2022
孕前优生健康检查目标人群覆盖率 (%)	Coverage Rate of Target Population for Pre-pregnancy Eugenic Checkups (%)	100.00	97.33
产前筛查率 (%)	Prenatal Screening Rate (%)	95.64	93.39
新生儿死亡率 (‰)	Neonatal Mortality Rate (‰)	0.91	0.67
婴儿死亡率 (‰)	Infant Mortality Rate (‰)	1.50	1.26
5岁以下儿童死亡率 (‰)	Mortality Rate of Children under 5 (‰)	2.03	1.93
3岁以下儿童系统服务率 (%)	Rate of Systematic Service for Children under 3 (%)	96.96	96.66
7岁以下儿童健康服务率 (%)	Rate of Health Service for Children under 7 (%)	99.37	99.24
5岁以下儿童肥胖率 (%)	Obesity Rate of Children under 5 (%)	3.26	3.29
5岁以下儿童超重率 (%)	Overweight Rate of Children under 5 (%)	10.73	11.25
5岁儿童乳牙龋患率 (%)	Rate of Deciduous Tooth Caries for Children of 5 Years Old (%)		58.50
0-6岁儿童眼保健和视力检查覆盖率 (%)	Coverage Rate of Eye Care and Optic Examination for Children of 0-6 Years (%)	99.25	98.91
卡介苗疫苗接种率 (%)	Rate of Inoculation of BCG Vaccines (%)	99.54	99.01
脊髓灰质炎疫苗接种率 (%)	Rate of Inoculation of Poliomyelitis Polio Vaccines (%)	99.98	99.98
百白破疫苗接种率 (%)	Rate of Inoculation of Pertussis, Diphtheria and Tetanus Vaccines (%)	99.99	99.97
含麻疹成分疫苗接种率 (%)	Rate of Inoculation of Vaccines with Measle Ingredients (%)	99.99	99.90
普惠性幼儿园覆盖率 (%)	Coverage Rate of Inclusive Kindergartens (%)	93.00	91.00
少先队实践教育营地(基地)数量 (个)	Number of Practice Education Camps (Bases) for Young Pioneers (unit)	306	313
少年法庭数量 (个)	Number of Juvenile Courts (unit)	21	21

资料来源：北京市卫生健康委员会、北京市教育委员会、共青团北京市委员会、北京市高级人民法院。
Source: Beijing Municipal Health Commission, Beijing Municipal Education Commission, China Communist Youth League Beijing Committee, The High People's Court of Beijing Municipality.

主要统计指标解释

参加职工基本养老保险人数 指报告期末按照国家法律、法规和有关政策规定参加企业职工基本养老保险并在社保经办机构已建立缴费记录档案的职工人数，包括中断缴费但未终止养老保险关系的职工人数和参加基本养老保险的离休、退休和退职人员的人数。不包括只登记未建立缴费记录档案的人数。

参加职工基本医疗保险人数 指报告期末按国家有关规定参加基本医疗保险的人数。包括参加保险的职工人数和退休人员数。

参加失业保险人数 指报告期末按照国家法律、法规和有关政策规定参加了失业保险的城镇企业事业单位的职工及地方政府规定参加失业保险的其他人员的人数。参加失业保险人数为参加失业保险的职工人数。

参加工伤保险人数 指报告期末参加工伤保险的职工人数。

参加生育保险人数 指报告期末参加生育保险的职工人数。

参加农村新型合作医疗人数 指截止报告期末乡镇已参加农村新型合作医疗的总人数。农村新型合作医疗制度是由政府组织、引导、支持，农民自愿参加，集体、个人和政府多方筹资，以大病统筹为主的农民医疗互助共济制度。

城市居民最低生活保障人数 指报告期末家庭平均收入在当地规定的最低生活保障线以下的城镇居民数。包括“三无”对象、失业人员和在职、下岗、退休人员等。

农村居民最低生活保障人数 指报告期末在建立农村最低生活保障制度的地区，得到当地政府或集体给予最低生活保障的农业人口家庭人数。

律师 指受聘参加律师事务所工作，提任法律顾问、刑（民）事代理人、刑事辩护人，办理非诉讼事件、解答法律询问，代写法律事务文书等主要从事律师业务的专职法律工作者和兼职律师。

公证人员 指在国家公证机关依法办理公证事务的司法人员。包括公证员、助理公证员和在公证处工作的其他人员。

调解人员 指人民调解委员会担负调解民间一般民事纠纷和轻微违法行为所引起的纠纷的工作人员。包括调解委员会的委员和调解小组调解员。

参加城乡居民养老保障人数 指报告期末参加城乡居民养老保险和享受老年保障福利养老金的人数合计。

市人大代表中女性比例 每一届当选的市人大代表中女代表中所占比例。

普通高中在校生中女生所占比例 指普通高中中具有学籍并在本学年初进行学籍注册的学生数中女生人数占总学生数的比例。

中等职业教育在校生中女生所占比例 指具有中等职业教育学籍并在本学年初进行学籍注册的学生总数中女生所占比例。

高等职业本专科在校生中女生所占比例 指具有高等职业教育本专科学籍并在本学年初进行学籍注册的学生总数中女生所占比例。

高等学校在校生中女生所占比例 指高等学校中具有高等职业本专科、普通本科、研究生、成人本专科、网络本专科学籍并在本学年初进行学籍注册的学生总数中女生所占比例。

孕产妇系统服务率 指年内孕产妇系统管理人数与活产数之比。

宫颈癌人群筛查率 指适龄妇女(35—64岁)中接受宫颈癌筛查的妇女所占比例。

乳腺癌人群筛查率 指适龄妇女(35—64岁)中接受乳腺癌筛查的妇女所占比例。

艾滋病母婴传播率 指艾滋病病毒(HIV)感染孕产妇所生儿童中因母婴传播途径感染的人数所占的比例。

开展婚姻家庭服务指导的婚姻登记机构比例 指在婚姻登记机构中，开展了婚姻家庭服务指导相关业务的婚姻登记机构所占比例。

法律援助妇女人数 指年满 14 周岁及以上女性公民年内获得法律援助机构组织提供的法律援助案件辩护、代理等服务的人次。

孕前优生健康检查目标人群覆盖率 指年内孕前优生检查总人数与计划怀孕夫妇人数之比。适用范围是孕前优生健康检查目标人群。

产前筛查率 指年内孕产妇产前筛查人数与产妇数之比。

新生儿死亡率 指年内出生至 28 天内(0—27 天)死亡的新生儿人数与活产数之比。

婴儿死亡率 指年内不满 1 周岁的婴儿死亡人数与活产数之比。

5岁以下儿童死亡率 指年内不满5周岁的儿童死亡人数与活产数之比。

3 岁以下儿童系统服务率 指该统计年度内 3 岁以下儿童在本年度内按年龄要求接受生长监测或4:2:2 体格检查（身高和体重等）的总人数与某年某地 3 岁以下儿童数之比。

7岁以下儿童健康服务率 指该统计年度内7岁以下儿童接受 1 次及以上体格检查（身高和体重等）的总人数与某年某地 7 岁以下儿童数之比。

5 岁以下儿童肥胖率 对照 WHO 标准的身高（长）别体重参考值，计算 5 岁以下儿童在该统计年度内至少有一次测量身高（长）别体重大于或等于同年龄标准人群身高（长）别体重中位数加 2 个标准差的人数与其年某地 5 岁以下健康管理人数之比。

5 岁以下儿童超重率 对照 WHO 标准的身高（长）别体重参考值，计算 5 岁以下儿童在该统计年度内至少有一次测量身高（长）别体重大于或等于同年龄标准人群身高（长）别体重中位数加 1 个标准差，且小于同年龄标准人群身高（长）别体重中位数加 2 个标准差的人数与某年某地 5 岁以下健康管理人数之比。

5 岁儿童乳牙龋患率 指 5 岁儿童根据乳牙龋坏牙数（dt）计算的患龋人数占总受检人数的百分率。参照国家第四次口腔健康流行病学调查方法完成抽样和现场调查。

0—6 岁儿童眼保健和视力检查覆盖率 指年内 0—6 岁儿童眼保健和视力检查人数占 0—6 岁儿童的百分比。

纳入国家免疫规划的疫苗接种率 指年内实际接种某国家免疫规划疫苗（某剂次）人数占应接种该国家免疫规划疫苗（该剂次）人数的百分比。

普惠性幼儿园覆盖率 指公办幼儿园和普惠性民办幼儿园（班）在园（班）幼儿数占在园（班）幼儿总数的百分比。

少先队实践教育营地（基地）数量 指街道（社区）、乡镇（村）少先队组织利用辖区内的各类党群阵地、文化场馆、社会资源建设的少先队校外实践教育营地（基地）数量。

少年法庭数量 指人民法院为维护未成年人合法权益、预防矫治未成年人犯罪而建立的少年法庭数量。

Explanatory Notes on Main Statistical Indicators

Number of People Participating in Basic Pension Insurance for Employed Persons refers to the number of employed persons participating in basic pension insurance for enterprise employed persons and keeping insurance premium payment records with social security organizations in accordance with provisions in national laws, rules and relevant policies at the end of reporting period, including the number of employed persons suspending the payment of insurance premium without terminating the pension insurance relation as well as retired employed persons participating in basic endowment insurance, excluding the number of persons only registered but having no insurance premium payment records.

Number of People Participating in Basic Medical Insurance for Employed Persons refers to the number of persons participating in basic medical insurance programs at the end of the reporting period in accordance with relevant national regulations, including the number of employed persons and retired persons participating in the insurance.

Number of People Participating in Unemployment Insurance refers to the number of employed persons in urban enterprises and public institutions participating in unemployment insurance programs at the end of the reporting period in accordance with provisions in national laws, rules and relevant policies, as well as other persons specified by local governments to participate in unemployment insurance. The number of people participating in unemployment insurance program is the number of employees employed persons who participate in unemployment insurance.

Number of People Participating in Work-related Injury Insurance refers to the number of employed persons participating in work-related injury insurance programs at the end of the reporting period.

Number of People Participating in Maternity Insurance refers to the number of employed persons participating in maternity insurance programs at the end of the reporting period.

Number of People Participating in New-type Rural Cooperative Medical Care refers to the total number of rural residents who have participated in the new-type rural cooperative medical care programs at the end of the reporting period. The new-type rural medical care system is a system of mutual aid in medical care for rural residents that is organized, guided and supported by the government, in which the rural residents voluntarily participate. It is a system of multi-party financing by collective entities, individuals and the government, and is mainly based on social pooling for serious disease.

Number of Residents Receiving Subsistence Allowances in Urban Areas refers to the number of urban residents whose average family income is below locally provided minimum living standard at the end of the reporting period, including elderly persons, minors, psychotic patients and disables who have no statutory guardian, no fixed pocketbook, no labor ability, unemployed persons, on-the-job persons, laid-off persons, and retired persons, etc.

Number of Residents Receiving Subsistence Allowances in Rural Areas refers to the number of persons in agricultural families covered by subsistence allowances of local government or collective entities in an area where rural minimum living standard guarantee system is established, at the end of reporting period.

Lawyer refers to a full-time legal worker and part-time lawyer joining a law firm, serving as a legal consultant, criminal (civil) proxy, criminal counsel, handling non-lawsuit events, answering legal questions, writing legal documents for others, and other lawyer business.

Notary refers to any judicial person handling notarization matters in national notarization agencies according to laws, including notaries, assistant notaries, and other personnel working in notarization offices.

Mediator refers to working personnel responsible for mediating general civil disputes as well as disputes caused by slightly illegal acts in any people's mediation committee, including members of people's mediation committees and mediators of mediation teams.

Number of People Participating in Pension Security for Urban and Rural Residents refers to total number of people participating in pension insurance for urban and rural residents and enjoying old age security benefit pension at the end of the reporting period.

Share of Females in Deputies to Municipal People's Congress refers to the share of female deputies in the elected deputies to the Municipal People's Congress of each session.

Share of Female Students in Total Enrollment in Regular Senior Secondary Schools refers to the share of female students in the total number of enrolled students in regular senior secondary schools who have student status and have registered their student status at the beginning of this academic year.

Share of Female Students in Total Enrollment in Schools for Secondary Vocational Education refers to the share of female students in the total number of enrolled students who have the student status for secondary vocational education and have registered their student status at the beginning of this academic year.

Share of Female Students in Total Enrollment of Undergraduates and Junior College Students in Higher Vocational Schools refers to the share of female students in the total number of enrolled students who have the student status for undergraduates and junior college students for higher vocational education and have registered their student status at the beginning of this academic year.

Share of Female Students in Total Enrollment in Institutions of Higher Education refers to the share of female students in total number of enrolled students in institutions of higher education who have the student status for higher vocational undergraduates and junior college students, general undergraduates, postgraduates, adult undergraduates and junior college students, or undergraduates and junior college students enrolled in Internet-based courses, and have registered their student status at the beginning of this academic year.

Rate of Systematic Service for Pregnant and Lying-in Women refers to the ratio of the number of people under the management of the system for pregnant and lying-in women to the number of live births in the year.

Screening Rate of Cervical Cancer Population refers to the proportion of women undergoing cervical cancer screening in the women of appropriate age (aged between 35 and 64 years old).

Screening Rate of Breast Cancer Population refers to the proportion of women undergoing breast cancer screening in the women of appropriate age (aged between 35 and 64 years old).

Mother-to-Child Transmission Rate of AIDS refers to the proportion of newborns infected due to mother-to-child transmission in the newborns given birth by the pregnant and lying-in women infected with HIV.

Share of Marriage Registration Agencies Providing Guidance on Marriage and Family Services refers to the proportion of marriage registration agencies carrying out marriage and family service guidance related service in the marriage registration agencies.

Number of Women Receiving Legal Aid refers to the person-times of legal aid case defense, representation and other services provided by legal aid organizations and received by female citizens aged 14 and above in the year.

Coverage Rate of Target Population for Pre-pregnancy Eugenic Checkups refers to the ratio of total number of couples having pre-pregnancy eugenic checkups to the total number of couples preparing for pregnancy in the year. The scope of application is the target population for pre-pregnancy eugenic checkups.

Prenatal Screening Rate refers to the ratio of number of pregnant and lying-in women undergoing prenatal screening to the total number of lying-in women in the year.

Neonatal Mortality Rate refers to the ratio of the number of newborns who die within 28 days (0-27 days) after birth to the number of live births in the year.

Mortality Rate of Infants refers to the ratio of deaths of infants under one year old to the number of live births in the year.

Mortality Rate of Children Under 5 Years Old refers to the ratio of deaths of children under 5 years old to the number of live births in the year.

Rate of Systematic Service for Children Under 3 Years Old refers to the ratio of the total number of children under 3 years old who have undergone growth monitoring or a 4:2:2 physical examination (height and weight, etc.) required by age during the statistical year to the number of children under 3 years old in a given year and a given area, within the statistical year.

Rate of Health Service for Children Under 7 Years Old refers to the ratio of the total number of children under 7 years old who have undergone physical examination (height and weight, etc.) for one or more times during this statistical year to the number of children under 7 years old in a given year and a given area.

Obesity Rate of Children Under 5 Years Old refers to the ratio of the number of children under 5 years old who have a measured weight for height (length) that is greater than or equal to the median of standard weight for height (length) of children of the same age plus 2 standard deviations, for at least one time during the statistical year, to the number of children under 5 years old with healthy weight management in a given year and a given area, calculated by reference to the standard reference value of weight for height (length) of WHO.

Overweight Rate of Children Under 5 Years Old refers to the ratio of the number of children under 5 years old who have a measured weight for height (length) that is greater than or equal to the median of standard weight for height (length) of children of the same age plus 1 standard deviation and is less than the median of standard weight for height (length) of children of the same age plus 2 standard deviations, for at least one time during the statistical year, to the number of children under 5 years old with healthy weight management in a given year and a given area, calculated by reference to the standard reference value of weight for height (length) of WHO.

Rate of Deciduous Tooth Caries for Children of 5 Years Old refers to the percentage of children of 5 years old with caries calculated in terms of the number of decayed deciduous tooth (dt) in the total number of children of 5 years old undergoing examination. Sampling survey and field survey are completed by reference to the methods of the fourth national oral health epidemiological survey.

Coverage Rate of Eye Care and Optic Examination for Children of 0-6 Years Old refers to the percentage of children of 0-6 years old undergoing eye care and optic examination in the total number of children of 0-6 years old in the year.

Rate of Inoculation of Vaccines Included in National Immunization Program refers to the percentage of people actually vaccinated against a national immunization program vaccine (a dose) in the number of people supposed to be vaccinated against the said national immunization program vaccine (the said dose) in the year.

Coverage Rate of Inclusive Kindergartens refers to the percentage of children enrollment in public kindergartens and inclusive private kindergartens (classes) in the total number of children enrollment in all kindergartens (classes).

Practice Education Camps (Bases) for Young Pioneers refer to the number of off-campus practice education camps (bases) for Young Pioneers built by sub-district (community), township (village) Young Pioneers Organization by making use of the positions of various party groups, cultural venues, and social resources within the jurisdiction.

Number of Juvenile Courts refers to the number of juvenile courts established by the people's courts to protect the legitimate rights and interests of minors, and prevent and correct minor crimes.

24

开发区
DEVELOPMENT ZONES

简要说明

一、主要内容

本章资料主要反映北京市开发区基本情况、招商、生产情况，重点介绍了北京经济技术开发区和中关村国家自主创新示范区的主要情况。

二、统计范围

根据 2012 年《国务院关于同意调整中关村国家自主创新示范区空间规模和布局的批复》，自 2013 年起，中关村国家自主创新示范区的统计范围在原有的海淀园、丰台园、昌平园、电子城科技园、亦庄园、德胜园、雍和园、石景山园、通州园和大兴生物医药产业基地的基础上，增加了平谷园、门头沟园、顺义园、房山园、密云园、怀柔园和延庆园七个园区。同时，“电子城科技园”更名为“朝阳园”；“德胜园”更名为“西城园”；“雍和园”更名为“东城园”。

2023 年中关村国家自主创新示范区统计范围调整为在中关村国家自主创新示范区内注册的规模(限额)以上六类企业法人单位,包括:1.证书在有效期内的国家高新技术企业；2.工业企业；3.应用高技术进行设计、施工以及技术装备的建筑业企业；4.符合国家统计局高技术服务业、科技服务业、生产性服务业目录的服务业企业；5.符合国家统计局文化及相关产业企业；6.境内外上市企业及新三版、地方四板挂牌企业。

北京首都国际机场临空经济区于2022年4月29日揭牌，由原北京天竺综合保税区和原北京临空经济核心区 2 个单位整合组建而成。

中关村国家自主创新示范区亦庄园在中关村国家自主创新示范区与北京经济技术开发区中为重叠部分。

Brief Introduction

I. Main Content

Statistics in this chapter mainly show the basic condition, attraction of investment and production of development zones in Beijing, the business invitation, capital contribution, investment, and production status. This chapter mainly focuses on the situation of Beijing Economic-Technological Development Area and Zhongguancun National Independent Innovation Demonstration Zone.

II. Scope of Statistics

According to the *Official Reply of the State Council on Approving the Adjustment of Spatial Scale and Layout of Zhongguancun National Innovation Demonstration Zone* issued in 2012, Since 2013, the statistical scope of Zhongguancun National Independent Innovation Demonstration Zone has been enlarged to include Pinggu Sub-park, Mentougou Sub-park, Shunyi Sub-park, Fangshan Sub-park, Miyun Sub-park, Huairou Sub-park and Yanqing Sub-park to supplement Haidian Sub-park, Fengtai Sub-park, Changping Sub-park, Electronic Science & Technology Park, Yizhuang Sub-park, Desheng Sub-park, Yonghe Sub-park, Shijingshan Sub-park, Tongzhou Sub-park and Daxing BioPharma Industry Base. At the same time, Electronic Science & Technology Park was renamed Chaoyang Sub-park, Deshengyuan Sub-park into Xicheng Sub-park and Yonghe Sub-park was renamed Dongcheng Sub-park.

The statistical scope of Zhongguancun National Independent Innovation Demonstration Zone was adjusted in 2023 to include six types of enterprises above designated size that were registered inside the Zhongguancun National Independent Innovation Demonstration Zone, including: 1. national high-tech enterprises with their certificates being within the validity period; 2. industrial enterprises; 3. construction enterprises that apply high technology for design, construction and technical equipment; 4. enterprises of the service sector that are in line with the catalogue of high-tech services, science and technology services and production services of the National Bureau of Statistics of China; 5. enterprises of cultural industry and related industries that meet the stipulations of the National Bureau of Statistics of China; 6. listed enterprises both at home and abroad as well as the NEEQ listed enterprises and the listed enterprises in regional equity trading market.

The Beijing Capital International Airport Economic Zone, integrating the two units of the former Beijing Tianzhu Free Trade Zone and the former Beijing Airport Economic Core Zone, was inaugurated on April 29, 2022.

Data of Zhongguancun Yizhuang Sub-park is counted in both Zhongguancun National Independent Innovation Demonstration Zone and Beijing Economic-Technological Development Area.

24-1 开发区基本情况(2023年)
BASIC STATISTICS ON DEVELOPMENT ZONES (2023)

项　目		Item		2023
开发区个数	(个)	Number of Development Zones	(unit)	3
区规划总面积	(公顷)	Total Planned Area of Development Zones	(hectare)	49448.6
总收入	(亿元)	Total Revenue	(100 million yuan)	94204.4
工业总产值(当年价格)	(亿元)	Gross Output Value of Industry		12438.3
		(at current prices)	(100 million yuan)	
利润总额	(亿元)	Total Profits	(100 million yuan)	10117.1
应缴税金	(亿元)	Total Taxes Payable	(100 million yuan)	2645.1

注：本表中的开发区仅包括国家级开发区情况，下同。
Note: Development zones in this table include those at state level only, the same below.

24-2 开发区土地规划情况(2023年) STATISTICS ON LAND PLANNING OF DEVELOPMENT ZONES(2023)

单位：公顷 (hectare)

名　　称	Item	规划总面积 Total Planned Area
国家级开发区	**State-level Development Zone**	**49448.6**
北京经济技术开发区	Beijing Economic-Technological Development Area	6579.9
中关村国家自主创新示范区	Zhongguancun National Independent Innovation Demonstration Zone	48816.0
海 淀 园	Haidian Sub-park	17432.2
丰 台 园	Fengtai Sub-park	1763.1
昌 平 园	Changping Sub-park	5140.7
朝 阳 园	Chaoyang Sub-park	2610.2
亦 庄 园	Yizhuang Sub-park	7505.0
西 城 园	Xicheng Sub-park	999.6
东 城 园	Dongcheng Sub-park	603.3
石景山园	Shijingshan Sub-park	1324.4
通 州 园	Tongzhou Sub-park	3434.5
大 兴 园	Daxing Sub-park	2322.0
平 谷 园	Pinggu Sub-park	508.4
门头沟园	Mentougou Sub-park	189.0
房 山 园	Fangshan Sub-park	1573.0
顺 义 园	Shunyi Sub-park	1207.7
密 云 园	Miyun Sub-park	1000.8
怀 柔 园	Huairou Sub-park	711.0
延 庆 园	Yanqing Sub-park	491.2
北京首都国际机场临空经济区	Airport Economic Zone near the Beijing Capital International Airport	1557.7

注：中关村国家自主创新示范区亦庄园数据在中关村国家自主创新示范区与北京经济技术开发区中为重叠部分。

Note: Data on Yizhuang Sub-park of Zhongguancun National Independent Innovation Demonstration Zone are overlapped in Zhongguancun National Independent Innovation Demonstration Zone and Beijing Economic-Technological Development Area.

24-3 开发区经营情况(2023年)
OPERATING STATISTICS ON DEVELOPMENT ZONES (2023)

名称	Item	自年初累计 Accumulative Number from Year-beginning	
		总收入 (万元) Total Revenue (10000 yuan)	利润总额 (万元) Total Profits (10000 yuan)
国家级开发区	**State-level Development Zone**	**1111768473**	**115572593**
北京经济技术开发区	Beijing Economic-Technological Development Area	207184370	13189694
中关村国家自主创新示范区	Zhongguancun National Independent Innovation Demonstration Zone	873792220	102029404
海淀园	Haidian Sub-park	380657939	37030991
丰台园	Fengtai Sub-park	48976691	5304719
昌平园	Changping Sub-park	30143509	2909377
朝阳园	Chaoyang Sub-park	46708179	7238199
亦庄园	Yizhuang Sub-park	170503086	14971727
西城园	Xicheng Sub-park	46306198	7139555
东城园	Dongcheng Sub-park	38024106	17411353
石景山园	Shijingshan Sub-park	35321335	3813251
通州园	Tongzhou Sub-park	10084818	1362643
大兴园	Daxing Sub-park	11275695	574916
平谷园	Pinggu Sub-park	1089312	142852
门头沟园	Mentougou Sub-park	8614761	140817
房山园	Fangshan Sub-park	10657892	384934
顺义园	Shunyi Sub-park	20948381	2389560
密云园	Miyun Sub-park	6244800	424977
怀柔园	Huairou Sub-park	5663749	636295
延庆园	Yanqing Sub-park	2571768	153239
北京首都国际机场临空经济区	Airport Economic Zone near the Beijing Capital International Airport	30791883	353496

注：1. 中关村国家自主创新示范区与北京经济技术开发区、北京首都国际机场临空经济区存在重复单位，在国家级开发区汇总时已剔除重复部分。
2. 中关村国家自主创新示范区统计范围为在中关村国家自主创新示范区内注册的规模(限额)以上六类企业法人单位，其他开发区统计范围为规模(限额)以上法人单位。

Note: a) There are repetitive units among Zhongguancun National Independent Innovation Demonstration Zone, Beijing Economic-Technological Development Area, and Airport Economic Zone near the Beijing Capital International Airport. The repetitive parts have been eliminated when summarizing the data on state-level development zones.
b) The statistical scope of Zhongguancun National Independent Innovation Demonstration Zone include six types of enterprises above designated size that were registered inside the Zhongguancun National Independent Innovation Demonstration Zone,while the statistical coverage for other development zones covers the corporate units above designated size.

24-4 北京经济技术开发区主要经济指标
MAIN ECONOMIC INDICATORS OF BEIJING ECONOMIC-TECHNOLOGICAL DEVELOPMENT AREA

项目		Item		2023	2022
规划面积	(公顷)	Area Planned	(hectare)	6579.9	6579.9
开发区生产总值	(亿元)	Gross Output Value	(100 million yuan)	2501.9	2456.4
工业总产值		Gross Output Value of Industry		4967.2	5128.7
(当年价格)	(亿元)	(at current prices)	(100 million yuan)		
销售(营业)收入	(亿元)	Sales (Business) Revenue	(100 million yuan)	20718.4	20276.9
利润总额	(亿元)	Total Profits	(100 million yuan)	1319.0	1330.0
进出口总值	(亿美元)	Total Value of Imports and Exports	(USD 100 million)	241.3	259.0
出　口		Exports		69.3	72.4
进　口		Imports		172.0	186.6
一般公共预算收入	(亿元)	General Public Budget Revenue	(100 million yuan)	377.3	372.4
实际利用外商直接投资额	(亿美元)	Amount of Foreign Direct Investment		11.1	3.9
		Actually Utilized	(USD 100 million)		
固定资产投资增速	(%)	Growth Rate of Investment in Fixed Assets	(%)	-17.4	10.7
从业人员期末人数	(人)	Year-end Number of Employed Persons	(person)	487651	475342
从业人员工资总额	(亿元)	Total Wages of Employed Persons	(100 million yuan)	956.5	910.8

注：1.工业总产值(当年价格)、销售(营业)收入和利润总额指标的统计范围为规模(限额)以上法人单位。
2.进出口总值、出口、进口、一般公共预算收入、实际利用外商直接投资额自2023年起调整为亦庄新城口径。
3.一般公共预算收入为地方级口径。

资料来源：北京经济技术开发区经济发展局、经济社会调查队。

Note: a)The statistics on gross output value of industry (at current prices), sales (business) revenue and total profits cover the legal entities above designated size.
b)The data on total value of imports and exports, exports, imports, general public budget revenue and actual use of foreign direct investment have been adjusted to be of the calibers of BDA New Town since 2023.
c)The data on general public budget revenue are based on the local level standards.

Source: Bureau of Economy and Development and Economic and Social Survey Team of Beijing Economic-Technological Development Area.

24-5　中关村国家自主创新示范区企业经营及科技活动情况(2008-2023年)
OPERATING ACTIVITIES AND SCIENTIFIC AND TECHNOLOGICAL ACTIVITIES OF ENTERPRISES IN ZHONGGUANCUN NATIONAL INNOVATION DEMONSTRATION ZONE (2008-2023)

项　目	Item	2008	2009	2010	2011	2012	2013	2014	2015
总收入　(亿元)	**Total Revenue　(100 million yuan)**	**10222.4**	**13004.6**	**15940.2**	**19646.0**	**25025.0**	**30497.4**	**36057.6**	**40811.9**
技术收入	Technological Revenue	1693.4	2093.6	2478.3	2845.9	3403.1	4032.4	4837.7	6623.6
产品销售收入	Products Sales Revenue	5229.2	5923.6	6889.6	7809.4	8741.2	10788.4	12474.2	13300.0
商品销售收入	Goods Sales Revenue	2398.9	3689.4	5032.2	7161.9	10077.4	11339.6	12832.6	13339.5
其他收入	Other Revenues	900.9	1298.0	1540.1	1828.9	2803.4	4337.0	5913.1	7548.9
利润总额　(亿元)	**Total Profits　(100 million yuan)**	**726.3**	**1122.4**	**1298.9**	**1533.9**	**1788.6**	**2264.8**	**3031.5**	**3404.5**
专利情况	**Statistics on Patents**								
期末有效发明专利数　(件)	Number of Effective Inventions at the End of the Period　(piece)	9836	11611	13988	15232	23198	35000	44870	63171
当年专利授权数　(件)	Number of Patents Granted in the Year　(piece)	9050	10512	13151	12951	17969	22308	25065	32327

注:2023年中关村示范区统计范围调整为在中关村国家自主创新示范区内注册的规模(限额)以上六类企业法人单位。统计范围调整后，2023年数据与往年数据不可比，下同。

Note: The statistical scope of Zhongguancun Demonstration Zone was adjusted in 2023 to include the six types of enterprises above designated size that were registered inside Zhongguancun National Independent Innovation Demonstration Zone. After the adjustment of statistical scope, the data for 2023 are incomparable to that of the previous years, the same below.

24-5　续表　Continued

项　目	Item	2016	2017	2018	2019	2020	2021	2022	2023
总收入　(亿元)	**Total Revenue　(100 million yuan)**	**46047.6**	**53025.8**	**58830.9**	**66422.2**	**72276.4**	**84402.3**	**87462.9**	**87379.2**
技术收入	Technological Revenue	7580.4	9369.6	11174.3	13450.8	16027.4	20419.4	22502.6	24888.7
产品销售收入	Products Sales Revenue	14752.5	15934.2	17058.7	19085.2	19784.8	23524.5	20676.1	19611.4
商品销售收入	Goods Sales Revenue	14522.4	16406.1	17878.0	20253.9	21752.8	23682.0	24616.7	21491.6
其他收入	Other Revenues	9192.3	11315.9	12719.9	13632.3	14711.4	16776.5	19667.5	21387.4
利润总额　(亿元)	**Total Profits　(100 million yuan)**	**3732.5**	**4321.1**	**4413.3**	**4182.6**	**6344.7**	**7725.3**	**6901.0**	**10202.9**
专利情况	**Statistics on Patents**								
期末有效发明专利数　(件)	Number of Effective Inventions at the End of the Period　(piece)	82890	114469	141486	170772	186511	206767	267471	288664
当年专利授权数　(件)	Number of Patents Granted in the Year　(piece)	37629	46046	56374	61221	74928	90434	98300	82262

24-6 中关村国家自主创新示范区企业经营活动情况 STATISTICS ON OPERATING ACTIVITIES OF ENTERPRISES IN ZHONGGUANCUN NATIONAL INDEPENDENT INNOVATION DEMONSTRATION ZONE

单位：亿元 (100 million yuan)

项　　目	Item	2023	2022
工业总产值(当年价格)	Gross Output Value of Industry (at current prices)	12040.5	13190.4
总收入	Total Revenue	87379.2	87462.9
技术收入	Technological Revenue	24888.7	22502.6
产品销售收入	Products Sales Revenue	19611.4	20676.1
商品销售收入	Goods Sales Revenue	21491.6	24616.7
其他收入	Other Revenues	21387.4	19667.5
利润总额	Total Profits	10202.9	6901.0
减免税总额	Reduced and Exempted Tax	930.4	1264.0
#增值税	Value Added Tax	243.7	331.7
所得税	Income Tax	680.2	748.3
应交增值税	Value Added Tax Payable	1239.3	1028.3
出口总额	Total Value of Exports	3345.8	3202.3

24-7 中关村国家自主创新示范区企业研发活动情况 STATISTICS ON RESEARCH AND DEVELOPMENT ACTIVITIES OF ENTERPRISES IN ZHONGGUANCUN NATIONAL INDEPENDENT INNOVATION DEMONSTRATION ZONE

项　　目	Item	2023	2022
研究开发活动情况	**Statistics on Research and Development Activities**		
研究开发人员合计 (人)	Total Number of Research and Development Personnel (person)	778225	1005583
#全职人员	Full-time Personnel	684844	904721
研究开发费用合计 (亿元)	Total Research and Development Costs (100 million yuan)	4494.1	4952.4
#人员人工费用	Labor Cost	2396.9	2695.6
委托外部研究开发费用 (亿元)	Costs of Research and Development Conducted by External Units Entrusted (100 million yuan)	719.5	704.9
#委托境外机构	Entrusted Overseas Institution	7.2	13.7
研究开发产出情况	**Research and Development Output**		
专利情况	Statistics on Patents		
期末有效发明专利数 (件)	Number of Effective Inventions at the End of the Period (piece)	288664	267471
当年专利授权数 (件)	Number of Patents Granted in the Year (piece)	82262	98300
论文、著作情况	Statistics on Papers and Writings		
发表科技论文 (篇)	Number of Published Scientific Papers (piece)	14377	16910
技术改造和技术获取情况	**Technical Renovation and Acquisition**		
技术改造经费支出 (亿元)	Expenditures on Technical Renovation (100 million yuan)	6.6	11.0
引进境外技术经费支出 (亿元)	Expenditures on Introduction of Foreign Technologies (100 million yuan)	11.3	2.8
引进境外技术的消化吸收经费支出 (亿元)	Expenditures on Absorption of Imported Foreign Technologies (100 million yuan)	0.1	1.1
购买境内技术经费支出 (亿元)	Expenditures on Purchasing Domestic Technologies (100 million yuan)	8.8	6.6

24-8 中关村国家自主创新示范区企业人力资源情况
STATISTICS ON HUMAN RESOURCES OF ENTERPRISES IN ZHONGGUANCUN NATIONAL INDEPENDENT INNOVATION DEMONSTRATION ZONE

单位：人 (person)

项　目	Item	2023	2022
从业人员年末人数	**Year-end Number of Employed Persons**	**2848322**	**2790210**
#留学归国人员	Returned Students Studying Abroad	65462	63209
按文化程度分	**By Educational Background**		
#博士及以上	Doctor's Degree and above	28315	31727
硕　士	Master's Degree	408805	399185
大　本	Undergraduates	1340940	1385864
大　专	Junior College	536094	527386
按年龄分	**By Age**		
#29岁及以下	29 years and below	799970	837137
从业人员平均人数	**Average Number of Employed Persons**	**2903558**	**2816894**

24-9 中关村国家自主创新示范区企业财务状况
FINANCIAL STATUS OF ENTERPRISES IN ZHONGGUANCUN NATIONAL INDEPENDENT INNOVATION DEMONSTRATION ZONE

单位：亿元 (100 million yuan)

项　目	Item	2023	2022
资产总计	Total Assets	254436.7	198746.6
流动资产合计	Total Current Assets	122100.7	98721.7
累计折旧	Accumulative Depreciation	3588.1	10885.9
负债合计	Total Liabilities	139725.8	121923.9
所有者权益合计	Total Owners' Equity	114710.8	76821.1
实收资本	Paid-in Capital	43044.7	36549.8

主要统计指标解释

累计招商项目企业个数 指自开始至报告期末累计招商入区，并经工商管理机关注册取得法人营业执照的企业个数。

总收入 指企业全年的生产产品销售收入、技术性收入和与本企业产品相关的商品的销售收入、其它收入等各种收入的总和，总收入等于主营业务收入加上其他业务收入。总收入应按不含增值税的价格计算，不包括补贴收入、营业外收入、投资收益。

出口总额 指直接出售给外商的产品、商品、技术或服务的总金额。包括来料加工装配出口，境外技术合同实现金额及在国内以外汇计价的商品出售和技术服务的总额等。

留学归国人员 指出国学习，取得学位的归国人员。

Explanatory Notes on Main Statistical Indicators

Accumulated Number of Enterprises Involved in Business Inviting Programs refers to the total number of enterprises invited to development zones and awarded with business licenses for legal persons from the administration for industry and commerce from the beginning to the end of the reporting period.

Total Revenue refers to the sum of income earned by enterprises across the year from sales of their own products, technological income, and income from selling commodities related to their own products, and other income. Total revenue is the sum of main business income and other business income. Total revenue shall be calculated at VAT-excluded prices, and exclude subsidies, non-operating income and return on investment.

Total Export refers to the total amount of products, commodities, technologies or services directly sold to foreign traders. It includes the value of export of investor's raw materials processed and assembled, the value of technical contracts completed at abroad, and the total value of domestic commodity sales and technical services measured in foreign currency.

Returned Students Studying Abroad refer to persons who have come home after studying abroad and been conferred with academic degrees.

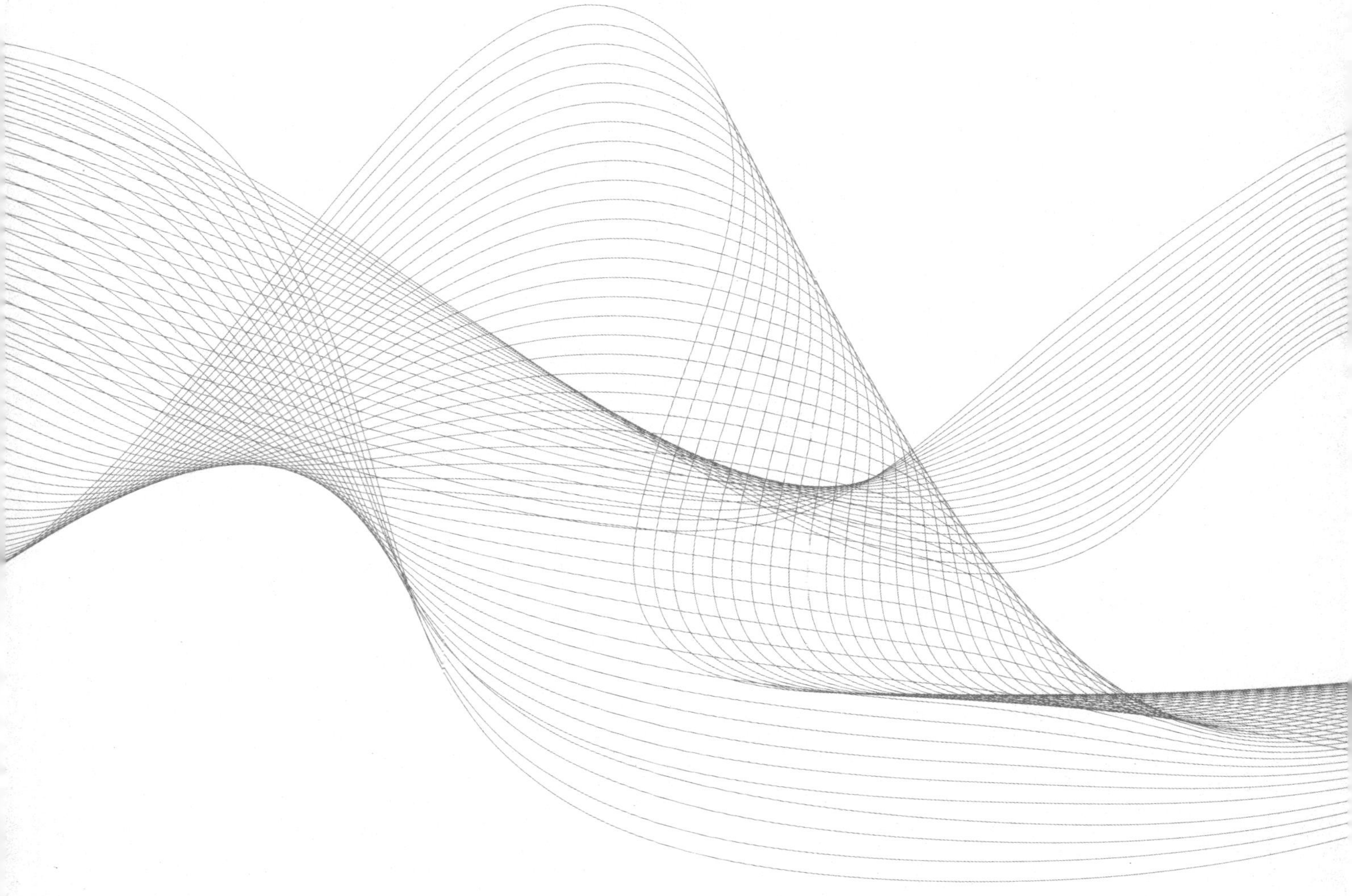